Chile

THE ROUGH GUIDE

There are more than one hundred and fifty Rough Guide titles covering destinations from Amsterdam to Zimbabwe

Forthcoming titles include

Cuba • Dominican Republic • Las Vegas • Sardinia • Switzerland

Rough Guide Reference Series

Classical Music • Drum 'n' Bass • European Football • House
The Internet • Jazz • Music USA • Opera • Reggae
Rock Music • World Music

Rough Guide Phrasebooks

Czech • Dutch • European • French • German • Greek • Hindi & Urdu
Hungarian • Indonesian • Italian • Japanese • Mandarin Chinese
Mexican Spanish • Polish • Portuguese • Russian • Spanish • Swahili
Thai • Turkish • Vietnamese

Rough Guides on the Internet

www.roughguides.com

ROUGH GUIDE CREDITS

Text editors: Ann-Marie Shaw and Samantha Cook
Series editor: Mark Ellingham
Editorial: Martin Dunford, Jonathan Buckley, Jo Mead, Kate Berens, Amanda Tomlin, Paul Gray, Helena Smith, Judith Bamber, Kieran Falconer, Orla Duane, Olivia Eccleshall, Ruth Blackmore, Sophie Martin, Geoff Howard, Claire Saunders, Gavin Thomas, Alexander Mark Rogers, Polly Thomas, Joe Staines, Lisa Nellis, Andrew Tomičić (UK); Andrew Rosenberg, Mary Beth Maioli (US)
Production: Susanne Hillen, Andy Hilliard, Link Hall, Helen Ostick, Julia Bovis, Michelle Draycott, Anna Wray, Katie Pringle, Robert Eyers
Cartography: Melissa Baker, Maxine Burke, Nichola Goodliffe, Ed Wright
Picture research: Louise Boulton, Catherine Marshall
Online editors: Alan Spicer, Kate Hands (UK); Kelly Cross (US)
Finance: John Fisher, Gary Singh, Ed Downey
Marketing & Publicity: Richard Trillo, Simon Carloss, Niki Smith, David Wearn, Jemima Broadbridge (UK); Jean-Marie Kelly, Myra Campolo (US)
Administration: Tania Hummel, Charlotte Marriott, Demelza Dallow

PUBLISHING INFORMATION

This first edition published October 1999 by Rough Guides Ltd, 62–70 Shorts Gardens, London WC2H 9AB.
Distributed by the Penguin Group:
Penguin Books Ltd, 27 Wrights Lane, London W8 5TZ
Penguin Books USA Inc., 375 Hudson Street, New York 10014, USA
Penguin Books Australia Ltd, 487 Maroondah Highway, PO Box 257, Ringwood, Victoria 3134, Australia
Penguin Books Canada Ltd, 10 Alcorn Avenue, Toronto, Ontario, Canada M4V 1E4
Penguin Books (NZ) Ltd, 182–190 Wairau Road, Auckland 10, New Zealand
Typeset in Linotron Univers and Century Old Style to an original design by Andrew Oliver.
Printed in England by Clays Ltd, St Ives PLC
Illustrations in Part One and Part Three by Edward Briant.
Illustrations on p.1 & p.443 by Henry Iles

512pp – Includes index
A catalogue record for this book is available from the British Library
ISBN 1-85828-410-4

Chile

THE ROUGH GUIDE

written and researched by

Melissa Graham, Christopher Sainsbury and Richard Danbury

with additional accounts by

Harry Adès and Jan Fairley

THE ROUGH GUIDES

THE ROUGH GUIDES

TRAVEL GUIDES • PHRASEBOOKS • MUSIC AND REFERENCE GUIDES

We set out to do something different when the first Rough Guide was published in 1982. Mark Ellingham, just out of university, was travelling in Greece. He brought along the popular guides of the day, but found they were all lacking in some way. They were either strong on ruins and museums but went on for pages without mentioning a beach or taverna. Or they were so conscious of the need to save money that they lost sight of Greece's cultural and historical significance. Also, none of the books told him anything about Greece's contemporary life – its politics, its culture, its people, and how they lived.

So with no job in prospect, Mark decided to write his own guidebook, one which aimed to provide practical information that was second to none, detailing the best beaches and the hottest clubs and restaurants, while also giving hard-hitting accounts of every sight, both famous and obscure, and providing up-to-the-minute information on contemporary culture. It was a guide that encouraged independent travellers to find the best of Greece, and was a great success, getting shortlisted for the Thomas Cook travel guide award, and encouraging Mark, along with three friends, to expand the series.

The Rough Guide list grew rapidly and the letters flooded in, indicating a much broader readership than had been anticipated, but one which uniformly appreciated the Rough Guide mix of practical detail and humour, irreverence and enthusiasm. Things haven't changed. The same four friends who began the series are still the caretakers of the Rough Guide mission today: to provide the most reliable, up-to-date and entertaining information to independent-minded travellers of all ages, on all budgets.

We now publish more than 150 titles and have offices in London and New York. The travel guides are written and researched by a dedicated team of more than 100 authors, based in Britain, Europe, the USA and Australia. We have also created a unique series of phrasebooks to accompany the travel series, along with an acclaimed series of music guides, and a best-selling pocket guide to the Internet and World Wide Web. We also publish comprehensive travel information on our web site:

www.roughguides.com

HELP US UPDATE

We've gone to a lot of effort to ensure that the first edition of *The Rough Guide to Chile* is accurate and up-to-date. However, things change – places get "discovered", opening hours are notoriously fickle, restaurants and rooms raise prices or lower standards. If you feel we've got it wrong or left something out, we'd like to know, and if you can remember the address, the price, the time, the phone number, so much the better.

We'll credit all contributions, and send a copy of the next edition (or any other Rough Guide if you prefer) for the best letters. Please mark letters: "Rough Guide Chile Update" and send to:

Rough Guides, 62–70 Shorts Gardens, London WC2H 9AB, or
Rough Guides, 375 Hudson St, 9th floor, New York, NY 10014.
Or send email to: mail@roughguides.co.uk
Online updates about this book can be found on Rough Guides' Web site at www.roughguides.com

THE AUTHORS

Melissa Graham first got hooked on Latin America while studying Spanish American literature and history as part of a modern languages degree at Cambridge University. She has since travelled widely in the Andean countries of Chile, Peru and Ecuador, where she has developed a passion for the region's landscapes and people, and a loathing for lomo con papas fritas. She is currently researching the forthcoming *Rough Guide to Ecuador.*

In a bid for freedom, **Richard Danbury** escaped his job as a barrister in 1998 and headed off to South America, a continent he'd first visited in the early 1990s. This trip produced a book, *The Inca Trail* (Trailblazer Publications), and, strengthened by the realization that you can actually enjoy your work, he started writing for *The Rough Guide to Chile.* He now works for the BBC and lives in London with Melissa and his arthritic 17-year-old cat.

Since graduating with a fine art degree more years ago than he cares to admit, **Christopher Sainsbury** has – among other things – worked as expedition photographer with Operation Drake and Operation Raleigh, served time as a ship's cook, survived cerebral malaria, been an extra in *The Blue Lagoon* with Brooke Shields, and visited several hundred Chilean churches while researching part of the *Cambridge Encyclopedia of Vernacular Architecture.* In 1990 he moved to Chile where he helped set up a travel agency and pioneered local tours in the south. He is currently renovating his old house in the Chilean Lake District, which is in grave danger of collapsing on top of him.

ACKNOWLEDGEMENTS

In Chile, the authors would like to thank all the members of Sernatur who gave their time and assistance and also all the Conaf *guardaparques*, from Arica to Punta Arenas, who without exception shared their knowledge and provided willing and enthusiastic help in researching the country's national parks and reserves. Back home, thanks are owed to Sam Cook for getting the book off to a great start and to Ann-Marie Shaw for bringing it all together, getting it through some difficult times and giving it a superb edit (the banana pancakes are on their way). Thanks also to Kate Berens for wading in with lots of help at the deep end, Ed Wright and The Map Studio, Romsey, Hants for the maps, Eleanor Hill for picture-editing, Katie Pringle for cool, calm typesetting, and Russell Walton for proofreading.

Melissa and Richard: we are grateful to Rolf Wagner from Sernatur, Santiago, for his very best efforts on our behalf, and José Manuel Rogers from the Corporación de Promoción Turística de Chile for his assistance. Also in Santiago, special thanks to Natalia Fetherston-Dilke for her friendship and invaluable help; Oscar, Lucas and Bruno Modiano for reminding us of the delights of *Thomas the Tank Engine*; and Simon and Allison Hosking for their much-appreciated hospitality. Further south, in the wilds of the Carretera Austral, thanks to Victor and Felipe and to Kate Holloway from the Alerce Lodge, and Pablo Negri from the Termas de Puyuhuapi for a great day's fishing. Finally, a big hello to Wayne and to Operation Raleigh. In addition, thanks **from Melissa** to: Fernando Leña and Paola Díaz from Santiago for their friendship and flow of helpful emails; Jaime Letelier for a room and unforgettable Valparaíso views; Janet Miller for letting me pick her brains; and Sra Gabriela Morales from Sernatur, Aisén, for her kind help. Finally thanks to Richard, as always, for all your help, and all the happy times. **From Richard**: Patricio Lanfranco and Lake Sagaris for lunch, conversation and a warm welcome in Huerquehue; in Pucón Sra Rosa Maria Echenique, Paul Connolly and Desmond Sutton, and of course all at ¡école!. Thanks to Eduardo at Lago Ranco, Michel Peyron on the road and in Chiloé, Adrian Turner and Caroline Morgado in Puerto Montt. A particular thank you to the staff at Sernatur in Punta Arenas who put up with coming back again and again with more and more obscure questions. And Melissa, *se van tiñendo con tu amor mis palabras. Todo lo ocupas tú, todo lo ocupas.*

This book is dedicated to the memory of Ignacio Modiano.

CONTENTS

• CHAPTER 3: EL NORTE CHICO 145–180

• CHAPTER 4: EL NORTE GRANDE 181–232

• CHAPTER 5: THE CENTRAL VALLEY 233–271

• CHAPTER 6: THE LAKE DISTRICT 272–332

• CHAPTER 7: CHILOÉ 333–353

• CHAPTER 8: THE CARRETERA AUSTRAL 354–384

• CHAPTER 9: CHILEAN PATAGONIA AND TIERRA DEL FUEGO 385–416

• CHAPTER 10: THE PACIFIC ISLANDS 417–442

PART THREE CONTEXTS 444

LIST OF MAPS

MAP SYMBOLS

Motorway
Road
Minor road
Steps
Path
Unpaved road
Railway
Ferry route
National border
Chapter division boundary
River
Airport (international)
Airport (domestic)
Bus stop
Cable car or funicular
Ski resort
Metro station
Accommodation
Restaurant or bar
Campsite
Point of interest
Spa or hot springs
Viewpoint
Waterfall
Lighthouse
Castle
Cliffs
Caves
Mountain range
Mountain peak
Volcano
Guardería (ranger station)
Refugio (mountain lodge)
Tourist office
Post office
Telephone office
Hospital
Building
Church (town maps)
Church (regional maps)
Cemetery
Park
National park
Beach
Glacier or icefield

INTRODUCTION

A long, narrow sliver of land, clinging to the edge of a continent, Chile has often drawn attention to itself for its wholly implausible shape. Seen in the pages of an atlas, the country's outline strikes you as aberrant and fantastical: almost 4000km in length (the equivalent of Scotland to Nigeria), and with an average width of just 180km, the very idea of it seems absurd. Once on Chilean soil, however, these boundaries make perfect sense, and visitors quickly realize that Chile is a geographically self-contained unit. The Andes, the great mountain range that forms its eastern border, are a formidable barrier of rock and ice which cuts the country off from Argentina. The Atacama desert, a thousand-kilometre stretch of parched wasteland separates it from Peru to the north. And to the west, only a few islands dotted in the Pacific Ocean break the waves that roll onto Chile's coast from Australasia.

All this has created a country distinct from the rest of South America, and one that defies many people's expectations of an Andean country. It is Westernized, relatively affluent, and – with the exception of the infamous military regime of the 1970s and 1980s – boasts a long tradition of political stability and orderly government. It is, without doubt, one of the safest and most relaxing South American countries to travel in. Its police are uncorrupt, helpful and reliable. Its buses are comfortable and run on time. Its people are warm, hospitable and generous.

Above all, though, it is for its remote and dizzyingly beautiful landscapes that visitors head to Chile. With its population of fifteen million largely confined to a handful of major cities, and a land area three times greater than the UK's, much of Chile is covered by vast tracts of scarcely-touched wilderness – places where you can be days from the nearest tarred road, and where it's not unusual to stumble upon steaming hot springs, gleaming white salt flats or emerald lakes, and have them all to yourself. Few countries, moreover, can match the astounding contrasts of scenery you'll find here, ranging from the driest desert in the world to immense icefields and glaciers. Spread between these extremes is a kaleidoscope of panoramas, taking in sun-baked scrubland, lush vineyards and orchards, virgin temperate rainforest, dramatic fjords and bleak Patagonian steppes. Towering over it all is the long, jagged spine of the Andes, punctuated by colossal peaks and smouldering volcanoes.

You can experience this wilderness in whatever style you choose – Chile is not a developing country, and you don't have to slum it while you're here. There are plenty of modest, inexpensive accommodation options and camping facilities up and down the country, while those on a more generous budget will find some luxurious, beautifully designed lodges in spectacular locations, particularly in the south. Whatever your budget, you'll probably want to take advantage of the numerous possibilities for outdoor activities, whether it be jeep rides, bird-watching, skiing, horse trekking, wine tours, hiking, volcano-climbing, sea kayaking, white-water rafting or fly-fishing – all offered by an increasing number of local outfitters, and comprehensively detailed in this book. If you have less active plans in mind, you can sit back and take in Chile's scenery from various ferry rides in the south, or on organized bus tours from most of the main cities. However you do it, you won't be disappointed.

Where to go: some highlights

Given the country's great size, and the huge distances that separate the main attractions, it's important to give careful thought to your itinerary before you go. If you want to experience both the northern and southern extremes, you should invest in an air pass, unless you're prepared to spend many hours sitting on a bus, or are in the country for an extended period. Otherwise, most visitors with just two or three weeks to

PERU
BOLIVIA
PARAGUAY
ARGENTINA
CHILE
N
Easter Island (Chile)
Arica
Iquique
Calama
Antofagasta
Copiapó
La Serena
Viña del Mar
Valparaíso
Santiago
Juan Fernandez Archipelago (Chile)
Talca
Chillán
Concepción
PACIFIC
OCEAN
Temuco
Valdivia
Osorno
Puerto Montt
I. de Chiloé
Chaitén
Arch. de los Chonos
Puerto Aisén
Coyhaique
Golfo de Penas
Cochrane
I. Wellington
Falkland Islands (UK)
Puerto Natales
Straits of Magellan
Punta Arenas
Tierra del Fuego
Cape Horn
0
500 km

play with tend to choose between heading north or south from Santiago, even then singling out a few chosen targets, rather than trying to fit everything in. Something else to bear in mind is that, on the whole, Chile's cities are not that exciting, and are best used as a jumping off point to get out into the backcountry. In light of this, you should seriously consider renting a vehicle for at least part of your trip, as public transport to some of the most beautiful areas, including many national parks, can be non-existent. We discuss each region's highlights in greater detail in the chapter introductions; what follows is a brief summary of the attractions of each area.

Santiago, though boasting some fine monuments, museums and restaurants, is not to everyone's taste, with its ceaseless noise and traffic, and heavy pollution, and two or three days here is enough for most visitors. The capital is handy for visiting some of the country's oldest **vineyards**, while a string of splendid beaches, as well as the romantic port of **Valparaíso** and fashionable resort of **Viña del Mar**, also sit on its doorstep.

North of Santiago, highlights include the handsome colonial city of La Serena, the lush, deeply rural **Elqui valley**, and another succession of idyllic **beaches**, all contained within the brittle, semi-arid landscape of the **Norte Chico**. At the northern edge of this region, the tidy little city of **Copiapó** serves as a springboard for excursions to the white sands and turquoise waters of **Bahía Inglesa**, one of the country's most attractive seaside resorts, and east into the cordillera, where you'll find the mineral-streaked volcanoes of **Parque Nacional Nevado de Tres Cruces**, and the dazzling **Laguna Verde**. Further north, the barren **Atacama desert**, stretching over 1000km into southern Peru, presents an unforgettable, if forbidding, landscape, whose attractions number ancient petroglyphs (indigenous rock art), abandoned nitrate ghost towns and a scattering of fertile, fruit-filled oases. Up in the Andes, the vast plateau known as the **altiplano**, as high and remote as Tibet, encompasses snow-capped volcanoes, bleached-white salt flats, lakes speckled pink with flamingos, grazing llamas, alpacas and vicuñas, tiny whitewashed churches, and native Aymara communities. The best points to head for up here are **Parque Nacional Lauca**, reached from the city of Arica, and **Parque Nacional Volcán Isluga**, reached from Iquique.

South of Santiago, the chief appeal of the lush **Central Valley** is its swaths of orchards and vineyards, dotted with stately haciendas, while further south, the famous, much-visited **Lake District** presents a picture-postcard landscape of perfect, conical volcanoes (including the exquisite **Volcán Osorno**), iris-blue lakes, rolling pastureland and dense native forests, perfect for hiking. A short ferry ride from Puerto Montt, at

CHILE'S REGIONS

Administratively, Chile is divided into thirteen regions, numbered one to twelve (with the addition of the Metropolitan region). We've listed each region by number and name below, followed by the regional capital in parentheses.

I Tarapacá (*Iquique*)
II Antofagasta (*Antofagasta*)
III Atacama (*Copiapó*)
IV Coquimbo (*La Serena*)
V Valparaíso (*Valparaíso*)
Metropolitana de Santiago
VI Libertador General O'Higgins (*Rancagua*)
VII Maule (*Talca*)
VIII Bío Bío (*Concepción*)
IX Araucanía (*Temuco*)
X Los Lagos (*Puerto Montt*)
XI Aisén (*Coihaique*)
XII Magallanes y Antartida Chilena (*Punta Arenas*)

the southern edge of the Lake District, the **Chiloé** archipelago is a quiet, rural backwater, famous for its rickety houses on stilts, old wooden churches, and rich local mythology. Back on the mainland, south of Puerto Montt, the **Carretera Austral** – a 1000km-long unpaved "highway" – carves its way through virgin temperate rainforest, and past dramatic fjords, one of which is the embarkation point for a 200-kilometre boat trip out to the sensational **Laguna San Rafael glacier**. Beyond the Carretera Austral, cut off by the **Campo de Hielo Sur** (southern icefields) lies **Chilean Patagonia**, a country of bleak windswept plains bordered by the magnificent granite spires of the **Torres del Paine** massif, Chile's single most famous attraction, and a magnet for hikers and climbers. Across the Magellan Strait, **Tierra del Fuego** sits shivering at the bottom of the world, a remote land of a harsh, desolate beauty.

Finally, there are Chile's two Pacific possessions: the little-visited **Isla Robinson Crusoe**, part of the Juan Fernández Archipelago, sporting dramatic volcanic peaks covered with dense vegetation; and remote **Easter Island**, famed for its mysterious statues and fascinating pre-historic culture.

When to go

The **north** of the country can be comfortably visited at any time of year, though if you're planning to rent a 4WD and tour the altiplano, note that the unpredictable weather phenomenon known as the **Bolivian Winter** (or *invierno altiplánico*) can produce heavy, sporadic rainfall between December and February (the height of summer), washing away roads and disrupting communications.

In the **centre** and **south** of the country, you should avoid the months of June to September (unless you plan to go skiing), when heavy snowfall often blocks access to the mountains, including many national parks. The peak summer months are January and February, but as accommodation rates and crowds increase in equal measure, you'd be better off coming in November, December or March, when the weather is often just as good.

DAYTIME TEMPERATURES (°C) AND AVERAGE MONTHLY RAINFALL (MM)

	Jan	Feb	Mar	Apr	May	June	July	Aug	Sept	Oct	Nov	Dec
Arica												
Av temp	21	22	21	20	18	16	15	14	16	18	19	20
Rainfall	1	0	0	0	0	0	0	3	0	0	0	2
Antofagasta												
Max temp	24	24	28	21	19	18	17	17	18	19	21	22
Min temp	17	17	16	14	13	11	11	11	12	13	14	16
Rainfall	0	0	0	0	0	3	5	4	0	3	0	0
Santiago												
Max temp	29	29	27	23	18	14	15	17	19	22	26	28
Min temp	12	11	9	7	5	3	3	4	6	7	9	11
Rainfall	3	3	5	13	64	84	76	56	31	15	8	5
Valdivia												
Max temp	23	23	21	17	13	11	11	12	14	17	18	21
Min temp	11	11	9	8	6	6	5	4	5	7	8	10
Rainfall	66	74	132	234	361	550	394	328	208	127	125	104
Punta Arenas												
Max temp	14	14	12	10	7	5	4	6	8	11	12	14
Min temp	7	7	5	4	2	1	-1	1	2	3	4	6
Rainfall	38	23	33	36	33	41	28	31	23	28	18	36

PART ONE

THE BASICS

GETTING THERE FROM THE USA AND CANADA

While US travellers are not exactly spoiled for choice when it comes to flights to Chile, they shouldn't find it too hard to get a fairly convenient flight to its international airport in Santiago. Several airlines offer daily non-stop flights, including American Airlines, United and Lan Chile, the Chilean national airline. Typical APEX fares from the US are: from New York/Newark US$1085 (low season)/US$1185 (high season); from Miami US$990/1105; from Chicago US$1115/1225; and from LA US$1225/1340.

In summer 1998, however, Continental entered the market, offering a daily non-stop service from Newark, with connections from other US and Canadian cities. This sparked off special promotional offers on flights from the US to Santiago, with the following low season round-trip fares available at the time of writing: from New York US$529; from Miami US$719; from Chicago US$879; from LA US$969.

Approximate flying times from the US to Santiago are: from Miami 8 hours 15 minutes; from LA 12 hours 45 minutes; and from the New York area 10 hours.

FLIGHTS FROM CANADA

There's even less choice if you're flying from Canada to Chile, with only Canadian Airlines offering daily flights from Toronto via Miami and from Vancouver via Los Angeles and Lima (with connections from other major Canadian cities). However, you shouldn't have much problem finding a connecting flight with a US carrier or with LanChile from all the major cities.

Sample fares from Toronto are CDN$1580 (low season)/1685 (high season); from Vancouver CDN$1865/1975.

Approximate flying times from Canada to Santiago are: from Toronto 10 hours 45 minutes; from Vancouver 16 hours.

SHOPPING FOR TICKETS

Barring special limited promotional sales, the cheapest of the airlines' published fares is usually an **Apex** ticket, although this will carry certain restrictions: you may have to book – and pay – up to 21 days before departure, spend at least seven days abroad (maximum stay three months), and you tend to get penalized if you change your schedule. It's worth remembering that most cheap return fares involve spending at least one Saturday night away and that many will only give a percentage refund if you need to cancel or alter your journey, so make sure you check the restrictions carefully before buying a ticket.

You can normally cut costs further by going through a **specialist flight agent** – either a **consolidator**, who buys up blocks of tickets from the airlines and sells them at a discount, or a **discount agent**, who in addition to dealing with discounted flights may also offer special student and youth fares and a range of other travel-related services such as travel insurance, car rental, tours and the like. Bear in mind, though, that penalties for changing your plans can be stiff. Some agents specialize in **charter flights**, which may be cheaper than anything available on a scheduled flight, but again departure dates are fixed and withdrawal penalties are high (check the refund policy). If you travel a lot, **discount travel clubs** are another option – the annual membership fee may be worth it for benefits such as cut-price air tickets and car rental.

A further possibility is to see if you can arrange a **courier flight** – most likely departing from Miami – although the hit-or-miss nature of these makes them most suitable for the single traveller who travels light and has a very flexible schedule. A couple of courier "associations" (courier-flight brokers) are listed in the box overleaf.

Regardless of where you buy your ticket, **fares** will depend on the season. In the case of flights to Chile, what this amounts to is basically a blackout on the cheaper fares over the major holiday period (Christmas and the New Year – from around Dec 10 to Jan 10).

If Chile is only one stop on a longer journey, you might want to consider buying a **Round-the-World (RTW) ticket**. Some travel agents can sell you an "off-the-shelf" RTW ticket that will have you touching down in several cities. Others will have to assemble one for you, which can be tailored to your needs but is apt to be more expensive. A sample itinerary would be: LA–Lima/overland on your own/Santiago–Paris/overland on your own/Amman–Cairo–Bombay/overland on your own/Katmandu–Bangkok–LA (US$2400–2500). A cheaper, though no less exotic, alternative is the **Circle Pacific ticket**. For example: New York or LA–Santiago–Easter Island–Auckland–Sydney–LA (around US$2040). Finally, Lan Chile offers its own **Pacific Circle fares**. A sample routing, allowing a stopover on Easter Island, would be LA–Santiago–Papeete–Honolulu–LA (US$1645).

Note also that flying on weekends, with some airlines, may add around US$60/CDN$90 to the round-trip fare; price ranges quoted assume mid-week travel, are round-trip, exclude taxes (again around US$60/CAN$90) and are subject to availability and change.

AIR PASSES

Lan Chile offers special **Visit Chile Fares** in the form of coupon **air passes**, available to anyone

AIRLINES AND AGENTS

AIRLINES

American Airlines (☎1-800/433-7300; *www.americanair.com*). *Daily non-stop service from Miami and Dallas/Fort Worth with connections from other major cities in the US and Canada.*

Canadian Airlines (☎1-800/665-1177 in Canada, ☎1-800/426-7000 in US; *www.cdnair.ca*). *Daily flights from Toronto via Miami and from Vancouver via Los Angeles and Lima with connections from other major Canadian cities.*

Continental Airlines (☎1-800/231-0856; *www.flycontinental.com*). *Daily non-stop service from Newark with connections from other major cities in the US and Canada.*

Lan Chile (☎1-800/735-5526; *www.lanchile.com*). *Daily non-stop service from Miami and, via Lima (with a free stopover allowed on the APEX fare quoted above) from New York or LA.*

United Airlines (☎1-800/538-2929; *www.ual.com*). *Daily non-stop service from Miami with connections from other major cities in the US.*

DISCOUNT AGENTS, CONSOLIDATORS AND TRAVEL CLUBS

Air Courier Association, 191 University Blvd, Suite 300, Denver, CO 80206 (☎303/215-0900 or 1-800/282-1202; *www.aircourier.org*). *Courier flight broker.*

Airtech, 588 Broadway, Suite 204, New York, NY 10017 (☎212/219-7000 or 1-800/575-8324; *www.airtech.com*). *Standby seat broker; also deals in consolidator fares and courier flights.*

Council Travel, Head Office, 205 E 42nd St, New York, NY 10017 (☎212/822-2700 or 1-800/226-8624; *www.ciee.com*). *Nationwide specialists in student travel, with branches in San Francisco, Los Angeles, Boulder, Washington DC, Chicago and Boston.*

High Adventure Travel, 353 Sacramento St, Suite 600, San Francisco, CA 94111 (☎415/912-5600 or 1-800/350-0612; *www.highadv.com*). *Round-the-World and Circle Pacific tickets. Web site features interactive database.*

International Association of Air Travel Couriers, 8 South J St, PO Box 1349, Lake Worth, FL 33460 (☎561/582-8320; *www.courier.org*). *Courier flight broker.*

STA Travel, 10 Downing St, New York, NY 10014 (☎212/627-3111 or 1-800/777-0112; *www.sta-travel.com*). *Other branches in Los Angeles, Chicago, San Francisco, Philadelphia, Boston, etc. Worldwide discount travel firm specializing in student/youth fares; also student IDs, travel insurance, car rental, train passes, etc.*

TFI Tours International, 34 W 32nd St, New York, NY 10001 (☎212/736-1140 or 1-800/745-8000). *Consolidator.*

Travel Avenue, 10 S Riverside, Suite 1404, Chicago, IL 60606 (☎1-800/333-3335). *Discount travel company.*

Travel Cuts, 187 College St, Toronto, ON M5T 1P7 (☎416/979-2406 or 1-800/667-2887; *www.travelcuts.com*). *Canadian discount travel organization, with branches in Montréal, Vancouver, Calgary, Winnipeg and Edmonton.*

Unitravel, 11737 Administration Drive, St Louis, MO 63146 (☎314/569-0900 or 1-800/325-2222). *Consolidator.*

not resident in Chile. These must be bought outside the country and can be used for internal flights between Santiago, Arica, Iquique, Antofagasta, Temuco, Puerto Montt and Punta Arenas. The price is US$250 (quoted in US dollars, though Canadians will pay the equivalent) for the first three coupons, then US$60 for each additional coupon. (If your international flight is with a carrier other than Lan Chile, then the price is US$350/80). A total of six tickets is permitted per air pass. There's a maximum stay of one month and the first coupon must be used within fourteen days of arrival in Chile.

SPECIALIST TOUR OPERATORS

Aside from Patagonian "adventure" packages combining Chile and Argentina (offered by, among others, Wilderness Travel and Mountain Travel Sobek) there's a fair range of exclusively Chilean tours to choose from. For instance, you could take a two-night city break in Santiago including hotel and round-trip fare from Miami for US$1080 (4th Dimension Tours) or celebrate New Year 2000 with twelve days' trekking in the Torres del Paine National Park for a land-only price of US$2995 (REI Adventures). Before you book, check whether any domestic flights involved are included in the fare.

All prices quoted in the box below exclude taxes and are subject to change. Accommodation is based on single person/double occupancy. Unless stated otherwise, round-trip flights are from Miami. Expect to pay supplements of roughly US$100–130 (from New York or Chicago), US$200–250 (from Los Angeles), and so on.

TOUR OPERATORS

Abercrombie & Kent International, Inc., 1520 Kensington Rd, Oak Brook, IL 60523 (☎630/954-2944 or 1-800/323-7308; *www.abercrombiekent.com*). *Upmarket South America packages plus independent travel service.*

Anglatin, Ltd, 132 E Broadway, Suite 733, Eugene, OR 97401 (☎541/344-7023 or 1-800/485-7842; *www.anglatin.com*). *Offers ten-day tours of Patagonia and the Lake District from US$1717 (land only), and a few educationally slanted packages such as the ten-day "Wineries, Wine & Cuisine" tour from US$2295 (land only).*

4th Dimension Tours, 7101 SW 99th Ave, Suite 106, Miami, FL 33173 (☎1-800/343-0020; *www.4thdimension.com*). *City breaks, cruises, ski packages and so on. Highlights include the nine-day "The Best of Chile" from US$2220 (land/air), skiing in Valle Nevado from US$1733 for nine days (land/air); seven-night cruise on the* Terra Australis *from US$1556 (cruise and local air from Santiago).*

International Gay Travel Association (☎1-800/448-8550). *Trade group with lists of gay-owned or gay-friendly travel agents, accommodations and other travel businesses.*

Mountain Travel Sobek, 6420 Fairmount Ave, El Cerrito, CA 94530 (☎1-888/MTSOBEK; *www.mtsobek.com*). *Trips to Chile which also take in Argentina, including the seventeen-day "Trekking the Paine Circuit" from US$2995, and the thirteen-day "Rafting the Bio-Bio" from US$2725 (both land only).*

Ponce de Leon Travel, 7325 W Flager St, Second Floor, Miami, FL 33144 (☎305/266-5827 or 1-800/826-4845). *Ski, spa, cruise and customized packages, including the three-day "Classic Santiago, Valparaíso and Viño del Mar" from US$217 (with optional horseback riding, river rafting, wine tasting extras), and a four-day trip to Easter Island from US$338 (both land only). This is one of the more interesting tour operators, though it doesn't have any of the US travel seals of approval (ASTA etc).*

REI Adventures, PO Box 1938, Sumner, WA 98390 (☎1-800/622-2236; *www.rei.com/travel*). *"A Hike in Patagonia" – twelve days from US$2295 (land only).*

Safaricentre, 3201 N Sepulveda Blvd, Manhattan Beach, CA 90266 (☎310/546-4411 or 1-800/624-5342 in California, ☎1-800/223-6046 rest of US, ☎1-800/233-6046 in Canada; *www.safaricentre.com*). *Wide range of packages, including a four-day Patagonian cruise from US$980; six days in the Atacama desert from US$995.*

Saga Road Scholar Tours, Saga International Holidays Ltd, 222 Berkeley St, Boston, MA 02116 (☎1-800/621-2151). *Learning adventures for senior travellers, such as "Chile: From Glacial Peaks to Pacific Shores" – 13 nights from US$2799 (land/air), with optional three-night extension to Easter Island for US$999.*

Wilderness Travel, 1102 Ninth St, Berkeley, CA 94710-1211 (☎510/558-2488 or 1-800/368-2794; *www.wildernesstravel.com*). *Argentina/Chile trips including the 16-day "Sea Kayaking in Tierra del Fuego" from US$2795, and "Pucón to Paine – Hiking in the Southern Andes" from US$2795 (both land only).*

INSURANCE

Before buying an **insurance policy**, check that you're not already covered. Some homeowners' or renters' policies are valid on vacation, and credit cards (particularly American Express) often include some medical or other insurance, while Canadian provincial health plans typically provide limited overseas medical coverage. Holders of official student/teacher/youth cards are entitled to accident coverage and hospital inpatient benefits – the annual membership is far less than the cost of comparable insurance. Students may also find that their student health coverage extends during the vacations and for one term beyond the date of last enrolment.

After exhausting the possibilities above, you might want to contact a specialist **travel insurance** company; your travel agent can usually recommend one, or see the box.

The best **premiums** are usually to be had through student/youth travel agencies – STA policies, for example, come in two forms: with or without medical coverage. The current rates are US$45/35 (for up to 7 days), US$60/45 (8–15 days), US$110/85 (1 month); US$140/115 (45 days); $165/135 (2 months); US$50/35 (for each extra month). If you're planning to do any "dangerous sports" (skiing, mountaineering, etc), be sure to ask whether these activities are covered: some companies levy a surcharge.

Most North American travel policies apply only to items lost, stolen or damaged while in the custody of an identifiable, responsible third party – hotel porter, airline, luggage consignment, etc. Even in these cases you will have to contact the local police within a certain time limit to have a complete report made out so that your insurer can process the claim.

TRAVEL INSURANCE COMPANIES

Access America ☎1-800/284-8300
Carefree Travel Insurance ☎1-800/323-3149
STA Travel ☎212/627-3111 or 1-800/777-0112
Travel Assistance International ☎1-800/821-2828
Travel Guard ☎1-800/826-1300
Travel Insurance Services ☎1-800/937-1387

GETTING THERE FROM BRITAIN AND IRELAND

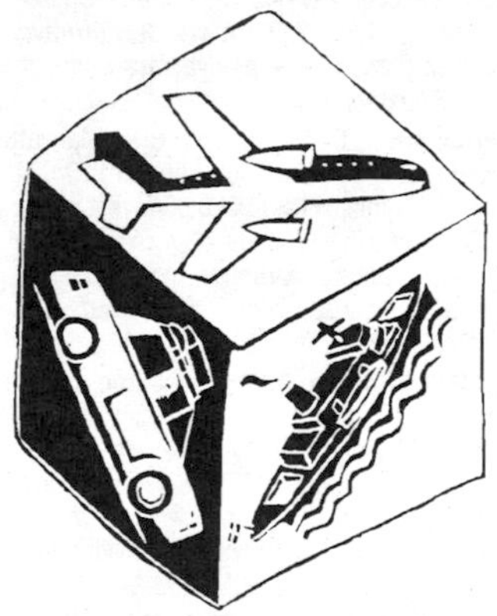

There was a time when the best way to get to Chile was on one of the regular passenger steamships from Liverpool to Valparaíso. These days, your only realistic option is to fly into Santiago. The most expensive time to travel is December, July and August; outside these months, most fares fall into the low-season bracket, with November being a particularly good time to look for special offers. In general, low-season return fares start from around £490, high-season fares from around £600.

FLIGHTS FROM BRITAIN

At least twelve airlines offer regular **scheduled flights** from Britain to Santiago. None of them is direct, and as a rule you'll have to choose between flying via another European city, or via the US (the latter is marginally cheaper). An important point to consider when shopping for tickets is that if you go directly through an airline you'll be offered what they call their "published fares", which are usually vastly more expensive than the "net fares" they sell to certain flight agents (known as consolidators). For instance, Air France's cheapest ticket is presently £1159 when booked through the airline itself, but around half that when booked through an agency; similarly, KLM's "published fares" start at £1000, while a ticket booked through an agency will cost around £570. In short, it's nearly always cheaper to book your flight through a **specialized or discount flight agency**. We've listed several in the box below, but it's also worth checking the travel sections of London's *Time Out* and the national Sunday newspapers, or phoning the Air Travel Advisory Bureau (☎0171/636 5000) for a list of discount agents. You should always shop around, though, as some agencies can offer exceptionally good one-off deals.

In addition to fares, it's also worth paying attention to the **routings** used by the different airlines – in particular, check how many stops are involved, and how long you'll have to spend in transit (note that transit in the US can be especially uncomfortable, often with limited toilet facilities and no access to the airport shops). The shortest and most convenient routings are offered by British Airways, which flies non-stop from London Gatwick to Buenos Aires, where you catch a connection to Santiago, and Iberia, which has recently introduced non-stop flights from Madrid to Santiago (a total travelling time of 16hr 35min with both airlines). Of the other European airlines, KLM has the least appealing routing, with stops in Amsterdam, Sao Paulo and Buenos Aires. Going via the US, United offers the worst connections, involving two stops, usually in Washington and Miami.

AIRLINES AND ROUTINGS

Aerolineas Argentinas, 54 Conduit St, London W1R 9FD (☎0171/494 1001; *www.aerolineas.com.ar*). *Daily flights to Santiago via Madrid and Buenos Aires, with free stopovers in the latter.*

Air France, 10 Warwick St, London W1R (☎0845 0845 111; from Eire ☎01/605 0383; *www.airfrance.fr*). *Flies four times a week from London, Birmingham, Manchester and Dublin, via Paris.*

American Airlines, 15 Berkeley St, London W1X 5AE (☎0345/789789); 54–57 Lower Mount St, Dublin 2 (☎01/602 0550); *www.aa.com. Daily flights to Santiago from London and Dublin via Miami, with possible alternative routings and stopovers in Newark, Chicago, Boston or Dallas.*

Avianca, Linen Hall, Suite 246, 162–168 Regent St, London W1R 5TA (☎0990/767747; from Eire ☎01/280 2641; *www.avianca.com.co*). *Columbian airline, flying non-stop from London to Bogotá, where you overnight (and can stopover) followed by a non-stop flight to Santiago.*

British Airways (☎0345/222111; from Eire ☎0141/222 2345; *www.british-airways.com*). *Three or four flights a week from London Gatwick to Buenos Aires, then on to Santiago. Booking through central reservations is very expensive; it's cheaper to go through its subsidiary company, British Airways Travel Shops (see box overleaf).*

Continental, First Floor, Beulah Court, Albert Road, Horley, Surrey RH6 7HP (☎0800/776464; from Eire ☎1800/321324; *www.continental.com*). *Daily flights from London, Glasgow, Manchester, Birmingham, Dublin and Shannon to Newark, New Jersey (free stopovers), where you catch a connection to Santiago. Transit can be lengthy.*

Iberia, Venture House, 27–29 Glasshouse St, London W1R 6SU (☎0171/830 0011 or 0990/341341); 54 Dawson St, Dubin 2 (☎01/677 9846); *www.iberia.com. Non-stop flights from Madrid to Santiago, four times a week, with connections from London, Manchester and Dublin. One free stopover allowed.*

KLM, ticket office at Terminal 4, Heathrow (☎0990/750900; *www.klm.nl*). *Three flights a week, via Amsterdam, Sao Paulo and Buenos Aires. The advantage is that you can fly to Amsterdam from 21 points in the UK and Ireland.*

Lan Chile, Premiere House, 3 Betts Way, Crawley, West Sussex RH10 2GB (☎01293/596607; *www.lanchile.cl*). *Daily flights from London, Manchester and Birmingham via Madrid, sometimes entailing a long wait in Madrid.*

Lufthansa, 7–8 Conduit St, London W1R 9TG (☎0345/737747; from Eire ☎01/844 5444; *www.lufthansa.co.uk*). *Flies five times a week from London or Dublin via Frankfurt and Buenos Aires.*

United Airlines, 7–8 Conduit St, London W1R 9TG (☎0845/844 4777; *www.ual.com*). *Two flights a day from London; rather a long haul, via Washington and Miami. Stopovers cost £25.*

Varig Brazilian Airlines, 61 Conduit St, London W1R 0HG (☎0171/287 3131; *www.varig.com.br*). *Four times a week from London, via Río or Sao Paulo, with stopovers en route.*

Apart from trying to minimize the length of the flight, another reason to scrutinize the routings is that many airlines allow you to break your journey and take **stopovers** on the way – sometimes for free, sometimes for a charge of around £25 to £50. Interesting potential stopovers include Buenos Aires (Aerolineas Argentinas), Bogotá (Avianca), Sao Paulo or Río (Varig) in South America; Newark, Boston, Chicago, Miami, Dallas and Washington (American, Continental and United) in the USA; and Madrid (Iberia, Lan Chile) and Paris (Air France) in Europe.

While considering the merits of the various airlines, however, you should bear in mind that if you plan to take **internal flights** or buy an **airpass** for travel in Chile (see below), then it may be worth your while flying to Santiago with Lan Chile, which offers discounts on internal flights and airpasses when bought in the UK in conjunction with a transatlantic ticket. Also, if you plan to visit Easter Island, note that your ticket there from Santiago will be considerably cheaper when bought in conjunction with a Lan Chile transatlantic flight (see p.425).

AIR PASSES

Given the immense distances involved in travelling through Chile, it makes a lot of sense to buy an airpass – this way you can cover virtually the whole country, from Arica to Punta Arenas, with-

FLIGHT AND DISCOUNT AGENTS

Apex Travel, 59 Dame St, Dublin 2 (☎01/671 5933). *General budget fares agent.*

British Airways Travel Shops, 156 Regent St, W1R 6LB (☎0171/434 4700); 1 Fountain Centre, Fountain St, Belfast BT1 6ET (☎01232/326566); with branches nationwide. *A subsidiary of British Airways, but classed as a travel agency and so able to offer special discount fares.*

Flight Finders International, 13 Baggot St Lower, Dublin 2 (☎01/676 8326). *Helpful and reliable discount fare outlet.*

Joe Walsh Tours, 69 Upper O'Connell St, Dublin 2 (☎01/872 2555); 8–11 Baggot St, Dublin 2 (☎01/676 3053); 117 Patrick St, Cork (☎021/277959). *Long-established, efficient specialist in discount flights.*

Journey Latin America, 12–13 Heathfield Terrace, Chiswick, London W4 4JE (☎0181/747 8315); 51–63 Deansgate, Manchester M3 2BH (☎0161/832 1441); *www.journeylatinamerica.co.uk. Knowledgeable and helpful staff, good at sorting out stopovers and open-jaw flights. Also does package tours (see opposite).*

The London Flight Centre, 131 Earls Court Rd, London SW5 9RH (☎0171/244 6411); 47 Notting Hill Gate, London W11 3JS (☎0171/727 4290); Shop 33, The Broadway Centre, Hammersmith Tube, London W6 9YE (☎0181/748 6777). *Discount flights around the world.*

Major Travel, 28–34 Fortress Rd, London NW5 2HB (☎0171/393 1060). *Reliable discount agent, often with very low fares to Santiago.*

North South Travel, Moulsham Mill Centre, Parkway, Chelmsford, Essex CM2 7PX (☎01245/492882). *Friendly, competitive travel agency, offering discounted fares worldwide – profits are used to support projects in the developing world.*

Passage to South America, Fovant Mews, 12 Noyna Rd, London SW17 7PH (☎0181/767 8989). *Good South American specialist, offering low-cost fares and helpful advice.*

South American Experience, 47 Causton St, London SW1P 4AT (☎0171/976 5511). *Mainly a discount flight agent but also offers a range of tours, plus a very popular "soft landing package".*

STA Travel, 38 Store St, London WC1E 7BZ (☎0171/361 6262; *www.statravel.co.uk*), with branches nationwide. *Worldwide specialist in low-cost flights and tours, with special discounts for students and under-26s.*

Trailfinders, 42–50 Earls Court Rd, London W8 6FT (☎0171/938 3366); 4–5 Dawson St, Dublin 2 (☎01/677 7888), with branches nationwide. *Long-established flight agent offering a wide range of cheap fares.*

Usit Campus, 52 Grosvenor Gardens, London SW1W 0AG (☎0171/730 8111; *www.usitcampus.co.uk*), with branches nationwide. *Student/youth travel specialist, with outlets also in YHA shops and on university campuses all over Britain.*

Usit Now, Fountain Centre, College St, Belfast BT1 6ET (☎01232/324073); 19 Aston Quay, Dublin 2 (☎01/602 1777 or 677 8117), with branches across Ireland. *Student and youth specialist, though other customers are also welcome.*

out the interminably long bus journeys. Lan Chile's "Visit Chile" airpass lasts for a month and allows you to take three internal Lan Chile or Ladeco flights anywhere in the country, with the option of buying up to three extra flights. The pass can only be bought outside South America; if you buy it in conjunction with a Lan Chile transatlantic flight, it's exceptionally good value at US$250, plus US$60 per extra flight; if you're flying to Chile with another airline, the pass costs US$350, plus US$80 per extra flight. (The pass is priced in US dollars and converted to sterling according to the day's exchange rate.) You have to specify the route and dates of travel when you buy the pass, but you can change the flight dates and times when you're out there at no extra cost. If, however, you need to change the routing there's a charge of US$30 per change.

PACKAGES AND ORGANIZED TOURS

There's no denying that independent travel in Chile requires a certain amount of forward-planning, particularly if you want to cover a large area of the country in a relatively short trip. If time's tight, or you simply don't want the hassle of organizing everything yourself, you can arrange everything before you go with a number of excellent, knowledgeable specialists – such as Journey Latin America or South American Experience – who'll put together a package for you including flights, transfers, accommodation and excursions.

SPECIALIST TOUR OPERATORS

Austral Tours, 120 Wilton Rd, London SW1V 1JZ (☎0171/233 5384). *Small company offering a seventeen-day tour in northern and southern Chile, plus tailor-made itineraries. Especially good at organizing special interest holidays, based around wine tours, fishing, trekking and archeology.*

Dragoman, 98 Camp Green, Debenham, Stowmarket, Suffolk IP14 6LA (☎01728/861127; *www.dragoman.co.uk*). *A range of South American overland trips, including a new line with all accommodation in hotels rather than in tents. Regular slide shows in London.*

Encounter Overland, 267 Old Brompton Rd, London SW5 9JA (☎0171/370 6845; *www.encounter.co.uk*). *One of the oldest overland companies going; its programme includes a nine-week trip from Santiago to Quito.*

Exodus, 9 Weir Rd, London SW12 0LT (☎0181/675 5550; *www.exodustravels.co.uk*). *Well-run, small-group trekking holidays in southern Chile and Argentina, plus a number of overland trips that include Chile in the itinerary.*

Explore Worldwide, 1 Frederick St, Aldershot, Hants GU11 1LQ (☎01252/319448; *www.explore.co.uk*). *Reasonably priced group tours in Chile's far south and Lake District.*

Guerba Expeditions, Wessex House, 40 Station Rd, Westbury, Wiltshire BA13 3JN (☎01373/826611). *UK branch of Canadian GAP Adventures, whose programme includes a three-week tour of southern Chile and Argentina.*

Hayes and Jarvis, Hayes House, 152 King St, London W6 0QU (☎0181/222 7844). *This well-known tour operator offers a two-week tour of southern Chile and Argentina, with the option of a five-day extension to northern Chile.*

Journey Latin America (see opposite for addresses). *Long-established company offering a range of unescorted packages, small-group trips with a tour leader, and tailor-made itineraries; covers both the north and south of Chile. Fairly expensive, but of a very high standard.*

Passage to South America (see opposite for address). *Specializes in organizing tailor-made holidays, and also offers a useful three-night accommodation package for your arrival in Santiago.*

South American Experience (see opposite for address). *Organizes flights, tailor-made packages, local excursions (such as to Santiago's vineyards) and offers an excellent "soft landing package" which includes three nights' accommodation and airport transfer on arrival.*

Tucan Travel, Top Deck House, 131–135 Earls Court Rd, London SW5 9RH (☎0171/370 4555). *Group holidays in southern Chile and Argentina, plus a range of overland expeditions in South America.*

World Expeditions, 4 Northfields Prospect, Putney Bridge Rd, London SW18 1PE (☎0181/870 2600; *www.worldexpeditions.com.au*). *UK branch of the very professional Australian tour company, offering a range of trekking, climbing and photographic tours in Chile and Argentina, plus adventure cruises to Antarctica.*

This inevitably works out more expensive than if you did everything on your own, but it does cut down on potential hitches and delays. Other package options include travelling with an escorted group, taking an overland tour (in huge trucks – usually as part of a longer trip through South America) and, perhaps the most rewarding, special-interest tours incorporating activities like trekking, bird-watching, wine-tasting and mountain-biking.

INSURANCE

It's essential to have **travel insurance** to cover loss of possessions and money as well as the cost of all medical and dental treatment. Bank and credit cards (particularly American Express) often have certain levels of medical or other insurance included, especially if you use them to pay for your trip. Note that very few insurers will arrange on-the-spot payments in the event of a major expense or loss; you'll usually be reimbursed only after going home, so keep all receipts and official papers. In all cases of loss or theft of goods, you should contact the local police to have a report made out so that your insurer can process the claim.

Travel insurance schemes (basic cover for Chile starts from around £35 a month, fully comprehensive cover from around £55) are sold by almost every travel agent or bank, and by **specialist insurance companies**. Cover varies, but a standard policy will cover the cost of cancellation and curtailment of flights, medical expenses, travel delay, accident, missed departures, lost baggage, lost passport, personal liability and legal expenses. Before you take out a policy, it's worth checking out the "all risks" section of your **home contents insurance** (if you have one), as these often cover items like photographic equipment for loss or theft abroad, which will save you paying additional premiums on your travel insurance. Also, if you have a **Barclaycard** and use it to pay for your flights, ask for details of its "Travel Accident Insurance and International Rescue" service, which can help provide emergency cash. In additional to the specialist companies listed below, check out the policies offered by Journey Latin America, Campus Travel and STA Travel (see p.8).

UK TRAVEL INSURANCE COMPANIES

Columbus, 17 Devonshire Square, London EC2M 4SQ (☎0171/375 0011).

Endsleigh Insurance, Cranfield House, 97–107 Southampton Row, London WC1B 4AG (☎0171/436 4451).

Inter Assurance, 16 West St, Farnham, Surrey GU9 7DR (☎0800/9171091).

Marcus Hearne & Co Ltd, 65–66 Shoreditch High St, London E1 6JL (☎0171/739 3444).

Worldwide, The Business Centre, 1–7 Commercial Rd, Tonbridge, Kent TN12 6YT (☎01892/833338).

GETTING THERE FROM AUSTRALIA AND NEW ZEALAND

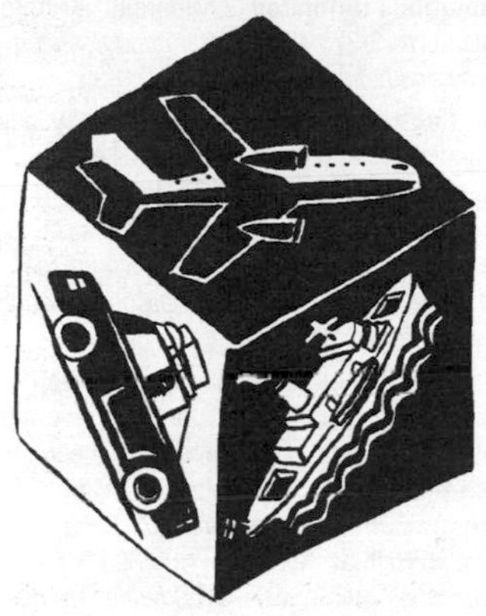

Although there are only a couple of airlines that fly to Santiago, the going is pretty straightforward – all follow the same route across the Pacific and cost much the same –with Qantas, Air New Zealand and Ansett Airlines teaming up with Lan Chile and Aerolineas Argentinas to offer several flights a week via Auckland, Papeete and Easter Island. As flying time is around 20 hours you may want to take advantage of the free stopover allowed each way.

Tickets purchased direct from the airlines can often work out more expensive than a round-the-world (RTW) fare. Travel agents offer the best deals and have the latest information on limited special offers, such as free stopovers and fly-drive/accommodation packages. Flight Centres and STA (which offer fare reductions for ISIC cardholders and under 26s) generally offer the lowest fares and can also assist with visas.

Airfares vary throughout the year, and depend on both the season (defined as high from December to February, and low the rest of the year) – generally working out between A/NZ$200–300 – and duration of stay (tickets are available for 21 days, 45 days, ninety days, six months and one year, with 45- and ninety-day tickets the best value for money).

Seat availability on most international flights out of Australia and New Zealand is often limited, so it's best to book several weeks ahead.

FROM AUSTRALIA

Most flights are out of Sydney (you'll pay the same from Melbourne, Canberra and Brisbane, but expect to pay A$150–200 more from Cairns, Adelaide and Hobart and A$300–500 more from Perth and Darwin).

The lowest fares are with Air New Zealand–Lan Chile whose 45-day tickets cost between A$1670 and A$1899 depending on season, with 90-day tickets costing A$2470–2799; and Ansett–Aerolineas which charges A$1699–1950 for 45 days and A$1950–2150 for 90 days. Qantas–Lan Chile/Qantas–Aerolineas fares are marginally higher at A$1710–1999 for 45 days and A$2199–2499 for 90 days.

FROM NEW ZEALAND

Flights generally leave from Auckland, with 45-day fares on both Air New Zealand–Lan Chile/Aerolineas priced from NZ$1699–1999, depending on season. However the best 90-day deals are with Aerolineas (NZ$1999), while Air New Zealand–Lan Chile are quite a bit more at NZ$2399–2699.

AIR PASSES

If you intend to cover a fair amount of the country there are several **air passes** that can be purchased with your international ticket. Lan Chile's "Visit Chile Pass", for example, can be used for internal flights between Santiago, Arica, Iquique, Antofagasta, Temuco, Puerto Montt and Punta Arenas. It is valid for one month, and you have to buy at least three coupons, but no more than six, before you leave your home country. The price (priced in US dollars and converted according to the day's exchange rate) is US$250 for the first three coupons, then US$60 for each additional coupon, as long as your international ticket is with Lan Chile; travelling with another airline means you'll pay US$350 for the first three and US$80 for each additional coupon.

ROUND-THE-WORLD TICKETS

If you intend to take in Chile as part of a world trip, a round-the-world (**RTW**) ticket offers the

AIRLINES AND ROUTINGS

Aerolineas Argentinas Australia (☎02/9283 3660); NZ (☎09/379 3675). *Twice-weekly flights from Auckland via Papeete, Easter Island and Buenos Aires: team up with Qantas/Ansett from major cities in Australia via Sydney.*

Air New Zealand Australia (☎13 2476); NZ (☎09/357 3000). *Three flights a week to Santiago from major cities in Australasia via Auckland, Papeete and Easter Island.*

Ansett Airlines Australia (☎13 1767); NZ (☎09/307 5378). *Several flights a week to Auckland from major cities in Australia, with onward connections to Santiago via Papeete and Easter Island on Aerolineas.*

Lan Chile Airlines Australia (☎02/9299 5599 or 1800/221 572); NZ (☎09/309 8673). *Twice-weekly flights to Santiago from Auckland via Papeete and Easter Island: team up with Qantas/Air New Zealand from major cities in Australia.*

Qantas Australia (☎13 1211); NZ (☎09/357 8900 or 0800/808 767). *Several connecting flights a week from major cities in Australia to Auckland: with onward connections to Santiago via Papeete and Easter Island on Lan Chile/Aerolineas*

DISCOUNT TRAVEL AGENTS

Anywhere Travel, 345 Anzac Parade, Kingsford, Sydney (☎02/9663 0411). *General airfare discounters.*

Budget Travel, 16 Fort St, Auckland (☎09/379 2099 or 1800/808 040); other branches around the country. *Established airfare discounter.*

Destinations Unlimited, 3 Milford Rd, Milford, Auckland (☎09/373 4033). *Offer good deals on airfares and holidays.*

Flight Centres Australia: Circular Quay, Sydney, plus branches nationwide (☎13 1600); NZ: National Bank Towers, 205–225 Queen St, Auckland (☎09/309 6171); plus branches countrywide. *Generally the best discounts worldwide, good range of London tours and accommodation. Friendly helpful staff.*

STA Travel Australia: 732 Harris St, Ultimo, Sydney; 256 Flinders St, Melbourne; other offices instate capitals and major universities (nearest branch ☎13 1776, fastfare telesales ☎1300/360 960; *www.statravelaus.com.au*). NZ: Travellers Centre, 10 High St, Auckland (☎09/309 0458); and branches countrywide. *Worldwide fare discounts for independent travellers, students and under-26 discounts.*

Thomas Cook, 175 Pitt St, Sydney; 257 Collins St, Melbourne; plus branches in other state capitals (nearest local branch ☎13 1771); NZ: 96 Anzac Ave, Auckland (☎09/379 3920); and branches throughout Australia and New Zealand. *Good range of tours.*

Trailfinders, 8 Spring St, Sydney (☎02/9247 7666); 91 Elizabeth St, Brisbane (☎07/3229 0887). *Specializing in low cost airfares and accommodation.*

Tymtro Travel, Level 8, 130 Pitt St, Sydney (☎502/9223 2211 or 1300/652 969). *Competitive discounts on fares and holidays.*

best value for money. Lan Chile and Aerolineas combine with numerous airlines and allow four stops within South America including Santiago, from A$2199/NZ$2499 to A$3299/NZ$3699. A typical itinerary would take you, in addition to Sydney, Auckland, Papeete and Easter Island, via either Kuala Lumpur/Bangkok/Hong Kong, Los Angeles, London, Frankfurt/Vienna, Buenos Aires and Rio.

TOUR OPERATORS

If you prefer to have all the arrangements made for you before you leave, the specialist **tour operators** in the box opposite can help you plan your trip – from booking a few nights' accommodation in Santiago to arranging fully escorted Chilean wilderness trips to the northern desert regions or south to Patagonia and the Lake District. Most tours don't include airfares from Australasia, though specialists can usually assist with flight arrangements. In turn, many of the tours opposite can also be arranged through your local travel agent.

INSURANCE

Travel insurance is available from most travel agents (see opposite) or direct from insurance companies for periods ranging from a few days

TOUR OPERATORS

Adventure Associates, 197 Oxford St, Bondi Junction, NSW (☎1800/222 141). *Independent and escorted small-group tours, city stopovers and cruises around Chilean Patagonia* and a *selection of archeological/natural history tours from Santiago.*

Adventure Specialists, 69 Liverpool St, Sydney 2000 (☎02/9261 2927 or 1800/634 465). *Agents for a myriad of adventure wholesalers with interests throughout South America.*

Adventure World, 73 Walker St, Sydney (☎02/9956 7766 or 1800/221 931); branches in Melbourne, Brisbane, Adelaide and Perth; 101 Great South Rd, Remuera, Auckland (☎09/524 5118). *Agents for a number of wholesalers who can arrange accommodation, air passes, tours and cruises in Chile as well as three-day stopovers in Easter Island from A$292 twin-share.*

Contours, 466 Victoria St, North Melbourne 3051 (☎1800/331 378). *Specialists in tailored city stopover packages and tours, including self-drive tours through the Lake District and a ten-day budget tour of Patagonia using local buses and staying in cheap to mid-range hotels. Prices start at A$1500 twin-share.*

Peregrine, Second Floor, 258 Lonsdale St, Melbourne (☎1800/331 124); 132 Wickham St, Fortitude Valley, Brisbane (☎07/3854 1022); First Floor, 862 Hay St, Perth (☎08/9321 1259); NZ agent Adventure World (see above). *Established adventure company and agents for a variety of wholesalers who operate extended small group tours through South America, with accommodation in tents, huts or basic village hotels (from A$3655). Also seventeen-day wine tours of Chile visiting the growing districts of Cachapoal, Maipo and Maul.*

Pride Travel, 254 Bay St, Brighton, Melbourne (☎03/9596 3566 or 1800/061 427; Sydney ☎1800/808 698). *Lesbian and gay operator which can tailor specific holidays.*

South American Experts, 82 Elizabeth St, Sydney (☎02/9235 3522). *Can arrange airfares, accommodation, group and independent tours and travel.*

South American Adventures, 169 Unley Rd, Unley, Adelaide (☎08/8272 2010). *Experienced in general travel to and around Chile.*

The Surf Travel Co., 2/25 Cronulla Plaza, Cronulla Beach, Sydney (☎02/9527 4722 or 1800/687 873); 7 Danbury Drive, Torbay, Auckland (☎09/473 8388); *www.surftravel.com.au. A well-established surf company that arranges holidays at the best surf beaches.*

World Expeditions, Level 3, 441 Kent St, Sydney 2000 (☎02/9264 3366), also branches in Melbourne and Brisbane. *Offer a number of adventure walking holidays from A$5295.*

to a year or even longer. Most policies are similar in premium and coverage – but if you plan to indulge in high-risk activities such as mountaineering, bungee jumping or scuba diving, check the policy carefully to make sure you'll be covered.

A typical policy for Chile will cost: A$130/NZ$145 for two weeks, A$190/NZ$210 for a month or A$280/NZ$310 for two months.

TRAVEL INSURANCE COMPANIES

Cover More, 9/32 Walker St, North Sydney (☎02/9202 8000 or 1800/251 881).

Ready Plan, 141 Walker St, Dandenong, Melbourne (☎03/9791 5077 or 1800/337 462); 10/63 Albert St, Auckland (☎09/379 3208).

UTAG, 122 Walker St, North Sydney (☎02/9956 8399 or 1800/809 462).

RED TAPE AND VISAS

Most foreign visitors to Chile do not need a visa, with the exception of citizens of New Zealand (at a cost of NZ$87) and a small number of other countries including Cuba, Russia and African countries – check with your local Chilean consulate. If you *do* need one, you'll have to submit an application to your consulate, along with your passport and a full written itinerary.

> **ARRIVAL TAX**
>
> Chile has introduced an arrival tax for American (US$45), Canadian (US$50) and Australian (US$20) citizens in reciprocation of similar taxes levied on Chilean citizens arriving in these countries.

Visitors of all nationalities are issued with a **tourist entry card** (*Tarjeta de Turismo*) on arrival in Chile, which is valid for ninety days, and can be extended once for a further ninety days. It will be checked by the International Police at the airport or border post when you leave Chile – if it's expired you won't be allowed to leave the country until you've paid the appropriate fine at the nearest Intendencia (up to US$100 depending on the number of days past the expiry date). If this happens when you're trying to fly out of the international airport in Santiago, you'll have to go back downtown to Moneda 1342 (Mon–Fri 9am–1pm; ☎2/672 5320). If at any time during your stay in Chile you **lose** your card, you should ask for a duplicate immediately either from the Fronteras department of the Policía Internacional, General Borgoño 1052, Santiago (☎2/698 2211) or from the Extranjería department of the Intendencia in any provincial capital (addresses are in the box below). There's no charge for replacing lost or stolen cards. If, however, you want to **extend** it, you've got two choices. You can either pay US$100 and have it extended at the Intendencia of Santiago or any provincial capital. Or you can simply leave the country and re-enter, getting a brand new ninety-day *Tarjeta de Turismo* for free. The latter is usually far cheaper and certainly more interesting – from Santiago, for instance, you could take the very scenic seven-hour bus ride to Mendoza in Argentina, and there are many other opportunities for border crossing up and down Chile.

Note that a tourist card does not allow you to undertake any **paid employment** in Chile – for

> **INTENDENCIAS**
>
> **Antofagasta**: Arturo Prat 384 (☎55/281260, fax 266055)
>
> **Concepción**: Aníbal Pinto 442 (☎41/225347, fax 230247)
>
> **Copiapó**: Los Carrera s/n (☎52/212727, fax 212460)
>
> **Coyhaique**: Plaza 485 (☎67/231000, fax 231494)
>
> **Iquique**: Costanera s/n (☎57/426106, fax 424244)
>
> **La Serena**: Arturo Prat 350 (☎51/224421, fax 212190)
>
> **Puerto Montt**: Décima Región 480 (☎65/252720)
>
> **Punta Arenas**: Bories 901 (☎61/221675)
>
> **Rancagua**: Plaza de los Héroes (☎72/225781, fax 222528)
>
> **Santiago**: Moneda 1342 (☎2/672 5320, fax 698 0510)
>
> **Talca**: 1 Oriente 1190 (☎71/225965, fax 225060)
>
> **Temuco**: Bulnes 590 (☎45/212616, fax 213064)
>
> **Valparaíso**: Melgarejo 669, Eighteenth Floor (☎32/213047, fax 212679

this, you need to get a work visa before you enter the country, which can either be arranged by your employer in Chile, or by yourself on presentation (to your embassy or consulate) of an employment contract authorized by a Chilean public notary. You can't swap a tourist card for a work visa while you're out there, which means that legally you can't just go out and find a job – though many language schools are happy to ignore the rules when employing language teachers. Other points to note are that **under-18s** travelling to Chile without parents need written parental consent authorized by the Chilean Embassy, and that minors travelling to Chile with just one parent need the written, authorized consent of the absent parent.

CHILEAN EMBASSIES AND CONSULATES ABROAD

AUSTRALIA

Embassy: 10 Culgoa Circuit, O'Malley, ACT 2606 (☎02/6286 2430).

Consulate: Level 18, National Mutual Building, 44 Market St, Sydney 2000 (☎02/9299 2533).

CANADA

Embassy: 50 O'Connor St #1413, Ottawa, ON K1P 6L2 (☎613/235-4402).

Consulates: 2 Bloor St W, #1801, Toronto, ON M4W 3E2 (☎416/924-0106); 1010 Sherbrooke St W #710, Montréal, PQ H3A 2R7 (☎514/499-0405); 1185 W Georgia St, #1250, Vancouver, BC V6E 4E6 (☎604/681-9162).

NEW ZEALAND

Embassy: 19 Bolton St, Wellington (☎04/471 6270).

UK

Embassy and Consulate: 12 Devonshire St, London W1N 2DS (☎0171/580 6392).

US

Embassy: 1732 Massachusetts Ave, Washington, DC 20036 (☎202/785-1746 or 785-1747).

Consulates: 1732 Massachusetts Ave, Washington, DC 20036 (☎202/785-3159); Public Ledger Building, Suite 444, Chestnut & Sixth St, Philadelphia, PA 19106 (☎215/829-9520); 1360 Post Oak Blvd, Suite 2330, Houston, TX 77056 (☎713/963-9066); 875 N Michigan Ave, Suite 3352, Chicago, IL 60611 (☎312/654-8780); 1110 Brickell Ave, Miami, FL 33131 (☎305/373-8623); 866 United Nations Plaza #302, New York, NY 10017 (☎212/355-0612); 870 Market St #1062, San Francisco, CA 94102 (☎415/982-7662).

MAPS, INFORMATION AND WEB SITES

Chile maintains no tourist offices abroad, but you can sometimes get limited tourist information, including a glossy manual, at the Chilean Embassy in many countries. Alternatively, some of the tour companies who specialize in the region, like South American Experience or Exodus (see p.9), prepare fact sheets on the countries they visit, and their brochures will at least give you an idea of what the main tourist attractions look like. Another good source of information is the *Chile Information Pack* produced by the South American Explorers' Club (a US-run non-profit organization that provides services to travellers in South America); it costs US$6.50 for non-members and US$4.50 for members, and can be paid for by credit card using the club's online order form (*www.samexplo.org*) or by fax (607/277 6122). One of the best ways of getting pre-trip information is via the Internet, with a number of Web sites offering hard facts, titbits and question-and-answer forums. Finally, you can buy maps before you go (see box opposite for a list of retailers), though you'll find a better selection in Santiago.

TOURIST INFORMATION

Chile's government-run tourist board is called **Sernatur** (short for Servicio Nacional de Turismo). There's a large and very helpful office in Santiago (see p.69), plus branches in every provincial capital in Chile. They produce a huge amount of material, including themed booklets on camping, skiing, national parks, beaches, thermal springs and so on; for some reason these are often kept out of sight, so you'll have to specifically ask to see everything they've got. In smaller towns you're more likely to find a municipal **Oficina de Turismo**, sometimes attached to the Municipalidad (town hall), and usually with a very limited supply of printed information to hand out. If there's no separate tourist office it's worth trying the **Municipalidad** itself – it sometimes stocks a few maps and leaflets, and at the very least can deliver over-the-counter advice. Another source of information is the excellent series of **Turistel guidebooks**, published annually by the Chilean phone company, CTC, and available at numerous pavement kiosks in Santiago and CTC offices in Chilean cities. They come in three volumes, covering the north, the centre and the south, and give extremely detailed information on even the tiniest of places, with comprehensive street plans and road maps. Unfortunately they're not translated into English, though some kiosks in Santiago still sell copies of the one-off translation made in 1992.

MAPS

No two **road maps** of Chile are identical, and none is absolutely correct. The bulk of errors lie in the representation of dirt roads; some maps mark them incorrectly as tarred roads, some miss a random selection of dirt roads out altogether, and some mark them quite clearly where nothing exists at all. Most drivers end up using two or three different maps, cross-referencing them to spot the errors. The most reliable and complete road map is probably the one produced by **Turistel**, printed in the back of its guides to Chile (see above) and also published in a separate booklet. **Sernatur** produces a good fold-out map of the whole of Chile, called the *Gran Mapa Caminero de Chile*, on sale at the main office in Santiago, and an excellent map of the north, called the *Mapa Rutero Turístico Macroregión Norte*, free from Sernatur offices in Santiago and the north (ask, as they're rarely on display). Other useful maps include Auto Mapa's *Rutas de Chile*, and Lonely Planet's *Road Atlas of Chile*, both distributed internationally.

MAP AND GUIDE OUTLETS

As well as over-the-counter sales, most of the outlets listed below allow you to order and pay for maps by mail, over the phone and sometimes via the Internet.

AUSTRALIA AND NEW ZEALAND

The Map Shop, 16a Peel St, Adelaide, SA 5000 (☎08/8231 2033).

Mapland, 372 Little Bourke St, Melbourne, VIC 3000 (☎03/9670 4383).

Perth Map Centre, 884 Hay St, Perth, WA 6000 (☎08/9322 5733).

Specialty Maps, 58 Albert St, Auckland (☎09/307 2217).

Travel Bookshop, Shop 3, 175 Liverpool St, Sydney, NSW 2000 (☎02/9261 8200).

Worldwide Maps and Guides, 187 George St, Brisbane (☎07/3221 4330).

UK AND IRELAND

Blackwell's Map and Travel Shop, 53 Broad St, Oxford OX1 3BQ (☎01865/792792; *www.blackwell.co.uk*).

Daunt Books, 83 Marylebone High St, London W1M 3DE (☎0171/224 2295); 193 Haverstock Hill, London NW3 4QL (☎0171/794 4006).

Easons Bookshop, 40 O'Connell St, Dublin 1 (☎01/873 3811).

Fred Hanna's Bookshop, 27–29 Nassau St, Dublin 2 (☎01/677 4754).

Heffers Map Shop, 3rd Floor, Heffers Stationery Department, 19 Sidney St, Cambridge CB2 3HL (☎01223/568467; *www.heffers.co.uk*).

James Thin Melven's Bookshop, 29 Union St, Inverness IV1 1QA (☎01463/233500; *www.jthin.co.uk*).

John Smith and Sons, 57–61 St Vincent St, Glasgow, G2 5TB (☎0141/221 7472; *www.johnsmith.co.uk*).

The Map Shop, 30a Belvoir St, Leicester LE1 6QH (☎0116/247 1400).

National Map Centre, 22–24 Caxton St, London SW1H 0QU (☎0171/222 2466; *www.mapsworld.com*).

Newcastle Map Centre, 55 Grey St, Newcastle upon Tyne NE1 6EF (☎0191/261 5622).

Stanfords, 12–14 Long Acre, London WC2E 9LP (☎0171/836 1321); Campus Travel, 52 Grosvenor Gardens, London SW1W 0AG (☎0171/730 1314); British Airways, 156 Regent St, London W1R 5TA (☎0171/434 4744); 29 Corn St, Bristol BS1 1HT (☎0117/929 9966); *sales@stanfords.co.uk*

The Travel Bookshop, 13–15 Blenheim Crescent, London W11 2EE (☎0171/229 5260; *www.thetravelbookshop.co.uk*).

USA AND CANADA

ADC Map and Travel Centre, 1636 lSt NW, Washington, DC 20006 (☎202/628-2608 or 1-800/544-2659).

Book Passage, 51 Tamal Vista Blvd, Corte Madera, CA 94925 (☎415/927-0960).

The Complete Traveler 3207 Fillmore St, San Francisco, CA 94123 (☎415/923-1511; *www.completetraveler.com*).

The Complete Traveller Bookstore, 199 Madison Ave, New York, NY 10016 (☎212/685-9007).

Elliot Bay Book Company, 101 S Main St, Seattle, WA 98104 (☎206/624-6600 or 1-800/962-5311; *www.elliotbaybook.com\ebbco*\).

Forsyth Travel Library, 226 Westchester Ave, White Plains, NY 10604 (☎1-800/367-7984).

International Travel Maps & Books, 552 Seymour St, Vancouver, BC V6B 3J6 (☎604/687-3320; *www.itmb.com*).

Map Link Inc., 30 S La Patera Lane, Unit 5, Santa Barbara, CA 93117 (☎805/692-6777; *www.maplink.com*).

Open Air Books and Maps, 25 Toronto St, Toronto, ON M5C 2R1 (☎416/363-0719).

Phileas Fogg's Books & Maps, #87 Stanford Shopping Center, Palo Alto, CA 94304 (☎1-800/533-FOGG; *www.foggs.com*).

Rand McNally, 444 N Michigan Ave, Chicago, IL 60611 (☎312/321-1751); *www.randmcnally-store.com* **Note**: *Rand McNally now has more than 20 stores across the US; call ☎1-800/234-0679 for the address of your nearest store, or for direct mail maps.*

Sierra Club Bookstore, 6014 College Ave, Oakland, CA 94618 (☎510/658-7470; *www.sierraclubbookstore.com*).

Travel Books & Language Center, 4437 Wisconsin Ave, Washington, DC 20016 (☎1-800/220-2665).

Traveller's Bookstore, 22 W 52nd St, New York, NY 10019 (☎212/664-0995 or 1-800/755-8728; *www.travellersbookstore.com*).

Ulysses Travel Bookshop, 4176 St-Denis, Montréal H2W 2M5 (☎514/843- 9447; *www.ulysses.ca*).

You can pick up free and usually adequate **street plans** in the tourist office of most cities, but better by far are those contained in the Turistel guidebooks, with a map for practically every town and village you're likely to want to visit. You can buy street-indexed maps of Santiago from bookshops and kiosks, but the most comprehensive A–Z of Santiago appears in the back of the CTC phone directory.

The Instituto Geográfico Militar produces 1:50,000 **topographic maps**, but these can only be bought from its office at Dieciocho 369 in Santiago. They're very expensive too, at about US$15 each – a cheaper alternative is to photocopy A4-size sections of them in the map room of Santiago's Biblioteca Nacional (see p.80). Another problem with the IGM maps is that footpaths are rarely marked. Instead, the best ones to use for **hiking** are the new series of JLM maps (*jmattassi@interactiva.cl*), which cover some of the main national parks, produced in collaboration with Conaf, and available in bookshops and some souvenir or outdoor stores.

WEB SITES

Chile has embraced the **Internet** with much enthusiasm, and any Web search on "Chile" will produce thousands of matches. We've listed a few of them below, but these are really just a starting point for what can easily turn into hours of surfing.

WEB SITES

Chilean Patagonia *www.chileaustral.com* Easy-to-use site dedicated to tourism in Chilean Patagonia, including city guides, national parks, hotels, weather forecasts and lots more.

Easter Island
www.netaxc.com/~trance/rapanui.html A short introduction to Easter Island's history and attractions, with great pictures and lots of links.

www.pbs.org.wgbh.nova.easter Put together by a team of archeologists, this slick site with excellent graphics guides you around Easter Island, with background on its history, archeology and "mysteries".

El Mercurio *www.mercurio.cl* The long-established, rather conservative daily newspaper online in Spanish.

General info *www.chiptravel.cl* First-rate site (partly funded by the government) with a vast range of useful information, from bus timetables to nightlife listings. Make this your first stop.

Government of Chile *www.segegob.cl* Official government Web site, with email links to various ministries.

Hotel list *www.chile-hotels.com* A long list of Chilean hotels with online booking facilities, plus brief descriptions of the towns and cities.

Lan Chile *www.lanchile.cl* Check out timetables and fares on the Lan Chile national flight network.

Sernatur *www.segegob.cl/sernatur/inicio.html* The national tourist board's site, with pages on national parks, major tourist attractions, history, culture and food.

South American Explorers Club *www.samexplo.org* Excellent site belonging to the long-established non-profit organization providing services for scientists, explorers and travellers in South America, with travel advisories and warnings, trip reports, a bulletin board and sensibly indexed links with other sites.

Sunsite Chile Weblink *sunsite.dcc.uchile.cl* Very useful page set up by the Universidad de Chile with links to many other sites, grouped in themes like news, government, law, tourism, weather and so on.

Tourist info *www.turismochile.cl* Descriptions of the major attractions in each region, with some historical and cultural background.

Wines of Chile *www.winesofchile.com* A comprehensive list of Chilean wine producers and their products; short on glossy graphics and critical reviews but lots of information there.

COSTS AND MONEY

Chile has a strong, stable economy with a relatively low rate of inflation, usually around the eight percent mark. Though not as high as in Argentina, prices are more in line with those in Europe and North America than in neighbouring Andean countries like Peru and Bolivia.

CURRENCY AND EXCHANGE RATES

The basic unit of currency is the **peso**, represented by the $ sign (and by the CH$ in this book, for clarity). Notes come in 500, 1000, 5000 and 10,000 denominations, while coins come in 1, 5, 10, 50 and 100 peso bits. There's a chronic shortage of change in Chile, and trying to pay for something small with a CH$10,000 note, and sometimes even a CH$5000 note, invariably results in the shopkeeper scurrying around, desperately trying to beg change from his neighbours. It's a good idea to break up these larger notes whenever you can – in big supermarkets and post offices, for instance – and keep a stock of loose change and small notes on you at all times. Many hotels, particularly the more expensive ones, accept US dollars cash (and will give you a discount for paying this way; see p.27). Apart from this, however, it's more common to pay for everything in **local currency**, and most places, including the majority of restaurants and shops, won't accept anything else. You may, however, come across prices quoted in the mysterious "**UF**". This stands for "*unidad de fomento*" and is an index-linked monetary unit that is adjusted (minutely) on a daily basis to remain in line with inflation. It's normally reserved for dealing with large sums of money, and the only time you're likely to come across it is if you rent a vehicle (your liability, in the event of an accident, will probably be quoted in UFs on the rental contract). You'll find the **exchange rate** of the UF against the Chilean peso in the daily newspapers, along with the rates for all the other currencies.

EXCHANGE RATES

You can check current exchange rates and convert figures on *www.xe.net/currency*

US$1	CH$480
CAN$1	CH$328
A$1	CH$317
NZ$1	CH$268
UK£1	CH$774

BASIC COSTS

US DOLLARS

We've given prices in **US dollars** below, to help you get an idea of basic costs before you're familiar with the local currency. Note, however, that you'll use Chilean pesos to pay for just about everything out there, with the exception of some hotels which also accept US dollars.

On the whole, Chile is an expensive country compared to the rest of South America. Typical **accommodation** prices are usually around the US$15 mark for a bottom-end double room; US$40 for a mid-range double with private bath; and anything from US$70 per room in a smart, attractive hotel. **Eating** out can also be pricey, particularly in the evening – it depends a lot on where you are, but a typical beef steak and french fries plus mineral water in an ordinary, local restaurant will often cost around US$8. You can save money by having the set lunchtime menus offered in most restaurants, usually at very reasonable prices, though this can get rather repetitive after a while. Another way to keep the costs down is to eat in the fast-food outlets you'll find in most towns and cities. Thankfully, **transport**, at least, is still inexpensive, with long-distance buses offering particularly good value – for instance, the 2000km-journey from Santiago to Arica costs around US$40. In general, then, you'll need to allow at least US$180 a week to get by on a tight budget; at least US$300 a week to live a little more comfortably, staying in mid-range hotels and eating in restaurants most days; while it would take from US$700 a week to live in luxury, staying in the more upmarket hotels and eating in the best restaurants. For details on **tipping**, see the "Directory" on p.59.

HIDDEN COSTS: IVA

The most widespread hidden cost in Chile is **IVA** (*Impuesto al Valor Agregado*), a tax of eighteen percent added to most goods and services. Although most prices include IVA, there are many irritating exceptions – some tourist shops, for instance, quote prices without IVA, and even some restaurants have a discreet "prices do not include IVA" at the bottom of their menu. Hotel rates sometimes include IVA and sometimes don't; as a tourist, you're supposed to be exempt from IVA if you pay for your accommodation in US dollars, but it's quite a complicated system – see p.27 for more details. Car rental is almost always quoted without IVA, which really jacks the end price up. If in doubt, you should always clarify whether a price quoted to you, from souvenirs to room rates, includes IVA.

CHANGING MONEY AND GETTING CASH

By far the easiest and most convenient way to get cash is to withdraw it at an **ATM**, using your credit card or debit card. In Chile, all ATMs carry the "Redbank" sign, and you'll find them in most of the major towns and cities dotted along the Panamericana. They usually accept both Visa and Mastercard, or any other cards linked to the Plus or Cirrus systems. The most obvious advantage is that you can get money out at any time of day in a matter of seconds; it would be unwise, however, to rely solely on ATMs – mainly in case your card's stolen – and you should always have a back-up source of funds, preferably **travellers' cheques**. These should always be in US dollars and though most brands are accepted, it's best to be on the safe side and take one of the main brands like American Express, Citibank or Thomas Cook. You can't use them like cash, and will have to change them in a **casa de cambio** (exchange bureau), usually for a small commission. Most *casas de cambio* are open from Monday to Friday between 9am and 5.30pm, usually closing for a couple of hours at lunchtime; some also open Saturday mornings. However, while there are numerous *casas de cambio* in Santiago, and usually one or two in the larger provincial cities, they're by no means in all towns and cities, which

RECEIVING WIRED MONEY

For the address of the nearest agent where you can collect money wired to you in Chile, call ☎800/200102 or 2/639 6346) for Western Union agents, and (☎800/203711) for Moneygram agents. We've listed a few below.

	Western Union	Moneygram
Antofagasta:	Chilexpress, Condell 2739 (☎55/227377)	Afex, Latorre 2670 (☎55/268709)
Arica:	Chilexpress, 21 de Mayo 814 (☎58/255171)	
Iquique:	Correos, Bolívar 458 (☎57/264228)	Afex, Serrano 396 (☎57/414324)
Puerto Montt:	Chilexpress, Antonio Varas 437 (☎65/252002)	Afex, Av Diego Portales 516 (☎65/256604)
Punta Arenas:	Chilexpress, Bories 911 (☎61/247662)	Afex, Rosa 886 (☎61/220730)
Santiago:	Chilexpress, Agustinas 1139 (☎2/382 4800)	Afex, General Holley 158 (☎2/233 6156)
Temuco:	Chilexpress, Vicuña Mackenna 557 (☎45/214084)	Afex, Arturo Prat 427 (☎45/238824).

is fairly limiting. Note that it's normally either impossible or prohibitively expensive to change cash and travellers' cheques at **banks**. Where banks come in useful is for getting a **cash advance** against a credit card, but this usually involves hours of queueing and waiting around. Another way of getting emergency cash is to have it **wired** to you, with the money usually available for collection (in local currency) within twenty minutes of being sent. It's a very expensive option, however, and is only really suitable as a last resort. Rates at Western Union Money Transfer (UK☎0800/833833; US ☎1-800/325-6000) start at £14/US$20 for £50–100/US$75–150, going up, on a sliding scale, to £105/US$150 for £3000/US$4500. Moneygram (☎0800/894887) has slightly cheaper rates, and operates from all UK post offices.

CREDIT CARDS

It's always a good idea to travel with at least one credit card – for emergencies, for placing deposits on car rental and for the occasional splurge in a smart hotel or restaurant. Visa and Mastercard are the most widely accepted; American Express and Diner's Card are considerably less useful. Note that you'll often be asked to produce ID when you pay for goods in a shop by credit card, and you should be prepared for some delays as staff wait for authorization for the transaction. You'll rarely be able to pay by card in the cheaper hotels and restaurants. If you're taking several credit cards out with you, it's worth taking out a **card protection insurance** before you leave home, so that if your cards are lost or stolen you only need to ring the card insurers, who will see to it that all your cards are cancelled, and can arrange for emergency cash to be sent to you. Card protection schemes are offered by most banks and card issuers, and normally cost around £10/US$15 a year. If you don't have this type of insurance, make sure you keep a written record of your card account numbers and the lost/stolen card telephone numbers in a safe place, separate from your wallet.

GETTING AROUND

Travelling in Chile is easy, comfortable and, compared to Europe or North America, inexpensive. Most of the population travels by bus, and it's such a reliable, affordable option that you'll probably do likewise. However, internal airlines, catering primarily for business passengers, are handy for covering long distances in a hurry. The country has a good road network with a low volume of traffic away from the major towns which makes driving a fast and relatively stress-free way of getting around. In recent years Chile's rail network has fallen into decline and only an ever-shrinking service operates south of Santiago. South of Puerto Montt there are limited ferry services which provide a slow but scenic way of travelling as far as Puerto Natales.

BY AIR

Chile is a country of almost unimaginable distances (it's over 5000km by road from Arica to Punta Arenas) which makes **flying** by far the quickest and most convenient way of taking in both its northern and southern regions in a single trip. It's also a surprisingly inexpensive way of getting about, thanks to fierce competition between the two main **domestic airlines** – Lan Chile-Ladeco and Avant – that serve the country's numerous regional airports.

The largest outfit is **Lan Chile** (☎600/600 4000), which besides offering the widest choice of domestic flights is Chile's principal long-haul carrier, and the only one with flights to Easter Island (see p.425). **Ladeco** (☎600/661 3000) recently became a subsidiary of Lan Chile, but maintains its own aircraft and staff. Fares are identical, and flights with both companies can be booked on a single ticket (allowing you, for instance, to fly out with Lan Chile and back with Ladeco). Their **tarifa supereconómica**, available on selected flights with a minimum of seven days' advance purchase, is exceptionally good value – a return ticket from Santiago to Puerto Montt, for instance, costs CH$46,000 on this tariff, compared to CH$75,000 one-way at the normal tariff. Another good-value option is their **Visit Chile airpass** which can be used on three internal flights within a one-month period. Note that the pass can only be bought outside Chile – for more details, see p.4, p.9 and p.11.

A relative newcomer, established in 1996, **Avant** (☎2/290 5050 or 600/500 7000) serves all the main domestic airports from Arica to Punta Arenas. It's affiliated to Tur Bus, Chile's largest long-distance bus company, and flights can be booked at most Tur Bus ticket offices. Its fares are extremely competitive, which makes it very popular, and flights should be booked as far in advance as possible.

Air taxis and regional airlines operate regular services to smaller destinations between Puerto Montt and Puerto Williams, but they are susceptible to weather delays and won't fly without a minimum number of passengers (usually six people). Two companies also fly out from Santiago to Isla Robinson Crusoe, 650km off the mainland – for more details, see p.420.

GETTING INTO TOWN

Getting between Chile's airports and its city centres is fast, cheap and easy. Most of the main airports have dedicated **bus services** into the centre, or **minibus transfers** which drop off passengers at their hotels (at a cost of around CH$3000). The smaller airports, without these services, are always well stocked with taxis, and tend to be only a few kilometres outside the city centre, keeping the cost of a taxi ride down. Only Santiago has flights leaving and departing at really antisocial hours, served by 24-hour minibus transfers.

MAIN DOMESTIC AIRPORTS

Antofagasta	☎55/268831
Arica	☎58/211116 or 211259
Balmaceda	☎67/272104
Calama	☎55/311331
Copiapó	☎52/218681
Iquique	☎57/412373
La Serena	☎51/224711
Puerto Montt	☎65/252019
Punta Arenas	☎61/214259
Santiago	☎2/601 9001
Temuco	☎45/214896

BY BUS

Chile's long-distance **buses** offer an excellent service, far better than their European or North American counterparts – thanks mainly to the enormous amount of legroom available on many routes. Facilities depend less on individual companies than on the class of bus you travel on, with prices rising according to comfort level. A **pullman** (not to be confused with the large bus company of the same name) or **clásico** contains standard semi-reclining seats; a **semi-cama** has seats with twice the amount of leg room, and which recline a good deal more; while a **salón cama**, at the top of the luxury range, has wide seats (just three to a row) which recline to an almost horizontal position. Most companies offer a choice of all three types of bus, particularly on their longer journeys. All buses have chemical toilets and most supply soft drinks. Some overnight services include meals or snacks while others stop at restaurants where set meals might be included in the ticket price. Videos, piped music and bingo games are also common in-transit attractions (or irritations).

Thanks to the intense competition and price wars waged between the multitude of bus companies, **fares** are extremely low. It always pays to compare fares offered by the different companies serving your destination, as you'll almost certainly find one offering a special deal. This price-comparing is easily done at the central **terminal** used by long-distance buses in most cities, where you'll find separate booking offices for each company (though Tur Bus and Pullman Bus, the two largest companies, often have their own separate terminals close to the main terminal). Some towns, however, don't have a central terminal, in which case buses leave from their company offices which are normally clustered together in the town centre. Due to the popularity of bus travel, you should always try to buy your ticket at least a few hours in advance, and preferably the day before travelling, especially if you plan to travel on a Friday. An added advantage of buying ahead is that you'll be able to choose a seat either by the aisle or window and, more impor-

USEFUL BUS VOCABULARY

Bus terminal	*Terminal de buses*, or *rodoviario*	Left luggage	*Custodia*
Ticket	*Pasaje*	What time does the bus leave?	*¿A qué hora sale el bus?*
Seat	*Asiento*	What time does the bus arrive?	*¿A qué hora llega el bus?*
Aisle	*Pasillo*	How long does the journey take?	*¿Cuánto tiempo demorra el*
Window	*Ventana*		
Luggage	*Equipaje*		

tantly, the side of the bus you sit on. Even with air conditioning, seats on the sunny side can get extremely hot and you may find yourself peeking at the scenery through a curtain.

When it comes to **boarding**, make sure that the departure time written on your ticket corresponds exactly to the time indicated on the little clock on the bus's front window, as your ticket is valid only on the bus it was booked for. Your luggage will be safely stored in lockers under the bus and the conductor will issue you with a numbered stub for each article. Soon after departure – and it cannot be stressed forcefully enough that Chilean buses leave with obsessive punctuality – the conductor will check your ticket and leave you with a stub which must be kept until the end of your journey.

Be warned that if travelling north of Santiago on a very long distance route, or crossing an international border, the bus and all luggage will be searched by Ministry of Agriculture officials, and all sandwiches, fresh fruit and vegetables will be destroyed – while you stand waiting, usually in the cold night temperatures.

SAMPLE CLÁSICO BUS FARES FROM SANTIAGO

Arica:	CH$20,000	US$41
Antofagasta:	CH$15,000	US$31
La Serena:	CH$8000	US$17
Concepcion:	CH$6000	US$12.5
Temuco:	CH$8000	US$17
Puerto Montt:	CH$10,000	US$21

LOCAL BUSES, COLECTIVOS AND TAXIS

Local buses, often called *micros*, connect city centres with residential outskirts, and with nearby villages. These buses are often packed, and travelling with a large rucksack can be a problem, particularly if your journey coincides with students going to or from college, or with market day. Buses sticking to the confines of the town or city usually ply up and down the principal thoroughfares, and around the central square – the main points of the route and final destination are displayed on the inside of the front window, but it always helps to carry a street map and be able to point to where you're trying to get to. Buses that leave the city for the countryside normally depart from their own *terminal rural*, which is usually next door or close to the Mercado Municipal (market building).

For some journeys, a faster alternative is provided by **colectivos**, which are shared taxis operating along a fixed route with fixed fares, normally only slightly more expensive than the local buses. Most *colectivos* look exactly like normal taxis (apart from being all black, not black and yellow), and have their route or final destination marked on a board on their roof – though in some cities, *colectivo* services are operated by bright yellow cars, often without a roof-board.

Taxis are normally black with a yellow roof, and in the bigger cities can be flagged down very quickly on the street. Alternatively, you can usually find them on or near the central square, as well as outside bus terminals and train stations. Although Chilean taxi drivers are normally very honest, it's worth checking to see that the meter has been turned on before you start a journey. Fares are clearly shown in the windscreen – they vary from city to city but are reasonable compared to North American or European prices.

BY TRAIN

Some fifty years ago, Chile possessed a huge network of railways, particularly in the far north where hundreds of kilometres of lines transported the region's nitrate ore down to the ports to be shipped abroad. Now that the nitrate days are over, no national railways operate north of Santiago, and what lines are left south of the capital are forever shrinking, unable to compete with the speed, low fares and punctuality offered by buses. In 1998 the slow, romantic train from Santiago to Puerto Varas was discontinued, and today only three daily trains pull out of Santiago's grand Estación Central, heading for Chillán, Concepción and Temuco. The daytime trains offer two standards of compartment – *economía* and *salón* – while the overnight trains to Temuco and Concepción offer the added choice of *cama* and *dormitorio*, the latter in two-berth cabins in a classic 1920s carriage.

DRIVING

While Chile's towns and cities are linked by plenty of buses, most visitors are here for the country's wilderness areas which are often difficult, and sometimes impossible, to reach on public transport. Many remote attractions are visited by tour companies operating out of the nearest major city, but for more independence, your best bet is to **rent a vehicle**. To do this, you need to be at least 21 years old and have a major credit card so you can leave a blank voucher as a guarantee. You're allowed to use your national licence but you're strongly advised to bring, in addition, an **international licence** – Chile's *Carabineros* (police officers), who frequently stop drivers to check their documents, are often suspicious of unfamiliar foreign licences, and are always happier when dealing with international ones. **Traffic regulations** are strictly enforced in Chile and the wearing of seatbelts is compulsory. The **speed limit** is 50km per hour or less in urban areas and 100km per hour on highways, and radar speed traps are commonplace. If an oncoming vehicle flashes its headlights, you're being warned of *Carabineros* lurking ahead. If you do get pulled over, exercise the utmost courtesy and patience, and under no circumstances do or say anything which could possibly be interpreted as bribery (see also "Trouble and Crime", p.45).

RENTAL OUTLETS AND COSTS

Several international car-rental companies have offices throughout Chile, including Hertz, Avis, Budget and First. In addition to these, you'll find an abundance of local outlets which are often, but by no means always, less expensive than the international firms. The cost of car rental is much higher in Chile than in North America, and more on a par with European prices. Rates can vary quite a lot from one company to another and it's always worth phoning as many as possible to compare prices. **Basic saloon cars** go from around US$250 to US$400 per week, while a 4WD **jeep** or **pick-up truck** can cost anything from US$350 to US$600-plus per week (less for non-4WD). Most outlets have lower rates if you're renting for a month or longer. Make sure that the price they quote includes IVA (Chilean sales tax), insurance and unlimited mileage. Your rental contract will almost certainly be in (legal and convoluted) Spanish – get the company to take you through it and explain everything. In most cases your liability, in the event of an accident, is normally around the US$500 mark (it'll be quoted in UFs; see p.19) and costs over this amount will be covered in total by the company.

DRIVING IN TOWNS

Just about all Chilean towns are laid out on a grid plan, which makes navigating them pretty easy. However, the country is obsessed with **one-way traffic** systems, and you'll find that many streets in even the smallest towns are one-way only, the

CAR RENTAL AGENCIES ABROAD

UK AND IRELAND

Avis ☎0990/900500; Eire ☎01/874 5844
Budget ☎0800/181181; Eire ☎0800/973159
Hertz ☎0990/996699; Eire ☎01/676 7476

AUSTRALIA AND NEW ZEALAND

Avis ☎1800/225 533; NZ ☎09/526 2847
Hertz ☎13 3039; NZ ☎09/309 0989.

US AND CANADA

Avis ☎1-800/331-1084
Budget ☎1-800/527-0700
Dollar ☎1-800/800-6000
Hertz ☎1-800/654-3001
National ☎1-800/CAR-RENT

USEFUL CAR VOCABULARY

Car	*Auto*	Insurance	*Seguro*
Jeep	*Jeep*	Damages excess	*Deducible*
Pick-up truck (double/single cabin)	*Camioneta (doble/simple cabina)*	Petrol (leaded/unleaded)	*Gasolina/bencina (con/sin plomo)*
4WD	*Doble tracción* or *Quatro por quatro* (4x4)	Petrol station	*Gasolinera*
		Jerry can	*Bidón*
Non-4WD	*Tracción single* or *Dos por dos* (2x2)	Highway	*Carretera*
		To rent	*Arrendar*
Unlimited kilometres	*Kilometraje libre*	Car rental outlet	*Rentacar*

direction of traffic alternating with each successive street. The direction is usually indicated by a white arrow above the street name on each corner; if in doubt, look at the direction of the parked cars. **Parking** is normally allowed in most downtown streets (but on one side only), and around the Plaza de Armas (central square). You'll invariably be guided into a space by a wildly gesticulating *guarda-auto* – a boy or young man who will offer to look after your car (quite unnecessarily) in return for a tip, normally of a couple of hundred pesos or so. In larger towns there's a small half-hourly charge for parking on the street, administered by eagle-eyed traffic wardens who slip tickets under your wipers every thirty minutes then pounce on you to collect your money before you leave (a small tip is expected, too). If you can't find a space to park in, keep a look out for large "estacionamiento" signs by the pavement, indicating private car parks, normally at around CH$500–600 an hour.

DRIVING ON HIGHWAYS

The Panamerican highway, which runs through Chile from the Peruvian border to the southern tip of Chiloé, is known alternately as *Ruta 5*, *la Panamericana*, or *el longitudinal*, with *sur* or *norte* often added on to indicate which side of Santiago it's on. In common with other paved highways, much of it is single carriageway, and traffic often builds up behind slow-moving long-distance lorries. For this reason there's a lot of mad overtaking on Chilean highways, and you should drive very defensively – slowing down, for instance, as you approach blind corners or brows of hills, just in case you find yourself face to face with an oncoming vehicle on your side of the road. The number of roadside shrines is a sobering reminder of the potential consequences of not taking these risks seriously.

COMMON CHILEAN ROAD SIGNS

Peligro	Danger
Desvío	Detour
Resbaladizo	Slippery surface
No adalantar	No overtaking
Curva peligrosa	Dangerous bend
Reduzca velocidad	Reduce speed
Sin berma	No hard shoulder

BACKCOUNTRY AND ALTIPLANO DRIVING

You'll probably find that most places you want to get to are reached by dirt road, for which it's essential to rent a suitable vehicle – namely a **jeep** or **pick-up truck**. On regular dirt roads you can usually get away without 4WD, but you should always try to a get a vehicle with the widest, sturdiest tyres and highest clearance you can afford. For **altiplano driving**, however, you should really pay the extra to have 4WD (again with the sturdiest tyres and highest clearance) as you can come across some dreadful roads up there, hundreds of kilometres from the nearest town. Make sure, too, that you take two spare tyres, not one, and that you always carry more than enough petrol (work it out yourself then add lots – don't rely on what the guys in the rental shop say), plus a funnel or tube for siphoning. It can be difficult to navigate in the altiplano, with so much open space and so few landmarks – a good tip is to make a careful note of your kilometre reading as you go along, so you can chart your progress over long roads with few markers. Despite this tone of caution, it has to be emphasized that altiplano driving is among the most rewarding adventures that Chile offers.

Finally, a general point on **tyre punctures**. This is such a common occurrence in Chile that even the smallest towns have special workshops (bearing signs saying "vulcanización") where they are quickly and cheaply repaired.

HITCHING

While we don't recommend **hitching** as a safe way of getting about, there's no denying that it's widely practised by Chileans themselves – in the summer it seems like every student in Chile is sitting beside the road with their thumb out, and in rural areas it's not uncommon for entire families to hitch a lift whenever they need to get into town. For backpackers, the large number of pick-up trucks on the road means there's a better chance than normal of being given a lift, as these vehicles have plenty of room to ditch your packs (and yourselves) in the back. Overseas tourists are much more likely to be given a lift if they identify themselves as such, as nearly everyone in Chile can trace their ancestry back to one European country or another, and many are keen to share their heritage with visitors from the fatherland. In general, you'll have a much better chance of getting a lift on a quiet rural road than on the Panamericana, where no one wants to stop for fear of being overtaken by slow-moving lorries. In this case, your best bet is to find a lift from parked traffic at a busy *servicentro* (motorway services).

BY FERRY

South of Puerto Montt, where the mainland breaks up into an archipelago, a network of ferries operates through the fjords, inlets and channels of Chile's far south, making a far more scenic and romantic alternative to flights and long-distance buses. Two of these, in particular, are very popular with tourists: one from Puerto Montt to Chacabuco and the San Raphael glacier, the other between Puerto Montt and Puerto Natales. The two main ferry companies are privately run **Navimag** and state-run **TransMarChilay**, which is due to be privatized late 1999; it's not clear to what extent this will affect prices, but TransMarChilay claims that the routes won't be tampered with. Both companies' ships transport cargo, vehicles and passengers, and are functional rather than luxurious. In addition to these two main routes, there are ferry links with Quellón on Chiloé, and with Chaitén, on the Carretera Austral, as well as a number of shorter routes forming a "bridge" along various points of the Carretera Austral (full details given on p.357). There's also a ferry trip across Lago Todos Los Santos, in the Lake District, connecting Petrohué with Peulla, near the Argentinean border, operated by Andina del Sud (see p.322).

FERRY COMPANIES

Navimag
(www.australis.com)

Puerto Montt: Angelmó 2187 (☎65/253318, fax 258540).

Puerto Natales: Pedro Montt 262 (☎61/411421, fax 412229).

Punta Arenas: Av Independencia 840 (☎61/224256, fax 225804).

Santiago: Av El Bosque Norte 0440, eleventh floor (☎2/442 3120, fax 203 5025).

TransMarChilay

Chacabuco: O'Higgins, s/n (☎ & fax 67/351144).

Chaitén: Corcovado 266 (☎65/731272, fax 731282).

Coyhaique: 21 de Mayo 417, second floor (☎67/231971, fax 232700).

Puerto Montt: Angelmó 2187 (☎65/270416, fax 270415).

Quellón: Costanera, s/n (☎65/680511, fax 680513).

Santiago: Agustinas 715, oficina 403 (☎ & fax 2/633 5959).

Andina del Sud

Puerto Montt: Varas 437 (☎65/257797, fax 270035).

Puerto Varas: Del Salvador 72 (☎65/232811, fax 232511).

MAIN FERRY ROUTES: AN OVERVIEW

Petrohué–Peulla, across Lago Todos Los Santos: Five hours; daily crossings (year-round) with Andina del Sud. See p.322.

Puerto Montt–Chacabuco: Twenty-four hours; two sailings per week with Navimag (year round) and TransMarChilay (year-round). See p.330 and p.373.

Puerto Montt–Chacabuco–Laguna San Rafael: Five days, four nights (returning to Puerto Montt); one or two sailings per week with Navimag and TransMarChilay (Dec–March). See p.330 and p.375.

Puerto Montt–Chaitén: Ten hours; three or four sailings per week with Navimag (Jan–March); one per week with TransMarChilay (year-round). See p.330 and p.364.

Puerto Montt–Puerto Natales: Four days, three nights; one or two sailings per week with Navimag (year-round). See p.330 and p.404.

Quellón–Chacabuco: One sailing per week with TransMarChilay (year-round). See p.352 and p.373.

Quellón–Chaitén: Five hours; four sailings per week with Navimag (Jan–March); one per week with TransMarChilay (year-round). See p.352 and p.364.

ACCOMMODATION

On the whole, the standard of accommodation in Chile is not that great and many visitors feel that prices are high for what you get, especially in mid- and upper-range hotels. Bottom-end accommodation starts at around US$15 for a double room, while you'll have to pay around US$40 for a double room with private bath in a decent mid-range hotel, and anything from US$70 for a smart, upmarket hotel. There's usually a wide range to choose from in the major tourist centres and the cities on the Panamericana, but in more remote areas you'll invariably have to make do with basic *hospedajes* (modest rooms, often in family homes). Most places include a small breakfast – bread roll, jam and instant coffee – in the price of the room, but you shouldn't always count on this, as some will charge extra for breakfast, and others won't serve it at all.

Note that the price of accommodation in the main tourist centres increases dramatically in **high season** – January and February –

IVA DISCOUNTS

Room rates are supposed to be quoted inclusive of IVA (a Chilean goods and services tax of 18 percent) but you should always check beforehand ("*¿está incluido el iva?*"). Many mid- and most upper-range hotels give you the opportunity of paying for your accommodation in US dollars (with cash or, if they're set up for it, by credit card) which exempts you from paying IVA. Note, however, that hotels are not obliged to offer this discount – they need to set up the right paperwork to do so, which is something some of them seem incapable of getting round to. Many will even deny the existence of such a scheme. Often, though, if they can't take off IVA, they'll offer you a discount of ten percent if you pay cash.

ACCOMMODATION PRICE CODES

Prices are for the cheapest **double room** in high season. At the lower end of the scale, **single travellers** can expect to pay half this rate, but mid- and upper-range hotels usually charge the same for a single as for a double. Note that the price of accommodation in many tourist centres drops significantly outside January and February.

① Less than US$10/CH$4800
② US$10–20/CH$4800–9600
③ US$20–30/CH$9600–10,080
④ US$30–50/CH$10,080–24,000
⑤ US$50–75/CH$24,000–36,000
⑥ US$75–100/CH$36,000–48,000
⑦ US$100–150/CH$48,000–72,000
⑧ over US$150/over CH$72,000

particularly in seaside resorts, where it can as much as double. Outside high season it's always worth trying to negotiate a discount, wherever you are. A simple *"¿tiene algo un poco más económico?* ("do you have anything a little cheaper?") or *"¿me puede dár un discuento?"* ("could you give me a discount?") will often get you a lower price on the spot. It's rarely necessary to make **advance reservations**, unless you've got your heart set on a particular hotel or *residencial*, in which case it can be a good idea to phone a few days in advance – especially if you plan to stay at the weekend, even more so if it's in striking distance of Santiago.

HOTELS

Chilean hotels are given a one- to five-star rating by Sernatur (the national tourist board), but this only reflects facilities and not standards, which vary widely from hotel to hotel. In practice, then, a three-star hotel could be far more attractive and comfortable than a four-star and even a five-star hotel; the only way to tell is to go and have a look, as even the room rates aren't a reliable indication of quality. In general, **mid-range hotels** fall into two main categories: large, old houses with spacious, but sometimes tired, rooms; and modern, purpose-built hotels, usually with smaller rooms and better facilities. You'll always get a private bathroom with a shower (rarely a bath), hot water and towels, and either an ancient black and white TV or, in the more modern places, cable TV with dozens of English-language channels. As the price creeps up there's usually an improvement in decor and space, and at the upper end of the price range you can expect room service, a mini bar (*"frigobar"*), a private safe, a hotel restaurant, private parking and sometimes a swimming pool. The standards of **upmarket hotels** can still vary quite dramatically, however – ranging from stylish, contemporary city hotels or charming, characterful *haciendas* to grim, impersonal monoliths catering for businessmen. Finally, a word of warning on **motels**, which are usually not economical roadside hotels, but places where unmarried couples go to have sex.

RESIDENCIALES

Residenciales are the most widely available, and widely used, accommodation option in Chile. As with hotels, standards can vary enormously, but in general *residenciales* offer simple, mod estly furnished rooms, usually off a corridor in the main house (often with no outside windows), or else in a row arranged around the back yard or patio. They usually contain little more than a bed (or up to four single beds), a rail for hanging clothes and a bedside table and lamp, though some provide more furniture (perhaps a writing desk and chair), and a few more comforts, like a

SOME ACCOMMODATION TERMS

Una habitación doble	Twin room
Una habitación matrimonial	Room with double bed
Una habitación sencilla/single (pronounced "singlay")	Single room
Baño privado	Private bathroom
Baño compartido	Shared bathroom
Agua caliente (todo el día)	Hot water (all day)

TV or a thermos for making tea or coffee. Most, but not all, have shared baths – note that you'll usually have to light the water heater (*calefón*) to get hot water, each time you take a shower. Where places differ is in the upkeep or "freshness" of the rooms: some of the really cheap rooms are dank and damp, with peeling paint and saggy beds, while others, though still very simple, have good bed linen, walls that are painted every summer, and a clean, swept, feel to them. Some of the slightly more expensive *residenciales* are very pleasant indeed, particularly those large, nineteenth-century houses with waxed wooden floorboards and floor-to-ceiling windows that open onto balconies. While some *residenciales* cater exclusively to tourists, many, especially in the mining towns of the north, fill mainly with workmen, so you can't always expect to meet fellow travellers where you're staying.

HOSPEDAJES AND CASAS DE FAMILIA

The distinction between a *residencial* and an *hospedaje* or *casa de familia* is often blurred. On the whole, the term **hospedaje** implies something rather modest, along the lines of the cheaper *residenciales*, while a **casa de familia** (or *casa familial*) offers, as you'd expect, rooms inside a family home – sometimes just four or five rooms left vacant by grown-up children; other times in an extension added onto the main house. It's nothing like staying with a family, however, and the relationship between the guest and the owner is no different from that in a *residencial*. *Casas de familia* don't normally have a sign at the door, and if they do it usually just says "*Alojamiento*" ("lodgings"); more commonly, members of the family might go and meet tourists at the bus station, handing out photocopied fliers or cards. These places are perfectly safe and you shouldn't worry about checking them out, though it's always wise to see a room before committing yourself to staying there. Sometimes you'll find details of *casas de familia* at tourist offices, as well, such as the one in Valparaíso, which hands out a long printed list of them.

CABAÑAS

Cabañas are a very Chilean enthusiasm, and you'll find them in tourist spots up and down the country, particularly by the coast. They are basically holiday chalets and are geared towards families, usually with a fully equipped kitchen area, a sitting/dining area, one double bedroom and a second bedroom with bunks. They range from the very rustic to the distinctly grand, complete with daily maid service. They're often quite expensive at full rate (at least US$60) and the price is normally the same for two people as it is for five. That said, as they're used predominantly by Chileans, their popularity tends to be limited to January and February and sunny weekends, and outside these times demand is so low that you can normally get a very good discount. If there are just two of you, you have a particularly strong case for arguing the price down. Many *cabañas* are in superb locations, right by the ocean, and it can be wonderfully relaxing to self-cater for a few days in the off-season – cooking the fresh fish you bought in the local market, sipping your gin and tonic on the veranda looking out to sea.

REFUGIOS

Many of the ranger stations in the national parks have a limited number of bunk beds available for tourists, at a charge of around US$10 per person. Known as **refugios**, these places are very rustic – often a small, stone-built hut – but they usually have flushable toilets, hot running water, clean sheets and heavy woollen blankets. Some of them, such as those at the Salar de Surire and Lago Chungará, are in stunning locations; conditions in these places can be very inhospitable, however, and there's no doubt that a *refugio* offers a good deal more comfort and shelter than camping. Most *refugios* are open year-round, but if you're travelling in winter or other extreme weather conditions it's best to check with the regional Conaf office in advance. While you're there, you can reserve beds in the *refugio*, as the Conaf staff will radio their colleagues and let them know when you're arriving. This is highly advisable if you're relying solely on the *refugio* for accommodation, but if you're travelling with a tent as a back-up it's not really necessary to book ahead.

CAMPING

There are lots of opportunities for **camping** in Chile, though it's not always the cheapest way to sleep. If you plan to do a lot of camping, the first thing you should do is equip yourself with the **camping guide** published by Turistel, which has details of every campsite in Chile. Official sites range from plots of land with minimal facilities to swanky grounds with hot showers and private barbecue grilles. The latter, often part of holiday complexes in seaside resorts, can be very expensive (around CH$15,000/US$31), and are usually only open between December and March.

It's also possible to camp **wild** in the countryside, but you'll really need your own transport if you plan to do this in remote areas. You should also bear in mind that most national parks don't allow camping outside designated areas, to protect the environment. Instead, they tend to have either rustic camping areas administered by Conaf (very common in northern Chile), costing about US$10 per tent, or else smart, expensive sites run by concessionaires (more common in the south). As for **beaches**, some turn into informal, spontaneously erected campsites in the summer months, while it's strictly forbidden to camp on others, and you'll be moved on by *Carabineros* if you try. If you do end up camping wild on the beach or in the countryside, do bury or pack up your excrement, and take all your refuse with you when you leave. Note that butane gas and sometimes Camping Gaz are available in hardware shops in most towns and cities. If your stove takes white gas, you need to buy *bencina blanca*, which you'll find either in hardware stores or, more commonly, in pharmacies.

For details of camping in Chiles's **national parks**, see p.51.

WHICH STOVE?

If you plan to camp in Chile, an important consideration is the type of **stove** you bring. The best sort is probably the basic Camping Gaz model, as butane cylinders are widely available in hardware stores (*ferreterías*) and general stores in most Chilean cities, and there's less that can go wrong with them, though butane gas can fail or burn low at high altitudes. White gas (*bencina blanca*) is much more difficult to come by, though it's sometimes available in hardware shops, supermarkets and pharmacies. Stoves that take unleaded petrol are liable to clog up with impurities contained in Chilean petrol, so you should always carry spare parts with you. Multi-fuel stoves are a good alternative, though, again, always carry a couple of spare generators in case of clogging.

HEALTH

On the whole, Chile is a fairly risk-free country to travel in, as far as health problems are concerned. No inoculations are required, though you might want to consider a typhoid and hepatitis-A jab, as a precaution. Check, too, that your polio and tetanus boosters are up-to-date. Most travellers experience nothing more serious than the odd stomach upset while adjusting to unfamiliar micro-organisms in the food and water, and many suffer nothing at all.

PHARMACIES AND HOSPITALS

Chile is well endowed with **pharmacies** (*farmacias*) – in Santiago and other major cities you'll find one on just about every street corner, and even smaller towns usually offer at least a handful to choose from. They're invariably stocked with a vast range of medicines, many of which can be purchased over the counter with no doctor's prescription; if you anticipate having to buy medication, make a note of its generic name, as brand names are likely to be different. If you need to see a doctor, your best bet is to make an appointment at the outpatient department of the nearest **hospital**, usually known as a *clínica*. The majority of *clínicas* are private, and expensive, so it's essential to ensure that your travel insurance provides good medical cover. An initial consultation will set you back around CH$15,000–20,000, and the cost of treatment can be astronomical. As with North American hospitals, you can pay for it all by credit card, but make sure you get all the details you need to claim it back on your travel insurance.

DISEASE

Although it's highly unlikely that you'll contract any of the following diseases, it's important that you are, at least, aware of them, and take appropriate precautions where necessary. For up-to-date information on disease outbreaks, check the US Center for Disease Control's Web site (*www.cdc.gov*).

Rabies, though only a remote risk, does exist in Chile. If you get bitten or scratched by a dog you should seek medical attention *immediately*; the disease can be cured, but only through a series of stomach injections administered before the onset of symptoms (which can appear within 24 hours or lay dormant for months, and include irrational behaviour, fear of water and foaming at the mouth). There is a vaccine – a course of three injections that has to be started at least a month before departure – but it's expensive and doesn't prevent you from contracting rabies, though it does buy you time to get to hospital.

Cholera – transmitted through contaminated water – occasionally breaks out in rural areas, but tends to be very localized, restricted to communities living in poor conditions with inadequate sanitation facilities and limited access to health care. As a tourist, it's unlikely you'll go anywhere near these places, but if you suspect you're infected (symptoms include watery diarrhoea, explosive vomiting and fever) it's easy to treat, provided you get to a doctor immediately and keep drinking large quantities of bottled or boiled water. There's no point getting a cholera inoculation as the cholera germ has become resistant to the vaccine, which is generally acknowledged to be worthless.

Hantavirus – a rare virus with a high fatality rate carried by long-tailed rats – has been around for years, but wasn't identified until 1993 in the southwest USA. It's now recognized to be a pan-American virus, and has been monitored in Chile since 1995. Forty cases have been recorded since then (most of them concentrated in rural areas of the south) of which 28 were fatal. After 25 cases broke out in 1997, the government mounted a massive public health campaign to control the spread of the disease, which is contracted by inhaling or swallowing dust contaminated with infected rats' faeces or urine, and whose symptoms include fever, headache, intestinal pain and acute respiratory problems. Thanks to increased public awareness and a huge research programme carried out by the US Center for Disease Control, Hantavirus is no longer a serious threat in Chile, but as the disease is still incurable it pays to follow the Ministry of Health's guidelines. In short, if you're camping, always do so in areas free of rubbish, dense weeds or heaps of logs or firewood (places where rats tend to nest and breed); use a hermetically sealed tent with no holes in it; keep all food completely sealed and out of reach of rats; and don't leave unwashed dishes lying around. If you're renting a rustic *cabaña* that looks as if it hasn't been inhabited for a while, open all doors and windows and let it ventilate for thirty minutes before you occupy it, then check carefully for any signs of rat excrement (while covering your mouth with a handkerchief). If you find any, all surfaces should be sprayed with disinfectant, before being swept, dusted and aired – the virus does not survive on exposure to chlorine and sunlight.

HIV and AIDS are not widespread in Chile, and are mainly concentrated in the poorer suburbs of Santiago and Valparaíso, Chile's largest port. Condoms (*condónes*) are available in most pharmacies, but you have to ask for them as there's no self-service. In both state and private hospitals, all blood is screened, and only disposable needles are used to give injections.

FOOD AND WATER

In general, **food** is hygienically prepared in Chile, posing no threats to your health. Until recently, restaurants were prohibited from serving uncooked vegetables that grow at ground level (like lettuce and beetroot), considered at risk from being irrigated with contaminated water, but this ban has been lifted as the risk has been virtually eliminated. However, many people (particularly middle-class Santiago housewives) still take the precaution of "disinfecting" their raw vegetables at home, with special products specifically designed for this purpose sold alongside fruit and vegetables in supermarkets. You may want to do likewise, but there's no need to go overboard as the risk of buying contaminated food is extremely small, and as long as you wash all fresh produce thoroughly, you shouldn't have any problems.

Shellfish, on the other hand, should be treated with the utmost caution. Every year, a handful of people die in Chile because they inadvertently eat bivalve shellfish contaminated by red tide, or *marea roja*, an algae which becomes toxic when the seawater temperature rises. The Chilean government monitors the presence of *marea roja* with extreme diligence, and bans all commercial shellfish collection when the phenomenon occurs. There is no health risk when eating in restaurants or buying shellfish in markets, as these are regularly inspected by the health authorities, but it's extremely dangerous to collect shellfish for your own consumption unless you're absolutely certain that the area is free of red tide. Note that red tide affects *all* shellfish, cooked or uncooked.

Tap water almost everywhere is clean and safe, but can cause diarrhoea to unfamiliar stomachs. Most travellers prefer to avoid this by drinking bottled mineral water, which is widely available in restaurants, grocery stores and supermarkets. If you're travelling in remote areas, you may find that only well water or stored rainwater is available; which should be boiled for a minimum of five minutes (ten minutes at high altitudes) or treated with chemical sterilization tablets. The same applies to stream water that may have been contaminated by animals or humans.

ALTITUDE SICKNESS

Anyone travelling in Chile's northern **altiplano**, where altitudes commonly reach 4500m – or indeed anyone going higher than 3000m in the cordillera – needs to be aware of the risks of **altitude sickness**, locally known as *soroche* or *apunamiento*. This debilitating and sometimes dangerous condition is caused by the reduced atmospheric pressure and corresponding reduction in oxygen that occurs around 3000m above sea level. Basic symptoms include breathlessness, headaches, nausea and extreme tiredness, rather like a bad hangover. There's no way of predicting whether or not you'll be susceptible to the condition, which seems to strike quite randomly, affecting people differently from one ascent to another. You can, however, take steps to avoid it by ascending slowly, and allowing yourself to **acclimatize**. In particular, don't be tempted to whizz straight up to the altiplano from sea level, but spend a night or two acclimatizing en route. You should also avoid alcohol and salt, and drink lots of water.

If you want to be really sure, you can also take a preventive drug called **acetazolamide** (125mg twice daily), starting a day before you ascend, and continuing for a further three or four days. This effectively speeds up acclimatization, but has the added effect of making you urinate a lot, and produces a tingling sensation in your fingers and toes. You might prefer to carry it only as a precaution, as it also relieves symptoms once you've developed them at altitude. Though available over the counter in pharmacies in Santiago and the north, note that acetazolamide is in most countries a prescription-only drug, as it can be dangerous for people with a heart condition. If in doubt, stick to the bitter-tasting **coca leaves** chewed by most locals in the altiplano (where they're widely available at markets and village stores), to ease the headaches and sense of exhaustion.

Although extremely unpleasant, this basic form of altitude sickness is essentially harmless, and passes after about 24 hours (if it doesn't, descend at least 500m). However, in its more serious forms, altitude sickness can be dangerous and even life-threatening. One to two percent of people travelling to 4000m develop **HAPO** (high altitude pulmonary oedema), caused by the build-up of liquid in the lungs. Symptoms include fever, an increased pulse rate, and coughing up white fluid; sufferers should descend immediately, whereupon recovery is usually quick and complete.

Rarer, but more serious, is **HACO** (high altitude cerebral oedema), which occurs when the brain gets waterlogged with fluid. Symptoms include loss of balance, severe lassitude, weakness or numbness on one side of the body and a confused mental state. If you or a fellow traveller display any of these symptoms, descend immediately, and get to a doctor; HACO can be fatal within 24 hours.

SUNSTROKE

In many parts of Chile **sunburn** and **dehydration** are a major threat. This is obviously more of a problem in the excessively dry climate of the north, but even in the south of the country, it's easy to underestimate the strength of the summer sun, undiluted by Chile's clear, pollution-free air. To prevent sunburn, take a high-factor **sunscreen** and wear a **hat**. It's also essential to drink plenty of fluids, and always carry large quantities of **water** with you if you're out hiking in the sun. As you lose a lot of salt when you sweat, add more to your food, or take a rehydration solution (if you don't have any, add half a teaspoonful of salt and four tablespoons of sugar to a litre of bottled water). Too much sun can often lead to **diarrhoea**, and it's always a good idea to carry an over-the-counter treatment like Imodium.

HYPOTHERMIA

Conversely, **hypothermia** is another potential enemy, especially at high altitudes and in Chile's far southern reaches. Because early symptoms can include an almost euphoric sense of sleepiness and disorientation, your body's core temperature can plummet to danger level before you know what has happened. Chile's northern deserts have such clear air that it can drop to -20°C at night, which makes you very vulnerable to hypothermia while sleeping if proper precautions aren't taken. Patagonia's average summer temperatures of 15°C, with occasional highs of 28°C, can give a false sense of security in an area where it snows and rains without warning. Even in clear weather, winds can exceed 100kph and it only takes an inadvertent soaking while crossing a stream for the wind chill factor to induce hypothermia within a matter of minutes. Even if you're just going out for a short walk, always be prepared for the worst the weather can throw at you and carry an emergency supply of high-energy food as well as a dry change of clothes. Always take suitable clothing and equipment if travelling in the desert or altiplano – down clothing and sleeping bags are ideal, as they pack up small and light during the heat of the day, but provide lots of warmth when you need it. Also, avoid camping alone – there's safety in numbers. If you get hypothermia, the best thing to do is take your clothes off and jump into a sleeping bag with someone else. This is absolutely serious – sharing another person's body heat is the most effective way of restoring your own. If you're alone, or have no willing partners, then get out of the wind and the rain, remove all wet or damp clothes, get dry, and drink plenty of hot fluids.

EATING AND DRINKING

Given the vast range and superior quality of the country's raw produce, Chilean food is something of a disappointment. The main problem is a lack of variety and imagination, as so many restaurants, up and down the country, offer the same boring, limited menu of fried chicken, fried beef and fried fish, usually served with chips or rice. That's not to say, however, that you can't eat well in Chile. One notable exception to the general dreariness of Chilean restaurant food is the country's fish and seafood, which ranks among the best in the world. Other alternatives include the various traditional dishes, often called *comida típica* or *comida criolla*, still served in old-fashioned, family-oriented restaurants known as *picadas*. Furthermore, most cities have a couple of upmarket "international" restaurants, where the staple meats and fishes are prepared more elaborately and imaginatively, with varying degrees of success.

On the whole, eating out in Chile tends to be fairly **expensive**, even in simple, local restaurants where you can expect to pay around CH$3000–5000 (US$6–10) for standard main courses. If you're aiming to keep costs down, you may find yourself resorting to the many **fast-food** outlets spread throughout the country, specializing in hotdogs, burgers and cheap pizzas. You could also head for the **municipal markets** found in most towns, which besides offering an abundance of cheap, fresh produce, are usually dotted with stalls selling basic bargain meals of soup or fried meat and rice. Another trick is to join the Chileans and make **lunch** your main meal of the day, when many restaurants offer a fixed-price *menú del día*, which is always much better value than their à la carte options.

As for the other meals of the day, **breakfast** at most *residenciales* and hotels is usually a simple affair of toasted breadrolls, jam and tea or coffee, though if your hosts are inclined to pamper you, this will be accompanied by ham, cheese and (most bizarrely) cake. The great tradition of **onces** – literally "elevenses" but served, like afternoon tea, around 5 o'clock – is a light snack consisting of bread, ham, cheese and biscuits when taken at home or, when out in a *salon de té*, huge fruit tarts and cakes. Apart from during their annual holidays or at weekends, relatively few Chileans go out to **dinner**, which leaves most restaurants very quiet through the week (note, also, that most places don't open before 8pm for dinner). Finally, one legacy of the influx of German immigrants in the nineteenth century is the country's obsession with **German food** – cake, for instance, is known everywhere as *küchen*, and Chile's largest and most popular restaurant chain is *Bavaria*, specializing in Teutonic plates piled high with grilled meat.

FISH AND SEAFOOD

With a 3700km-long coastline to hand, it's no surprise that **fish** and **seafood** are central to the Chilean national diet (there's even a fish stew, *caldillo de congrio*, immortalized in a poem by Pablo Neruda). The range and quality are outstanding, particularly of seafood, which equals anything found in Galicea or Newfoundland. The widest choice is available on the coast of the *litoral central* and Norte Chico, where a string of fishing villages serve the day's catch in the little **marisquerías** (fish restaurants) clustered around the *caleta* (fish quay). Here, you'll find, depending on the season, *albacora* (albacore), *corvina* (sea bass), *congrio* (a firm-fleshed, white fish), *lenguado* (sole), *reineta* (similar to lemon sole) and *merluza* (hake), as well as *almejas* (clams), *choritos* (mussels) *camarones* (prawns), *jaiva* (crab) and *ostras* (oysters), to mention some of the more familiar types of shellfish. Among the less familiar are *erizos* (sea urchins) and *picorocos* (huge barnacles with tentacles peering out their shells). Even if you're not normally adventurous with seafood, you should persuade yourself to experiment; one of the most delicious dishes, and a good one to start with, is *machas a la parmesana* – pink clams, lightly baked in their shells and covered with parmesan cheese. Another typical – and very tasty – dish is *ceviche* (raw fish marinaded in lemon juice).

Down in the south you'll find some of the above with a few further additions: the delicious, lobster-like *centolla* (king crab) is a Patagonian speciality, while freshwater trout and salmon are widely available in the cold waters of Aisén. Around Puerto Montt and Chiloé you should also try the local speciality of *curanto* – a fish and shellfish broth (with the curious addition of chicken and sausage) served out of huge, steaming cauldrons. Look out, too, for *cancato*, a filleted fish topped with cheese, tomato and sausage, like a pizza, before being cooked over an open fire in a special grill.

Finally, a note of caution: you should never collect shellfish from the beach to eat, unless you know for sure that the area is free of red tide (an algae that makes shellfish toxic, causing death within a few hours of consumption; see p.32). There is no danger of eating shellfish contaminated by red tide in restaurants.

MEAT DISHES

Chileans are also big meat eaters, with **beef** featuring prominently on most restaurant menus and family dinner tables. The summertime **asado** (barbecue) is a national institution, giving Chilean men, who normally never step foot in the kitchen, the chance to roll up their sleeves and demonstrate their culinary prowess. Always slow, leisurely affairs, accompanied by lots of Chilean wine, *asados* take place not only in back gardens, but also in specially-equipped picnic areas that fill to bursting on summer weekends. In the south, where the weather is less reliable, large covered grilles known as *quinchos* provide an alternative venue, where meat is often cooked on long skewers in the Brazilian style. The restaurant equivalent of an *asado* is the **parillada** – a mixture of grilled steaks, chops and sausages (in the best places cooked over charcoal), sometimes served on a hot grill by your table. Following beef in the popularity stakes is **chicken**, which is usually served fried, but can also be had roasted in the oven, or spit-roasted. Chilean chickens are nearly all corn-fed, and are delicious when well cooked – in Arica, in the far north, owing to the locally based chicken breeding industries, succulent, spit-roasted chicken is widely available, and inexpensive, while in central Chile, *pollo al coñac* is a popular, and very tasty, chicken casserole, served in large clay pots with brandy and cream. **Pork** chops also feature on many restaurant menus, but **lamb** is hardly ever available, except in the Lake District where it's a local speciality.

TRADITIONAL FOOD

There's a wide range of older, traditional dishes – usually a fusion of indigenous and Hispanic influences – that are still very much a part of Chilean home cooking and can, with a little luck and effort, be found in the small, old-fashioned restaurants that survive in the hidden corners of town or out in the countryside. Though recipes vary from region to region, depending on the local produce available, there are a few core staples, including sweetcorn and potatoes. **Sweetcorn** forms the basis of two of the most traditional Chilean dishes: **humitas** – mashed corn, wrapped in corn leaves and steamed – and **pastel de choclo**, a pie made of mince or chicken topped by sweetcorn and sugar and baked in the oven. The **potato**, meanwhile, is such an important staple in the Chilean diet that it's acquired its own mythology and folklore (see box, overleaf). Another great traditional dish (or snack) is the **empanada**, as symbolic as the national flag, although it was introduced by the Spanish and is popular throughout South America. Baked or fried, large or small, sweet or savoury, *empanadas* (which are not unlike Cornish pasties) can be filled with almost anything, but the most traditional filling is minced beef, onions, an olive and a portion of hard-boiled egg.

Also very typical are numerous **soups** and **broths**, of which the most famous, cropping up as a starter on many a set meal, is **cazuela**. Named after large Spanish saucepans, *cazuela* is celebrated as much for its appearance as for its taste, with ingredients carefully chosen and cooked to retain their colour and texture: pale yellow potato, orange pumpkin, split rice, green beans, peas and deep yellow sweetcorn, served on a large soup plate with a piece of meat on the bone swimming in stock and sprinkled with parsley and coriander. Other favourite one-pot broths include **caldillo**,

TRADITIONAL SOUPS AND STEWS

Caldillo Vegetables cooked in meat stock, somewhere between a stew and a soup

Caldo Quite bland, simple meat stock or consommé with a little added salt

Caldo de Gallo Nothing to do with chickens, or cockerels (*gallo*), this is sheeps' testicles, cut into star shapes and arranged in a broth. It's meant to cure impotence

Charquicán Meat (dried) stew

Chupe Thick fish or shellfish stew, with added butter, breadcrumbs and cheese

Crema Cream soup made predominately with flour or egg yolks to produce a smooth, thick consistency

Guiso Stew made with blood from a whole sheep, salt pork and vegetables or seaweed

Locro Meat and vegetable stew

Tomaticán Tomato and vegetable stew believed to improve one's singing voice.

Zarzuela Seafood stew

very similar to cazuela but with fish instead of meat, and **escabechado**, a stew made with fish steaks that have been fried then soaked in vinegar. Doubtless because it is so economical, **offal** enjoys a long (though waning) history in Chilean cookery – slaughtermen in Santiago's original Matadero Municipal were given all the offal from the results of their daily labour, which formed the basis of a traditional stew, *caldo de Matadero*, while further south, the area around Rancagua is still famous for its roadside vendors with their bowls of cold pigs' trotters and knuckles.

POTATOES

The **potato** is such an important staple in the Chilean diet – appearing in countless culinary guises and with over 200 names for endemic species – that it's surrounded by folk tradition and superstition. Nowhere is this more true than Chiloé, where potatoes must be sown during a waning moon in August or September unless large *macho* specimens are required for seeds, in which case they are sown at the full moon. Neighbours help each other in every aspect of cultivation and this communal labouring is known as a *minga*. There are three main mingas, *quechatún*, the turning of the earth, *siembra de papa*, the planting, and *cosecha* or *sacadura*, the harvest.

Amongst the mythology and traditional customs associated with the potato are magic stones (*piedras cupucas*) which are found on cerro Chepu, a hill near Ancud in Chiloé where they have been hidden by witches (*brujos*). Made of a porous silicone these stones are either male or female and they are carefully guarded until the potato plants bloom and then the flowers are placed on them and burnt as a sacrifice. Other myths relate that a small silver lizard, *el Lluhay*, feeds on the flowers and anyone who can catch one is guaranteed good fortune, while a maggot, *la coñipone*, that lives in the root ball will prevent babies from crying when placed under their pillow.

POPULAR AND TRADITIONAL WAYS OF EATING POTATOES

Chuañe Balls of grated raw potato which have been wrapped in *nalca* (a rhubarb-like plant) leaves and cooked.

Chuchoca Mashed potato mixed with flour and pig fat, plastered onto a long, thick wooden pole (*chochoquero*) and cooked over an open fire.

Colao Small cakes made from potato, wheat, pork fat and crackling cooked in hot embers.

Mallo de papas Potato stew.

Mayo de papas Peeled, boiled potatoes mashed with onions, chillies, pepper and pig fat.

Mayocan A potato, seaweed and dried shellfish stew traditionally eaten for breakfast.

Milcao Small cakes of grated and mashed potato which are steamed like dumplings, baked or deep fried.

Pan de papas Baked, flat, round cakes of mashed potato mixed with flour, eggs and pig fat.

Papas rellenas Sausage-shaped rolls of mashed potato mixed with flour and filled with meat or shellfish.

Pastel de papas A baked dish with alternating layers of mashed potato and meat or shellfish topped with more potato.

FAST FOOD

All of Chile's towns are well endowed with greasy-spoon cafés and snack bars – usually known as *fuentes de soda* or *schoperías* – serving draught beer and cheap fast food. This usually consists of **sandwiches**, which are consumed voraciously by Chileans of all ages and social standing – indeed one variety, the **Barros Luco** (beef and melted cheese) is named after an ex-president who is said to have devised the combination. Chilean sandwiches are dauntingly large, and the layers of ingredients which ooze out from a roll or bap make them impossible to eat with any degree of delicacy. The choice of fillings is firmly meat-based, with most options revolving around **churrasco** – a thin cut of griddle-fried beef, rather like a minute steak – served with a variety of toppings, including tomato, mashed avocado, runner beans, lettuce, cheese, fried egg, chopped chillies, and mayonnaise (Club sandwiches will probably contain them all).

Chile is also the unlikely home of the **hot dog** or *completo*. Sitting all by itself in a bun the hot dog is simply called a *vienesa* but it grows into an *especial* when mayonnaise is squeezed along the top, and the addition of avocado makes it a *dinámico*. It is not until the sausage is buried under extra sauerkraut and chopped tomato that it becomes completely *completo*.

DRINKING

Soft **fizzy drinks** (*gaseosas*) can be found everywhere in Chile, particularly Coca Cola, Sprite and Fanta. Bottled **mineral water**, too, is widely available, but most restaurants only stock the fizzy variety (*con gas*) – if you want still water (*sin gas*), you'll probably have to buy it from a supermarket. **Coffee**, in Chile, is nearly always instant Nescafé, even in the most upmarket restaurants, and it's virtually impossible to find good, real coffee (if you're on the lookout for it, ask for *café-café*, or *café de grano*, but the chances are that most people won't know what you're talking about). By the same token, Chileans just haven't got the hang of making **tea**, which is nearly always served lukewarm and weak. If you take your tea with milk, beware of asking for *té con leche*, as this will simply be a cup of hot milk and a teabag. Similarly, if you ask for tea with *un poco de leche*, you'll probably get half milk and half water – for just a dash of milk, English-style, it's best not to say anything until your (milkless) tea has been brought to you, and then ask, as an afterthought, for a little milk. **Herbal teas**, however, are widely available and come in countless flavours, some of which are internationally recognizable, while others are made from native plants. The most popular varieties are *manzanilla* (camomile), *menta* (mint) and *boldo* (a fragrant native plant). Where Chile really comes into its own, though, is with the delicious, freshly squeezed **fruit juices** (*jugos naturales*) available in many bars, restaurants and roadside stalls, especially in the fruit-producing regions of the Central Valley, and a few northern oases like Pica. Another home-grown drink is **mote con huesillo**, sold at numerous roadsides throughout the Central Valley and Lake District in summer. *Mote* is boiled or soaked barley grain and *huesillos* are sun-dried peaches, though this sweet, gooey drink can be made with any fresh soft fruit.

Chilean **beer** doesn't come in many varieties, with Crystal and Escudo dominating the choice of bottled lagers, and Schop being the only brand of draught beer available. There's always a good selection of **wine**, on the other hand (see p.102), though the choice on restaurant lists is usually limited to a handful of producers, and in no way reflects the vast range of wines produced for export. Regarded as the Chilean national drink, **pisco sour** is a tangy, refreshing aperitif made from *pisco* (a white brandy made from distilled Moscatel grapes – see box on p.168), freshly squeezed lemon juice and sugar. Coming a close second as Chile's favourite cocktail, **Vaina** is based on the strong sweet wine known as *vino anejo*, mixed with sweet vermouth, brandy and cacao, all shaken together with icing sugar and egg yolk.

You may also come across a number of **regional specialities**, including *chicha de manzana* (apple cider), made at home by every *huaso* in the Central Valley. Further south, in the Lake District, a traditional element of many drinks is *harina tostada* (toasted maize flour), used by the Mapuches since pre-Spanish days. Today, it's still common to see Mapuches sitting around a table with a large jug of frothy coffee-coloured liquid, which is dark beer mixed with *harina tostada*. It's also mixed with cheap wine made from dessert grapes, among other drinks, and is usually stocked by the sackful at local Lake District bars.

UNDERSTANDING CHILEAN MENUS

BASICS

Aceite	Oil
Ají	Chilli
Ajo	Garlic
Arroz	Rice
Azúcar	Sugar
Huevos	Eggs
Ketchup (pronounced "ketchoo")	Tomato sauce
Leche	Milk
Mantequilla	Butter
Mermelada	Jam
Miel	Honey
Mostaza	Mustard
Pan	Bread
Pimienta	Pepper
Sal	Salt

SOME COMMON TERMS

A la parilla	Grilled
A la plancha	Lightly fried
A lo pobre	Served with chips, onions and a fried egg
Ahumado	Smoked
Al horno	Oven-baked
Al vapor	Steamed
Asado	Roast
Asado al palo	Spit-roasted, barbecued
Crudo	Raw
Frito	Fried
Pastel	Paste, purée, mince
Picante	Spicy hot
Pil-pil	Very spicy
Puré	Mashed
Relleno	Filled or stuffed

MEALS

Agregado	Side order
Almuerzo	Lunch
Cena	Dinner
Comedor	Dining room
Cuchara	Spoon
Cuchillo	Knife
Desayuno	Breakfast
La carta	The menu
La cuenta	The bill
Menú del día	Fixed-price set meal
Onces	Afternoon tea
Plato vegetariano	Vegetarian dish
Tenedor	Fork

MEAT (CARNE) AND POULTRY (AVES)

Bistec	Beef steak
Carne de vacuno	Beef
Cerdo	Pork
Chuleta	Cutlet, chop (usually pork)
Churrasco	Griddled beef, like a minute steak
Conejo	Rabbit
Cordero	Lamb
Escalopa Milanesa	Breaded veal escalope
Filete	Fillet steak
Jamón	Ham
Lechón, cochinillo	Suckling pig
Lomo	General term for steak of indiscriminate cut
Pato	Duck
Pavo	Turkey
Pollo	Chicken
Ternera	Veal
Vienesa	Hot dog sausage

OFFAL (MENUDOS)

Chunchules	Intestines
Guatitas	Tripe
Hígado	Liver
Lengua	Tongue
Patas	Feet, trotters
Picante de conejo	Curried rabbits'innards
Riñones	Kidneys

FISH (PESCADO)

Albacora	Albacore (a small, white-fleshed tuna)
Anchoveta	Anchovy
Atún	Tuna
Bacalao	Cod
Bonito	Pacific bonito, similar to tuna
Ceviche	Strips of fish "cooked" in lemon juice and onions
Congrio	A large, superior member of the cod family, erroneously translated as conger eels on menus
Corvina	Related to the sea bass
Lenguado	Sole
Merluza	Hake
Reyneta, reineta	Similar to lemon sole
Salmón	Salmon
Trucha	Trout

SEAFOOD (MARISCOS)

Almeja	Clam, cockle	*Mariscal*	Mixed shellfish, served chilled
Calamar	Squid	*Mejillón*	Mussel
Camarón	Prawn	*Ostión*	Scallop
Centolla	King crab	*Ostra*	Oyster
Choro, chorito	Mussel	*Paila marina*	Thick fish and seafood stew
Erizo	Sea urchin	*Picoroco*	Giant barnacle with a single crab-like claw
Langosta	Lobster	*Piure*	Scarlet-red, kidney-shaped animal that lives inside a hairy mud ball and has an extremely high iodine content. Very popular
Langosta de Isla de Pascua	Spiny lobster	*Pulpo*	Octopus
Langosta de Juan Fernández	Crayfish, rock lobster		
Langostino	Crayfish, red crab		
Loco	Abalone		
Macha	Razor clam		

VEGETABLES (VERDURAS)

Aceitunas	Olives	*Chucrut*	Sauerkraut	*Papa*	Potato
Alcachofa	Artichoke	*Chumbera*	Prickly pear	*Papas fritas*	Chips (French fries)
Cebolla	Onion	*Espinaca*	Spinach	*Poroto verde*	Green, French, runner bean
Champiñón	Mushroom	*Lechuga*	Lettuce	*Tomate*	Tomato
Choclo	Maize, sweetcorn	*Palmito*	Palm heart	*Zapallo*	Pumpkin
		Palta	Avocado pear		

SALADS (ENSALADAS)

Ensalada Chilena	Tomatoes, shredded onion and vinaigrette	*Ensalada Rusa*	Diced vegetables and peas mixed in a thick mayonnaise
Ensalada primavera	Hard-boiled eggs, sweet corn, peas, carrot, beetroot, salsa americana	*Ensalada surtida*	Mixed salad
		Palta Reina	Avocado pear filled with chicken

SANDWICHES (SANWICHES)

Ave mayo	Chicken and mayonnaise	*Completo*	Hotdog, sauerkraut, tomato, avocado, mayonnaise
Ave sola	Chicken	*Diplomático*	Beef, egg and melted cheese
Barros Jarpa	Ham and melted cheese	*Especial*	Hotdog with mayonnaise
Barros Luco	Beef and melted cheese	*Hamburguesa*	Hamburger
Churrasco solo	Griddled beef, like a minute steak		

FRUIT (FRUTAS)

Albaricoque	Apricot	*Frambuesa*	Raspberry	*Naranja*	Orange
Castaña	Chestnut	*Frutilla*	Strawberry	*Pera*	Pear
Cereza	Cherry	*Higo*	Fig	*Piña*	Pineapple
Chirimoya	Custard apple	*Limón*	Lemon	*Plátano* or *banana*	Banana
Ciruela	Plum	*Manzana*	Apple		
Durazno	Peach	*Membrillo*	Quince		

DESSERTS (POSTRES)

When desserts are described as being in juice (*al jugo*) or syrup (*en almíba*), they are going to come out of a tin.

Flan	Crème caramel	*Manjar*	Very sweet caramel, made from condensed milk
Helado	Ice cream	*Panqueque*	Pancake
Küchen	Flan, cake	*Torta*	Tart
Macedonia	Fruit salad		

DRINKS AND BEVERAGES

Note that, owing to the Chileans' compulsive use of the diminutive (*ito* and *ita*), you'll hardly ever be asked if you want a *té* or *café*, but rather a *tecito* or *cafecito*, which tends to throw people at first.

ALCOHOLIC DRINKS

Beer	*Cerveza*
Champagne	*Champán*
Cider	*Chicha*
Wine (red/white)	*Vino* (*tinto/blanco*)

HOT DRINKS

Coffee	*Café*
Decaff	*Descafeinado*
Hot chocolate	*Chocolate*
Herbal tea	*Aguita de hierba*
Tea	*Té*

SOFT DRINKS

Fizzy drink	*Gaseosa*
(in a can/bottle)	(*en lata/botella*)
(draught)	(*de máquina*)
Juice (pure)	*Jugo* (*natural*)
Juice (syrup)	*Nectar*
Water	*Agua*
Mineral water	*Agua mineral*
(sparkling)	(*con gas*)
(still)	(*sin gas*)

COMMUNICATIONS – POST, PHONES AND EMAIL

Chile's postal service, Correos de Chile, is fairly dependable and efficient, and overseas mail sent even from remote areas generally reaches its destination within a couple of weeks. You'll also find it extremely easy to make international phone calls and send faxes from most Chilean towns, though Internet access for sending emails is not yet very common, apart from in the far south.

POST

The Chilean **postal service** is very reliable for international mailings, but can be surprisingly erratic for domestic mailings. A letter from Santiago takes about five days to reach Europe, a little less to reach North America. Allow a few extra days for letters mailed from other towns and cities. Post offices are marked by a blue Correos sign, and are usually on or near the Plaza de Armas of any town; post boxes are yellow, and bear the blue Correos symbol. You can have letters mailed to you at the central post office of any town, using the poste restante system, known as **Lista de Correos** in Chile. The letters should be addressed: Sr/Sra/Srta FULL NAME (last name in capitals), Lista de Correos, Correo Central, CITY OR TOWN, Chile. The names of recipients are typed out in alphabetical order, sorted by last name, and posted up on a board. There are separate lists for men and women, which is why it helps to have a Sr or Sra/Srta in front of your name – otherwise, you should check both lists carefully, whatever your gender. Another thing to bear in mind is that if a middle name is included, this is often taken to be the first part of your surname (Chileans have two last names, one taken from the father and another from the mother) so a letter addressed to George Thomas Marrs would probably be filed under T, and not M. Once you've located your name, jot down the number next to it and present it, along with your passport, to the staff at the counter, along with a small fee (about 50¢ per letter). Unclaimed letters are kept for thirty days and then returned to the sender – it's a good idea to ask the sender to put *your* home address on the back of the envelope instead of theirs, so you'll end up with the letter eventually, even if you miss it in Chile.

An alternative to the Lista de Correos is to use the **American Express mail collection** service, though this is limited to Santiago, and the office (c/o Turismo Cocha, El Bosque Norte 0430) is far less convenient than the Correos Central. Letters should be addressed with your full name, followed by Cliente de American Express (just to avoid confusion); in theory, you're supposed to be an American Express customer to use this service, but no one seems to check.

TELEPHONES

Chilean phone services are the best on the continent, with excellent lines and cheap rates, but getting to grips with the many ways you can use them can be quite a challenge. There's no single national telecommunications company, but a number of private companies, known as carriers, or *portadores*, dominated by **Entel** and **CTC**. Stiff competition between the companies means that prices are low and constantly changing – check the daily papers for up-to-the-minute tariffs (but note that these published rates only apply to private lines, and not public phones).

Each carrier has its own access code (see box). Public telephones are programmed to connect automatically to whichever carrier owns the booth, so there's no need to dial the access code unless you want to choose a different carrier. In this case, dial your chosen carrier's code, then, for inter-regional calls, dial the national area code and number, or, if you're making an international call, dial a single 0, followed by the country code and phone number. If you *don't* want to change carrier, you simply enter the full area code for an inter-regional call (preceded by a 0), and 00 for an international call (followed by the phone number you want to dial). Complicated.

CARRIER CODES

Entel (123)
CTC (188)
Chilesat (171)
BellSouth (181)
VTR (120)
Lusatel (155)
Carrier (121)

The two main types of public phone you'll find on the streets belong to CTC and, less commonly, Entel. CTC's phones are the green and turquoise ones. Some only accept coins, but many accept prepaid **CTC phonecards** (*tarjetas telefónicas*), which you can buy from news kiosks, corner shops and CTC offices, and which generally use a cheaper rate than calls from a *centro de llamadas* (see below). It's a very practical way to phone abroad, and it's worth stocking up on phonecards in major cities, as you can't always buy them in small towns and villages. Entel's phones are the shiny chrome ones. These don't take cards, but you can buy a prepaid "**Entel ticket**", which you use by dialling an access number, given in the instructions on the card, pressing 2, then keying in the card's unique number (revealed by scratching away the gold foil), followed by the number you want to dial. You can use the ticket several times over, until its value runs out. In some ways they're more practical than CTC cards, as you can use them on any type of phone, not just an Entel one.

Besides calling from public phone booths, you can also use call centres, or **centros de llamadas**. There are dozens of these in most cities, and some of them offer exceptionally cheap rates – particularly the small private ones which are more likely to have "promotions" and "special offers". The catch, however, is that in most *centros de llamadas* you can't set a time limit for the call, so you have to be really careful about not talking too long, as you can quickly run up a huge bill. Note that you can normally send and receive **faxes** in these *centros*, as well as in many small shops, which advertise the service with signs on the window.

A final option is to take an **international calling card**. Generally billed to your home phone account or credit card, these are very handy and easy to use, but in the case of Chile, usually work out more expensive than buying a Chilean phonecard or using a *centro de llamadas*.

INTERNATIONAL CALLING CARDS

UK
BT Charge Card ☎0800/345600
AT & T Global Calling Card ☎0500/626262
Mercury Calling Card ☎0500/100505

NORTH AMERICA
AT & T Global Calling Card ☎1-800/382-5610
Sprint ☎1-800/800 0008
MCI ☎1-800/444 2162

AUSTRALIA
Telstra Telecard ☎1800/626 008

NEW ZEALAND
Telecom Calling Card ☎04/382 5818

INTERNET SERVICES

Given the number of companies and individuals who use the Internet, and the resources the main telecommunications companies are pouring into promoting it, there are surprisingly few cybercafés in Chile, especially in comparison with neighbouring Peru. That said, access points are slowly springing up in the main cities, led by Entel which often has a public Internet terminal at its *centros de llamadas*. You can check the location of many cybercafés in Chile (and around the world) on *cybercaptive.com*.

THE MEDIA

With its long tradition of independence, Chile's print media is of a very respectable quality, with two major dailies, whose contents include a good spread of international news. TV, on the other hand, is of generally poor quality, dominated by dreadful soaps and gameshows – though the daily weather slot is an unexpected highlight, as it zooms down the length of Chile, with excellent graphics representing the different geographical features. The radio is even worse than the television, though some of the very rural stations provide a fascinating insight into local communities.

THE PRESS

The Chilean **press**, always resistant to government interference, has managed to uphold a strong tradition of editorial freedom ever since the country's first newspaper, *La Aurora*, was put together by an anti-royalist friar on an imported printing press in 1812, during the early days of the independence movement. One year before *La Aurora* folded in 1827, a new newspaper, *El Mercurio*, went to press in Valparaíso, and has been in continuous publication ever since (despite the best efforts of the Allende government in the early Seventies), making it the longest-running newspaper in the Spanish-speaking world. Emphatically conservative, and owned by the powerful Edwards family in Santiago, *El Mercurio* is considered to be the most "serious" of Chile's dailies, with the most comprehensive coverage of international news. The other major daily is *La Nación*, which tends to be pro-government.

In addition to these two main newspapers, Chile produces a plethora of racy **tabloids** such as *La Segunda* and the afternoon *Ultimas Noticias* (also part of the Edwards empire), as well as *¡Hola!*-style clones, including *Cosas* and *Novidades*. For a more edifying read, try the selection of *Private Eye*-style satirical papers, such as *Condorito*, which provide the best examples of Chile's free press culture. In Santiago you'll find a wide range of foreign papers on offer, as well as the locally produced, English-language *News Review*, while in the south the *Diario Austral* (another Edwards product) usually has at least a brief section on international news, as well as useful listings of regional festivals and events. In the Lake District you might come across *El Cóndor*, a German-language paper first published in Argentina sixty years ago. Until recently it was the only periodical in the world still printing in Gothic typeface but, due to the failing vision of its loyal readers, the paper has adopted a style that's easier on the eye. All these newspapers and magazines are sold at **pavement kiosks** found on the street corners of most towns, where they hang together like a patchwork curtain, clipped together with clothes pegs.

TELEVISION

Almost every household in Chile owns a **television**, which tends to be permanently switched on at a very high volume. The cult of the television is also very much in evidence in bars, cafés and the less expensive restaurants, which are often dominated by enormous screens in the corner of the room. Cable TV is widespread, offering around forty to sixty channels that frequently show US films and popular series like *Friends* and *Cheers* in English with Spanish subtitles, most commonly on the Cinecanal, Cinemax and Sony channels. CNN is always on offer (as is the omnipresent MTV) but BBC World has very limited availability.

Of the seven terrestrial channels (curiously numbered 2, 4, 5, 7, 9, 11 and 13), top choice is Channel 7, the state-owned Televisión Nacional, which makes the best programmes in Chile, including decent documentaries. Among the others are the independent Universidad Católica (very conservative, with a daily *Mensaje Cristiano*) and the network stations Megavisión (lots of dubbed American films) and La Red (mainly youth-oriented). Lunchtime and evening **news coverage** – shown on 4, 7, 9, 11 and 13 – is quite good but invariably starts with football highlights followed by road accidents and bloody shootings no matter what earth-shattering events have occurred in the rest of the world. Otherwise, soap operas, game shows and talent contests predominate, reaching an excruciating climax with *Sábado Gigante*, a truly dreadful talent contest beamed from Miami where Chileans get flown to compete against Mexicans, Puerto Ricans and anyone else who can speak Spanish. Popping up in endless commercials, peering down from advertising hoardings, and plastered over food packaging, the show's indefatigable and larger-than-life compere, Don Francisco, is a national institution whose popularity reaches its zenith each December when he hosts the annual *Teletón* event, which raises money for good causes.

RADIO

There is a compulsive Chilean habit, particularly prevalent amongst the owners of the country's quietest rural bars, of turning the **radio** on as soon as you walk through the door. Outside towns and cities, radio reception is poor and even when there's a clear FM music station its limited play list will make you glad to be just passing through. **News stations** are very rare and when the reception is good you can hear the pages of newspapers being turned as a monotone voice reads one article after another, interrupted periodically by voiced-over jingles telling you that "if you are not informed you cannot have an opinion". Rather a reassuring Chilean institution in this age of instant worldwide communications is the radio station which provides remote rural communities with their sole **message service**. Sitting in a quiet backwoods bar, locals bend an ear for news of family and friends and catch up on the latest developments of ongoing sagas that could easily be scripts for a soap opera.

OPENING HOURS AND HOLIDAYS

Most shops and services are open Monday to Friday 9am to 1pm and 3pm to 6 or 7pm; and on Saturday until 2pm. Supermarkets normally stay open at lunchtime and may close as late as 9pm on weekdays and Saturdays. Large shopping malls are often open all day on Sundays. Banks have more limited opening hours, usually Monday to Friday 9am to 2pm, but *casas de cambio* tend to use the same opening hours as shops.

Museums are nearly always shut on Mondays, and are sometimes free on Sundays. Many **tourist offices** are only open Monday to Friday through the year, with a break for lunch, but in summer (usually between December 15 and March 15) they increase their weekday hours and open on Saturday and sometimes Sunday – their hours are subject to frequent change, however, and those that we've listed in the *Guide* may no longer be correct by the time you visit. **Post offices** don't close at lunchtime on weekdays and are open on Saturdays from 9am to 1pm.

Note also that **February** is the main holiday month in Chile, when there's an exodus from the big cities to the beaches or the Lake District, leaving some shops and restaurants closed.

PUBLIC HOLIDAYS

Apart from the statutory public holidays which are recognized nationwide, shops and offices will be closed for certain local festivals and on national and local election days when the country comes to an almost complete standstill for 24 hours from midnight to midnight.

NATIONAL PUBLIC HOLIDAYS

January 1 New Year's Day (*Año nuevo*)

Easter (*Semana Santa*) with national holidays on Good Friday, Easter Saturday and Easter Sunday

May 1 Labour Day (*Día del Trabajo*)

May 21 *Combáte Naval de Iquique*. A Remembrance Day celebrating the end of the War of the Pacific after the naval victory at Iquique

June 15 Corpus Christi

June 29 San Pedro y San Pablo

August 15 Assumption of the Virgin

September 11 Public holiday marking the military coup which deposed the democratic government in 1973

September 18 National Independence Day (*Fiestas Patrias*), in celebration of the first provisional government of 1810

September 19 Armed Forces Day (*Día del Ejército*)

October 12 Columbus Day (*Día de la Raza*), marking the discovery of America

November 1 All Saints' Day (*Todos los Santos*)

December 8 Feast of the Immaculate Concepcion

December 25 Christmas Day (*Navidad*)

TROUBLE AND CRIME

Chile is probably the safest South American country to travel in, and violent crime against tourists is almost unheard of. The kind of sophisticated tactics used by thieves in neighbouring Peru and Bolivia are very uncommon in Chile, and the fact that you can walk around without being gripped by paranoia is one of the country's major bonuses.

That's not to say, of course, that you don't need to be careful. On the contrary, opportunistic pick-pocketing and petty thieving is rife in Santiago and major cities like Valparaíso, Arica and Puerto Montt, and you should take all the normal precautions to safeguard your money and valuables, paying special attention in bus terminals and markets – wear a money belt, and keep it tucked inside the waistband of your trousers or skirt, out of sight, and don't wear flashy jewellery, flaunt expensive cameras or carry a handbag. It's also a good idea to keep photocopies of your passport, tourist card, driving licence, air tickets and credit card details separate from the originals – whether it's safer to carry the originals with you or leave them in your hotel is debatable, but whatever you do, you should always have some form of ID on you, even if this is just a photocopy of your passport.

Out of the cities, there's no fear of banditry or general lawlessness, as there is in many parts of South America. Chile's police force, the **Carabineros**, have the whole country covered, with stations in even the most remote areas, particularly in border regions. In general, the *Carabineros* are helpful, reliable and scrupulously courteous to foreign travellers, with an extremely low level of corruption – *never* offer a bribe to a policeman, as you will cause offence and make the situation worse. If you're robbed and need a police report for an insurance claim, you should go to the nearest *Carabineros retén* (station) where details of the theft will be entered in a log book. You'll be issued with a slip of paper with the record number of the entry, but in most cases a full report won't be typed out until your insurance company requests it.

Street demonstrations have become a way of life in Chile since the military coup, always heating up during court appearances and debates in the Senate or Congress relating to human rights abuses during the military government. Another cause of protest has been the detainment of General Pinochet in the United Kingdom, following his arrest there in October 1998. Demonstrations frequently get out of control, and the police invariably respond with strong-arm measures including the use of tear gas and batons – you'd be wise to steer well clear of the local Plaza de Armas (or Plaza Italia in Santiago) if you're in town when one's taking place.

Something else to avoid is taking photographs of **naval vessels** and **military areas**, including prisons – this is illegal, and you will have your film confiscated. Certain sensitive international border areas also have photographic restrictions, particularly between Arica and the Peruvian frontier which is full of mine fields and tank emplacements.

EMERGENCY TELEPHONE NUMBERS

Carabineros 133
Investigaciones 134
Ambulance 131
Fire 132
Coastguard 137
Air rescue 138

SPORT, ENTERTAINMENT AND FESTIVALS

The Chileans are not a particularly exuberant people (especially compared to their Argentinean neighbours) and the country's entertainment scene sits firmly on the tame side of the fence. That said, passions are roused by several national enthusiasms – chiefly football and rodeo, which at their best are performed with electrifying skill and theatricality, wrapped up in a fantastic atmosphere. Local and national fiestas are another opportunity for the Chileans to let their hair down, and usually include a good deal of flag waving, dancing, singing, drinking and eating of *empanadas*. If your Spanish is good, you'll also be entertained

MAJOR FESTIVALS

For more on altiplano fiestas and ceremonies, see p.218.

January

20 *San Sebastián* Spaniards brought the first wooden image of San Sebastián to Chile in the seventeenth century. After á Mapuche raid on Chillán, the image was buried in a nearby field, and no one was able to raise it. The saint's feast day has become an important Mapuche festival, especially in Lonquimay, where it's celebrated with horse racing, feasting and drinking.

February

1–3 *La Candelaria* Celebrated throughout Chile since 1780, when a group of miners and muleteers discovered a stone image of the Virgin and child while sheltering from an inexplicable thunderstorm in the Atacama. Typical festivities include religious processions and traditional dances.

End of the month *Festival Internacional de la Canción* Glitzy and wildly popular five-day festival held in Viña del Mar's open-air amphitheatre, featuring performers from all over Latin America and broadcast to most Spanish-speaking countries in the world.

April

Easter *Semana Santa* (Holy Week). Among the nationwide Easter celebrations, ones to look out for include Santiago's solemn procession of penitents dressed in black habits, carrying crosses through the streets, and La Ligua's parade of mounted *huasos* followed by a giant penguin.

First Sunday after Easter *Fiesta del Cuasimodo* In many parts of central Chile, *huasos* parade through the streets on their horses, often accompanied by a priest sitting on a float covered in white lilies.

May

3 *Santa Cruz de Mayo.* Throughout the altiplano, ceremonial villages celebrate the cult of the cross, inspired in the seventeenth century by the Spaniards' bewildering obsession with crosses, which they carried everywhere, erected on hillsides and even carved in the air with their fingers. The festivities have strong pre-Christian elements, often including the sacrifice of a llama.

13 *Procesión del Cristo de Mayo.* A huge parade through the streets of Santiago bearing the *Cristo de Mayo* – a sixteenth-century carving of Christ whose crown of thorns slipped to its neck during an earthquake, and which shed tears of blood when attempts were made to put the crown back in place.

June

13 *Noche de San Juan Bautista* An important feast night, celebrated by families up and down the country with a giant stew, known as the *Estofado de San Juan.* In Chiloé, an integral part

by the characteristic fast-thinking humour evident throughout Chilean culture, from the teasing jokes of young waiters and bar staff, through to the sophisticated word-plays that pepper the country's theatre, music and literature.

FOOTBALL

El fútbol reigns supreme as Chile's favourite sport and the top *futbolistas* are modern-day folk heroes whose exploits are frequently splashed across the front pages of the newspapers.

Introduced by British immigrants in the early 1800s, football in Chile can trace its history back to the playing fields of the Mackay School, one of the first English schools founded in Valparaíso, and its heritage is reflected in the names of the first clubs: Wanderers, Everton, Badminton, Morning Star and Green Cross.

Everton and Wanderers are still going strong but the sport is now dominated by the Santiago teams of Colo Colo, Universidad Católica and Universidad de Chile. Matches featuring any of these teams are guaranteed a good turn-out and a great atmosphere. There's rarely any trouble, with whole families coming along to enjoy the fun. In Santiago (unquestionably the best place to watch a match), tickets to see the main teams play cost around CH$3000–5000 (US$6–10) at the bottom end, going up to CH$35,000 (US$73) for the most expensive seats. If you can't make it to a match, you'll still see plenty of football on the huge TVs that dominate most cafés and bars, including European games shown on cable channels (you may notice, too, that widespread expo-

of the feast are roasted potato balls called *tropones*, which burn the fingers and make people "dance the *tropón*" as they jig up and down, juggling them from hand to hand.

29 *Fiesta de San Pedro* The length of Chile's coast, fishermen decorate their boats and take the image of their patron saint out to sea – often at night with candles and flares burning – to pray for good weather and large catches.

July

12–18 *Virgen de la Tirana* The largest religious festival in Chile, held in La Tirana, in the Norte Grande, and attended by over 80,000 pilgrims and hundreds of costumed dancers (see p.212).

16 *Virgin del Carmen* Military parades throughout Chile in honour of the patron saint of the armed forces; the largest are in Maipú, on the southern outskirts of Santiago, where San Martín and Bernardo O'Higgins defeated Spanish Royalists in 1818.

August

21–31 *Jesús Nazareno de Caguach* Thousands of Chilotés flock to the archipelago's tiny island of Caguach to worship a two-metre-high figure of Christ, donated by the Jesuits in the eighteenth century.

September

18 *Fiestas Patiras* Chile's Independence Day is celebrated throughout the country with street parties, music and dancing.

October

First Sunday *Virgen de las Peñas* Numerous dance groups and over 10,000 annual pilgrims from Chile, Peru, Bolivia and Argentina make their way along a tortuous cliff path to visit a rock carving of the Virgin in the Azapa valley, near Arica. There are many smaller festivals in other parts of Chile, too.

November

1 *Todos los Santos* (All Saints Day) Traditionally, this is the day when Chileans tend their family graves. In the north, where Aymara customs have become entwined with Christian ones, crosses are often removed from graves, and left on the former bed of the deceased overnight. Candles are kept burning in the room, and a feast is served for family members, past and present.

2 *Día de los Muertos* (All Souls Day) A second vigil to the dead is held in cemeteries, with offerings of food and wine sprinkled on the graves. In some Norte Grande villages, there's a tradition of reading a liturgy, always in Latin.

December

8 *La Purísima* Celebrated in many parts of Chile, the festival of La Purísima is at its liveliest in San Pedro de Atacama, where it's accompanied by traditional Aymara music and dancing.

23–27 *Fiesta Grande de la Virgen de Andacollo* Over 100,000 pilgrims from all over the north come to Andacollo, in the Norte Chico, to worship its Virgin and watch the famous masked dancers (see p.153).

sure to English football has led many young Chileans to refer to an Englishman as a *húligan* rather than a *gringo*).

Football hardly has a **season** in Chile because apart from the league games played between March and December, there are numerous other competitions of which the Copa de Libertadores is the most important, so you'll be able to catch the action whatever time of year you visit.

HORSE RACING

There are two very different types of **horse racing** in Chile: conventional track racing, known as *hípica*, and the much rougher and wilder *carreras a la chilena*. **Hípica** is a sport for rich Santiaguinos, who don their tweeds and posh frocks to go and watch it at the capital's Club Hípico and Hipódromo Chile, which have races throughout the year. The most important of these are the *St Leger* at the Hipódromo Chile on December 14, and the *Ensayo* at the Club Hípico on the first Sunday in November.

Carreras a la chilena are held anywhere in the country where two horses can be found to race against each other. Apart from the organized events which take place at village fiestas, these races are normally a result of one *huaso* betting another that his horse is faster. Held in any suitable field, well away from the prying eyes of the *Carabineros*, the two-horse race can attract large crowds who bet heavily on the outcome, and enterprising local families who set up food and drink stalls. After a track is marked out with a piece of string, both horses and riders mill around giving each other the evil eye for an hour or more. When the race begins, the tension is palpable as the two men and their beasts pit their strength and skill against each other, and the crowd is frozen in silence until the winner crosses the finishing post, whereupon it breaks out into loud, raucous whooping.

RODEO

Rodeos evolved from the early colonial days when the cattle on the large *estancias* had to be rounded up and branded or slaughtered by *huasos* (Chilean "cowboys" or horsemen). The feats of horsemanship required to do so soon took on a competitive element, which eventually found an expression in the form of rodeos. Even though ranching has long declined in Chile, organized rodeos remain wildly popular, with many free competitions taking place in local stadiums (known as *medialunas*) throughout the season, which runs from September to April. Taking in a rodeo not only allows you to watch the most dazzling equestrian skills inside the arena, but also to see the *huasos* decked out in all their traditional gear, ponchos, silver spurs and all. Added to this, the atmosphere is invariably excellent, with lots of whooping families and excited kids, and plenty of food and drink afterwards. For a fuller account of rodeos, see the box on p.237.

CUECA

Huasos are also the chief performers of **cueca**, Chile's national dance – a curious cross between thigh-slapping English morris dancing and smouldering *Sevillanas*. Its history can in fact be traced to the African slave dances, which were also the basis of the Argentinean samba and Peruvian *zamacueca*, and were introduced into Chile by a battalion of Negro soldiers in 1824. During the War of Independence, Chileans adopted their own forms of these dances known as *la Chilena*, *la Marinera* and *el Minero* which eventually became a national victory dance known simply as the *cueca*. Although there are regional variations, the basic elements remain unchanged, consisting of couples strutting around each other in a courtship ritual, spurs jingling and handkerchiefs waving over their heads. The men are decked out in their finest *huaso* gear, while the women wear wide skirts and shawls. In the background, guitar-strumming musicians sing romantic ballads full of patriotic sentiments. If you are going to a fiesta and want to take part in a *cueca*, remember to take along a clean white handkerchief.

FESTIVALS

Most of Chile's **festivals** are held to mark religious occasions, or to honour saints or images of the Virgin, but the fascinating thing about them is the strong element of pre-Spanish, pre-Christian rites, particularly in the Aymara communities of the Norte Grande and the Mapuches of the south. Added to this is the influence of colourful folk traditions rooted in the Spanish expeditions of exploration and conquest, colonization and evangelism, slavery and revolution. Because of the country's singular geography, the forms of celebrating fiestas have evolved in quite different ways in different regions. In the altiplano of the **Norte Grande**, Aymara herdsmen celebrate Catholic feasts and ancient cults alike with ritual dancing, and often the offering of sacrificial llamas.

In **central Chile**, the influence of colonial traditions is very pronounced. Since the days of the conquest, an important ingredient of any fiesta was the verbal sparring between itinerant bards called *payadores* who would compose and then try to resolve each other's impromptu rhyming riddles. The custom is kept alive at many fiestas in Central Valley, where young poets spontaneously improvise *lolismos* and *locuciones*, forms of jocular verse which are quite unintelligible to an outsider. These rural fiestas always culminate in an energetic display of *cueca* dancing, washed down with plenty of wine and *chicha* – reminiscent of the entertainment organized by indulgent *hacienda*-owners for their peons.

In the **south**, the solemn Mapuche festivals are closely linked to mythology, magic and faith healing, agricultural rituals, and supplications to gods and spirits. Group dances (*purrún*) are performed with gentle movements and participants either move round in a circle or advance and retreat in lines. Most ceremonies are accompanied by mounted horn players whose four-metre-long bamboo instruments, *trutrucas*, require enormous lung power to produce a note. Other types of traditional wind instrument commonly played at such events include a small pipe (*lolkiñ*), flute (*pinkulwe*), cow's horn (*kullkull*) and whistle (*pifilka*). Of all Mapuche musical instruments, the most important is the sacred drum (*kultrún*), which is only used by faith healers (*machis*).

THE CHILEAN HUASO

"Of the many cowboys of the Americas, none remains as shrouded in mystery and contradiction as Chile's *huaso*", says Richard Slatta in *Cowboys of the Americas*. Certainly the *huaso* holds a special place in Chile's perception of its national identity, and has become a potent symbolic figure over the years. But the definition and identity of the *huaso* is somewhat confused, and subject to multiple, wildly differing interpretations. The one you're most likely to come across as a traveller is that of the "gentleman rider", the middle-class horseman who, while not a part of the landed elite, is a good few social rungs up from the landless labourer. This is the *huaso* you'll see in *cueca* performances (see opposite) and at rodeos, mounted on a fine-blooded steed and dressed in richly woven ponchos, silk sashes, high-heeled Cordova-leather boots and large silver spurs. This version of the *huaso* has evolved from a Spanish archetype – the dignified country gentleman and his horse – imported, along with cattle and horses, by the conquistadors. While not exactly a fiction, these gentlemen riders (labelled "postcard huasos" by Slatta) are, nonetheless, part of a romanticized image of the Chilean countryside, and are a far cry from the far larger and perhaps more authentic group of huasos who carried out the real horse-work on the land. More akin to the Argentine *gaucho* and the Mexican *vaquero*, this other type of *huaso* was a landless, badly paid, poorly dressed ranch-hand, who worked on the large haciendas during the cattle round-up season. His prototype developed during the early years of the colony – with the creation of the immense landed estates, and the introduction of livestock-breeding – and by the eighteenth century was a fundamental cog in the rural economy. Despite the harsh reality of his lifestyle, the lower-class *huaso* is also the victim of myth-making, frequently depicted as a paragon of virtue and happiness – loyal to his master, honest, hard-working and at one with the land.

All types of *huaso*, whatever their social status, were renowned for their outstanding horsemanship. One visiting Englishman in the nineteenth century described, with astonishment, the skilful Chilean cowboys who could "throw their lasso at full speed and entangle and secure the wildest animal". They were also marvelled at for their practice of training their horses to stop dead in their tracks at a single command, a technique known as *la sentada*. A skill mastered by *huasos* in the southern Central Valley (and borrowed from Argentinian gauchos) was that of the *bolas* – three stones or metal balls attached to long leather straps, that were hurled at animals and wrapped around their legs, bringing them to the ground. Huasos also developed a whole host of equestrian games and contests including the *juego de cañas* (jousting with canes), the *tiro al gallo* (a mounted tug-of-war) and *topeadura* (a side-by-side pushing contest). Today, these displays have a formal outlet in the regular rodeos (see p.237) that take place throughout the Central Valley. As for the working *huaso*, you'll still come across him in the back roads of rural central Chile, herding livestock, often wearing a broad-rimmed *huaso* hat, and occasionally a brightly hued poncho.

NATIONAL PARKS AND RESERVES

Some eighteen percent of Chile's mainland territory is protected by the state under the extensive Sistema Nacional de Areas Silvestres Protegidas (National Protected Wildlife Areas System), which is made up of thirty national parks, thirty-eight national reserves and eleven natural monuments. These inevitably include the country's most outstanding scenic attractions, but while there are provisions for tourism, the main aim is always to protect and manage native fauna and flora. Given Chile's great biodiversity, these vary tremendously from one region to another, and park objectives are as diverse as protecting the flamingo populations of the altiplano lakes to monitoring glaciers off the southern fjords. Other important functions include preventing poaching (for instance of vicuñas in the altiplano) and guarding against forest fires. All protected areas are managed by the Corporación Nacional Forestal (better known as Conaf), established in 1972 as part of the Ministry of Agriculture.

DEFINITIONS AND TERMS

National parks (*parques nacionales*) are generally large areas of unspoilt wilderness, usually featuring fragile endemic ecosystems. They include the most touristed and scenically beautiful of the protected areas, and often offer walking trails, and camping areas. **National reserves** (*reservas nacionales*) are areas of ecological importance which have suffered some degree of natural degradation; there are fewer regulations to protect these areas, and "sustainable" commercial exploitation (such as mineral extraction) is allowed to take place. **Natural monuments** (*monumentos naturales*) tend to be important or endangered geological formations, or small areas of biological, anthropological or archeological significance. In 1976, two tree species, the araucaria and alerce, were awarded the status of natural monument. In addition to these three main categories, there is a small number of **nature sanctuaries** (*sanctuarios de la naturaleza*) and **protected Areas** (*areas de protección*), usually earmarked for their scientific or scenic interest. It is not difficult for the government to change the status of these areas, and national parks have been known to be downgraded so that their resources could be commercially exploited.

In addition to these state-owned parks, there's an important private initiative, **Parque Pumalín**

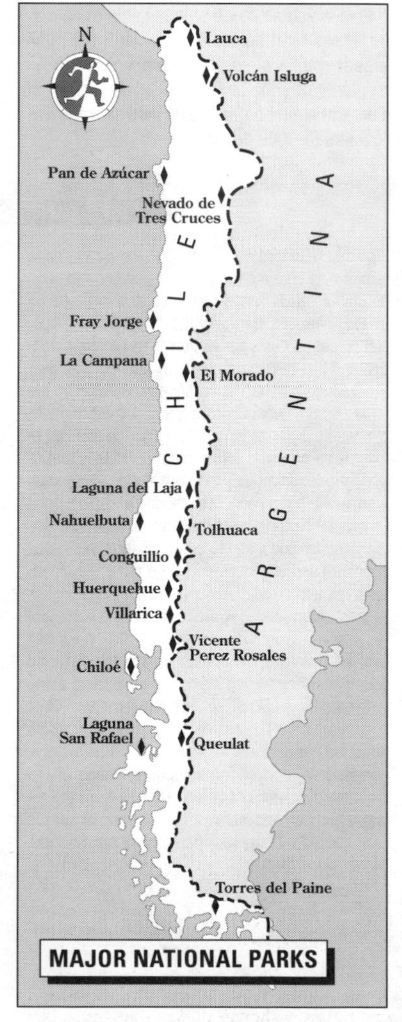

(see p.361), just south of Puerto Montt, which contains some of the most luxuriant native forest in the country.

PARK ADMINISTRATION

The administration of Chile's protected areas is highly centralized, with all important decisions coming from **Conaf's head office** in Santiago. This is a good place to visit before heading out of the capital (for the address, see p.69), as you can pick up brochures and basic maps of all the parks, and buy several publications on native flora and fauna. In addition, each regional capital has a Conaf headquarters, which is useful for more practical pre-visit tips, such as on road conditions and hiking possibilities. The parks and reserves are staffed by Conaf **guardaparques** (park wardens), who live in rustic ranger stations (called *guarderías*) and can be immediately identified by their green uniform and green peaked cap bearing the Conaf symbol. Chilean *guardaparques* are almost without exception friendly, enthusiastic and dedicated to their job, despite working extremely long hours under difficult conditions for little pay. They're often out of their stations all day, patrolling the park for poachers or other hazards, or monitoring the various programmes set up to recuperate declining wildlife populations or flora with conservation problems. Most parks are divided into several areas, known as "sectors" (*sectores*), and the larger ones have a small *guardería* in each *sector*.

VISITING THE PARKS

No **permit** is needed to visit any of Chile's national parks; you simply turn up and pay your **entrance fee**, which is usually between CH$1000 and CH$2500. Ease of **access** differs wildly from one park to the next – a few have paved highways running through them, while others are served by appalling dirt tracks that are only passable for a few months of the year. Typically, though, parks are reached by rough, bumpy dirt roads, and getting to them often involves renting a vehicle or booking transport through a local tour company, as around two thirds of national parks can't be reached by public transport.

Arriving at the park boundary, you'll normally pass a small hut (called the "*Conaf control*") where you pay your entrance fee and pick up a basic map (usually photocopied, and poor quality). Some of the larger parks have more than one entrance point, served by different access roads. The main ranger station is always separate from the hut, sometimes just a few hundred metres away, sometimes several kilometres. The station contains the rangers' living quarters and administrative office, and often a large map or scale model of the park, marking all the trails. The more popular parks also have a **Centro de Información Ambiental** attached to the station, with displays on the park's flora and fauna and, in high season, slide shows and talks (*charlas*).

Nearly all parks have **camping** areas: in some, these are rustic sites, with basic facilities, run by Conaf who charge around CH$4000 to CH$8000 per tent; in other parks, particularly in the south, Conaf gives licences to **concessionaires**, who operate campsites and *cabañas*, which tend to be very expensive. Some of the more remote national parks, especially in the north, have small **refugios** attached to the ranger stations – these are usually rustic, stone-built huts containing around eight to ten bunk beds (from CH$5000 per person), hot showers and gas stoves. Some of these are in the most stunning locations, such as the *refugios* looking across the Salar de Surire (see p.231), and across Lago Chungará to Volcán Parinacota (see p.230).

ADVENTURE TOURISM

Much of Chile is a paradise of untamed wilderness, and it's no surprise that what the Chileans call "adventure tourism" is one of the main reasons why people come here. The range of outdoor activities on offer is enormous, taking in skiing, surfing, volcano-climbing, white-water rafting, fly-fishing and horse riding. Although Chile's tourism industry is traditionally geared up to Argentinian holiday-makers who come to lie on the beaches, an increasing number of operators and outfitters are wising up to the potential of organized adventure tourism, offering one- or multi-day guided excursions.

Many of these companies are based in Pucón, in the Lake District, with a good sprinkling of other outfitters spread throughout the south. There are fewer opportunities for outdoor activities in the harsh deserts of the north, where altiplano jeep trips and mountain biking are the main options. If you plan to do any adventurous activities, be sure to check that you're covered by your **travel insurance**, or take out specialist insurance where necessary.

RAFTING AND KAYAKING

Numerous narrow rivers hurtling down from the Andes to the ocean provide Chile with some excellent **white-water rafting** opportunities. These include two top "world class" rafting rivers: the great **Bío Bío**, on the southern edge of the Central Valley, and, down by the Carretera Austral, the **Futaleufú**, the venue of the Rafting World Championships in 2000. Both of these rivers feature class III to V rapids (out of a grading of I to VI, with VI being commercially unraftable), as well as a spectacular backdrop of volcanoes, waterfalls and lush native forest.

Trips range in length from one to eight days and, in the case of the Bío Bío, sometimes include the option of climbing 3160m Volcán Callaquén. **Prices** are normally around US$100 for a day's rafting, US$350 for a three-day trip (with all camping equipment and food provided), going up to US$1500–2000 for all-inclusive ten-day packages, with added excursions. As well as these challenging rivers, gentler alternatives exist on the **río Maipo** close to Santiago, the **río Trancura** near Pucón, and the **río Petrohue** near Puerto Varas. The Maipo makes a good day-trip from Santiago while the last two are just half-day affairs, and can usually be arranged on the spot, without advance reservations. In general, all rafting trips are extremely well organized, but you should always take great care in choosing your outfitter – this activity can be very dangerous in the hands of an inexperienced guide.

THE ANDES FROM THE SKY

For an unforgettable experience and heart-stopping views over the Andean peaks near Santiago, you could go on a "Flying Adventure Tour", including **hot-air balloon** rides and flights in **cockpit biplanes** and **gliders**. For more information, contact Sportstour at Moneda 970, fourteenth floor, Santiago (☎2/696 3100, fax 698 2981).

Chile's white-water rapids also make fantastic **kayaking**, though this is less developed as an organized activity – your best bet is probably to contact one of the US-based outfitters that have base camps on the Bío Bío and Futaleufú (see box on p.56 for contacts). The very wide range of rapids on Chile's rivers, from II to V+, means there's something to suit all levels of experience and abilities, and because they can all be easily portaged, novices can go along with experts. **Sea kayaking** is becoming increasingly popular in Chile, generally in the calm, flat waters of Chile's southern fjords, though people have been known to kayak around Cape Horn. Note that the Chilean navy is very sensitive about any foreign vessels (even kayaks) cruising in their waters, and if you're planning a trip through military waters, you'd be wise to inform the Chilean consulate or embassy in your country beforehand.

HIKING

For the most part, Chile is a very empty country with vast swaths of wilderness offering potential for fantastic hiking (and concealing no dangerous animals or snakes). Chileans, moreover, are often reluctant to stray far from their parked car when they visit the countryside, and you'll find that most trails without vehicle access are blissfully quiet. However, the absence of a national enthusiasm for hiking also means that, compared to places of similar scenic beauty like California, British Columbia and New Zealand, Chile isn't particularly geared up to the hiking scene, with relatively few long-distance trails (given the total area) and a shortage of decent trekking maps. That said, what *is* on offer is superb, and ranks among the country's most rewarding attractions.

The **north** of Chile, with its harsh climate and landscape, isn't really suitable for hiking, and most walkers head for the lush native forests of Chile's **south**, peppered with waterfalls, lakes, hot springs and volcanoes. The best trails are nearly always inside **national parks** or reserves, where the *guardaparques* are a good source of advice on finding and following the paths, and should *always* be informed if you plan to do an overnight hike (so that if you don't come back, they'll know where to search for you). The majority of trails are for half-day or day hikes, though some parks offer a few long-distance hikes, sometimes linking up with trails in adjoining parks. The level of path-maintenance and signing

WHERE TO HIKE

For those who want to plan a trip around a few hikes, we refer you to the following accounts in the *Guide*:

Parque Nacional Chiloé (p.348)
Parque Nacional El Morado (p.104)
Parque Nacional Huerquehue (p.290)
Parque Nacional La Campana (p.106)
Parque Nacional Queulat (p.370)
Parque Nacional Tolhuaca (p.268)
Parque Nacional Valdivia, Sector Quetrupilán (p.294)
Parque Nacional Vicente Perez Rosales (p.322)
Reserva Nacional Río Los Cipreses (p.239)

varies greatly from one park to another, and many of the more remote trails are indistinct and difficult to follow. Some parks allow wild **camping**, while others have a series of rustic camping areas that you're required to stick to – check with the *guardaparque*. If you do camp (and this is the best way to experience the Chilean wilderness) note that forest and bush fires are a very real hazard, and take great care when making a campfire (having checked beforehand that they're allowed). Also, never chop or break down vegetation for fuel, as most of Chile's native flora is endangered.

By far the most popular destination for hiking is **Torres del Paine** in the far south, which offers magnificent scenery but fairly crowded trails, especially in January and February. Many quieter, less well-known alternatives are scattered between Santiago and Tierra del Fuego, ranging from narrow paths in the towering, snow-streaked central Andes, to hikes up to glaciers off the Carretera Austral.

If you go hiking, it's essential to be well-prepared – always carry plenty of water, wear a hat and sun block for protection against the sun and carry extra layers of warm clothing to guard against the sharp drop of temperatures after sundown. Even on day hikes, take enough supplies to provide for the eventuality of getting lost, and always carry a map and **compass** (or *brújula*, preferably bought in the southern hemisphere or adjusted for southern latitudes). Also, make a conscious effort to help preserve Chile's environment – where there's no toilet, **bury human waste** at least 20cm under the ground and 30m from the nearest river or lake; take away or burn all your **rubbish**; and use specially designed eco-friendly **detergents** for use in lakes and streams.

CLIMBING

The Andean cordillera, running the whole length of Chile, offers numerous mountaineering possibilities, from day-trips for novices to challenging peaks for experts. In the **far north** of Chile, there are several volcanoes over 6000m, including Volcán Parinacota (6330m), Volcán Llullaillaco (6700m) and Volcán Ojos del Salado (6950m). Although ropes and crampons aren't always needed, these ascents are suitable only for experienced climbers, and need a fair amount of independent planning, with only a few companies offering guided excursions. There are several challenging, technical climbs in the **central Andes**, including Volcán Marmolejo (6100m) and Volcán Tupungato (6750m). Although just across the border in Argentina, the continent's highest peak, Cerro Aconcagua (6980m), is usually approached from Santiago, from where several companies offer guided expeditions, normally taking fifteen to twenty days, costing from US$1500 per person.

In the **south** of Chile, in the Lake District, two volcanoes have developed into major tourist attractions: Volcán Villarica (2840m) and Volcán Osorno (2652m), which you can climb in a day without previous experience, with one of several tour companies. Further south, the most popular climbs are Cerro Torre (3100m) and Cerro Paine Grande (3248m) in Parque Nacional Torres del Paine, but beware that climbing in this park involves paying a fee of CH$40,000 per person.

Elsewhere in Chile there are no climbing fees, but there's a lot of tedious bureaucracy to get through before you can climb. To go up any mountain straddling an international border (which means most of the high Andean peaks), you need advance **permission** from the **Dirección de Fronteras y Límites** (DIFROL), Fourth Floor, Bandera 52, Santiago (☎2/671 4110, fax 697 1909). To get this, write to or fax DIFROL with the planned dates and itinerary of the climb, listing full details (name, nationality, date of birth, occupation, passport number, address) of each member of the climbing team, and your dates of entry and exit from Chile. Authorization will then be sent or faxed to you on a piece of paper which you

USEFUL CLIMBING CONTACTS

Federación de Andinismo, Almirante Simpson 77, Providencia, Santiago (☎2/222 0799, fax 635 9089). *This friendly organization runs mountaineering courses, sells equipment, can put you in touch with guides and offers knowledgeable, helpful advice. It also helps out foreigners trying to arrange climbing authorization.*

British Mountaineering Council, 177–179 Burton Rd, Manchester M20 2BB, UK (☎0161/445 4747, fax 445 4500). *Produces a very useful information sheet on mountaineering, and also provides specialist insurance for members.*

American Alpine Club, 710 Tenth S, Suite 100, Golden, CO 80401, USA (☎303/384-0110, fax 384-0111). *A good source of pre-trip advice.*

must present to Conaf before ascending (if the peak is not within a national park, you must take the authorization to the nearest *Carabineros* station). If your plans change while you're in Chile, you can usually amend the authorization or get a new one at the *Gobernación* of each provincial capital.

FLY-FISHING

Chile is one of the world's great fly-fishing destinations, its crystal-clear waters teeming with rainbow, brown and brook **trout**, and silver and Atlantic **salmon**. These fish are not native, but were introduced for sport in the late nineteenth century; since then, the wild population has flourished and multiplied, and is also supplemented by generous numbers of escapees from local fish farms. The fishing **season** varies slightly from region to region, but in general runs from November to May.

Traditionally, the best sport-fishing was considered to be in the Lake District, but while this region still offers great possibilities, attention has shifted to the more remote, pristine waters of **Aisén**, where a number of classy fishing lodges have sprung up, catering mainly for wealthy North American clients. Fishing in the Lake District is frequently done from river boats, while a typical day's fishing in Aisén begins with a ride in a motor dinghy through fjords, channels and islets towards an isolated river. You'll then wade upstream to shallower waters, usually equipped with a light six or seven weight rod, dry flies and brightly coloured streamers. Catches weigh in between 1 and 3kg – but note that many outfitters operate only on a catch and release basis, so don't count on being able to cook them for your supper.

Costs range from a reasonable US$70 per person for a day in the more visited waters of the Lake District (including full equipment hire and boat transport), to around US$400 per day to fish the scarcely-touched waters of Aisén with top-notch guides. You may also need to get yourself a **licence** (CH$6300 for the whole country), widely available at town halls and specialist fishing shops, though many outfitters supply this as part of the package. To find out more about fly-fishing in Chile, contact the government agency **Servicio Nacional de Pesca** at Yungay 1737, piso 4, Valparaíso, Chile (☎32/214371, fax 259564).

SKIING

Chile has the best skiing in South America and on high altitude slopes, many argue that the very dry powder snow – known as "champagne snow" – is of a quality found nowhere else. The **season** is from June to September, with August marking the busiest period. Conveniently, the best slopes and resorts are just 40km from Santiago: neighbouring **El Colorado**, **La Parva** and **Valle Nevado** can easily be skied on a day-trip from the capital, while classy **Portillo** lies within comfortable striking distance for a weekend visit, 149km north. One-week all-inclusive **packages** at these places start at around US$800 per person in low season, and about twice that much in high season; for more details on these ski centres, see p.105.

Nothing else in Chile can match the resorts near Santiago, though the **Termas de Chillán** ski centre, 480km south, isn't too far behind, and offers the added advantage of steaming thermal pools for après-ski relaxation. Added to this, the fledgling, rustic ski-centres dotted down the Andes south of Santiago make a fun and much cheaper alternative to the main resorts: examples include **Chapa Verde**, near Rancagua (see p.238); **Antuco**, near Concepción (see p.265); **El Fraile**, near Coihaique (see p.380); and **Cerro Mirador**, near Punta Arenas (see p.397).

HORSE TREKKING

Exploring Chile's dramatic landscapes on **horseback** is a highly memorable experience, though organized treks for tourists are only slowly taking off. The best possibilities are around **Santiago**, and in the **Central Valley**, where riding has been a way of life for centuries, and horses are sleek, fit and strong. Here, groups of riders make their way up to remote mountain passes, framed by soaring, jagged peaks, sloping pastures, and clear rivers. In addition to the spectacular scenery, you can also expect to see condors and other birds of prey circling around the peaks. Trips are usually from three to seven days, guided by local *arrieros*, who herd cattle up to high pastures in springtime, and know the mountain paths intimately. You normally spend about five or six hours in the saddle each day, broken up by a lengthy *asado* (barbecue) cooked over an open fire, and washed down with plenty of Chilean wine. At night, you sleep in tents transported by mules, and will be treated to the most breathtaking display of stars. The only disadvantage of riding treks in the central Andes is that, due to the terrain, you're unlikely to get beyond a walk, and cantering is usually out of the question. If you want a faster pace, opt for the treks offered by some companies in **Patagonia**, where rolling grasslands provide plenty of opportunity for gallops – though the weather can often put a dampener on your trip.

Most outfitters only offer a few multi-day trips between December and March, and these need to be booked well in advance, as demand often exceeds supply. Casual, one-day riding trips, however, can be arranged on the spot in many Central Valley mountain villages for around CH$20,000 a day – Conaf rangers can often help you find an *arriero* for the day, especially in Parque Nacional El Morado, Reserva Nacional Río de los Cipreses and Reserva Nacional Altos del Lircay.

SURFING

Chile does not spring to mind as a major surfing destination, but its beaches are pulling in an increasing number of in-the-know enthusiasts from North America, who come to ride the year-round breaks that pound the Pacific shore. By unanimous consent, the **best breaks** – mainly long left-handers – are concentrated around **Pichilemu**, near Rancagua, which is the site of the annual National Surfing Championships (quite a small affair). However, apart from the relatively small community of hard-core Chilean surfers, there's not much of a home-grown "scene", and renting boards can be quite problematic (your best bet is at Pichilemu's Surf Shop at Aníbal Pinto, esquina Ortúzar; ☎72/841236). Another slight deterrent is the temperature of the water, cooled by the Humboldt Current to around 14°C, making at least a 3mm wetsuit essential.

MOUNTAIN BIKING

For most of Chile's length there are extremely good and little-used dirt roads perfect for **cycling** – although the numerous potholes mean it's only worth attempting them on a **mountain bike**. For a serious trip, you should bring your own bike or buy one in Santiago – **renting** something of the quality required can be difficult to arrange. An alternative is to go on an organized biking excursion, where all equipment, including tents, will be provided.

The most popular cycling route is the **Carretera Austral** from Puerto Montt to Cochrane, which takes you through awe-inspiring scenery – but be prepared for spells of dismal weather along the way. Cycling around the relatively flat **altiplano** in the far north is an incredible way to experience the region's solitude and beauty, though it's definitely more suited to an organized trip with a support vehicle. Otherwise, it's difficult to arrange transport up there (though mining lorries sometimes give lifts to cyclists), and the total absence of drinking water and extreme fluctuations of temperature mean you have to carry a very heavy load. During the summer, cycling in **Patagonia** and **Tierra del Fuego** is made almost impossible by incessant and ferociously strong winds.

Your major problem, however, will be getting hold of spare parts when you need them. Chileans are not great cyclists, so bike shops tend to be found only in Santiago and a few major cities. Your best bet is to visit such a shop, befriend the owner, and if you get into difficulty, call for parts to be sent as cargo on a long-distance bus. When on the road, bear in mind that long stretches are bereft of accommodation options and even the most basic services, so you must be completely self-sufficient and prepared for a long wait if you require assistance.

Some bus companies will not transport bicycles unless you wrap frame and wheels separately in cardboard. Entering the country you may well find that customs officials enter details of your bicycle in your passport to prevent you from selling it.

ADVENTURE TOURISM OPERATORS AND OUTFITTERS

Below we give a selection of operators and outfitters for various outdoor activities. The list is by no means comprehensive, and new companies are constantly springing up to add to it – you can get more details from the relevant regional Sernatur office.

ALL-ROUNDERS

Altué Expediciones, Encomenderos 83, Las Condes, Santiago (☎2/232 1103, fax 233 6799). *Reliable, slick operation whose options include rafting the río Maipo, Aconcagua and Ojos del Salado expeditions, and three- to seven-day horse treks.*

Azimut 360, Arzobispo Casanova 3, Providencia, Santiago (☎62/735 8034). *Franco-Chilean outfit with a young, dynamic team of guides and a wide range of programmes, including mountain biking in the altiplano, Aconcagua expeditions, and climbs up Chile's highest volcanoes.*

Cascada Expediciones, Orrego Luco 054, Providencia, Santiago (☎2/234 2274, fax 233 9768; *cascada@ibm.net*). *One of the early pioneers of adventure tourism in Chile, with a particular emphasis on activities in the Andes close to Santiago, where it has a permanent base in the Cajón del Maipo. Programmes include rafting and kayaking the río Maipo, horse treks in the high cordillera, hiking and one-day mountain biking excursions.*

WHITE-WATER RAFTING

See also Cascada Expediciones *and* Altué Expediciones, *listed above.*

Bío Bío Expedetions, PO Box 2028, Truckee, CA 96160, USA (☎562/246-7238, fax 582-6865; *www.bbxrafting.com*). *Headed by Laurence Alvarez, the captain of the USA's World Championships rafting team, this experienced and friendly outfit offers ten-day packages on the Bío Bío and Futaleufú, plus one- to three-day excursions down the latter. They can be booked in Chile by* Aquamotion, *Imperial 0699, Puerto Varas (☎65/232747), in the UK by* Adrift *at 140–142 High St, Wandsworth, London SW18 4JJ (☎0181/874 4969) and in New Zealand by* Adrift, *PO Box 310, Queenstown (☎03/442 1615).*

Grado Diez, Huelén 222, oficina 31, Providencia, Santiago (☎2/234 4130, fax 234 4138; *gradodie.z001@chilnet.cl*). *Long-established Chilean rafting company offering trips down the río Maipo plus three- and five-day trips down the Bío Bío and Futaleufú.*

Trancura, O'Higgins 211-C, Pucón (☎45/441189). *Major southern operator with high standards and friendly guides, offering rafting excursions down the río Trancura (1 day) and the Bío Bío (3 days).*

KAYAKING

Al Sur Expediciones, Del Salvador 100, Puerto Varas (☎ & fax 65/232300; *alsur@telsur.cl*). *One of the foremost adventure tour companies in the Lake District, and the first one to introduce sea kayaking in the fjords south of Puerto Montt.*

Bío Bío Expedetions (see above). *This rafting outfitter also rents out kayaks to experienced kayakers, who accompany the rafting party down the Bío Bío or Futaleufú.*

¡ecole!, Urrutia 592, Pucón (☎ & fax 45/441675; *trek@ecole.mic.cl*). *Ecologically-focused tour company offering, among other activities, sea kayaking classes and day outings in the fjords south of Puerto Montt, and around Parque Pumalín, from its Puerto Montt branch.*

Expediciones Chile, 333 Earl's Rd, Bryson City, NY 12404, USA (☎704/488-9082, fax 488-2112; *office@kayakChile.com*). *River kayaking catering to all levels of experience, especially seasoned paddlers, operated by former Olympian kayaker, Chris Spelius.*

Onas, Blanco Encalada 599, Casilla 78, Puerto Natales (☎61/412707; *onas@chileaustral.com; www.chileaustral.com/onas*). *Sea kayaking excursions in the remote, bleak waters of Patagonia.*

CLIMBING

See also Azimut 360 *and* Altué Expediciones *in "All-rounders" for details of tours up Volcán Osorno, see p.324, and Volcán Villarica, p.287.*

Amerindian Concept, Ladrilleros 105, Puerto Natales (☎61/410678, fax 410169; *amerindi@entelchile.net*). *A range of mountaineering and ice-climbing programmes in the Torres del Paine region, plus mountaineering courses. A very good company.*

Mountain Service, Paseo Las Palmas 2209, Providencia, Santiago (☎2/233 0913, fax 234 3438; *mountainservice@chilnet.cl*). *An experienced, specialist company, dedicated to climbing Aconcagua, the major volcanoes and Torres del Paine.*

FLY-FISHING

For a list of guides and lodges on and around the Carretera Austral, see box on p.368.

Bahía Escocia Fly Fishing, Lago Rupanco (☎64/371515). *Small, beautifully located lodge with fly-fishing excursions run by a US–Chilean couple. Can also book with English-run* Travellers *in Puerto Montt* (☎65/262099, fax 258555; *gochile@entelchile.net*).

Cumilahue Lodge, PO Box 2, Llifen (☎63/481015, fax 481360). *Very expensive packages at a luxury Lake District lodge run by Adrian Dufflocq, something of a legend on the Chilean fly-fishing scene.*

Off Limits Adventures, Fresia 273, Pucón (☎45/441210, fax 441604; *offlimitspucon@hotmail.com*). *Half-day and full-day excursions, plus fly-fishing lessons. One of the more affordable options.*

Patagonia Adventure Lodges, 445 Milan Drive, Suite 220, San José, CA 95134, USA (☎408/432-8600, fax 432-1190); Hube 418, El Bolson, RN 8430, Argentina (☎9/449 3280); *www.patadv.com. US-based company offering all-inclusive packages (seven days minimum), with accommodation in a range of luxury lodges in Chilean and Argentinean Patagonia.*

Turismo Aventur, J Nogueira 1255, Punta Arenas (☎61/243354, fax 241197). *A relative newcomer, offering fishing packages in almost untouched Patagonian waters, based at an attractive, rustic lodge.*

SKIING

Full details of the resorts near Santiago are given on p.105.

Sportstour, Moneda 970, Fourteenth Floor, Santiago (☎2/696 3100, fax 698 2981; *sportstour@chilnet.cl*). *Among a wide-ranging national programme, this travel agent offers fully-inclusive ski packages at the resorts near Santiago, and the Termas de Chillán ski centre.*

HORSE TREKKING

See also Cascada Expediciones *and* Altué Expediciones *in "All-rounders", opposite.*

La Posada Expediciones, 1 Norte 2280, Talca (☎71/243833, fax 243822). *Local outfit offering three-day horse treks in Reserva Nacional Altos del Lircay, through native forests and up to high mountains.*

Pared Sur, Juan Esteban Montero 5497, Las Condes, Santiago (☎2/207 3525, fax 207 3159; *paredsur@chilnet.cl*). *In addition to its extensive mountain biking programme, Pared Sur offers a one-week horse trek through the virgin landscape of Aisén, off the Carretera Austral.*

Rancho de Caballos (☎45/441575, fax 441604). *German-owned ranch in the Lake District, near Pucón, offering a range of treks from three to nine days.*

Ride World Wide, 58 Fentiman Rd, London SW8 1LF (☎0171/735 1144, fax 735 3179; *www.rideworldwide.co.uk*). *UK-based company that hooks up with local riding outfitters around the world. In Chile, it offers a range of horseback treks from eight days to two weeks in the central cordillera, the Lake District and Patagonia. Groups are limited to six or eight people.*

Terracotta Excursions, Agustinas 1547, departamento 705, Santiago (☎2/698 8121, fax 696 1097; *terracot@intercity.cl*). *Run and guided by a Santiago woman, this young company makes an alternative to the more traditional, slightly macho* huaso *outfits. It offers a range of treks from one to eight days in the Andes and coastal mountains near Santiago.*

MOUNTAIN BIKING

See also Azimut 360 *and* Cascada Expediciones *in "All-rounders".*

Pared Sur, Juan Esteban Montero 5497, Las Condes, Santiago (☎2/207 3525, fax 207 3159; *paredsur@chilnet.cl*). *Pared Sur has been running mountain bike trips in Chile for longer than anyone else (over 12 years). Its list includes a wide range of programmes throughout the whole of the country.*

CRAFTS AND SHOPPING

While there's no denying that the handicrafts (*artesanía*) produced in Chile are nowhere near as diverse or colourful as in neighbouring Peru or Bolivia, you can still find a range of beautiful souvenirs that vary from region to region, usually sold in *ferias artesenales* (crafts markets) on or near the central squares of the main towns. As for day-to-day essentials, you'll find just about everything you need, from sun block to contact lens solution, in the main towns up and down the country.

ARTESANIA AND OTHER SOUVENIRS

The finest and arguably most beautiful goods you can buy in Chile are the items – mainly jewellery – made of **lapis lazuli,** the deep-blue semi-precious stone found only in Chile and Afghanistan. The best place to buy these is in the Bellavista area of Santiago (see p.83); note that the deeper the colour of the stone, the better its quality. Though certainly less expensive than lapis exports sold abroad, they're still pricey, with a reasonable-quality choker, for instance, costing anything from CH$30,000 (US$60).

Most *artesanía* is considerably less expensive. In the **Norte Grande**, the most common articles are hand-knitted alpaca sweaters, gloves and scarves, which you'll find in altiplano villages like Parinacota, or down in Arica and Iquique. The quality is usually fairly low grade, but they're inexpensive and very attractive all the same. In the **Norte Chico**, you can pick up some beautiful leather goods, particularly in the crafts markets of La Serena; you might also be tempted to buy a bottle of pisco, to re-create that pisco sour experience back home – though you're probably better off getting it at a supermarket in Santiago before you leave, to save yourself carting it about. The **Central Valley**, as the agricultural heartland of Chile, is famous for its *huaso* gear, and you'll find brightly coloured ponchos and stiff straw hats in the numerous working *huaso* shops. The highlight in the **Lake District** is the traditional Mapuche silver jewellery, while the **far south** is a good place to buy chunky, colourful knitwear.

A range of these goods can also be bought in the major crafts markets in **Santiago**, notably at Los Dominicos market. Also worth checking out are Santiago's little **flea markets** (see p.97), where you can pick up some wonderful objects, like old South American stirrups and spurs, pre-War of the Pacific maps and English bric-a-brac left over from the nitrate era.

ESSENTIALS

Chile is well stocked in just about all of the essential day-to-day goods you may need to replenish while travelling. Pharmacies are particularly well-stocked, and you'll have no difficulty buying things like tampons, condoms, contact lens supplies and toiletries, as well as an astonishing range of over-the-counter medicines. Slide film can be more difficult to come by outside Santiago and the major cities, so it's worth bringing a decent stock along with you. Ordinary film is widely available in most cities and not so expensive. English-language books aren't widely available, even in Santiago, and there are very few travellers' book-exchanges around – so bring enough reading material to keep you going. There's also a very poor selection of outdoor gear and camping equipment in Chile, so try to bring everything you need for the weather conditions you'll be travelling in.

DIRECTORY

ADDRESSES These are nearly always written with just the street name (and often just the surname, if the street's named after a person) followed by the number: for example Prat 135. Avenues (Avenidas) however, usually get a mention at the start of the address, e.g. Avenida 21 de Mayo 553. Buildings without a street number are suffixed by s/n, short for *sin número* ("without a number").

BARGAINING Hard haggling is neither commonly practised nor expected in Chile, though a bit of bargaining is in order at many markets, particularly when buying *artesanía*. It's also worth trying to bargain down the price of hotel rooms (of whatever category), especially outside the peak months of January and February.

DISABLED TRAVELLERS Chile makes very few provisions for people with disabilities, and travellers with mobility problems will have to contend with a lack of lifts, high curbs, dangerous potholes on pavements and worse.

EARTHQUAKES You can expect to experience a few mild tremors during your stay in Chile – if you feel the ground move slightly, don't be alarmed as it's highly unlikely to be a fully fledged earthquake. If, however, you're unlucky enough to be caught in one, don't panic (remember that buildings in this country are designed to withstand earthquakes) and whatever you do, don't run out into the street as this is how most injuries and fatalities are caused. Instead, stand under a doorway, which is the strongest part of a building. Note that lights will automatically go off if the quake is over 5 on the Richter scale.

ELECTRICITY 220V/50Hz is the standard throughout Chile. The sockets are two-pronged with round pins (as opposed to the flat pins common in neighbouring countries).

GAY LIFE Chileans do not have a very liberal attitude towards homosexuality, which is frowned upon and pretty much kept under wraps. However, while physical displays of affection between gay couples on the street would be likely to turn heads, gay people are unlikely to suffer any direct abuse or harassment in Chile.

LAUNDRY Towns with a lot of students or itinerant workers have plenty of laundries but otherwise they can be few and far between. Chilean laundries are not self-service, and charge by the kilo – usually a very low rate. Your clothes are rarely sent back terribly clean, however, as the laundries are loath to use hot water.

TAMPONS All the major brands are widely available in supermarkets and small shops, along with sanitary towels.

TELEPHONE JACKS Chile uses international standard telephone jacks (the same as those in the USA), compatible with all standard fax and email connections.

TIME DIFFERENCES From the first Saturday in October until the second Saturday in March, Chile is four hours behind GMT, and six hours behind for the rest of the year.

TIPPING It's customary to leave a ten percent tip in restaurants – service is rarely included in the bill. You are not, however, expected to tip taxi drivers.

TOILETS You'll find few public toilets (*baños*) in Chilean squares or on street corners; instead, every bar and café has one which, unless a sign proclaims it *exclusivo por clientes*, passers-by can use on payment of fifty pesos. In bus stations, large shops and most busy commercial premises there is an attendant who collects a fee and dispenses toilet paper (*papel higiénico*), normally referred to by the brand name Confort. Be warned that Chileans have a particularly unpleasant custom of leaving used toilet paper in an open box or bucket next to the toilet, to prevent the flushing system from blocking up.

WOMEN Chilean men – especially groups of young workmen on the street – take great pleasure in making revolting kissing noises at unaccompanied young women as they walk past. Faced with the same woman accompanied by a man, however, they wouldn't make a sound. Fair-haired or obviously gringo-looking women are most vulnerable, but even *Chilenas* find themselves the focus of this unwanted attention. Most of them just walk past and ignore them, and you'll probably find it easiest to do likewise. Apart from this irritating but essentially harmless habit, you're unlikely to find Chile a threatening place as a single woman traveller, and if you stray from the main tourist circuits you'll find yourself continually befriended by local families who feel dreadfully sorry for you, having to take a holiday alone.

PART TWO

THE GUIDE

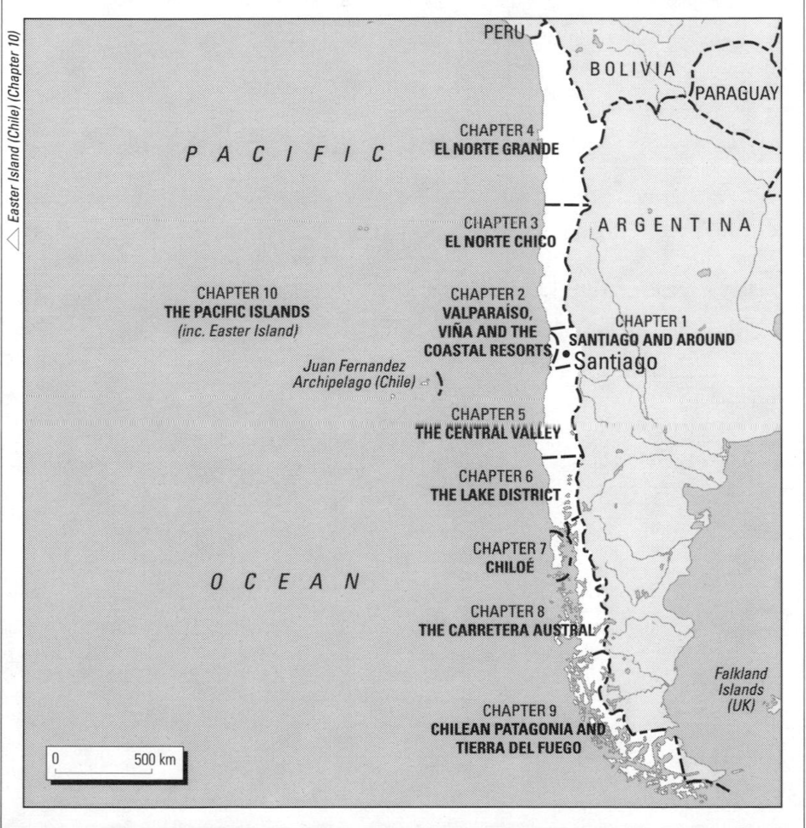

CHAPTER ONE

SANTIAGO AND AROUND

Set on a wide plain near the foot of the Andes, **Santiago** boasts one of the most dazzling backdrops of any capital city in the world. The views onto the towering cordillera after a rainstorm's cleared the air are magnificent, especially in winter when the snow-covered mountains rise behind the city like a giant white rampart against the blue sky. Unfortunately, such vistas are few and far between, as these same mountains prevent winds from shifting the air trapped over the plain, leaving it thickly polluted with diesel fumes. As a result, Santiago is frequently covered by a dense blanket of smog through which the Andes can be only dimly perceived – a smudged, tantalizing shadow of their real selves.

The city itself is a great, sprawling metropolis of five million people – that's more than a third of the population of Chile. It's divided into thirty-two autonomous *comunas*, most of them squat, flat suburbs, stretching ever further out from the centre. Downtown Santiago, in contrast, is compact and manageable, and while not exactly beautiful has a pleasant, enjoyable atmosphere, especially when the sun shines and all of life pours out

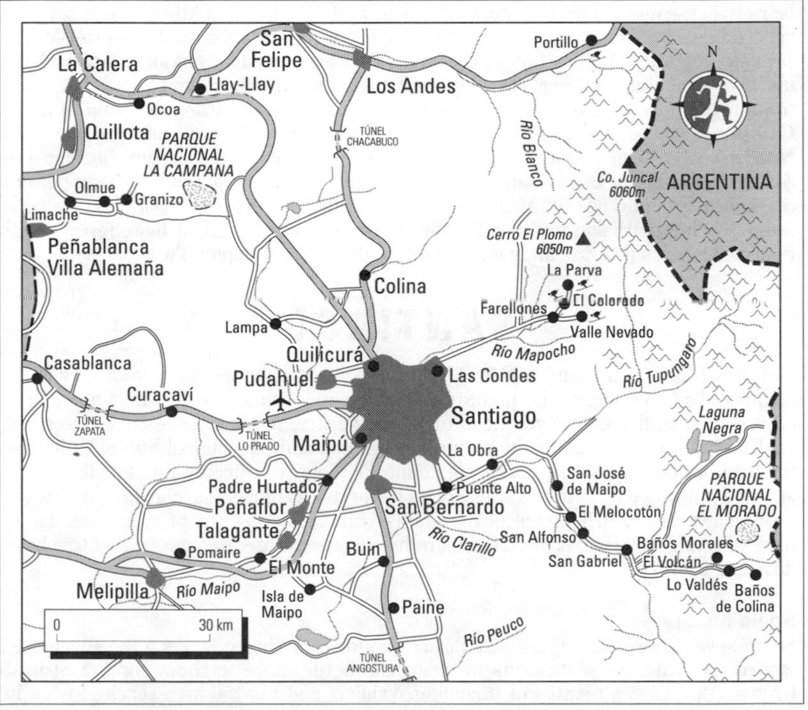

onto the streets. Part of its appeal comes from the fact that it's so green: tall, luxuriant trees fill the main square and line the riverbank, and exotically landscaped parks provide instant refuge from the traffic-choked roads. Above all, though, it's the all-pervading sense of energy that makes the place so atmospheric, with crowds of Santiaguinos constantly milling through narrow streets packed with shoe-shiners, fruit barrows, news kiosks and sellers of everything from coathangers to plastic plugs.

Architecturally, it's a bit of a hotchpotch, thanks to a succession of earthquakes and a spate of undisciplined rebuilding in the Sixties and Seventies. Ugly office blocks and dingy *galerías* compete for space with beautifully cared-for colonial buildings, while east of the centre Santiago's economic boom is reflected in the glittering new skyscrapers and international hotels of the *comunas* of Providencia and Las Condes. These different faces are part of a wider set of contrasts – between the gleaming, modern metro, for example, and the decrepit, fume-belching buses; between the American-style shopping malls in the *barrios altos* and downtown's shabby, old-fashioned shops; and, most significantly, between the well-heeled, briefcase-clutching professionals and the scores of impoverished street traders struggling to make a living. It's not a place of excesses, however: homelessness is minimal compared to many other cities of this size, and there's no tension in the air or threat of violence. On the whole it's a good introduction to the country and its people, offering a pleasing choice of museums, markets, restaurants and nightspots, wrapped up in a friendly, if noisy, environment.

Most travellers stay here for just a few days before launching into far-flung trips to the north or south, but if you've time to spare you'd do well to use Santiago as a base while exploring the surrounding region; some targets make easy day-trips, while others demand a couple of days or so. With the Andes so close and so accessible, you can be right in the mountains in an hour or two; in winter people go **skiing** for the day, with special buses laid on to and from the resorts; in warmer months the **Cajón del Maipo** (a deep canyon cutting into the high cordillera) offers fantastic trekking, horseback riding and white-water rafting. Heading west towards Valparaíso, you'll also find great trekking opportunities in the arid coastal mountains of **Parque Nacional La Campana**, where you can easily do a day's walking without seeing another soul. Nearby villages can provide a relaxing antidote to Santiago's constant din, like **Los Andes** to the north, or **Pomaire** to the west, famous for its incredibly cheap pottery. Still more tempting are the many **vineyards** within easy reach of Santiago, some of them offering tours and tastings. Finally, there are some excellent **beaches** about an hour and a half's bus ride away – for more on these, see Chapter Two.

SANTIAGO

How much time you spend in **SANTIAGO** depends on the length of your stay in the country; it's by no means the highlight of Chile, and if time's really short a couple of days should suffice before you head off to the spectacular landscapes of the north or south. That said, Santiago is the cultural, economic and educational hub of Chile, and the best place to get to grips with the country's identity – dipping into its vibrant theatre and music scene; getting a sense of its history in its museums; checking out its varied restaurants and striking up conversations with the wide variety of people you'll meet here will really help you scratch beneath the surface and get the most out of this kaleidoscopic country.

Some history

Some seven years after Francisco Pizarro conquered Cuzco in Peru, he dispatched **Pedro de Valdivia** southwards to claim and settle more territory for the Spanish Crown. After eleven months of travelling, Valdivia and his 150 men reached what he considered to be a suitable site for a new city, and, on February 12, 1541, officially founded "Santiago de la Nueva Extremadura" at the foot of a rocky hill he'd named Santa Lucía. A native population of Picunches was scattered around the region, but this didn't deter Valdivia from getting down to business: with great alacrity the main square was established and the surrounding streets were marked out with a string and ruler, a fort was built in the square (thus named "Plaza de Armas") and several other buildings were erected. Six months later they were all razed to the ground in a Picunche raid.

The town was doggedly rebuilt to the same plans, wedged into the triangle of land bounded by the Mapocho River to the north, its southern branch to the south and Santa Lucía hill to the east. It began to take on the shape of a new colonial capital, but nine years after founding it the Spaniards shifted their attention to Arauco in the south, in search of gold, and Santiago became something of a backwater. Following the violent Mapuche uprising in 1553 (see p.449), however, the Spaniards were forced to abandon their towns south of the Bío Bío, and many returned to Santiago. Nonetheless, growth continued to be very slow: there were no easy riches to be had from gold or silver, so settlers were never large in number, and what opportunities the land offered were thwarted by strict trade restrictions imposed by Spain. Moreover, expansion was repeatedly knocked back by **earthquakes**, which shook the city at alarmingly regular intervals.

Santiago started to look like a real capital during the course of the eighteenth century, as trade restrictions were eased, more wealth was created, and the population increased. However, it wasn't until after independence in 1818 that expansion really got going, as the rich clamoured to build themselves glamorous mansions and the state erected beautiful public buildings like the Teatro Municipal and the congress building; a visitor who returned to Santiago after a nine-year absence commented, "What a transformation! So many palaces! What architectural majesty and beauty!"

As the city entered the twentieth century it began to push eastwards into the new *barrio alto* and north into Bellavista. The horizontal spread has gone well beyond these limits since then, gobbling up outlying towns and villages at great speed; Gran Santiago now stretches about 35km north to south and 40km east to west. Its central zones have shot up vertically, too, particularly in Providencia where the showy high-rise buildings reflect the country's rapid economic growth over the past decade. Despite this dramatic transformation, however, the city's central core still sticks to the same street pattern marked out by Pedro de Valdivia in 1541, and its first public space, the Plaza de Armas, is still at the heart of its street life.

The **telephone code** for Santiago is ☎2

Arrival

Santiago is undoubtedly one of the easiest and least intimidating South American capitals to **arrive** in. Connections from the airport, bus terminals and train station to downtown are frequent and straightforward, and while you should take normal precautions you're unlikely to be hassled or feel threatened while you're finding your feet.

By air

International and domestic **flights** arrive at Arturo Merino Benítez airport in Pudahuel, some 26km northwest of Santiago. The smart international terminal has a **Sernatur** information desk (daily 9am–9pm; ☎601 9320) in the baggage reclaim hall, where staff

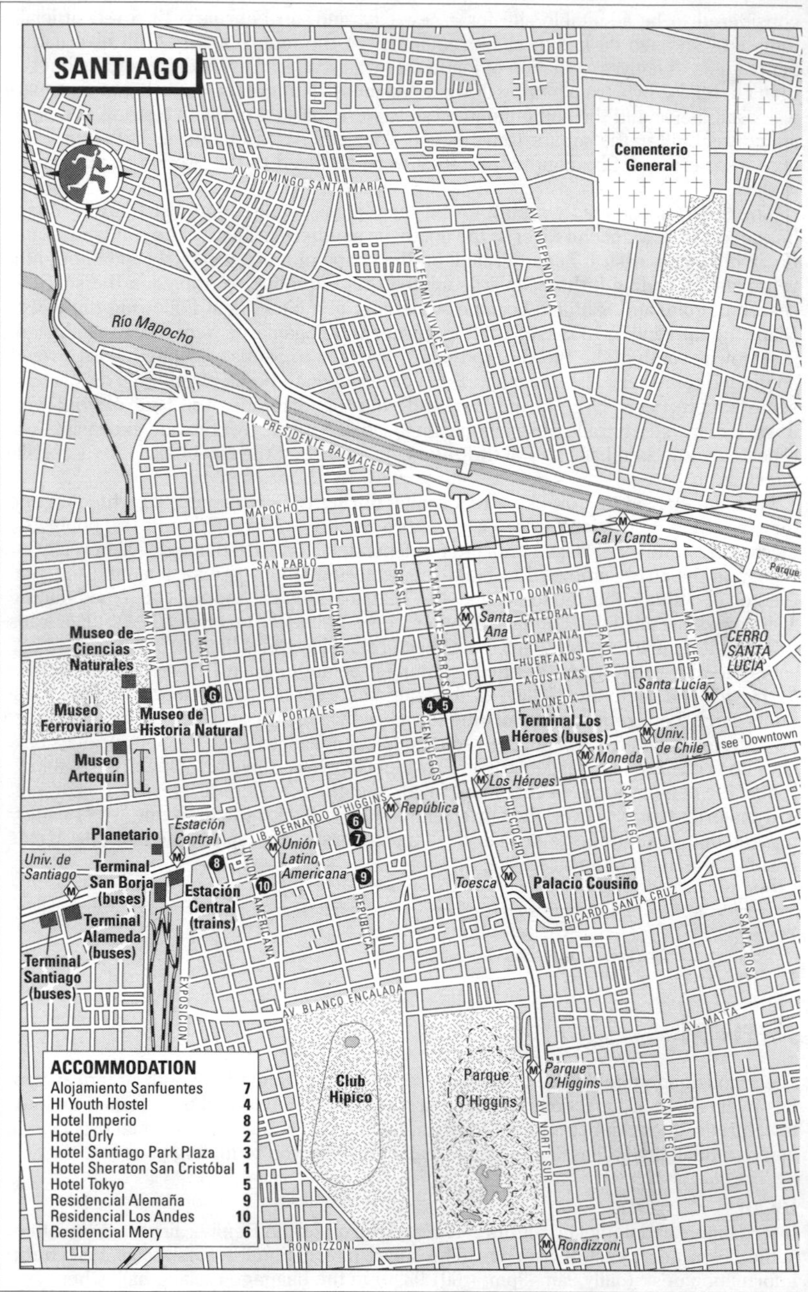
SANTIAGO
N
Cementerio General
AV. DOMINGO SANTA MARIA
AV. FERMIN VIVACETA
AV. INDEPENDENCIA
Río Mapocho
AV. PRESIDENTE BALMACEDA
MAPOCHO
Cal y Canto
Parque
SAN PABLO
BRASIL
ALMIRANTE BARROS
SANTO DOMINGO
CATEDRAL
COMPANIA
HUERFANOS
AGUSTINAS
MONEDA
Santa Ana
BANDERA
MAC IVER
CERRO SANTA LUCIA
Santa Lucía
MATUCANA
MAIPU
CUMMING
Museo de Ciencias Naturales
Museo Ferroviario
Museo de Historia Natural
Museo Artequín
AV. PORTALES
CIENFUEGOS
Terminal Los Héroes (buses)
Univ. de Chile
see 'Downtown
Moneda
Los Héroes
República
LIB. BERNARDO O'HIGGINS
DIECIOCHO
SAN DIEGO
Planetario
Estación Central
Unión Latino Americana
Univ. de Santiago
Terminal San Borja (buses)
Estación Central (trains)
Terminal Alameda (buses)
Terminal Santiago (buses)
UNION AMERICANA
REPUBLICA
Toesca
Palacio Cousiño
RICARDO SANTA CRUZ
SANTA ROSA
EXPOSICION
AV. BLANCO ENCALADA
AV. MATTA
Club Hipico
Parque O'Higgins
AV. NORTE SUR
SAN DIEGO
RONDIZZONI
Rondizzoni
ACCOMMODATION
Alojamiento Sanfuentes 7
HI Youth Hostel 4
Hotel Imperio 8
Hotel Orly 2
Hotel Santiago Park Plaza 3
Hotel Sheraton San Cristóbal 1
Hotel Tokyo 5
Residencial Alemaña 9
Residencial Los Andes 10
Residencial Mery 6

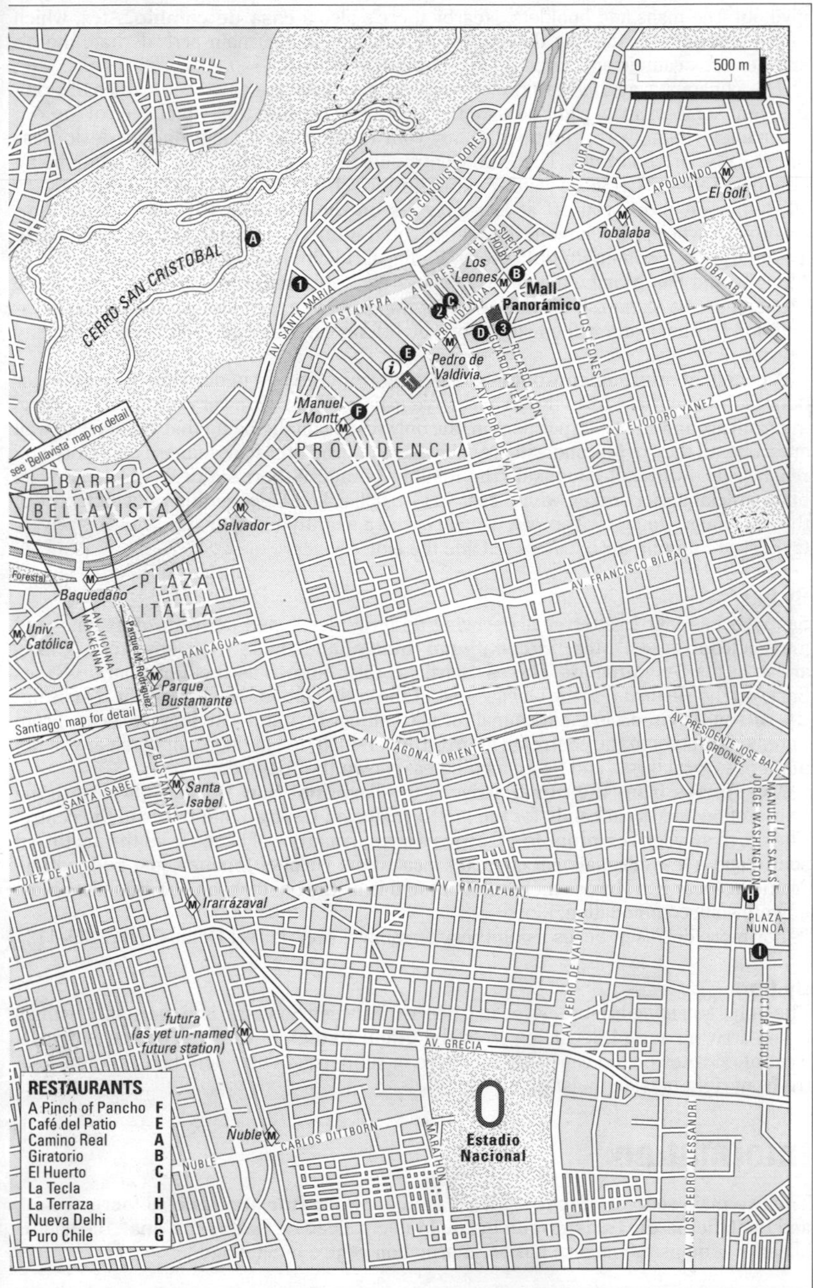
0 500 m
CERRO SAN CRISTOBAL
AV. SANTA MARIA
LOS CONQUISTADORES
COSTANERA
ANDRES BELLO
SUECIA
HOLBI
AV. PROVIDENCIA
Los Leones
Mall Panorámico
Pedro de Valdivia
RICARDO LYON
GUARDIA VIEJA
AV. PEDRO DE VALDIVIA
VITACURA
APOQUINDO
El Golf
Tobalaba
AV. TOBALABA
LOS LEONES
AV. ELIODORO YANEZ
Manuel Montt
PROVIDENCIA
see 'Bellavista' map for detail
BARRIO BELLAVISTA
Salvador
Forestal
Baquedano
PLAZA ITALIA
Univ. Católica
AV. VICUNA MACKENNA
Parque M. Rodriguez
RANCAGUA
Parque Bustamante
Santiago' map for detail
AV. FRANCISCO BILBAO
AV. DIAGONAL ORIENTE
AV. PRESIDENTE JOSE BATLE Y ORDONEZ
JORGE WASHINGTON
MANUEL DE SALAS
SANTA ISABEL
BUSTAMANTE
Santa Isabel
DIEZ DE JULIO
AV. IRARRAZABAL
Irarrázaval
PLAZA NUNOA
DOCTOR JOHOW
AV. PEDRO DE VALDIVIA
'futura' (as yet un-named future station)
AV. GRECIA
Estadio Nacional
Ñuble
CARLOS DITTBORN
NUBLE
MARATHON
AV. JOSE PEDRO ALESSANDRI
RESTAURANTS
A Pinch of Pancho F
Café del Patio E
Camino Real A
Giratorio B
El Huerto C
La Tecla I
La Terraza H
Nueva Delhi D
Puro Chile G

give out free maps and booklets. Nearby there's also a **casa de cambio**, Afex, which offers poorer rates than its downtown branch. Out in the main arrivals hall, there's another Afex cambio and three **ATMs**, one on each level.

The cheapest way to get to the city centre is by **bus**, with two companies offering frequent services from right outside the arrivals gate; note that whichever of the two companies you go with, you need to buy your ticket from the appropriate desk (near the exit) before boarding. The blue Centropuerto bus probably has the edge, being cheaper (about CH$650) and running more frequently (7am–11.30pm; every 10–30min); it drops you off at **Los Héroes** on the Alameda (the city's main thoroughfare), where you can join the metro, catch numerous buses, or flag down a taxi. Tour Express (6am–midnight; every 30min; CH$1000) takes you to the corner of Moneda and San Martín, a couple of blocks east of Los Héroes, and a short walk to Moneda metro station. Both buses call at the domestic terminal as well as the international terminal, and will usually drop you off anywhere along their route to the city centre.

A couple of **minibus companies**, operating from the row of desks by the exit, offer door-to-door services from the airport to your hotel. These are very good value, charging from around CH$2500 per person, the only disadvantage being that you have to wait around until they're full, and will probably have to drop other passengers off before you reach your own hotel. Alongside the minibus counters there's a desk where you can book official airport **taxis**, which cost CH$10,000–14,500, depending on which part of the city you're going to. You can usually agree a slightly cheaper rate with the private taxi drivers touting for business outside the exit.

By bus

Santiago has four bus terminals serving a highly developed network of national and international buses. Most **international buses**, and those from **southern Chile**, arrive at the **Terminal de Buses Santiago** (also known as the Terminal de Buses Sur), on the Alameda, a few blocks west of the train station. Next door, the **Terminal de Buses Alameda** is the terminal for all Pullman Bus and Tur Bus journeys. From here, you can get to the centre by metro (Universidad de Santiago), or catch any of the numerous local buses and taxis hurtling east down the Alameda.

Most **buses from the north** arrive at the **Terminal San Borja**, right next to the train station and again handy for the metro (Estación Central) and buses to the centre. The much smaller **Terminal los Héroes** serves a mixture of buses from the north and south, and a few international ones; it's located on Tucapel Jiménez, just north of the Alameda (near Los Héroes metro station) and is a short and cheap taxi ride from most downtown accommodation.

For more details of buses using these terminals, see "Travel Details" on p.109–113.

By train

The only remaining train services in Chile are between Santiago and the south, with all trains arriving at and departing from the grand **Estación Central** on the Alameda, west of downtown. You can take the metro or numerous buses and taxis into the centre from right outside the station.

Information

The two main sources of tourist information are **Sernatur**, the national tourist board, and the **Oficina de Turismo** run by the Municipalidad de Santiago. **Conaf**, the national parks administration, also has an information centre in Santiago.

Sernatur

The **Sernatur** office is west of the city centre at Av Providencia 1550, between Manuel Montt and Pedro de Valdivia metro stations (Dec–March Mon–Fri 9am–8pm, Sat 9am–2pm; April–Nov Mon–Fri 9am–6pm, Sat 9am–1pm; ☎236 1416). It offers a range of free booklets on Santiago's attractions, accommodation and restaurants, and the staff, usually English-speaking, can answer most questions about services and facilities in the city. It's also a good place to stock up on information on the rest of Chile, with lists of accommodation in all the other regions, as well as some themed booklets like *Parques Nacionales, El Norte, El Sur, Playas, Skiing* and *Camping*; you have to ask for them, though, as they're usually kept out of sight. While you're here you should also pick up a copy of *What's On*, a free monthly publication with a useful section on current exhibitions and cultural events – it's also distributed in the municipal tourist office (see below) as well as many hotels.

Oficina de Turismo

Far more conveniently located – in the Casa Colorada, just off the Plaza de Armas at Merced 860 – the Municipalidad de Santiago's **Oficina de Turismo** (Mon–Fri 10am–6pm; ☎632 7783) has free maps, a range of booklets (including the excellent *Historical Heritage of Santiago*) and friendly, competent staff. There's also a **kiosk** on Ahumada (Mon–Fri 9.30am–8.30pm, Sat 11am–3pm & 5–8pm, Sun 11am–3pm), between Agustinas and Huérfanos, where you can buy street-indexed maps of the city, or pick up basic ones for free. Free **guided walking tours** of Santiago leave from the kiosk in summer – check with the staff inside for times.

Conaf

For information on Chile's national parks, visit **Conaf** at Av Presidente Bulnes 291 (Mon–Fri 9am–1pm & 2–4.30pm; ☎390 0125), where you can buy detailed information sheets (CH$100) on all the national parks and reserves, as well as books on native flora and fauna, and other mementos.

City transport

You'll probably spend most time in the city centre, which is entirely walkable, but for journeys further afield you'll find public transport cheap and abundant. For trips along the main east–west axis formed by the Alameda and its extensions, the **metro** is quickest. The city and suburbs are also served by thousands of **buses**, while **colectivos** offer a quick way out of the centre into surrounding districts. Regular **taxis** are numerous and inexpensive, and are in many cases the most convenient way to get about.

The metro

Santiago's spotless **metro** system (daily 6am–10.30pm) is modern, efficient and safe. Of the three lines, Line 1 is the most useful (and crowded) running east–west under the Alameda and Avenida Providencia. Line 2 runs north–south from Cal y Canto, by the Mapocho river, down to Lo Ovalle, crossing Line 1 at Los Héroes, and is useful for visiting Palacio Cousiño, Parque O'Higgins and the Franklin market. The recently constructed Line 5 (which has beaten Lines 3 and 4 from the drawing board to reality) runs south from Baquedano to La Florida.

Fares are the same for any length of journey, but fall into three different price brackets according to the time of day: *alta* (7.15–9am & 6–7pm; CH$240), *media* (9am–6pm, 7–9pm & weekends; CH$190) and *baja* (6.30–7.15am & 9–10.30pm; CH$130). Cheaper

rates (CH$220 for *alta*, and CH$170 for *media*) are available if you buy the *boleto valor* (CH$2000), a single ticket from which each journey's fare is deducted until it runs out.

Buses

Santiago has one of the highest bus densities in the world, with over 14,000 of them choking the streets. City buses are called **micros**, and are nearly all yellow. The most widely used form of transport in Santiago, they're very cheap – about CH$180 a ride – and run from 5am to around midnight. They're also bewildering to the uninitiated – there's no bus route map available, and it was only recently that proper bus stops were introduced in the city. They do at least stick to fixed routes, and the destination and main points of the route are displayed on the front window. They're most useful for going along the Alameda – as a general rule, buses displaying *Estación Central* will take you west, while those displaying *Providencia* or *Apoquindo* are safe for going east. If you're not sure where to get off, ask the driver (*¿me puede avisar cuando estamos a . . .?*) and you'll no doubt find everyone else on the bus keeping an eye out for you.

Taxis

Santiago has more **taxis** than New York City, and in the centre you'll have no trouble flagging one down in moments. They're black with yellow roofs, and have a small light in the top right-hand corner of the windscreen that's lit when the taxi is available. Fares are low and are displayed on the window – usually CH$150 when the meter's started and CH$60 every 200m; you're not expected to add a tip. Drivers are allowed to charge more at night, so check the rate on the window before you begin the journey as night rates can vary. Note that taxi drivers aren't tested on their knowledge of the city's streets in order to get a licence; if you're going somewhere out of the way, it's best to check where it is beforehand (there's a good A–Z in the back of the phone book). Make sure, also, that the meter is reset at the start of your journey.

Colectivos

Santiago's **colectivos** looks like ordinary taxis except they're black all over and have a sign on the roof displaying their destination. They travel along fixed routes, mostly from the centre out to the suburbs, and are only slightly more expensive than buses. Plaza Baquedano (also called Plaza Italia) is the starting point of many *colectivo* routes.

Accommodation

There's plenty of **accommodation** in Santiago to suit most budgets, though *really* cheap places are thin on the ground and tend to be pretty squalid. Most of the city's low-price rooms are small, simple and sparsely furnished, often without a window but usually fairly clean. Moving up a notch or two you'll find more comfort in many of the small, moderately priced hotels, though you need to choose carefully as some of them can be dismal. Upmarket hotels are abundant, especially in Providencia, ranging from good-value independent outfits to luxurious international chains. Prices in Santiago don't usually fluctuate much during the course of the year, although a few hotels charge more in summer (Nov–Feb). In addition to the hotels listed below, there's a large, modern HI **youth hostel** at Cienfuegos 151 (☎671 8532), a five-minute walk from Los Héroes metro station, which charges around CH$5000 for a dorm bed. All the following hotels and *residenciales* are marked on the map on p.66–67 or 75.

Central Santiago

This is where the museums, monuments and other attractions are located, so it makes sense to sleep here too – there are some good, inexpensive options dotted about and lots of mid-range hotels of varying cost and attractiveness.

City Hotel, Compañía 1063 (☎695 4526, fax 695 6775). Old, once-grand hotel just off the Plaza de Armas, past its heyday but retaining a certain romantic charm. Some rooms have parquet floors and old leather armchairs; those at the back are quietest. ⑤.

Hotel Carrera, Teatinos 180 (☎698 2011, fax 672 1083). Imposing five-star hotel overlooking the Palacio de la Moneda, with a flash rooftop pool and restaurant, but disappointing rooms. Non-guests can use the bar, worth it for the fantastic views, especially as the sun's going down. ⑧.

Hotel Cervantes, Morandé 631 (☎696 7966, fax 696 5318). The rooms here are dated and vary in quality, but on the whole are clean and pleasant enough; all have private bath. ④.

ACCOMMODATION PRICE CODES

Prices are for the cheapest double room in high season. At the lower end of the scale, single travellers can expect to pay half this rate, but mid- and upper-range hotels usually charge the same for a single as for a double. For more information see p.27 in Basics.

① Less than US$10/CH$4800
② US$10–20/CH$4800–9600
③ US$20–30/CH$9600–10,080
④ US$30–50/CH$10,080–24,000
⑤ US$50–75/CH$24,000–36,000
⑥ US$75–100/CH$36,000–48,000
⑦ US$100–150/CH$48,000–72,000
⑧ over US$150/over CH$72,000

Hotel España, Morandé 510 (☎ & fax 696 6066). Ancient and rather decrepit rooms with private bath and dank wallpaper; fairly clean, however, and all with outside windows. ③.

Hotel Forresta, Victoria Subercaseaux 353 (☎ & fax 639 6262). Excellent hotel with bright, fresh rooms, smart bathrooms and lovely views onto the trees of Santa Lucia. There's also a piano bar on the top floor. ④–⑤.

Hotel Gran Palace, Huérfanos 1178, piso 10 (☎671 2551, fax 695 1095). Decent if slightly cramped rooms with good bathrooms, above the Gran Palace cinema (take the lift near the ticket office up to the 10th floor). Its restaurant has huge windows giving onto the rooftops of Santiago, and to the Andes. ④.

Hotel Libertador, Av Bernardo O'Higgins 853 (☎639 4211, fax 633 7128). Large Seventies-style hotel opposite the Iglesia San Francisco, with spacious, comfortable rooms, all with TV and bath. Also has a rooftop terrace with sun lounges and a plunge pool. ⑤.

Hotel Majestic, Santo Domingo 1526 (☎695 8366, fax 697 4051). Distinctive green and cream building in a quiet corner of town, about a 15min walk from the Plaza de Armas. The interior has been lavishly adorned by the Indian owner, and the restaurant serves good Indian food. Small outdoor pool and garden, and free parking. ⑤.

Hotel Metrópoli, Sótero del Río 465 (☎672 3987, fax 695 2196). Clean, spacious rooms, with lots of natural light but in need of a lick of paint. The best thing about this place is its constant supply of hot water and amazingly powerful showers. Located in a quiet alley off Catedral. ④.

Hotel Nuevo Valparaíso, Morandé 791 (☎671 5698). The rooms are so cheap here that many gringos (especially language teachers) rent them by the month. They're not bad for the price, and there's a kitchen, though you need to bring your own utensils. The area's OK but creeping towards the red-light district. ②.

Hotel París, París 813 (☎ & fax 639 4037). Popular budget hotel, tucked behind the Iglesia San Francisco. Most rooms have private bath, and there's a little interior patio where you can take breakfast. The friendly and trustworthy *dueña* runs a discreet "by the hour" business in some of her rooms. Good place to meet other travellers. ③.

Hotel París Nuevo, París 813 (☎ & fax 639 4037). New addition to the original hotel next door, with smart, comfortable rooms and immaculate bathrooms. Best-value hotel in Santiago in this price range, and a good choice for a couple of nights' comfort at the start or end of your trip. ④.

Hotel Sao Paulo, San Antonio 357 (☎ & fax 639 8031). Slightly musty rooms, but they're well cared-for, with spotless bathrooms; good value for such a central location. ④.

Hotel Vegas, Londres 49 (☎632 2498, fax 632 5084). Whitewashed, pseudo-Moorish mansion, excellently located in the Paris-Londres *barrio*. The rooms are disappointingly characterless, but neat and quiet. Friendly staff. ④.

Residencial Londres, Londres 54 (☎ & fax 638 2215). Best budget choice in Santiago – clean, light rooms in a lovely old building with parquet floors and period features, very central but also quiet. Rooms are in heavy demand, with singles particularly hard to come by. Doubles (but not singles) can and should be reserved in advance. ③.

Residencial Santo Domingo, Santo Domingo 735 (☎639 6733). Beautifully restored nineteenth-century mansion with marble steps, polished oak floors, unfeasibly high ceilings and two interior patios. The rooms themselves are basic and a little gloomy, but very clean. Curiously few travellers here, and used mainly by Chilean workmen and families. ③.

Around San Pablo and San Martín

There's a cluster of very cheap places to stay in the northwest corner of downtown, concentrated on calles San Pablo and San Martín. The area, which falls into the red-light district, is a bit seedy at night but fine by day. Some hotels are used for prostitution, others are just plain grim, but the following are safe and reliable.

Alojamiento Sra Nera, 651 Armúnatategui (☎696 2459). Unsigned *residencial* with a friendly owner, lots of plants and adequate rooms. ③.

Hotel Caribe, San Martín 851 (☎696 6681). A small facade conceals a huge building with a maze of corridors and thirty or so rooms, each with three to four beds (and nothing else). Friendly, trustworthy staff, lots of backpackers and one of the cheapest night's sleep in town. ②.

Hotel Oleca, San Pablo 1265 (☎698 3683). Dark hotel with basic rooms – two beds and a sink – among the cleanest in this price range; run by two friendly women. This part of San Pablo is busier and safer than a couple of blocks west. ②.

Providencia and Las Condes

There's a lot of accommodation in the swanky districts of Providencia and Las Condes, most of it very expensive and geared towards foreign business travellers. Providencia, in particular, has some good restaurants and a lively, though gringo-dominated, nightlife scene.

Hotel Orly, Pedro de Valdivia 027, Providencia (☎231 8947, fax 252 0051). Small hotel (23 rooms) in an old, recently remodelled building. Friendly, personal service and excellent breakfasts. A good choice in this price range. ⑥.

Hotel Santiago Park Plaza, Ricardo Lyon 207, Providencia (☎233 6363, fax 233 6668). Luxurious, old-fashioned hotel, with a sumptuous lobby, elegant decor and attentive staff. ⑧.

Hotel Sheraton San Cristóbal, Av Santa Maria 1742, Providencia (☎233 5000, fax 232 8000). Vast, first-class hotel nestling into the slopes of San Cristóbal, on the northern bank of the Mapocho. Tennis courts, outdoor and indoor pool, extravagant decor and prices to match. Its restaurant, *El Cid*, is excellent. ⑧.

Hyatt Regency, Av Kennedy 4601, Las Condes (☎218 1234, fax 218 2279). The poshest, plushest and most expensive hotel in Santiago, in a landmark, glass-plated building in the heart of Las Condes. ⑧.

Los Héroes to Estación Central

The *barrios* west of downtown are mainly residential, characterized by quiet, leafy streets and elegant old houses – many of which have been converted into inexpensive hotels or *residenciales*. The centre is easily reached by bus or metro along the Alameda.

Alojamiento, Sanfuentes 2258 (☎699 2938). Nameless establishment offering basic, airy rooms on a quiet street. Good value. ②.

Hotel Imperio, Av Lib Bernardo O'Higgins 2876 (☎689 7774, fax 689 2916). Comfortable, well-equipped hotel offering eighty rooms on the Alameda; rather dated but well cared-for and good value. ④–⑤.

Hotel Tokyo, Almirante Barroso 160 (☎698 4500). Small, spotless hotel full of Japanese art and interesting furniture. Its large garden makes a peaceful retreat from Santiago's noise, especially in summer when you can lounge on the deck chairs. ④.

Residencial Alemaña, República 220 (☎671 2388). Immaculate budget accommodation on an attractive, tree-lined avenue. All meals available. There's no sign at the door. ③.

Residencial Los Andes, Union Americana 134 (☎ & fax 689 4271). Dusty old rooms around a central patio, rather run-down but in a romantic kind of way. Use of kitchen. Some rooms with private bath. ②.

Residencial Mery, Pasaje República 36 (☎ & fax 696 8883). Spotless rooms in a pleasant, cheerfully decorated *residencial* on a quiet alley round the corner from República metro. ③.

The City

Santiago isn't a city that demands major sightseeing, and you can get round many of its attractions on foot in two or three days – a walk around the compact downtown core might take in the changing of the guard at the **Palacio de la Moneda**, the excellent **Museo Chileno de Arte Precolombino**, a look inside the evocative **Museo Colonial** and a climb up **Cerro Santa Lucía**, while less strenuous activities could include lunch at the exhilarating **Mercado Central**, or just sitting in the **Plaza de Armas** with an ice cream and a book. North of downtown, on the other side of the Mapocho river, it's an easy funicular ride up **Cerro San Cristóbal** whose summit provides unrivalled views for miles around. At its foot, **barrio Bellavista** is Santiago's "Latin quarter", replete with small cafés and restaurants and the former **house of Pablo Neruda**, now an intriguing museum. West of the centre, the once glamorous *barrios* housing Santiago's moneyed classes at the turn of the century make rewarding, romantic wanders, and contain some splendid old mansions, including the sumptuous **Palacio Cousiño**. Moving east into the *barrios altos* of Providencia and Las Condes, the tone is newer and flasher, and there's less to draw you out here; notable exceptions, however, include the beautiful **Museo de Artes Decorativos**, and the highly enjoyable market at **Los Dominicos**.

Plaza de Armas

The **Plaza de Armas** is the epicentre of Santiago, both literally – it's where all distances to the rest of Chile are measured from – and symbolically. It was the first public space laid out by Pedro de Valdivia when he founded the city in 1541 and quickly became the nucleus of Santiago's administrative, commercial and social life. This is where the young capital's most important seats of power – the law courts, the governor's palace, and the cathedral – were built, and where its markets, bullfights, festivals and other public activities took place. Four and a half centuries on (and even while diggers have moved in to build a new metro station, due to be completed in 2000), this is still where the city's pulse beats loudest and half an hour's people-watching here makes for perhaps the best introduction to Santiago.

These days the open market space has been replaced by flower gardens and numerous trees; palms, poplars and eucalyptus tower over benches packed with giggling schoolchildren, gossiping old men, lovers, tourists, indulgent grandmothers and shop girls on their lunch break. Forlorn photographers stand about with their old box cameras and mangy props – a toy lion to sit reluctant toddlers on, and a llama that looks more dead than alive; thirsty dogs hang around the fountain; shoe-shiners polish the feet of dour businessmen clutching *El Mercurio*; and ancient-looking chess players hold sober tournaments inside the bandstand. All against a backdrop of constant noise supplied by stamp-sellers, singers and evangelical preachers. Meanwhile, a constant ebb and flow of people mills in and out of the great civic and religious buildings enclosing the square.

Correo Central and Municipalidad

On the northwest corner of the Plaza de Armas stands the candyfloss-coloured **Correo Central**, whose interior, with its tiered galleries crowned by a beautiful glass roof, is every bit as impressive as its elaborate facade. It was built in 1882 on the foundations of what had been the Palacio de los Gobernadores (governors' palace) during colonial times, and the Palacio de los Presidentes de Chile (presidential palace) after independence. Now given over to more mundane affairs, this is where you'll come to send postcards home and where you can pick up poste restante (see p.40). It also houses a moderately interesting **Museo Postal** (Mon–Fri 9am–5pm; free) on the second level, which consists mainly of a collection of stamps from around the world.

In the same block, on the northeast corner of the square, is the pale, Neoclassical edifice of Santiago's **Municipalidad**. The first *cabildo* (town hall) was erected on this site back in the early seventeenth century, and also contained the city's prison. Several reconstructions and restorations have taken place since then, most recently in 1895. A curious feature of the current building is that its basement is still divided into the original cells of the old prison, which are now used as offices. Note the city's coat of arms on the central pediment above the flags; it was donated by King Carlos V in 1552 to consolidate Santiago's status as a city.

Museo Histórico Nacional

Wedged between the Correo and the Municipalidad is the splendid **Palacio de la Real Audiencia**, an immaculately preserved colonial building that's borne witness to some

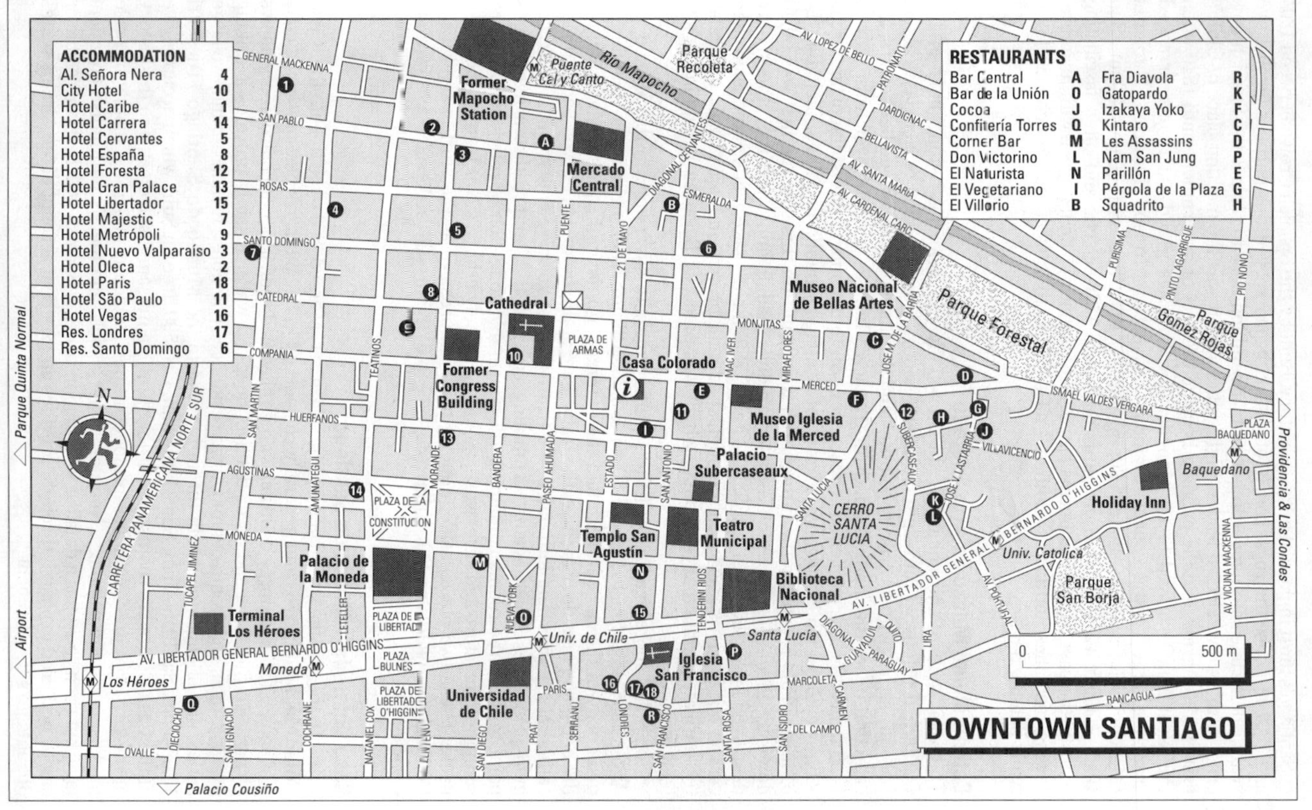
DOWNTOWN SANTIAGO
0
500 m
ACCOMMODATION
Al. Señora Nera 4
City Hotel 10
Hotel Caribe 1
Hotel Carrera 14
Hotel Cervantes 5
Hotel España 8
Hotel Foresta 12
Hotel Gran Palace 13
Hotel Libertador 15
Hotel Majestic 7
Hotel Metrópoli 9
Hotel Nuevo Valparaiso 3
Hotel Oleca 2
Hotel Paris 18
Hotel São Paulo 11
Hotel Vegas 16
Res. Londres 17
Res. Santo Domingo 6
RESTAURANTS
Bar Central A
Bar de la Unión O
Cocoa J
Confitería Torres Q
Corner Bar M
Don Victorino L
El Naturista N
El Vegetariano I
El Villorio B
Fra Diavola R
Gatopardo K
Izakaya Yoko F
Kintaro C
Les Assassins D
Nam San Jung P
Parillón E
Pérgola de la Plaza G
Squadrito H
Providencia & Las Condes
Parque Quinta Normal
Airport
Palacio Cousiño
Río Mapocho
Parque Recoleta
Puente Cal y Canto
Former Mapocho Station
Mercado Central
Cathedral
Plaza de Armas
Former Congress Building
Casa Colorado
Museo Iglesia de la Merced
Museo Nacional de Bellas Artes
Parque Forestal
Parque Gomez Rojas
Palacio Subercaseaux
Teatro Municipal
Templo San Agustín
Biblioteca Nacional
Cerro Santa Lucia
Iglesia San Francisco
Universidad de Chile
Palacio de la Moneda
Terminal Los Héroes
Holiday Inn
Parque San Borja
Plaza Baquedano
Baquedano
Univ. Catolica
Santa Lucía
Univ. de Chile
Moneda
Los Héroes
Plaza de la Constitucion
Plaza de la Libertad
Plaza Bulnes
Plaza de Libertad O'Higgins
Av. Libertador General Bernardo O'Higgins
Carretera Panamericana Norte Sur
Av. Santa Maria
Av. Cardenal Caro
Av. Lopez de Bello
Av. Vicuña Mackenna
Av. Portugal

of Santiago's most important turns of history. Built by the Spanish Crown between 1804 and 1807 to house the royal courts of justice, it had served this purpose for just two years when Chile's first government junta assembled here to replace the Spanish governor with its own elected leader. Eight years later it was the meeting place of Chile's first ever Congress, and the building became the seat of government until 1846 when President Bulnes moved to La Moneda. The Palacio's grand old rooms, arranged around a large central courtyard, today house the **Museo Histórico Nacional** (March–Dec Tues–Sun 10am–5.30pm; Jan & Feb Tues–Sat 10am–5.30pm, Sun 10am–1.30pm; CH$500, free on Sun), crammed with eclectic and often fascinating relics of the past. Military uniforms and suits of armour jostle for space with furniture, sewing machines and ladies' clothes – all of it fun to look at, but too chaotic to be really illuminating.

Cathedral and Museo de Arte Sagrado

The west side of the square is dominated by the grandiose stone bulk of the **Cathedral** (Mon–Sat 9am–7pm, Sun 9am–noon). A combination of Neoclassical and Baroque styles, with its orderly columns and pediment, and its ornate bell towers, the cathedral bears the mark of **Joaquín Toesca** who was brought over from Italy in 1780 to oversee its completion. Toesca went on to become the most important architect of colonial Chile, designing many of Santiago's public buildings, including La Moneda. This is actually the fifth church to be built on this site; the first was burnt down by Picunches just months after Valdivia had it built, and the others were destroyed by earthquakes in 1552, 1647 and 1730. Inside, take a look at the main altar, carved out of marble and richly embellished with bronze and lapis lazuli. Note also the intricately crafted silver frontal, which was made by Bavarian Jesuits in the sixteenth century.

You'll find more examples of the Jesuits' exquisite silverwork in the **Museo de Arte Sagrado** (Mon 10.30am–1.30pm & 3.30–6.30pm; free) tucked away behind the main body of the cathedral. To find the entrance, go down the passage belonging to the bookshop next door to the cathedral; a gate at the bottom takes you back into the cathedral grounds, and into one of Santiago's most evocative courtyards, where languid palm trees brush against crumbling colonial architecture. From here, signs point to the three rooms containing the museum's collection of religious paintings, sculpture, furniture and silverwork, including a finely crafted silver lectern and tabernacle. These two pieces aside, none of it's as impressive as the stuff in the Museo Colonial in the Iglesia San Francisco (see p.81), but still makes for a rewarding browse.

Casa Colorada – Museo de Santiago

Just off the southeast corner of the plaza, at Merced 860, you'll find the **Casa Colorada**, built in 1769 and generally considered to be Santiago's best-preserved colonial house. The two-storey mansion with its clay-tiled roof, its row of balconied windows giving onto the street and its distinctive, deep-red walls certainly provides a striking example of an eighteenth-century town residence. The house is built around two large patios, one of which you walk through to get to the **Museo de Santiago** (Tues–Fri 10am–6pm, Sat 10am–5pm, Sun 11am–2pm; CH$500, free on Sun) which occupies five of the Casa Colorada's rooms. This rather humble museum is dedicated to the history of the city from pre-Columbian to modern times, which is illustrated mainly by scale models, maps and paintings. None of it's very slick, and there's no English commentary, but each room has a detailed information panel in Spanish which, if you're able or can be bothered to plough through, provides an excellent account of the various stages of Santiago's development.

Museo Chileno de Arte Precolombino

A stone's throw from the southwest corner of the Plaza de Armas, on the corner of Compañía and Bandera, stands the beautifully restored Real Casa de la Aduana (the old royal customs house) which now houses the **Museo Chileno de Arte Precolombino** (Tues–Sat 10am–6pm & Sun 10am–2pm; CH$1500, Sun free). Unquestionably Santiago's best museum, it brings together over two thousand pieces representing some eighty pre-Columbian peoples of Latin America. The collection spans a period of about five thousand years and covers regions from present-day Mexico down to southern Chile, brilliantly illustrating the artistic wealth and diversity of the continent's many pre-Columbian cultures. Good layout and lighting set off the delicate beauty of the exhibits, and the whole thing's a very manageable size. The permanent collection is displayed in four rooms arranged around a central courtyard, each one dedicated to a different cultural area.

Area Mesoamérica

Walking through the large double doors off the hall you'll find yourself in the **Area Mesoamérica**, corresponding to present-day Mexico, Guatemala, Honduras, El Salvador and parts of Nicaragua. Right in front of you is one of the most startling pieces in the museum: a statue of **Xipe-Totec**, the god of Spring, represented as a man covered in the skin of a monkey, exposing both male and female genitalia. At the time of the Spanish conquest, the cult of Xipe-Totec was widespread throughout most of Mesoamerica, and was celebrated in a bizarre ritual in which a young man would cover himself with the skin of a sacificial victim, and wear it until it rotted off, revealing his young, fresh skin and symbolizing the growth of new vegetation from the earth. Another eye-catching object, further up the room on the left, is the elaborately ornamented **incense burner**, used by the Teotihuacán culture (300–600 AD) to pray for rain and good harvests. The face carved in the middle represents a rain god, and when the incense was burning, the smoke would escape from his eyes. Standing at the far end of the room, by the exit, is a huge slab of stone, whose **bas-relief carvings** depict a hulking, armed warrior with two small figures at his feet. It originally formed part of an immense Maya structure, built between 600 and 900 AD.

Area Intermedia

In this region, covering what is now Ecuador, Colombia, Panama, Costa Rica and Nicaragua, the continent's oldest pottery was produced, as well as some exquisite goldwork. Pottery made its first appearance in the Americas around 3000 BC on the coast of Ecuador, where it was created by the agricultural and fishing communities of the Valdivia culture. Among the museum's best examples of **Valdivia pottery** is the gorgeous little female figurine with a big, round belly and childlike face, thought to have been used for fertility rites carried out at harvest time. Other female representations include the Tumaco-La Tolita carving of a woman with her head thrown back, laughing, and the Bahía-Jama carving of a mother suckling her child at her breast – both images date from 500 BC to 500 AD, and both are touchingly naturalistic. Note also the wonderful **cocoa leaf-chewing figures** known as *coqueros*, carved with a tell-tale lump in their mouth by the Capulí culture (500 BC–500 AD). As well as pottery, this *sala* contains some beautiful **gold objects**, such as the miniature, finely-worked carvings produced by the Vegaguas and Diquis cultures (700–1550 AD) featuring images of frightening monsters and open-jawed, long-fanged felines.

Area Andina

Covering the central Andean region (today's Peru and western Bolivia), this room is distinguished by its superb **textiles**, retrieved from ancient graves and immaculately preserved, thanks to the darkness of the tombs and the dryness of the Andean desert. Hanging by the door as you go in is a fragment of painted cloth depicting three human figures with fanged jaws – this is the oldest textile in the museum, produced by the Chavín culture almost 3000 years ago, and still in astonishingly good condition. At the opposite end of the room is the striking Chimú tapestry (1100–1470 AD), densely illustrated with repeating geometric motifs in stunning, vividly preserved colours. Besides the textiles, the room also features the highly expressive work of the Moche culture (100 BC–800 AD), including copper figurines and masks, now a gorgeous jade-green colour, and a series of polished ceremonial pots decorated with images of animals, faces and houses.

Area Surandina

The final room is the **Area Surandina**, corresponding to modern Chile and northwest Argentina. Among the most striking pieces on display are the huge **ceramic urns** of the Aguada culture (600–900 AD), painted with bold geometric designs incorporating fantastic, often feline, images. Look out too for the wooden and stone **snuff trays**, carved by the San Pedro people of northern Chile between 300 and 1000 AD, and used with small tubes to inhale hallucinogenic substances. The curious thing on the wall that looks like a grass skirt is a relic from the Incas, who made it all the way down to central Chile during their expansion in the fifteenth century. Known as a **quipú**, it consists of many strands of wool attached to a single cord, and was used to keep various records – such as of taxes collected – by means of a complex system of knots tied in the strands.

Ahumada, Huérfanos and around

The southeast corner of downtown Santiago contains the city's busiest pedestrian thoroughfares, Ahumada and Huérfanos, and a miscellany of attractions. Running south from the west side of the Plaza de Armas to the Alameda, **Paseo Ahumada** is a seething mass of people at every moment of the day. Walking down, you'll pass sombre doorways leading into labyrinthine shopping arcades, *confiterías* serving preposterously large cream cakes and, between Agustinas and Moneda, the famous **Café Caribe** and **Café Haiti**, where sharp-suited businessmen enjoy the thrill of being served their *cortados* and *expresos* by scantily-clad waitresses. Take a moment to pop into the **Banco de Chile**, between Huérfanos and Agustinas; its vast hall, polished counters and beautiful old clock have changed little since the bank opened in 1925.

Paseo Huérfanos crosses Ahumada at right angles, one block south of the plaza, and is lined with numerous banks and cinemas. Several places of interest are dotted amongst the shops, office blocks and *galerías* of the surrounding streets. You could start with the **Basilica de la Merced**, a towering, Neo-Renaissance structure on the corner of Merced and Mac Iver, with a beautifully carved eighteenth-century pulpit. Attached to the church is a small **musuem** (Tues–Fri 10am–1pm & 3–6pm; CH$500) where, among the usual crucifixes and other religious paraphernalia, you'll find a collection of Easter Island artefacts, including a wooden **rongorongo tablet**, carved in the undeciphered Easter Island script – one of just 29 left in the world (see p.428).

From here, head south for two blocks and turn right at Agustinas, where you'll find the dazzling white facade of the **Teatro Municipal**, a splendid French Neoclassical building, all arches and columns and perfect symmetry. This has been the capital's most prestigious venue for ballet, opera and classical music since it was inaugurated in 1857. It's worth asking to have a look around inside; the main auditorium is quite a sight, with its sumptuous red upholstery and crystal chandeliers. Standing opposite the theatre, and mirroring its cool, smooth whiteness, is the **Mansión Subercaseaux**, built at the turn of the century for one of Santiago's wealthiest families, and now occupied by a bank. A little further along, at the corner of Agustinas and Estado, loom the green walls and yellow columns of the **Templo de San Agustín**, dating from 1608 but extensively rebuilt since then. The chief interest within its highly decorative interior is the wooden carving of Christ, just left of the main altar as you face it, known as the *Cristo de Mayo* and the subject of an intriguing local legend. The story goes that the crown of thorns around the figure's head slipped down to its neck during the 1647 earthquake, and that when someone tried to move the crown back up to its head, the carved face of Christ began to bleed, and the ground started to shake. For this reason, the crown has remained untouched ever since, still hanging around the neck.

La Moneda, the Ex Congreso Nacional and the Tribunales de Justicia

The best approach to the **Palacio de la Moneda** is from the northern side of the vast, paved Plaza de la Constitución, three blocks east and south of the Plaza de Armas. From here you can appreciate the perfect symmetry and compact elegance of this low-lying Neoclassical building, spread across the entire block. It was built between 1784 and 1805 by the celebrated Italian architect Joaquin Toesca, with the purpose of housing the royal mint. This role was to be short-lived, however, and after some forty years it became residential palace for the presidents of Chile, starting with Manuel Bulnes in 1848, and ending with Carlos Ibáñez del Campo in 1958. At this point it stopped being used as the president's home, but it continues to be the official seat of government. **Guided tours** around the palace are ridiculously complicated to arrange; you need either to fill in a form in one of the underground offices on the Morandé side of the square (this is part of the maze of subterranean corridors and meeting rooms created by Pinochet and nicknamed *el bunker*; to find the entrance, look out for a policeman standing guard); or else you can send a written request to the Dirección Administrativa, Palacio de la Moneda, making sure to give your full name and passport number. Either way, you need to do it at least twenty days before you want to visit, and you need to give a telephone number you can be reached on, to be told whether or not permission has been granted. If you do get on a tour you'll be shown around some grand state rooms and be given an interesting talk on the history of the building, but whether it's really worth all the trouble is debatable. Far easier is to come and watch the **changing of the guard** in front of the palace at 10am on alternate days, when hundreds of green-uniformed soldiers in high black boots march around the square to the rather jolly Chilean national anthem.

North of the Plaza de la Constitución, at the corner of Morandé and Compañía, are another couple of impressive public buildings. The most beautiful, from the outside, is the white, temple-like **Ex Congreso Nacional**, set amidst lush gardens. This is where Congress used to meet, until it was dissolved on September 11, 1973, the day of General Pinochet's coup d'état (see p.456). In 1990, following the end of the military regime, a new congress building was erected in Valparaíso; this one currently houses the Cancillería (foreign ministry). On the southern side of Compañía, spanning the whole block, is the **Tribunales de Justicia**, an imposing Neoclassical building housing the highest court in Chile, the Corte Suprema. You'd never guess it from the outside but this austere building conceals one of the most beautiful interiors in the city: you walk in to find yourself in a long, narrow hall running the length of the building, topped by a stunning glass and metal vault three floors above, and flooded with natural light. If you want to take photos, you need to get permission from the *Secretaria* on the first floor.

Along the Alameda

Officially the Avenida del Libertador Bernardo O'Higgins, Santiago's most vital east–west artery is universally known as **"la Alameda"**, a word of Arabic origin meaning "poplar-lined avenue with areas for recreation". It began life as "La Cañada" when a branch of the Mapocho was sealed off shortly before independence, and a roadway was created over the old river bed. A few years later, when the Supreme Director Bernardo O'Higgins decided that Santiago required an *alameda*, La Cañada was deemed the best place to put it: "There is no public boulevard where people may get together for honest relief and amusement during the resting hours, since the one known as Tajamar, because of its narrowness and irregularity, far from being cheerful, inspires sadness. La Cañada, because of its condition, extension, abundance of water and other circumstances, is the most apparent place for an *alameda*."

Three rows of poplars were promptly planted along each side, and the Alameda was born, soon to become *the* place to take the evening promenade. Since those quieter times the boulevard has evolved into the city's biggest, busiest, noisiest and most polluted thoroughfare, made up of a sea of yellow *micros* moving as one organic mass, all screeching brakes, frenetic horns and choking fumes. Still, it's an unavoidable axis and you'll probably spend a fair bit of time on it or under it: the main metro line runs beneath it, and some of Santiago's most interesting landmarks stand along it.

Cerro Santa Lucía and around

The lushly forested **Cerro Santa Lucía** is the most imaginative and exuberant piece of landscaping in Santiago. Looking at it now, it's hard to believe that for the first three centuries of the city's development this was nothing more than a barren, rocky outcrop, completely ignored despite its historical importance – for it was at the foot of this hill that Santiago was officially founded by Valdivia, on February 12, 1541. It wasn't until 1872 that the city turned its attention to Santa Lucía once more, when the *intendente* of Santiago, Vicuña Mackenna, enlisted the labour of 150 prisoners to transform it into a grand public park. Almost Gaudíesque in appearance, with its swirling pathways and baroque terraces and turrets, this is a great place to come for panoramic views across the city, even when they're veiled behind a layer of smog. If slogging up the steps doesn't appeal, there's a free lift on the western side of the park, by the junction with Huérfanos. While it's always busy and safe by day, you should note that several muggings have been reported here after dark, so hanging around to watch the sun go down, though tempting, isn't advisable.

Immediately west of the hill stands the massive **Biblioteca Nacional**, one of the largest libraries in Latin America (and handy for its free loos inside), while to the east, set back from the Alameda, is the quiet, arty quarter centred on **Plaza Mulato Gil de Castro** (daily: 10am–2pm, Sat also 7pm–2am), at the corner of Merced and Lastarria. This small cobbled square, enclosed by old buildings housing artists' workshops, galleries, an antiquarian bookshop, a café-restaurant and a tiny archeological museum (same hours as above), is one of the nicest places in Santiago to go and sit with a book over a coffee. The bohemian atmosphere continues down Lastarria, with its string of trendy restaurants (see p.89), and its arts cinema and café, *El Biógrafo*, filled with students from the nearby Universidad Catolica.

Iglesia San Francisco and Barrio París-Londres

Looking west from the Biblioteca Nacional, you can't miss the **Iglesia San Francisco**, highly conspicuous with its towering red walls jutting out into the street. This is the oldest building in Santiago, erected between 1586 and 1628 and the survivor of three great earthquakes. Take a look inside at the **Virgen del Socorro**, a small polychrome carving (rather lost in the vast main altar) brought to Chile on the saddle of Pedro de Valdivia in 1540 and credited with guiding him on his way, as well as fending off Indian attackers by throwing sand in their eyes. For all its age and beauty, the most remarkable feature of this church is its deep, hushed silence; you're just metres from the din of the Alameda but those buses seem a million miles away.

The monastery adjacent to the church houses the **Museo Colonial** (Tues–Sat 10am–1pm & 3–6pm, Sun 10am–1pm; CH$500), where you'll find a highly evocative collection of paintings, sculpture, furniture and other objects dating from the colonial period, most of it religious and a good deal of it created in Peru, the seat of colonial government. Note the immense eighteenth-century **cedar door** of the first room you come to off the cloisters; carved into hundreds of intricately designed squares, this is one of the museum's most beautiful possessions. Inside, you'll find another arresting sight: a gigantic painting of the **genealogical tree of the Franciscan Order** consisting of 644 miniature portraits. Other highlights to look out for include the **Cristo Chilote**, a small wooden image of Christ on the cross, carved in Chiloé in 1780, bearing unmistakeably South American features; a roomful of delicately crafted **locks**; and, squeezed into the Gran Sala, a collection of 54 paintings depicting the **life and miracles of St Francis of Assisi**, quite overwhelming in their sheer size and number.

If you turn left as you leave the museum, you'll find yourself on calle Londres which intersects with calle París to form the **Barrio París-Londres**, tucked behind the Iglesia San Francisco on what used to be the monastery's orchards. These sinuous, cobbled streets lined with crumbling mansions and cheap hotels look like a little chunk out of Paris's Latin Quarter. Created in 1923 by a team of architects, the *barrio* is undeniably attractive but feels incongruous; it's also odd the way it's made up of just two streets, and simply stops at the end of them.

Universidad de Chile to Los Héroes

Back on the Alameda, walking west, you'll come to the yellow-washed walls of the **Universidad de Chile**, a fine French Neoclassical building dating from 1863. Opposite is the **Bolsa de Comercio**, Santiago's stock exchange, housed in a flamboyant, French Renaissance-style building that tapers to a thin wedge at the main entrance. One block further along you reach Plaza Bulnes, flanked by the **tomb** and massive **equestrian statue of Bernardo O'Higgins** to the south, and to the north by the grey stone outline of the **Palacio de la Moneda** (see p.79), sitting with its back to the Alameda. As you continue west past the 128m-high telecommunications tower known as the **Torre Entel,** you enter what was once the preserve of Santiago's moneyed elite, with several glorious old turn-of-the-century mansions serving as reminders – look out for the **Palacio Irarrázabal** on the south side of the Alameda between San Ignacio and Dieciocho, the **Palacio Ariztía** a little further on and, next door to the latter, the **Palacio Errázuriz**, the oldest and finest of these Alameda mansions, and now the Brazilian Embassy. You're now standing opposite the triumphant **Monumento a los Héroes de la Concépción**, an imposing statue, which borders the junction of the Alameda with the Avenida Norte Sur (the Panamericana), and is where metro lines 1 and 2 intersect.

A detour to Palacio Cousiño

If you take Line 2 to Toesca, one stop south of Los Héroes, you can make a highly recommended detour to the **Palacio Cousiño** (Tues–Fri 9.30am–1.30pm & 2.30–5pm, Sat & Sun 9.30am–1.30pm; CH$800) at Dieciocho 438 (turn left out of Toesca station). This was and remains the most magnificent of the turn-of-the-century palaces, the one that dazzled Santiago's high society by the sheer scale of its luxury and opulence. It was built between 1870 and 1878 for doña Isidora Goyenechea, the widow of Luis Cousiño who'd amassed a fortune with his Lota coal mines and Chañarcillo silver mines. All the furnishings and decoration were shipped over from Europe, especially France, and top European craftsmen were brought over to work on the house. The first floor was burnt to ashes in 1968, but the ground floor remains totally intact, and provides a wonderful close-up view of turn-of-the-century European craftsmanship at its best: Italian hand-painted tiles; Bohemian crystal chandeliers; mahogany, walnut and ebony parquet floors; a mosaic marble staircase; and French brocade and silk furnishings are just a few of the splendours of the *palacio*. Visits are by guided tour, in Spanish or English, and last about forty minutes.

West to Estación Central

West of Los Héroes, the Alameda continues its path through the once-wealthy neighbourhoods that were abandoned by Santiago's well-heeled earlier this century, when the moneyed classes shifted to the more fashionable east side of town. After falling into serious decline, these areas are finally coming into their own again, as a younger generation has started renovating decaying mansions, opening up trendy cafés and bookshops and injecting a new vigour into the streets. One of the most beautiful of these districts, on the northern side of the Alameda, between Avenida Brasil and Avenida Ricardo Cumming, is **Barrio Concha y Toro**, a jumble of twisting cobbled streets leading to a tiny round plaza with a fountain in the middle – possibly the most romantic spot in Santiago. Further north you'll find **Barrio Brasil**, one of the liveliest of the newly revived neighbourhoods, centred around the large, grand Plaza Brasil full of children playing among the old silk-cotton and lime trees.

A few blocks west stands one of the Alameda's great landmarks: the stately **Estación Central**, featuring a colossal metal roof that was cast in the Schneider foundry in Creuzot, in 1896. It's the only functioning train station left in the city, with regular services to the south of Chile. Right opposite is the **Planetarium** (Wed & Fri 7pm, Sat 3.30pm, 5pm & 7pm, Sun noon, 3.30pm, 5pm & 7pm; CH$1800; ☎681 2171 for confirmation of performance times) which puts on high-tech audiovisual shows with astronomical themes.

Along the río Mapocho

Besides the Alameda, the other major axis binding the old city is the **río Mapocho**, filled with the muddy brown waters from the melted snow of the Andes. There are few historic buildings along here, as frequent floodings deterred riverside development until the Mapocho was canalized in 1891. Nonetheless, several city landmarks stand out, including the flamboyant Mercado Central, the now defunct Estación Mapocho and the elegant Palacio de Bellas Artes.

Mercado Central and Feria Municipal

If you follow calle Puente north from the Plaza de Armas you'll reach the **Mercado Central** (daily 6am–4pm) close to the river's southern bank. This huge metal structure, prefabricated in England and erected in Santiago in 1868, contains a very picturesque fruit, vegetable and fish market that's worth a place on everyone's itinerary. The highlight is the fish stalls, packed with glistening sea bass and salmon, buckets of salt-crusted oysters, mussels and clams, and unidentifiable crustaceans out of which live things with tentacles make occasional appearances. Overhead, rows of pink and grey fish hang from hooks, and white-coated fishmongers turn gutting and filleting into an art form. The best time to come here is at lunchtime when you can feast at one of the many **fish restaurants** dotted around the market; the cheapest are those on the outer edge, but it's worth paying the extra to sit amongst the colour and atmosphere of the central hall. See p.34 for more on seafood.

True market addicts should cross the river and, by way of the sweetly perfumed **Mercado de Flores**, head for the gargantuan **Feria Municipal**, set a couple of blocks back from the riverbank opposite the Mercado Central. There's no pretty architecture here, and no tourists either; just serious shoppers and hundreds of stalls selling the whole gamut of Central Valley produce, from cows' innards and pigs' bellies to mountains of potatoes and onions, at a fraction of the price charged in the Mercado Central. Work your way to the back of the building and out into the maze of canopied stalls behind. This is mainly wholesale, and the quantities of fresh fruit on display here are simply breathtaking: table after table piled high with raspberries, grapes, pears, apples, kiwis, plums, nectarines and peaches – all dappled by the sunlight poking through the awnings.

Estación Mapocho

Just west of the Mercado Central, right by the river, is the immense stone and metal **Estación Mapocho**, built in 1912 to house the terminal of the Valparaíso–Santiago railway line. Sadly this service no longer runs, though there's constant talk of reviving it; meanwhile, the station is used as a cultural centre, housing exhibitions, plays and concerts which never quite manage to fill its beautiful, vast interior. You can walk in and have a look inside, worth it if only for the view of its great copper, glass and marble roof; you'll also find a craft shop, restaurant and bookshop off the main hall. The only time the station is full of the bustle and activity it deserves is the last week of November, when it stages the **Feria Nacional del Libro**, one of the continent's most important book fairs.

Parque Forestal and Museo de Bellas Artes

The **Parque Forestal**, stretching along the southern bank of the Mapocho between Puente Recoleta and Puente Pío Nono, was created at the turn of the century on land that was reclaimed from the river after it was canalized. Lined with long, perfectly straight rows of trees and lampposts, it provides a picturesque setting for the **Palacio de Bellas Artes** (Tues–Sat 10am–7pm, Sun 10am–6pm; CH$400), built to commemorate the centenary of Chilean independence. The palacio houses the **Museo de Bellas Artes** and **Museo de Arte Contemporáneo**, composed of predominantly Chilean works from the beginning of the colonial period onwards. The quality is mixed, and it could be argued that none of the paintings equals the beauty of the building's vast white hall with its marble statues bathing in the natural light pouring in from the glass and iron ceiling. The palacio is noted, however, for putting on excellent temporary exhibitions.

Barrio Bellavista and Cerro San Cristóbal

Head across the Pío Nono bridge at the eastern end of the Parque Forestal and you'll find yourself in the main street (also called Pío Nono) of **Barrio Bellavista**. Nestling between the northern bank of the Mapocho and the steep slopes of Cerro San Cristóbal, Bellavista is a warren of quiet, leafy streets lined with brightly coloured houses, steeped in a village-like atmosphere. It was originally known as *La Chimba*, which means "the other side of the river" in Quechua, and grew into a residential area when Santiago's population started spilling across the river in the nineteenth century. Today it has a reputation for being the capital's bohemian quarter, thanks in part to the fact that Pablo Neruda lived here, along with several other artists, writers and intellectuals. It's packed with restaurants, many of them small and atmospheric, and on Thursday, Friday and Saturday nights the district becomes one of Santiago's main nightlife centres. Another attraction is the evening handicraft market that spreads along the length of Pío Nono at weekends and is a good place to come for gifts or souvenirs. You might also be tempted by the dozens of lapis lazuli outlets running along Avenida Bellavista, between Puente Pío Nono and Puente del Arzobispo, but be warned that this semi-precious stone is not cheap, and there are few bargains to be found. There's no metro in Bellavista itself, but it's a short walk from Baquedano metro.

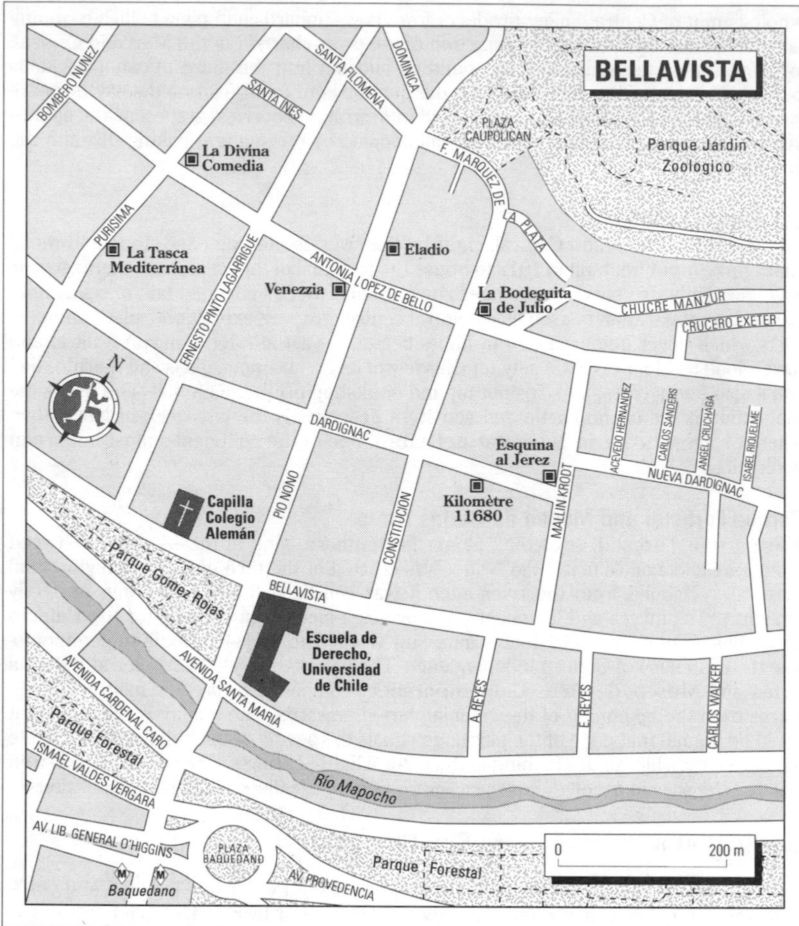

La Chascona

Tucked away in a tiny street at the foot of Cerro San Cristóbal – at Marquéz de la Plata 0192 – you'll find **La Chascona**, the house that Pablo Neruda shared with his third wife, Matilde Urrutia, from 1955 until his death in 1973 (guided tours Tues–Sun 10am–1pm & 3–6pm; CH$1000 in Spanish, CH$2000 in English or French). It was named "La Chascona" ("tangle-haired woman") by Neruda, as a tribute to his wife's thick red hair. Today, it's the headquarters of the Fundación Neruda which has painstakingly restored this and the poet's two other houses – *La Sebastiana* in Valparaíso (see p.124) and *Isla Negra*, about 90km down the coast (see p.137) – to their original condition, opening them to the public for visits. This house is split into three separate sections that climb up the hillside, and is packed to the rafters with objects collected by Neruda, illuminating his loves, enthusiasms and obsessions. Beautiful African carvings jostle for space with Victorian dolls, music boxes, paperweights and coloured glasses; the floors are littered with old armchairs, stools, a rocking horse, exotic rugs and a sleeping toy lion. There are numerous references to Neruda's and Mathilde's love for each other, such as the bars on the windows in which their initials are entwined and lapped by breaking waves, and the portrait of Mathilde by Diego Rivera, which has the profile of Neruda hidden in her hair. The third and highest level houses Neruda's library, containing over nine thousand books, as well as the diploma he was given when awarded the Nobel Prize for Literature in 1971, and a replica of the medal.

Cerro San Cristóbal

A trip up to the summit of **Cerro San Cristóbal** is one of the highlights of a stay in Santiago, particularly on clear, sunny days when the views over the city and to the Andes are quite stunning. The hill is, in fact, a spur of the Andes, jutting into the heart of the capital and rising to a peak of 860m, a point that's marked by a giant 22-metre-high statue of the *Virgen de la Inmaculada*. The easiest way to get up is to take the **funicular** from the station at the north end of Pío Nono in Bellavista (Mon–Fri 9.45am–8pm, Sat & Sun 9.45am–8.30pm; CH$900 return, CH$1500 return including cable car). It stops first at the **Jardín Zoológico** (Tues–Fri 10am–6pm, Sat & Sun 10am–7pm; CH$1600) – an old-fashioned sort of zoo full of dull-eyed creatures, including two soporific tigers in a small cage – and then continues up to the Terraza Bellavista where you get out. From here it's a short but steep walk up to the huge white Virgin where you'll be rewarded with fine views over Santiago's suburbs vanishing into hazy mountains. Back down at Terraza Bellavista, a path leads west to the **teleférico** (cable car) station known as Estación Cumbre (joint ticket with funicular; see above). This provides hair-raising rides across to Estación Tapahue, then descends to Estación Oasis at the foot of the hill (and a long walk from anywhere). Get off at Tapahue for the expensive but fabulous open-air **Piscina Tapahue** (Nov–March Tues–Sun 10am–7pm; CH$4000), or to switch cable cars to return to Estación Cumbre.

Parque Quinta Normal and its museums

About 1km north of the Estación Central, the **Parque Quinta Normal** is perhaps the most elegant and peaceful of Santiago's parks. It was created in 1830 as a place to introduce and acclimatize foreign trees and plants to the city – Chileans from the nineteenth century onwards have been very fond of filling their public squares with many types of trees, and most of these have had to be imported from abroad. Today the park is packed with some beautifully mature examples: Babylonian willows, Monterey pine, cypress and poplars, to name just a few. Additional attractions include a pond with rowing boats for hire, and four museums. The best way to get here is to take the metro to Estación Central, then a bus or taxi up Avenida Matucana.

Museo Nacional de Historia Natural

The grand, Neoclassical building near the park entrance on Matucana houses the **Museo Nacional de Historia Natural** (Tues–Sat 10am–5.30pm, Sun noon–5.30pm; CH$400). Founded in 1830 and occupying its present building since 1875, this is the oldest natural history museum in Latin America and still one of the most important. It's worth a visit for the colossal skeleton of a blue whale mounted in the vast entrance hall, and for the noteworthy Easter Island collection on the second level, featuring a *moai*, an upturned "topknot", or "hat", and the famous Santiago Staff inscribed with the mysterious, undeciphered rongorongo script (see p.428). Another highlight, on the ground level, is the five-hundred-year-old frozen body of a child, found at an altitude of 5400m on Cerro Plomo (near Santiago) in 1954, and thought to be a sacrificial victim. Otherwise, a lack of funds has forced the museum to concentrate more on its role as an academic centre than as a place to inform and entertain the public, and the remaining displays amount to moth-eaten dioramas of Chilean landscapes and a roomful of stuffed birds.

Museo de Ciencia y Tecnología

A short distance west of the natural history museum, you'll find the **Museo de Ciencia y Tecnología** (Tues–Fri 10am–5pm, Sat & Sun 11am–6pm; CH$500). Far more modern and high-tech in feel, it's geared primarily towards kids, demonstrating the basic principles of physics with entertaining, hands-on gadgets and displays.

Museo Ferroviaro

Follow the road down towards the southern park gate, on Avenida Portales, and you'll reach the shiny black steam engines belonging to the outdoor **Museo Ferroviaro** (Tues–Fri 10am–5pm, Sat & Sun 11am–6pm; CH$500, CH$1000 for photo permit). The museum consists of fourteen pristine locomotives dating from 1893 to 1940, including a splendid Kitson-Meyer, manufactured in England in 1909 and shipped over to Chile where it served the famous trans-Andean service from Los Andes to Mendoza in Argentina until 1971. Another highlight is the luxurious wood-panelled presidential train, built in 1911 for Ramón Barros Luco – if you ask nicely you'll be allowed to climb on board.

Museo Artequín

The wildly colourful glass and metal building standing opposite the park's Avenida Portales entrance was originally the Chilean pavilion in the Universal Exhibition in Paris, 1889. It now contains the extraordinary **Museo Artequín** (Tues–Sun 10am–5pm; CH$500) – short for Arte en la Quinta – which aims to bring people, especially schoolchildren, closer to art by exposing them to reproductions of the world's greatest paintings in a relaxed, unintimidating environment. They're all here, from El Greco and Delacroix through to Andy Warhol and Jackson Pollock, and copious plastic information cards tell you all about the artists and their work.

Parque O'Higgins

Perhaps the best reason to come to the spacious **Parque Bernardo O'Higgins**, a couple of kilometres or so southeast of the Quinta Normal, is to soak up the Chilean family atmosphere, as it's one of the most popular green spaces in the city. It was originally the Parque Cousiño, commissioned by Luis Cousiño, the entrepreneurial millionaire, in 1869, and *the* place to take your carriage rides in the late nineteenth century. These days working-class families and groups of kids flock here on summer weekends to enjoy the picnic areas, outdoor pools (very crowded), roller rink, basketball court and the gut-churning rides of **Fantasilandia**, an outdoor amusement park (Sat & Sun 11am–9.30pm, plus July & Sept Mon–Fri 2.30–9.30pm, Jan & Feb Tues–Fri 3–9.30pm, closed when raining; CH$4000). The park also features **El Pueblito**, a collection of adobe buildings typical of the Chilean countryside and housing several cheap restaurants, some craft stalls and a handful of small museums. The best of these is the **Museo del Huaso** (Tues–Fri 10am–5pm, Sat & Sun 10am–2pm; free), dedicated to the Chilean cowboy, or horseman, with displays of spurs, saddles, ponchos and hats, and a big photo of the pope decked out in a poncho when he visited the museum in April 1987 (he came to give Mass at the chapel next door). There's also a tiny shell museum, an insect museum and a not very exciting aquarium. See p.49 for more on Chile's *huasos*.

Los barrios altos: Providencia, Las Condes and beyond

The *barrios* east of the city centre spreading into the foothills of the Andes are home to Santiago's moneyed elite; the further you go and higher you get the richer the people and bigger the houses. It's hard to believe that up until the beginning of this century there was virtually no one here; it was for its isolation and tranquillity that the Sisters of Providencia chose to build their convent on what is now Avenida Providencia in 1853. Then, following a slow trickle of eastbound movement, there was a great exodus of wealthy families from their traditional preserves west of the city over to the new *barrio alto* in the 1920s, where they've been entrenched ever since. The *barrio* you're most likely to visit is **Providencia**, as it's home to Sernatur, various adventure tourism and skiing outfits and a thriving nightlife scene. Further east in **Las Condes** the atmosphere is more residential, and apart from a few notable exceptions such as the **decorative arts museum** and **Los Dominicos market** there's less to pull you out here. If you've access to a car, however, or meet some Chileans who offer to give you a sightseeing tour (not uncommon), it can be quite fun to drive around the fabulously wealthy uptown *barrios* like **La Dehesa**; you could even just sit on a bus to the end of Avenida Las Condes to watch the Andes get closer and closer, and feel the city creep higher and higher.

Providencia

You can walk east along the Alameda to the centre of **Providencia** in about twenty or thirty minutes from the Universidad Católica, but it's far easier to take the metro (to Manuel Montt, Pedro de Valdivia or Los Leones, depending on which stretch you want to get to) or hop on a *micro*. Providencia's oldest building is the yellow-washed **Iglesia de Nuestra Señora de la Divina Providencia**, founded in 1853 and lending its name to the district that grew up around it. Opposite, occupying a former fruit and vegetable market, is **Sernatur** (see p.69), and a few blocks east of here you're into the commercial heart of Providencia, with its stylish stores and elegant cafés. Many travellers complain that it's bland and faceless, while others appreciate the modern shopping facilities, such as the **Mall Panorámico**. There's also a concentration of **restaurants and bars** around here, notably on Holley and Suecia – mostly full of Chilean yuppies, foreign expats and tourists, they're not to everyone's taste but are undeniably good meeting places.

Las Condes

Just east in **Las Condes**, the shops and office blocks gradually thin out into a more residential district, punctuated with the odd giant shopping mall, such as **Alto Las Condes**, Av Kennedy 901 (daily 10am–10pm). This proudly promotes itself as "*el Shopping Center más moderno de Latinoamérica*", and with its 240 shops (including JC Penney) and pristine, antiseptic interior, it may be right. If this appeals, note that a free shuttle bus runs twice-daily from most major hotels to the mall and back (☎229 1383 for times). In addition, most of the buses running along the Alameda displaying "Las Condes" on the window will stop near the mall.

Just opposite the mall at Av Kennedy 9350 is an altogether more compelling reason for coming out here: Casa Lo Matta, the main house of an eighteenth-century hacienda, now housing the fabulous **Museo de Artes Decorativas** (Tues–Fri 10am–5.30pm, Sat 11am–5.30pm, Sun 2–5.30pm; CH$500). The collection, which includes silverwork, paintings, ceramics, textiles, sculpture and furniture, is beautifully displayed in two large rooms of the old house. The ground floor is dedicated mainly to the silver collection which includes some gorgeous, delicately worked cups and tubes for drinking maté, and – in prim contrast – a Victorian silver tea set from England. Upstairs you'll find ivory carvings, fourteenth-century oriental rugs, a magnificently carved oak wardrobe, nineteenth-century Bohemian crystal and Sèvres and Royal Doulton porcelain. The best pieces, perhaps, are the colonial Spanish coffers, made of polished wood inlaid with ivory in beautiful, Moorish-influenced geometric patterns. You can get here via a footbridge from the rear entrance of the mall, or if you're coming straight from Santiago, on bus #388 (marked "Lo Barnechea") from Estación Mapocho.

About ten blocks south of Alto las Condes, at the eastern end of Avenida Apoquindo, is **Los Dominicos** market (Tues–Sun 11am–7.30pm), a large and lively craft fair held in a sort of mock village. You'll find a wide range of beautiful handicrafts – made in workshops on site and sold at the stalls – as well as antiques, books, fossils, a restaurant, and live music and dancing at weekends. Next door is the **Iglesia Los Dominicos**, built by Toesca in the late eighteenth century; the church is usually locked, but you can admire its attractive colonial architecture from the gardens between 4pm and 8pm on weekdays. Buses marked "Apoquindo" come here from the Alameda, or you can take the metro out to Estación Militar then get a *colectivo* (under the bridge next to the station).

Eating

Santiago could make a serious bid for the title of fast-food capital of the world, with a proliferation of uninviting **chains** like *McDonald's*, *Max Beef*, *Lomito'n* and *Pollo Stop* spread around the city, along with the hundreds of **fuentes de soda** offering cheap snacks (usually hot dogs or fried meat sandwiches), beer and TV football. Add to these the numerous **stand-up snack bars** on the south side of the Plaza de Armas, and you've got a pretty comprehensive picture of the budget food scene in Santiago. For not much more you can eat more heartily and healthily in some of the old-fashioned **bars**, or local **picadas** (inexpensive traditional canteens) which serve typical Chilean basics like *pastel de choclo*, *humitas* and *cazuela*.

There's also an enormous choice of **restaurants**, from the humble to the outstanding, taking in many different types of cuisine including Asian, Arabic, Spanish, Peruvian, French and Italian. Some of these are modestly priced but the majority are quite expensive, except at **lunchtime** when many places offer a good-value fixed-price **menú del día** or **menú ejecutivo**. For this reason a lot of restaurants, particularly downtown, tend to be packed out at lunchtime but fairly quiet (sometimes empty) in the evening, at least during the week. In most places there's no need to **book ahead**; where it's advisable, we've included a phone number.

Santiago is not a café city, but there are a number of **coffee shops** catering to the great tradition of *onces* (afternoon tea). The influence of Chile's German immigrants is very much in evidence here, with many places serving delicious *küchen* and strudel. If you just want to rest your legs and replenish your energies with a drink, you could also try the many bars and restaurants that act more like cafés by day. For more on food and drink, including menu translations, see pp.34–40.

Budget food

In addition to the sandwich bars in the Plaza de Armas and ubiquitous fast-food outlets, you could try the following options.

Bar Central, San Pablo 1063, between Puente and Bandera. Popular local bar with a huge TV and a good choice of bargain lunches, including all the usual meat and fish dishes.

Bella Pizza, Estado 125 and 159 (near Alameda). Filling low-priced pizzas served until midnight every night.

Chez Henry, south side of Plaza de Armas. Large delicatessen serving good ready-made hot and cold meals to take away, as well as fresh fruit, ice cream and other goodies. Closed Sun.

Corner Bar, corner of Moneda and Bandera. Old-fashioned bar with lots of polished brass, old mirrors and dark wood, offering typical inexpensive dishes like *churrasco, lomo* and *empanadas*. Closed Sun pm.

Dominó, 1016 Agustinas. The most popular sandwich bar in Santiago, distinguished by its fresh, good-quality fillings. Closed Sun.

Don Simón, Pío Nono 262. Cheapest choice in Bellavista, offering *cazuela* for an amazing CH$900. All the other favourites are here as well, like *pollo con papas fritas* (chicken and chips), and *lomo a lo pobre* (steak and egg); prices go up after 8pm. Closed Sun pm.

Food Garden, in *galería* on Huérfanos between Estado and San Antonio. Burgers, pizzas and other plastic food from a collection of outlets around a central eating area. Closed Sun.

Restaurants

Most of Santiago's **restaurants** are concentrated in a few areas of town, notably Calle Lastarria (just east of Cerro Santo Lucía), Bellavista and Providencia; there are also some imaginative places springing up in Barrio Brasil and on Plaza Nuñoa (see p.92). Perhaps the most memorable place for lunch in all of Santiago is the Mercado Central (see p.82), whose central hall is lined with *marisquería*, the most famous being *Donde Agusto*. Note that most restaurants are closed on Sunday evenings.

Downtown

Bar de la Unión, Nueva York 11, near to the Bolsa. Old wooden floors, shelves of dusty wine bottles and animated, garrulous old men make this a really atmospheric place to come for a drink or a meal. The food's tasty (lots of fish) and good value, and the servings are generous. Closed Sun pm.

Cocoa, Lastarria 297 (☎632 1272). Tiny Peruvian restaurant in a painted wooden building off a pretty courtyard. The food is expensive but excellent, with the sort of complex seasonings and mixtures of ingredients you just don't get in Chilean food. Try the *Costa Verde* (deep-fried prawns and chicken in BBQ sauce) or *filete a la mantequilla de ají peruano* (fillet steak with chilli butter sauce). Great pisco sours, too. Closed Sat lunch and Sun pm.

Confitería Torres, corner of Alameda and Dieciocho, near Los Héroes (☎698 6220). Open since 1879, this is the oldest restaurant in Santiago; don't come here for the food (overpriced meat and fish) but for the dark, wood-panelled walls, the old, tarnished mirrors, the sagging chairs and the fabulous atmosphere. At weekends there's live tango from around 10.30pm. Closed Sun.

Don Victorino, Lastarria 138. The food (pastas, fish and meat) is not the best on this street, but it's one of the prettiest and most intimate places to eat in, especially at the tables next to the little fountain on the terrace. Closed Sat lunch and Sun pm.

El Villorio, San Antonio 676, north of Santo Domingo. Large restaurant serving excellent *carnes asadas*; if you're really hungry go for *La Kilo y Medio,* one and a half kilos of meat on a plate. There's a rather cheesy live music and dance show at weekends, from 11pm. Closed Sun pm.

Fra Diavola, París 836, near *Residencial Londres*. Busy canteen sort of place offering superb-value fixed-price lunches with a daily-changing menu (usually Italian-influenced). Closed Sat and Sun.

Gatopardo, Lastarria 192, opposite Biógrafo cinema. Very classy restaurant with a beautiful interior featuring lots of modern art and an atrium supported by eight tree trunks from the south of Chile. Good, imaginatively prepared food including a range of Bolivian specialities and an excellent lunchtime salad bar. Live jazz at weekends in winter. Closed Sat lunch and Sun.

Izakaya Yoko, Merced 456, near corner with Mosqueto. Attractive Japanese canteen offering good, authentic food at unbeatable prices; try one of their enormous bowls of soup with noodles, or the superb sushi that melts in your mouth. Closed Sun.

Kintaro, Monjitas 460. Another Japanese gem, a bit cleaner and tidier than *Izakaya Yoko*, with great-value fixed-price lunches. If you want to choose from the menu, they've got a bookful of photos to help you out. Closed Sun.

La Habana Vieja, Tarapaca 755, between Santa Rosa and San Francisco. Large hall containing a restaurant, a small dance floor and a stage, best at the weekend when there's live Latin music with dancing. The mid-priced menu includes Cuban staples like cassava, yellow rice and black beans, and fried plantains. Closed Sun.

Les Assassins, Merced 297, near corner of Lastarria (☎638 4280). Small, informal restaurant with lots of charm, serving traditional French food at reasonable prices. Very popular, so you'd be wise to reserve at weekends. Closed Sun.

Nam San Jung, Santa Rosa 24, near the Alameda. Humble Korean restaurant serving succulent, marinated meat dishes which slowly cook in front of you on a small gas stove at your table. Presided over by the delightful Sra Lee who, with a little prompting, will sing you Korean songs on her karaoke machine.

Parillón, Merced 734, between Mac Iver and San Antonio. One of a dying breed of spit-and-sawdust bar-restaurants serving really traditional Chilean food – *riñon al jerez* (kidneys in sherry sauce), *arrollado* (rolled pork), *lengua maya* (tongue with mayonnaise) and *guatitas* (tripe). No frills but plenty of atmosphere. Closed Sun.

Squadritto, Rosal 332, on east side of Cerro Santa Lucía. Good Italian food in a very stylish, slightly formal restaurant. Closed Sat lunch and Sun.

Bellavista

Eladio, Pío Nono 241. One of the best places in the city for a big hearty steak. Friendly, relaxed and eternally popular. Closed Sun pm.

Kilomètre 11680, Dardignac 0145. Large, cheerful restaurant with one of Santiago's best-stocked wine cellars. As good for snacks – try the excellent *tabla de quesos* or *carpaccio* – as for the more usual hearty steak and chips, the other house speciality. Closed Sun pm.

La Bodeguita de Julio, Antonia López de Bello 0108, at corner with Constitución. Down-to-earth Cuban restaurant with live music and a real party atmosphere every Friday and Saturday night. Tues–Sat from 7pm.

La Divina Comedia, Purísima 215. Friendly, reasonably priced Italian restaurant, extravagantly decorated with frescoes corresponding to whichever room you're in: Hell, Heaven or Purgatory. The salmon *carpaccio* is well worth a try. Closed Sun.

La Esquina al Jerez, Mallinkrodt 102. Giant hanging hams and posters of bullfighters make an evocative backdrop for some excellent Spanish food, including *pulpo a la gallega* (octopus) and *cordero asado* (roast lamb). Order the plate of mixed tapas (chorizo, tortilla, garlic mushrooms, serrano ham and cheese) and you won't have room for anything else. Closed Sun pm.

La Tasca Mediterranea, Purísima 165. Cosy, popular restaurant serving Mediterranean-influenced dishes, with live flamenco and Latin music at weekends. Closed Sun pm.

Venezzia, Pío Nono 200. A former haunt of Pablo Neruda, this old-fashioned bar-restaurant has been around for decades, and has more charm and atmosphere than many of its smarter rivals. The food is mainly grills, sandwiches and other traditional snacks.

Providencia

A Pinch of Pancho, General del Canto 45, near Manuel Montt metro. Attentive staff, a mellow atmosphere and excellent North American dishes, including New England chowder, BBQ spare ribs, Cajun chicken and desserts to die for.

Camino Real, also known as the *Enoteca*, on Cerro San Cristóbal (☎232 3381; take a taxi). A really special place to come for a splurge, offering magical views, especially at night when the city lights spread out below like a blanket of diamonds. The menu's imaginative, featuring dishes like sea bass in champagne sauce with fettucine, and there's an excellent choice of wine.

Giratorio, 11 de Septiembre 2250, near Los Leones metro. Santiago's only revolving restaurant is inevitably touristy, serving expensive "international" food; one floor down, though, there's an unrevolving restaurant called *La Estancia*, far cheaper and less formal, and with much the same views.

Mikado, Francisco Bilbao 1933 (☎225 2947; take a taxi). Upmarket Japanese restaurant specializing in *teppanyaki*. Watch the food being chopped and sliced in front of you at lightning speed, and

SANTIAGO'S VEGETARIAN RESTAURANTS

Chilean food revolves firmly around meat and fish, and vegetarians will probably tire of the few meat-free staples like humitas and empanadas de queso quite quickly. Santiago does, however, offer a handful of good vegetarian restaurants serving modern, imaginative veggie food at low prices. Don't be surprised to find these places packed out at lunchtime, as they're as popular with local, meat-eating office workers as with anyone else.

Café del Patio, Providencia 1670, in courtyard next to *Phone Box Pub*, near Sernatur. Mainly sandwiches, salads and stir-fries served by bohemian waitresses dressed in black; has a pretty outdoor patio. Closed Sat pm and Sun.

El Huerto, Orrego Luco 054, Providencia. The best veggie restaurant in Santiago, with a mouthwatering range of seasonal dishes; its Greek salad and gazpacho are especially recommended in summer. Note that the main restaurant is indoors, next door to the café section, which doesn't offer the full menu. Closed Sun.

El Naturista, Moneda 846, near Estado. The original pioneer of vegetarian food in Santiago, this large, inexpensive restaurant attracts a huge, frenetic crowd at lunchtime; if there's no room, try the stand-up bar on the ground floor. Also has a branch in Providencia, at Orrego Luco Sur 42. Closed Sat pm and Sun.

El Vegetariano, Huérfanos 827, in *galería* near corner of San Antonio. An extensive, good-value menu, including excellent milkshakes and desserts (the apple pancakes are especially gorgeous). Upstairs is very pleasant with its stained-glass windows and overhead sunlight. Closed Sat pm and Sun.

cooked on a hotplate at your table, usually with a bit of juggling thrown in for good measure. Expect to shell out for the experience. Mon–Sat from 7pm.

Nueva Delhi, Guardia Vieja 156. Fairly expensive Indian restaurant, festooned with bright cloths and wall hangings. The food's very good, with a special recommendation going to the *corvina Nueva Delhi* (sea bass marinaded in ginger). Closed Sun pm.

Other parts of town

La Tecla, Doctor Johow 320, south side of Plaza Nuñoa. The best pancakes in Santiago, served to a background of smooth jazz music in an intimate, attractive restaurant. Closed Sun pm.

La Terraza, Jorge Washington 58, Plaza Nuñoa. Lovely, mellow restaurant with a large terrace, serving typical meat and fish dishes and snacks; fills with a young, trendy crowd, especially at weekends. Closed Sun pm.

Puro Chile, Maipú 636, between Compañía and Huérfanos, three blocks east of Quinta Normal (☎681 9355). Really funky restaurant full of hip, good-looking types. It's in an old building with a modern, very imaginative interior divided into three sections: a bar for drinking, a restaurant, and a *ceviche* bar. At weekends they lay out a range of top-quality wines you can buy by the glass. Closed Sun.

Cafés and bakeries

Santiago has a curious and eclectic range of **cafés**, from homely coffee shops full of weary housewives through to trendy North American-owned chains serving Seattle-style coffee and baguette sandwiches. There's also an alarming number of **stand-up coffee bars** staffed by skimpily clad waitresses serving middle-aged businessmen.

Au Bon Pain, Bandera 92 (opposite La Bolsa) and Providencia 1936, among other branches. This minimalist, North American chain is one of the few places in Santiago where you can get a filter coffee (*café de grano*). Great pastries and sandwiches, too.

Café Caribe, Ahumada 120, or **Café Haiti,** Ahumada 140. Two of several stand-up coffee bar chains dotted about the city specializing in young waitresses in short, tight dresses.

Café Colonia, Mac Iver 161, between Moneda and Agustinas. Large café where matronly waitresses in German costume serve the best cakes, tarts, *küchen* and strudel in Santiago. It's been going for some fifty years and remains a perennial favourite with Santiago's housewives.

Café Paula, Ahumada 343. Not big on style or atmosphere, but a good place to rest your legs downtown, especially in summer when you can sit outside and watch the world spin by.

Café Virtual, Alameda 145. This huge, futuristic Internet-equipped café-bar is part of the Alameda Cultural Centre; there are lots of terminals and plenty of tables for non-Netting customers. Good food available, and frequent weekend jazz performances.

Copelia, in Galería Drugstore, Providencia 2211, near Los Leones metro. Very popular *salon de té* serving mouthwatering iced coffee and delicious cakes and pastries.

Pérgola de la Plaza, Plaza Mulato Gil de Castro, off Lastarria. Laid-back, arty café-restaurant (see p.80) on a lovely cobbled courtyard – one of the nicest corners in the city to unwind over a cup of coffee.

Tavelli, Andrés de Fuenzalida 34, off Av Providencia. Large, busy café in the same mould as the nearby *Copelia*, with two outside terraces, good coffee and wonderful ice creams.

Drinking and nightlife

Santiago is no Buenos Aires or Río. It is not a seven-nights-a-week party town, and compared to other Latin capitals can seem rather tame. That said, Thursdays, Fridays and Saturdays get pretty lively to compensate for the lack of activity during the week, and huge, buzzing crowds pour into the streets and bars of the nightlife *zonas*. These fall into three main areas – Bellavista, Providencia and Nuñoa – each with a distinct flavour and clientele. **Bellavista**, a short walk from Baquedano metro stop, is the most picturesque, with its colourful night-time market running the length of the main street. Though increasing numbers of loud discos are springing up on Pío Nono, the area is characterized by its small, informal restaurants, many of them putting on live music after 11pm, usually guitar music, *boleros* or Latin (for a night out in Bellavista, consult the restaurant listings on p.90). **Providencia**, particularly around the junction of Suecia and Holley, is packed with slick, American-style bars that pull in a huge crowd of professional types, including lots of expats and foreign visitors. It tends to be fairly lively through the week, as well, filled with the after-work crowd. Drinks are much more expensive here, although most places offer happy hours; many of them also have live music at weekends, typically cover bands doing pop or rock favourites. The nearest metro station is Los Leones. **Nuñoa** is very different again. This is where you'll find Santiago's "underground" scene, where the bars and cafés lining the main square are filled with nonchalant students in ripped black jeans and leather jackets. Nuñoa also has a couple of good live music venues, including Santiago's only jazz club. Take a blue Métrobus from Salvador metro station to the Plaza Nuñoa.

These are the main areas for drinking, though you'll find a number of other places scattered around the city – around Plaza Brasil, for example, or in Las Condes. When it comes to dancing, Santiago's **nightclubs** are more widely dispersed, some of them quite a drive away. The ones we've listed below are all reasonably central, easily reached by taxi (and some of them on foot). The club scene is notoriously difficult to pin down – places drift in and out of fashion, and open up and close down in an apparently random manner. The ones below should be reliable, but it's a good idea to seek advice from locals (bar staff are usually helpful). Prices at the most fashionable clubs are very high, up to CH$8000 per person, affordable only to the more affluent young Chileans.

In the event of a mega-famous band playing in Santiago they'd probably perform in the Estado Nacional. This is quite rare, however, and most South American and national bands play in smaller **venues**, which makes for a lot more atmosphere. For details of who's playing where and when, check the listings section (under "Recitales") of Friday's *El Mercurio* or *La Tercera del Día*, or visit *la Feria del Disco* at Ahumada 286, where performances are advertised and tickets for them sold. Good national bands to look out for include Inti Illimani, Congreso, La Ley, Sexual Democracia and Los Jaivas.

Whatever you decide to do, you should bear in mind that at the weekend things don't liven up until quite late in Santiago – from around 10 or 11pm in restaurants, and from about midnight to 1am in clubs.

Bars and live music

Santiago's **bar scene** takes in a vast range of styles, from dusty, mahogony-panelled corner bars full of ancient regulars, through to ultra-trendy, architect-designed spaces selling designer beers. **Live music**, too, can take in anything from romantic folk songs to Britpop covers.

Downtown

777, also known as **El Siete**, Alameda 777, across from Iglesia San Francisco. Huge old rooms covered in graffiti and packed with grungy students; serves cheap beer and very interesting snacks like pigs' trotters sandwiches.

Café-Berri, Rosal 321. Small, old-fashioned bar-café hidden away on a little street east of Santa Lucía. Friendly Basque staff and a young crowd give this place a great atmosphere, even midweek. Well worth seeking out.

El Biógrafo, Corner of Lastarria and Villavicencio. Lively, attractive bar next door to the arts cinema, inevitably peopled by arty, intellectual types. Good food on offer, too.

Bellavista

Café Público, Pío Nono 389. Attractive and quiet bar-café that also serves delicious home-made pastas and other light meals.

La Casa en el Aire, Antonia López de Bello 0125. Named after Neruda's poem *Voy a hacerte una casa en el aire*, this bar-café is one of the nicest places in Bellavista to enjoy a drink and a chat; mellow live music at weekends, with occasional poetry recitals thrown in.

La Fábrica, Asunción 426. Trendy, central pub-venue, with a small dance floor and regular live music taking in everything from metal to folk. Around CH$6000 for concerts.

Libro-Café Mediterráneo, Purísima 161. Laid back café next door to its sister restaurant, *La Tasca Mediterráneo*. Soft music and lighting, books scattered about for your perusal, and a relaxed clientele. Hugely popular at weekends.

Manifesto, Dardignac 0175. Futuristic bar with lots of wrought iron, uncomfortable seats, a breathtaking selection of foreign beers, and a tendency to be either very full or very empty.

Tomm, Bellavista 098, at corner with Constitución. Loud, invariably packed pub-venue, one of the best places to see established national bands. CH$3000 at weekends.

Providencia

Boomerang, Holley 2285. Loud music, expensive cocktails and lots of gringos. Very fashionable.

Boston Pub, Holley 2291. Often has live music midweek as well as weekends – usually classic American and British covers like Simon and Garfunkel and the Beatles.

Brannigan's, Suecia 035. One of the more restrained bars in Providencia, where the music's rarely loud enough to rule out conversation. Good atmosphere.

Electric Cowboy, Guardia Vieja 35. Lively Tex-Mex saloon stocking an excellent range of spirits, including Irish and Scottish whiskies and Caribbean rums. Live blues and country at weekends.

Mister Ed, Suecia 0152. Noted for putting on good live music at weekends, often well-known national bands. Get here before 10pm or there'll be no room left. Midweek it's a relaxing place to come for a drink.

Phone Box Pub, Providencia 1670, near Sernatur. Amusing if not entirely convincing replica of a British pub (run by a South African) complete with exposed beams, dart boards and beer mats stuck up everywhere. The entrance is through a red British phone box.

Wunderbar, Holley 92. This metallic, minimalist bar really breaks the Providencia mould, especially on Friday and Saturday nights when it turns into a techno dance floor packed with a trance-like crowd. Only serves beer. Free entry.

Nuñoa

Batuta, Jorge Washington 52, Plaza Nuñoa. Dark room with a bar and a dance floor; no trendy decor but a great, grungy atmosphere. Hosts established and new bands (usually Fridays). Saturday works as a disco. Don't dress smart. CH$3000.

Café de la Isla, Irarrázaval 3465. Popular place for chilling out with a drink to a background of Caribbean and Latin rhythms.

Café Nuñoa, J D Cañas 1675. Art gallery-cum-café in a beautiful old house – a good place to relax and chat into the early hours of the morning. Delicious pancakes served, too.

Club de Jazz, Av José Pedro Alessandri 85, one block south of the plaza. Comfortable, relaxed and friendly with loads of atmosphere and an invariably excellent line-up of Chilean and international jazz musicians. Live music Thurs, Fri and Sat. CH$3000.

Las Lanzas, Humberto Trucco 25, Plaza Nuñoa. This traditional old bar-restaurant, with its tables spilling onto the pavement, is *the* classic drinking spot in Nuñoa. It's also a good place to eat, offering a range of fish dishes at amazingly low prices. The drinks are cheap too.

Other parts of town

Blondie, Alameda 2879, north side, near ULA metro. Popular student hangout close to the university; loud music and dancing, with lots of Pixies, Cures and Ministry. CH$3000.

La Ferria, Av Portales 2655, next to Quinta Normal. Interesting, stripped-down structure with lots of bare wood and a mellow, studenty atmosphere. Good snacks available, and a separate area for dancing. Open weekends only.

Nightclubs, discos and salsatecas

Santiago's nightclubs tend to be the preserve of the city's more affluent teenagers, and are well out of most young people's price range. In addition to the clubs listed below, *La Fábrica*, *Tomm*, *Wunderbar*, *Batuta*, *Blondie* and *La Ferria* (listed under "Bars and live music" above) are also popular places to go dancing.

El Tucán Salsateca, Pedro de Valdivia 1783. Long-established *salsateca* favoured by serious *salseros*. Not conducive to getting up and having a go if you've never done it before.

Gente, Apoquindo 4900, Las Condes. Large nightclub stretching over three floors; formerly super-hip, now slightly dated, though it may well be on course for a revival.

Heaven, Recoleta 345, a few blocks north of the Mapocho, west of Bellavista. Scaffolding-like stairs and balconies, a smallish dance floor and good sound and lights. Very trendy. CH$4000.

La Maestra Vida, Pío Nono 380, Bellavista. Small, crowded *salsateca* with a friendly atmosphere – no need to feel shy about practising your salsa here. CH$2500.

Laberinto, Vicuña Mackenna 915, near Irarrázaval. Very stylish, very contemporary club spread over various levels, galleries and passages of an old converted warehouse. Plays a mixture of house, indie and rock to cool young things in jeans. CH$7000.

Oz, Chucre Manzur 5, Bellavista, off Antonio López de Bello. Ridiculously popular and expensive in equal measure, this is *the* place to go and strut your stuff in Santiago right now. Plays a mixture of techno, rock and pop. CH$8000.

The arts and entertainment

Chile is noted in Latin America for the quality and range of its **theatre**, and Santiago is of course the best place to see it. Performances are staged in the many theatres and cultural centres dotted about the city, and take in everything from time-honoured classics to contemporary and experimental works. While it clearly helps to be fluent in Spanish to get the most out of Chilean theatre, anyone can enjoy the visual comedies put on by outfits like Circus OK, whatever the state of their Spanish. **Classical music** is performed in a number of venues including theatres, cultural centres and churches; in particular you should check out the cheap midday concerts at the Teatro Municipal from around June to December. This is the most prestigious venue in Santiago for music, **dance** and **opera** and although it tends to be fairly conservative in its repertoire, it occasionally puts on innovative new productions, usually from abroad. **Cinema** is very popular in Santiago, with a concentration of movie theatres on Huérfanos downtown, and several newer, modern ones in Providencia and Las Condes. Most films shown are mainstream US imports, usually in the original version with Spanish subtitles, but there are a number of **arts cinemas** showing less commercial films and old movies. Nearly all cinemas have a half price policy on Wednesdays attracting huge crowds – get there early to queue, or buy your ticket earlier in the day.

There's a frustrating lack of decent **listings information**: although all the Friday newspapers include comprehensive details of what's on at the weekend, none gives descriptions or synopses to help you work out what you're interested in (especially crucial when it comes to theatre). The best is probably *La Tercera*'s Friday supplement, though many Santiaguinos prefer the "Wiken" section that comes with Friday's *El Mercurio*. If you aren't able to buy one of the Friday papers, the tourist kiosk on Ahumada keeps a copy of *La Tercera*, and the daily papers give cinema listings for that day. You could also try *What's On*, a free monthly publication distributed in tourist offices and hotels, with an incomplete but descriptive listings section at the back. Finally, a word on **prices**; most entertainment is quite affordable, with theatre and concert tickets commonly going for about CH$2000 or CH$3000. Even the Teatro Municipal offers inexpensive ballet and opera from CH$2000 for national productions, or from CH$7000 for international productions, though the better seats are of course considerably more expensive (as much as CH$59,000 for international opera).

Cinemas

Huérfanos is the main downtown cinema street; you'll find all the latest mainstream releases here (plus one or two soft porn films with ridiculous titles like *Depravadas Ardientes*). The sound quality isn't always brilliant, but the Lido at no. 680, the Hoytes at no. 727, the Rex at no. 735, the Huérfanos at no. 930 and the Gran Palace at no. 1176, are all reliable. For non-mainstream movies – known as "*cine arte*" – try the following:

Centro de Extensión de la Universidad Católica, Alameda 390 (☎635 1994). Especially good for older films, often presented in themed programmes like "Fifty Years of the Cannes Festival" or "Spanish Film Week".

Cine Alameda, Alameda 139, near Plaza Baquedano (☎639 2479). Comfy, well-arranged seats and a fast-changing, wide-ranging choice of foreign films.

Cine El Biógrafo, Lastarria 181 (☎633 4435). Old favourite in this trendy, restaurant-lined street. Shows mainly current European films.

Cine Normandie, Tarapacá 1181 (☎697 2979). A reputation for obscure contemporary European films.

Theatre

We've listed some of the main theatres below, but quality performances are staged in many different venues, including various multipurpose cultural centres and sometimes in the open-air amphitheatre of the Palacio de Bellas Artes. Ask in the Sernatur kiosk on Ahumada for recommendations, check the weekend listings and keep an eye out for anything involving Rosita Nicolet (actress), Alejandro Goic (director), Andrés Pérez (director), Jorge Díaz (playwright) and Benjamín Galemiri (playwright). The best time to experience Chilean theatre is in January, when Santiago hosts an enormous **theatre festival**, known as Ene Teatro. During the rest of the year, many theatres are only open from Thursday to Saturday. Ticket prices are usually very reasonable, around CH$3500–6000.

Sala Antonio Varas, Morandé 25 (☎696 1200). Belongs to the Universidad de Chile, and is the home of Chile's national theatre company, Teatro Nacional Chileno. Puts on a mixture of contemporary and classical works, usually of a high standard, paying special attention to Latin American playwrights.

Teatro Bellavista, Dardignac 0110 (☎735 6264). Long-established and reliable Bellavista theatre, usually staging modern, foreign plays, often comedies.

Teatro Circus OK, Providencia 1176 (☎235 1822). *Café-concert* offering a selection of highly visual and usually comic works, often combining dance, music and sometimes circus acts or mime.

Teatro El Conventillo, Bellavista 173 (☎777 4164). Great modern space with seats close up to the stage, creating an intimate atmosphere. Usually puts on contemporary comedies.

Teatro la Comedia, Merced 349 (☎639 1523). Home of the ICTUS theatre company, known for its high standards of acting and often innovative approach to direction.

Teatro la Feria, Crúcero Exeter 0250 (☎737 7371). Funky decor, and a reputation for highly watchable comedies.

Classical music, dance and opera

As well as the three main venues listed below, classical concerts are also performed in many churches (often for free) and cultural centres – look under "música selecta" in the listings papers. Traditionally, the season lasts from March to December.

Teatro Municipal, Agustinas 749 (☎639 0282). Santiago's most prestigious venue, offering a menu of classical concerts, ballet and opera in a splendid old building.

Teatro Oriente, Pedro de Valdivia, between Costanera and Providencia (☎232 1360). Classical concerts performed by Fundación Beethoven and visiting orchestras from May to October. Information and tickets at 11 de Septiembre 2214, oficina 66 (☎251 5321).

Teatro Universidad de Chile, Providencia 043 (☎634 4746). Another established venue for ballet and classical music, both national (principally the Orquésta Sinfónica de Chile) and foreign.

Shopping and markets

Santiago is a curious place to go **shopping**. Downtown is packed with small, old-fashioned shops dedicated to weird and wonderful things like panty girdles and industrial-sized food processors, as well as an astonishing number of pharmacies. One of the first things that strikes you about these shops is that everything's kept behind the counter, with no scope for browsing or touching. Managing to buy something can be quite a challenge: you first have to convey what you want to one of the assistants, who'll give you a ticket showing the amount you need to pay; you then go to the cash desk where you pay for the goods and get your ticket stamped; finally, you take the stamped ticket to another desk where you exchange it for (hopefully) what you asked for. Another oddity about downtown shopping is the warren of arcades, or *galerías*, that seem to lurk behind every other doorway, most of them gloomy and uninviting. Providencia and Las Condes, on the other hand, sport a slick array of fashionable boutiques and modern, American-style malls – better shopping, perhaps, but far less interesting.

Artesanía: crafts, knitwear and lapis lazuli

Avenida Bellavista, between Puente Pío Nono and Puente del Arzobispo. A string of workshops and salesrooms selling jewellery and other objects made of lapis lazuli.

Comercializadora Nacional de Artesanías, Estación Mapocho. Smart handicraft shop, selling musical instruments, wooden bowls, lapis lazuli, ceramics, carvings and textiles.

Feria Santa Lucía, opposite Cerro Santa Lucía. Fairly large market selling crafts, clothes and lapis lazuli.

Los Dominicos market, next to Iglesia Los Dominicos in Las Condes (Tues–Sun 11am–7.30pm). Excellent market with over two hundred stalls selling knitwear, ceramics, glass objects, books, antiques and lots more; see p.88 for details on how to get there.

Books, magazines, records and CDs

Books, Providencia 1652, in courtyard next to *Phone Box Pub*, near Sernatur. Secondhand English books, mainly best sellers and obscure text books.

Feria del Disco, Ahumada 286. The best place to buy Chilean and world music.

Feria del Libro, Huérfanos 623 (☎639 6621). Largest bookshop in Santiago, with an excellent choice of Spanish-language novels, reference books and maps.

Librería Inglesa, Huérfanos 669, local 11. Fairly good choice of Penguin paperbacks and other English-language books; very expensive, though.

Libro's, San Antonio 236, local 815, and Pedro de Valdivia 039, Providencia. A small range of English-language paperbacks and a truly impressive selection of magazines, including *The Face*, *Wired*, *GQ* and *Gramophone* (plus a few bizarre titles like *Tattoo Magazine*).

Shopping malls

Alto Las Condes, Av Kennedy 9001, Las Condes (daily 10am–10pm). Huge, modern shopping mall with 240 shops, including JC Penney. Connected to downtown by a free shuttle bus (☎229 1383 for times).

Arauco Outlet Mall, Américo Vespucio 399 (Mon–Sat 10am–9pm, Sun 11am–9pm). Low-cost clothes direct from the manufacturer. Shuttle buses from Ecuador metro station.

La Dehesa, El Rodeo with La Dehesa (Mon–Sat 9.30am–9pm, Sun 10am–9pm). Small, very upmarket shopping centre, reached on buses #200, #201 or #202 from the Alameda.

Parque Arauco, Av Kennedy 5413, Las Condes (Mon–Sat 10am–9pm, Sun 11am–9pm). Gets insanely busy at weekends. Frequent shuttle buses from Estación Militar metro.

Flea markets and antiques

Anfiteatro Lo Castillo, Candelería Goyenechea 3820, Vitacura (Mon–Fri 10am–2pm & 4–8pm, Sat 10am–2pm). About twenty serious antiques dealers on the ground floor. Expensive.

Anticuarios de Mapocho, in the red warehouse on corner of Brasil and Matucana, near Parque de los Reyes (Sat & Sun 9am–8pm). Lots of antique furniture, musical instruments, books and bric-a-brac – a wonderful place to browse.

Franklin Market, near Franklin metro (Sat & Sun 9am–7pm). Enormous and very lively market running the length of two parallel streets, Franklin and Bío Bío. There's a lot of rubbish at the bottom end, near the metro, but if you walk about five blocks up to the junction with Victor Manual, there's a great flea market on the Franklin side, and lots of antiques stalls off Bío Bío.

Food and drink

Comercial San Agustín, Puente 828. Huge liquor store stocking all kinds of wines and spirits at bargain prices. A good place for Chilean wine and pisco if you know what you want.

Confites Larbos, Estado 26. Beautiful, old-fashioned shop selling fine wines, spirits and fancy foodstuffs (including small packets of Earl Grey teabags, very useful if you're sick of the Chilean variety).

The Wine House, El Bosque Norte 0500, Las Condes. Good service and advice on quality wines, both Chilean and European.

Listings

Airlines Aero Perú, 5th floor, Fidel Oteíza 1593 (☎274 3434); Aeroflot, 23rd floor, Agustinas 640 (☎331 0244); Aerolíneas Argentinas, Moneda 756 (☎639 3922); Air France, Agustinas 1136 (☎672 5333); Alitalia, 10th floor, Alameda 949 (☎698 3336); American Airlines, Huérfanos 1199 (☎671 3553); Avant, Huérfanos 885 (☎639 9012) and Pedro de Valdivia 041 (☎252 5300); Avianca, 6th floor, Moneda 1140 (☎695 4105); British Airways, 3rd floor, Isidora Goyenechea 2934 (☎232 9560); Canadian, 3rd floor, Huérfanos 666 (☎639 3058); Cubana, 2nd floor, Fidel Oteíza 1971 (☎274 1819); Ecuatoriana, 25th floor, Alameda 949 (☎696 4251); Fast Air, Apoquindo 4944 (☎228 8003); Iberia, 8th floor, Bandera 206 (☎671 4510); KLM, 2nd floor, San Sebastián 2839 (☎233 0111); Lacsa, 7th floor, Fidel Oteíza 1921 (☎209 7477); Ladeco, Huérfanos 1157 (☎633 8343); Lan Chile, Agustinas 640 (☎362 3211); Lloyd Aero Boliviano, Moneda 1170 (☎671 2751); Lufthansa, 16th floor, Moneda 760 (☎630 1000); Pluna, 16th floor, Alameda 949 (☎696 8400); Saeta, 16th floor, Moneda 970 (☎630 1676); SAS, 7th floor, Suecia 0119 (☎233 3585); Swissair, 15th floor, Estado 10 (☎633 7014); United Airlines, 23rd floor, Alameda 949 (☎699 0555); Varig, Miraflores 156 (☎639 5976); Viasa, 6th floor, Tenderini 82 (☎639 5001).

Airport information ☎676 3149 or 690 1900.

American Express To change travellers' cheques and cash: Agustinas 1360 (☎699 3919); for mail collection and other services: Turismo Cocha, El Bosque Norte 0430 (☎230 1000).

Banks, cambios and ATMs There's an abundance of ATMs downtown, especially on Huérfanos between Ahumada and Mac Iver; other streets to try are Moneda, Agustinas and Morandé. To change cash and travellers' cheques, head for the cluster of *cambios* on Agustinas, between Ahumada and Bandera; a few to try are: Exprinter, Agustinas 1074 (the only one to change US dollars travellers' cheques at the same rate as cash, with no commission; closed Sat); Afex, Moneda 1148 (travellers' cheques of all currencies and no commission; open Sat am); Transpacific, Agustinas 1028 (US dollars cheques only; no commission); Alfa, Agustinas 1052 (one percent commission on travellers' cheques of all currencies). In Providencia, try Afex at Pedro de Valdivia 044 and General Holley 158. Of the few banks that are useful for foreign exchange, Citibank, (many branches including Ahumada 280 and Huérfanos 770) charges no commission for changing US dollars into pesos.

Bike rental Lys, Miraflores 541 (☎633 7600), including guided excursions into the Andes on mountain bikes.

Camera repairs Harry Müller, office 402, Ahumada 312, and various repair shops on lower floor of the *galería* at Merced 832, next to the Casa Colorada.

Car rental Avis, airport (☎690 1382) and Guardia Vieja 255 (☎331 0121); Budget, airport (☎601 9421) and Francisco Bilbao 3028 (☎204 9091); Chilean Rent a Car, Bellavista 0183 (☎ & fax 777 7758); Costanera, Andrés Bello 1255 (☎235 7835, fax 236 1391); Diamond, airport (☎211 2682) and Manquehue Sur 841 (☎212 1523); Dollar, airport (☎601 9743) and Santa Magdalena 163 (☎233 2945); Hertz, Andrés Bello 1469 (☎235 9666); Just, Helvecia 228, Las Condes (☎232 0900); Lacroce, Vitacura 5480 (☎219 1258, fax 242 2687); Lys, Miraflores 541 (☎633 7600); Toluka, Isabel La Católica 5019, Las Condes (☎207 3837, fax 207 5711).

Dental clinics Agrupación Alem Dental Suecia, 13th floor, Suecia 42, near Los Leónes metro (☎232 3889); Agrupación Medica Apoquindo, 2nd floor, Apoquindo 4100, near Alcantara metro (☎207 1031).

Embassies and consulates Argentina, Miraflores 285 (☎633 1076); Australia, Gertrudis Echeñique 420 (☎228 5065); Austria, 3rd floor, Barros Errázuriz 1968 (☎223 4774); Belgium, dept 1104, Providencia 2653 (☎232 1071); Bolivia, Santa Marí 2796 (☎232 8180); Brazil, embassy at Alonso Ovalle 16665 (☎698 2347), consulate at Mac Iver 225 (☎639 8867); Canada, 12th floor, World Trade Centre, Nueva Tajamar 481 (☎362 9660); Denmark, Santa María 0182 (☎737 6056); Finland, Office 71, Sótero Sanz de Villalba 55 (☎232 0456); France, Condell 65 (☎225 1030); Germany, 7th floor, Agustinas 785 (633 5031); Israel, San Sebastian 2812 (☎246 1570); Italy, Clemente Fabres 1050 (☎223 2467) Japan, 19th floor, Providencia 2653 (☎232 1807); Netherlands, Las Violetas 2368 (☎223 6825); New Zealand, Isidora Goyenechea 3516, Las Condes (☎231 4204); Norway, Vespucio Norte 548 (☎228 1024); Panama, Del Inca 5901 (☎220 8286); Peru, Andrés Bello 1751 (☎232 6275); South Africa, 16th floor, 11 de Septiembre 2353 (☎231 2862); Spain, 4th floor, Providencia 329 (☎40239); Sweden, 4th floor, Torre San Ramón, 11 de Septiembre 2353 (☎231 2733); Switzerland, office 1602,

Providencia 2653 (☎232 2693); UK, El Bosque Norte 0125 (☎231 3737); USA, embassy at Andrés Bello 2800 (☎232 2600), consulate at Merced 230 (☎710133).

Emergencies Ambulance ☎131; firemen (*bomberos*) ☎132; police (*Carabineros*) ☎133.

Hospitals Clínica Indisa, Santa María 01810, Providencia (☎225 4555); Clínica Las Condes, Lo Fontecilla 441, Las Condes (☎211 1002); Clínica Las Lilas, Eleodoro Yáñez 2087, Providencia (☎225 2001); Clínica Santa María, Santa María 0410 (☎777 8024); Clínica Universidad Católica, Lira 40, downtown (☎633 4122).

Internet access The longest established cybercafé in town is the futuristic *Café Virtual*, Alameda 145, with plenty of terminals, plus a bar and restaurant. Otherwise you could try Entel at Morandé 315 (just one terminal) and newly opened SCAI Club (which also sells maps and outdoor gear) at Rosas 1339, near the corner with Amunategui.

Language courses Recommended places offering Spanish language courses include: Centro Chileno Canadiense, Av Thayer Ojeda 0191 (☎ & fax 334 1089); Instituto Chileno-Británico, Santa Lucía 124 (☎638 2156, fax 632 6637); Instituto Chileno-Norteamericano, Moneda 1467 (☎696 3215, fax 697 0365); Instituto de Idiomas Polyglot, Villavicencio 361 (☎639 8078, fax 632 2485); Linguatec Language Center, Los Leones 439 (☎233 4356, fax 234 1380).

Laundry American Washer, Monjitas 646, near corner with Miraflores (Mon–Sat 9am–8pm); Lava Flash, Santa Rosa 95, near corner with Ovalle (Mon–Sat 9am–9pm).

Maps Topographical maps on all parts of Chile available at the Instituto Geográfico Militar, Dieciocho 369, near Toesca Metro; largest scale 1:50,000 (CH$6000); you can also photocopy A4-size sections of these at the Sala de Mapas in the Biblioteca Nacional. You'll also find a good section of road maps for sale at the Feria del Libro, Huérfanos 623.

Newspapers There are numerous newspaper kiosks around town; those at the corner of Huérfanos and Banderas sell a breathtaking range of foreign papers, from the *London Evening Standard* to *Het Parool*. The *Chilean News Review* – a weekly English-language newspaper published in Santiago every Wednesday – is also widely available.

Opticians Contalent, 2nd floor, Agustinas 715 (☎639 3238); Opticas Moneda Rotter, Moneda 1152 (☎698 0714) and Huérfanos 1029 (☎698 0465); Optica Rotter & Krauss, Ahumada 324 (☎698 7213) and Estado 273 (☎638 3295).

Outdoor equipment Patagonia Sport, Almirante Simpson 77 (Mon–Fri 11am–1pm & 5–8pm). A range of mountaineering and camping equipment, in the same building as the Federación de Andinismo.

Pharmacies There's a pharmacy on just about every street corner downtown. Farmacias Ahumada (☎222 4000) have a number of 24hr branches, including Av Portugal 155, downtown, and El Bosque 164 in Providencia; they'll also deliver to your hotel, for a small charge.

Post office Correo Central, Plaza de Armas (Mon–Fri 8am–7pm, Sat 8am–2pm). Other branches include Moneda 1155, near Morandé; Exposición 51, next to Estación Central; 11 de Septiembre 2239, near Sernatur.

Swimming pools Piscina Tapahue (Nov–March Tues–Sun 10am–7pm; CH$4000), near Tapahue *teleférico* station on Cerro San Cristóbal, is large and beautiful, but expensive; Piscina Antilén (Dec–March daily except Tues 10am–6pm; ☎232 6617), also on Cerro San Cristóbal, is in the same mould but harder to reach by public transport. Parque O'Higgins (☎556 9612) has a large outdoor pool which is much more affordable but gets quite crowded. There's an Olympic-size pool in Parque Arauco (☎212 4376) behind Parque Arauco shopping centre, near Estación Militar metro.

Telephone centres Entel's biggest and newest branch is at Morandé 315, between Huérfanos and Compañía; it's air-conditioned, quiet, has plenty of phones and provides access to the Internet. You can also send and receive faxes here (☎360 9447); they'll keep them for a month. Smaller Entel offices are at Huérfanos 1141, near corner with Morandé; Mall del Centro, Puente 689, near Mercado Central. CTC's *centros* include those at Universidad de Chile and Moneda metro stations, Monjitas 760, Moneda 1151, and Pasaje Matte, by the Casa Colorada. One *centro de llamadas* offering consistently cheap rates is Centro El Bosque, at Encomenderos 106, near Tobalaba metro.

Train information ☎689 5199/5401/5718.

Travel agents There are countless travel agents downtown, among them: Andina del Sud, 3rd floor, Bombero Ossa 1010, very friendly and professional, good for international flights and package holidays inside and outside Chile; Andy Tour, Agustinas 1046 (☎695 2254), for good-value packages in

South America, especially to Peru and Argentina; ACE Turismo, 15th floor, Alameda (☎696 0391), reliable all-rounders; Rapa Nui, 9th floor, Huérfanos 1160 (☎672 1050), for mainly international flights – not Easter Island specialists as the name suggests. There are plenty in Providencia as well, including: Chilean Travel Services, 1st floor, Antonio Bellet 77 (☎251 0400), professional all-rounders, and Turavión, Andrés de Fuenzalida 18 (☎231 7100), strong on international flights. All the above offer city tours and regional excursions; for adventure tourism in the region, see box on p.54.

AROUND SANTIAGO

Santiago is close to some fine, and frequently overlooked, attractions, from national parks and thermal springs to sleepy villages and lush vineyards. Closest at hand for a short jaunt is the southwest suburb of **Maipú**, whose colossal temple draws a steady stream of visitors, while an hour or so beyond lies the tiny village of **Pomaire**, famous for its pottery. East of the city, the obvious attraction is the **Andes**, with the **Cajón del Maipo** providing good access into the cordillera, leading to the small but spectacular **Parque Nacional El Morado**. In winter, **skiing** is another possibility, with several excellent resorts just ninety minute's drive from the capital. **Wineries** form another of the area's highlights, with some of Chile's oldest and most famous vineyards within easy striking distance, often offering tours and tastings. North of Santiago, you could head for the colonial town of **Los Andes**, surrounded by picturesque villages and mountain scenery. Further afield, on the way to (and easily approached from) the sea port of Valparaíso (see p.117), **Parque Nacional La Campana** offers fantastic hiking, and really deserves a couple of days to be fully enjoyed. All these places are served by frequent buses; details are given in the text and in "Travel Details" on p.108.

Maipú

The working-class suburb of **MAIPÚ**, 10km southwest of central Santiago, is home to one of the most eye-catching, though perhaps not the most beautiful, buildings in Chile: the **Templo Votivo de Maip Maipú** (daily 8.30am–7.30pm). This towering, monolithic and almost futuristic edifice – all harsh vertical lines from the front, and sweeping curves from the back – is built on the site of the Battle of Maipú, where Spanish Royalists were finally defeated by San Matín's liberating army on April 5, 1818. To mark the victory, commander-in-chief Bernardo O'Higgins vowed to erect a temple in honour of the Virgin of the Carmen, the patron saint of Chile. The pink, crumbling ruins of this first temple are still standing on the front esplanade, dwarfed by the scale of the modern version, which was started in 1944 and still isn't fully completed. The concrete interior has a raw, gloomy feel to it, only partially relieved by the stained-glass windows. Attached to the north side of the temple is the more inviting **Museo del Carmen** (Tues–Fri 9am–1pm, Sat 10am–1pm, Sun 10am–1pm & 3–6pm; CH$400), which houses an eclectic mix of colonial and ecclesiastic objects including tapestries, silverware, coffers, paintings, documents, furniture and horse-drawn carriages. To get to Maipú, take a *micro* (marked "Templo") from the Alameda at Teatinos, or a *colectivo* from Armunátegui; either way, it's a half-hour journey.

Pomaire

A further 50km southwest, the tiny, ramshackle village of **POMAIRE** was one of the "*pueblos de indios*" created by the Spanish in the eighteenth century in an attempt to control the native population. Its inhabitants quickly built up a reputation for their **pot-**

tery, and to this day Pomaire devotes itself almost exclusively to this craft. The village consists of little more than one long street packed with dozens of workshops selling a vast range of pots, bowls and Chilean kitchenware that the English vocabulary has no words for. It's nearly all made from the same brown clay that the area's so rich in, though a few potters have started to work in white clay (Juana Gonzalez at no. 442 has some beautiful examples). Most of the shops work to the same designs, but this doesn't make a browse any less appealing. Another draw is the chance to see the potters at work (except on Mondays, their day off), as they shape the clay by hand at the wheel. If you decide to buy, don't bargain too hard – it's very cheap as it is, and profit margins aren't high, as you can see from the basic living conditions in the village.

Pomaire has also built up a reputation for its good, traditional **restaurants** (some of them specializing in giant 1½-kilo empanadas); *Los Naranjos* and *San Antonio* are especially recommended. To get here from Santiago, take any of the **Melpilla buses** (every 15min) from the Terminal San Borja, behind the Estación Central, and ask to be set off at the side road to Pomaire (one hour from Santiago along Ruta 78, one and a half hours via Talagante). From here, *colectivos* run into the village, or you can walk it in about half an hour.

Cajón del Maipo

The **CAJÓN DEL MAIPO** is a beautiful river valley carved out of the Andes by the río Maipo. Served by a good paved road (for 48km of its 70km length) and punctuated with a string of hamlets offering tourist facilities, it's one of the most popular weekend escapes from the capital. The mouth of the *cajón* is just 25km southeast of Santiago, at Las Vizcachas; here the scenery is lush and gentle, and as you climb into the valley you'll pass vineyards, orchards, and roadside stalls selling locally produced fruit, and signs advertising home-made *küchen*, *miel* (honey) and *chicha* (cider). Twenty-five kilometres on, you reach the administrative centre of the valley, **SAN JOSE DE MAIPO**, a small town that was founded in 1791 following the discovery of nearby silver deposits. It's quite attractive with its single-storey adobe houses and old, colonial church; if you want to **stay**, try *Residencial Inesita* at Comercio 19321 (☎2/861 1012; ③). Drivers should note that this is the last place along the road where you can fill up with petrol.

The Cajón del Maipo is easily reached from Santiago: blue and white Cajón del Maipo **buses** (☎2/861 1518) leave from a small terminal outside Parque O'Higgins, near the metro, with four buses daily going as far as El Volcán, and less frequent services to Baños Morales (daily Jan & Feb; weekends only Oct–March).

San Alfonso

Some 15km beyond San José, you get to **SAN ALFONSO**, a lovely place to head if you just want to unwind for a few hours in beautiful mountain scenery. For longer stays, it offers a good choice of **accommodation** – *Hostería Los Ciervos*, by the roadside (☎2/861 1581; ④), has a gorgeous, flower-filled terrace and a little swimming pool, while *Residencial España*, next door (☎2/861 1543; ③) is simpler, but very clean, with an excellent restaurant. Down by the river, the *Cascada de las Animas* complex (☎2/861 1303; ②–⑤) is set in a park with log cabins and camping areas, as well as a fabulous outdoor pool and a restaurant overlooking the steep river gorge. It also offers **horse riding** trips into the Andes, and **white-water rafting** down the Maipo, though you should really arrange this in advance at the Santiago office at Orrego Luco 054, Providencia (☎2/234 2274), above *El Huerto* restaurant. There's a good walk from here up to the 20m **waterfall** (called the *Cascada de las Animas)* on the other side of the river, taking about ninety minutes; ask at the complex's reception for permission to cross the bridge.

CHILEAN WINE

Wine has been produced in Chile ever since the first Catholic missionaries planted vines in the 1540s, so they could give the Eucharist. No doubt the Spanish colonists had less spiritual motives in following their lead, and small-scale production became common throughout Chile's Central Valley. However, it wasn't until 1851 that the first proper winery was established, when Silvestre Ochagavía imported a range of vine cuttings from France. His timing couldn't have been better, for only a few years later the dreaded phylloxera pest began to devastate vine stocks across Europe. Today, Chile is the only major wine-growing country in the world to have remained free from phylloxera, thanks to the formidable natural barriers that surround the country, and, more recently, to rigorous import controls.

Ochagavía's new winery set in motion a spate of vineyard-planting in central Chile, mostly by Santiago's old moneyed families, who also erected fine mansions and parks next to their vines. The most prestigious and beautiful of these were in the Maipo valley, southeast of the capital, where the well-drained, lime-rich soils and temperate climate present perfect conditions for grape-growing. The industry grew steadily throughout the twentieth century, but undemanding domestic tastes ensured that producers never had to try too hard, a fact reflected in the mediocre, unambitious wines that dominated the Chilean market. Things changed fast, however, when the innovative Spanish producer, Miguel Torres, arrived on the scene in the 1980s, ushering in an era of modernization. Suddenly, stainless steel vats were invested in and new methods of ageing were introduced, accompanied by rapid improvements in wine quality. The quest for progress and innovation has continued ever since, and these days Chilean wines are considered to be among the most exciting in the New World, and are winning regular prizes in the international arena.

In 1995 the Chilean government introduced an official appellation system, with five demarcated regions: Atacama, Coquimbo, Aconcagua, Central Valley and Southern Region. Most of the quality wines are produced in the Central Valley (of which, for the purposes of appellation, Santiago is classed as a part), which is subdivided into the four lateral valleys of Maipo (including the Santiago area), Rapel, Curicó and Maule. The principal grape varieties in this region are Cabernet-Sauvignon, Merlot, Chardonnay and Sauvignon Blanc. West of Santiago, the Casablanca area (part of the Aconcagua delimitation) is producing excellent Chardonnays, considered by many to be the finest whites in the country. In general, Chilean wines are characterized by their very fruity flavours and often by their vanilla tones. The better reds are oak-aged and full-bodied, and the whites are fresh and clean. Unfortunately, the best Chilean wines are exported, and those available in most restaurants are produced specifically for the domestic market. That said, you can still find some very pleasing, and great-value wines in Chile: of the reds, try Concha y Toro's Casillero del Diablo, Cousiño Macul's Don Matias and Antiguas Reservas, Santa Rita's Casa Real and Medalla Real, and Undurraga's Cabernet Sauvignon Reserva; for whites, try Canepa's Finisimo Blanco, Casablanca's Sauvignon Blanc, Caliterra's Chardonnay, and Cousiño Macul's Chardonnay. The best wine merchant in Santiago is The Wine House, El Bosque Norte 0500, Las Condes (☎2/232 7257).

On to Baños Morales and Lo Valdés

Moving on from San Alfonso the scenery becomes increasingly rugged and wild as you climb higher into the Andes. By the time you reach **SAN GABRIEL**, 48km from the start of the valley road at Las Vizcachas, the steep walls of the valley are dried-out reds and browns. This uninteresting hamlet marks the end of the asphalt road, which continues as a very poor dirt track for another 22km to Lo Valdés. To carry on, you have to go through a *Carabineros* checkpoint, so make sure you've got all your driving documents and passport with you. Unless you're in a 4WD you should expect to go *very* slowly from this point onwards. **EL VOLCÁN**, at km 56, is as far as the telephone lines go up the valley – it has a public phone, but little else, as the village was practically wiped out by a landslide some years ago. By now the scenery is really dramatic as you

WINE TOURS NEAR SANTIAGO

Santiago is within easy reach of some of the oldest wineries in Chile, several of which offer tours and tastings. Those by the río Maipo, in particular, are beautifully located, with large swaths of emerald-green vines framed by the snow-capped cordillera, and bright-blue skies. Harvesting takes place in March, and if you visit during this month you'll see the grapes being sorted and pressed – a real extravaganza of colours and smells. If you want to visit a vineyard you should phone and book the day before. We've listed three of the most easily reached wineries below, all of which are accessible by public transport. You can also visit them on tours organized by several travel agents, including Sportstour, 14th Floor, Moneda 970 (☎2/549 5200), ACE Turismo, 16th Floor, O'Higgins 949, between Ahumada and Estado (☎2/360 0350), and Maxi Tour, Moneda 812 (☎2/632 9298). It's expensive doing it this way, though, starting at around CH$10,000 per person. The vineyards themselves make no charge for their tours.

Concha y Toro, Virginia Subercaseaux 210, Pirque (☎2/853 0042). Tours in English Mon–Fri 10am, noon & 3.30pm; Sat 10am & noon. This handsome vineyard was founded in 1883 by don Melchor Concha y Toro, and in 1994 became the first ever winery to trade on the New York Stock Exchange. It's Chile's largest wine producer, with nine vineyards spread around the Central Valley. The tours take you round the original bodega, with its countless oak barrels and huge stainless steel vats, and end up at the sales room where you can buy bottles and tastings at CH$500 a glass. To get here, go first to Puente Alto, either by *micro* #399 from the Alameda at San Francisco, or by *colectivo* from the *Hotel Crowne Plaza*; then, from the plaza at Puento Alto, go to the vineyard either by *micro* "El Principal" or by taxi.

Cousiño Macul, Av Quillín 7100, Peñalolen, Santiago (☎2/284 1011). Tours Mon–Sat 11am; Feb closed Fri. Set on an exceptionally beautiful estate, this vineyard was founded in 1871 by Luís Cousiño, owner of the Lota coal mines and the splendid Palacio Cousiño (see p.81). It's still owned and managed by the Cousiño family, who possess the oldest and largest collection of red wines in Chile, which you get a glimpse of on the tour (in Spanish only). Fewer visitors make it here than to Concha y Toro, which gives the tours a more intimate feel. Another bonus is the free tastings at the end, as well as the 15 percent discount on all bottles. To get here, take *micro* #390 or #391 from the Alameda, and ask to be dropped at the corner of Tobalaba and Quillín.

Undurraga, antiguo camino a Melpilla, km 34 (☎2/817 2346). No fixed time for tours – ring to arrange one. Still run by the Undurraga family, the vineyard was established in 1885, complete with mansion and park. It's a large, modern winery, and you're likely to be shown round not by a smiling public relations guide, but by someone who's directly involved in the wine-making, which makes it a whole lot more engaging. There are no tastings at the end, however, though you can buy from the sales room. The winery's a thirty-minute bus ride from Santiago – take a Flota Talagante or Autobuses Melpilla bus to Melpilla (not via the autopista) from the Terminal San Borja (every 15min), and ask the driver to drop you off at the vineyard.

snake between 4000m-high mountains coloured with jagged mineral-patterns of violet, cream and blue.

About 12km on, a short track branches left across a rudimentary bridge to **BANOS MORALES**, the site of an uninviting thermal pool that's reputed to be good for rheumatism and arthritis. Despite its spectacular location, this is quite a grim little village, with a half-finished, slightly derelict feel to it. It is, however, the closest base to the beautiful, jagged-peaked **Parque Nacional El Morado**, and offers a number of **residenciales**, none of them very comfortable: *Residencial Díaz* (no phone; ③) is the only one that stays open all year; *Los Chicos Malos* (☎2/288 5380; ③) and *Hostería Baños Morales* (☎2/226 9826; ③) are open in January, February and at Easter. There's also an unofficial **camping** area along the road by the river. If your budget allows it, head instead for the secluded and very comfortable *Refugio Alemán* (☎ & fax 2/220 7610; ⑤), at **Lo Valdes**, about 1km beyond the fork to Baños Morales. From here the road deteriorates into an even poorer track, but continues for a further 11km to **Baños de Colina**, a series of natural thermal pools carved into the mountainside; for all their remoteness they can get horribly crowded in summer weekends, but otherwise are blissfully empty.

Parque Nacional El Morado and the Cajón del Morado

A path from the bus stop in Baños Morales leads to the Conaf hut at the entrance to **PARQUE NACIONAL EL MORADO** (Oct–April daily 8.30am–6pm; CH$1000), 1km from the village. The park's single 8km trail follows the río Morales through a narrow valley that ends at the glacier that feeds the river. Towering above the glacier, and visible from almost all points along the trail, is the magnificent silhouette of El Mirador del Morado (4320m) and, just behind, El Morado itself (5060m). Apart from the first half-hour, the path is fairly level and not hard going, though you may find yourself feeling breathless as you gradually climb in altitude. About 5km beyond the Conaf hut you reach a small **lake**; you're allowed to camp here, and there's a toilet and water pump, though there's talk of moving this camping area closer to the park entrance because of fear of landslides. Once past the lake the path is less defined, but it's easy enough to pick your way through the stones to the black, slimy-looking **glacier** three kilometres beyond, at an altitude of 2500m. It takes about two and a half to three hours to walk here from the start of the trail; an alternative way to arrive is on **horseback** (CH$6000 with a guide, from Baños Morales or outside the Conaf hut). There are also guided riding treks up the neighbouring **Cajón del Morado**, which runs parallel to the río Morales, a few kilometres east, and leads to a huge glacier towering over a chocolate-coloured lake full of great chunks of ice. It takes three hours to get there on horseback (CH$10,000) and about eight hours to walk, though you may be able to hitch a lift with a 4WD which can get within half an hour's walk of the lake. If you plan to walk, make sure you have a good map and a compass, and have a word with the Conaf ranger first, as the route isn't obvious.

Los Andes

There's nothing wildly exciting about **LOS ANDES**, but this old colonial town with its narrow streets and lively main square is an agreeable place to while away an afternoon, and makes a convenient base for day-trips to the ski resort of Portillo (see opposite). Eighty kilometres north of Santiago, on the international road to Mendoza, Argentina, it's set in the beautiful Aconcagua valley, framed by the foothills of the Andes. The surrounding region is very fertile, and as you approach Los Andes from Santiago you'll pass vineyards and numerous peach and lemon orchards. About 10km short of the town, the **Santuario de Santa Teresa de los Andes** is a huge, modern church built in 1987 to house the remains of **Santa Teresa**, who became Chile's first saint when she was canonized in 1993. Her shrine attracts thousands of pilgrims each year, especially on July 13, her feast day.

You can find out more about the saint in the **Monasterio del Espíritu Santo**, a simple brick building on Avenida Santa Teresa in Los Andes, where she taught until her death in 1920, at the age of nineteen. A small museum upstairs (Tues–Sun 10am–noon & 3–5pm; CH$500) exhibits an assortment of memorabilia, including photos and clothes. Almost opposite, the **Museo Arqueológiquo** (Tues–Sun 10am–5.30pm; CH$500) has an impressive collection of pre-Columbian pottery, petroglyphs and skulls, and an astonishing mummy from the Atacama desert. Almost everything's labelled in Spanish and English, and the enthusiastic curator (who speaks good English) will give you a free guided tour if you ask. Six blocks east, on

SKIING NEAR SANTIAGO

Santiago is only 40km from some of the best skiing in South America. You don't need to have to have come specially prepared to take advantage of this – equipment hire and transport to the slopes are very easy to arrange, and the runs are close enough to the capital to make day-trips perfectly feasible. The season normally lasts from mid-June to mid-October, with snow virtually guaranteed from mid-July to the first week in September. The biggest concentration of skiing is provided by three resorts based around the service village of **Farellones**, a ninety-minute drive from Santiago along a paved, serpentine road. Farellones itself, sitting high in the Andes at the foot of Cero Colorado, is a straggling collection of hotels and apartments. It's connected by paved roads to the ski resorts of El Colorado, 4km north, La Parva, 2km further on, and Valle Nevado, a winding 14km east. **El Colorado** – also reached from Farellones by ski lift – is the largest of the resorts, with nineteen lifts and 22 runs, covering a wide range of levels. Elevations range from 2430m to 3330m. The resort's base is known as Villa El Colorado, and includes several apart-hotels, restaurants and pubs. Neighbouring **La Parva** has a reputation for exclusivity, and is used mainly by rich Santiaguinos. The skiing, however, is considered to be excellent, with some very challenging runs, reaching an altitude of 3630m. The resort has thirty pistes and fourteen lifts, but very limited accommodation facilities, as most people who come here have their own chalets. **Valle Nevado**, connected to La Parva by ski lift, is a luxury resort with three first-class hotels and some very good restaurants. It has 27 runs, with a maximum altitude of 3670m, and eight lifts.

As well as the resorts near Farellones, there's also **Portillo**. Set on the international road from Los Andes to Mendoza, in Argentina, it's a classy place, with no condominiums and just one hotel – the luxurious *Hotel Portillo* (☎ & fax 2/699 2575; ⑦), perched by the shores of the Laguna del Inca. The runs are good too, ranging from 2510m to 3350m in elevation, and there are twelve lifts, as well as a snow-making machine. However, it's too far from Santiago (149km) to do comfortably in a day, and the hotel, which caters principally to vacationing Argentinians, only likes to take week-long bookings. All of the resorts described above have ski schools with English-speaking instructors, and equipment rental outlets.

PRACTICALITIES

The least expensive way to go skiing is to stay in Santiago and go up for the day. A number of **minibus** companies offer daily services to the resorts during the ski season, including Ski Total (☎2/246 6881), which also rents out equipment and clothes. It's based at oficina 42 in the lower-ground level of the Edificio Omnium shopping mall at Av Apoquindo 4900, four blocks east of Estación Militar metro (any *micro* to Las Condes or Apoquindo will drop you there). Buses leave at 8am daily for El Colorado, La Parva and Valle Nevado, returning to Santiago at the end of the day; advance reservations are essential. A return ticket costs around CH$5000, with full equipment rental an additional CH$10,000. If you intend to drive up yourself, note that traffic is only allowed up the road to Farellones until noon, and back down to Santiago from 2pm onwards; chains are often needed as well, and can be rented on the way up. Each resort has its own **lift ticket**, which costs from CH$13,000 on weekdays and CH$16,000 at weekends; there is no common ticket for all three resorts, but La Parva and Valle Nevado sell a joint ticket from around CH$15,000 weekdays and CH$19,000 at weekends.

If you want to stay, you've got several **accommodation** options. At Farellones you could try cosy *Hotel Tupungato* (☎2/218 2216, fax 299 7519; ⑤) or the *Refugio Club Andino* (☎2/222 5843; ④). The choice in El Colorado includes upmarket *Hotel Posada Farellones* (☎2/246 0660; ⑥) and *Villa Palomar* (☎2/232 3407, fax 233 6801; ⑥). The only place to stay in La Parva is at the *Condominio Nueva La Parva* (☎2/211 4400, fax 220 8510; ⑦). Valle Nevado's hotels are all very upscale, and include the grand *Hotel Valle Nevado* (☎2/698 0103, fax 698 0698; ⑦). Ski Total can give advice on accommodation, and make bookings for you. All of the ski resorts have their administrative offices in Santiago: El Colorado is at the Edeficio Omnium, oficina 47, Av Apoquindo 4900, Las Condes (☎2/246 3344, fax 206 4078); La Parva is at La Concepción 266, oficina 301, Providencia (☎2/264 1466, fax 264 1575); Valle Nevado is at Gertrudis Echeñique 441, Las Condes (☎2/206 0027, fax 208 0695); and Portillo is at Roger de Flor 2911, Las Condes (☎2/231 3411, fax 231 7164).

the corner of Freire and Rancagua, **Cerámica Cala** is worth dropping in on – this family-run business sells pretty, hand-painted ceramics to retailers throughout Chile, and you can ask to see the artisans at work in their factory, and visit the small sales room. Other than this, the best thing to do in Los Andes is hang out in one of the cafés lining the square and watch the world go by or, if you're feeling energetic, climb **Cerro de la Virgen**, the hill rising behind the town. It takes about an hour to reach the top following the path from the picnic site on Independencia; the views are wonderful, especially just before sunset when the whole valley is bathed in a clear, golden light.

Practicalities

Frequent **buses** for Los Andes run out of Terminal Los Héroes in Santiago, dropping you at the bus station on Membrillar, one block east of the main square; most of them stop at the Santuario de Santa Teresa en route. There's a helpful **Oficina de Turismo** (Mon–Fri 8.30am–2pm & 3–5.30pm) next door to the Municipalidad at Esmeralda 526; if it's closed, try the **Sernatur** kiosk (daily 10am–6pm) round the corner on Avenida Santa Teresa, next to the Esso station. If you want to **stay**, *Residencial O'Higgins* at O'Higgins 470, near the square (no phone; ②) is probably the best budget choice; for more comfort try *Residencia Italiana* at Rodríguez 76 (☎34/423544; ④), an attractive old house with pleasant rooms (but shared bath). *Hotel Plaza* at Esmeralda 367 (☎34/421169, fax 426029; ⑤) has well-equipped, but dowdy, rooms off the square, and its own pool. For **eating**, the French-owned *Comédie Française* at Papudo 375 serves good-value French food, with live music at weekends; the restaurant in *Hotel Plaza* is more traditional, and very popular. For snacks, or **drinking**, there are a cluster of bars and cafés on the square and down Esmeralda.

Parque Nacional La Campana

Set in the dry, dusty mountains of the coastal range, **PARQUE NACIONAL LA CAMPANA** (June–Sept daily 8am–5pm; Oct–May daily 8am–6pm; CH$700) is a wonderful place to come hiking, and offers some of the best views in Chile. From the 1880m-high summit of Cerro La Campana you can see the Andes on one side and the Pacific Ocean on the other – in the words of Charles Darwin, who climbed the mountain in 1834, Chile is seen "as in a map". Another draw is the chance to see a profusion of **Chilean palms** in their natural habitat; this native tree was all but wiped out in the nineteenth century, and the Palmar de Ocoa, a grove in the northern section of the park, is one of just two remaining places in the country where you can find wild palms. You can also expect to see eagles and giant hummingbirds and, if you're lucky, mountain cats and foxes.

The park is located 110km northwest of Santiago, and about 60km east of Valparaíso. It's divided into three "sectors" – Ocoa, Granizo and Cajón Grande – each with its own entrance and Conaf control. **Sector Ocoa**, on the northern side of the Park, is where you'll find the palm trees – literally thousands of them. **Sector Granizo** and **Sector Cajón Grande** are both in the south of the park, close to the village of **Olmué**; this is the part to head for if you want to follow Darwin's footsteps and climb **Cerro La Campana**. While it's possible to get to Parque Nacional La Campana on a day-trip from Valparaíso, Viña or even, at a push, from Santiago, you should count on spending a couple of nights here to get the most out a visit. There are **camping** areas in all three sectors, and plenty of **accommodation** in Olmué.

THE PALMA CHILENA

The curious miniature coconuts sold at roadside stalls throughout the central region in winter are not imported from tropical countries, but are the fruit of Chile's very own native palm tree, the **palma chilena**. It's the southernmost species in the world, and grows very slowly, producing its first fruit after eighty years (some of those in the Palmar de Ocoa are over 300 years old). The mountains and ravines of this region used to be covered with thousands of these palms, but when Chileans developed a taste for the treacle produced from their sap during the eighteenth and nineteenth centuries, they were felled almost to extinction, since the sap could only be extracted after the tree was chopped down. Charles Darwin wrote this account after his visit in 1834:

> *These palms are, for their family, ugly trees. Their stem is very large, and of a curious form, being thicker in the middle than at the base or top. They are excessively numerous in some parts of Chile, and valuable on account of a sort of treacle made from the sap. On one estate near Petorca, they tried to count them, but failed, after having numbered several hundred thousand. Every year in August very many are cut down, and when the trunk is lying on the ground the crown of leaves is lopped off. The sap then immediately begins to flow from the upper end, and continues doing so for some months... A good tree will give 90 gallons, and all this must have been contained in the vessels of the apparently dry trunk.*

These days, the only places left in Chile where the palms are "excessively numerous" are the Palmar de Ocoa, and the Palmar de Cocolán, in Cachapoal.

Getting to the park

To get to **Sector Granizo** and **Sector Cajón Grande** you should aim for the gateway village of **Olmué**, reached via a long, roundabout route from Santiago, but far more directly from Valparaíso. There are direct **buses** from both directions: from Santiago, Buses Golondrina (☎2/778 7082) run every thirty minutes out of terminal San Borja; from Valparaíso's Playa Ancha, Ciferal Express (☎32/953317) run six times a day almost to the park entrance. If you're coming from Santiago **by car**, the quickest route is via Casablanca, Villa Alemana and Limache. Don't be tempted to take the short route from Tiltil to Olmué across the Cuesta La Dormida – this is very scenic but unsuitable unless you're in a 4WD. From Olmué it's a further 9km to the park; regular buses (every 15min) run from the main square to **Granizo**; the last bus stop is a fifteen-minute walk from the Conaf hut in Sector Granizo, and a forty-minute walk from Sector Cajón Grande.

Sector Ocoa is approached on a gravel road branching south from the Panamericana about halfway between Llaillay and Hijuelas; coming from Llaillay, it's the left turn just before the bridge across the río Aconcagua. Any northbound bus along the Panamericana will drop you at the turn-off, but from here it's a 12km hike to the park entrance, with minimal hitching opportunities.

Accommodation in Olmué

An agreeable village in a fertile valley, **OLMUÉ** has a good choice of places to stay, many of them with pools. Cheapest is *Residencial Sarmiento*, Blanco Encalada 4647 (☎33/441263; ③), with clean, simple rooms, most with bath, in a traditional adobe building. *Hostería El Copihué*, Portales 2203 (☎ & fax 33/441544; ⑤) has a nice pool, beautiful gardens full of vines and flowers and a good restaurant. Rooms at *Scala de Milán*, Prat 5058 (☎33/441414; ④) are a little tired, but again there's a good pool. About halfway along the road to the park, *Hostería Aire Puro*, Av Granizo 7672 (☎33/441381; ⑤) has well-equipped *cabañas*, great views from its restaurant, and the obligatory pool.

HIKING IN PARQUE NACIONAL LA CAMPANA

There are some very scenic walks in the park, most of them along good, well-maintained trails. The photocopied maps given away at the Conaf hut aren't very clear, so you should try to get hold of an *Instituto Geográfico Militar* map (see p.99) before you come if you plan to do some serious walking. If you're on a day-hike you must get back to the Conaf control before it closes (5pm in winter, 6pm in summer); if you plan to camp in the park, inform the *guardaparque* when you sign in. Finally, there aren't many water sources along the trails so bring plenty of water with you.

Sector Granizo

The well-marked 9km-long **Sendero el Andinista** up Cerro La Campana is the most popular, and possibly the most rewarding, trek in the park. It's quite hard-going, especially the last one and a half hours, when it gets very steep, but the views from the top are breathtaking. Allow at least four and a half hours to get up and three to get down. **Sendero Los Peumos** is a pretty, 5km walk (about three hours) up to the Portezuelo Ocoa, through gentle woodland for the first half, followed by a fairly steep climb. Three paths converge at the Portezuelo; you can either go back the way you came; take the right-hand path (Sendero Portezuelo Ocoa; see below) down through the Cajón Grande to that sector's Conaf control (about three hours); or follow the lefthand path (Sendero El Amasijo) through Sector Ocoa to the northernmost park entrance (a further four hours; best if you're camping as there's no accommodation at the other end).

Sector Cajón Grande

The only path starting at this sector is the **Sendero Portezuelo Ocoa**, a 7km trail (about three hours) through beautiful woods with natural *miradores* giving views down to the Cuesta La Dormida. From the Portezuelo Ocoa, at the end of the path, you can link up with other paths as described above.

Sector Ocoa

Sendero La Cortadero makes a lovely day-hike through lush palm groves to a 35m-high waterfall, most impressive in early spring. The 9km path is mainly flat; allow about seven hours there and back. **Sendero El Amasijo** is a 14km trail following the Estero Rabuco (a stream) through a scenic canyon, before climbing steeply to the Portezuelo Ocoa. Most walkers make this a cross-park trek, continuing to Granizo or Cajón Grande (see above). Fast, fit walkers should be able to do it in a day, but it's more relaxing if you camp overnight.

travel details

Sitting as it does right in the middle of the country, Santiago is the transportation hub of Chile. All national transport networks lead to and from the capital, and most journeys between the north and south of Chile involve a change or at least a stop there. There are limited **train** services to the south and regular **flights** to most Chilean cities, but by far the greatest majority of transport services are provided by **buses**, run by a bewildering number of private companies. These operate out of four terminals: the Terminal de Buses Santiago, also called the Terminal del Sur (☎779 1385); the Terminal de Buses Alameda (☎778 0808); the Terminal San Borja (☎776 0645); and the Terminal Los Héroes (☎697 4178; metro Los Héroes). While you can normally turn up and buy a ticket for travelling the same day, it's better, if you can, to buy it a day in advance, just to be on the safe side, especially at weekends. In the days around Christmas, New Year's Eve and Easter, you should buy your ticket several days in advance.

Buses

BUSES FROM THE TERMINAL SANTIAGO

This terminal, close to the Universidad de Santiago metro station, is used by buses going to the south of the country, to international destinations and to some seaside resorts on the central coast. It's the largest and most chaotic of the terminals, with over a hundred companies operating out of it.

South of Santiago

Services down the Panamericana from this terminal are provided by all the major companies, including Bus al Sur (☎779 2305), Buses Lit (☎779 5710), Cóndor Bus (☎779 3721), Fénix Pullman (☎776 3253), Tas Choapa (☎779 4694), Tur Bus (☎776 3133), and many others.

To	*Frequency*	*Distance*	*Duration*
Chillán	30 daily	407km	5hr 45min
Concepción	20 daily	519km	7hr 30min
Curicó	every 15min	194km	2hr 45min
Los Angeles	30 daily	517km	7hr 20min
Los Lagos	14 daily	835km	12hr
Osorno	20 daily	913km	13hr
Pucón	15daily	789km	11hr 30min
Puerto Montt	20 daily	1016km	14hr
Puerto Varas	20 daily	996km	16hr 30min
Rancagua	every 20min	87km	1hr 30min
San Fernando	every 10min	142km	2hr
Talca	every 30min	257km	3hr 40min
Talcahuano	20 daily	535km	7hr 45min
Temuco	30 daily	677km	9hr
Valdivia	15 daily	839km	12hr
Villarica	20 daily	764km	11hr

To the central coast

You can get buses to the coastal resorts of the *litoral central* from this terminal with Bahía Azul (☎776 2604), Condor Bus (☎779 3721), Pullman Lit (☎521 7198), Robles (☎779 1526), Bus Pullman Sur (☎779 5243) and Sol del Pacífico (☎776 2604). Additional services to the coast leave from the nearby Terminal Alameda (see overleaf) and the Terminal San Borja (see p.112). All these destinations are within 170km of Santiago.

To	*Frequency*	*Duration*
Algarrobo	every 20min	2hr (via Casablanca); 2hr 30min (via Cartagena)
Cartagena	every 20min	1hr 30min
Concón	every 45min	2hr 45min
El Quisco	every 20min	2hr 15min
El Tabo	every 20min	2hr
Horcón	every 30min	2hr 40min
Isla Negra	every 20min	2hr 10min
Maitencillo	every 30min	2hr 45min
Quintero	every 45min	3hr
San Antonio	2 daily	1hr 45min
Santo Domingo	2 daily	1hr 50min
Valparaíso	every 30min	1hr 40min
Viña del Mar	every 30min	1hr 50min

International buses

The main companies serving international destinations are Ahumada (☎779 5243), Cata (☎779 3660), Chile Bus (☎776 5557), El Rápido (☎779 0316), Expreso Brújula (☎776 2642), Pluma (☎779 6054) and Tas Choapa (☎779 4925). The most frequent services are to Mendoza and Buenos Aires in Argentina, but there are also direct buses to La Paz in Bolivia (Chile Bus), Tacna and Lima in Peru (Tas Choapa and El Rápido), Sao Paulo and Rio in Brazil (Chile Bus and Pluma), Montevideo in Uruguay (Tas Choapa and El Rápido) and Asunción in Paraguay (Expreso Brújula).

To	*Frequency*	*Duration*
Asunción	2 weekly	30hr
Buenos Aires	2 weekly	20hr
Lima	4 weekly	50hr
Mendoza	25 daily	7hr
Montevideo	1 weekly	28hr
Rio de Janeiro	3 weekly	60hr
Sao Paulo	3 weekly	52hr
Tacna	4 weekly	30hr

BUSES FROM THE TERMINAL ALAMEDA

One of the exits from the Universidad de Santiago metro leads directly into this terminal, which is used only by Tur Bus and Pullman Bus, Chile's two largest bus companies.

North of Santiago

To	*Frequency*	*Distance*	*Duration*
Antofagasta	20 daily	1361km	20hr
Arica	5 daily	2062km	29hr
Calama	7 daily	1574km	22hr 30min
Caldera	20 daily	870km	13hr
Chañaral	10 daily	968km	14hr
Copiapó	20 daily	801km	12hr
Coquimbo	10 daily	465km	6hr 45min
Iquique	5 daily	1853km	25hr
La Ligua	every 20min	153km	2hr 30min
La Serena	20 daily	474km	7hr
Los Vilos	1 daily	229km	3hr 20min
Mejillones	1 daily	1462km	21hr
Ovalle	6 daily	412km	6hr
Tal Tal	1 daily	1114km	16hr
Tocopilla	10 daily	1549km	22hr
Vallenar	15 daily	660km	9hr 30min

South of Santiago

To	*Frequency*	*Distance*	*Duration*
Chillán	every 30min	407km	5hr 45min
Concepción	20 daily	519km	7hr 30min
Curicó	every 30min	194km	2hr 45min
Los Angeles	every 30min	517km	7hr 20min
Los Lagos	15 daily	835km	12hr
Osorno	20 daily	913km	13hr

Pucón	10 daily	789km	11hr 30min
Puerto Montt	20 daily	1016km	14hr
Puerto Varas	20 daily	996km	16hr 30min
Rancagua	every 20min	87km	1hr 30min
San Fernando	every 20min	142km	2hr
Talca	every 20min	257km	3hr 40min
Talcahuano	20 daily	535km	7hr 45min
Temuco	every 45min	677km	9hr
Valdivia	15 daily	839km	12hr
Villarica	15 daily	764km	11hr

To the central coast

All these destinations are within 170km of Santiago.

To	*Frequency*	*Duration*
Algarrobo	every 30min	2hr (via Casablanca); 2hr 30min (via Cartagena)
Cachagua	6 daily	2hr 30min
Cartagena	every 30min	1hr 30min
El Quisco	every 30min	2hr 15min
Isla Negra	every 30min	2hr 10min
Papudo	17 daily	3hr
Valparaíso	every 15min	1hr 40min
Viña del Mar	every 15min	1hr 50min
Zapallar	11 daily	2hr 45min

BUSES FROM THE TERMINAL LOS HÉROES

Just north of the Plaza de los Héroes, this is the most central of the bus terminals, and has a mixture of north-bound, southbound and international buses. The terminal is used by just eight companies: Buses Ahumada (☎696 9798); Cruz del Sur (☎696 9324); Fenix (☎696 9321); Flota Barrios (☎696 9311); Libac (☎698 5974); Pullman del Sur (☎673 1967); Tas Choapa (☎696 9326); and Tramacá (☎696 9839).

North of Santiago

To	*Frequency*	*Distance*	*Duration*
Antofagasta	12 daily	1361km	20hr
Arica	4 daily	2062km	29hr
Calama	8 daily	1574km	22hr 30min
Copiapó	22 daily	801km	12hr
Coquimbo	every 15min	465km	6hr 45min
Guanaqueros	1 daily (summer only)	432km	6hr
Iquique	4 daily	1853km	25hr
La Serena	every 15min	474km	7hr
Los Andes	every 15min	80km	1hr 20min
Los Vilos	9 daily (summer only)	229km	3hr 20min
Ovalle	12 daily	412km	6hr
Pichidangui	6 daily (summer only)	190km	3hr
San Felipe	every 30min	94km	1hr 30min
Tongoy	4 daily (summer only)	417km	6hr 45min
Vallenar	19 daily	660km	9hr 30min

South of Santiago

To	*Frequency*	*Distance*	*Duration*
Ancud	2 daily	1106km	18hr 30min
Castro	2 daily	1191km	11hr 50min
Chillán	9 daily	407km	5hr 45min
Concepción	2 daily	519km	7hr 30min
Curicó	9 daily	194km	2hr 45min
Los Angeles	6 daily	517km	7hr 20min
Osorno	15 daily	913km	13hr
Puerto Montt	12 daily	1016km	14hr
Puerto Varas	6 daily	996km	16hr 30min
Rancagua	9 daily	87km	1hr 30min
San Fernando	3 daily	142km	2hr
Talca	3 daily	257km	3hr 40min
Talcahuano	2 daily	535km	7hr 45min
Temuco	11 daily	677km	9hr
Valdivia	8 daily	839km	12hr

International buses

To	*Frequency*	*Duration*
Asunción	2 weekly	30hr
Bariloche	1 daily	20hr
Buenos Aires	3 daily	22hr
Lima	1 weekly	50hr
Mendoza	4 daily	7hr
Montevideo	1 weekly	24hr

BUSES FROM THE TERMINAL SAN BORJA

This modern, well-organized terminal is set at the back of a shopping mall behind the Estación Central (from the metro, follow the signs carefully to exit at the terminal). This is the main departure point for buses to the north of Chile, particularly for long-distance buses going right up to Iquique and Arica. There are several regional buses, as well, and some services to the coastal resorts.

To	*Frequency*	*Distance*	*Duration*
Antofagasta	23 daily	1361km	20hr
Arica	20 daily	2062km	29hr
Calama	6 daily	1574km	22hr 30min
Caldera	9 daily	870km	13hr
Chañaral	3 daily	968km	14hr
Copiapó	15 daily	801km	12hr
Coquimbo	every 30min	465km	6hr 45min
Iquique	15 daily	1853km	25hr
La Ligua	5 daily	153km	2hr 30min
La Serena	every 30min	474km	7hr
Los Andes	every hour	80km	1hr 20min

Los Vilos	8 daily	229km	3hr 20min
Mejillones	2 daily	1462km	21hr
Olmué	every 30min	180km	2hr 40min
Ovalle	15 daily	412km	6hr
San Felipe	every hour	94km	1hr 30min
Tocopilla	2 daily	1549km	22hr
Vallenar	8 daily	660km	9hr 30min
Vicuña	2 daily	540km	7hr 45min

To the central coast

The main companies with services to the coast are Buses Quintero (☎778 7069), Condor Bus (☎696 5551) and Pullman Bus Costa (☎779 2569). All these destinations are within 170km of Santiago.

To	***Frequency***	***Duration***
Algarrobo	every hour	2hr (via Casablanca); 2hr 30min (via Cartagena)
Cartagena	every hour	1hr 30min
Concón	every 30min	2hr 45min
El Quisco	every hour	2hr 15min
El Tabo	every hour	2hr
Isla Negra	every hour	2hr 10min
Maitencillo	every 30min	2hr 45min
Quintero	every 30min	3hr
Valparaíso	4 daily	1hr 40min
Viña del Mar	every 30min	1hr 50min

Trains

There's scarcely anything left of Chile's passenger rail network, which has been whittled down to just three daily services from Santiago: a morning train to Chillán, a night train to Temuco and another night train to Concepción. All trains leave from the Estación Central (☎689 5199) on the Alameda, by the metro stop of the same name.

TRAINS FROM SANTIAGO

To	***Frequency***	***Duration***
Chillán	3 daily	5hr
Concepción	1 daily	9hr
Curicó	1 daily	2hr 20min
Linares	1 daily	4hr
Parral	1 daily	4hr 20min
Rancagua	2 daily	1hr
San Fernando	1 daily	1hr 45min
Talca	2 daily	3hr 20min
Temuco	1 daily	12hr
Victoria	1 daily	10hr 20min

Flights

There are plenty of flights out of Santiago's Aeropuerto Arturo Merino Benitez (☎601 9709) to all the major cities up and down the country. It's best to reserve your ticket as far in advance as possible, as the cheaper fares tend to get booked up long before the flight. Your best bet is to go to a travel agent (see p.99) who'll be able to give you a rundown of all the different options available. To get to the airport from downtown, you can take a Centropuerto bus from Los Héroes or a Tour Express bus from Mondeda and San Martín; another good-value alternative is to book a door-to-door minibus transfer the day before you travel – try Transfer (☎777 7707) or Delfos (☎226 6020).

FLIGHTS FROM SANTIAGO

To	*Frequency*	*Duration*
Antofagasta	11 daily	2hr
Arica	8 daily	3hr 30min
Balmaceda (Coyhaique)	3 daily	3hr
Calama	5 daily	2hr direct; 3hr via Antofagasta
Concepción	9 daily	1hr
Copiapó	5 daily	2hr
Iquique	11 daily	2hr 20min
La Serena	4 daily	1hr
Osorno	2 daily	1hr 45min
Puerto Montt	7 daily	1hr 40min
Punta Arenas	6 daily	4hr
Temuco	6 daily	1hr 15min
Valdivia	2 daily	2hr 20min

CHAPTER TWO

VALPARAÍSO, VIÑA AND THE COASTAL RESORTS

Of Chile's 4000-kilometre coastline, the brief central strip between Santo Domingo and Papudo is the most visited and most developed. Known as *el litoral central* by Chileans and promoted as the "Chilean Riviera" in many tourist brochures, this 140-kilometre stretch boasts bay after bay lined with gorgeous, white-sand beaches and a string of some twenty resorts of varying size and character. In the centre, **Valparaíso** and **Viña del Mar** sit next door to each other, geographical neighbours but light years apart in look and feel. Viña is Chile's largest and ritziest beach resort and, with its high-rise condominiums, its casino, its seafront pizzerias and its bronzed, beautiful sunbathers, could be almost any international resort in the world. Valparaíso, on the other hand, has a style all its own, with its ramshackle, brightly painted houses spilling chaotically down the hills to the sea. This is Chile's biggest port and is wonderfully atmospheric, though bereft of decent beaches. For these you need to head north or south where you can find anything from disco-packed pleasure grounds to tiny, secluded coves – if you know where to go (and where to avoid).

Closest to Santiago are the resorts **south of Valparaíso**, which are busier and more developed – though **Laguna Verde** and **Quintay**, bypassed by the coast road, feel very remote outside high season. Further south, between **Algarrobo** and **San Antonio**, there's an almost uninterrupted string of *cabañas*, villas and small resorts, but most of the development is low-level and low-scale, and it's still possible to find places with charm and a soul – in the village of **Las Cruces**, for example, or at **Cartagena**, a lively seaside town full of colourful houses and twisting streets. The huge port of **San Antonio** is the only place on the *litoral* south of Valparaíso that doesn't rely on tourism for its livelihood, and merits a visit for its massive fish quay lined with excellent restaurants.

Heading **north from Viña** you leave most of the concrete behind at **Concón**. From **Quintero** up, the coast begins to look more rugged and feels distinctly wild and windswept by the time you reach **Maitencillo**, where brown, sandstone cliffs tower above a huge, white beach. The stretch from here to Papudo is the most beautiful of the *litoral*, as the road clings to the cliff edge, giving views down to empty coves and thundering surf. Not even the new wave of villas and second-home complexes that's sprung up along here in the last year or two has managed to spoil **Zapallar**, the most graceful and harmonious of all the resorts, or **Papudo**, a small fishing town dramatically hemmed in by its steep, green hills.

It's worth noting that most Chileans take their annual holiday in February when all the resorts, large and small, are unbearably crowded. They also get busy at weekends in December and January, but outside these times are remarkably unvisited. November and March are probably the **best months** to be here, as the weather is usually perfect and the beaches virtually deserted, especially midweek, though winter can be even more romantic when the resorts wear a forlorn, abandoned look and you can go for blustery walks along the empty beaches. From April to October **accommodation rates** are considerably lower, sometimes up to half those suggested in our price guide,

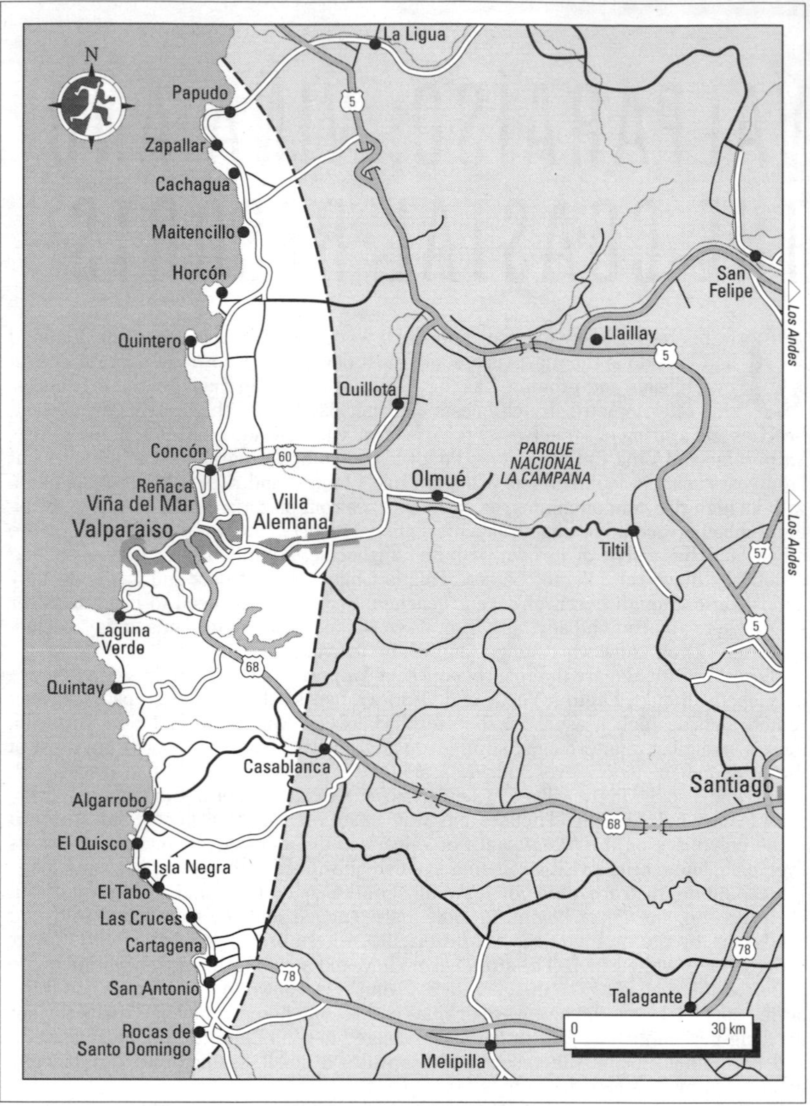

and even in November, December and March you should be able to negotiate a discount midweek. Most beaches are safe for **swimming**, though you should definitely stay out of the water if a red flag's displayed; you might also be put off by the cold **Humboldt current** that sweeps up the Pacific from the Antarctic coast, leaving the water chilly even in the height of summer. Something you should not miss out on, though, is the exquisite **seafood** available all along the coast – head for the little restau-

ACCOMMODATION PRICE CODES

Prices are for the cheapest **double room** in high season. At the lower end of the scale, **single travellers** can expect to pay half this rate, but mid- and upper-range hotels usually charge the same for a single as for a double. For more information see p.27 in Basics.

① Less than US$10/CH$4800
② US$10–20/CH$4800–9600
③ US$20–30/CH$9600–10,080
④ US$30–50/CH$10,080–24,000
⑤ US$50–75/CH$24,000–36,000
⑥ US$75–100/CH$36,000–48,000
⑦ US$100–150/CH$48,000–72,000
⑧ over US$150/over CH$72,000

rants by the *caleta* where the local fishermen bring in their catch or, if you're renting a *cabaña* with its own kitchen, be adventurous and buy your supper from the market to cook for yourself.

Finally a word on **transport**: there are numerous daily buses from Santiago to Valparaíso and Viña, and several direct services from the capital to most of the other resorts (see pp.109–113). From Valparaíso or Viña you can catch buses to all the resorts in the *litoral*. The stretch between Algarrobo and San Antonio is also served by frequent local buses, while from Quintero to Papudo there are only a few local connections daily.

Valparaíso

Valparaíso es un montón, un racimo
de casas locas
Pablo Neruda

Spread over an amphitheatre of hills encircling a wide bay, **VALPARAÍSO** is perhaps the most memorable city in Chile. Its most striking feature is its houses – a mad, colourful tangle of them tumbling down the hills to a narrow shelf of land below. Few roads make it up these gradients and most people get up and down on the city's fifteen "lifts" or *ascensores*, a collection of ancient-looking funiculars that slowly haul you up to incredible viewpoints. The lower town, known as *el plan*, is a series of narrow, traffic-choked streets packed with shops, banks, offices and warehouses, crowded round the quays and port that once made Valparaíso's fortune.

The bay was chosen as the site of the new colony's port as early as 1542, when Pedro de Valdivia decided it would "serve the trade of these lands and of Santiago". Growth was slow, however, owing to trading restrictions imposed by the Spanish Crown, but when Latin American trade was liberalized in the 1820s, following independence, Valparaíso started to come into its own. Located as it was on the shipping route from Europe to America's Pacific Coast, it became the main port of call and resupply centre for ships after they rounded Cape Horn. As Chile's own foreign trade expanded with the silver and copper booms of the 1830s, the port became ever more active, but it was the government's innovative creation of public warehouses where merchants could store goods at low prices that really launched Valparaíso into its economic ascent.

Foreign businessmen, particularly British ones, flocked to the city where they ran trading empires built on copper, silver and nitrate. The wealth and influence of these men extended well beyond mining exports: they financed railways, trams and canals as well as electricity, telephone and gas networks and by the late nineteenth century had turned Valparaíso into the foremost financial and commercial centre of Chile. The city outstripped Santiago in most urban developments, producing its own daily newspaper, banks and stock exchange long before the capital. Even as it prospered, though,

Valparaíso continued to be dogged by the kind of violent setbacks that had always punctuated its history, from looting pirates and buccaneers through to earthquakes and fires. On March 31, 1866, following Chile's entanglement in a dispute between Spain and Peru, the Spanish admiralty bombarded Valparaíso from its harbour for three hours, wreaking devastation on the city. It took a long time to rebuild it, but worse was still to come. On August 16, 1906, a colossal earthquake practically razed the city to the ground, killing over 2000 people. The disaster took a heavy toll on Valparaíso's fortunes, which never really recovered. Eight years later, the opening of the Panama canal signalled the city's inexorable decline.

Today, Valparaíso's heyday is long gone, and the city wears a run-down, moth-eaten air. That said, it's still a vital working port – the biggest in Chile – shifting five million tonnes annually, and has been the seat of Congress since President Aylwin's inauguration in 1990. As the capital of the Fifth region, it also has its share of galleries and museums, but the city's chief attractions lie in its crumbling, romantic atmosphere and its extravagant geography.

Arrival, information and orientation

Buses from Santiago (every 10min from the Terminal Alameda) and other major cities pull in at the Terminal Rodoviario on the eastern end of Pedro Montt, opposite the Congress building; there are **left luggage** lockers (buy a token from the news kiosk next to the lockers), though your bus company will probably store bags in its office. From here it's about a twenty-minute walk into the old town; plenty of *micros* also go into the centre from right outside the station. There's also a regional **train** service to Valparaíso from Viña del Mar, dropping you right next door to the port.

Information

The well-run municipal **oficina de turismo** hands out lists of accommodation and will sometimes ring to see if there are vacancies. There's a helpful branch at the **bus station** (Dec 15–March 15 daily 10am–2pm & 3–7pm; March 16–Dec 14 Tues–Sun 10am–6pm; no phone), while in the centre the main branch is at the **town hall**, Condell 1490 (Mon–Fri 8.30am–2pm & 3.30–5.30pm; ☎32/251071), with additional kiosks at **Muelle Prat**, by the port (Dec 15–March 15 daily 10am–2pm & 3–7pm; 16 March–14 Dec Thurs–Sun 10am–6pm) and in **Plaza Victoria** (Dec 15–March 15 10am–2pm & 3–7pm).

Orientation and getting around

The eastern end of town around the bus terminal is of limited interest; best head west to the **old town** which stretches along a narrow strip of land between Plaza Victoria and Plaza Aduana. Countless **micros** (and an electric trolley bus) run east and west through the city: those displaying "Aduana" on the window will take you west through the centre, past the port, while those marked "P. Montt" will take you back to the bus station. To climb up the hills, the easiest thing to do is use the **ascensores**; some bus routes also take you to the upper town, and you can take **colectivos** from Plazuela Ecuador. **Taxis** are numerous and inexpensive and can easily be flagged down on the street.

Accommodation

There's plenty of **accommodation** in Valparaíso, the bulk of it simple and inexpensive. If you're on a short visit it's probably easiest to stay near the bus terminal and get buses in and out of the centre, but if you plan to stay for more than a couple of days it's worth seeking out a room with a view up on the hills. It's a good idea to phone ahead to check vacancies, as accommodation isn't concentrated in a single area, but spread all over the city.

Alojamiento Ezno & Martina, Quebrada Verde 192, Playa Ancha (☎32/288873). Out of the centre, but the reward is the friendliest welcome in town and a truly beautiful house – its attic room has windows on all sides and splendid views. Take bus #1, #2, #5, #6 or #17 from outside the bus terminal and ask to be dropped at the colegio María Auxiliadora, opposite the house. ④.

Alojamiento Hilda Rubilal, Pedro Montt 2881 (☎32/253358). Basic but light, airy rooms a few steps from the bus station, opposite the Congress building. Those at the front are very noisy. ③.

Alojamiento Juan Carrasco, Abtao 668, Cerro Concepción (☎32/210737). Big old house next to the Lutheran church in a beautiful, hilltop location, a short walk from Ascensor Concepción. Spotless rooms (a couple with great views, others with no outside windows) and the use of a kitchen. A good choice. ③.

Alojamiento Mónica Venegas, Av Argentina 322B (☎32/215673). Simple, immaculate rooms with the smell of fresh bread wafting in from the bakery next door. Those on the top floor are very quiet. Handy for the bus station. ③.

Alojamiento Monique Markowicz, subida Artillería 105, Cerro Artillería (☎32/283790). A tiny, gem of a place offering superb views from its three rooms, and a glassed-in balcony where you can have breakfast. It's halfway up the stairway next to Ascensor Artillería. ②.

Alojamiento Sra Silvia, Pasaje Quinta 70 off Av Argentina (☎32/216592). Rather out of the way, in a tiny alley next to the paroquía San Juan Bosque, but the rooms are clean and peaceful, some of them opening onto a small patio. Plenty of buses into town from Avenida Argentina. ③.

Brighton Bed & Breakfast, Pasaje Atkinson 151, Cerro Concepción (☎ & fax 32/223513). Stylish decor and fantastic views at this small hotel in one of the prettiest corners of town, with an outdoor terrace looking onto the bay. Take Ascensor Concepción and head for the bright yellow building on the corner. ⑤.

Hotel Casa Baska, Victoria 2449 (☎32/234036). Quiet, elegant rooms (some with large French windows and balconies) in a beautifully renovated old building. One of the nicest hotels in Valparaíso; has its own parking. ④.

Hotel Garden, Serrano 501 (☎32/252776). Ancient, neglected building with some interesting features (check out the beautiful domed ceiling in reception) and spacious, no-frills rooms. ②.

Hotel Lancaster, Chacabuco 2362 (☎32/217391). Old hotel, not as fresh as it could be but with lots of character. The front rooms are bright and spacious, with small balconies, while the back ones have no outside windows. ④.

Hotel Reina Victoria, Plaza Sotomayor 190 (☎32/212203). Clean but very basic rooms with shared bath in a fine old building in the heart of town. Noisy. ②.

Residencial Dinamarca, Dinamarca 535, Cerro Cárcel (☎32/259189). Very clean, well-maintained *residencial* just down from the prison. Some rooms have private bath and TV at no extra cost. Take a bus or *colectivo* up Ecuador or Cumming. ②.

The City

Valparaíso isn't really about museums and "sights" but about losing yourself in labyrinthine streets and magnificent panoramas. Unfortunately you'll also have to contend with a certain amount of noise, pollution and general shabbiness, which for some people overshadow the city's charms. But take a **boat ride** round the harbour (especially as the sun's going down and its rays fall into every fold of the hills); go up two or three **ascensores**; check out the colourful old residential quarters of **cerros Alegre** and **Concepción**, and don't miss the views by night, when the city's million flickering lights are reflected in the ocean like a basket of pearls – and you're sure to fall under Valparaíso's spell.

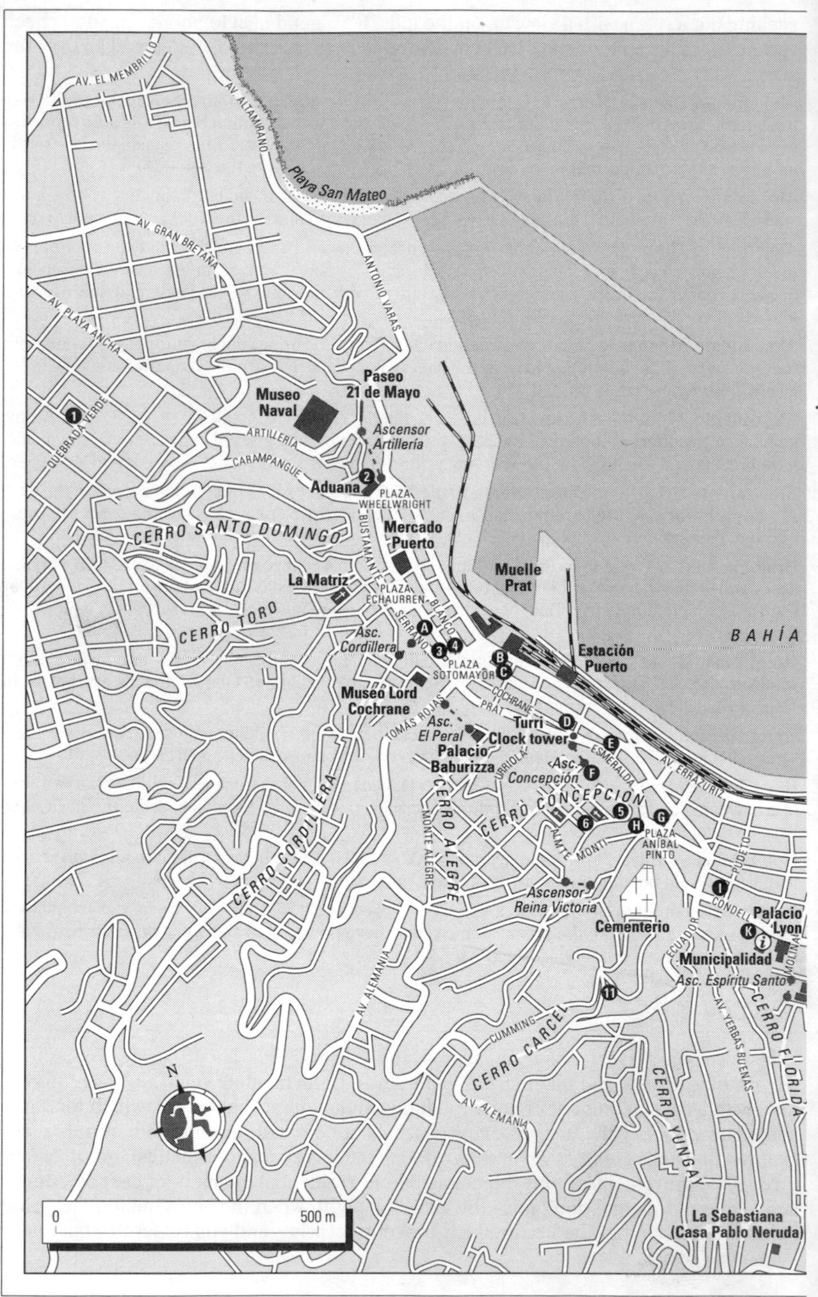
AV. EL MEMBRILLO
AV. ALTAMIRANO
Playa San Mateo
AV. GRAN BRETAÑA
ANTONIO VARAS
AV. PLAYA ANCHA
Paseo
21 de Mayo
Museo
Naval
QUEBRADA VERDE
ARTILLERÍA
Ascensor
Artillería
CARAMPANGUE
Aduana
PLAZA
WHEELWRIGHT
CERRO SANTO DOMINGO
Mercado
Puerto
BUSTAMANTE
Muelle
Prat
La Matriz
PLAZA
ECHAURREN
BLANCO
SERRANO
CERRO TORO
Asc.
Cordillera
PLAZA
SOTOMAYOR
BAHÍA
Estación
Puerto
Museo Lord
Cochrane
COCHRANE
PRAT
TOMÁS ROJAS
Asc.
El Peral
Turri
Clock tower
Palacio
Baburizza
ESMERALDA
URRIOLA
Asc.
Concepción
AV. ERRAZURIZ
CERRO CONCEPCIÓN
CERRO CORDILLERA
CERRO ALEGRE
MONTE ALEGRE
ALMTE MONTT
PLAZA
ANÍBAL
PINTO
PUDETO
Ascensor
Reina Victoria
CONDELL
Palacio
Lyon
Cementerio
ECUADOR
Municipalidad
MOLINA
Asc. Espíritu Santo
AV. ALEMANIA
CUMMING
CERRO CARCEL
AV. YERBAS BUENAS
CERRO FLORIDA
CERRO YUNGAY
AV. ALEMANIA
N
0
500 m
La Sebastiana
(Casa Pablo Neruda)

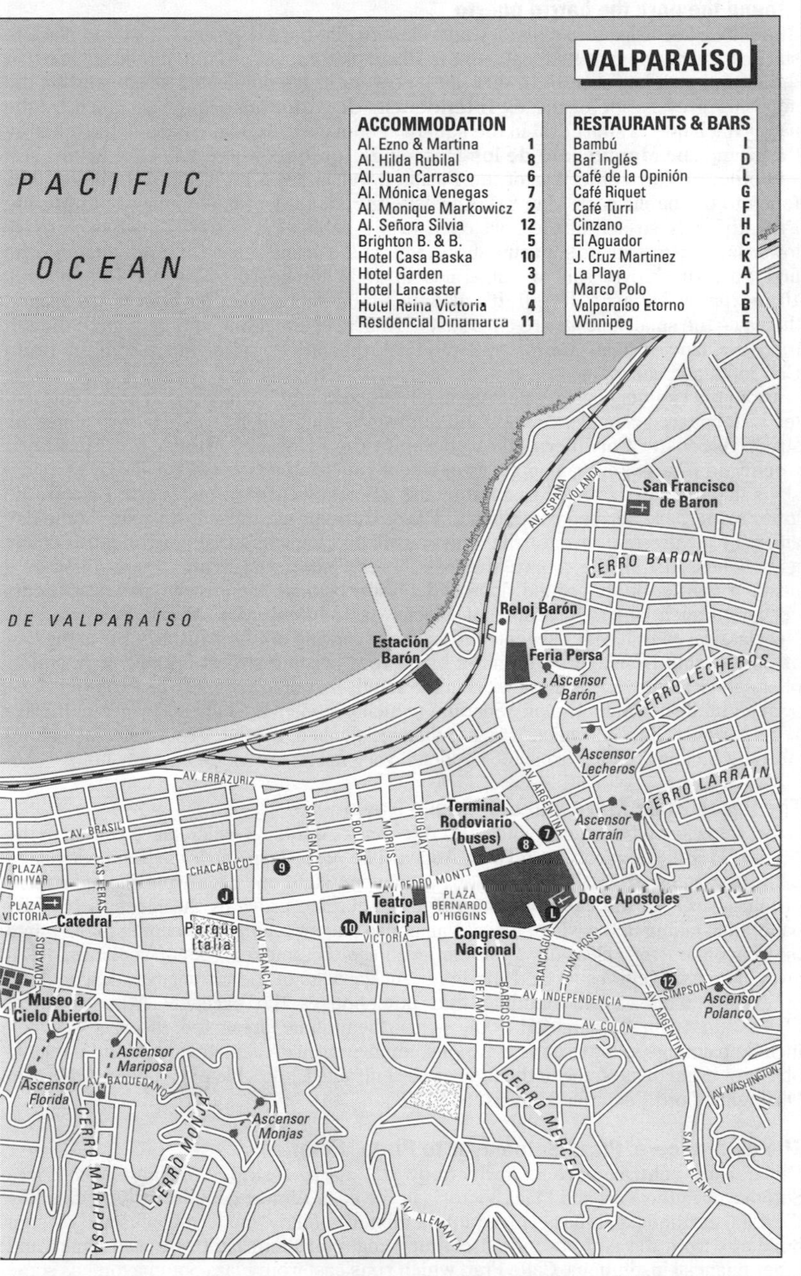
VALPARAÍSO
ACCOMMODATION
Al. Ezno & Martina 1
Al. Hilda Rubilal 8
Al. Juan Carrasco 6
Al. Mónica Venegas 7
Al. Monique Markowicz 2
Al. Señora Silvia 12
Brighton B. & B. 5
Hotel Casa Baska 10
Hotel Garden 3
Hotel Lancaster 9
Hotel Reina Victoria 4
Residencial Dinamarca 11
RESTAURANTS & BARS
Bambú I
Bar Inglés D
Café de la Opinión L
Café Riquet G
Café Turri F
Cinzano H
El Aguador C
J. Cruz Martinez K
La Playa A
Marco Polo J
Valparaíso Eterno B
Winnipeg E
PACIFIC OCEAN
DE VALPARAÍSO
San Francisco de Baron
CERRO BARON
Reloj Barón
Estación Barón
Feria Persa
Ascensor Barón
CERRO LECHEROS
Ascensor Lecheros
CERRO LARRAIN
Ascensor Larraín
Terminal Rodoviario (buses)
Doce Apostoles
Congreso Nacional
Teatro Municipal
PLAZA BERNARDO O'HIGGINS
Parque Italia
Catedral
PLAZA BOLIVAR
PLAZA VICTORIA
Museo a Cielo Abierto
Ascensor Mariposa
Ascensor Florida
Ascensor Monjas
Ascensor Polanco
CERRO MARIPOSA
CERRO MONJA
CERRO MERCED
AV. ERRÁZURIZ
AV. BRASIL
CHACABUCO
AV. PEDRO MONTT
VICTORIA
AV. INDEPENDENCIA
AV. COLÓN
AV. ARGENTINA
AV. ESPAÑA
YOLANDA
SAN IGNACIO
S. BOLIVAR
MORRIS
URUGUAY
LAS HERAS
EDWARDS
AV. FRANCIA
RETAMO
BARROSO
RANCAGUA
JUANA ROSS
SIMPSON
AV. WASHINGTON
SANTA ELENA
AV. ALEMANIA
AV. BAQUEDANO

Around the port: the barrio puerto

At the heart of Valparaíso's history and identity, the **barrio puerto** is a good place to start exploring the city. Its focal point is **Plaza Sotomayor**, a large public square that the city council has seen fit to turn into a car park. It's dominated at one end by the imposing grey facade of the **ex-Intendencia de Valparaíso** (now occupied by the navy, which does a short drill in the square at 6pm every weekday) and at the other by the triumphant **Monumento de los Héroes de Iquique**, where statues of Arturo Prat and other heroes of the War of the Pacific tower above a crypt housing their tombs (open to the public each May 21). Opposite the monument is the gateway to **Muelle Prat**, the only stretch of the port open to the public. It's geared almost exclusively towards tourists, with its souvenir shops, tourist kiosk and replica of *el Santiaguillo*, the first Spanish ship to sail to Valparaíso in 1536 (on-board tours Dec–March daily 10am–2pm & 3–7pm; CH$300). It's also the embarkation point for **boat rides** around the bay – the small *lanchas* are cheapest (CH$500, every 20min until nightfall), though there's a fancier boat, *Maité* (☎32/691112), that offers rides into the night (from CH$2500) and cocktails.

From the ex-Intendencia, calle Serrano leads west into the oldest part of the city, dotted with battered chandlers' shops and dubious-looking sailors' bars. Halfway along the street, **Ascensor Cordillera** takes you up to the red-walled **Museo del Mar Lord Cochrane** (Tues–Sun 10am–6pm; free) where you'll find an impressive display of model ships that belonged to Lord Cochrane, and a magnificent view out to sea. Back in the lower town, Calle Serrano continues to **Plaza Echuarren**, the oldest square in the city and very picturesque save for the whisky-swilling characters that permanently occupy its benches. Just off the square, the iron structure of the **Mercado Puerto** houses a bustling market on its ground floor and several popular, inexpensive fish restaurants upstairs (lunch only). A couple of blocks east, **Iglesia La Matriz** – a graceful, Neoclassical church with a seventeenth-century carving of Christ inside – sits at the foot of Cerro Santo Domingo surrounded by narrow, twisting streets full of colour, atmosphere and a slightly menacing feel; this is a rough part of town, not to be explored alone or at night. If you continue along Serrano (which becomes Bustamente) you reach Plaza Wheelwright (also known as Plaza Aduana), flanked by the large, colonial-looking **Aduana** building, dating from 1854 and still very much a working customs house.

The Paseo 21 de Mayo and the Museo Naval

A few steps from the Aduana you'll find **Ascensor Artillería** which takes you up to the **Paseo 21 de Mayo** on Cerro Playa Ancha. The *paseo* (esplanade) is the most visited in the city, and sports a row of uninspiring souvenir stalls and a fairly permanent stream of tourists. Of all the viewpoints in the city, this one provides the most spectacular panorama, taking in the whole bay of Valparaíso and sweeping 20km north to the punta de Concón; on very clear days you can even see the smokestacks of Ventanas, 45km away. The *paseo* curves around the luxuriant gardens of the former Naval School, an impressive whitewashed building that now houses the excellent **Museo Naval** (Tues–Sun 10am–5.30pm; CH$500), whose beautifully presented displays – which include paintings, photographs, weapons, uniforms, nautical instruments and personal objects – bring to life some of the figures so central to Chile's history, such as Ambrosio O'Higgins, Lord Cochrane and Arturo Prat.

The central core: Plaza Sotomayor to Plaza Victoria

Valparaíso's **central core** is formed by the narrow strip stretching from Plaza Sotomayor in the west and Plaza Victoria in the east. Almost completely devastated by the 1906 earthquake, it has evolved into a mixture of ugly, modern blocks and elegant buildings from the early twentieth century, many of them built to house banks and other financial institutions. Calle Prat, which runs east from Plaza Sotomayor, has some

LOS ASCENSORES DE VALPARAÍSO

Most of Valparaíso's fifteen *ascensores*, or funicular "lifts", were built in the late nineteenth or early twentieth century to provide a link between the lower town and the new residential quarters that were spreading up the hillsides. Appearances would suggest that they've scarcely been modernized since, but despite their rickety frames and alarming noises they've so far always proved safe and reliable. What's more, they nearly all end up at a panoramic viewpoint. The *ascensores* operate every few minutes from 7am to 11pm, and cost CH$70 a go. Here are a few of the best, listed from east to west:

Ascensor Barón This *ascensor* has windows on all sides, so you get good views as you go up. Inaugurated in 1906, it was the first to be powered by an electric motor, still in perfect working order. At the top, you're allowed into the machinery room where you can watch the giant cogs go round as they haul the lift up and down. There's also a display of photos of all the *ascensores* in the town. The entrance is hidden away at the back of a clothes market, Feria Persa el Barón, off the seaward end of Avenida Argentina.

Ascensor Polanco The most picturesque *ascensor*, and the only one that's totally vertical. It's approached through a cavernous, underground tunnel and rises 80m through a yellow wooden tower to a balcony that gives some of the best views in the city. A narrow bridge connects the tower to Cerro Polanco with its flaking, pastel houses in varying states of repair. Ascensor Polanco is on calle Simpson, off Avenida Argentina (opposite Independencia).

Ascensor Concepción (also known as Ascensor Turri) Hidden in a small passage opposite the Turri clock tower, this was the first *ascensor* to be built, in 1883, and was originally powered by steam. It takes you up to a beautiful residential area, well worth a visit (see p.124); just by the upper entrance you'll find *Café Turri* on calle Prat, a great place to sit and admire the views over a coffee or a meal.

Ascensor El Peral Next door to the Tribunales de Justicio, just off Plaza Sotomayor, this *ascensor* leads to one of the most romantic corners of the city: Paseo Yugoslavo, a little esplanade looking west onto some of Valparaíso's most beautiful houses, and backed by a flamboyant mansion housing the Museo de Bellas Artes. It's worth walking from here to Ascensor Concepción – see our map on p.125.

Ascensor Artillería Always busy with tourists, but highly recommended for the stunning views at the top, from the Paseo 21 de Mayo. It was built in 1892 to transport cadets to and from the naval school at the top of the hill, now the site of the Museo Naval. It's located on Plaza Wheelwright, next to the Advana building.

good examples – take a look inside the **Banco O'Higgins** opposite the Turri clock tower, originally the Banco de Londres and dripping with bronze and marble brought over from England. Next door to the bank, **Ascensor Concepción** (also known as Ascensor Turri) provides access to Cerro Concepción, a pretty residential area that was once the preserve of English businessmen. Further east, **Plaza Anibal Pinto** is an attractive cobbled square overlooked by a couple of the city's oldest restaurants. From here, the main drag continues along calle Condell where you'll find the Municipalidad at no. 1490 and, just beyond, **Palacio Lyon**, a splendid mansion dating from 1881 (one of the few to survive the earthquake) and now housing the **Museo de Historia Natural** (Tues–Sat 10am–1pm & 2–6pm, Sun 10am–2pm; CH$500). This cash-starved museum tries hard to inform and entertain but its displays can't help looking dowdy and outdated. The central theme is "el mar de Chile" and topics covered include the chemical, physical and biological aspects of the sea, marine flora and fauna (look out for the caseful of stuffed penguins) and the influence of the sea on pre-Hispanic cultures. The cellars of the building have been converted into the **Galería Municipal de Arte** (Mon–Sat 10am–7pm; free) which puts on temporary art exhibitions; the entrance is on Condell, separate from the museum's.

Condell ends at **Plaza Victoria**, a large tree-filled square where most of Valparaíso seems to come to chat and sit in the sunshine. It's flanked, on its eastern side, by the Gothic-looking **Iglesia Catedral de Valparaíso** whose simply decorated interior includes a delicate ivory carving of Christ, a Moretto painting and, most intriguingly, a marble urn (in the crypt) containing the heart of Diego Portales, the famous Chilean statesman. If you want to visit the cathedral, ask in the administrative office at the north side of the building, on Chacabuco (Mon–Fri 10am–1pm & 4–6.30pm). From the square, calles Molina and Edwards lead to the **Museo a Cielo Abierto**, a circuit of narrow streets and passageways painted with seventeen huge, bold murals by art students of the Universidad Católica and finished off by renowned Chilean artists. There's a lot of abstract, geometric stuff, and it's all colourful and eye-catching, but the area has a rough feel to it which doesn't encourage you to linger.

La Sebastiana – casa de Neruda

Of Pablo Neruda's three houses open to the public, **La Sebastiana** is perhaps the most enjoyable to visit (Tues–Sun 10.30am–2.30pm & 3.30–6pm; CH$1000), not least because it attracts the fewest crowds, and you're not forced to take a guided tour so can amble around at your own pace. The poet moved into the house in 1961 with Matilde Urrutia, his third wife. Perched high on a hill, giving dramatic views over the bay, it was his "*casa en el aire*" and although he spent less time here than in his other homes, he imprinted his style and enthusiasms on every corner of the house. After the 1973 coup it was repeatedly vandalized by the military but has been meticulously restored by the Fundación Neruda, which opened it as a museum in 1992. Its narrow, sinuous passages and bright colours seem to mirror the spirit of Valparaíso, and the countless bizarre objects brought here by Neruda are simply astonishing, from the embalmed Venezuelan Coro-Coro bird hanging from the ceiling of the dining room to the wooden horse in the living room, taken from a merry-go-round in Paris. The house is located at Ferrari 692, off Avenida Alemaña; to get there, take bus Verde Mar D from Plazuela Ecuador, or Verde Mar O from Avenida Argentina or Plaza Aduana and ask to be set off at the casa de Neruda.

Cerros Alegre and Concepción

The hilltop residential quarter spread over **cerros Alegre** and **Concepción** is a rambling maze of steep streets and small alleys lined with elegant, brightly painted houses and flamboyant mansions clinging precipitously to the hillside. It grew up as the enclave of Valparaíso's immigrant businessmen, particularly the English, who left their legacy in street names like Leighton, Templeman and Atkinson, and the Germans, whose influence can be seen in the many half-timbered, shuttered houses dotted about the area. There are two points of access from the lower town; **Ascensor Concepción** (see p.123), opposite the Turri clock tower in calle Prat, takes you up to **Paseo Gervasoni** on Cerro Concepción, while **Ascensor El Peral** (see p.123), next to the Tribunales de Justicia just off Plaza Sotomayor, takes you up to Cerro Alegre's **Paseo Yugoslavo**, one of the most attractive and peaceful corners of town. A good way to explore the area is to walk between the two *ascensores*: the Oficina de Turismo has produced a leaflet with a suggested **walking tour** which takes you through some narrow alleys and hidden passageways – see our map, opposite, for the route.

Arriving at Paseo Yugoslavo you'll see an extravagant, four-storey mansion right behind the esplanade. This is **Palacio Baburizza**, built in 1916 for a nitrate baron and now the home of the **Museo de Bellas Artes de Valparaíso** (Tues–Sun 10am–6pm; free), a hushed, scarcely visited museum with a collection of nineteenth and twentieth century Chilean and European art. It's a mixed bag, but worth a visit for the evocative paintings of an earlier Valparaíso by artists such as Juan Mauricio Rugendas, Alfred

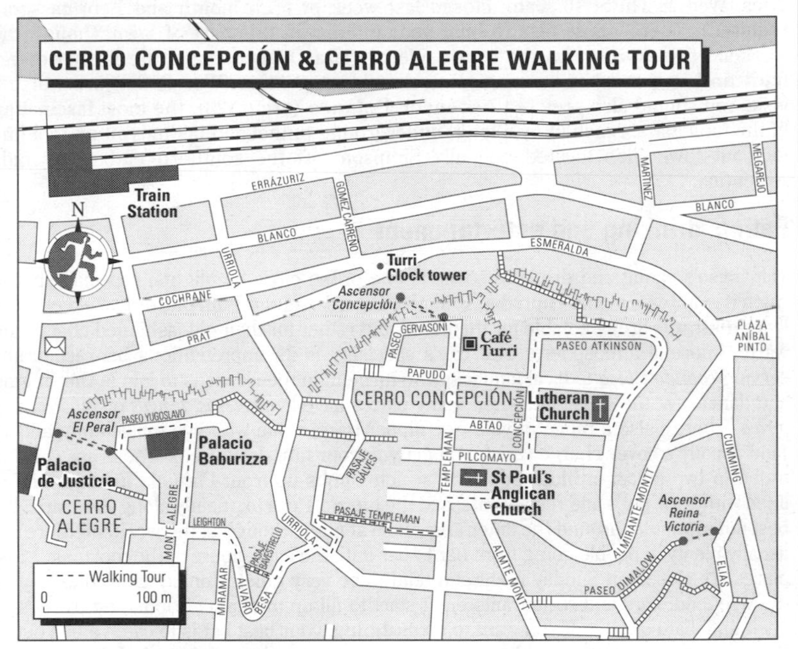

Helsby, Thomas Somerscales and, most notably, Juan Francisco González. Lighter in tone and in some ways more rewarding, the **Casa Mirador de Lukas** (Tues–Sun 10.30am–2pm & 3.30–6pm; CH$500) is a few steps from the other point of arrival, at Paseo Gervasoni 448. This little museum pays homage to *El Mercurio*'s great satirist and cartoonist, known simply as Lukas, who possessed a sharp talent for capturing the spirit of his country in the hilarious drawings he produced between 1958 and 1988, many of which are displayed here. A walk around Cerro Concepción should also include a visit to **Paseo Atkinson**, an esplanade giving great views and lined with pretty houses whose tiny front gardens and window boxes recall their original English owners. From here you can see the tall tower of the **Lutheran church**, a distinctive, green-walled structure built in 1897; a block or so behind you'll find the towerless **St Paul's Anglican Church** (built in 1858) whose solemn interior contains a huge organ donated by Queen Victoria in 1903.

Around the Congreso Nacional

The first thing that hits you as you emerge from the bus station is the huge, aggressive outline of the **Congreso Nacional**, described by Collier and Sater in their *History of Chile* as "half neo-Babylonian, half post-modernist atrocity". It was actually one of Pinochet's projects, which perhaps explains its heavy-handed style, but the dictator relinquished power before it was completed and its life began on March 11, 1990, when President Aylwin was sworn in as President and congress resumed its activities after a sixteen-year absence – away from the capital for the first time. It's not, in fact, as impregnable as it looks, and members of the public are allowed to go in and watch congress in session (senate Tues & Wed 4pm, Thurs 10am; deputies

Tues, Wed & Thurs 10.30am; closed last week of each month and Feb; passport required). There's little else to hold your interest in this part of town, though the weekend **flea market** on the south side of Plaza O'Higgins and the lively **flower, fruit and veg market** running along Avenida Argentina (Wed & Sat) are worth a visit. You should also seek out **Ascensor Polanco** (see p.123), the most fascinating of the funiculars, reached by a long, underground tunnel and taking you up to a fine look-out tower: it's located on calle Simpson, off the southern end of Avenida Argentina.

Eating, drinking and entertainment

Valparaíso's eating and drinking scene is one of the city's highlights, especially if you catch it in full swing on a Thursday, Friday or Saturday night. With one or two exceptions, its **restaurants** aren't notable for their food, but rather for their old-fashioned charm and warm, informal atmosphere. The city's speciality is its unpretentious bar-restaurants serving *comida típica* to local families, who turn out in their dozens to join in the singing and dancing at the weekend, when many places have live *boleros, tangos* or *música folklórica*. There's also a range of younger, hipper **bars**, some with live music and dancing (and usually a cover charge which will get you your first drink free). These are concentrated in two areas: **subida Ecuador**, which climbs up from Plazuela Ecuador and is lined with bars, pubs and restaurants; and the **barrio Puerto**, mainly along Errázuriz. It's best not to wander around the latter area alone at night, though at the weekend there are usually plenty of people going from bar to bar until the early hours of the morning. Most places are closed on Sunday night and tend to be very quiet Monday to Wednesday; at the weekend, bars and restaurants don't start to fill up until after 10pm, and many stay open until 5am or later. If you want to go **clubbing**, your best bet is to catch a bus out to Reñaca, a suburb of Viña that has something of a monopoly on the local nightclub scene (see p.141). If you're after something a little more cultural, check out the programme at the **Teatro Municipal**, on the corner of Pedro Montt and Plaza O'Higgins, which puts on regular theatre, music and dance performances. As for **cinema**, the Metroval, Pedro Montt 2111, shows mainstream releases, and art movies are frequently shown in various cultural centres – check the back of *El Mercurio de Valparaíso* for details.

Cafés and snacks

Babestrello, Av Uruguay 426, on Plaza O'Higgins, opposite the bus terminal. Spacious coffee shop serving sticky cakes and coffee, and hot toast and jam – a good place for breakfast.

Café Riquet, Plaza Aníbal Pinto. Old-fashioned café-restaurant that's virtually frozen in time – it's been going for 75 years and the chef's been here for 58 of them. Come for coffee, snacks and breakfast.

Café-Arte Mirador, Paseo 21 de Mayo (top exit of Ascensor Artillería). Small, arty café with sweeping views across the bay and a changing display of paintings by local artists. Closed Tuesday mornings.

Marco Polo, Pedro Montt 2199, opposite Parque Italia. Large, inexpensive Italian cafeteria not far from the bus terminal, serving hearty lunches and snacks.

Pastelería Stefani, Condell 1608, Plaza Victoria. Exquisite strawberry tarts and other delights, as well as a small stand-up bar where you can eat your cake with a coffee.

Tentazione, Pedro Montt 2484. Typical, TV-dominated *fuente de soda* serving filling, cheap meals; handy for the bus station.

Vitamin Service, Pedro Montt 1746, off Plaza Victoria. Delicious fruit juices and tasty sandwiches – perfect for replenishing your energies.

Restaurants

Anita, Mercado Puerto, upper level. Busy, no-frills *marisquería* serving fresh fish and shellfish at reasonable prices. The *paila marina* is especially recommended. Lunch only.

Bambú, Pudeto 450, off west end of Condell. Good-value vegetarian food – mainly omelettes, salads and soups – in a central location.

Café de la Opinion, Juana Ross 50, behind the Congreso Nacional. Elegant, contemporary restaurant with a gramophone in the *comedor* on which they'll play old 45 jazz records, if you ask. Appetizing Mediterranean-influenced food, imaginatively prepared, catering mainly to the congress crowd. Not too expensive.

Café Turri, paseo Gervasoni, by upper exit of Ascensor Concepción (☎32/259198). Classy restaurant with an outdoor terrace and superb, panoramic views, especially magical at night. Excellent, if traditional, meat and fish dishes (main courses around CH$6000); also works as a café through the day. Highly recommended.

El Aguador, Blanco 698, underneath *Valparaíso Eterno*. Colourful vegetarian canteen with a limited choice but decent food. Lunch only; closed weekends.

J. Cruz Martínez, Condell 1466, in side alley next to Municipalidad (☎32/211225). An extraordinary place, more like a museum than a restaurant, packed to the gills with china, old clocks, musical instruments, crucifixes and more. Famous for its filling, inexpensive *chorrillana* and *pan con carne mechada* – not to be missed on any account.

Bar-restaurants

Cinzano, Plaza Aníbal Pinto. Hugely popular place with a fantastic weekend atmosphere when it fills with locals and ageing crooners singing sentimental ballads.

El Bar Inglés, Cochrane 851 (rear entrance at Blanco 870). Long-standing favourite, very popular for lunch though more expensive than its old-fashioned, crumbling decor might suggest.

La Playa, Serrano 567. An atmospheric place with a long, mahogany bar, dark wood-panelled walls and big old mirrors. Live music and open until 7am at the weekend.

¡Proa al cañaveral! Errázuriz 304, towards the Mercado Puerto. Nautically themed seafood restaurant, with glass-covered ships' wheels for tables and life rings on the walls. Live music and dancing upstairs at the weekend, when there's a CH$600 cover.

Valparaíso Eterno, corner of Blanco and A Señoret (one block east of Plaza Sotomayor). Dark rooms decorated with graffiti and wooden collages of the city's *ascensores* and houses. Live music at weekends until late and a *salsateca* in the basement; very popular with all ages.

Winnipeg, Esmeralda 1083, near Turri clock tower. Stylish restaurant-bar-café with polished floors, bright yellow walls and high ceilings. Serves Spanish food and generously filled hot sandwiches (*bocas calientes*); quite frantic at lunchtime but very mellow by night.

Pubs and bars

Azul Galería Bar, Ecuador 167. Dark, blue-walled place full of candlelit tables and a very laid-back crowd. Inexpensive drinks, and live jazz at the weekend.

Barparaíso, Errázuriz 1042. Funky bar with a dance area downstairs overlooked by a dimly lit balcony where you can hang out and drink. Plays a mixture of rock, Latin and dance music; popular with students. Cover CH$3000.

La Piedra Feliz, Errázuriz 1054, near junction with Blanco. Really mellow place with creaky wooden floors and plenty of tables to sit at and chat. There's live jazz on Tuesdays, *boleros* on Wednesdays, and various types of music at the weekend. Cover CH$2000.

Mr Egg, Ecuador 57. Huge, crowded pub famous for its two-litre glasses of beer (*copónes*). Lots of teenagers and loud music. There's a *Mr Egg* disco opposite the pub with a CH$2500 cover.

Pancho Pirata, Pudeto 489, off west end of Condell. Lively cellar-pub with stone walls and an intriguing, pirate-themed decor. One of the most popular drinking holes in town. Open Thursday to Saturday.

MOVING ON FROM VALPARAÍSO

Intercity and **international buses** leave from the Terminal Rodoviario (every 10min **to Santiago**). You can also get buses **up and down the coast** from the terminal, mainly with Sol del Pacífico (☎32/288577), Pullman Bus Costa (☎32/250858) and Mirasol (☎32/235985). To get **to Viña del Mar**, pick up a *micro* anywhere along Pedro Montt; they're very frequent and take about fifteen minutes, twice that time in bad traffic; alternatively take a train from the station next to Muelle Prat, off Plaza Sotomayor (every 15–30min), or even a boat from Muelle Prat (CH$1000). The Oficina de Turismo at the Municipalidad keeps timetables of all bus services. For more information see "Travel Details" on p.144.

Trolebar, subida Cumming 93. A magical little bar with bubbles shooting up and down the window, working models of two of Valparaíso's *ascensores* moving up and down their hills, and a doorway leading into a trolley bus. Open Thursday to Saturday.

Valparaíso Liverpool, Ecuador 130. Disco-bar with pictures of the Beatles and live bands doing Britpop covers – feels very out of place but it seems to go down well. Cover CH$1500.

Listings

Airlines Aerolíneas Argentinas, Pasaje Ross 149 (☎32/217049); Air France, Cochrane 667 (☎32/213249); Alitalia, Pasaje Ross 149 (☎32/250906); American Airlines, Esmeralda 940 (☎32/257777); Ladeco, Esmeralda 973 (☎32/216355); Lan Chile, Esmeralda 1048 (☎32/251441); Viasa, Pasaje Ross 149 (☎32/217049).

Banks and exchange The main financial street is Prat, where you'll find plenty of banks with ATMs and *cambios*, including Exprinter at no. 895 and New York at no. 659. Of the banks, the Banco de Santiago is the best for currency exchange. There's an ATM on Pedro Montt, one block west of the bus terminal, and at Condell 1481, near the Municipalidad.

Car rental Comveq Rent a Car, Argentina 850 (☎32/212153); Mach Viña, Las Heras 428 (☎32/259429); Transportes Arellano, Patricio Lynch 333 (☎32/282013); Union Rent a Car, Independencia 2771 (☎32/213927).

Laundry Las Heras 554 (two blocks west of Plaza Victoria).

Post office Correo Central on Plaza Sotomayor, between Cochrane and Prat.

Telephone offices Entel, Condell 149, opposite the Municipalidad (Mon–Fri 8.30am–10pm, Sat 10am–9pm, Sun 11am–8pm); CTC, Plaza Victoria (daily 8.30am–midnight).

Viña del Mar

A fifteen-minute bus ride is all it takes to exchange the chaotic alleys of Valparaíso for the tree-lined avenues and manicured lawns of **VIÑA DEL MAR**. This fast-paced town is Chile's largest and most fashionable beach resort, drawing thousands of Chileans and Argentinians to its sands each summer. In many ways it's indistinguishable from countless other international resorts with its oceanfront condominiums, scores of bars and restaurants and glitzy casino, but lurking in the older corners of the town are reminders of a graceful and dignified past, in the form of extravagant palaces, elegant villas and sumptuous, luxuriant gardens. Many of these date from the late nineteenth century when Viña del Mar, at that stage a large hacienda, started to be subdivided into plots that were sold or rented to the wealthy families of Valparaíso and Santiago who came to spend their summers by the sea, emulating the fashion in Europe. The early decades of the twentieth century saw the arrival of many more visitors: hotels were built, restaurants opened, a casino installed – and Viña's fate was sealed. Devoted as it is to tourism, Viña has plenty of accommodation, plenty of restaurants and the best shops and services in the region. It's also very easy to get to from Santiago, and can be a relaxing place to bum around for a couple of days at the beginning or end of your holiday. But, whatever Chileans tell you – and they will – Viña is not the most beautiful city in Chile, and the sun doesn't always shine here.

Arrival, information and orientation

Intercity buses from Santiago (every 10min from Terminal de Buses Alameda) and elsewhere arrive at the **bus terminal** at the eastern end of Avenida Valparaíso; best take a taxi to wherever you're staying, or a *micro* from the back of the terminal along Arlegui towards the centre and the sea. **From Valparaíso** you can get here by boat, train or *micro*: **boats** drop you off at *Hotel Miramar* and Muelle Vergara; the **train station** is centrally located, one block south of Plaza Vergara; and **micros** come down calle Viana, parallel to the railway tracks, and turn into Plaza Vergara.

Information

The most convenient place to go for tourist information is the **Oficina de Turismo**, just off the northwest corner of Plaza Vergara, next door to the post office (Dec 15–March 15 Mon–Fri 9am–2pm & 3–9pm, Sat 10am–1.30pm & 3–9pm; March 16–Dec 14 Mon–Fri 9am–2pm & 3–6pm, Sat 10am–2pm; ☎32/883154); it gives out maps and comprehensive lists of hotels and *residenciales*. The **Sernatur** office (Jan & Feb Mon–Fri 8.30am–7pm, Sat 10am–7pm, Sun 10am–2pm; March–Dec Mon–Fri 8.30am–1pm & 2.30–5pm; ☎32/882285) is helpful and well stocked with maps and pamphlets, but very difficult to find. It's at Av Valparaíso 507, on the third floor of an office block with a big Coca Cola sign on the roof; the block is set back from the main street, next door to an amusement arcade on the corner of Valparaíso and Echevers. There's also a **Conaf** information office (Mon–Thurs 9am–5.30pm, Fri 9am–4.30pm; ☎32/670315) at Alvarez 2760, opposite Chorillos train station (take the train for one stop, or a taxi).

Orientation

Viña del Mar falls into two quite separate sections, divided by the **Estero Marga Marga**, a filthy riverbed that cuts through the town to the ocean. South of the Marga Marga is the old part of town, Viña's lively commercial centre with the **Plaza Vergara** (also known as the **Plaza de Viña**) and **Avenida Valparaíso** at its core. North of the river, the grid-patterned streets are named simply "North", "East" or "West": those parallel to the Marga Marga are 1 Norte, 2 Norte and so on, ascending in number the further away they are from the river. Streets intersecting them at right angles, running parallel to the coast are known as Oriente (east) or Poniente (west) depending on which side of Avenida Libertad they're on; the first street east of Libertad is 1 Oriente, the second is 2 Oriente, and so on, the same system applying on the other side. This northern section has access to the main **beaches**, and is where you'll find most of the **restaurants** and **bars** catering to tourists.

Accommodation

Viña offers an enormous choice of places to stay, from dingy hovels to five-star hotels. All the **budget accommodation** is in the southern part of town, particularly on Agua Santa and Von Schroeders, and the side streets off Avenida Valparaíso. **Smarter options**, though spread all over town, are especially abundant on the northern side.

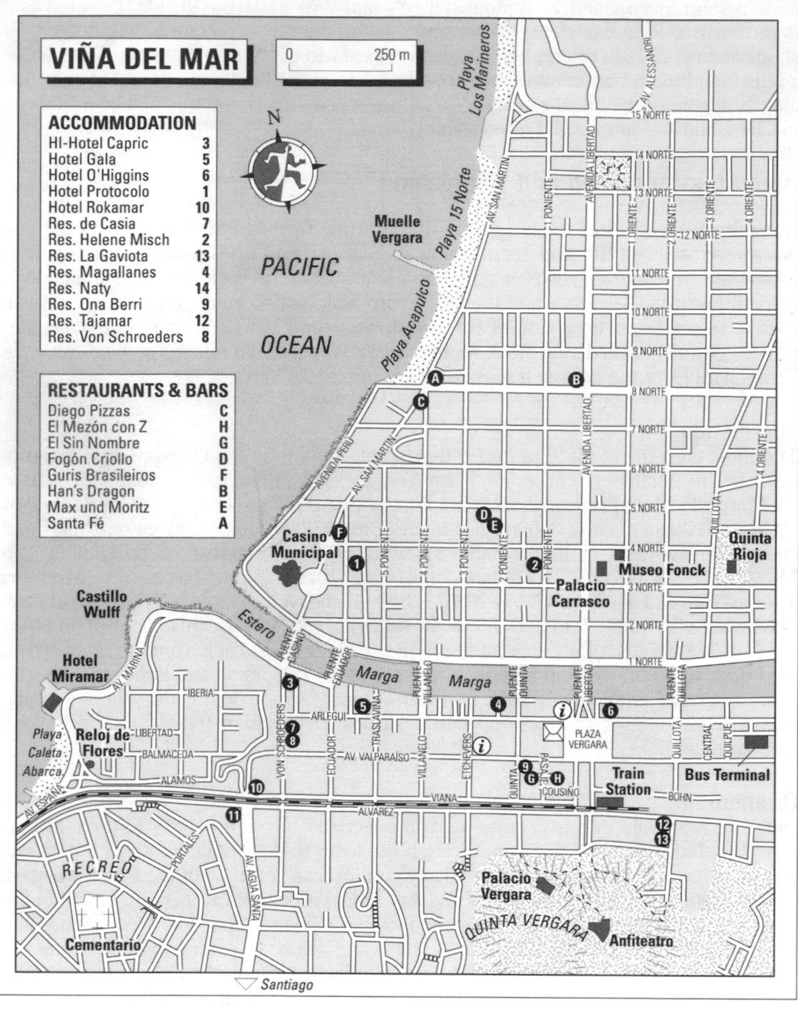

Only a few places offer sea views, as the ocean front is taken up by residential condominiums. Prices drop significantly outside January and February.

Habitaciones Adriana de Calderón, Batuco 147. Clean, comfortable rooms owned by a very welcoming couple; located on a quiet street near the bus terminal. ③.

HI-Hotel Capric, Von Schroeders 39 (☎32/978295). Curious HI hostel offering simple rooms off a courtyard and smarter ones with private bath in the adjacent *Hotel Capric*, where you'll also find the reception. ③.

Hotel Gala, Arlegui 273 (☎32/686688, fax 689568). Large, luxurious hotel featuring lots of modern art and contemporary decor. Rooms very spacious and light, with good views. ⑦.

Hotel Miramar, Caleta Abarca (☎32/626677, fax 665220). Superb location on a promontory jutting into the sea, with a swimming pool surrounded by crashing waves. Spacious rooms, great views and impossible prices. ⑧.

Hotel O'Higgins, Plaza Vergara (☎32/882016, fax 883537). Grand, 1930s hotel with a sumptuous lobby and dining room but slightly faded rooms. ⑥.

Hotel Protocolo, 5½ Poniente 253 (☎32/694696). Small, eight-room hotel offering good quality accommodation in a quiet street close to the sea. ⑤.

Hotel Rokamar, Viana 107 (☎ & fax 32/690019). Smart, newly furnished and well-equipped rooms in an elegant old building; reasonable value for the standard. ⑤.

Residencial De Casia, Von Schroeders 151 (☎32/971861). Adequate, fairly clean rooms; may be let out to students between March and December. ③.

Residencial Helene Misch, 1 Poniente 239 (☎32/971565). Attractive *residencial*, run by the same family for fifty years; quiet, comfortable rooms and a well-tended front garden where you can have breakfast. ④.

Residencial La Gaviota, Alcalde P. Nieto 0332, at corner with Alvárez (☎32/974439). Friendly atmosphere and bright if slightly run-down rooms in this beautiful old house by the rail line. Free parking. ②.

Residencial Magallanes, Arlegui 555 (☎32/685101). A quiet, dusty place, set back from the main road. Clean but old rooms, and somewhat overpriced; has its own parking. ④.

Residencial Naty, Agua Santa 16 (☎32/661720). Noisy but spacious budget rooms with the use of a large kitchen, a few blocks from the Playa Caleta Ábarca. ③.

Residencial Ona Berri, Valparaíso 618 (☎32/688187). Large *residencial* with tired but adequate rooms in a central location; some have large windows and balconies, and a few have private bath. There's usually space here. ③.

Residencial Tajamar, Alvarez 334 (☎32/974404). Reasonable rooms with bath and TV in a lovely old villa near the train station; not all the rooms have outside windows. ④.

Residencial Von Schroeders, Von Schroeders 153 (☎32/689974). Basic and rather shabby *residencial*, possibly the cheapest in town. ②.

The City

Most people come to Viña for its 3.5km of beaches, though be warned that they are impossibly crowded in January and February, and this stretch of the ocean tends to be quite polluted. There are, however, a number of appealing distractions from the sand and sea: the **Quinta Vergara** – an extravagant subtropical park – more than justifies the town's sobriquet of "Ciudad Jardín" for the town, along with the Conaf-run **Jardín Botánico**, a short bus ride from the centre. There are some handsome old residences to admire, notably the **Palacio Rioja**, whose opulent interior is preserved intact, and the **Palacio Vergara** (in the Quinta Vergara) which now houses the **Museo de Bellas Artes**. Another worthwhile museum is the **Museo Fonck**, which has some good pre-Columbian and Easter Island collections. All of these can easily be visited in a couple of days.

Plaza Vergara and Avenida Valparaíso

Viña's centre is marked by the large, green **Plaza Vergara**, full of tall, stately trees and surrounded by some fine, early twentieth-century buildings including the **Teatro Municipal** (the imposing Neoclassical building with a sweeping flight of steps leading to a grand entrance), the stately **Hotel O'Higgins**, and the Italian Renaissance-style **Club de Viña**, an exclusive gentlemen's club (opposite Fallabella). You'll also find a string of ponies and traps hanging around the square, on which you can take tours around the town (CH$6000 for 30min). The south side of the square borders **Avenida**

Valparaíso, Viña's main commercial street, lined with shops, malls and fast-food outlets, and constantly bustling with people. Most of its activity is in the five blocks between the plaza and calle Ecuador, lined with modern, attractive shops and *galerías*, far better than those in downtown Santiago. There's also a good **feria artesenal** in pasaje Cousiño, a narrow passage off the south side of the avenue, just west of Plaza Vergara.

The beaches and around

Viña's most central beach, and the only one south of the Marga Marga, is the **Playa Caleta Abarca**, a sheltered, sandy bay at the eastern end of calle Viana. Just off the beach, at the foot of Cerro Castillo, you'll find the much-photographed **Relój de Flores**, a large clock composed of colourful bedding plants and working dials. From here, the promenade continues north past the neo-Gothic **Castillo Wulff**, its spire and turrets jutting into the sea. Built in 1906 for a nitrate and coal baron, it now houses the **Museo de la Cultura del Mar** (Tues–Sat 10am–1pm & 2.30–6pm, Sun 10am–2pm; CH$400) founded in honour of Salvador Reyes Figueroa, the writer and maritime historian, displaying his collections of nineteenth-century furniture, books, paintings and nautical objects. One of the most striking features of the house is a glass-floored passage where you can stand and watch the waves breaking under your feet.

Just beyond the museum you come to the **Estero Marga Marga** – follow it inland a couple of blocks to reach the bridge that crosses it. On the other side, the **Casino Municipal** sits in the middle of its finely landscaped gardens, skirted by the coast road, **Avenida Perú** which (once past the casino gardens) is lined by high-rise condominiums, ice-cream parlours and restaurants. A pedestrian promenade runs alongside the ocean but there's no sand here, just a stretch of rocks. A few blocks north, Avenida Peru swerves inland to make way for the long unbroken strip of sand stretching for over 3km towards Reñaca. Though effectively one single beach, different sections of it are given different names: just north of Avenida Peru is **Playa Acapulco**, followed by **Playa Mirasol**, then **Playa Los Marineros**, and finally **Playa Larga**. To get to the beaches, take any of the Reñaca or Concón buses from Puente Libertad, and get off at 10 or 12 Norte for Playas Acapulco and Mirasol, or ask the driver to set you off on the coast road for the beaches further north.

Quinta Vergara and the Museo de Bellas Artes

If you make only one detour from the beach, make it to the **Quinta Vergara** (daily 7am–7pm), an exceptionally beautiful park filled with exotic, subtropical trees and surrounded by wooded hills. Since the early days of the colony, this was the site of the *casa patronal* of the Hacienda Las Siete Hermanas, owned by the prominent Carerra family. Around 1840, the hacienda was bought by the rich Portuguese businessman, Francisco Alvarez, whose wife – an amateur botanist – set out to fill her gardens with rare plants and trees. Their son, Salvador Alvarez, was a seaman and brought back exotic species from his voyages to the Far East, many of which still survive in the immaculately maintained gardens. Besides walking through the avenues and groves, you can follow paths up the hillsides, or walk round to the amphitheatre where concerts are regularly performed, including the rather dreadful Festival Internacional de la Canción, a rather kitsch and spangly pop festival that takes place every February.

In the centre of the park sits the **Palacio Vergara**, a dazzling, whitewashed Venetian-style palace built in 1906 for Blanca Vergara de Errázuriz (granddaughter of the above-mentioned Salvador, and daughter of José Francisco Vergara, who organized the official foundation of Viña in 1874). The palace is now home to the **Museo de Bellas Artes** (Tues–Sun 10am–2pm & 3–6pm; CH$300) which has a decent spread of Chilean and European paintings from the fifteenth to nineteenth centuries, including works by

Rubens, **Poussin** and a portrait by **Tintoretto** (no. 25) of a Venetian gentleman, whose startling blue eyes and delicately lit face really stand apart from the other works. The park and museum are located two blocks south of the Plaza Vergara, across the railway tracks.

Palacio Rioja and Palacio Carrasco

North of the Marga Marga at Quillota 214 you'll find the **Palacio Rioja**, built in the style of an eighteenth-century French château, its very grand entrance reached by two stairways sweeping up to a semicircular loggia. It was built in 1906 for don Fernando Rioja Medel, a Spanish millionaire who owned the Banco Español among other enterprises. His family lived in the building until 1956, when it was acquired by the Municipalidad which now runs it as a reception centre and a **museum** (Tues–Sun 10am–2pm & 3–6pm; CH$500). The entire ground floor is perfectly preserved and provides a fascinating close-up view of early twentieth-century luxury, with its *belle époque* furniture and glittering ballroom. In summertime, the *Conservatoria de Música* (which occupies the former servants' quarters in the basement) gives concerts in the palace – check in the Oficina de Turismo for details.

Nearby, at Libertad 250, is the **Palacio Carrasco**, an elegant, three-storey building designed in a French Neoclassical style by the same architect responsible for the Palacio Rioja. It's also owned by the Municipalidad, which runs it as the **Centro Cultural de Viña del Mar**, putting on a lively programme of exhibitions, plays and talks. The building also houses the municipal library and the city's historical archives.

Museo Sociedad Fonck

Just round the corner from the Palacio Carrasco, at 4 Norte 784, the **Museo Fonck** (Tues–Fri 10am–6pm, Sat & Sun 10am–2pm; CH$400) has one of the most important Easter Island collections in Chile, as well as some interesting pre-Hispanic exhibits and a modest natural history collection – though note that all the displays are poorly labelled, and there's no English-language explanation. One of the museum's best pieces stands in the garden, by the entrance: a giant stone *moai*, brought to Chile from Easter Island by the Sociedad Fonck in 1950, and one of just six that exist outside the island. Inside, the three ground-floor rooms dedicated to Easter Island include displays of wooden and stone carvings of those long, stylized faces (some of them around 500 years old), as well as jewellery, weapons, household and fishing utensils, and ceremonial objects. The rest of the ground floor contains the pre-Hispanic collections, including some delicate Mapuche silverwork, musical instruments and bearded masks, and the 3000-year-old mummy of a small, huddled child found in an ancient burial site south of Arica. Upstairs, the natural history section has some rather unsettling displays, among them a caseful of scorpions illustrated by photos of limbs deformed by their venom and an embalmed two-headed lamb, born in Casablanca in 1950 and surviving for just one week.

Jardín Botánico Nacional

Set in a sheltered valley surrounded by sun-baked hills, the Conaf-run **Jardín Botánico Nacional** (Tues–Sun 10am–6.30pm; CH$350) contains 3000 plant species from Chile, other Latin American countries, Europe and Asia. It's just six kilometres from the centre of Viña but feels far more remote – a short walk along its quiet paths and you feel you're right out in the countryside. The Jardín is a ten-minute bus ride (#20, eastbound) from calle Viana.

Eating, drinking and entertainment

Viña's **restaurants** are among the most varied outside the capital, and while they're almost without exception geared towards tourists, the quality's usually good, and they offer some welcome alternatives to the *comida típica* you're restricted to in most other places. Most, however, are fairly expensive, and if you're on a tight budget you'll have to make do with the fast-food outlets on avenidas Valparaíso and San Martín. **Nightlife** tends to be seasonal, reaching a heady peak in January and February when everyone heads for the nightclubs and bars of **Reñaca**, a suburb further up the coast (see p.141 for details). In summer, *micros* run to and from Reñaca right through the night. In winter the partying dies out, and the focus shifts back to Viña. The grand **Teatro Municipal** (☎32/681739) puts on theatre, classical music and dance performances, and there's an excellent arts **cinema**, the Cine Arte on the Plaza Vergara (through the passage off the west side of the square). For mainstream movies, check out the Olimpio at Quinta 294, the Premier at Quillota 898 and the Rex at Valparaíso 758.

Restaurants

Café Santa Fé, corner of San Martín and 8 Norte. Tex-Mex restaurant with an attractive outdoor patio and colourful decor; good food and generous portions, especially the fajitas, which are enough for two people.

Diego Pizzas, corner of San Martín and 8 Norte. Large, sunny restaurant near the ocean offering a huge choice of pizzas, all of them delicious and most of them expensive.

El Mezón con Z, Pasaje Cousiño 9, off Av Valparaíso. Stylish, studenty Spanish tapas bar and restaurant, with live music or comedy every night in summer, and at weekends in winter.

El Sin Nombre, Pasaje Cousiño 12, off Av Valparaíso. Downmarket bar-restaurant that would look more at home in Valparaíso; serves cheap grills and fried fish, and has live music or comedy at weekends.

Fogón Criollo, 5 Norte 476, near corner with 2 Poniente. Upmarket "*comida típica Chilena*" in a phoney *huaso* restaurant; the food, though, is outstanding – try the spicy pork *arollados*, or the *conejo escabechado* (a rabbit casserole).

Guris Brasileiros, San Martín 304, opposite casino gardens. Quite pricey Brazilian restaurant specializing in delicious skewered meat dishes.

Han's Dragon, corner of Libertad and 8 Norte. Excellent Chinese restaurant specializing in *sizzling platos estilo Hong Kong*. Extremely good-value fixed-price meals, as well – highly recommended.

Marisquería Isabel, calle Mercado, opposite the Mercado Municipal. Local restaurant serving authentic, inexpensive fish dishes.

Max und Möritz, 2 Poniente 377, near corner with 5 Norte. Large, tavern-style restaurant stuffed with German wine bottles, beer mats, maps and posters, and serving the most succulent meat dishes imaginable.

Bars and nightclubs

Coyote Cantina Discotheque, Arlegui 829. One of the most fashionable dance spots in Viña, playing mainstream disco music to a youngish crowd.

El Burro, Pasaje Cousiño, off Av Valparaíso. Large, dark pub that turns into a disco after midnight.

El Colmao, 4 Norte 124, near corner with 6 Poniente. Cheap beer and a lovely outdoor terrace at this mellow bar. Fills with a relaxed, studenty crowd.

El Gato de la Luna, Arlegui 396. Local bar with a good atmosphere; live music and dancing at weekends.

Hotel Gala, Arlegui 273. Stylish hotel bar, a good place for sipping cocktails to soothing jazz sounds.

In, Playa Caleta Abarca. Typical beachfront resort disco, pulsating with sun-tanned teenagers.

Manhattan, Arlegui 302. Popular nightclub, with a more local feel to it than those in Reñaca.

MOVING ON FROM VIÑA

Buses **up the coast** (Central Placeres or Sol del Pacífico) don't stop at the bus terminal, but at Avenida Libertad (just north of Puente Libertad), with frequent services to Reñaca, Concón and Quintero, and several daily to Horcón, Maitencillo, Zapallar and Papudo. *Colectivos* also pass this way en route to Reñaca, Concón and Quintero. To go **down the coast**, your best bet is to catch a bus from **Valparaíso** (see p.117), reached by any *micro* (every 10min) marked "Puerto" or "Aduana" from Plaza Vergara or Arlegui. You can also get to Valparaíso by train (every 15–30min) from the station at the corner of Bohn and Sucre, just south of Plaza Vergara, or by boat from Muelle Vergara. **Intercity buses** leave from the bus terminal on Avenida Valparaíso, two blocks east of Plaza Vergara (**to Santiago** every 15min, 6am–9.30pm), along with **buses to Mendoza** in Argentina (daily 8.30am). For more information see "Travel Details" on p.114.

Listings

Banks and exchange Most banks and *cambios* are on Arlegui: of the *cambios*, try Afex at no. 641, Cambio Andino at no. 644 or Guiñazú Cambios at no. 684. Banks on Arlegui (all with ATMs) include Banco Bhif at no. 665 and Banco Osorno at no. 501; other useful banks are Banco Sudamericano, Plaza Vergara 103, Banco Crédito e Inversiones at Valparaíso 193 and Citibank at 1 Norte 633.

Bookshops Eurotex, in Galería Paseo del Mar, Valparaíso 554, for English-language fiction. Second-hand English novels (mostly best-seller types) available in Contactolibros, Vonn Schroeders 181.

Car rental Anditour, Viana 31 (☎32/971996); Bert Rent a Car, Libertad 892 (☎32/681151); Euro Renta a Car, *Hotel O'Higgins*, Plaza Vergara (☎32/883559); Flota Verschae, Libertad 1030 (☎32/974235); Prodaro, 5 Norte 551 (☎32/970186).

Laundry Lavarapido, Arlegui 440, three blocks west of Plaza Vergara.

Post office Correos de Chile is next to the Oficina de Turismo, between Plaza Vergara and Puente Libertad.

Telephone offices Several offices, located at: Valparaíso 628, near pasaje Cousiño; corner of Valparaíso and Villanelo; Valparaíso 510; and 14 Norte 1184.

South to Santo Domingo

Given that the coastal resorts **south of Valparaíso** are closer to, and more easily reached from, Santiago than those further north, it's not surprising that they're among the busiest and most developed of the *litoral central*. Most of them are strung along the 40km coast road, stretching from the rather sprawling, family-oriented **Algarrobo** down to the exclusive **Rocas de Santa Domingo**. In between, and linked by numerous *micros* and *colectivos*, is a trail of little seaside towns packed full of hotels, cabañas and *marisquerías*, most of them sitting on long, golden-sand beaches. Despite its dependence on tourism, this stretch of coastline is not without its charms, especially in the older places like **Cartagena** and **Las Cruces**, whose nineteenth-century houses and narrow streets give them the air of faded Victorian seaside resorts. Another attraction is **Isla Negra**, the site of Pablo Neruda's extraordinary house, now a museum. You might also consider heading for the little chunk between Algarrobo and Valparaíso, not yet connected to the coast road, where the tiny resorts of **Laguna Verde** and **Quintay** are as deserted as you could wish for outside the summer months.

Laguna Verde

Some 18km south of Valparaíso, the coast curves in to another, smaller bay, sheltering the tiny settlement of **LAGUNA VERDE**. Hemmed in by steep, green hills, its golden beach is strikingly beautiful, though marred by an ugly thermoelectric plant on the south side of the bay, and a line of pylons running behind. The small community here serves the local electricity and logging industries, and the place has a rough-edged, neglected feel to it, its ramshackle houses spread along a few dirt roads. That said, it's a quiet, peaceful spot to lie by the ocean, and makes an easy day-trip from Valparaíso, forty minutes away **by bus** (Central Placeres #3, every 30min from the corner of Victoria and Rancagua, behind the congress building). Should you want **to stay**, *Camping los Olivios* (no phone; Sept–March) is nicely situated in an olive grove, or you could try the basic *Hostería Laguna Verde* (☎32/348035; ③) at the northern end of the town. For **eating**, there are a couple of snack bars and food stores, but little else.

Quintay

Until recently reached only by a poor dirt track, **QUINTAY** is now served by a newly paved road that brings an increasing number of in-the-know visitors to its superb beach each summer. It's still, however, a low-key, family sort of place, and outside high season feels wonderfully remote. It falls into two areas, the *caleta* and the beach, separated by a long walk. From the road off the main square, a path leads down to the **caleta**, a tiny, picturesque cove full of colourful fishing boats and once the site of a whaling station (locals claim the whales have started to come back into the bay). This is the place to head for at lunchtime, when you can feast at excellent **marisquerías** like *El Rey del Congrio* (on the path down), run by the same wizened old woman for as long as anyone can remember, or the smart, new *Restaurant Caleta Quintay* down by the boats.

Further from the centre, reached by a track branching south of the asphalt road coming into the village (20–30min on foot from the *plaza*), the sheltered **Playa Grande** is among the most attractive of the *litoral central* beaches, with powdery sand and a dramatic backdrop of pine-covered hills. *Hostería Playa Grande* (☎2/271 7317; ④) offers smart **accommodation** just off the beach; otherwise you'll have to stay in the village where you'll find good-value rooms at *Residencial Mónica* (☎32/362090; ③) on Avenida Teniente Merino, approaching the track to the *caleta*. From Valparaíso, you can get here by **bus** with Ciferal Express (☎32/362101; 3 daily from the corner of Colón and Argentina) and Buses Mirasol (☎32/235985; 2 daily from the terminal), as well as **colectivos** from behind the terminal.

Algarrobo

ALGARROBO is probably the most popular family resort of the *litoral central*, but with a trail of modern hotels dominating the coastline it can't be said to be the most attractive. Nonetheless, it has a number of good **beaches**, including the gorgeous horseshoe bay of El Canelo, on the southern side of the promontory used by the marina. It also has a **penguin sanctuary**, on the rocky islet just off the promontory, visited in summer by *lanchas* from the Club Deportivo. Wrapping up the town's attractions are the **Iglesia de la Candelaria**, a red-walled adobe church built in 1837 in the traditional style of a colonial rural chapel, and the **Cascadas de San Jerónimo**, a series of waterfalls forming natural pools you can bathe in, reached after a half-hour walk through a lushly vegetated ravine (take a bus north along the coast road and ask the driver to drop you off at the puente San Jerónimo, just north of the path).

Algarrobo has a **tourist information kiosk** just off Playa Las Cadenas (Jan & Feb daily 9am–10.30pm; March–Dec Sat & Sun 9am–7pm; no phone) and, opposite, a **bank** with an ATM. The cheapest **rooms** are in the grotty *Residencial Colonial,* just north of the church at Carlos Alessandri 1468 (no phone, ③); opposite, the spotless *Residencial Vera* (☎35/481131; ④) is much nicer, with some rooms backing right onto the beach. Further south, at no. 2156, *Hotel Costa Sur* (☎35/481151; ⑤) has comfortable rooms with bath. There are several down-to-earth **places to eat** on the beach near the tourist kiosk, including the Spanish-run *La Gamba,* Carlos Alessandri 1915.

El Quisco and El Punto de Tralca

Four kilometres south of Algarrobo, **EL QUISCO** is a busy string of hotels, holiday homes, restaurants and bars spread along the coast road. Its **beach** is long and attractive, with a little *caleta de pescadores* that supplies good, fresh fish to the nearby restaurants. The *Gran Hotel Italia* on the main road at Isidoro Bubournais 413 (☎ & fax 35/471631; ④) has comfortable **rooms**, nice gardens and a pool, and you'll find cool, quiet rooms at the immaculate *Residencial San Pedro,* San Pedro 094 (☎35/472158; ③). There are a couple of good if unimaginatively named **fish restaurants**, including *Caleta Miramar,* down by the *caleta,* and *La Caleta* up on the main road.

EL PUNTO DE TRALCA, the next bus stop south, is the site of eight blocks of granite sitting on the headland, carved into giant faces by a group of French sculptors in honour of Pablo Neruda. Their sad, haunted look is accentuated by all the litter blowing around and the graffiti scribbled over them. The hill leads down to a rocky promontory and a long beach sweeping in a thin crescent around the bay.

Isla Negra

The tiny hamlet of **ISLA NEGRA** was put firmly on the map when **Pablo Neruda** moved into a half-built house on the beach in 1939. On and off, Neruda spent the next forty years of his life enlarging his house and filling it with the strange and beautiful objects he ceaselessly gathered from far-flung corners of the world. The Fundación Neruda – acting on the wishes of the poet's widow, Matilde Urrutia – has transferred Neruda's and Matilde's graves to its garden and operates the house as a **museum** (guided tours in English or Spanish, Dec 15–March 11 Tues–Sun 10am–8pm; March 12–Dec 14 Tues–Fri 10am–2pm & 3–6.30pm, Sat & Sun 10am–6.30pm; closed for maintenance two unfixed weeks in May; CH$1000, or CH$2000 for English guide; ☎35/461284). Inside, its winding passages and odd-shaped rooms are crammed full of exotic objects like ships' figureheads, Hindu carvings, African and Japanese masks, ships in bottles, sea shells, butterflies, coloured bottles, Victorian postcards and a good deal more. It's an extraordinary place, spoiled only by the hurried, regimented pace of the tours.

There's little else to Isla Negra save a small, pretty beach and a couple of handicraft stalls in the main square, but if you want to stay you'll find good-value **rooms** at *Pensión Guillermina* (☎35/461090; ③) on the main road by the bus stop (ask in *Café-Bar Cali*), and comfortable *cabañas* at *La Flor de Isla Negra* (☎35/461043; ④) on the same road at no. 4160.

El Tabo

Just 2km south of Isla Negra, **EL TABO** is a small seaside resort with a handful of hotels and restaurants, and two beaches. **Playa Chépica** is large and filled with soft, fine sand but is slowly being spoiled by encroaching development; **Playa el Caleuche**, to the north, is a tiny, rugged beach with lovely views – the rest of the coast is completely hidden from sight, and all you can see are rocks and ocean. There's a delightful

PABLO NERUDA

While teaching in Temuco in 1916, the Chilean poet Gabriela Mistral – who would later become the first Latin American to win the Nobel Prize for Literature – came across a twelve-year-old boy called Neftalí Reyes, the son of a local railwayman. Less than ten years later this same Neftalí – now a tall, pale and impoverished young man who wandered the streets of Santiago dressed in a swirling cape and a wide sombrero – was making his own name in the world of poetry, under the pseudonym of Pablo Neruda. The coincidental meeting of the two is striking, for Neruda was, of course, to become Chile's second Nobel Laureate, in 1971. He published his first collection of poems, *Crepusculario*, in 1923 at his own expense, selling his furniture and pawning the watch given to him by his father to cover the costs. Success came quickly and when, the following year, he published a slim volume of sensual, tormented verses under the title of *Veinte Poemas de Amor y una Canción Desesperada* ("Twenty love poems and a song of despair") he suddenly found himself, at the age of twenty, with one of the fastest-growing readerships on the continent.

Despite the success of *Veinte Poemas*, Neruda still needed to earn a living to fund his writing, and so, aged twenty-four, he began his career as Chilean consul in Rangoon, the first of many posts. It seems ironic that this most "Chilean" of poets, whose verses are imprinted with the forests, rain, sea, lakes and volcanoes of southern Chile, and whose countrymen love him as a man of their soil, should have spent so much of his adult life far from his native land. His years in Rangoon, Colombo, Jakarta and Singapore were often intensely lonely, but also coloured with vivid episodes, not least the many sexual adventures he fondly recalls in his *Memoirs*. The most dramatic of these was his love affair with a woman in Rangoon who called herself Josie Bliss. Described by Neruda as his "Burmese panther . . . a love-smitten terrorist capable of anything", she was a jealous and possessive lover who would sometimes terrorize him with her silver dagger. When he was transferred to Ceylon, he left secretly, without telling her, but she turned up on his doorstep several months later, carrying a bag of rice (believing it grew only in Rangoon) and a selection of their favourite records. Neruda's outright rejection of her was to haunt him for many years, and Josie Bliss makes several appearances in his poems.

During his time in Asia, Neruda's poetry (published in the collection *Residencia en la Tierra*) was inward-looking, reflecting his experience of dislocation and solitude. His posts in Barcelona (1934) and Madrid (1935–36), however, marked a major turning point

little **bar-restaurant** down here, *El Caleuche* (closed Mon), providing excellent seafood against a perfect backdrop.

If you want to stay, you'll find clean, sunny **rooms** (some overlooking the sea) at *Residencial El Mar,* Av el Mar 1111 (☎35/461232; ③), and smart rooms around an attractive courtyard at *Hostería Montemar* at Carlos Mockenberg 406, off Playa Chépica (☎35/461904; ④). There are a few other hotels and restaurants up on the main road by the bus stop, including *Rengo*, a good-value, old-fashioned fish restaurant. Also worth a look up here is Alta Marea, at Serrano 45, a **bookshop** and small publishing house dedicated to publishing and selling the works of contemporary Chilean poets.

Las Cruces

Nestling between two hills, its houses spilling down to a small, sandy bay, **LAS CRUCES** is one of the prettiest resorts south of Valparaíso. Its popularity dates from the early twentieth century when it was linked to Cartagena by a horse-drawn "railway" in 1911. Some of the grand mansions from those early days are still dotted about the hillside, such as the English-style Castilo Negro, and the Casa Pacheco, down by the beach. A footpath from the beach leads north to the **Punta el Lacha**, a promontory giving fabulous views up to the Punta de Tralca and down to Santo Domingo.

in his life and his work: with the outbreak of the Spanish Civil War, and the assassination of his close friend, García Lorca, Neruda became intensely committed to active politics. As consul for emigration, he threw himself into the task of providing Spanish refugees with a safe passage to Chile, and at the same time sought to give his poetry a meaningful "place in man's struggle", with *España en el Corazón*. On returning to Chile he became a member of the Communist Pary, and was elected senator for Antofagasta and Tarapacá regions, a role he took very seriously, tirelessly touring the desert pampas to talk to the workers. His politics were to land him in serious trouble, however, when newly elected president González Videla, who had enlisted Neruda's help in managing his presidential campaign, switched sides from left to right, and outlawed Communism. When Neruda publicly attacked Videla, the president issued a warrant for his arrest, and he was forced into hiding. In 1949 the poet was smuggled across a southern pass in the Andes on horseback, and spent the next three years in exile, mainly in Europe.

It was during his years of exile that Neruda met the woman who was to inspire some of his most beautiful love poetry: Matilde Urrutia, whom he was later to marry. Neruda had been married twice before: first, briefly, to a Dutch woman he'd met as a young consul in Rangoon; and then for eighteen years to the Argentinian painter, Delia del Carril. The poet's writings scarcely mention his first wife, nor their daughter – his only child – who died when she was just eight years old, but Delia is described as "sweetest of consorts, thread of steel and honey. . . my perfect mate for eighteen years". It was so as not to wound Delia that *Los Versos del Capitán* – a book of passionate love poems written for Matilde on their secret hideaway in Capri – was published anonymously. Nonetheless, when the order for his arrest was revoked three years after his return to Santiago in 1940, Neruda divorced Delia and moved into *La Chascona*, in Santiago, and then to *Isla Negra* with Matilde. Based in Chile from now on, Neruda devoted himself to politics and poetry almost in equal measure. His dedication to both causes found its reward at the same time: in 1970, Salvador Allende, whose presidential campaign Neruda had tirelessly participated in, was elected president at the head of the socialist Unidad Popular. Then, the following year, Neruda was awarded the Nobel Prize for Literature. His happiness was to be short-lived, however. Diagnosed with cancer, and already bedridden, the poet was unable to withstand the shock brought on by the 1973 military coup, which left his dear friend Allende dead. Less than two weeks later, on September 23, Neruda died in Santiago with Matilde at his side.

Hotel Villa Trouville, just off the beach (☎35/633 9192; ④) has good **rooms** with bath, kitchen and excellent views (especially from no. 9, the corner room). For something a little more economical, try the spotless *La Posada* at Av Errázuriz 804 (☎35/233520; ④) or *Residencial Alvarez* (☎35/212729, ④) down by the beach, which also has a popular **restaurant**.

Cartagena

CARTAGENA is a colourful and rather flamboyant little seaside town made up of narrow, twisting streets and unruly houses clinging to the hills around the bay. Unlike most of the resorts, it doesn't feel lonely or abandoned outside high season – indeed, the time to come here is *not* January and February when the town is swollen by some 400,000 visitors, but rather the warm, balmy months just before or after, when the place is lively but not frenetic.

In the upper town, the palm-filled Plaza de Armas is flanked by the Municipalidad, which houses an **Oficina de Turismo** in its basement (Dec 15–March 15 daily 8am–1.30pm & 2–8pm; March 16–Dec 14 same hours but closed Sat & Sun; ☎35/450319). From here, winding streets and stairways lead down to the **Playa Chica**, south of the square, and the **Playa Grande**, to the north, connected by a busy promenade lined with handicraft stalls, amusement arcades and good-value **fish restaurants**

– try *Fafra* on the Playa Chica, or *Montemar, El Tiburón* or *Pato Santis* on the Playa Grande.

There's an abundance of simple, inexpensive **accommodation** spread all over town, including (just down from the square) *Residencial El Refugio*, Av Cartagena 50 (☎35/450586; ②), the *Gran Hotel*, Casanova 170 (☎35/450381; ③), with fine views over the bay from its *comedor*, and (down towards Playa Chica) *Residencial Condell*, Condell 176 (in Santiago, ☎2/271 2777; ②), with spotless rooms, a few with sea views. If you're after more comfort, *Residencial Violeta*, Condell 140 (☎35/450372; ④) offers modern rooms and a pool, while *Hotel La Bahia* on Playa Chica (☎35/450534; ④) has comfortable rooms and cabins (no sea views) right by the beach. There's also a municipal **campsite** at the far end of Playa Grande.

San Antonio

Compared to its neighbours, the busy working port of **SAN ANTONIO**, 112km south of Valparaíso, is refreshingly indifferent to tourism. True, there's a beach and a few hotels in the southern suburb of **Llolleo**, 4km down the coast, but San Antonio's real attraction is its bustling **fish quay** where a huge market sells row upon row of glistening fish and every type of *Crustacea* imaginable, and dozens of fishermen rush about in yellow plastic overalls. You can observe all this activity from one of the little *marisquerías* by the market, safe in the knowledge that your lunch is only a few hours dead. The quay is across the railway tracks south of the main square.

Another reason you might want to visit San Antonio is to use its **banks** – the first south of Algarrobo. You'll find several with an **ATM** on Avenida Centenario, off the main square. A short bus ride from Cartagena, San Antonio is best visited on a lunchtime excursion and it's unlikely you'll want to stay. If you do need a **room**, though, try the small, pleasant *Hotel Casablanca* opposite the port at 21 de Mayo 280 (☎35/212290; ③–④).

Rocas de Santo Domingo

Marking the end of the coast road and the southern extreme of the *litoral central*, **ROCAS DE SANTO DOMINGO** is less a holiday resort and more an exclusive residential area by the sea. Formerly an empty wasteland on the southern bank of the río Maipo, it was designed and built from scratch in the 1940s following a nationwide architectural competition. Fifty years on, it still feels slightly artificial, its gardens too manicured, its streets too tidy. The beach however, is superb, stretching 20km south of the town, backed by nothing but sand dunes; even in the height of summer you don't have to walk far to escape the crowds. There are only two **hotels** in Santo Domingo, both of them expensive: *Hotel Rocas Santo Domingo*, La Ronda 130 (☎35/444356, fax 444494; ⑤) and *Apart-Hotel Pidra del Sol*, Av Pacífico 010 (☎ & fax 35/283011; ⑤). The sand dunes further south, however, make a perfect place for unofficial **camping**.

North to Papudo

North of Viña, a good road meanders up the coast to the small fishing town of **Papudo** and beyond, hugging the oceanside in some stretches, dipping inland in others. It's far quieter than the southern coast road, and very beautiful in some parts, particularly the northern reaches towards Papudo as you approach the parched hills and rugged outlines of the Norte Chico. From Viña there are countless local buses to the busy neighbouring resorts of **Reñaca** and **Concón**, and regular but less frequent services to the other resorts, further north; most can also be reached directly from Santiago (see "Travel Details" on p.109). Unless you've got your own vehicle, your best option is to pick one or two places and head for these, rather than count on resort-hopping up the coast, which is slow and tiresome on public transport, and doesn't offer enough variety to be worth the effort.

Reñaca

Six kilometres north of Viña, heavily developed **REÑACA** is a 1.5-kilometre stretch of coast swamped by bars, restaurants and ugly apartment blocks built in tiers up the hillside. It's also the favoured resort of Chile's beautiful young things (it's the teen equivalent of Viña) who flock to its long beach by day and its bars and discos by night. **Accommodation** here is very expensive, with the exception of a pleasant campsite up on Santa Luisa 401 (☎32/832830); it's quite a steep walk from the beach but you can take the Concón bus up and down the hill. Otherwise, you're better off staying in Viña and coming in by *micro*, but if Reñaca's charms prove truly irresistible you could try *Cabañas Central*, Central 171 (☎32/833695; ⑤), or *Piero's Hotel*, overlooking the beach at Segunda 95 (☎32/830280; ⑦). Reñaca's **discos** are also expensive (average cover about CH$6000) but remain resolutely popular throughout the summer season; the most fashionable include *Neverland* on Playa Las Salinas, just south of Reñaca, *Cocodrilo*, a little further along the coast at Borgoño 13101 and *Kamikaze*, in from the coast at Vicuña Mackenna 1106.

Concón

From Reñaca there are two roads to **CONCÓN**, 10km north, one clinging to the scenic rocky coastline (passing a small sea lion colony off *El Mirador de los Lobos Marinos*), the other – followed by most buses – running inland, on the other side of the immense sand dunes rising steeply from the sea.

Concón's a funny sort of place, part concrete terraced apartment blocks, part elegant villas with flower-filled gardens, and part run-down, working-class fishing village. The most interesting bit of town is **La Boca**, the ramshackle commercial centre at the mouth of the río Aconcagua. The *caleta* here was used to export the produce of the haciendas of the Aconcagua valley in the nineteenth century and is now a bustling fish quay, lined with modest, down-to-earth **marisquerías**, many with freshly caught fish hanging up for sale over the counter. They all serve first-rate seafood, *La Perla del Pacífico* particularly standing out.

The beach at La Boca, the **Playa de Concón**, is rather sad-looking, though if you cross the bridge over the Aconcagua and follow a path branching off from the railway tracks, you'll reach the vast **Playa de Ritoque**, stretching 11km north to Quintero, gloriously empty save for its north and south extremes. The most developed and popular beaches are **Playa Amarilla** and **Playa Negra**, south of La Boca. Concón makes an easy day-trip from Viña, but if you want **to stay** over you could try *Hostal Casa Rosada*, Pedro de Valdivia 514 (☎32/813040; ④), or the faded seafront *Hotel Internacional* on Playa Amarilla (☎32/811915; ⑤); there's also a well-maintained **campsite** a short walk north of the bridge over the Aconcagua and wonderfully isolated outside high season.

Quintero

Spread over a rocky peninsula studded with horseshoe bays of soft, white sand, **QUINTERO** is an attractive place to spend a day or two lying on the beach – though not in high season, when its small coves bulge with busloads of day-trippers from Santiago. From the pier at the end of the seafront avenue, a coastal footpath laces its way through pine and eucalyptus trees, past tiny beaches with romantic names like *Playa el Duranzo* and *Playa Los Enamorados*. The path ends at *la Cueva del Pirata* at the tip of the peninsula, its walls decorated with bizarre graffiti portraits of Mother Theresa, Albert

Einstein, Jimi Hendrix and other luminaries of the twentieth century. From here, climb the steps to the lookout point, where huge slabs of rock plunge into the ocean – a fine place to sit and watch the sun go down, surrounded by crashing waves and spray.

You'll find inexpensive **rooms** at *Residencial Casa de Piedra*, a beautiful old red-brick house at Luís Cousiño 2076 (☎32/930196; ③) and *Residencial María Alejandra*, close to the main square at Lord Cochrane 157 (☎32/930266; ③). If you want sea views and a private bath, try *Brazilian Suites*, 21 de Mayo 1336 (☎32/930590; ④), which also offers *talasoterapía* – bathtubs filled with warm sea water, apparently with therapeutic qualities. For sheer luxury, head for the *Hotel Yachting Club* at Luís Acevedo 1736 (☎32/930061, fax 931557; ⑥), a stylish hotel looking onto the ocean whose rooms have floor to ceiling windows. *Restaurant Victoria*, up near the Hotel Yachting Club at Vicuña Mackenna 1460, is the best **place to eat**, offering good-value home cooking and terrific views. Quintero has a **bank** with an ATM, near the Municipalidad on Avenida 21 de Mayo.

Horcón

A chaotic tumble of houses straggling down the hill to a rocky bay, **HORCÓN** is a charming and picturesque if slightly tatty fishing village. In summer it's taken over by artisans selling jewellery and leatherware on the beach and unfeasible numbers of young Chileans who come to chill out for the weekend – this is the alternative Reñaca, catering to the hippieish element of Chile's youth. Outside these heady months, Horcón takes on a quieter air: old men sit around the *caleta* and talk about the weather, and not a great deal seems to happen. The beach in front of the village is narrow and uninviting but a short walk along pasaje Miramar (opposite the CTC office) takes you to **Playa Cau-Cau**, a lovely, sheltered beach surrounded by wooded hills: lying on it, and eating in the excellent, good-value **marisquerías** clustered around the *caleta* is pretty much all there is to do here. If this appeals, you'll find good, comfortable **rooms** at *Arancibia* (☎32/796169; ④) down by the waterfront, and *Alojamiento Juan Esteban*, pasaje Miramar 2 (☎32/796056; ③), and tireder ones at *Habitaciones Helia Gonzalez*, pasaje Miramar 03 (☎32/796050; ③), through an alley next to no. 05.

Maitencillo

Stretching four kilometres along one main street, **MAITENCILLO** is little more than a long, narrow strip of holiday homes, *cabañas* and hotels strung along the shoreline, catering to families from the capital attempting to get away from it all. The chief reason for coming here is the **Playa Aguas Blancas**, a superb white-sand beach sweeping 5km south of the village, backed by steep sandstone cliffs. The only **accommodation** at this southern extreme is *Cabañas Donde Julian*, Aguas Blancas 078 (☎ & fax 32/771091; ⑥; bargain hard outside high season), offering a handful of spacious cabins looking right onto the ocean. Towards the northern end of the shore, your best bet is *Residencial Abanico* at Av del Mar 664 (☎32/771141; ④), with comfortable rooms and private bath. You'll find excellent, imaginative **seafood** at *La Pajarera*, towards the southern end of Avenida del Mar (and linked by funicular to *Marbella Resort*, an exclusive, Club Med-type complex sitting on top of the cliff), while *Restaurant La Caleta*, just off Playa La Caleta, is more homespun and less expensive. Best of all, if you're in a *cabaña* with a kitchen, choose your supper from the hooks of fish and buckets of clams, oysters and mussels at the morning market by the *caleta*, and cook it yourself.

Cachagua

CACHAGUA is home to one of the most beautiful beaches of the *litoral*, a wide expanse of golden sand curling round the bay, backed by gentle hills. It's further blessed by an almost total absence of holiday homes and *cabañas* on the land off the beach, which is instead given over to a golf course. Just off the coast, the Isla de los Pingüinos is a **penguin sanctuary** which local fishermen sometimes offer to take tourists to – accept at your peril, for the smell is truly nauseating. What little **accommodation** Cachagua offers is up in the village, back from the beach: Sra Albertina Sepúlveda, who runs the bazaar at Cachagua 658 (☎33/771044; ③), and Sra Juana Ormeño at Nemesio Vicuña 250 (☎33/771034; ③) both offer simple, adequate rooms. For **eating**, you'll have to make do with the uninspiring fries and grills dished up at *Donde Juanito*, Cachagua 264 and *El Pollo con Chaleco*, nearby on the other side of the road.

Zapallar

Certainly the classiest, and possibly the most attractive of the *litoral*'s resorts, **ZAPALLAR** is set on a sheltered, horseshoe bay backed by lushly wooded hills where luxurious holiday homes and handsome old mansions nestle between the pine trees. Relaxing on the beach is the principal attraction, but you could also spend half an hour strolling along the coastal path around the bay, or walking up Avenida Zapallar, admiring its turn-of-the-century mansions. A more strenuous possibility would be to climb the 692m-high **Cerro Higuera** that rises sharply between Zapallar and Papudo: the path, starting across the main road behind the tennis club, is very difficult to find, but the views from the top are superb. You can go down the other side, to Papudo, where you can catch a *micro* back to Zapallar; allow about three hours up, and a couple to get down.

If you feel like splashing out, the stylish *Hotel Isla Seca* (☎33/711508, fax 711502; ⑥) up by the main road, at the northern end of the bay, offers good-quality **rooms**, its own pool and magnificent views, while *Hostal Villa Alicia*, Moisés Chacón 280 (☎33/741176; ④), is a good deal simpler but comfortable enough. Also, the woman in the shop next to the bus stop might be able to let you know who's renting private rooms in the town. There's an excellent but pricey **restaurant** at the *Hotel Isla Seca*, and a superbly situated little fish restaurant, *Chiringuito*, down by the *caleta* at the southern tip of the bay (Dec–Feb daily; March–Nov closed all day Mon & Tues–Thurs eves).

Papudo

PAPUDO is the northernmost resort of the *litoral central*, giving way to deserted coves and sporadic fishing villages scattered up the coast of the Norte Chico. Development here hasn't been as graceful as in neighbouring Zapallar, and several ugly buildings mar the seafront. That said, the steep hills looming dramatically behind the town are undeniably beautiful, and the place has a friendly, local atmosphere, particularly outside high season. The best beach is the long **Playa Grande** by the municipal park – in fine weather you can hire horses here and go for exhilarating rides across the sands.

Papudo has a wealth of good-value **accommodation** centred mainly around the square and on Fernández Concha, branching off from it. The cheapest is the dilapidated *Hotel Plaza* (☎33/791240; ③; closed April–Dec); other options include *Residencial Armandini*, Fernández Concha 525 (☎33/791139; ④); *Hotel Moderno* at no. 150 (☎33/791114; ④; rooms in main building best); and *La Abeja* by the beach at Chorrillos 36 (☎ & fax 33/791116; ④), all of them clean and with private bath. Papudo is also home to the most offbeat **restaurant** along the entire coast: *El Barco Rojo* on Playa Grande, owned by a hip young Parisian who arranges funky jazz and Latin concerts in his restaurant by night.

travel details

Buses

Valparaíso to: Algarrobo (every 15min; 1hr 10min); Arica (16 daily; 29hr); Casablanca (every 15min; 30min); Copiapó (6 daily; 12hr); Coquimbo (11 daily; 6hr 45min); El Quisco (every 15min; 1hr 20min); El Tabo (every 15min; 1hr 30min); Iquique (16 daily; 25hr); Isla Negra (every 15min; 1hr 25min); La Serena (16 daily; 7 daily); Laguna Verde (every 30min; 40min); Maitencillo (1 daily; 1hr 40min); Olmué/Granizo (every 10min; 1hr); Papudo (3 daily; 2hr); Puerto Montt (4 daily; 18hr); Quintay (5 daily; 45min); Quintero (3 daily; 1hr); San Antonio (every 15min; 1hr 40min); Santiago (every 10min; 1hr 40min); Temuco (3 daily; 10hr 20min); Zapallar (3 daily; 1hr 45min).

Viña del Mar to: Arica (2 daily; 29hr); Concón (every 10min; 10min); Copiapó (11 daily; 12hr); Horcón (every 60min; 1hr); Iquique (6 daily; 25hr); La Serena (14 daily; 7hr); Maitencillo (every 60min; 1hr 20min); Papudo (3 daily; 1hr 45min); Puerto Montt (4 daily; 18hr); Quintero (every 40min; 45min); Reñaca (every 10min; 25min); Santiago (every 10min; 1hr 40min); Zapallar (every 60min; 1hr 30min).

CHAPTER THREE

EL NORTE CHICO

Chile's "little north" is a land of rolling, sun-baked hills streaked with sudden river valleys that cut across the earth in a flash of green. It's what geographers call a "transitional zone", its semi-arid scrubland and sparse vegetation marking the transformation from the fertile heartland to the barren Atacama desert. The **NORTE CHICO** has no official delimitation but is usually considered to start somewhere around the río Aconcagua, just north of Santiago, and to end at the río Copiapó, some 700km further north. In between, a series of rivers – notably the Choapa, the Limarí, the Elqui and the Huasco – flow year-round from the Andes to the coast, allowing the surrounding land to be irrigated and cultivated. The result is spectacular: lush, emerald-green terraces laden with olives, apricots and vines snake between the brown, parched walls of the valleys, forming a sensational visual contrast. The most famous product of these valleys is **pisco**, a white, aromatic brandy distilled from sun-dried grapes and treasured by Chileans as their national drink (though it probably originated in Peru).

Far more than agriculture, though, it's **mining** that's really shaped the Norte Chico's growth, giving birth to towns, ports, railways and roads, and drawing large numbers of settlers to seek their fortune here. **Gold** was mined first by the Incas for ritual offerings, and then intensively by the Spaniards until the end of the eighteenth century. Next came the great **silver** bonanza of the nineteenth century, when a series of dramatic silver strikes – some of them accidental – set a frenzy of mining and prospecting in motion, propelling the region into its heyday. Further riches and glory came when the discovery of huge **copper** deposits turned the Norte Chico into the world's largest copper producer from the 1840s to 1870s. Still the most important regional industry, its presence is most visible up in the cordillera, where huge mining trucks hurtle around the mountain roads, enveloped in clouds of dust.

The largest population centre (and most fashionable seaside resort) is **La Serena**, its attractive, colonial-style architecture and lively atmosphere making it one of the few cities of the north worth visiting for its own sake. It also makes a good base for exploring the beautiful **Elqui Valley**, immortalized in the verses of the Nobel laureate Gabriela Mistral, and home to luxuriant vines and idyllic riverside hamlets. Also within easy reach of La Serena, **Parque Nacional Fray Jorge** has its own coastal microclimate that supports a small, damp cloudforest – rather mangy compared to the great forests of the south but quite extraordinary in this landscape of brittle shrubs and cactus plants. Another botanical wonder is the famous *desierto florido* or **flowering desert** that appears when the normally dry earth sprouts vast expanses of vibrantly coloured flowers after heavy winter rains – a rare, unpredictable phenomenon that occurs on average once every four to eight years.

Perhaps the most seductive attraction of the Norte Chico is its string of superb **beaches**, many of them tantalizingly visible from the Panamericana as you head north from Santiago. The most accessible are located south of La Serena, including **Los Molles**, **Pichidangui**, **Los Vilos**, **Tongoy** and **Guanaqueros**, all of them excellent. Beyond La Serena the highway veers inland for the next 350km, coming back to the coast near **Bahía Inglesa**, famous throughout Chile for its turquoise waters. About 70km inland from here, **Copiapó** is the northernmost city of the Norte Chico. A tidy,

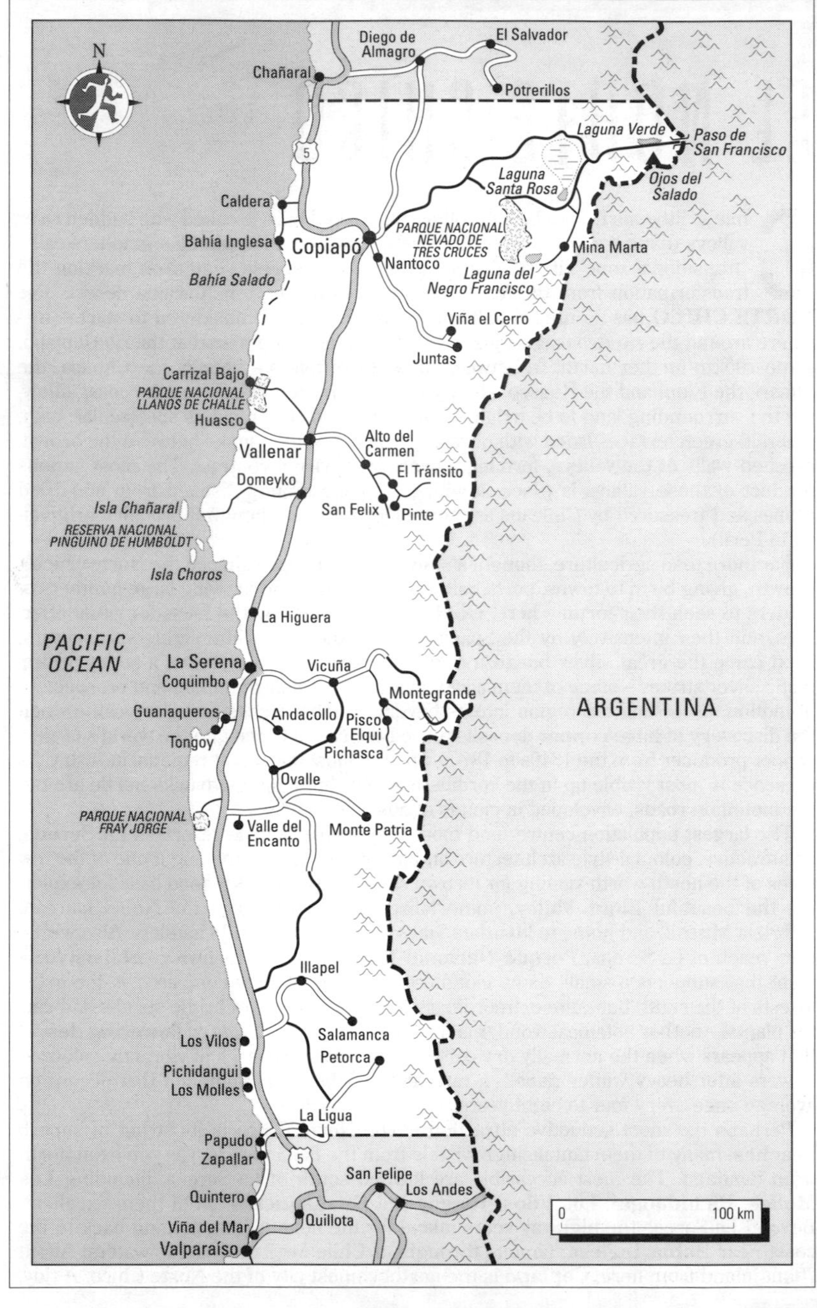
N
Diego de Almagro
El Salvador
Chañaral
Potrerillos
5
Laguna Verde
Paso de San Francisco
Laguna Santa Rosa
Ojos del Salado
Caldera
Bahía Inglesa
Copiapó
PARQUE NACIONAL NEVADO DE TRES CRUCES
Nantoco
Mina Marta
Bahía Salado
Laguna del Negro Francisco
Viña el Cerro
Juntas
Carrizal Bajo
PARQUE NACIONAL LLANOS DE CHALLE
Huasco
Vallenar
Alto del Carmen
El Tránsito
Domeyko
Isla Chañaral
San Felix
Pinte
RESERVA NACIONAL PINGUINO DE HUMBOLDT
Isla Choros
La Higuera
PACIFIC OCEAN
La Serena
Vicuña
Coquimbo
Montegrande
ARGENTINA
Guanaqueros
Andacollo
Pisco Elqui
Tongoy
Pichasca
Ovalle
PARQUE NACIONAL FRAY JORGE
Valle del Encanto
Monte Patria
Illapel
Salamanca
Los Vilos
Petorca
Pichidangui
Los Molles
La Ligua
Papudo
Zapallar
5
San Felipe
Los Andes
Quintero
0
100 km
Viña del Mar
Quillota
Valparaíso

ACCOMMODATION PRICE CODES

Prices are for the cheapest **double room** in high season. At the lower end of the scale, **single travellers** can expect to pay half this rate, but mid- and upper-range hotels usually charge the same for a single as for a double. For more information see p.27 in Basics.

① Less than US$10/CH$4800
② US$10–20/CH$4800–9600
③ US$20–30/CH$9600–10,080
④ US$30–50/CH$10,080–24,000
⑤ US$50–75/CH$24,000–36,000
⑥ US$75–100/CH$36,000–48,000
⑦ US$100–150/CH$48,000–72,000
⑧ over US$150/over CH$72,000

compact place, it serves as a useful springboard for excursions into the high cordillera, where the **Parque Nacional Nevado de Tres Cruces**, the **Volcán Ojos de Salado** and **Laguna Verde** present some of Chile's most magnificent and least-visited landscapes, taking in snow-capped volcanoes, bleached-white salt flats and azure lakes.

Heading north from Santiago

North of Santiago, the Panamericana weaves its way through lush valleys that gradually take on the sunburnt, semi-arid tones of the Norte Chico. Evidence of farming and habitation peter out, and soon you're in wild, open country where the only signs of life are the numerous goats that roam the hills. The first town you come to is **La Ligua**, set 6km back from the highway, which at this point turns towards the coast.

La Ligua

The turn-off from the highway to **LA LIGUA** is announced by groups of energetic white-coated women trying to tempt you to buy their "*dulces de La Ligua*" – sweet, sugary cakes unaccountably famous throughout Chile. A bustling agricultural town, La Ligua's chief appeal is its setting, enfolded as it is by undulating hills that take on a rich honey glow in the early evening sunlight. There is no particular reason to stop off here but if you do, be sure to visit the **Museo de La Ligua** at Pedro Polanco 698 (Tues–Fri 9am–1pm & 3–6.30pm, Sat 10am–2pm; CH$250); its well-presented displays include the skeleton and reconstructed burial site of a thirty-year-old Diaguita woman, ritually burned in the late sixteenth century. You could also pay a visit to the working *huaso* shop on the corner of Esmeralda and Condell, which stocks a vast range of cowboy goods, from ponchos and hats to belts, spurs and saddles. The town's remaining attractions are limited to an artisans' market on the main square and countless shops selling woollen clothes of questionable taste (La Ligua is famous not only for its *dulces* but also for its knitwear). Should you want to stay you'll find smart, spacious **accommodation** at *Hotel Anchimallen*, Ortiz de Rozas 694 (☎ & fax 33/711696; ⑤) and clean budget rooms at *Residencial Aconcagua*, Esmeralda 173 (☎33/711145; ②). There's not much choice in the way of restaurants – try *Montemar* at Portales 699, or *Antares* at Portales 404, for basic meat dishes and pizzas.

The coast

Once past La Ligua, the Panamericana steers towards the coast and follows it for some 200km before dipping inland again, towards Ovalle. This stretch of highway takes you past a succession of glorious, white-sand **beaches** dotted with a few fishing villages and

LA QUINTRALA

Famous today for its confectionery and knitwear, La Ligua was once notorious throughout the colony as the home of one of Chile's darkest figures: doña Catalina de Los Ríos y Lispergeuer, or "**La Quintrala**". Descended from one of the soldiers who formed Pedro de Valdivia's original band of colonizers, she was born in 1600 and inherited the large Hacienda de La Ligua. The female Lispergeuers were already known for their violent natures: Catalina's grandmother had murdered her husband by pouring mercury into his ears as he slept, and her mother had whipped one of her stepdaughters to death and attempted to poison the Governor of Chile. Catalina proved herself to be more than their equal when, at the age of 23, she murdered her father by serving him a poisoned chicken. The following year she killed a Knight of the Order of St John, after having seduced him, and forced one of her servants to "confess" to the crime, for which he was hanged. Curiously, her bloody tendencies seemed to vanish during her twenty-four-year-marriage to Captain Alonso Campofrío Carvajal – only to return with added fervour when she became a widow at the age of fifty. It was at this point that she embarked on her most brutal period, regularly whipping and torturing her numerous slaves, often to the point of death. In 1660 the Bishop of Santiago appealed to the Real Audiencia (Royal Court) to intervene and investigate her behaviour. The enquiry concluded that she had murdered 39 people on her estate, without counting the murders committed before her marriage. La Quintrala evaded justice to the end, however, by dying before the charges could be brought against her. Today, in rural areas near La Ligua, her name still strikes fear into the hearts of children, warned by their mothers that if they are naughty La Quintrala will come to get them.

small resorts, for the most part completely deserted except in January and February when rows of tents are spontaneously erected along the coast, forming huge, improvised campsites. The road is also dotted with vendors waving grotesque **goat's carcasses** at passing cars, and stalls selling home-made cheeses, a regional speciality.

Los Molles and Pichidangui

Some 40km on from La Ligua, past a string of deserted, pristine coves, **LOS MOLLES** is a small fishing village-cum-holiday resort set on a fine beach curving around a wide, sheltered bay. There's some good walking to be done here, particularly along the shore north of the *caleta* where you'll find curious rock formations looming out of the sea, and hidden caves – look out, in particular, for the thundering spray of the Puquén, a blowhole formed by underground tunnels. There's not much to do in the village itself, but since most people come here to chill out quietly by the ocean for a couple of days, this isn't really a problem. If you want to **stay**, there are a number of *cabañas* on the road running parallel to the shore: try *Cabañas Lourdes* (☎33/791783; ④) for two-bed cabins, or *Cabañas Rukalauken* (no phone; ⑤), a couple of doors down, for smarter, larger ones. There's also an excellent seafront **restaurant**, *La Pirata*, serving extremely fresh fish and seafood.

Ten kilometres further up the coast, **PICHIDANGUI**'s beach is up there with Chile's finest. Set 4km back from the Panamericana, the sudden sight of it as you reach the coastal avenue is quite stunning – seven kilometres of white, powdery sand fringed by deep-green eucalyptus trees. There's virtually no beachfront development to spoil the view, and the little town wisely holds back from the shoreline, clinging to the rocky peninsula south of the bay. There's not a lot to do in town, but there's plenty of **accommodation**: *Residencial Lucero*, at the corner of Albacora and Dorado (☎53/531106; ③), has good-value rooms with and without bath, while *La Rosa Nautica*, at Dorado 120 (☎53/531133; ⑤), offers more luxury and a good **restaurant**. Down in the eucalyptus woods backing onto the beach there are *cabañas* – try *Bahía Marina* (☎53/531120; ⑤) – and an excellent **campsite**, *Camping el Bosque* (☎53/531030; CH$8000 per site).

There are **bus services** to Los Molles and Pichidangui from Santiago's Terminal Santiago (Condor Bus; ☎2/779 3721) and from Valparaíso (Buses La Porteña, which leave from the company's office at Molina 366; ☎32/216568).

Los Vilos

Local legend has it that **LOS VILOS**, 30km north of Pichidangui, takes its name from the Hispanic corruption of "Lord Willow", a British pirate who was shipwrecked on the coast and decided to stay. It later became notorious as a danger spot where highway robbers held up horse-drawn carriages travelling between Santiago and La Serena, relieving their occupants of all their belongings, sometimes murdering them for good measure. These days it's a lively, cheerful seaside town that makes a great place to spend a couple of days by the sea without paying over the odds, with a wide choice of inexpensive *residenciales* and restaurants. The flip side of its affordability, however, is that it gets unfeasibly packed in January and February, when over 20,000 visitors descend on the place. Inevitably, the town's chief attraction is its long golden **beach**, but you could also pass an hour or two taking a boat trip around the harbour, wandering around the **fish market** on the *caleta*, or walking out to the **Isla de los Lobos**, a 1500-strong seal colony 200m off the coast, reached by a five-kilometre jeep track just south of the bay.

Los Vilos has a summertime **Oficina de Turismo** (Jan & Feb Tues–Sun 10am–2pm & 6–10pm) near the pier, housed in the Municipalidad on Avenida Caupolicán, the town's main street. Also on this street, at no. 693, *Residencial Central* (no phone; ②), offers decent budget **rooms**, some with sea views. You could also try clean, antique-filled *Residencial Vienesa* at Av Los Vilos 11 (☎53/541143; ③), or the dilapidated but pleasant *Hotel Bellavista* (☎53/541073; ③) opposite the *caleta* at Rengo 020, with a resident parrot wandering the corridors. *Hostería Lord Willow* (☎53/541037; ④), overlooking the beach at Av Los Vilos 1444, offers smarter but overpriced rooms with private bath, while nearby, just off Caupolicán, *Campomar* (☎53/541049; ②) is an institutional-looking but well-equipped **campsite** on calle Campusano. For reliable **seafood**, try *Costanera*, overlooking the bay at Purén 080, the restaurant at *Hotel Bellavista* or the little *marisquerías* opposite the fish market. *Casa de Piedra* on the Panamericana, near the Shell station, is a more upmarket alternative, offering fish and seafood in elaborately prepared sauces. **Buses** to Los Vilos leave from Santiago's Terminal Santiago (Condor Bus; ☎2/779 3721) and La Serena (several companies, including Lasval Incabus ☎51/224795 and Tas Choapa ☎51/225959).

Ovalle and around

North of Los Vilos, the Panamericana follows a trail of lonely *caletas* before straying inland, reaching – 160km up the road – a lone sign pointing to **OVALLE**, 37km east. Most people are happy to give this rather dull agricultural town a miss, though, if you've a couple of days to spare, you might consider using it as a base for exploring the deeply rural and scarcely visited Limarí valley, which holds a few low-key attractions. East of Ovalle, a winding dirt road climbs slowly into the mountains, passing an ancient petrified wood at **Pichasca**. West, you'll find a concentration of rock carvings in the **Valle del Encanto**, a luxurious hot springs resort at the **Termas de Socos** and the impressive cloudforest reserve of **Parque Nacional Fray Jorge**, attracting an increasing number of visitors.

The Town

Ovalle's centre is marked by the expansive lawns and luxuriant trees of the **Plaza de Armas**, lined with nineteenth-century Phoenix palms and rows of jacaranda.

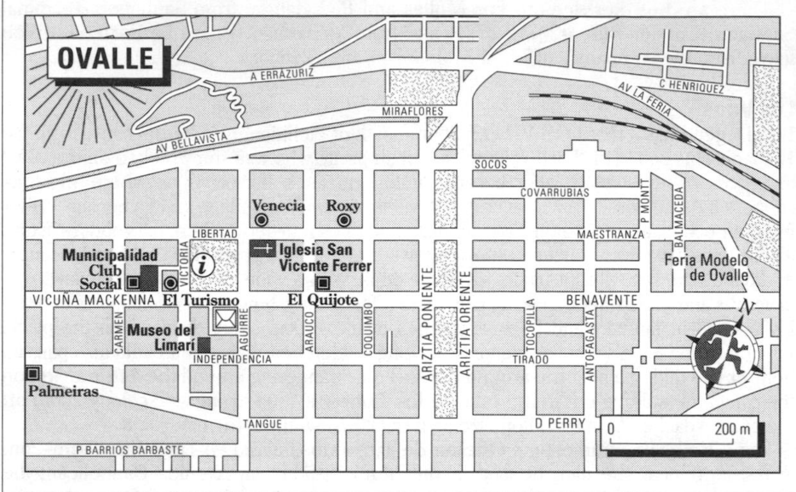

Dominating the east side of the square, the **Iglesia San Vicente Ferrer** is a large, colonial-style church built in 1849, with thick, white adobe walls, only recently repaired from the damage caused by the earthquake of 1997. The streets around the square are narrow and traffic-choked, and flanked by typical single-storey adobe houses. One of these streets, Libertad, has a couple of good traditional **leather shops** (opposite *Hotel Roxy*) where you'll find finely crafted belts, wallets, bags and *huaso* (cowboy) gear. Ovalle's **Museo del Limarí** (Mon–Fri 9am–1pm & 2–6pm, Sat & Sun 9am–1pm; CH$500) stands on the northeast edge of town in the grand old building that once housed the train station, and holds an 1800-piece collection of **Diaguita pottery**. Famed for its exquisite geometric designs painted in black, white and red onto terracotta surfaces, it was produced by the Diaguita people who inhabited the Norte Chico between 900 and 1500 AD. Around a third of the collection suffered some form of damage during the 1997 earthquake, and it remains to be seen how successful the repairs will be. Not far from the museum, about ten blocks east of the plaza (take an eastbound *micro* along Vicuña Mackenna), you'll find a huge, ramshackle iron hangar that houses the **Feria Modelo de Ovalle** (Mon, Tues, Fri & Sat 6am–4pm). Lively and colourful, this is the largest fresh-produce market in the north of Chile and is definitely worth a visit; you can pick up fantastic home-made cheeses (including some alarmingly pungent goats' cheese) as well as delicious dried figs and a vast range of fruit and vegetables.

Practicalities

Arriving by **bus** you'll be dropped at your bus company's office, as there's no single terminal (most bus companies are on Avenida Aritzía, three blocks west of the Plaza de Armas). For limited **tourist information**, try the small *turismo* kiosk on the west side of the plaza (no fixed hours) or the Municipalidad, round the corner at Vicuña Mackenna 441 (Mon–Fri 8.30am–2pm; ☎53/620955). Ovalle has a lot of **accommodation**, though most of it has seen better days. A notable exception is the spruce *Hotel El Turismo*, at Victoria 295 (☎ & fax 53/623536; ⑤), offering spacious, well-kept rooms in a handsome old building with its own restaurant and parking. For something more economical, your best bet is *Hotel Roxy* at Libertad 155 (☎53/620080; ③), with comfortable if dated rooms ranged around a large, brightly painted patio filled with flowers, chairs and a cageful of blackbirds; further towards the plaza, at no. 261, *Hotel Vencia* (☎53/620968; ③) has a friendly *Señora* and a row of spotless but dark rooms off a long corridor.

Most of Ovalle's **restaurants** limit themselves to the standard meat and fish dishes you find everywhere else in Chile – which is frustrating, considering this is the fresh-produce capital of the North. The *Club Social de Ovalle*, at Vicuña Mackenna 400, is the best of a disappointing bunch, with good fish and seafood (keep an eye out for the local river prawns when they're in season). *Palmeiras*, at Independencia 606, serves traditional meat and fish in a large hall that fills with live music and dancing at weekends, while *El Quijote*, at Arauco 294, is an intimate, bohemian sort of restaurant, with political graffiti and poetry on the walls, and an inexpensive menu featuring staples like *cazuela* and *lomo*. There are no *cambios* in Ovalle, but you'll find an **ATM** on the plaza, at the corner of Vicuña Mackenna and Victoria.

Pichasca

East of Ovalle, a rough, unpaved road meanders through the fertile valley, skirting – 12km out of town – the deep-blue expanse of water formed by the **Recoleta dam**, one of three dams that irrigate the Limarí valley. About 50km up the road, past a string of tiny hamlets, a side road to San Pedro de Pichasca dips down across the river leading, just beyond the village, to the Conaf-run **Monumento Natural Pichasca** (daily 8.30am–4.30pm; CH$1000), the site of a "petrified wood". As you arrive at the parking area, two paths diverge: the right-hand path leads north to a hillside scattered with stumps of **fossilized tree trunks**, some of them imprinted with the shape of leaves; the left-hand, or southern, path leads down to an enormous **cave** formed by an eighty-metre gash in the hillside topped by a massive overhanging rock. Archeological discoveries inside the cave point to human habitation some 10,000 years ago. It's possible to get to the turn-off to San Pedro de Pichasca on a bumpy, rickety **bus** from Ovalle's Feria Modelo, on market days (see opposite), but this involves walking 3km from the main road to the site entrance, and then a further 2km to the cave and fossil remains. If you're **driving**, you could visit Pichasca as part of a longer tour through the valley, continuing perhaps to Vicuña (see p.164) across a breathtaking mountain pass, or to Andacollo (see p.153), again through wonderful scenery.

Valle del Encanto and Termas de Socos

Nineteen kilometres west of Ovalle, a heavily pot-holed dirt road leads 5km south of Ruta 45 into a dry, dusty ravine known as the **Valle del Encanto** (daily 8am–6pm; CH$400). The site contains one of Chile's densest collections of **petroglyphs** – images engraved on the surface of rocks – carved mainly by the El Molle culture (see p.446) between 100 and 600 AD. Most of the images show geometric motifs or stylized human outlines, including faces with large, wide eyes and elaborate headdresses. There are about thirty petroglyphs in total, concentrated in two separate areas: one near the picnic tables, as you enter the site, and another reached by following the right-hand (western) path for about 1km. A few of the images are very striking, while others are faint and difficult to make out; the best time to visit is around 2–3pm, when the outlines are at their sharpest, unobscured by shadows. There's an erratically available free guide service, arranged on the spot when you turn up – if you can, it's worth taking advantage of this so as not to miss the most impressive petroglyphs. You're allowed to **camp** here for free, so long as you notify the *guardaparques* – it makes a hushed, tranquil spot, once the visitors have trickled away, with a stunning display of stars at night.

Back on the Panamericana, just south of the turn-off for Ovalle, a track leads 2km to the exclusive thermal baths complex of **Termas de Socos**. The main attraction is the 22°C outdoor pool, surrounded by palm and eucalyptus trees, wicker armchairs and huge potted ferns, and the cubicles containing private bathtubs where you can soak in hot thermal water, supposedly rich in medicinal properties. These are free if you're staying at the resort's studiously rustic **hotel** (☎ & fax 53/681021; ⑤); otherwise, there's a charge of CH$2800 for the pool, and CH$3000 for the baths. There's also an excellent but exorbitantly priced **campsite** (☎53/681013; CH$17,000 per site) with its own outdoor pool.

Parque Nacional Fray Jorge

A UNESCO world biosphere reserve since 1977, **PARQUE NACIONAL FRAY JORGE** (April–Nov Sat & Sun 8am–6pm, latest entry 4.30pm; Dec–March Mon & Thurs–Sun same hours; CH$1500) sits on the Altos de Talinay, a range of steep coastal hills plunging into the Pacific some 80km west of Ovalle and 110km south of La Serena. It extends over 10,000 hectares but its focal point, and what everyone comes to see, is the small **cloudforest** perched on the highest part of the sierra, about 600m above sea level. The extraordinary thing about this forest is how sharply it contrasts with its surroundings, indeed with everywhere else in the Norte Chico. Approaching it, you follow a dry dusty road through a charred landscape of cactus plants and brittle shrubs, and then, as you get closer to the coast, you notice patches of grey hovering over the sky. Suddenly, you're on what looks and feels like a Scottish hill, enfolded by cold, damp cloud and swirling mist. This is the **camanchaca**, the thick coastal fog that rises from the ocean and condenses as it meets the land, supporting a cover of dense vegetation like fern, bracken and myrtle trees, normally found only in the south of Chile. Close to the parking area, a one-kilometre path dotted with information panels guides you through a poorly labelled range of plants and trees on the crest of the hill – while you're here, look down to where the ocean should be and, if you're patient, you'll catch sudden glimpses of the crashing waves and little islets below, as the mist temporarily clears. At the end of the path you enter the **forest** proper, where a slippery, wooden boardwalk takes you through tall trees dripping with moisture. The whole trail takes less than half an hour to walk.

Practicalities

There's no public transport to the park so, unless you've got a rental car, your best bet is to arrange a trip by **taxi** (try Abel Olivares in Ovalle, ☎53/620352, or Transervice in La Serena, ☎51/212021) or take a **tour** from La Serena (see p.162). If you're **driving** there, allow about one and a half hours from Ovalle, a little more from La Serena. The park is reached by a dirt road that branches west from the Panamericana 14km north of the junction with Ruta 45 to Ovalle. From the turn-off, it's 18km to the park entrance, where you pay your fee and register your visit. From here it's a further 10km to the wood itself, and the road gets rough and extremely steep in some places. Three kilometres on from the Conaf control, there's a **picnic** and basic **camping** area (CH$5000 per site), with toilets and cold showers.

Ovalle to La Serena

Ovalle is separated from the busy city of La Serena, 88km north, by a series of gentle valleys and dried-out rivers, punctuated with the occasional abandoned mine and colonial mansion. The most direct, and most scenic, route between the two towns is along Ruta 43, from which a side road branches east to the charming pilgrimage centre of

Andacollo – a worthwhile detour. West of Ovalle, the Panamericana turns towards the ocean and skirts a string of small resorts that make a calmer and more attractive beach setting than the built-up coast at La Serena.

Andacollo

Enfolded by sun-bleached, rolling hills midway between Ovalle and La Serena, **ANDACOLLO** is a tidy little town of small adobe houses grouped around a long main street. It's been an important gold- and copper-mining centre ever since the Incas mined its hills in the sixteenth century, but is best known as the home of the **Virgen de Andacollo**, a small wooden carving that draws over 100,000 pilgrims to the town each year. Most of them arrive between December 23 and 26 to participate in the Fiesta Grande de la Virgen: four days of music and riotous dancing performed by costumed groups from all over Chile. Many of these dances have their roots in pre-Columbian rituals, such as the *bailes Chinos*, recorded in Spanish chronicles around 1580 and thought to have been introduced by the Incas during their occupation in the late fifteenth century. Quieter, less frenetic celebrations take place in the Fiesta Chica on the first Sunday in October.

If you miss the fiestas it's still worth coming to check out the two temples erected in honour of the Virgin. Largest and grandest is the **Basílica**, which towers over the main square in breathtaking contrast to the small, simple scale of the rest of the town. Built almost entirely of wood in a Roman–Byzantine style, its pale, cream-coloured walls are topped by two colossal 50m towers and a stunning 45m dome. Inside, sunlight floods through the dome, falling onto huge wooden pillars painted to look like marble. On the other side of the square stands the smaller, stone-built **Templo Antiguo**, dating from 1789. This is where the Virgin lives for most of the year, perched on the main altar, awaiting the great festival when she's transported to the Basílica to receive the petitions and prayers of the pilgrims. Her devotees have left her an astonishing quantity of gifts over the years, ranging from artificial limbs and wooden crutches to jewellery, badges, china vases, model boats and exam certificates, all displayed in the crypt of the Templo Antiguo as part of the **Museo de Andacollo** (daily 9am–12.30pm & 3–6.30pm; free).

THE VIRGIN OF ANDACOLLO

The true facts of the story of the Virgin of Andacollo – a 90cm carving considered to be singularly generous with her favours and miracles – have long been lost in mythology and legend. One popular version has it that the whereabouts of the carving was revealed to an Indian named Collo by a heavenly apparition who urged him to go and seek it crying "¡Anda, Collo, Anda!" ("Go, Collo, Go!"). A more credible theory is that the image was taken from La Serena by priests fleeing the city when it was attacked and destroyed by Indians in 1549. They buried the carving in the hills near Andacollo, where it was accidentally discovered by an Indian some time later. Old chronicles tell of a rudimentary chapel erected in Andacollo around 1580, presumably to house the image, and of celebratory dances carried out to worship it. In any event it seems that the image went missing some time in the seventeenth century, prompting Andacollo's parish priest, a Sr Bernardino Alvarez del Tobar, to organize a whip-round to pay for a new one to be made. The sum of 24 pesos was duly raised and dispatched to Lima, Peru, where a new image of the Virgin was carved and returned to Andacollo, receiving its inaugural blessing on the first Sunday of October, 1676. The loss of the original image was providential, for the new one turned out to have far greater miracle-working powers than its predecessor. The Virgin's fame spread far and wide, and an intense cult of devotion sprang up. In 1901 the image was recognized as officially "miraculous" by the Vatican, and the Virgin was crowned in a dazzling ceremony attended by five bishops and 10,000 pilgrims.

Practicalities

Getting to Andacollo is easy, either by bus or *colectivo* from Ovalle (2hr) or La Serena (1hr; see p.163); either way, the journey takes you through beautiful hill country. You'll find an **Oficina de Turismo** (March–Dec Mon–Fri 10am–12.30pm & 3–6pm; Jan & Feb Mon–Fri 10am–8pm, Sat 2–8pm, Sun 4–8pm) on the southern side of the square, opposite the Basílica. There's not a huge choice of **accommodation** here – *El Parrón* (☎51/431609; ②) at Urmeneta 773, offers reasonable, basic rooms, as does the comparable *Residencial La Criolita* (☎51/431553; ②) a few doors up at no. 713. For **food**, you could try *El Rincón Latino Pizza* at Urmeneta 159 which serves uninspiring pizzas and other snacks.

Tongoy and Guanaqueros

Some 60km north of the turn-off for Ovalle, a side road branches off the Panamericana for **TONGOY**, a popular family resort spread over a hilly peninsula. It has two attractive sandy **beaches**, the Playa Socos, north of the peninsula, and the enormous Playa Grande, stretching 14km south. While there are plenty of hotels, *cabañas* and restaurants, development has been low-key and low-level, and the place remains pretty and relatively unspoiled. There's a good choice of **accommodation**. Artist Paula Hernández has a few wooden and glass *cabañas* dotted up a hillside overlooking the bay, each one decorated with her own canvases; the entrance is at Costanera Sur 48 (☎51/391697; ④–⑤). Another characterful place is *Hotel Panorámco*, Av Mirador 455 (☎51/391944; ④–⑤), crammed with 1950s items including a great TV set and a stand-up hairdryer. Down by the beachfront at Serena 460, *Yacolen* (☎51/391772; ③) offers basic but clean rooms off the yard behind the restaurant, with the two end rooms overlooking the beach; 500m down Playa Grande, *Ripial* (☎51/391220; CH$5000 per site) is a quiet **campsite**, open year-round. Also on the beach, next to the *caleta*, you'll find a row of excellent little **restaurants** serving delicious seafood – try *Negro Cerro*, or *El Veguita*.

Fourteen kilometres north, **GUANAQUEROS** is a small, slightly shabby fishing town perched at the southern tip of a vast bay lined with a 17-kilometre white-sand beach. There's nothing in particular to do here, but if you like the idea of lazing undisturbed by the ocean for a day or two, then Guanaqueros is a good place to head. Even in the heaving height of summer, you can be sure to find your own stretch of empty sands just by walking a couple of kilometres up the bay – also a good place for unofficial **camping**. There are a few well-equipped but very expensive campsites on the beach, too, down by the road into the village; try *Complejo Turístico Federico Schaeffer* (☎51/395288; ④), which also offers upmarket *cabañas*. Considerably cheaper, *Hotel La Bahía* at Av Costanera 274 (☎51/395380; ③), offers simple, good-value **rooms** (mostly with shared bath) overlooking the bay. Guanaqueros has some good, down-to-earth **fish restaurants** – busy *El Pequeño*, in particular, is one of the best in the region. Another one to try is *Miramar*, a small place that fills with locals, or, in summer, the little *marisquerías* by the fish quay. There's frequent **transport** to Tongoy and Guanaqueros from: Ovalle (Buses Ossandon, Aristía Poniente 245; ☎53/620430); Coquimbo, 30km up the coast (Buses Ruta Costera, and Colectivos Alfamar); and La Serena a further 11km north (Buses Serenamar, Francisco de Aguirre 344, at Matta; ☎51/213658).

Coquimbo and La Herradura

Spread over a rocky peninsula studded with colourful houses, the busy port of **COQUIMBO** was established during colonial times to serve neighbouring La Serena, and became Chile's main copper exporter during the nineteenth century. Despite its undeniably impressive setting, the town has a slightly rough-edged, down-at-heel air, but is useful as an inexpensive base for La Serena's beaches, or for taking public transport to the nearby resorts of Guanaqueros and Tongoy.

Coquimbo's main street, Aldunate, runs parallel to the northern shore of the peninsula, at the foot of the steep hills that form the **upper town**, or *parte alta*. Several stairways lead from Aldunate up to lookout points giving sweeping views down to the port and across the bay; if you can't face the climb, take any *micro* marked "*parte alta*". The **Plaza de Armas**, in the middle of Aldunate, is dotted with park benches hogged, during the day, by legions of chattering old men and women, and is dominated by a single, unfeasibly tall, palm tree. North of the square, still on Aldunate, you'll find some of the city's finest houses, many of them carved in wood by English craftsmen during the prosperous mining era. A couple of blocks north of Aldunate, the Avenida Costanera runs along the shore, past the large **port**, the **terminal pesquero**, and along to the lively **fish market**. This area has been smartened up recently, and makes a nice place to stroll by the ocean.

The southern shore of the peninsula, known as **Guayacán**, has a sandy beach, dominated at one end by a huge mechanized port used for exporting iron. While you're here, take a look at the nearby **Iglesia de Guayacán**, a steel church designed by Eiffel, and the **British cemetery**, built in 1860 at the behest of the British Admiralty, and full of the graves of young sailors etched with heart-rending inscriptions like "*died falling from aloft*" (if the gates are locked, ask in the caretaker's house). Guayacán's beach curves south to that of La Herradura, which although long, golden and sandy is marred by its proximity to the Panamericana. That said, the night-time views across the bay to the tip of Coquimbo are superb, and if you want to spend a night or two at the seaside, La Herradura makes a convenient, cheaper alternative to La Serena's Avenida del Mar.

Practicalities

Coquimbo's busy **bus terminal** is on the main road into town, near the junction of Videla with Balmaceda. All the main north–south inter-city buses stop here, as do local buses to coastal resorts like Tongoy and Guanaqueros. You can also get to the resorts, and to Guayacán and La Herradura, by **colectivo** – they pick up behind the bus terminal and through the centre of town. There's a *casa de cambio*, Afex, at Melgarejo 1355, plus a couple of **ATMs** on Plaza Prat, on the Plaza de Armas, and at Aldunate 822. There's a good choice of **accommodation** in town, the best being *Hotel Lig*, at Aldunate 1577 (☎51/311171, fax 313717; ④), with bright, comfortable rooms and private parking. *Hotel Iberia*, just off Aldunate at Lastra 400 (☎51/312141, fax 326307; ③) has spacious rooms, with and without bath, in an attractive old building, while the best budget option is *Residencial Mi Casa*, at Varela 1653 (☎51/326919; ②) which offers small but spotless rooms and private parking close to the bus terminal. As for **eating**, head for the little *marisquerías* by the fish market for simple, cheap seafood lunches, or try *Pastissima* at Aldunate 927 for filling, reasonably priced Italian and Chilean food.

In **La Herradura**, *Hotel La Herradura*, just off the beach at La Marina 200 (☎ & fax 51/321320; ④) offers OK rooms at reasonable prices or, if you want the best views of the bay, head for *Hotel Bucaneros* (☎51/260315, fax 260842; ⑥) perched on a jetty projecting into the ocean. This is also where you'll find La Herradura's plushest **restaurant**, offering good but overpriced seafood and great views across to Coquimbo (best at night). Also looking out to sea, but with more modest prices, is the *Club de Yates*, a little further west along the beach.

La Serena

Sitting by the mouth of the río Elqui, 11km north of Coquimbo, **LA SERENA** is for many tourists their first taste of the Norte Chico, after whizzing straight up from Santiago. Three kilometres in from the modern, brassy coast lined with the apart-hotels and *cabañas* of Avenida del Mar, the city-centre is an attractive mix of pale colonial-style houses, carefully restored churches, craft markets tucked away on hidden squares and bustling crowds.

La Serena is Chile's second oldest city, with a history chequered by violence and drama. Founded by Pedro de Valdivia in 1544 as a staging post on the way to Peru, it got off to an unpromising start when it was completely destroyed in an **Indian attack** four years later. Undeterred, Valdivia had the city refounded in a new location the following year, but La Serena continued to lead a precarious existence, subjected to frequent and often violent raids by pirates, many of them British. The most famous of these buccaneers was **Sir Francis Drake**, who paid a visit to La Serena in 1578; the most notorious was **Bartholomew Sharp**, who sacked the city in a three-day rampage in December 1680, before burning it to the ground. Happier times arrived in the nineteenth century when the discovery of large silver deposits at Arqueros, just north of La Serena, marked the beginning of the region's great **silver boom**. These heady days saw the erection of some of the city's finest mansions and churches, as the mining magnates competed in their efforts to dazzle with their wealth.

It was the 1940s, though, that really shaped La Serena's architectural look when **Gabriela González Videla**, President of Chile and local Serenense, instituted his **"Plan Serena"**. One of the key elements of this urban remodelling scheme was the vig-

THE PACIFIC BUCCANEERS

La Serena was one of a string of ports on South America's Pacific seaboard to be regularly attacked and plundered by bands of buccaneers, out to loot the Spanish colonies of their gold, silver and other riches. The marauders – mainly British, but also French and Dutch – were positively encouraged in their actions by their own governments, who were intensely jealous of Spain's overseas possessions, and eager to undermine their rival's glory. The English were particularly dreaded, from their arrival on the scene in 1578 when Francis Drake sailed the *Golden Hind* through the Magellan Strait and up the coast of Chile. Drake's first port of call was Valparaíso where, besides ransacking the church for its silverware, he captured a Spanish ship containing 60,000 gold pesos and vast quantities of Chilean wine. Further north, he attempted to repeat his success at La Serena, but was thwarted by the fierce armed resistance mounted by its inhabitants. Peru yielded greater prizes, and when he returned to England, his ship heavy with booty, he was knighted by a jubilant Queen Elizabeth, who called him her "little pirate."

It wasn't until the second half of the sixteenth century, however, that the heyday of the Pacific buccaneers began in earnest. Among the most ruthless of the leaders was Captain Bartholomew Sharp who in 1680 attacked and captured La Serena, where his hungry crew feasted on "strawberries as large as walnuts". Silver, on the other hand, was almost nowhere to be found, and when the inhabitants refused to pay a ransom, the embittered Sharp set fire to the town, almost razing it to the ground. That night, by way of revenge, one of the Spaniards sent a servant to float out to Sharp's boat on an inflated horsehide and set fire to the stern, but the blaze was extinguished before any real damage could be done. Also known for his cruelty was Edward Davis, who arrived in La Serena in 1685. Unable to capture the town, he retreated to the Iglesia Santo Domingo which he looted and set on fire before fleeing the town.

As Britain and France established a more peaceful relationship with Spain towards the end of the seventeenth century, the plunderers no longer served their governments' ends, and the days of buccaneering drew to a close. Vivid memories of the terror they caused lived on for many years, however, and as late as 1835, Charles Darwin, while visiting La Serena, told of an old lady "who remarked how wonderfully strange it was that she should live to dine in the same room as an Englishman; for she remembered that twice as a girl, at the cry of "Los Ingleses", every soul, carrying what valuables they could, had taken to the mountains.

orous promotion of the Spanish colonial style, with facades restored or rebuilt on existing structures and strict stylistic controls imposed on new ones. Unimaginative and inflexible though some claimed these measures to be, the results are undeniably pleasing, and La Serena boasts an architectural harmony and beauty noticeably lacking in most Chilean cities. It's also surrounded by some rewarding places to visit. Close at hand, and with good bus and *colectivo* connections, are the excellent beaches at Tongoy and Guanaqueros (see p.154), and the glorious **Elqui valley**, one of the must-sees of the region. Further afield, the cloudforest reserve of **Parque Nacional Fray Jorge** and the penguin sanctuary at **Parque Nacional Pinguino de Humboldt** are not served by public transport, but can be visited with several **tour companies**.

Arrival and information

La Serena's **bus terminal** is a half-hour walk south of the centre. There's no direct bus from the terminal into town, but there are plenty of taxis, charging about CH$1000. Alternatively, you can flag down a *micro* from the Panamericana, a five-minute walk west. If you've flown in, you'll land at the **Aeropuerto Gabriela Mistral**, some 5km out of town, and served only by taxis.

Sernatur has an extremely helpful, well-stocked tourist office on the west side of the Plaza de Armas at Matta 461 (Jan & Feb Mon–Fri 8.45am–8.30pm, Sat & Sun 10am–2.30pm & 5.30–8.30pm; March–Dec Mon–Fri 8.45am–1.30pm & 2.30–5.30pm; ☎51/225199, fax 213956). There's also a municipal **Oficina de Turismo** at the bus terminal (Tues–Sat 9.30am–1pm & 3.30–9pm), and a **kiosk** on the corner of Prat and Balmaceda (Mon–Sat 11am–2pm & 4–7pm). For information on Parque Nacional Fray Jorge, Monumento Natural Pichasca and Parque Nacional Pinguino de Humboldt, visit **Conaf** (Mon–Fri 9am–1pm & 2.30–5pm; ☎51/225685), east of the centre on the corner of avenidas Colo Colo and Rodríguez.

Accommodation

You'll find a huge choice of well-located budget accommodation in the **centre**, plus a range of mid- to upmarket options. If you want to stay on **Avenida del Mar**, however, you're looking at fancy *cabañas* and hotels with pools which, even in winter when you can get them for less than half their February rates, are almost without exception very expensive.

Downtown

Casa de familia Adriana Jiliberto, (☎51/211287). Simple, comfortable rooms arranged around the large patio of an ageing but still magnificent nineteenth-century house. ③.

Casa de familia Alejandro Muñoz, Brasil 720 (☎51/211619). Quiet, attractive family home with good, clean rooms and access to a garden. No sign at the door; English and French spoken. ③.

Hotel Croata, Cienfuegos 248 (☎ & fax 51/224997). Excellent mid-priced choice, with modern rooms, laundry, parking and phone/fax services. ④.

Hotel El Cid, O'Higgins 138 (☎51/212692, fax 222289). Small hotel run by a Scots-Chilean couple, with well-furnished rooms around a flower-filled terrace. Highly recommended in this price category. ⑤.

Hotel Francisco de Aguirre, Cordovéz 210 (☎ & fax 51/222991). La Serena's plushest hotel, with stylish rooms in a handsome old building, and a poolside restaurant in summer. ⑦.

Hotel Londres, Cordovéz 550 (☎ & fax 51/214673). Clean and tidy rooms, some with private bath and others (better value) with just a washbasin. ③–④.

Hotel Los Balcones de Aragón, Cienfuegos 289 (☎51/225724 & fax 211800). Smart, upmarket rooms in a fine building with private parking. ⑥.

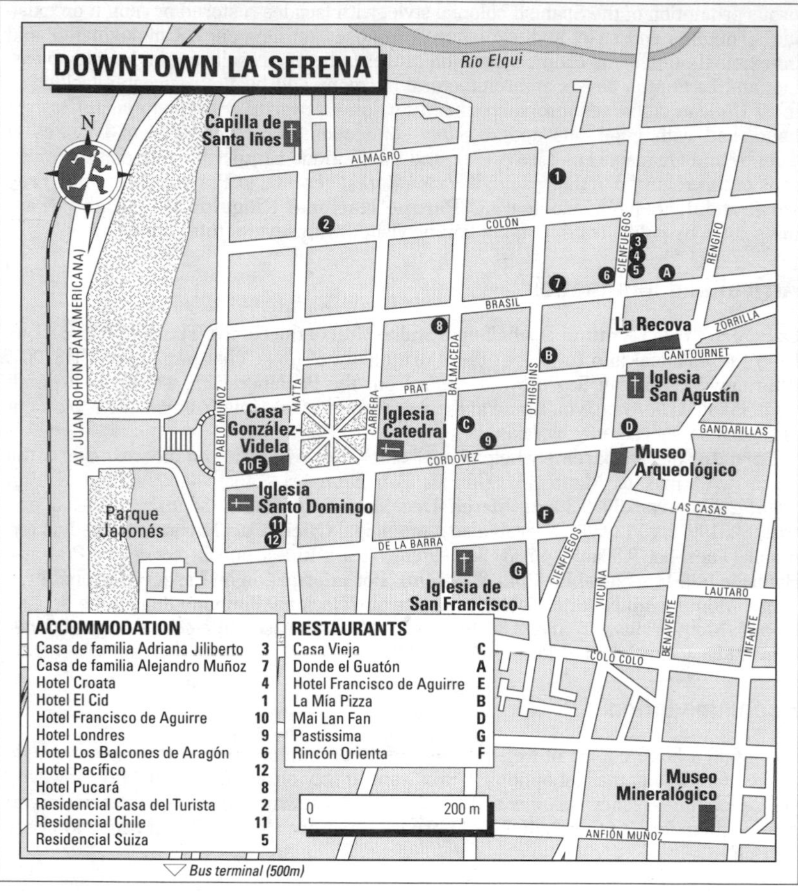

Hotel Pacífico, de la Barra 252 (☎51/225674). Ancient, rambling hotel with clean, basic rooms with and without bath, and friendly staff. ③.

Hotel Pucará, Balmaceda 319 (☎51/211966, fax 211933). Efficiently run hotel with spacious, comfortable but drab rooms and private parking. ⑤.

Residencial Casa del Turista, Colón 318 (☎51/223524). Light, airy rooms set around two large patios; good value. ②.

Residencial Chile, Matta 561 (☎51/211694). Simple, tidy and inexpensive rooms; a good budget choice. ③.

Residencial Suiza, Cienfuegos 250 (☎51/216092). Spotless, well-kept *residencial* with a fresh, modern feel – highly recommended. ④.

Avenida del Mar

Cabañas Alborada, no. 5695 (☎51/246124, fax 245589). One of the more reasonably priced options along here, offering small, clean *cabañas* with fully equipped kitchens. The reception is in the mini-market next door. ⑤.

Cabañas Celia Norero de Domínguez, down track off Av del Mar, behind *La Serena Club Resort* (☎51/212453, fax 213761). Old, well-equipped and very spacious *cabañas*, less expensive than most; good deals available out of season. ⑤.

Hostal del Mar, Cuatro Esquinas at Av del Mar (☎51/225559, fax 225816). Pleasant, well-furnished *cabañas* with a mid-sized pool, a short walk from the beach. ⑥.

Hostería La Serena, Av Francisco de Aguirre 0660, on the corner with Avenida del Mar (☎51/225745, fax 222459). Long-established hotel with a good pool and tennis courts, comfortable rooms and lots of brown 1970s furnishings. ⑤.

La Serena Club Resort, no. 1000 (☎51/221262, fax 217130). Huge, unattractive building but good rooms and decor, great views from the restaurant and a large pool. Occasional special three-night deals. ⑦.

Camping

Antares, calle Los Pescadores (☎51/243753, fax 245207). Outrageously expensive campsite with a sandy, grassy area to pitch your tents and a few tired *cabañas* for hire (⑤); CH$18,000 per site.

Hipocampo, opposite Playa el Corsario (☎ & fax 51/241316). Sixty-site campsite about 200m back from the beach, plus a few inexpensive, sparsely furnished huts (③); CH$14,000 per site.

Sol di Mare, Parcela 66 (☎51/312531). Lovely, grassy campsite down at the quieter end of the beach. Good facilities and lots of shade; CH$10,000 per site.

The City

La Serena has one or two good museums – including the noteworthy **Museo Arqueológico** – but the city's main appeal lies in just strolling the streets and squares, admiring the grand old houses, browsing through the numerous crafts markets, wandering in and out of its many churches and hanging out in the plaza. Another big attraction is the six-kilometre **beach**, flanked by the glitzy **Avenida del Mar**, and easily reached from downtown.

Museo Arqueológico

Entered through an imposing nineteenth-century portico on the corner of Cordovéz and Cienfuegos, La Serena's **Museo Arqueológico** (Tues–Fri 9am–1pm & 4–7pm, Sat 10am–1pm & 4–7pm, Sun 10am–1pm; CH$500, Sun free) boasts two outstanding treasures. First is its large collection of **Diaguita pottery** considered by many to be among the most beautiful pre-Columbian ceramics in South America. The terracotta pieces, dating from around 900 to 1500 AD, are covered in intricate geometric designs, painted in black and white and, in the later phases, red. Starting with simple bowls and dishes made for domestic use, the Diaguitas went on to produce elaborately shaped ceremonial pots and jars, often in the form of humans or animals, or sometimes both, such as the famous *jarros patos*, or "duck jars", moulded in the form of a duck's body with a human head. The museum's second gem is the giant stone statue, or **moai**, from Easter Island, "donated" to La Serena at the behest of President González Videla in 1952. Until recently it stood in a park on Avenida Colo Colo, covered in graffiti and urinated on by drunks. Then, as part of an exhibition of Easter Island art in 1996, it travelled to Barcelona where it was accidentally decapitated. Tragedy turned to good fortune, however, when the insurance money from the accident paid for a brand-new *sala* to be built for the statue in the archeological museum – which is where you'll find it today, standing on a raised platform against an azure backdrop, the joins at the neck hardly showing.

The rest of downtown

The two-storey adobe house sitting on the southwest corner of the Plaza de Armas was, from 1927 to 1977, home to Chile's erstwhile president, Gabriel González Videla, best

LA SERENA'S CHURCHES

There are a remarkable twenty-nine **churches** in La Serena, lending an almost fairy-tale look to the city. This proliferation of places of worship dates from the earliest days of the city, when all the religious orders established bases to provide shelter for their clergy's frequent journeys between Santiago and Lima (the viceregal capital). Unusually for Chile nearly all the churches are built of stone, and are all in mint condition. Grandest is the **Iglesia Catedral** dominating the east side of the Plaza de Armas. Its pale, stone walls date from 1844, when the existing church was finally pulled down after the damage wrought by the 1796 earthquake; inside, one of its more curious features is its wooden pillars, disguised to look like stone. Just off the opposite side of the square, on Cordovéz, the pretty **Iglesia Santo Domingo** was first built in 1673 and then again in 1755, after it was sacked by the pirate Sharp (see p.156). Attached to it is a convent and a little *plazuela* containing a stone fountain, originally used by priests to wash their hands, and said to be the oldest monument in the city. Standing at the corner of Balmaceda and de la Barra, the **Iglesia San Francisco** is one of La Serena's oldest churches, though the date of its construction is unknown, as the city archives were burnt in Sharp's raid of 1680. Its huge walls are one-metre thick, covered in a stone facade carved in fanciful baroque designs. Inside, the **Museo de Arte Religioso** (currently closed for restoration) contains a small but impressive collection of religious sculpture and paintings from the colonial period. Beautiful for its very plainness, the **Iglesia San Agustín**, on the corner of Cienfuegos and Cantournet, was originally the Jesuit church but was taken over by the Augustinians after the Jesuits were expelled from Chile in 1767. Built in 1755, its honey-toned stone walls were badly damaged in the 1975 earthquake, but have been skilfully restored. On the northern edge of town, overlooking the banks of the río Elqui, the **Capilla de Santa Inès** was built in the seventeenth century on the site of a rudimentary chapel erected by the first colonists. Heavily reconstructed in 1819, its thick white adobe walls recall the Andean churches of the northern altiplano.

known for outlawing the Communist party after using its support to gain power in 1946. Inside, a small and rather dull **museum** (Tues–Sat 9am–noon and 4–7pm, Sun 10am–1pm; CH$500) has an eclectic display of photos, objects, documents and paintings relating to the president's life and works, along with a section on regional history. More eye-catching, but not so central, is the **Museo Mineralógico** (Mon–Fri 9.30am–12.30pm; free) in the university, on Muñoz with Infante, where you'll find a large selection of glittering mineral rocks, many of them mined in the Norte Chico. Of La Serena's numerous **crafts markets**, the biggest and best is the bustling **La Recova**, occupying two large patios inside an arcaded building opposite the Iglesia San Agustín. The quality is generally high, and goods include finely-worked objects in *combabalita* (a locally mined marble), lapis lazuli jewellery, alpaca sweaters and sugared papaya. Backing onto the Panamericana, two blocks west of the Plaza de Armas, the **Parque Japonés** (daily 10am–6pm; CH$500) is an oasis of perfectly manicured lawns, ponds awash with water lilies, ice-white geese and little Japanese bridges and pagodas – unfortunately, the sense of peace and tranquillity it creates is undermined by the din of the highway.

Avenida del Mar

Stretching 6km round the rim of a wide, horseshoe bay, the **Avenida del Mar** is a serious collection of glitzy hotels, tourist complexes and *cabañas* that bulge with visitors for two months of the year and are otherwise empty. In January and February hundreds of cars inch their way up and down the avenue, bumper to bumper, and Chilean and Argentinian tourists pile onto the sandy beaches, which are clean and golden, but spoiled by the high-rise backdrop. The heaviest concentration of bodies is usually at the northern end, closer to the city, while the very southern end, where the Panamericana veers inland, is always quieter and less crowded. This bit also has the best views, looking directly onto the rocky peninsula studded with the houses of Coquimbo, La Serena's busy port (see p.154). While there's no bus or *colectivo* service along the Avenida del Mar, you can take a *micro* for Coquimbo from just about any street corner (if in doubt head for Avenida Francisco de Aguirre) and get off on the Panamericana either at Cuatro Esquinas or Peñuelas, both a short walk from the beach.

Eating, drinking and entertainment

There's a wide choice of **places to eat** in downtown La Serena, most of them unpretentious, unexceptional and not too expensive. Restaurants on the Avenida del Mar, on the other hand, tend to be more select and overpriced, though some offer excellent views and a lively holiday atmosphere. **Nightlife** downtown is surprisingly quiet, while the pubs and discos by the beach tend to be seasonal, reaching their heady zenith in January and February. There's a **cinema** at Cordovéz 399, Cine Centenario, which shows mainstream Hollywood films.

Restaurants in the centre

Casa Vieja, Balmaceda 432. Fairly good fish and meat dishes served in a pretty little interior patio. Closed Sun.

Donde el Guatón, Brazil 750. Lively and intimate restaurant serving the best *parilladas* in La Serena, with live, romantic *boleros* at weekends. Highly recommended.

Hotel Francisco de Aguirre, Cordovéz 210. If you're around in summer and fancy a splurge, this is the place to come, principally for its glamorous poolside setting. The French-influenced food is toothsome and well presented.

La Mía Pizza, O'Higgins 360. Delicious, inexpensive pizzas served in an attractive café-style place; also does breakfasts.

La Recova market, corner of Cienfuegos and Cantournet. Dozens of good-value *marisquerías* on the upper gallery of the handicrafts market – an excellent place for lunch.

Mai Lan Fan, Cordovéz 740. Reliable and inexpensive Chinese restaurant, popular with tourists.

Pastissima, O'Higgins 663. Large and supposedly Italian restaurant with surprisingly few pasta dishes, but good fish, shellfish, meat and pizzas.

Rincón Oriental, O'Higgins 570. La Serena's newest and smartest Chinese restaurant offering tasty food at reasonable prices.

Restaurants on Avenida del Mar

Il Pomodoro, near the casino. Beachfront Italian restaurant serving delicious but overpriced pizzas.

La Creperie, opposite Playa La Barca. Delicious crepes and snacks, and a lively atmosphere in this popular bar-restaurant. Closed Mon.

La Serena Club Resort, no. 1000. Attractive, brightly decorated restaurant with excellent ocean views and good, fairly pricey seafood.

Velamar, no. 2100. One of the best fish and seafood restaurants in La Serena; very fine food at commensurate prices. Closed Tues.

Cafés, bars and discos

5a Ola, Av del Mar, one block south of 4 Esquinas. Lively café-bar which gets very busy on summer evenings.

Bocaccio, Prat 490. Large and hugely popular café, good for ice cream, pizzas, snacks and drinks. Open until 3am.

Café del patio, Prat 470. La Serena's most atmospheric café-bar, with tables spread over a little patio and live jazz at weekends. A good, mellow place to spend an evening.

TOURS FROM LA SERENA

The two most popular tours from La Serena are to the **Elqui valley** (see p.164), taking in Vicuña, Montegrande and Pisco Elqui (all easily reached on public transport) and to the cloudforest reserve at **Parque Nacional Fray Jorge** (see p.152) about two hours' south of the city and not served by public transport. Other destinations include nearby **beaches** like Guanaqueros and Tongoy (see p.154); **Andacollo**, an important pilgrimage centre 54km south of La Serena (see p.153); the ancient petroglyph site of the **Valle del Encanto**, near Ovalle (see p.151); **Monumento Natural Pichasca**, where you'll find the remains of a "fossilized wood" (see p.151) and the **Reserva Nacional Pinguino de Humboldt**, a penguin sanctuary 120km northeast of La Serena. On Saturdays you can take tours to the international astronomical observatory of **Cerro Tololo** in the Elqui Valley (see box opposite). The **cost** of most tours is around CH$15,000 to 20,000 per person, usually for a full day. The following operators are all well-established and reliable:

Ciclomanía, Huanhuali 900 (☎ & fax 51/210172). Reasonably priced, eco-conscious mountain bike tours (half-day to two days) in the Elqui Valley and the foothills of the Andes. Nov–March.

Diaguitas Tour, Matta 510 on Plaza de Armas (☎ & fax 51/217265). All the main tours.

Explora Tours, Prat 567, office 8 (☎ & fax 51/219681). One-day tours to Parque Nacional Fray Jorge, including lunch in Tongoy.

Ingservitur, Los Lirios 300, Coquimbo (☎ & fax 51/260694). Popular, long-established company offering all the standard tours, including one to the Cerro Tololo observatory. Based in Coquimbo but will pick you up from your hotel in La Serena.

Trotamundo Expedition, Prat 544, office 305 (☎ & fax 51/228687). All the main destinations, including the penguin sanctuary, plus a long, exhausting trip to the Parque Nacional Nevado de Tres Cruces in the altiplano east of Copiapó (see p.179).

Turismo San Bartolomé, Balmaceda 417 (☎ & fax 51/221992). Efficiently run company offering the standard tours plus a range of more unusual ones, such as astronomical observation tours by night, and a visit to the small villages of the Limarí Valley.

Kamikaze, Av del Mar, near 4 Esquinas. Trendy, popular pub-disco attracting a range of ages.

Scratch, Av del Mar. Typical beach resort disco, with a predominantly young clientele.

Listings

Airlines Avant, Cordovez 309 (☎51/219275); Ladeco, Cordovéz 484 (☎51/225753); Lan Chile, Eduardo de la Barra 435 (☎51/221531).

Banks and exchange There are plenty of ATMs including on the Plaza de Armas, next to the cinema; on the corner of Prat and O'Higgins; and the corner of Cordovéz and Cienfuegos. For exchange, try Cambios La Portada, Prat 515 (daily 9am–11pm); Cambios Fides, Balmaceda 460, office no. 7; Casa de Cambio Maya, Portales 305; and Gira Tour, Prat 689.

Car rental Good-value saloon cars at Callegari, O'Higgins 672 (☎51/225714). There are many outlets on Av Francisco de Aguirre, including Avis at no. 68 (☎ & fax 51/227171); Bert at no. 312 (☎51/211475); Dollar at no. 58 (☎51/225714, fax 211688); Hertz at no. 225 (☎51/225471, fax 212166); and Oceanic at no. 62 (☎ & fax 51/214007). You could also try Budget at Balmaceda 3850 (☎ & fax 51/248200) and Daire at Prat 645 (☎ & fax 51/226933).

Laundry Ro-Ma at Los Carrera 654.

Post office The main Correo is on the west side of Plaza de Armas, on the corner of Prat and Matta.

Tarjeta de Turismo To replace lost tourist cards or extend your existing card go to the Intendencia at Prat 350 (☎51/224421).

MOVING ON FROM LA SERENA

Inter-city buses operate from La Serena's large, modern bus terminal on El Santo, southwest of the city centre. From here, there are frequent services to Santiago and all the main cities and towns of the north, plus a few services to regional destinations. Buses for the **Elqui valley** leave from the Plaza de Abastos on Esmeralda, just south of Colo Colo, about every 30min. To get to **Tongoy**, take a Serenamar bus from Av Francisco de Aguirre 344 (☎51/213658); the other **coastal resorts** are more easily reached from Coquimbo – to get there, take a *micro* from Avenida Francisco de Aguirre, or main south- and westbound streets. There are two **colectivo** services from La Serena, both operating from calle Domeyko, one block south of Iglesia San Francisco: Anserco, at no. 524 (☎51/217567) goes to Andacollo, Vicuña and Ovalle; Tasco, at no. 575 (☎51/224517) goes to Vicuña, Montegrande and Pisco Elqui. Regular **flights** to Santiago and the north are provided by Lan Chile, Ladeco and Avant (see "Listings" opposite).

Taxis 24-hour radio taxis on ☎51/211455.

Telephone offices Many in the centre, including at Cienfuegos 498; Cordovéz 446; and O'Higgins 536.

Travel agencies For airline tickets, try Viajes Val, Prat 540; Gira-Tour, Prat 689 or Viajes Torremolinos at Balmaceda 431. For tours and excursions in the region, see box opposite.

OBSERVATORIES

Thanks to the exceptional transparency of its skies, northern Chile is home to the largest concentration of astronomical **observatories** in the world. The region around La Serena, in particular, has been chosen by a number of international astronomical research institutions as the site of their telescopes, housed in white, futuristic domes that loom over the valleys from their hilltop locations. The research bodies that own the observatories include North American and European groups who need a base in the southern hemisphere, where the amount of sky that can be viewed is far greater than in the northern hemisphere (about a third of the sky seen here is never visible in the northern hemisphere). Some of the observatories offer guided tours, including the impressive **Cerro Tololo** Inter-American Observatory, whose four-metre telescope is currently the largest in the southern hemisphere (but, early in the new millennium, will be overtaken by Cerro Paranal's Very Large Telescope, near Antofagasta, which will be the largest in the world).

Cerro Tololo is 70km east of La Serena, reached by a side road branching south of the Elqui Valley road; free tours take place every Saturday at 9am and 1pm, and need to be booked several days in advance on ☎51/225415 (English-speaking), quoting the registration number of the vehicle you'll be arriving in. You'll be asked to pick up your visitor's permit from its offices in La Serena (up the hill behind the university, at Colina Los Pinos) the day before the tour, but it's easier if you arrange to pick it up at the observatory gates; alternatively, take a pre-booked tour from La Serena (see box opposite), which takes care of all the organization. Some 150km northeast of La Serena, reached by a side road branching east from the Panamericana, **La Silla** is the site of the European Southern Observatory's fourteen telescopes, including two 3.6-metre optical reflectors; visits take place on the first Saturday of each month, with advance bookings at its Santiago offices on ☎2/228 5006. Thirty kilometres north of Las Silla, the Carnegie Institute's observatory at **Las Campanas** contains four telescopes, with two 6.5-metre telescopes under construction as part of its Magellan Project; it can be visited on Saturdays, phoning ahead to book at its offices in La Serena (☎51/224680), located next to Cerro Tololo's offices on Colina Los Pinos. All of these tours, of course, take place during the day, and are strictly no-touching; a more hands-on experience is provided by the Municipalidad de Vicuña's small observatory on **Cerro Mamalluca**, 5km north of the town – for details, see p.165.

The Elqui valley

Quiet, rural and extremely beautiful, the **ELQUI VALLEY** pans east from La Serena and climbs into the Andes. Irrigated by canals fed by the Puclara and La Laguna dams, the valley floor is given over entirely to cultivation – of papayas, custard apples, oranges, avocados and, most famously, the vast expanses of vines grown to produce **pisco**. It's the fluorescent green of these vines that makes the valley so stunning, forming a spectacular contrast with the charred, brown hills that rise either side. To get the full visual impact you need to visit between September and March, but this is a gorgeous place to spend a couple of days at any time of year. Some 60km east of La Serena, **Vicuña** is the main town and transport hub of the Elqui valley. Moving east from here, the valley gets higher and narrower, and is dotted with tiny villages like **Montegrande** and the odd pisco distillery. The road from La Serena is paved for 105km as far as **Pisco Elqui**, a very pretty village that makes a great place to unwind for a couple of days, while if you really want to get away from it all, head for one of the rustic *cabañas* dotted along the banks of the **río Cochiguás** that forks east of the main valley at Montegrande.

GETTING ABOUT THE ELQUI VALLEY

Many tour companies in La Serena offer trips to the Elqui valley, but it's hardly worth it as public transport up and down the valley is so frequent and cheap. The two main **bus** companies are Frontera Elqui and Via Elqui-Megal; in **La Serena**, they use the terminal southwest of the centre at the Plaza de Abastos, on calle Esmeralda (just south of Colo Colo). Daily buses depart every half-hour for **Vicuña**, with about six of these continuing to **Montegrande** and **Pisco Elqui**. You can also take a **colectivo** from La Serena – Tasco runs every half-hour from Domeyko 575 (☎51/224517), for Vicuña, Montegrande and Pisco Elqui.

Vicuña

VICUNA, about a forty-minute-drive east from La Serena, is a neat and tidy agricultural town laid out around a large, luxuriantly landscaped square. It's a pleasant, easy-going place with a few low-key attractions, a good choice of places to stay and eat, and a major new public observatory on its doorstep. Life revolves firmly around the **plaza** which sports, at its centre, a huge stone replica of the **death mask** of Nobel prize-winning poet **Gabriela Mistral**, the Elqui valley's most famous daughter. On the square's northwest corner stands the **Iglesia de la Inmaculada Concepción**, topped by an impressive wooden tower built in 1909 – take a look inside at its vaulted polychrome ceiling painted with delicate religious images, and supported by immense wooden columns. Right next door, the eccentric **Torre Bauer** is a bright-red, mock-medieval tower prefabricated in Germany in 1905 and brought to Vicuña on the instructions of the town's German-born mayor, Adolfo Bauer; the adobe building supporting it houses the Municipalidad. Standing on the southern side of the square, the **Museo Entomológico** (Mon–Fri 10.30am–1.30pm & 3.30–7pm, Sat & Sun 10.30am–7pm; CH$400) hoards a fascinating collection of horror-movie creepie crawlies and exotic butterflies and shells.

Four blocks east of the square, at the end of Gabriela Mistral, the **Museo Gabriela Mistral** (Jan & Feb Mon–Sat 10am–7pm, Sun 10am–6pm; March–Dec Tues–Fri 10am–1pm & 3–7pm, Sat 10am–1pm & 3–6pm, Sun 10am–1pm; CH$500) displays pho-

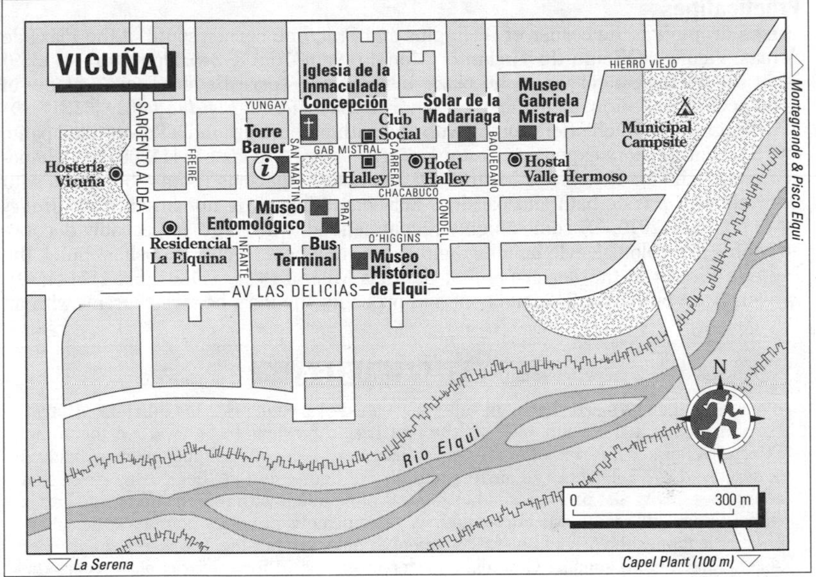

tos, prizes, articles and personal objects bequeathed to the city by the poet, and panels giving an account of her life and works. A few doors down at no. 683 is the **Solar de los Madariaga** (daily 11am–1pm & 3–5pm; CH$400), an old, colonial-style house preserved as a museum displaying a modest collection of nineteenth-century furniture and clothes. Another unassuming little museum is the **Museo Histórico de Elqui** (daily: March–Nov 10am–6pm; Dec–Feb 9am–8pm; CH$200) at Prat 90, which houses a curious jumble of pre-Columbian ceramics and nineteenth-century paraphernalia. Just out of town, across the bridge by the filling station, you'll find the **Planta Capel**, the largest pisco distillery in the Elqui valley. It offers free and very slick guided tours in English and Spanish (March–Dec Mon–Fri 9.30am–noon & 2.30–6pm, Sat 10am–12.30pm; Jan & Feb same hours plus Sun 10am–12.30pm), with free tastings and the chance to buy bottles and souvenirs at the end.

Five kilometres northeast of Vicuña, the recently opened **Cerro Mamalluca observatory** is the only observatory in Chile built specifically for public use. Run by the Municipalidad de Vicuña and featuring a 30cm Smith-Cassegrain telescope donated by the Cerro Tololo team, it runs two-hour **evening tours** (daily 8pm, 10pm & midnight; CH$3000) that start with a high-tech audiovisual talk on the history of the universe, and end with the chance to look through the telescope. You can expect to see a dazzling display of stars, planets, galaxies, nebulas and clusters, including Jupiter, Saturn's rings, the Orion nebula, the Andromeda galaxy, Sirius and lots more. These are aimed at complete beginners, but serious astronomers can arrange in-depth, small-group sessions (US$100) with two months' advance notice. The tours assemble half an hour before the scheduled slot at the observatory's administrative office in Vicuña, at Gabriela Mistral 260 (Mon–Sat 9am–10pm, Sun 10am–10pm; ☎51/411352, fax 411255; *obser_mamalluca@yahoo.com*; *www.angelfire.com/wy/obsermamalluca*), from where transport is provided to Cerro Mamalluca; advance reservations are essential, either by phone, fax, email or in person at the office.

Practicalities

Buses drop off at the corner of O'Higgins and Prat, one corner south of the Plaza de Armas. Vicuña's **Oficina de Turismo** (Mon–Fri 9am–1pm & 2–5.30pm; ☎51/411359) is on the northwest corner of the plaza, beneath the Torre Bauer. There's plenty of good **accommodation**, including the friendly *Residencial La Elquina* (☎51/411317; ③) at O'Higgins 65, which offers rooms with and without bath around a flower-filled patio, and the slightly more expensive *Hostal Valle Hermoso* (☎ & fax 51/411206; ③), a handsome old building at Gabriela Mistral 706, with clean spacious rooms (but some with no windows), private bath and parking. For something more upmarket, *Hotel Halley* (☎ & fax 51/412070; ④) comes highly recommended, with large, impeccably decorated rooms in a colonial-style building, and access to a pool. Vicuña's poshest hotel, the *Hostería Vicuña*, at the western end of Gabriela Mistral (☎51/411301, fax 411144; ⑥), is overpriced but has a fabulous pool and probably Vicuña's best restaurant, with an

GABRIELA MISTRAL

Even more than its pisco, the Elqui valley's greatest source of pride is **Gabriela Mistral**, born in Vicuña in 1889 and, in 1945, the first Latin American to be awarded the Nobel Prize for Literature. A schoolmistress, a spinster and a deeply religious woman, Mistral is perceived by Chileans as an austere and distant figure, and yet her poetry reveals an aching sensitivity and passion, and her life was punctuated with tragedy and grief. Lucila Godoy Alcayaga, as she was christened, was just three years old when her father abandoned the family, the first of several experiences of loss in her life. It was left to her older sister, Emiliana, to support Gabriela and her mother, and for the next eight years the three of them lived in the schoolhouse in the village of Montegrande where Emiliana worked as a teacher. At the age of fourteen, Gabriela started work as an assistant schoolteacher herself, in a village close to La Serena, where she taught children by day and workmen learning to read by night. It was here, also, that she took her first steps into the world of literature, publishing several pieces in the local newspaper under the pseudonyms of "Alguien" ("Someone"), "Soledad" ("Solitude") and "Alma" ("Soul"). When she was seventeen years old, Gabriela fell in love with Romelio Ureta, the only romantic love in her life. Three years later, Ureta committed suicide; in his pocket, a card was found bearing the name of Lucila Godoy.

The intense grief caused by Ureta's suicide was to inform much of Gabriela's poetry, to which she devoted her time with increasing dedication while supporting herself with a series of teaching posts. In 1914 she won first prize in an important national poetry competition with *Los Sonetos de la Muerte* (Sonnets of Death), and in 1922 her first collection of verses was published under the title of *Desolación* (Desolation), followed a couple of years later by a second collection, *Ternura* (Tenderness). Her work was received with international acclaim and, in recognition of this, the Chilean government offered Gabriela a position in the consular service, allowing her to concentrate almost exclusively on her poetry. As consul, she spent many years abroad, particularly in the USA, but her verses continued to look back to Chile, particularly her beloved Elqui valley, which she described as "a cry of nature rising amidst the opaque mountains and intense blue sky". Her most frequently recurring themes, however, were her love of children, and her sorrow at her childlessness.

Though never a mother, Gabriela did have her adored nephew "Yin Yin", who had been placed in her care when he was just nine months old. Once again, though, tragedy was to strike her life when, at the age of seventeen, Yin Yin committed suicide in Brazil, where Gabriela was serving as consul. It was a loss from which she never recovered, and for which her Nobel Prize, awarded two years later, could do little to console her. Gabriela outlived her nephew by twelve years, during which she continued to be regaled with international prizes, honorary degrees and other tributes, including the French Legion of Honour. She died in New York, aged sixty-seven, leaving the proceeds of all her works published in South America to the children of Montegrande.

unadventurous but good-quality meat- and fish-based menu. The municipal **campsite** (☎51/411713; CH$6000 per site), off the eastern end of Chacabuco, has lots of shade and a pool, but is poorly maintained. For **eating**, besides the *Hostería Vicuña* you could do worse than the *Club Social* at Gabriela Mistral 435, which serves typical Chilean meat and fish dishes, or*Halley*, across the road at no. 404, which has a large, attractive dining room and is a good place for Sunday lunch.

Montegrande

Thirty-four kilometres on from Vicuña (if you're driving, take the right turn for Paihuano at Rivadavia), **MONTEGRANDE** is a picturesque village with a pretty church standing on a surprisingly large square. The childhood home of Gabriela Mistral, Montegrande assiduously devotes itself to preserving her memory: her profile has been outlined in white stones on the valley wall opposite the plaza, and the school where she lived with and was taught by her sister has been turned into a **museum** (Tues–Sun 10am–1pm & 3–6pm; CH$500), displaying some of her furniture and belongings. Just south of the village, her **tomb** rests on a hillside, opposite the small **Capel plant** (free tours Jan & Feb daily 9.30am–6pm; March–Dec Mon–Fri 9.30am–noon & 2.30–6pm, Sat & Sun 2.30–6pm). Close by is the wacky **Galería de Arte Zen**, where you can admire esoteric art and have a tarot card reading. There's nowhere to stay in Montegrande – for accommodation, continue 4km along the main road to Pisco Elqui, or take the turn-off (from the fork by the Capel plant) for Cochiguás.

Pisco Elqui

PISCO ELQUI was known as La Unión until 1939 when Gabriel González Videla – later President of Chile – cunningly renamed it to thwart Peru's efforts to gain exclusive rights over the name "Pisco". An idyllic village with fewer than 500 inhabitants, it boasts a beautiful square filled with lush palm trees and flowers, overlooked by a colourful church with a tall, wooden tower. Locals sell home-made jam and marmalade in the square, and its abundant shade provides a welcome relief from the sun. Down by the main road, the **Solar de Pisco Elqui** is Chile's oldest pisco distillery, which today (considerably modernized) produces the famous Tres Erres brand; there are free **guided tours** (Mon–Sat 10.30am–12.30pm & 2.30–6.30pm) around the old part of the plant, with tastings at the end. You can also visit the 130-year-old private distillery at **Los Nichos**, 4km on from Pisco Elqui (daily 11am–1pm & 3–6pm); if there's no one there, ask in the red house next door.

Increasingly popular in summer, Pisco Elqui has plenty of good **places to stay**. The *Hotel Elqui* (☎51/451083; ③–④) on the main street, has eight immaculate rooms, some with balconies, in a charming old building with a pool. Alternatively try the *Hostería de Don Juan* (☎51/451087; ③) on Prat, a Gothic, Adams Family-type house full of nooks, crannies and antique furniture. The friendly, German-run *El Tesoro de Elqui* (☎ & fax 51/451958; ④) offers attractive, spotless *cabañas* and a gorgeous pool. There's also a **campsite**, *Los Olivios* (☎51/411338; CH$2000 per person), just off the main road, with shade and a small swimming pool. Pisco Elqui's best **restaurants** are in *Hotel Elqui*, which serves typical Chilean meat dishes on a large, vine-covered patio, and *El Tesoro de Elqui*, where you'll find excellent roast meats.

Along the río Cochiguás

Back in Montegrande, a rough, unpaved road branches off the main road, dips down the valley and follows the northern bank of the **río Cochiguás** a tributary of the Elqui.

PISCO

The fruity, aromatic brandy known as pisco is the undisputed national drink of Chile. Made from the distilled wine of muscatel grapes, it's produced in the transverse valleys of the Norte Chico, particularly the Elqui valley where consistently high temperatures, light, alkaline soil and brilliant sunshine combine to produce grapes with a high sugar content and low acidity, perfect for distillation. Some believe its name derives from the Quechua word "Pisku", which means "flying bird", others that it took its name from the small Peruvian port from where it was shipped, illegally, during colonial times. It's been enjoyed by Chileans for over four centuries, but it wasn't until the 1930s that it was organized into an effective commercial industry, starting with the creation, by the government, of a pisco *denominación de origen*. Shortly afterwards, a large number of growers, who'd always been at the mercy of the private distilleries for the price they got for their grapes, clubbed together to form co-operatives to produce their own pisco. The largest were the tongue-twisting *Sociedad Cooperativa Control Pisquero de Elqui y Vitiviniculo de Norte Ltda* (known as "Pisco Control") and the *Cooperativa Agrícola y Pisquera del Elqui Ltda* (known as "Pisco Capel"), today the two most important producers in Chile, accounting for over ninety percent of all pisco to hit the shops. The basic distillation technique is the same one that's been used since colonial times: in short, the fermented wine is boiled in copper stills, at 90°C, releasing vapours which are condensed, then kept in oak vats for three to six months. The alcohol – of 55° to 65° – is then diluted with water, according to the type of pisco it's being sold as: 30° or 32° for *Selección*; 35° for *Reservado*; 40° for *Especial*; and 43°, 46° and 50° for *Gran Pisco*. It's most commonly drunk as a tangy, refreshing aperitif known as **Pisco Sour**, an ice-cold mix of pisco, lemon juice and sugar. Further north, whisked egg white is added to this cocktail by the Peruvians, who also produce pisco – indeed, who consider their own to be the only authentic sort, and believe that the Chilean stuff is nothing short of counterfeit. The Chileans, of course, pass this off as jealousy, maintaining that theirs is far superior, and that pisco is a Chilean drink, not a Peruvian drink. Whatever its origins, and whoever produced it first, there's no denying that the Elqui valley pisco is a very fine spirit, worthy of the pride felt for it by Chileans up and down the country.

Dotted at intervals along the river bank are rustic *cabañas*, many of them offering holistic therapies and meditation classes. The small community of **Cochiguás**, 12km along the valley, was founded in the 1960s by a group of New Age hippies in the belief that the Age of Aquarius had shifted the earth's magnetic centre from the Himalayas to the Elqui valley. But don't let this put you off – the scenery is fabulous and the remoteness and tranquillity of the valley irresistible. If you're walking from the turn-off, you can easily reach the first set of *cabañas*, called *Spa Naturista* (☎51/451067; ⑤), 2km from the paved road. A further 3km along, friendly *El Albaricoque* (☎ & fax 51/230089; ④) offers rustic *cabañas* in a wood by the river, and good vegetarian food. About 13km from Montegrande you'll find luxurious but expensive *cabañas* at *Casa del Agua* (☎ & fax 51/411246; ⑤) set in six hectares of private land, spanning both sides of the river. At the very end of the road, 18km from Montegrande, *Camping Cochiguás* (☎51/327046; CH$6000) has 24 sites with picnic tables, and offers **horse-riding** tours of the valley.

Vallenar and around

North of La Serena, the Panamericana turns inland and heads towards the town of **VALLENAR**, 188km up the road. There are only a few sporadic signs of habitation in between, and nothing to tempt you off the highway save a possible detour down a 76-kilometre dirt track (opposite Domeyko) to the **Reserva Nacional Pinguino de Humboldt**, where you can take boat trips (CH$30,000 per boat) to Isla Chañaral, surrounded by bottle-nosed dolphins, and to Isla Choros, home to a colony of Humboldt penguins. Pushing on to Vallenar, you'll find a busy but somewhat run-down little town, that acts as a service centre for local mining and agricultural industries. Founded in 1789 by Governor Ambrosio O'Higgins, who named the city after his native Ballinagh in Ireland, it has little in the way of tourist attractions, but makes a convenient base for an excursion east into the fertile **upper Huasco valley**, laced with green vines and small pisco plants, or northwest towards the coast and the wild flowers of the **Parque Nacional Llanos de Challe**. The self-appointed "*capital del desierto florido*" (and vigorously promoted as such by the tourist authorities), Vallenar is also a good base for forays into the **flowering desert**, if you're here at the right time. As for the town itself, the **Museo del Huasco** (Mon–Fri 10am–1pm & 3–6.30pm, Sat 10am–1pm; CH$300) at Sargento Aldea 742 has some moderately diverting displays on indigenous cultures and photos of the flowering desert, and there's a municipal **swimming pool** one block east. There is also a **cinema** (with a dreadful sound system) at Prat 1094.

Practicalities

Vallenar's **bus terminal** is on Matta, six blocks west of the main square. The **Oficina de Turismo** (unfixed hours; ☎51/619215), however, is inconveniently located just off the Panamericana, on the side road into town – unless you're arriving by car, enquire instead at the Municipalidad on the north side of the Plaza de Armas. **Accommodation** in Vallenar is on the whole overpriced, but you'll find good budget rooms with private bath, set around a quiet patio, at *Residencial Oriental*, Serrano 720 (☎51/613889; ②). *Hostal Camino del Rey* at Merced 943 (☎51/613184; ③) has neat, box-like rooms with shared and private bath and its own parking, while the *Hotel Garra de León*, at Serrano 1052 (☎ & fax 51/613753; ⑤), has smart, very spacious rooms with air conditioning, cable TV and pristine bathrooms, plus its own car park. Of Vallenar's **restaurants**, the one at the *Hostería de Vallenar*, at Alonso de Ercilla 848, is surprisingly good, serving well-cooked meat and fish in imaginative sauces; you could also try *Bavaria* at Serrano 802 and *El Fogón* at Ramírez 934, for *parilladas*, or *Bocatto*, on the east side of the

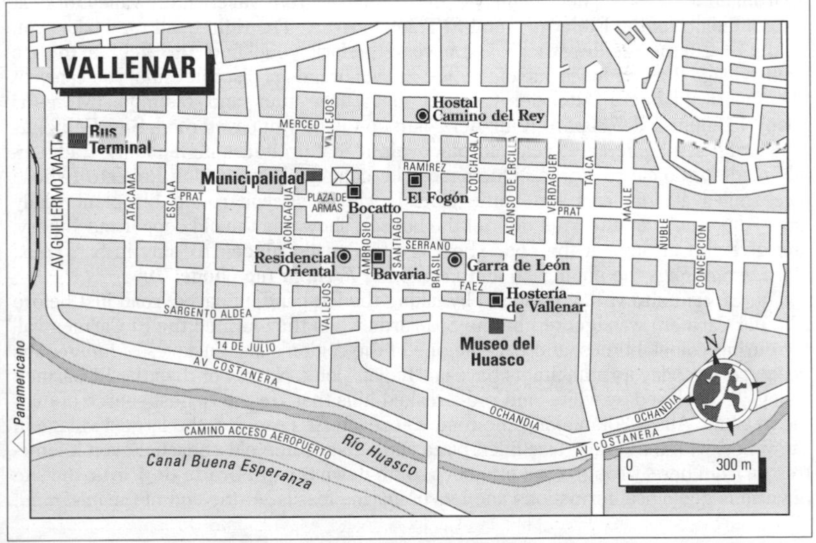

THE FLOWERING DESERT

Travelling up the Panamericana between Vallenar and Copiapó, you'll cross – on any ordinary day – a seemingly endless, semi-desert plain, sparsely covered with low shrubs and cactus plants. Take the same journey in spring after a heavy winter rainfall and you'll find, in place of the parched, brown earth, a fluorescent carpet of flowers, stretching into the horizon. This extraordinary transformation is known as the *desierto florido*, or "flowering desert", when unusually heavy rainfall (normally very light in this region) causes dormant bulbs and seeds, hidden beneath the earth, to sprout into sudden bloom from early September to late October. In the central strip, crossed by the highway, the flowers appear in huge single blocks of colour, formed chiefly by the purple *pata de guanaco* ("guanaco's hoof"), but also the yellow *coronas de fraile* ("monk's halo") and the blue *suspiro de campo* ("field's sigh"). On the banks of the *quebradas*, or ravines, that snake across the land from the cordillera to the ocean, many different varieties are mixed together, producing a kaleidoscope of contrasting colours. West, towards the coast, you'll also find large crimson swaths of the endangered *garra de león* ("lion's claw"), particularly in the Parque Nacional Llanos de Challe (see opposite), near Carrizal Bajo. There's no predicting the *desierto florido*, which is a relatively rare phenomenon – occurring most recently in 1983, 1987, 1991 and, most spectacularly, in 1997.

square, for pizzas. There are no *cambios* in Vallenar, but several **ATMs** on Prat, between Brasil and Alonso de Ercilla.

The upper Huasco valley

From Vallenar, a good paved road follows the río Huasco through a deep, attractive valley that climbs towards the mountains. The road weaves back and forth across the river, taking you through dry, mauve-coloured hills and green orchards and vineyards. About 20km from the town, you pass the enormous **Santa Juana dam** which, after a season of heavy rainfall, overflows into a magnificent waterfall that can be viewed close-up from an observation deck. Thirty-eight kilometres from Vallenar, the valley forks at the confluence of the El Carmen and El Tránsito rivers. The right-hand road takes you up the **El Carmen valley** where, just beyond the fork, you'll find **Alto del Carmen**, a pretty village that produces one of the best-known brands of pisco in Chile; you can visit the Planta Pisquera Alto del Carmen for a free tour and tastings (Mon–Fri 10am–12.30pm & 3–5.30pm). A further 26km up the now unpaved road, **San Félix** has a beautiful setting and a 95-year-old **pisco plant** that produces high-quality, traditionally made pisco called Horcón Quemado. The congenial owner, don Roberto (whose face smiles at you from the bottle labels), will guide you round his plant (daily 8am–8pm; knock on the front door of the house), show you the old copper machinery, and give you tastings at the end. There are two rustic **places to stay** in San Félix: *Pensión San Félix* (no phone; ②) and *Pensión La Fortuna* (no phone; ②).

The **El Tránsito valley** (reached by taking the left-hand, unpaved, road just before Alto del Carmen) was ignored by the Spaniards when they farmed the El Carmen valley during colonial times, and became one of the region's last enclaves of indigenous people; even today its inhabitants have an "Indian" look. Narrower than the El Carmen valley, it's enclosed by white- and red-streaked hills that are the richest source of marble in Chile. About 30km along the road you reach **El Tránsito**, the largest village in the valley, with a fragrant, tree-filled plaza and a handsome old church. Seven kilometres on from here, a rough road branches south down the **quebrada de Pinta**, the site of curious geological formations and lots of marine fossils. At the end of the *quebrada*,

5km from the turn-off, **Pinte** is a tiny oasis village with a beautiful white church surrounded by orange, lemon and lime trees; you can hire a guide here, Raquel Gallo, to show you the geological features of the area.

Parque Nacional Llanos de Challe and the northern beaches

If you have the good luck to be around while the desert's in bloom, head for the **PARQUE NACIONAL LLANOS DE CHALLE**, northwest of Vallenar, for the full impact of the phenomenon. This 45,000-hectare swath of coastal plains has been singled out for national park status because of the abundance of **garra de león** – an exquisite, deep-red flower in danger of extinction – that grow there during the years of the *desierto florido*. The area covered by the park is crossed by an 82-kilometre dirt road branching east from the Panamericana, 17km north of Vallenar, ending at **Carrizal Bajo**, a once-important mining port now home to a tiny fishing community made up of sixteen families. Three buses a week leave Vallenar for Carrizal Bajo (for details, check with Vallenar's Oficina de Turismo on ☎51/619215). If you have a 4WD, a tent and a taste for wilderness, you could follow the very rough track north of Carrizal Bajo up to Puerto Viejo, near Caldera and Copiapó – the deserted **beaches** along this stretch, particularly the northern half, are breathtaking, with white sands and clear, turquoise waters.

Copiapó

The thriving, prosperous city of **COPIAPÓ** sits in the flat basin of the Copiapó river valley, some 60km from the coast, 145km north of Vallenar. This is the last of the Norte Chico's "transverse valleys" and – with the exception of the río Loa which empties into the ocean near Iquique – the **río Copiapó** is Chile's northernmost river to flow all the way from the Andes to the Pacific. Beyond this valley the transformation from semi-desert to serious desert is complete, and the bare, barren Atacama stretches a staggering 1200km north into southern Peru. When Diego de Almagro made his long trek south from Cuzco in 1536, following the Inca Royal Road down the spine of the Andes, it was into this valley that he descended, recuperating from the gruelling journey at the *tambo*, or resting place, where Copiapó now stands. Known as "Copayapú" or "cup of gold", the valley had been occupied and cultivated by the Diaguita people from around 1000 AD and then from around 1470 by the Incas, who mined gold and copper here. Although Spanish *encomenderos* (see p.449) occupied the valley from the beginning of the conquest, it wasn't until 1744 that the city of Copiapó was founded, initially as San Francisco de la Selva. A series of random silver strikes in the nineteenth century, most notably at Chañarcillo, threw the region into a frenzied boom.

Today, following a period of decline at the beginning of the twentieth century, Copiapó is once more at the centre of a rich mining industry, revolving around copper, iron and gold. A lively, busy city of around 98,000 inhabitants, it has a fairly compact downtown core composed of typical adobe houses dotted with churches and the odd mansion, with a large, attractive square at its centre. While it's all perfectly pleasant, there isn't a great deal to do here and Copiapó's main use to travellers tends to be as a springboard for excursions into the surrounding region – primarily up to the lakes and volcanoes of **Parque Nacional Nevado de Tres Cruces** and nearby **Volcán Ojos de Salado** and **Laguna Verde**, all sitting high in the Andes, or west into the famously beautiful seaside resort of **Bahía Inglesa**. Closer at hand, the **Copiapó river valley** is a popular day-trip, and one of the most stunning examples of desert irrigation in Chile.

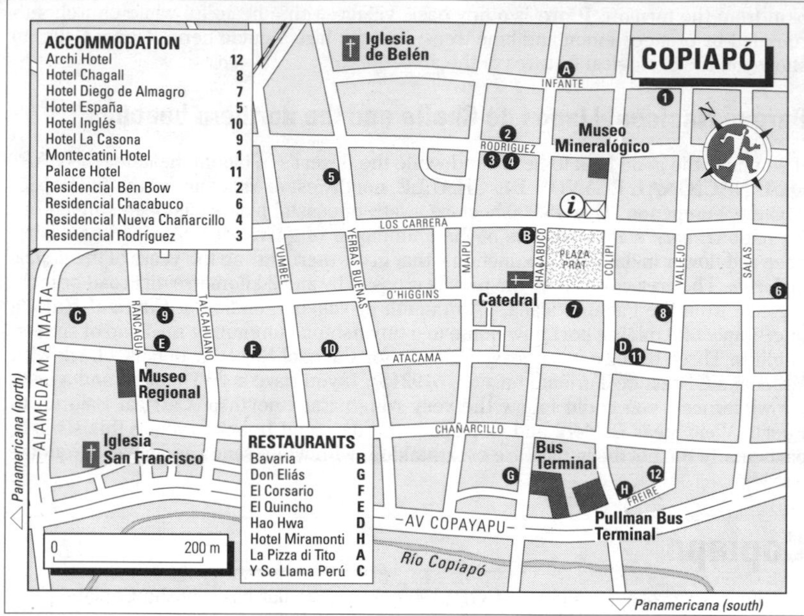

Arrival and information

Copiapó's main **bus terminal**, served by most inter-city buses, is centrally located on the corner of Freire and Chacabuco, three blocks south of Plaza Prat. Next door, also on Chacabuco, is the **Tur Bus terminal**, while one block east, on the corner of Freire and Colipí, is the gleaming new **Pullman Bus terminal**. The **airport** is 15km east of the city; there are no buses into the centre, but there's always a **minibus** there to meet arriving planes, which will take you into town for around CH$1500.

There's a well-organized, helpful **Sernatur** office (mid-Dec to Feb Mon–Fri 8.30am–8pm, Sat 10am–2pm & 4–7pm; March to mid-Dec Mon–Fri 8.30am–6pm; ☎52/212838) on the north side of Plaza Prat, at Los Carrera 691. **Conaf**, at Atacama 898 (Mon–Fri 9am–1pm & 2.30–5.30pm; ☎52/213404), will give you information on protected areas in Region IV, including Pan de Azúcar and Nevado de Tres Cruces national parks; it's also good source of information on road conditions in the altiplano.

Accommodation

Copiapó has an excellent choice of upmarket hotels offering the levels of comfort and service you would expect, but rarely get, for the price. Decent mid-priced options, on the other hand, are thin on the ground, but there are plenty of adequate budget rooms.

Archi Hotel, Vallejo, on the corner with Freire (☎ & fax 52/212983). Claims of "*elegancia y distinción*" are belied by the blue crushed velvet furnishings and worn-out rooms (all with private bath) of this neglected hotel. Passable, nonetheless, and handy for the bus station. Has its own parking. ③.

Hotel Chagall, O'Higgins 760 (☎52/213775, fax 211527). North American-style hotel with an attractive lobby and bar, spacious, new-looking rooms, smart baths, a good restaurant and private parking. ⑥.

Hotel Diego de Almagro, O'Higgins 656 (☎52/212075, fax 212076). Large, stylish hotel with contemporary decor, pool, sauna and parking. ⑥.

Hotel España, Yerbas Buenas 571 (☎52/217197, fax 217198). Overpriced rooms with private bath in the main building, and cheap, basic ones minus bath out the back. ③–④.

Hotel Inglés, Atacama 337 (☎52/212797, fax 211286). Simple rooms with polished wooden floors in a traditional adobe house built round a large patio with a veranda. A good budget choice. ③.

Hotel La Casona, O'Higgins 150 (☎52/217277, fax 217278). Small, charming and impeccably decorated hotel with an English-speaking owner. ⑤.

Montecatini Hotel, Infante 766 (☎52/211363, fax 217021). Bright, spacious rooms falling into two classes: smart, new "*ejecutivo*" and older but cheaper "*turista*", both with private bath. Has its own parking. ④–⑤.

Palace Hotel, Atacama 741 (☎52/212852). Reasonable but overpriced rooms with private bath around an attractive patio; try bargaining the rate down. ⑤.

Residencial Ben Bow, Rodriguez 541 (☎52/217634). Cramped but perfectly fine little rooms, among the cheapest in town. ②.

Residencial Chacabuco, O'Higgins 921 (☎52/213428). Simple but cared-for rooms off a patio. ②.

Residencial Nueva Chañarcillo, Rodriguez 540 (☎52/212368). Large, spick-and-span *residencial* with a busy turnover and a stern *señora*. ③.

Residencial Rodriguez, Rodriguez 528 (☎52/212861). Old and tired but clean budget rooms with a friendly owner and a noisy budgerigar. ②.

The City

The nucleus of Copiapó is the large, green **Plaza Prat**, lined with 84 towering old pepper trees planted in 1880. On the southwest corner of the square stands the mid-nineteenth-century **Iglesia Catedral**, designed by the English architect William Rogers, sporting a Neoclassical three-door portico, and topped by an unusual tiered wooden tower. Just off the northwest corner of the square, at the corner of Colopí and Rodriguez, the University of Atacama's excellent **Museo Mineralógico** (Mon–Fri 10am–1pm & 3.30–7pm, Sat 10am–1pm; CH$300) displays a glittering collection of over two thousand mineral samples from around the world, including huge chunks of malachite, amethyst, quartz, marble and onyx. Five blocks west of the square, at the corner of Atacama and Rancagua, the **Museo Regional** (Tues–Thurs 9am–12.45pm & 3–7.15pm, Fri 9am–12.45pm & 3–6pm, Sat 10am–12.45pm & 3–5.45pm, Sun 10am–12.45pm; CH$500) is also worth a visit, not least for the handsome mansion that houses it, the **Casa Matta**, built in the 1840s for one of Copiapó's wealthy mining barons. The museum's well-presented displays cover themes like the exploration of the desert, the development of mining, the war of the Pacific, pre-Columbian peoples of the region, and the Inca road system.

One block south and west of the museum, the imposing, red-walled **Iglesia San Francisco**, built in 1872, towers over a tiny square that is the site of a busy Friday market selling fresh produce and household items. The square's centre is marked by a statue of a rough-clad miner, tools in hand – none other than **Juan Godoy**, the goatherd who accidentally discovered the enormous silver deposits of nearby Chañarcillo in 1832, now honoured in Copiapó as a local legend. Just off the square, Avenida Matta leads north to the former **railway workers' residence**, a rather grand, Neoclassical building with a large pediment supported by tall wooden columns. Round the corner, a couple of blocks down Martínez (the extension of Atacama), the former **railway station**, built in 1854, houses a small but evocative **Museo Ferroviaro** (unfixed hours, usually open evenings; free) which displays photos and memorabilia of the Caldera–Copiapó railway, the first in Chile and third in South America. Not close to anything in particular, out at the corner of Yerbas Buenas and Infante, the **Iglesia de Belén** – built by the Jesuits during the colonial period and restored in 1856 by a wealthy local family – also deserves a visit, for its delicate, Neoclassical structure and dainty wooden tower.

Eating, drinking and entertainment

Copiapó has a reasonable but uninspiring choice of restaurants, most of them moderately priced. For **cheap snacks**, head for the row of cafés on Chacabuco, opposite the bus terminal – the best is *Don Elías*. The **nightlife** scene is not what you'd call swinging, but if you're set on having a dance you could try the city's trio of **discos**, made up of *Splash* at Juan Martínez 46, *Alai* at Maipú 279 and *Amadeo* on the corner of Maipú and Infante. There's a fairly large **cinema** with decent sound at Atacama 455.

Restaurants

Bavaria, west side of Plaza Prat. Conveniently located branch of the ubiquitous chain serving sandwiches, snacks and meat dishes.

El Corsario, Atacama 245. Attractive restaurant with tables around the interior patio of an old adobe house, offering traditional Chilean dishes like *pastel de choclo* and *humitas*.

El Quincho, Atacama, between Rancagua and Talcahuano. Large, dark restaurant specializing in hearty *parilladas*.

Hao Hwa, Colopí 340. Reliable, inexpensive Chinese restaurant, especially popular at lunchtime.

Hotel Miramonti, Ramón Freire 731, opposite Pullman Bus terminal. Elegant hotel restaurant serving good but quite expensive Italian food.

La Pizza di Tito, Chacabuco 710. Intimate Italian restaurant offering pizzas, pastas and good service.

Y se llama Perú, O'Higgins 12. One of the friendliest restaurants in Copiapó, offering moderately priced Peruvian food (meats marinaded in interesting, tangy sauces) that makes a change from normal Chilean cuisine. Sometimes has singing and dancing at the weekend.

TOURS FROM COPIAPÓ AND CALDERA

An increasing number of companies and individuals are offering tours out of Copiapó. The two main destinations are east into the cordillera, taking in **Parque Nacional Nevado de Tres Cruces** and sometimes **Laguna Verde** and **Ojos de Salado** (full day, from CH40,000; see p.179), and west to the **coast**, either to the beaches around **Bahía Inglesa** (half-day, from CH$10,000; see p.178), or north to **Parque Nacional Pan de Azúcar** (full-day, from CH$20,000; see p.184). Several companies also offer trips up the **Copiapó river valley** (half-day, from CH$10,000; see opposite). Note that those operators based in Caldera will pick you up in Copiapó, if that's where you're based, en route to the cordillera.

Aventurismo, Condominio Tupac Yupanqui 16, Caldera (☎ & fax 52/316395). Maximiliano Martínez has been taking tourists up to Ojos de Salado, Laguna Verde and around for longer than anyone else in the business. Friendly, professional and reliable.

Expediciones Puna Atacama, Piloto Marcial Arredondo 154 (☎52/212684, fax 211273). Tours primarily into the cordillera, but also to the Copiapó river valley and the coast.

Jeep Ecotour (☎52/216418). 4x4 jeep tours guided by a North American marine biologist to the coastal dunes and deserted beaches around Caldera, to Parque Nacional Pan de Azúcar and into the high cordillera.

Peruvian Tour, O'Higgins 12 (☎ & fax 52/212645). Small, family-run outfit offering customized jeep tours up into the altiplano and north to Parque Nacional Pan de Azúcar, or wherever else you want to go.

Taxinor (☎52/224951). Taxi trips to the coast, through the Copiapó valley and into the "flowering desert" when it's in bloom.

MOVING ON FROM COPIAPÓ

Copiapó has daily **bus services** to all the major cities between Santiago and Arica, as well as to local and regional destinations. **Inter-city** services are offered by all the main companies, including Flotta Barrios (☎52/213645), Pullman Bus (☎52/218676), Tas Choapa (☎52/213793), Tramacá (☎52/214007) and Tur Bus (☎52/212150). For **Caldera** and **Bahía Inglesa**, Recabarren has the most frequent service from the side street opposite the main terminal (about every 30min). Casther (☎52/218889) has around seven daily buses up the **Copiapó river valley**, which is also served by Abarán buses.

There are direct **flights** from Copiapó to Iquique, Calama, Antofagasta, La Serena and Santiago. The airport is 15km east of town; to get there, either take a taxi or arrange a minibus transfer with Cerro Mar (☎52/217155).

Listings

Airlines Avant, Colipí 350 (☎52/238962); Ladeco, Colipí 484, in Cosmocentre Plaza Real (☎52/217285); Lan Chile, Colipí 526 (☎52/213512).

Airport information ☎52/214360.

Banks and exchange There are several ATMs on the main square, including Corp Banca at Chacabuco 481 and BCI at Chacabuco 449. Casa de Cambio Fides is at Atacama 541, on the second floor of Galería Coimba.

Camping *Bencina blanca* (white gas) and butane gas are available at Ferretería el Herrerito, Atacama 699. Sparta, next to Entell on Plaza Prat, has a wide range of Camping Gaz appliances.

Car rental Good-value 4x4 jeeps and good service at Rodaggio, Colipí 127 (☎52/212153). Other firms include: Avis, Peña 102 (☎ & fax 52/213966); Budget, Colipí 50 (☎52/218802); First, Copayapú 923 (☎52/211290, fax 212369); Hertz, Copayapú 173 (☎52/213522); and Retablo, Los Carrera 955 (☎ & fax 52/219384).

Laundry Good, cheap service at Lavasuper, Mackenna 430, between O'Higgins and Carrera.

Post office Main Correo on the north side of Plaza Prat at Los Carrera 691.

Swimming Olympic-size swimming pool on Av Luis Flores; Piscina El Bosque (☎52/219522) at the corner of Cancha Rayada and San Martín.

Telephone centres CTC is at the corner of Los Carrera and Chacabuco; Entell is on the main square, at Colipí 500; Telex Chile, Atacama 499.

Travel agencies For flights etc, try Cobre Tours at O'Higgins 640 or Turismo Atacama at Los Carrera 716. For organized tours around Copiapó, see box opposite.

Around Copiapó

The region around Copiapó offers some of the most striking landscapes in Chile. To the west, **Bahía Inglesa**, near the port of **Caldera**, could be a little chunk of Capri, with its pristine sands studded with odd-shaped rocks rising out of the sea; further south, reached only in a 4x4, the coast is lined with wild, deserted **beaches** lapped by turquoise waters. To the east, the **río Copiapó valley** offers the extraordinary spectacle of emerald-green vines growing in desert-dry hills, while high up in the Andes, Chile is transformed into a world of salt flats, volcanoes and lakes, encompassed by the **Parque Nacional Nevado de Tres Cruces**, the **Volcán Ojos de Salado** and the blue-green **Laguna Verde**.

Copiapó river valley

Despite an acute shortage of rainfall, the valley of the río Copiapó is one of the most important grape-growing areas of Chile. This is thanks mainly to new irrigation techniques that have been developed over the past fifteen years, tapping into the valley's abundance of underground flowing water. The combination of computer-controlled irrigation and a hot, dry climate ensures an early harvest, with the grapes on US supermarket shelves by October. While the Copiapó valley is not quite as pastoral or picturesque as the Elqui valley, its cultivated areas provide, more than anywhere else in the north, the most stunning contrast between deep-green produce and parched, dry earth – from October to May, in particular, it really is a sight to behold.

The first stretch from Copiapó is quite dull, though you do pass some interesting landmarks, like the large country mansion and church at **Nantoco** (23km from the city), built in 1878 for one of Copiapó's rich mining magnates and now in a lamentable state of disrepair. At kilometre 34, hidden behind a dense covering of palm trees on the right-hand side, the **Casa de Jotabeche** is another grand nineteenth-century residence, this one belonging to the prominent essayist José Joaquín Vallejo, known as "Jotabeche", who lived here until his death in 1858. By the time you reach Los Loros, 64km from Copiapó, the valley has become narrower, greener and prettier. Los Loros makes a good place to stop for **lunch** – try Sra Herrera at no. 62 of the main street, Martínez (knock on the big yellow door), for good simple food served on a terrace overlooking the valley. Around 17km further on, a small track leads from the paved road up to **Viña del Cerro**, the heavily restored remains of a fifteenth-century Diaguita-Inca copper foundry, composed of the low stone walls of what was once the control centre, the workers' quarters and 26 circular smelting ovens that were powered by wind and carbon fuel. The site is in a dramatic location, commanding panoramic views over the surrounding vineyards.

From Copiapó's Terminal de Buses, Casther (☎52/218889) runs frequent **bus services** up and down the valley (2hr), which is served by a good, paved road. If you're being dropped off near the copper foundry, count on a ten- to twenty-minute uphill walk from the road.

Caldera

Just over 70km from Copiapó, **CALDERA** is a small, easy-going seaside town with a smattering of nineteenth-century buildings, a beach, a pier and a few good fish restaurants. Chosen as the terminus of Chile's first railway by mining and railway pioneer William Wheelwright, it became the country's second largest port in the last decades of the nineteenth century, when it exported all the silver extracted in the region's dramatic silver boom. Caldera's two ports are still busy – one exporting table grapes, the other exporting copper – but they don't dominate the bay, which remains fairly attractive and clean. The town itself is unassuming but pleasant; landmarks include the Gothic-towered **Iglesia de San Vicente** on the main square, built by English carpenters in 1862, and the former **train station**, down by the pier, dating from 1850 and looking a little sorry for itself these days. The **pier** down by the beach makes a nice place for a stroll, and is the starting point for **boat rides** around the bay in summer. Caldera's main **beach** is the sheltered, mid-sized Copiapina, while to the west of the pier, the large, windswept Playa Brava stretches towards the desert sands of the Norte Grande.

Practicalities

Caldera is a one-hour **bus** ride from Copiapó; the most frequent service is provided by Recabarren, from the side street opposite Copiapó's main terminal. **Sernatur** has a summertime kiosk (unfixed hours) on calle Gana, by the seafront; otherwise, try the Municipalidad on the plaza. The town has a reasonable spread of **accommodation**. The cheapest rooms – basic but clean and quiet – are at *Sra Marta's*, at Ossa Varas 461

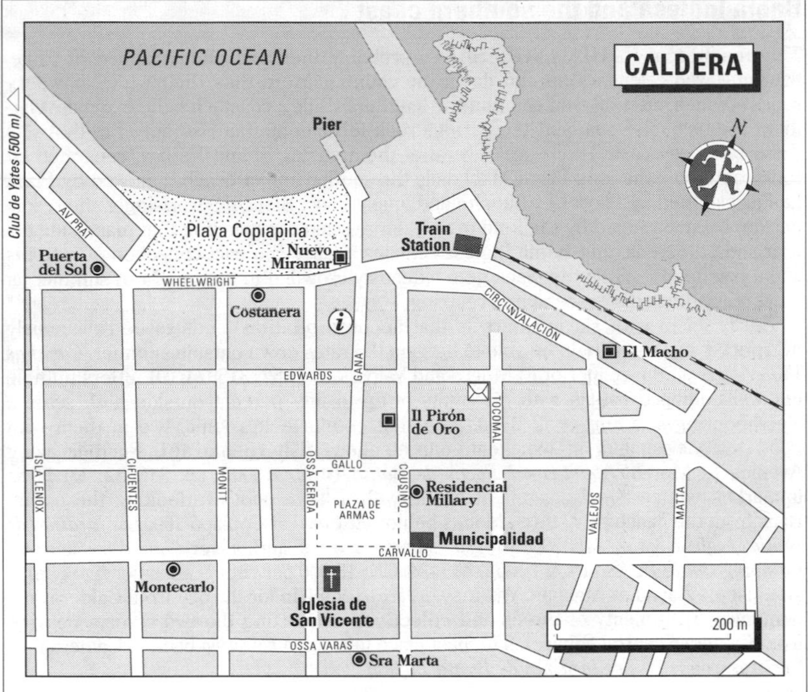

(☎52/315222; ②), while the nicest budget choice is probably *Residencial Millary* on the plaza at Cousiño 331(☎52/315528; ③), which offers simple, airy rooms without bath looking onto a leafy patio. For a step up in comfort, try *Montecarlo*, at Carvallo 627 (☎52/315388; ④), offering *cabaña*-type rooms with bath, TV, fridge and private parking. The similarly priced *Hotel Costanera*, on the seafront at Wheelwright 543 (☎ & fax 52/316007; ④) has spacious, clean rooms, some with sea views, and its own parking. Caldera's best hotel, the *Puerta del Sol*, at Wheelwright 750 (☎52/31505, fax 315507; ⑤), has a mix of smart and dowdy rooms, and an attractive outdoor restaurant and pool area.

Caldera's **restaurants**, specializing in fish and shellfish, offer better quality than its hotels. Best in town is the down-to-earth *Il Pirón de Oro* at Cousiño 218, which serves imaginatively prepared dishes, including exquisite dressed crab. *Nuevo Miramar* isn't quite as good (locals claim, disapprovingly, that they've started to use frozen fish), but has a better location, right on the beach, with wonderful ocean views. Also on the beach, out past the old railway station, no-frills *El Macho* is inexpensive and always busy with locals, while *Puerto Seguro*, right at the other end of the beach and part of the *Club de Yates*, is a smart, stylish place with great views but a little less atmosphere. You can finish off your evening at *Bartolomeo*, a mellow **pub-café** at Wheelwright 747, which often has live jazz, folk or blues at the weekend. There's a CTC **phone office** at Edwards 360, while the **post office** is up the road at no. 339. Caldera has no *cambios* or ATMs, but the BCI **bank** opposite the *Nuevo Miramar* will do a cash advance on Visa cards.

Bahía Inglesa and the southern coast

The **beaches** of **BAHÍA INGLESA** are probably the most photographed in Chile, adorning wall calendars up and down the country. More than their white, powdery sands – which, after all, you can find the length of Chile's coast – it's the exquisite clarity of the turquoise sea, and the curious rock formations that rise out of it, that sets these beaches apart. There are several of them strung along the bay, separated by rocky outcrops: the long Playa Machas is the southernmost beach, followed by Playa La Piscina, then by Playa El Chuncho and finally Playa Blanca. Surprisingly, the resort has not been swamped by the kind of ugly, large-scale construction that mars Viña del Mar and La Serena, and Bahía Inglesa remains a fairly compact collection of *cabaña*s and a few hotels. While the place gets hideously crowded in the height of summer, at most other times it's peaceful and relaxing.

The problem with staying here is that **accommodation** tends to be ridiculously overpriced, but you should be able to bargain the rates down outside summer. *Cabañas Villa Alegre*, at the corner of El Morro and Valparaíso (☎52/315074; ⑤), offers humble but well-equipped cabins with discounts of up to fifty percent outside high season. Neighbouring *El Coral* (☎52/315331; ⑤) has comfortable rooms, two of them with good sea views, and an excellent, unpretentious fish **restaurant**. Further along Avenida El Morro, *Apart-Hotel Rocas de Bahía* (☎52/316005, fax 316032; ⑥) is an upmarket, whitewashed apartment block, with a large pool overlooking the ocean. Back from the beachfront, three blocks behind *El Coral* at Copiapó 100, *Los Jardines de Bahía Inglesa* (☎52/315359; ⑤) has smart *cabañas* and a very good restaurant. *Camping Bahía Inglesa* (☎ & fax 52/315424; CH$15,000 per site) is an expensive **campsite** just off Playa Las Machas. You may prefer to come in for the day from Caldera, just 6km away, with plenty of **buses** and **colectivos** connecting the two resorts (leaving from Caldera's central square). The best place to catch a *colectivo* back to Caldera is at the crossroads by *Los Jardines de Bahía Inglesa*.

The southern coast

South of Bahía Inglesa, beyond the little fishing village of Puerto Viejo that marks the end of the paved road, the coast is studded with a string of **superb beaches** lapped with crystal-clear water, and backed by immense sand dunes. The scenery is particularly striking around **Bahía Salada**, a deserted bay indented with tiny coves some 130km south of Bahía Inglesa. A couple of the tour operators, including Gringotour (see box on p.174), will arrange excursions to these beaches, but to really appreciate the solitude and wilderness of this stretch of coast you're better off renting a jeep and doing it yourself.

Parque Nacional Nevado de Tres Cruces, Laguna Verde and Volcán Ojos de Salado

East of Copiapó, the Andes divide into two separate ranges – the cordillera de Domeyko and the cordillera de Claudio Gay – joined by a high basin, or plateau, that stretches all the way north to Bolivia. The waters trapped in this basin form vast salt flats and lakes towered over by enormous, snow-capped volcanoes, and wild vicuña and guanaco roam the sparsely-vegetated hills. This is a truly awe-inspiring landscape, conveying an acute sense of wilderness and space – appreciated more fully than around San Pedro de Atacama, for instance, thanks to the general absence of tourists. The number of visitors has started to increase, however, following the creation in 1994 of the new **Parque Nacional Nevado de Tres Cruces**, which takes in a dazzling white salt flat, the **salar de Maricunga**, two beautiful lakes, the **Laguna Santa Rosa** and **Laguna del Negro**

CHRISTOPHER SAINSBURY

Ancient and modern, Santiago

M. BARLOW, TRIP

Crowded hillside, Valparaiso

MELISSA GRAHAM

Coquimbo fishing boats

CHRISTOPHER SAINSBURY

Bofedal and volcanoes in the Parque Nacional Lauca

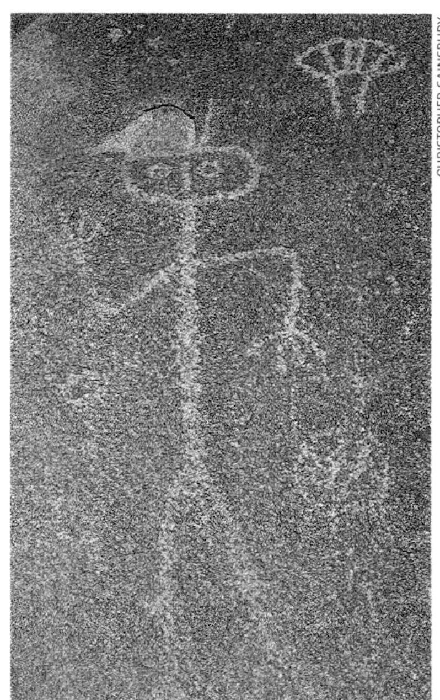

CHRISTOPHER SAINSBURY

Valle del Encanto petroglyph

MELISSA GRAHAM

Aymara woman, Enquelga

CHRISTOPHER SAINSBURY.

Parinacota church

CHRISTOPHER SAINSBURY

Alpaca and its young

CHRISTOPHER SAINSBURY

Valle de Chalinga

CHRISTOPHEF SAINSBURY

Pachicha, Atacama desert

CHRISTOPHER SAINSBURY

Puerto Varas rodeo

RICHARD DANBURY

Salar de Surire, altiplano

Francisco, and the 6753-metre volcano, **Tres Cruces**. Close to but not part of the park, by the border with Argentina, the stunning, blue-green **Laguna Verde** lies at the foot of the highest active volcano in the world, the 6893-metre **Ojos de Salado**. From Copiapó it's about a three-hour drive to Laguna Santa Rosa, and a six-hour drive to Laguna Verde. The dirt roads are normally passable from September or October to April or May and temperatures are low at all times of year, so take plenty of warm gear. There is no public transport to this area – for a list of agencies and individuals offering **tours** here, see p.174 & 54.

Parque Nacional Nevado de Tres Cruces

The bumpy road up to **PARQUE NACIONAL NEVADO DE TRES CRUCES** takes you through a brief stretch of desert before twisting up narrow canyons flanked by mineral-stained rocks. As you climb higher, the colours of the scoured, bare mountains become increasingly vibrant, ranging from oranges and golds to greens and violets. Some 165km from Copiapó, at an altitude of around 3700m, the road (following the signs to Mina Marta) reaches the first sector of the park, skirting the pale-blue **Laguna Santa Rosa**, home to dozens of pink flamingos. A track branching north of the road leads to a tiny wooden **refugio** (no bunk beds; floor space only) maintained by Conaf, on the western shore of the lake – a basic but convenient place to camp, with its own private views of the lake backed by the snow-capped **Volcán Tres Cruces**. Immediately adjacent, the gleaming white **Salar de Maricunga** is Chile's most southerly salt flat, and covers an area of over 8000 hectares. A two- to three-hour drive south from here, past Mina Marta, the park's second sector is based around the large, deep-blue **Laguna del Negro Francisco**, some 4200m above sea level, and home to abundant birdlife including wild ducks and flamingos. Towering over the lake, the 6080m **Volcán Copiapó** was the site of an Inca sacrificial altar. Conaf has its park headquarters and a large, comfortable **refugio** (③) about four kilometres from the lake; the *guardaparques* are very friendly and take visitors on educational excursions to the lake and around.

Laguna Verde and Volcán Ojos de Salado

The first, sudden sight of **LAGUNA VERDE** takes your breath away. The intense colour of its waters – green or turquoise, depending on the time of day – almost leaps out at you from the muted browns and ochres of the surrounding landscape. The lake is situated at an altitude of 4500m, about 250km from Copiapó on the "international road" to Argentina (follow the signs to Paso San Francisco or Tinogasta). At the western end, a small shack contains a fabulous **hot-spring bath**, where you can soak and take blissful refuge from the biting wind outdoors. The best place to camp is just outside the bath, where a stone wall offers some protection from the wind, and hot streams provide useful washing-up water. At the lake's eastern end there's a *Carabineros* checkpoint, where you should make yourself known if you plan to camp.

Laguna Verde is surrounded by huge volcanoes like Mulas Muertas, Incahuasi and the monumental **Ojos de Salado**. At 6893m, this is the highest peak in Chile and the highest active volcano in the world; its last two eruptions were in 1937 and 1956. A popular climb (between October and May), it's not technically difficult, apart from the last 50m which border the crater. The base of the volcano is a twelve-kilometre walk from the abandoned *Carabineros* checkpoint on the main road, and there are two *refugios* on the way up, one at 5100m and another at 5750m; if you need to arrange transport to the base, or a guide for the ascent, contact Maximiliano Martínez at Aventurisimo, in Caldera, on ☎ 52/316395 (see box on p.174). As it sits on the border with Argentina, climbers need to present written permission from the Dirección de Fronteras y Límites (see p.53) to the *Carabineros* before going up the volcano.

travel details

Buses

Copiapó to: Antofagasta (17 daily; 7hr); Arica (11 daily; 16hr); Calama (12 daily; 9hr 30min); Caldera (every 30min; 1hr); Chañaral (10 daily; 2hr); Iquique (12 daily; 13hr); La Serena (20 daily; 5hr); Los Vilos (2 daily; 8hr); Ovalle (6 daily; 5hr 30min); Santiago (22 daily; 12hr); Vallenar (10 daily; 1hr 45min); Valparaíso (6 daily; 12hr).

La Serena to: Antofagasta (16 daily; 11hr); Arica (8 daily; 18hr); Calama (14 daily; 12hr 30min); Chañaral (7 daily; 6hr); Copiapó (20 daily; 5hr); Iquique (9 daily; 16hr); Los Vilos (2 daily; 3hr); Montegrande (6 daily; 1hr 40min); Ovalle (18 daily; 1hr); Pisco Elqui (6 daily; 1hr 45min); Santiago (every 30min; 7hr); Vallenar (17 daily; 2hr 20min); Valparaíso (10 daily; 7hr); Vicuña (every 30min; 40min).

Ovalle to: Andacollo (4 daily; 2hr); Antofagasta (10 daily; 11hr); Arica (1 daily; 19hr); Calama (13hr); Chañaral (10 daily; 7hr); Copiapó (10 daily; 5hr); Iquique (2 daily; 19hr); La Serena (18 daily; 1hr); Los Vilos (6 daily; 2hr); Santiago (15 daily; 6hr); Tongoy (4 daily; 1hr 30min); Vallenar (5 daily; 4hr).

Vallenar to: Alto del Carmen (5 daily; 1hr); Antofagasta (10 daily; 9hr); Calama (10 daily; 11hr); Caldera (3 daily; 3hr); Chañaral (10 daily; 3hr 30min); Copiapó (10 daily; 1hr 45min); Iquique (2 daily; 14hr); La Serena (17 daily; 2hr 20min); Los Vilos (4 daily; 5hr 30min); Ovalle (5 daily; 4hr); Santiago (26 daily; 9hr 30min).

Flights

Note that some of the flight times given include stops.

Copiapó to: Antofagasta (1 daily; 2hr); Iquique (1 daily; 30min); La Serena (3 daily; 45min); Santiago (3 daily; 2hr).

La Serena to: Antofagasta (3 daily; 2hr 30min); Arica (1 daily; 1hr); Calama (2 daily; 3hr); Copiapó (5 daily; 1hr); Iquique (3 daily; 3hr 30min); Santiago (5 daily; 50min).

CHAPTER FOUR

EL NORTE GRANDE

Stretching away between the ocean and the great wall of the Andes, a seemingly endless belt of tawny sand, rock and mountain unfurls itself, more absolute and terrifying in its uncompromising aridity than the Sahara. The first glimpse of a strange land usually elates; but the sight of this grim desert oppresses the mind with a sense of singular desolation. . . It is only when the rays of the rising or setting sun kindle its sombre surface into the most gorgeous and improbable pink, purple, blue, crimson and orange that we feel the compelling fascination which all deserts exert.

Stephen Clissold, *Chilean Scrapbook.*

Austere, inhospitable and overwhelming in its vastness, the **NORTE GRANDE** occupies a full quarter of Chile's mainland territory, and contains a mere five percent of its population. Its single most outstanding feature is the **Atacama desert**, stretching 1200km from the río Copiapó to southern Peru; the driest desert in the world, it contains areas where no rainfall has ever been recorded. The landscape of this desert is not one of Arabian golden sand dunes, but rather of bare rock and gravel spread over a wide *pampa* or plain, almost shockingly barren. To the west, the plain is lined by a range of coastal hills that drop abruptly to a narrow shelf of land where most of the region's towns and cities – chiefly **Antofagasta**, **Iquique** and **Arica** – are scattered, hundreds of kilometres apart. East, the desert climbs gradually towards the cordillera, which rises to a high, windswept plateau composed of lakes and salt flats ringed with snow-capped volcanoes, forming a fabulous panorama.

It seems almost inconceivable that such a hostile land can support life, but for thousands of years the Norte Grande has been home to indigenous peoples who've wrested a living either from the sea or from the fertile oases that nestle in the Andean foothills. The excessive dryness of the climate has left countless relics of these people almost perfectly intact – most remarkably the **Chinchorro mummies**, buried on the desert coast near Arica some seven thousand years ago. It wasn't until the nineteenth century that the Europeans turned their attention to the Atacama, when it became apparent that the desert was rich in **nitrates** that could be exported at great commercial value. So lucrative was this burgeoning industry that Chile was prepared to go to war over it, for most of the Norte Grande at that time in fact belonged to Bolivia and Peru. The **War of the Pacific**, waged by Chile against Bolivia and Peru between 1878 and 1883, acquired for Chile the desired prize, and the desert pampas went on to yield enormous revenues for the next three decades. With the German invention of synthetic nitrates at the end of World War I, Chile's nitrate industry entered a rapid decline, but a financial crisis was averted when new mining techniques enabled low-grade copper, of which there are huge quantities in the Norte Grande, to be profitably extracted. Today, this mineral continues to play the most important role in the country's economy, accounting for forty percent of Chile's exports and making it the world's leading copper supplier.

Formidable and desolate as it is, the Norte Grande contains a wealth of superb attractions, and for many constitutes the highlight of a trip to Chile – particularly European travellers, who will find nothing remotely like it back home. The Pacific is lined by vast tracts of stunning **coastal scenery**, most strikingly presented by the towering cliffs and empty beaches of **Parque Nacional Pan de Azúcar**, near Chañaral. The **desert**

PERU
Visviri
PARQUE NACIONAL LAUCA
Tacna
Putre
Parinacota
Tambo Quemado
Socoroma
Arica
RESERVA NATURAL LAS VICUÑAS
San Miguel de Azapa
Salar de Surire
Enquelga
Colchane
Isluga
PARQUE NACIONAL VOLCAN ISLUGA
Pisagua
Tiliviche
Chusmiza
5
Huara
Mamiña
Humberstone
Pozo Almonte
Iquique
La Tirana
BOLIVIA
Cerro Pintados
Pica
RESERVA NACIONAL PAMPA DEL TAMARUGAL
Ollagüe
PACIFIC OCEAN
Tocopilla
Chuquicamata
Ayquina
Caspana
Maria Elena
Calama
Chiu Chiu
Gatico
Cobija
Pedro de Valdivia
Hornitos
Valle de La Luna
San Pedro de Atacama
Mejillones
Chacabuco
Toconao
Salar de Atacama
Camar
Baquedano
Juan López
Socaire
Antofagasta
Peine
5
ARGENTINA
N
Taltal
PARQUE NACIONAL PAN DE AZUCAR
El Salvador
0
150 km
Chañaral

ACCOMMODATION PRICE CODES

Prices are for the cheapest **double room** in high season. At the lower end of the scale, **single travellers** can expect to pay half this rate, but mid- and upper-range hotels usually charge the same for a single as for a double. For more information see p.27 in Basics.

① Less than US$10/CH$4800
② US$10–20/CH$4800–9600
③ US$20–30/CH$9600–10,080
④ US$30–50/CH$10,080–24,000
⑤ US$50–75/CH$24,000–36,000
⑥ US$75–100/CH$36,000–48,000
⑦ US$100–150/CH$48,000–72,000
⑧ over US$150/over CH$72,000

pampa itself impresses not only with its out-of-this-world geography, but also with a number of fascinating testimonies left by man. One of these is the trail of decaying nitrate **ghost towns**, including **Humberstone** and **Santa Laura**, easily reached from Iquique. Another are the immense images known as **geoglyphs** left by indigenous peoples on the hillsides and ravines of the desert – you'll find impressive examples at **Cerro Pintados**, south of Iquique, **Cerro Unitas**, east of Huara, and **Tiliviche**, between Huara and Arica. As you journey towards and up into the cordillera you'll come across gorgeous **oasis villages**, some – such as **Pica**, **Mamiña** and **Chusmiza** – with **hot springs**. Up in the Andes, the **altiplano** is undoubtedly the highlight of the north, with its dazzling lakes, salt flats and volcanoes, its abundance of wildlife and its tiny, whitewashed villages inhabited by native Aymaras. The main altiplano tourist base is **San Pedro de Atacama**, a pleasant oasis 314km northeast of Antofagasta, where numerous tour companies offer excursions to attractions like the famous **El Tatio geysers** and the **Valle de la Luna**. Further north, the stretch of altiplano between Iquique and Arica is home to countless wild vicuña and spectacular scenery, preserved in **Parque Nacional Lauca** and several adjoining parks and reserves. With the possible exception of **Arica**, the towns and cities of the far north are dreary and uninviting, but serve as unavoidable departure points for excursions into the hinterland.

Many of the Norte Grande's attractions can be reached by **public transport**, though to really explore the region you'll need to book some tours or, better still, rent a 4WD vehicle. Whatever your mode of transport, don't underestimate the distances involved in getting to most points of interest, particularly in the altiplano. It makes sense to isolate a few chosen highlights rather than try to see everything, which would be interminably time-consuming. Something else to bear in mind is the **Bolivian Winter** (see p.xiv), when sporadic heavy rains in the altiplano between December and February can wash roads away and seriously disrupt communications and access.

Parque Nacional Pan de Azúcar and beyond

North of Copiapó and Caldera (see p.176), the first stop on the Panamericana is **Chañaral**, a drab, uninviting town useful principally as a base for visiting **Parque Nacional Pan de Azúcar**, 30km up the coast. The park, with its towering cliffs and pristine beaches, certainly deserves a visit. Back on the highway, four hundred empty kilometres stretch north to the city of Antofagasta, broken only by the small, neglected fishing town of **Taltal**, 135km on from Chañaral.

Chañaral

Some 167km north of Copiapó, sitting by a wide, white bay and the Panamericana, **CHAÑARAL** is a rather sorry-looking town of grey houses staggered up a hillside.

Originally a small *caleta* used for shipping out the produce of an inland desert oasis, it still serves chiefly as an export centre, these days for the giant El Salvador copper mine, 130km east in the cordillera. Chañaral's huge beach was until recently notorious for the toxic wastes deposited by the mine, but these are now diverted to a properly managed site and the beach has been successfully cleaned up.

While Chañaral itself has absolutely nothing to tempt you off the Panamericana, it makes a useful base for visiting the far more appealing **Parque Nacional Pan de Azúcar**, just 30km north. Many north–south buses make a stop in the town, and those that don't will drop you off if you ask. There are a number of **accommodation** choices, including the basic but clean and light *Hotel La Marina* on the main street at Merino Jarpa 562 (no phone; ②; no hot water), and the good-value *Residencial Sutivan* at Comercio 365, at Chacabuco (☎52/489123; ③), with comfortable rooms at the back looking down to the ocean. The smartest place to stay is the *Hostería Chañaral*, at Müller 268 (☎52/480055, fax 480554; ④), which also has a pleasant **restaurant** offering good-quality meat and fish dishes. More economical options for eating include *Nuria* on the main square, opposite the church, and busy *El Rincón Porteño* at Merino Jarpa 567, both of which serve basic Chilean staples like fried fish and *lomo con papas* (steak and chips). Chañaral has no *cambios* or ATMs, but the BCI **bank** at Maipú 319 will give cash advances on Visa cards.

Parque Nacional Pan de Azúcar

PARQUE NACIONAL PAN DE AZÚCAR is a forty-kilometre strip of desert coast containing the most stunning coastal scenery in the north of Chile. Steep hills and cliffs rise abruptly from the shore, which is lined with a series of pristine sandy beaches, some of them of the purest white imaginable. Though bare and stark, these hills make an unforgettable sight as they catch the late afternoon sun, when the whole coastline is bathed in rich shades of gold, pink and yellow. The only inhabited part of the park is **CALETA PAN DE AZÚCAR**, 30km north of Chañaral, where you'll find a cluster of twenty or so fishermen's shacks as well as the Conaf information centre and a campsite (see below). Opposite the village, 2km off the shore, the **Isla Pan de Azúcar** is a small island sheltering a huge collection of marine wildlife, including seals, sea otters, plovers, cormorants, pelicans and over three thousand Humboldt penguins; you can (and should – it's well worth it) take a boat trip out to get a close look at the wildlife. Another highlight is the **Mirador Pan de Azúcar**, a lookout point 10km north of the village, giving fabulous panoramic views up and down the coast. More difficult to reach, and probably less rewarding, **Las Lomitas** is a 700m-high clifftop about 30km north of the village; it's almost permanently shrouded in mist and is the site of a large black net, or "fog catcher", that condenses fog into water and collects it below.

Practicalities

There are two **access roads** to the park, both branching off the Panamericana: approaching from the south, the turn-off is at the north end of Chañaral, just past the cemetery; from the north, take the turn-off at Las Bombas, 45km north of Chañaral. Both roads are bumpy but passable in a saloon car. There is no **public transport** to the park, but Chango Turismo (☎52/480668 or 480484) runs a twice-daily **bus** (CH$1500) to Caleta Pan de Azúcar from Chañaral; it leaves at 8am and 3pm from opposite the Pullman Bus terminal, at Freire 493, and returns from the park at 10am and 5pm (phone to confirm times). It also does **jeep tours** to the Mirador Pan de Azúcar (CH$5000) and Las Lomitas (CH$10,000).

The **Conaf information centre** (daily 8am–1pm & 2–6pm), near the village, offers maps, leaflets and souvenirs. This is where you pay your park fee (CH$3000) if you want to drive to the Mirador or Las Lomitas which can be reached only with a key to unlock the barrier across the access roads (walkers can nip round). You don't need to pay this fee to visit the rest of the park. A single concessionaire (☎ & fax 52/480539) provides **camping** areas (CH$6000 per site) on the beaches around the village and at Playa Piqueros, further south, as well as two beautifully located *cabañas* (④) on a secluded beach north of the village. Rough camping is not allowed in the park. You can buy fish and water in the village, otherwise you need to bring everything yourself. **Boat trips** to the island depart from the *caleta* and cost CH$3500 per person (minimum six people) or CH$21,000 per boat trip. It takes about ninety minutes to do the circuit; the best time is around 7 or 8am, or 6pm, when the penguins come out to eat.

Taltal

Chañaral and Antofagasta are separated by 400km of desert and one single town – **TALTAL**. Strung along a narrow shelf of land at the foot of the coastal mountains, Taltal was once an important nitrate port used for exporting the *caliche* (nitrate ore) brought down from the pampas by the Taltal Railway Company. Now a small, marginal fishing town, there's nothing very special about Taltal, but it makes a convenient place to break the long desert journey – take the (signed) 25-kilometre side road branching west off the Panamericana about 120km north of Chañaral. While you're there, take a wander down to the **old railway terminus** and port, to take a look at the former houses and offices of the Taltal Railway Company, clearly fine buildings in their heyday and now gently decaying. Also down here, in a small square at the corner of O'Higgins and Prat, stands one of the old **locomotives**, a shiny green "Kitson Meyer no. 59" containing, inside, a display of black and white photographs of Taltal during the nitrate era. You could also take a look in the **Museo de Taltal** (Mon–Fri 9.30am–1pm & 4–7pm; free) on Prat, just north of the plaza, where you'll find a poorly presented but interesting collection of archeological finds from the region, including ancient arrowheads and tools, and a tiny Chinchorro mummy (see p.224).

Should you wish to stay here, there's plenty of **accommodation** to choose from. *Taltal City*, at Ramírez 348 (no phone; ②), is probably the cheapest, with basic, clean enough rooms and a friendly owner; across the road, at no. 345, *Hotel Verdy* (☎55/611105; ③) has pleasant, airy rooms with and without bath. Down by the seafront, at Esmeralda 671, *Hostería Taltal* (☎55/611173; ④) has smart but overpriced rooms with sea views. There are some surprisingly good **restaurants** in town, serving fresh seafood; try the *Club de Taltal* in a large old building opposite the Municipalidad, off the plaza, or *Las Anclas*, by the sea at the corner of Martínez and Esmeralda. Several **bus companies** have offices in Taltal, including Tramacá and Tur Bus.

Antofagasta

The desert city of **ANTOFAGASTA** does not rank high on the Norte Grande's list of highlights, and many tourists bypass it altogether. However, as the regional capital, it boasts plenty of useful facilities – including banks, *cambios* and car-rental firms – and is a major transport hub. A Bolivian town until 1879, when it was annexed by Chile in the War of the Pacific, Antofagasta is now Chile's fifth-largest city. It's also one of the most prosperous, serving as an export centre for the region's great mines, most notably Chuquicamata (see p.194). Sitting on a flat shelf between the ocean and the hills, Antofagasta has a compact downtown core, made up of dingy, traffic-choked streets that sport a few handsome old public buildings, and a modern stretch spread along the coastal avenue. If you do end up here, you'll find plenty of places to stay and eat, while you attend to business in town. You could also make an easy day-trip to the more attractive seaside resort of **Juan López**, 38km north (see p.190), or even make this an alternative base. On the way, be sure to stop off at **La Portada**, a huge rock eroded into a natural arch, looming out of the sea.

Arrival and information

If you're arriving **by bus**, you'll be dropped at one of several bus terminals, most within easy walking distance of downtown accommodation. Coming in **by air**, you'll arrive at the Aeropuerto Cerro Moreno, 25km north of the city. From here, there are regular *colectivos* and infrequent *micros* to the centre or, easiest of all, you can take a minibus transfer directly to your hotel. For **tourist information**, head for the Sernatur office at Maipú 240 (Mon–Thurs 8.30am–1pm & 3–7.30pm, Fri 8.30am–1pm & 3–6.30pm; ☎ & fax 55/264044). For details on the protected areas around San Pedro de Atacama, visit the regional **Conaf office** at Av Argentina 2510 (Mon–Fri 9am–1pm & 2.30–5.30pm; ☎55/222250).

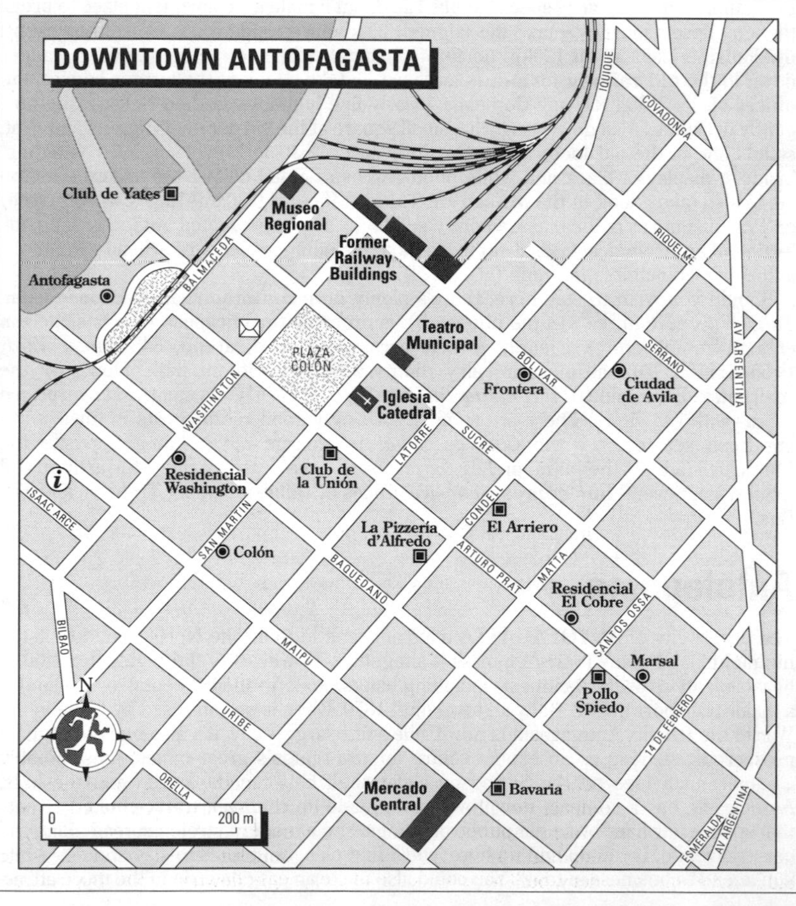

Accommodation

There's an abundance of **accommodation** in Antofagasta, but the range tends to jump from cheap and basic to expensive (and not necessarily good quality), with very few mid-priced options in between. Most places are in the downtown core, with the hotels on the coastal avenue catering mainly to business travellers.

Frontera Hotel, Bolívar 558 (☎55/281219). Best mid-range choice, offering spotless, modern rooms with private bath and cable TV. Some rooms can be noisy. ④.

Holiday Inn Express, Av Grecia 1490 (☎800/808080 or 55/228888). Recently built, super-clean American chain hotel, with pool and parking – a good place to pamper yourself if the desert is getting to you. It's on the coast road, out of town, but is connected to the centre by plenty of *micros*. ⑥–⑦.

Hotel Antofagasta, Balmaceda 2575 (☎55/268259, fax 264585). Large, venerable hotel overlooking the ocean, with well-furnished but overpriced rooms. ⑦.

Hotel Ciudad de Avila, Condell 2840 (☎55/221040). Simple, no-frills accommodation; most rooms have private bath and external windows. ③.

Hotel Colón, San Martín 2434 (☎55/261851, fax 260872). Reasonable-value, clean and fairly comfortable rooms with private bath. ④.

Marsal Hotel, Prat 867 (☎55/268063, fax 221733). Modern hotel offering spacious, comfortable rooms with private bath and parking. ⑤.

Residencial El Cobre, Prat 49 (☎55/225162). Huge *residencial* with 58 rooms, some airy and light, others dark and dingy. ②.

Residencial Washington, Washington 2480 (☎55/263592). Basic, cleanish rooms in a large old house near the main square. ②.

The City

All the historic buildings are in the downtown core, while scattered along the coast are a few small **beaches**, the **ruins** of a nineteenth-century silver refinery and **La Portada**, Antofagasta's beloved natural arch rising out of the sea.

Downtown

Antofagasta's centre is marked by the large, green **Plaza Colón**, dominated by a tall clock tower whose face is supposedly a replica of London's Big Ben. The square is surrounded by the city's administrative and public buildings, including the neo-Gothic **Iglesia Catedral**, built between 1906 and 1917. A couple of blocks northwest towards the port, spread along Bolívar, you'll find the magnificently restored nineteenth-century offices and railway terminus of the former Antofagasta and Bolivia Railway Company, complete with polished wooden verandas and dark-green stucco walls (but with no public access). Opposite, at the corner of Bolívar and Balmaceda, the old customs house, or **Aduana**, was built in 1866, and is the oldest building in the city. Inside, the **Museo Regional** (Tues–Sat 10am–1pm & 3.30–6.30pm, Sun 11am–noon; CH$500) houses an impressive mineral display downstairs and, upstairs, a collection of clothes, furniture and general paraphernalia dating from the nitrate era. At the opposite end of town, at the corner of Ossa and Maipú, the **Mercado Central** is a huge, crumbling pink and cream building selling fresh food and *artesanía*.

Along the coast

South of the city centre, the busy coastal avenue runs past a couple of tiny, coarse-sand **beaches**, first at the Balneario Municipal, then, much further south, at the Playa Huáscar – take *micro* #3 from Washington, near the square. Sitting on a hilltop a short distance inland, by the Universidad del Norte, the **Ruinas de Huanchaca** are the remains of an old Bolivian silver refinery, built to process the silver brought down from the Potosí mine (at that time the most important silver mine in South America), before being shipped out of Antofagasta. Looking at the square and circular walls of the complex from below, you could be forgiven for thinking they were the ruins of a pre-Columbian fortress; to get there, take *micro* #2, #4 or #10 from Prat. Sixteen kilometres north along the coast road, and an obligatory day-trip from Antofagasta, **La Portada** is a huge eroded arch looming out of the sea. Declared a national monument in 1990, it's something of a regional symbol, and its picture graces postcards and wall calendars all over Chile. To get there, take *micro* #15 from the Terminal Pesquero; or one of the Mejillones-bound minibuses leaving from Bazar Acuario at Latorre 2733, Bazar Mariela at Latorre 2727, or Bazar Mejillones, Latorre 2715 – all near the Tur Bus terminal. If you're driving, follow the coast road north and take the turn-off to Juan López, from where La Portada is well signed.

Eating, drinking and entertainment

Antofagasta's **restaurants** tend to be busy and lively, with a couple of classy establishments standing out among the grill houses and pizzerias. The nightlife scene, thanks mainly to the number of university students around town, is surprisingly vibrant, with some good **bars** to choose from and a choice of **dance spots** including *Disco Vox*, *Club Happy*, *Konigan's*, *Planet* and *New Popo's*, all on the coastal avenue south of town (take a taxi). There's a **cinema**, the Cine Nacional, at Sucre 731, and the modern **Teatro Municipal** is just off Plaza Colón, at the corner of Sucre and San Martín.

Restaurants

Bavaria, Santos Ossa 2424. The same pine decor, the same grilled meat, the same indifferent service you find in every other *Bavaria* in the country. At least you know what you're getting – and the food's not bad, after all.

Club de la Unión, Prat 474. Efficient service but average food (standard Chilean) in an attractive building with a balcony.

Club de Yates, Balmaceda 2705, at corner with Sucre. Elegant restaurant on the waterfront with ocean views and an expensive seafood-based menu, more imaginative than most.

El Arriero, Condell 2644. Lively atmosphere provided by two brothers who play old jazz tunes on the piano every night. Good *parilladas* and nice decor.

Hotel Antofagasta, Balmaceda 2575. The indoor dining room is empty and unatmospheric, but the outdoor terrace, overlooking the sea, is one of the nicest lunch spots in the city. Appetizing snacks and main meals at quite moderate prices.

La Pizzería d'Alfredo, Condell 2539. Popular, inexpensive pizzería with a little outdoor balcony where you can eat your meal alfresco.

Pollo Spiedo, Santos Ossa 2594. Cheap and tasty chicken roasted on the spit. Very popular.

Bar and cafés

Bar Picadillo, Av Grecia 1000. Eternally popular bar on the coastal avenue, near the university. Fills with a studenty crowd.

Café Caribe, Prat 482. Ordinary café serving good milkshakes, fruit juices and breakfasts.

Fiori di Gelatto, in *Hotel Nadine*, Baquedano 519. Delicious ice creams and a relaxing place for a sit down and a coffee during the day.

Nuevas Raíces, O'Higgins 1892. Mellow café-bar with live Andean or folk music every night, starting at around midnight.

Listings

Airlines American Airlines, Washington 2507 (☎55/221730); Avant, Prat 230 (☎55/452050); Iberia, Latorre 2508, office 2 (☎55/268994); Ladeco, Washington 2589 (☎55/269170); Lan Chile,

MOVING ON FROM ANTOFAGASTA

All the main bus companies have services from Antofagasta up and down the Panamericana, and to Calama. There's a municipal central terminal at Argentina 1155, from where several companies operate, including Carmelita, Libac and Ramos Cholele, but many companies operate instead out of their own separate terminal, including: Camus, Riquelme 513 (☎55/267424); Fenix, San Martín 2717 (☎55/268896); Fepstur, Riquelme 513 (☎55/222982); Flota Barrios, Condell 2782 (☎55/268559); Geminis, Latorre 3055 (☎55/251796); Kenny Bus, Arauco 4270 (☎55/262216); Los Corsarios, Latorre 2805 (☎55/282187); Pullman Bus, Latorre 2805 (☎55/262591); Tramacá, Uribe 936 (☎55/200124); Tur Bus, Latorre 2751 (☎55/266691). There are direct **flights** from Antofagasta to Calama, Iquique, Arica, Copiapó, La Serena and Santiago (see "Listings", below, for airlines). To get to the airport from downtown, order a minibus transfer to pick you up from your hotel, with Ladeco Express (☎800/205777) or Aerobus (☎55/262727), or take a taxi.

Washington 2552 (☎55/265151); Lufthansa, Copiapó 654 (☎55/263399); United Airlines, Balmaceda 2584 (☎55/224864).

Banks and exchange There are several ATMs on the central square and the main commercial streets like Prat, Washington and San Martín. You can change the major foreign currencies at Ancla at Baquedano 524, and US$ cash and travellers' cheques at Nortour, Baquedano 474.

Camping White gas (*bencina blanca*) and butane gas are available at Casa del Aseo, Matta 2578.

Car rental Avis, Balmaceda 2499 (☎ & fax 55/221073); Budget, Prat 206 (☎55/251745, fax 268959); First, Bolívar 623 (☎55/225777); Hertz, Balmaceda 2492 (☎55/269043); Iqsa, Balmaceda 2575 (☎ & fax 55/268323); La Portada, Prat 801 (☎55/263788, fax 263934); Lacaliza, Baquedano 300 (☎55/225370); Value, Sucre 220 (☎55/223330).

Laundry The only wet-wash laundry is inconveniently located out of town, at calle 14 de Febrero 1802, near the corner with O'Higgins.

Post office The main *correo* is on the central square, at Washington 2613.

Telephone offices Chilesat, Uribe 645; Chilexpress, corner of Prat and Washington (on Plaza Colón); CTC, Uribe 746; Entel, Baquedano 751; Startel, Baquedano 1984; Telex Chile, Washington 260; VTR, Prat 288.

Travel agencies There are many good, professional travel agencies downtown, including Australian-run Inti Tour, Baquedano 460 (☎55/266185, fax 260882); Tatio Travel Service, Washington 2513; and North Gate Tour, Baquedano 498.

North of Antofagasta: the coast road and the nitrate pampa

Heading north out of Antofagasta you've got the choice of two routes: the coast road (Ruta 1) to Iquique, via Tocopilla, or the Panamericana across the nitrate pampa. Taking the latter, you can either branch off for Calama and San Pedro de Atacama, or continue north to Iquique, passing close to the last remaining nitrate *oficinas* at Pedro de Valdivia and María Elena.

The coast road

Antofagasta is connected to Iquique, 492km further north (see p.203), by Ruta 1, the coast road used by most buses in preference to the Panamericana. Much of this coastline is heavily eroded, and the road twists around weird rock formations at the foot of huge cliffs. There are a couple of intriguing abandoned ports on the way, and two towns, **Mejillones** and **Tocopilla**, neither of them terribly interesting but useful for filling up with petrol, if you're driving.

Juan López

Just 38km from Antofagasta, **JUAN LÓPEZ** is an untidy but picturesque collection of pastel-coloured fishermen's shacks, scattered over a rocky headland. It's reached by a newly paved road (the same one for La Portada; see p.188) branching west of Ruta 1 about 14km north of Antofagasta, a very scenic drive that takes you past a vast, pearl-white beach, Playa Rinconada. In the village itself, you'll find a simple but charming hotel, the *Hostería Sandokan* (☎55/692031; ④) which has a *comedor* overlooking the ocean, and a staircase leading down to the beach (but no hot water in the showers). This is a wonderfully peaceful place to stay, except in January and February when the little resort is overrun with visitors.

Mejillones

There's very little to say about **MEJILLONES**, a rather dreary port 65km north of Antofagasta, but it makes a convenient lunch or petrol stop on the long drive up Ruta 1. Spread over several long streets running parallel to the shoreline, it's a fairly modern-looking town, though there are a few handsome old buildings dating from Mejillones' early days as a nitrate port. Right behind the main square, on the coastal avenue, there's a little promenade and a patch of sand. If you want to **eat** here, try *Abtao* at Las Heras 241 for good, fresh fish. There's no earthly reason to stay, but if you're stuck you'll find basic but clean **rooms** at *Residencial Marcela*, Borgoño 150 (☎55/621464; ②), more comfortable ones with and without bath at *Hotel Capitanía*, San Martín 410 (☎55/621542; ③–④), and smart, modern accommodation at *Hotel Costa del Sol* at Manuel Montt 086 (☎55/621590; ⑥).

Hornitos

Thirty-two kilometres north of Mejillones, **HORNITOS** is a long, powdery beach lined with exclusive holiday homes. The one place to **stay** and **eat** is the *Hostería Club Hornitos*, Av Hornitos 189 (☎55/233359 or 621586; ④), open only from December to March. Camping on the beach is strictly prohibited, a rule vigorously enforced by Hornitos' resident *Carabineros*, who clearly have nothing else to do with their time.

Cobija and Gatico

Scattered by the main road, 115km north of Antofagasta and 70km south of Tocopilla, are the half-decayed ruins of **COBIJA**. Looking at the crumbling shells that once were houses, it's hard to believe that this was Bolivia's first port, founded by the decree of Simón Bolívar in 1825 when there was nothing else on this coast. By 1860 it was a flourishing little town with over a thousand inhabitants, but was almost destroyed by a tidal wave in 1868 and a yellow fever epidemic the following year. With the emergence of Antofagasta as the region's main port, the last drops of lifeblood drained out of Cobija, and in 1907 its church was moved to Gatico and the town was abandoned. In addition to the ruins, there's a ransacked cemetery up by the road, full of body-shaped mounds of earth and a few open, empty coffins.

Ten kilometres north of Cobija the road passes more ruins, this time of **GATICO**, a former port that operated until 1930. An evocative reminder of its past is the huge *Casa de Huéspedes*, a grand, decaying hotel overlooking the sea – you can climb up the front entrance, wander around the empty rooms and admire the views from its veranda. Not far from the hotel are the rusty remains of the former railway terminus. Two kilometres north of Gatico, another abandoned **cemetery** stands right by the road, full of iron and wooden crosses bearing no names. It's all very atmospheric and melancholy.

Tocopilla

TOCOPILLA, 185km north of Antofagasta and 369km south of Iquique, is a busy industrial town with 25,000 inhabitants, two thermoelectric plants, a mechanized nitrate port and a railway terminus serving Chile's two remaining nitrate workings at María Elena and Pedro de Valdivia. Rather like Mejillones, it's a cheerless sort of place, although its setting, at the foot of steep hills looming over the town, is undeniably impressive. There is no reason to make a special trip here, but it's a handy place to stop over if you're driving along Ruta 1; it's also connected to Calama by a good 160-kilometre paved road, and some people like to head here for a day or two after a spell in the altiplano around San Pedro. Tocopilla has only a tiny, dark-sand beach, and there's not much to do in town except walk along the high street, 21 de Mayo, sit on a park bench in the pretty green plaza or go and take a look at the wooden Torre del Reloj, a clock tower dating from 1800, standing near the pier at the corner of Prat and Baquedano.

Accommodation, however, is plentiful and reasonably priced: try *Residencial Alvárez* at Serrano 1234, three blocks south of the plaza (☎55/811578; ③), for tidy rooms in a large old house with a patio, or bang opposite at no. 1243, the rambling *Hotel América* (☎55/812588; ③), for no-frills rooms with private bath. The good-value *Hotel Colonial*, on the main street at 21 de Mayo 1717 (☎55/811621; ③), has cramped but spotless new rooms with TV and private bath, while *Hotel Vicuña* at 21 de Mayo 2069 (☎55/812155; ④) offers spacious, light rooms around a patio with private bath and parking. There are plenty of **restaurants** on 21 de Mayo, including *Bavaria* and *Lucciano's Pizza*, four blocks north of the plaza; the nicest place to eat, though, is probably in the *Club de la Unión*, an attractive wooden building opposite the clock tower at the corner of Baquedano and Prat. On the same corner, there's an **ATM** at the BCI bank.

North of Tocopilla

The 369 kilometres that separate Tocopilla and Iquique are virtually uninhabited, with just a handful of tiny fishing *caletas* breaking the emptiness. Ruta 1 still clings to the shore, taking you past sporadic beaches that increase in number the further north you go. For the most part, though, there's no access from the highway down to the ocean. If you're driving this route, remember that Tocopilla is the last petrol stop before Iquique. You should also note that there's a customs checkpoint 154km south of Iquique, where all vehicles must be registered, and where items brought south from the Zona Franca are checked. For an account of Iquique, see p.203.

The nitrate pampa

Northwest of Antofagasta, the vast *pampa salitrera*, or **nitrate pampa**, pans across the desert towards the cordillera. Between 1890 and 1925 there were over eighty *oficinas* (workings) here, extracting the nitrate ore and sending it down to the ports by railroad. Some of them are still standing, abandoned and in ruins, including the atmospheric Chacabuco, crumbling in the desert heat. Two highways cross the pampa: the Panamericana, heading north, and Ruta 25, branching off northeast to the mining city of Calama. The former passes near to the most recently abandoned nitrate town, **Pedro de Valdivia**, and the last remaining nitrate town in Chile, **María Elena**, both of which can be reached on public transport.

Baquedano

Seventy kilometres northeast of Antofagasta, the Panamericana passes through **BAQUEDANO**, once an important railway junction, now a down-at-heel village. The rail tracks are still used by a few freight trains, but a large part of the station and workshops have been turned into an open-air **Museo Ferroviario** (daily 8am–12.30pm &

2–7pm; free) displaying many beautiful old locomotives, a couple of which you can climb aboard. If you want to stop for **lunch**, you'll find a couple of good-value canteens on the main road, opposite the railtracks.

Chacabuco

Thirty kilometres on from Baquedano, you reach the Carmen Alto junction. To the right, Ruta 25 goes to Calama, passing over twenty abandoned nitrate *oficinas*, many of them reduced to a few stone walls and a pile of rubble. To the left, the Panamericana continues north, passing **CHACABUCO**, just past the junction on the right-hand side. Built in 1922 and abandoned in 1940, this former nitrate town is now a national monument and a fascinating relic of the pampa's past. The rows of tiny terraced houses where the workers lived are still standing, along with the remains of the church, market and theatre. It's usually completely empty and is a decidedly eerie, even sinister, place to wander through, despite the blue sky and glare of the sun – especially when you consider that it was used as a concentration camp during the first two years of the Pinochet regime.

Pedro de Valdivia

Sixty-nine kilometres past the junction, a side road leads six kilometres from the Panamericana to **PEDRO DE VALDIVIA**, the newest "ghost town" on the pampa, abandoned only in 1996. It was created in 1931 by the Guggenheim brothers as their second large-scale nitrate plant, following the success of neighbouring María Elena (see below), established five years earlier. The plant itself is still working, and the huge chimneys belching out smoke form a dramatic backdrop to the deserted town. But it was too expensive to maintain two company towns, so the residents of Pedro de Valdivia were moved to María Elena, 36km further north. The architecture and layout are just like all the other ghost towns – small, whitewashed terraced houses, a plaza with a church, school and theatre – but the fact that it's so recently abandoned makes it, if anything, even more haunting. Wandering around the streets you stumble, here and there, across old shoes, a teddy bear left behind in the move, a forsaken bicycle and an empty children's playground.

María Elena

After driving past so many decaying, abandoned nitrate towns, it's quite uplifting to find one that's still alive and full of people. **MARÍA ELENA**, created in 1926, is the only inhabited nitrate town left in Chile, with a population of 7600. It's got exactly the same houses and buildings as the ghost towns, but its square is teeming with people. It's also home to an excellent little **archeological museum**, on the square (Mon–Sat 9am–1pm & 4–7pm, Sun 10am–1pm & 5–8pm; free). If he's there, get the director, don Claudio, to guide you through the displays, most of which he amassed himself, ranging from tombs, arrowheads and ceramics through to memorabilia from the local nitrate towns. You'll find basic **accommodation** at *Residencial Chacance*, Vicuña 437 (☎55/639123; ②), and **food** at the *Club María Elena* and the *Club Social No. 6*.

The Chug Chug geoglyphs

The Panamericana is crossed by a lateral road, Ruta 24, 107km north of the Carmen Alto junction. This is connected to Tocopilla, 60km west, and Chuquicamata, 66km east. Just short of 50km along the road for Chuquicamata, a sign points north to the **Chug Chug geoglyphs**, reached by a thirteen-kilometre dirt road that's just about passable in a saloon car. These consist of some three hundred images spread over several hills, many of them clearly visible from below, including circles, zoomorphic figures, human faces and geometric designs. It's an impressive site, and certainly deserves a visit if you're driving in the area.

Calama and Chuquicamata

Sitting on the banks of the río Loa, at an altitude of 2250m, **CALAMA** is a clean and modern if rather bland town, whose chief role is service centre and residential base for **Chuquicamata**, the massive copper mine 16km north. While it holds few attractions in its own right, it's a convenient place for sorting out money and laundry, and most visitors spend at least a night here on their way to or from San Pedro de Atacama, the famous oasis village and tourist centre 100km east.

Calama began life as a *tambo*, or resting place, at the intersection of two Inca roads, one running down the Andes, the other connecting the altiplano with the Pacific, and was visited by both Diego de Almagro and Pedro de Valdivia on their journeys into Chile. It was never heavily populated by pre-Hispanic peoples, who preferred nearby Chiu Chiu with its less saline water supply. The town took on a new importance, however, when it became a stop on the Oruro–Antofagasta railway in 1892, and its future was sealed with the creation of the Chuquicamata copper mine in 1911. Today, its busy streets are built around a surprisingly small and laid-back central core. Though there's little sightseeing to be done, you could pass a couple of hours in the **Parque El Loa**, where you'll find a mini reconstruction of Chiu Chiu's church and displays on local pre-Columbian history in the **Museo Arqueológico** (Tues–Fri 10am–1.30pm & 2.30–6pm, Sat & Sun 11am–6.30pm; CH$500). To get to the park, take a *colectivo* – #5 or #18 – on Vicuña Mackenna at Latorre, or *micros* #1b, #1c or #1d from Vivar at Mackenna.

Practicalities

Arriving by **bus** you'll be dropped at your bus company's office, as there's no single terminal. If you're **flying** to Calama you'll land at the Aeropuerto El Loa, 5km south of the centre – the only way into town from here is by taxi. **Trains** from Bolivia pull in at the conveniently located station, three blocks east of the plaza. There's an extremely helpful municipal **Oficina de Turismo** opposite the Municipalidad at the corner of Latorre and Vicuña Mackenna (Mon–Fri 9am–1pm & 3–7pm, Sat 9am–1pm; ☎55/345345), where you can get maps of the town and the altiplano around San Pedro. Calama has plenty of inexpensive **accommodation** – good budget choices include friendly *Hotel Claris Loa* at Granaderos 1637 (☎55/311939; ②), where you'll find basic but spotless rooms off a back yard; *Hotel Loa* at Abaroa 1617 (☎55/341963; ③) with lots of singles out the back, and a few doubles and triples in the main house; and *Residencial Toño* at Vivar 1970 (☎55/341185), offering simple rooms with good bed linen. Stepping up in comfort, *Hotel El Mirador* at Sotomayor 2064 (☎ & fax 55/340329; ⑤) is a lovely, small hotel with spacious rooms – including one with a Victorian cast iron bath – and attractive furnishings. At the top end of the scale, the *Park Hotel* at Camino al Aeropuerto 1392 (☎55/319900, fax 319901; ⑦) boasts elegant decor, a good restaurant and a swimming pool.

Calama has lots of **restaurants**, none particularly inspiring but most reasonably priced. *Club Croata*, on the plaza, offers decent if predictable food and a pleasant, mellow atmosphere, with candles on the table by night. A couple of doors along, *Pizzería d'Alfredo* is a modern, rather stylish pizza house with an all-glass wall looking onto the square, though the pizzas are pretty average. You'll find better Italian food, including delicious home-made pesto sauce, at *Tavola Caldo*, Vicuña Mackenna 2033, where you can eat on a pleasant outdoor terrace. On the edge of town, at Balmaceda 1504, *Adobes de Balmaceda* serves good-value *parilladas* in a large, attractive old house that really fills up for Sunday lunch. You'll find plenty of **ATMs** on Sotomayor, as well as a *cambio* at Tokori Tour, Latorre 2018, on the second floor. There are several **laundries**, including Lavexpress at Sotomayor 1867, and Universal at Antofagasta 1313.

Chuquicamata

Sixteen kilometres north of Calama, **Chuquicamata** is the world's largest open-pit copper mine and biggest single supplier of copper, producing 600,000 tonnes per year. Carved out of the ground like a giant, sunken amphitheatre, its massive proportions dwarf everything within it, making the huge trucks carrying the ore up from the crater floor – whose wheels alone are 4m high – look like tiny, crawling ants. Its size is the result of some ninety years of excavation, and its reserves are predicted to last at least another 45 years. Along with all of Chile's large-scale copper mines, or "*gran minería*" as they're called, Chuquicamata belongs to Codelco, the government-owned copper corporation. Codelco also maintains the adjacent company town, complete with its own school, hospital, cinema and football stadium, but plans are afoot to move the nine thousand workers and their families to Calama to make way for further excavation.

Regular *colectivos* leave for Chuquicamata from calle Abaroa, on Calama's main plaza, taking about twenty minutes; the driver will drop you by the café at the north end of JM Carrera, which is the starting point for **guided tours** (Mon–Fri 10am). To be sure of a place, you should get there by 9am, and even by 8.30am in February; as soon as you

MOVING ON FROM CALAMA

Most visitors are in Calama on their way to San Pedro, with regular bus connections provided by several companies, including Buses Frontera, with the most frequent service, at Antofagasta 2041 (☎55/318543); Buses Atacama, Abaroa 2105-B (☎55/314757); and Tramacá at Granaderos 3048 (☎55/340404). The inter-city bus companies are spread around town, with Flota Barrios at Ramírez 2298 (☎55/341497); Géminis at Antofagasta 2239 (☎55/341993); Pullman Bus at Sotomayor 1808 (☎55/319665); and Tur Bus at Balmaceda 1852 (☎55/341472). There are regular flights out of Calama to Santiago and the main northern cities, with Ladeco, Ramírez 1858 (☎55/312626), Lan Chile, at Latorre 1499 (☎55/341394), and Avant, Cobijo 2188 (☎55/343064). Finally, there's the famous 30-hour train to Oruro in Bolivia, across the spectacular salar de Uyuni; it leaves on Wednesdays at 11pm, with tickets (around CH$10,000) sold at Tramacá (see above).

arrive, register at the counter and you'll be given a token. There is no charge, though you are invited to make a small donation to a children's charity supported by the mine. The tours take place almost entirely on a bus, though you're allowed to get out at the viewpoint looking down to the pit. The rest of the tour takes you round the machinery yards and buildings of the plant, which you see from the outside only.

San Pedro de Atacama and around

One hundred kilometres southeast of Calama, **SAN PEDRO DE ATACAMA** is a little oasis village of narrow streets and adobe houses that has transformed itself, over the last ten years or so, into the travel mecca of northern Chile. Sitting at an altitude of 2400m between the desert and the altiplano, or *puna* (the high basin connecting the two branches of the cordillera), this has been an important settlement since pre-Hispanic times, originally as a major stop on the trading route connecting the llama herders of these highlands with the fishing communities of the Pacific. Later, during the nitrate era, it was the main rest stop on the cattle trail from Salta in Argentina to the nitrate *oficinas*, where the cattle were driven to supply the workers with fresh meat. Perhaps its current role as tourist centre, far from having been thrust upon it, is another example of San Pedro's ability to adapt to the times and find its own niche in which it can prosper.

The large numbers of gringos here can come as quite a shock if you've visited other parts of the northern Andes, like Parque Nacional Nevado de Tres Cruces, or Parque Nacional Isluga, where tourists are few and far between. Here in San Pedro they seem to be everywhere, and just about every other house has been turned into a *residencial*. That said, the result is not unpleasant, and the village still has a lot of charm and character, having been developed on a very local, human scale (with a couple of exceptions). On the whole, it's a small, friendly and laid-back place offering an excellent range of accommodation and restaurants. What's really great about San Pedro, though, is the concentration of **tour operators** offering very reasonably priced excursions into the altiplano. This can, of course, be a curse as well as a blessing, for it increases tourist traffic in the region to the point where it can be difficult to visit the awe-inspiring landscape of the *puna* in the kind of silence and isolation it really ought to be experienced in. But for sheer convenience and ease of access into spectacular wilderness areas, San Pedro can't be beat. The tours appear, moreover, to be responsibly managed and you'll see no rubbish littering the sites you're taken to, or any other signs of over-exploitation.

Arrival, information and orientation

Several **bus** companies have regular services from Calama to San Pedro (for details see box opposite); they all have different drop-off points, but these are all within a couple of blocks of the main square. This is where to head if you want to visit the very helpful **Oficina de Turismo** (Feb–March daily 10am–2pm & 3–9pm; ☎55/851126); if it's closed, try the Municipalidad, also on the square. San Pedro's main street is **Caracoles**, which is where you'll find the biggest concentration of accommodation, eating places and services. None of the village's houses has a street number.

Accommodation

There are around 25 places offering **rooms** in San Pedro, including a number of good-value, comfortable *residenciales* plus some classy, upmarket places for those on a more generous budget. There are also several **campsites**. If you're travelling alone and arrive at a busy time, you may have difficulty finding a **single room** in many *residenciales*, and will probably be asked to share with another traveller. Note that San Pedro

has electricity only until midnight and that, as a rule, only the more expensive hotels have their own generators.

Residenciales

Casa Corvatsch, Antofagasta s/n (☎55/851101). Swiss-owned *residencial* offering simple but immaculate rooms, including four singles, and reliable shared showers (hot water evenings only). A good budget choice. ③.

Hostal Puri, Caracoles s/n (☎55/851049). Attractive, colourful building but the rooms are cramped and very noisy, owing to next door's generator. ③.

Hostal Takha Takha, Caracoles s/n (☎55/851038). Small but neat, tidy and quiet rooms giving onto a pleasant garden. A good bet for singles. Also has spaces for camping. ③.

Residencial Chiloé, Domingo Atienza s/n (☎55/851017). Good simple rooms kept very clean by the friendly owner. ②–③.

Residencial Florida, Tocopilla s/n (☎55/851021). Basic but adequate rooms around a courtyard. No singles. ②.

Residencial Juanita, Plaza (☎55/851039). Pleasant and popular *residencial* on the square, with an agreeable terrace-restaurant attached. ③.

Residencial Rayco, Antofagasta s/n. Well-kept rooms around a patio with seating areas. Most rooms without bath but a few, more expensive ones, with. No singles. ③.

Hotels

Hostal Katarpe, Domingo Atienza s/n (☎55/851033). Excellent-value, comfortable rooms with private bath and all-night light. ④.

Hostería San Pedro, Solcor s/n (☎55/851011, fax 851048). Well-maintained, comfortable accommodation – mostly in little bungalows – and a fantastic swimming pool. The restaurant is very good, too. ⑥.

Hotel Explora, reservations in Santiago: Av America Vespucio Sur 80, Fifth Floor (☎2/206 6060, fax 228 4645; *www.interknowledge.com/Chile/explora*). Newly built exclusive hotel with fifty rooms (all with jacuzzi) built around three large patios, and four outdoor pools. Only all-inclusive packages are available of 3, 4 or 7 nights, based around hiking, horse riding, mountain biking and jeep tours. ⑦.

Hotel Kamal, Domingo Atienza s/n (☎ & fax 55/851030). Spacious, light and very attractive rooms, combining contemporary, spartan architecture with soft, warm rugs and plants. ⑥.

Hotel Tambillo, Antofagasta s/n (☎ & fax 55/851078). Reasonably priced hotel offering fresh, clean rooms and a dependable water supply. ④.

Hotel Terrantai, Tocopilla s/n (☎55/851140, fax 851037). Modern, stylish hotel with bare stone walls and minimalist wooden furniture. ⑥–⑦.

Hotel Tulor, Domingo Atienza s/n (☎ & fax 55/851027). Comfortable but small rooms with a friendly archeologist owner. There's a nice bar/restaurant attached. ⑤.

Camping

Camping Cunza, Antofagasta s/n (no phone). A fairly hard-ground campsite, with shade provided by a straw roof over each site; around CH$2000 per person.

Edén Atacameño, Tocanoa s/n (☎55/851154). Best campsite in San Pedro (around CH$1500 per person), with lots of trees, water and an outdoor kitchen. Also has a few basic rooms. ①.

The village

The focus of San Pedro is the little **plaza** at its centre, dotted with pepper trees and wooden benches. On its western side stands the squat white **Iglesia de San Pedro**, one of the largest Andean churches in the region. It's actually San Pedro's second church, built in 1744, just over 100 years after the original church was erected near the present site of the archeological museum. The bell tower was added towards the end of the nineteenth century, and the thick adobe walls surrounding the church were rebuilt in 1978. Inside, religious icons look down from the brightly painted altar, among them a stern-looking Saint Peter, the village's patron saint. Overhead, the sloping roof is made of rough-hewn reddish planks and rafters, bound together with leather straps. Opposite the church, on the other side of the square, the lopsided colonial-looking house known as the **Casa Incaica** is San Pedro's oldest building, thought to date from the earliest days of the colony. The southeast corner of the square is given over to an alley full of **artesanía** stalls, where you can buy alpaca knitwear and other souvenirs.

Just off the northeast corner of the square, the outstanding **Museo Arqueológico Padre le Page** (Jan & Feb daily 10am–1pm & 3–7pm; March–Dec Mon–Fri 9am–noon & 2–6pm, Sat & Sun 10am–noon & 2–6pm; CH$1000) should not be missed on any account. Named after the Belgian missionary (cum-archeologist) who founded it in 1955, it possesses over 380,000 artefacts gathered from the region around San Pedro, of which the best examples are displayed in eight "naves" arranged around a central hall. Charting the development, step by step, of local pre-Columbian peoples, the displays range from neolithic tools to sophisticated ceramics, taking in delicately carved wooden tablets and tubes used for inhaling hallucinogenic substances, and a number of gold and silver ritual masks used by village elders during religious ceremonies. There's no doubt, however, that the most arresting and compelling exhibits are the prehistoric mummies, most famously that of a young woman sitting with her knees huddled up to her chest, her skin all withered and leathery, but her hair still thick and black. She is known affectionately as "Miss Chile".

Eating, drinking and entertainment

San Pedro's **eating and drinking** scene is usually quite lively, thanks to the steady flow of young travellers passing through town. Just about every restaurant offers a fixed-price evening meal, with several choices of main course, usually including a vegetarian option. Many eating places double up as bars, sometimes with live music, while a couple of places also have **dancing**. The best time for partying in San Pedro is **June 29**, when the village celebrates its Saint's day with exuberant dancing and feasting.

Adobe, Caracoles s/n. Always-lively outdoor restaurant with a roaring fire lit every night. Uncomfortable seats but good atmosphere.

Banana Chávez, Caracoles s/n. Exquisite, freshly squeezed fruit juices and a range of appetizing snacks.

Café Francés, Caracoles s/n. Little two-table café run by a Frenchwoman, serving tasty sandwiches, coffee, cakes and other snacks.

Café Sonchek, Calama s/n. Quiet restaurant serving delicious soups and pastas on a lovely patio behind the main building.

Flórida, Tocopilla s/n. Unpretentious little restaurant serving simple but very good Chilean meals.

Hostería San Pedro de Atacama, Solcor s/n. One of the best menus in San Pedro, more expensive than most but worth it, though the atmosphere can be rather dull. Positioned on the edge of the village, away from the hurly burly of Caracoles.

Juanita, La Plaza. A popular choice, mainly because of its appealing location on the main square, perfect for people-watching. Simple, filling meals.

La Casona, Caracoles s/n. Informal and inexpensive, but arguably the best restaurant in San Pedro. The dining room is very elegant, inside a large, colonial-style house, and the menu is fairly imaginative.

La Estaka, Caracoles s/n. Rustic-looking restaurant-cum-bar with trendy young waiters and loud music, open from breakfast-time until 1am. Very popular.

Paacha, Domingo Atienza s/n. Large restaurant with an attractive interior, good food and regular Andean folk bands.

Tambo Cañavaral, Toconao s/n. San Pedro's most happening nightspot, with frequent live music (usually Andean) and plenty of drinking.

Tierra, Caracoles s/n. Tiny café specializing in home-made vegetarian food, including wholemeal bread, fruit pancakes, salads and cakes.

Listings

Banks and exchange There are no banks, but two *casas de cambio*, one at Toconao, opposite Planeta, and the other on Caracoles.

Bicycles You can rent mountain bikes at Sirio, on Caracoles, for very reasonable rates.

Laundry There's an inexpensive laundry at calle Licancabur s/n.

Post office The village *correo* is on Antofagasta, opposite the archeological museum.

Swimming pool There's a swimming pool (permanently open) at Pozo Tres, a 3km walk east of the village out of calle Padre Le Paige.

Telephone offices Entel is on the plaza, and CTC is just around the corner on Caracoles.

Around San Pedro

The landscape around San Pedro is really quite spectacular: vast desolate plains spread out for miles around, cradling numerous **volcanoes** of the most delicate colours imag-

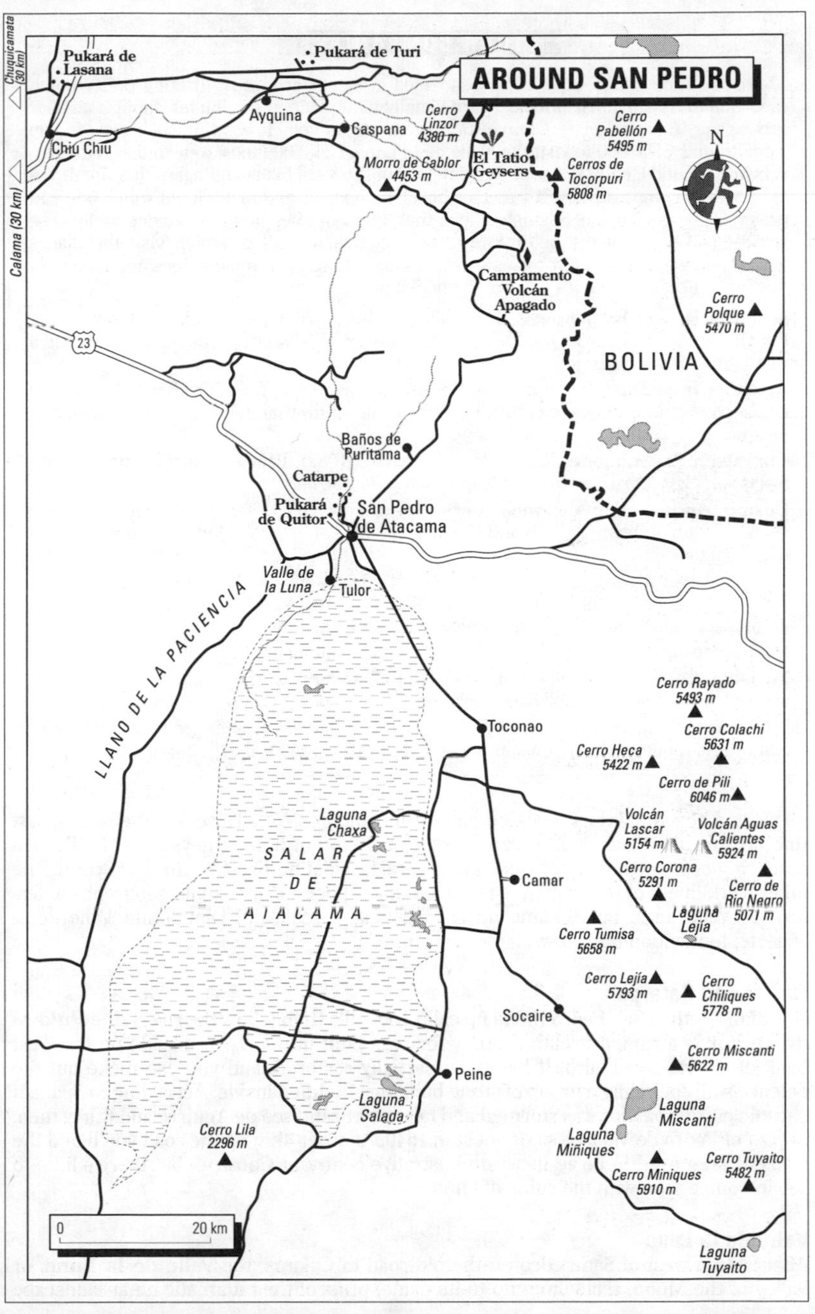
AROUND SAN PEDRO
N
Chuquicamata (30 km)
Calama (30 km)
Pukará de Lasana
Pukará de Turi
Ayquina
Caspana
Chiu Chiu
Cerro Linzor 4380 m
Morro de Cablor 4453 m
El Tatio Geysers
Cerro Pabellón 5495 m
Cerros de Tocorpuri 5808 m
Campamento Volcán Apagado
Cerro Polque 5470 m
BOLIVIA
23
Baños de Puritama
Catarpe
Pukará de Quitor
San Pedro de Atacama
Valle de la Luna
Tulor
LLANO DE LA PACIENCIA
Toconao
Cerro Rayado 5493 m
Cerro Colachi 5631 m
Cerro Heca 5422 m
Cerro de Pili 6046 m
Volcán Lascar 5154 m
Volcán Aguas Calientes 5924 m
Laguna Chaxa
SALAR DE ATACAMA
Camar
Cerro Corona 5291 m
Cerro de Rio Negro 5071 m
Laguna Lejía
Cerro Tumisa 5658 m
Cerro Lejía 5793 m
Cerro Chiliques 5778 m
Socaire
Cerro Miscanti 5622 m
Peine
Laguna Salada
Laguna Miscanti
Laguna Miñiques
Cerro Lila 2296 m
Cerro Miniques 5910 m
Cerro Tuyaito 5482 m
Laguna Tuyaito
0
20 km

TOUR COMPANIES

There are numerous **tour companies** based in San Pedro, most offering pretty much the same tours at similar prices. Tours usually take place in minibuses, though smaller groups may travel in jeeps. Competition keeps prices very low – you can expect to pay from around CH$3000 to visit the Valle de la Luna, CH$8000 for a tour to the Tatio geysers and around CH$18,000 for a full-day tour of the local lakes and oases. It's worth visiting several companies to get a feel for how they operate and to work out which one you prefer; if you don't speak Spanish, check that they can offer bilingual guides. Below is a selection of some of the better-known tour companies, all of which visit the places described over the next few pages – note, though, that if a company does not appear on this list, it doesn't mean it's not worth checking out.

Atacama Desert Expeditions, Tocopilla s/n (☎55/851045, fax 851037). Described by the Oficina de Turismo as the "VIP" tour company, this is pricier than most, but has a reputation for good service.

Atacama Inca Tour, Pedro de Valdivia, off La Plaza (☎ & fax 55/851062). One of the oldest companies in town, run by a local man with more than ten years' experience and inexhaustible enthusiasm. Recommended.

Corvatsch Expediciones, Caracoles s/n (☎55/851087). Efficient partnership between Swiss-run *Casa Corvatsch* and Chilean *Residencial Florida*.

Cosmo Andino Expediciones, Caracoles s/n (☎55/851069). Dutch-run company (hence Dutch, English, French and German spoken) offering guided treks in addition to the usual tours.

Desert Adventure, Caracoles s/n (☎ & fax 55/851067) in San Pedro; Latorre 1815 (☎55/344894) in Calama. Polished, professional and reliable – one of the most successful outfits in town, owned by a dynamic young Chilean woman.

Pachamama, Toconao s/n (☎55/851064). Reliable company with experienced guides.

Turismo Colque, Caracoles s/n (☎55/851109) Offers excellent-value three-day trips across the border to the Bolivian altiplano.

Turismo Ochoa, Toconao s/n (☎55/851022). The longest-established tour operator in San Pedro, though some complain it's no longer trying as hard as it might.

inable and beautiful **lakes** speckled pink with flamingos. You'll also find the largest **salt flat** in Chile, the Salar de Atacama, a whole field full of fuming **geysers** at El Tatio, a scattering of fertile **oasis villages**, and several fascinating **pre-Columbian ruins**. The other-worldliness of this region is reflected in the poetic names of its geographical features – Valle de la Luna, Llano de la Paciencia, Cuesta del Diablo and Valle de la Muerte, to mention but a few.

Quitor and Catarpe

Just 3km north of San Pedro (head up calle Tocopilla then follow the river), the **Pukará de Quitor** is a ruined twelfth-century fortress built into a steep hillside on the west bank of the río San Pedro. It has been partially restored, and you can make out the defence wall encircling a group of stone buildings huddled inside. According to Spanish chronicles, this *pukará* was stormed and taken by Francisco de Aguirre and thirty men, as part of Pedro de Valdivia's conquest in 1540. Another 4km up the road you'll find the ruins of what used to be an Inca administrative centre at **Catarpe**, but there's little to see in comparison with the ruins of Quitor.

Valle de la Luna

About 14km west of San Pedro on the old road to Calama, the **Valle de la Luna**, or Valley of the Moon, really lives up to its name, presenting a dramatic lunar landscape of wind-eroded hills surrounding a crust-like valley floor, once the bottom of a lake. An immense sand dune sweeps across the valley, easy enough to climb and a great place to sit and survey the scenery – if you're prepared to battle your way through the flying sand, you can even walk along its crest. The valley is at its best at sunset, when it's transformed into a spellbinding palette of golds, reds and honeys, but you'll have to share this view with a multitude of fellow visitors, as all San Pedro tour operators offer daily sunset trips here. A more memorable (but more demanding) experience would be to get up before day breaks and cycle to the valley, arriving at sunrise. The way there is straightforward: you follow Caracoles west out of San Pedro and at the end take the left-hand turn, following the old road to Calama directly to the valley. Remember to take plenty of water and sunscreen. Note that the valley is part of the Conaf-run Reserva Nacional Los Flamencos, and camping is not permitted.

Tulor

Nine kilometres southwest of San Pedro, **Tulor** is the site of the earliest example of settled habitation in the region, dating from around 800 BC. Buried beneath a sand dune for hundreds of years, this settlement has remained remarkably intact, and was discovered only in the mid-twentieth century by Padre Le Paige, founder of the Museo Arqueológico in San Pedro. Today, the uppermost parts of the walls are exposed, protruding from the earth, while the rest remains buried under the sand. Alongside, there are two reconstructions of these igloo-like houses.

The Salar de Atacama

Some 10km south of San Pedro you reach the northern edge of the **Salar de Atacama**, a 3000-square-kilometre basin covered by a vast crust of saline minerals. The largest salt flat in Chile, it's formed by waters flowing down from the Andes which, unable to escape from the basin, are forced to evaporate, leaving salt deposits on the earth. It's not a dazzling white like the Salar de Surire (see p.231), or Bolivia's Salar de Uyuni, but is fascinating all the same – especially when you get out and take a close look at the crust, which looks like coral reef, or ice shards, and clanks when you walk on it. The *salar* contains several small lakes, including **Laguna Chaxa**, home to dozens of flamingos, and the beautiful **Laguna Salada**, whose waters are covered with floating plates of salt. Many tour companies include a stop at the salt flat as part of a tour to the oases and lakes south of San Pedro.

The southern oases and lakes

Heading south from San Pedro, on the eastern side of the Salar de Atacama, you enter a region of beautiful lakes and tiny oasis villages. The first oasis you reach, 38km south, is **TOCONAO**, whose softwater stream enters the village through the **Quebrada de Jérez**, a steep, narrow gorge with figs and quinces growing on its southern banks. Though not as pretty as some of the other villages, Toconao does possess a handsome whitewashed bell tower dating from 1750, set apart from the main church. Some 35km further south you reach **CAMAR**, a tiny hamlet with just sixty inhabitants, set amidst lush green terraces. **SOCAIRE**, 15km beyond, is less picturesque, save for its little church set by a field of sunflowers. **PEINE**, reached by a track branching west from the "main road" between Camar and Socaire, has a mid-eighteenth century church and a large swimming pool, invariably full of squealing children.

Not far from Socaire, 4350m above sea level, **Laguna Miscanti** is one of the most stunning lakes in the region, its brilliant-blue waters almost leaping out at you. Adjacent is the much smaller **Laguna Miñeques** whose waters are a deep, dark blue; both lakes are protected areas, part of the Reserva Nacional Los Flamencos. Further south, pastel-coloured **Laguna Tuyaito** is home to dozens of flamingos, and is set against a fabulous backdrop of mineral-streaked mountains. Another lake visited on some tours is **Laguna Legía**, filled with emerald-green waters tinged white with salt deposits floating on the surface; like Tuyaito, it's also home to large numbers of flamingos.

The Tatio geysers

Getting to the **Tatio geysers**, 95km north of San Pedro, is quite an ordeal: first, you drag yourself out of bed in the dead of night, with no electric lights to see by; you then stand shivering in the street while you wait for your tour company to come and pick you up at 4am; and finally, you embark on a three-hour journey across a rough, bumpy road. Added to this is the somewhat surreal experience of finding yourself in a pre-dawn rush hour, part of a caravan of minibuses following each other's lights across the desert. But no one who goes there regrets it. At 4300m above sea level, El Tatio is the highest geyser field in the world. It's essentially a large, flat field containing countless blowholes full of bubbling water that, between around 6 and 8am, send billowing clouds of steam high into the air. At the same time, the geysers' spray forms pools of water on the ground that are streaked with silver as they catch the first rays of the sun. It's really a magnificent spectacle. You should take great care, however, when walking around the field; the crust of earth is very thin in some parts, and serious accidents can happen. You should also remember that it will be freezing cold when you arrive, though once the sun's out the place warms up quite quickly. There's a swimming pool near the geysers, visited by most tour companies, so remember to take your bathing suit. On the way back, some tour companies also pay a visit to the **Baños de Puritama** (CH$5000), a rocky pool filled with warm thermal water, 60km south of the geysers and run by Explora in San Pedro.

El Tatio to Calama

Spread between El Tatio and Calama is a series of charming oases and pre-Columbian remains, visited by several tour companies after a morning at the geysers. This is a good one to do on your final day, as you can store your luggage in the minibus and get dropped off at Calama, before the tour returns to San Pedro. About 45km west of El Tatio (by road) and one of the most beautiful oases in Chile, **CASPANA** sits in a fertile valley at the foot of a steep cliff. A small river runs through the valley, crossed by a little stone bridge which leads to the school and museum (Tues–Sun 9.30am–5.30pm; CH$400), where you'll find displays on Caspana's pre-Columbian origins. Across the river from the main village, perched high on a hill, the "pueblo viejo" is the site of the old church, dating from 1641, with steps leading up the bell tower. Not far from Caspana, **AYQUINA** is another picture-postcard village but is almost deserted, coming to life only for its fiesta on September 8. Its houses, made entirely of stone, are clustered around the church, which has a distinctive five-tiered bell tower. The village's main street leads to a *mirador* overlooking the deep canyon through which the río Salado runs, lined by dark-green terraces – a truly gorgeous view.

North of Ayquina, the twelfth-century **Pukará de Turi** was the largest fortified village ever built in the region, and was used as an administrative centre by the Incas towards the end of the fifteenth century. Today, you can still make out the outline of its streets and squares, and there are some half-standing circular towers. Heading west, towards Calama, you reach another twelfth-century *pukará*, the **Pukará de Lasana**, now partially restored and conserved as a national monument. Made up of narrow, maze-like streets laid out in a zigzag pattern, it's a fascinating place to wander. Eight kilometres south of Lasana, **CHIU CHIU** is a tidy, well-maintained village with one of the most beautiful Andean churches in Chile, built in 1674. A wide, squat whitewashed building, its adobe walls are over a metre thick, topped by a rough thatched roof. Perhaps most impressive are its massive doors, lined with cactus boards and decorated with leather cross-stitching. If you walk around the outside of the church building, within the thick white walls enclosing it, you'll find a tiny cemetery out the back. Chiu Chiu is just 33km east of Calama, so can also be visited as part of a tour from there.

Iquique

Dramatically situated at the foot of the 800-metre coastal cordillera, **IQUIQUE**, 390km north of Calama, is a sprawling, busy city, and capital of Region I. It started out as a small settlement of indigenous fishing communities, and during the colonial period became a base for extracting guano deposits from the coast. It continued to grow with the opening of a nearby silver mine in 1730, but its population never exceeded one hundred in the eighteenth century, and it wasn't until the great nineteenth-century nitrate boom that Iquique really took off as a city. Following its transferral to Chilean hands during the War of the Pacific (1878–83), Iquique became the "**nitrate capital**" of Chile – where the largest quantities of ore were shipped from, and where the wealthy nitrate barons based themselves, building opulent mansions all over the rapidly expanding city. By the end of the nineteenth century, Iquique was the wealthiest and most hedonistic city in Chile – it was said that more champagne was consumed here, per head, than in any other city in the world.

With the abrupt end of the nitrate heyday after World War I, Iquique's boom was over, and the grand mansions were left to fade and crumble as the industrialists took themselves back to Santiago. Fishing stepped in to fill the economic gap, and over the years Iquique has transformed itself into the world's leading exporter of fishmeal. This is a thriving and prosperous industry, but has the unfortunate effect of filling Iquique's streets with a distinctly unpleasant odour, noticeable all over the city, and particularly down by the waterfront. This, added to the general feeling of a city gone to seed, gives Iquique a gloomy, worn-out air. That said, its central square and main avenue conserve some splendid buildings from the nitrate era which, along with the city's beaches, are for many people a good enough reason to visit. Still more people, mainly Chileans, head here for the duty-free shopping at Iquique's Zona Franca, or "Zofri". It's more likely, however, that you'll find yourself here out of necessity rather than choice – Iquique is a convenient place to arrange excursions into the interior, whose attractions include the famous nitrate ghost towns of **Humberstone** and **Santa Laura**, the beautiful hot-springs oases of **Pica**, **Matilla** and **Chusmiza**, and the stunning altiplano scenery of **Parque Nacional Volcán Isluga**.

Arrival, information and city transport

Iquique's **bus terminal** is in a rather run-down quarter at the northern end of Patricio Lynch – best take a taxi to the centre, or wait for a *colectivo*. If you're arriving **by air**, you'll land at Diego Arecena airport, 40km south of the city. From here, you can get to the centre by bus, *colectivo* or regular taxi.

For **tourist information**, head for the well-stocked and very helpful Sernatur office (mid-March to mid-Dec Mon–Fri 8am–1pm & 3–6pm; mid-Dec to mid-March Mon–Fri 8am–7pm, Sat & Sun 10am–7pm; ☎57/427686) on the third floor of a large office block at Serrano 145, just off Plaza Prat. In high season it also has an office at Aníbal Pinto 436 (Dec 15–March 15 Mon–Fri 8am–7pm, Sat & Sun 10am–7pm). Note that a lot of its material is not on display, so ask the staff to show you what they've got.

With the exception of those from the bus terminal and airport, nearly all Iquique's **taxis** function like *colectivos*, with fixed, low fares but flexible routes. This is very handy for shuttling to and from the beach, or even going from your hotel to a restaurant. Find

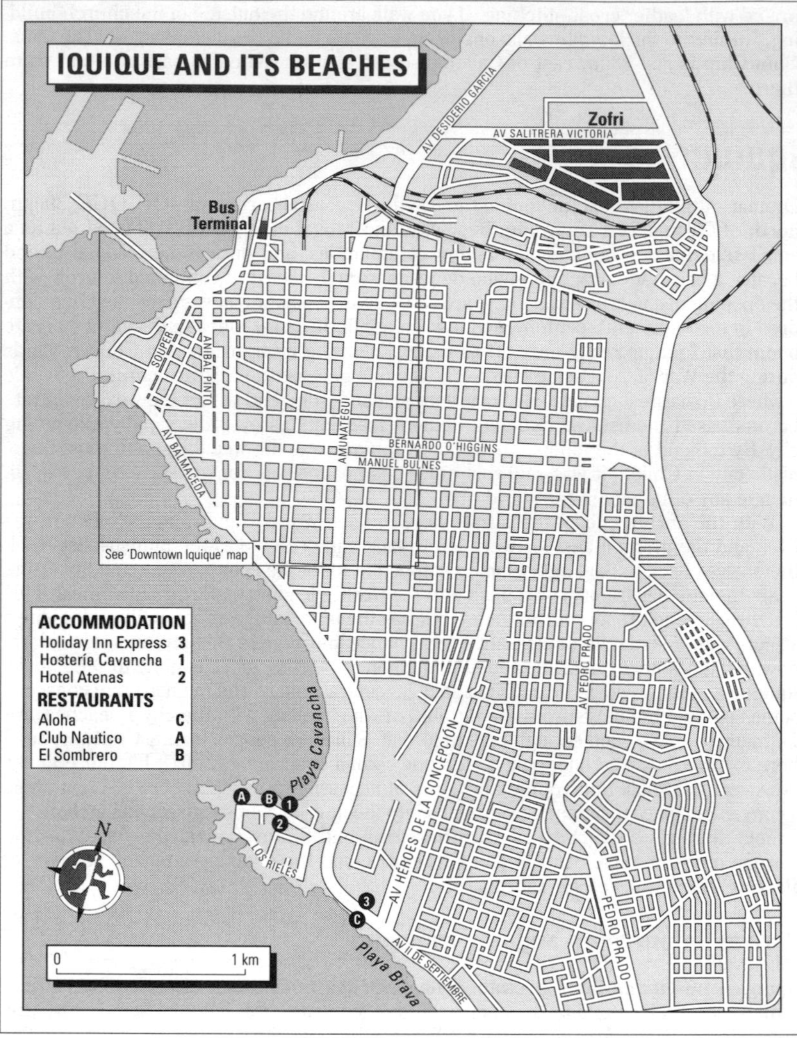

out from Sernatur or your hotel what the going rate is, and confirm this with the taxi driver before you get in.

Accommodation

Iquique is a popular holiday resort and offers an abundance of **accommodation**. The widest choice is in the centre, where you'll find cheap *residenciales* and smart hotels alike, while the hotels by the beaches are almost unanimously expensive – but worth it, perhaps, if you want a couple of days by the ocean. Both in the centre and by the beaches, always ask what the "best price" is, as many places will give discounts when pushed.

Downtown

Gianni Hotel, Ramírez 814 (☎57/416100). Modern, spacious rooms with large windows, TV and private bath. Could do with a lick of paint but pleasant all the same. ④.

Hostal Pleamar, Latorre 1036 (☎57/411840). Small but clean, quiet rooms with private bath and TV, giving onto a covered terrace with tables and chairs. Excellent value. ③.

Hotel Arturo Prat, A Pinto 695 (☎57/411067, fax 423309). Plush city-centre hotel with an elegant period front section containing the reception and restaurant, and modern rooms in tall blocks behind. Also has a small rooftop pool. ⑥.

Hotel Carlos Condell, Baquedano 964 (☎57/424467, fax 422920). Beautiful old timber building on the historic stretch of calle Baquedano; the rooms at the front are looking worse for wear but open onto a wonderful veranda; those at the back are small, dark and overpriced. ⑤.

Hotel Icaisa, Orella 434 (☎ & fax 57/428464). Smart downtown hotel with attractive furnishings, good rooms and a pool. Ask about "special offers" (*ofertas*). ⑥.

Hotel Inti Llank, Obispo Labbé 825 (☎57/412511, fax 413858). Friendly and efficiently run single-storey hotel offering 30 spacious, light rooms with private bath. Showing its age a little, but very clean. ④.

Hotel Obispo Labbé, Obispo Labbé 1272 (☎ & fax 57/416181). Simple but spotless rooms with private bath, not far from the beach. ③–④.

Hotel Riorsa, Vivar 1542 (☎ & fax 57/423823). Good-quality, well-maintained rooms with private bath, cable TV and a very helpful owner. On the southern edge of town, an easy walk from the beach. ④.

Residencial Casa Grande, Barros Arana 1071 (☎ & fax 57/426846). Decent budget rooms in the main house, with high ceilings and wooden floors, but those out back are cramped and dingy. ③.

Residencial El Turista, Juan Martínez 857 (☎57/422245). Large *residencial* with 55 cell-like rooms, most with windows, on two levels around a courtyard. A bit grotty but very cheap. ②.

Residencial José Luis, Ramírez 402. Bright, airy and fairly spacious rooms with shared bath – a good budget choice. ②.

Residencial Sol del Norte, Juan Martínez 852 (☎57/421546). Simple but clean rooms off a long corridor, with a very friendly *señora*. Recommended. ②.

The beaches

Holiday Inn Express, 11 Septiembre 1690 (☎57/433300). Impersonal but immaculate US chain hotel, with a pool, air conditioning and spacious rooms with ocean views (at the front). Special discounts Fri–Sun. ⑥.

Hostería Cavancha, Los Rieles 250 (☎ & fax 57/434800). Modern, 80-room hotel with tennis courts, swimming pool, a dining room overlooking the ocean and direct access to the beach. Rooms not as fresh as they could be. ⑥.

Hotel Atenas, Los Rieles 738 (☎ & fax 57/431100). Grand nitrate-era house with lots of character and beautifully furnished rooms with verandas. A modern annexe out the back has plainer, less expensive rooms. ⑥.

The City

Iquique falls into two quite distinct areas: **downtown**, which is where all the shops and services are located, as well as the old historic buildings, and the modern stretch along the **oceanfront**, given over almost entirely to tourism. The **Zofri** is just north of the centre, in an industrial area.

Downtown Iquique

The focus of town is the large **Plaza Prat**, dominated by the gleaming white **Teatro Municipal**, whose magnificent facade features Corinthian columns and statues repre-

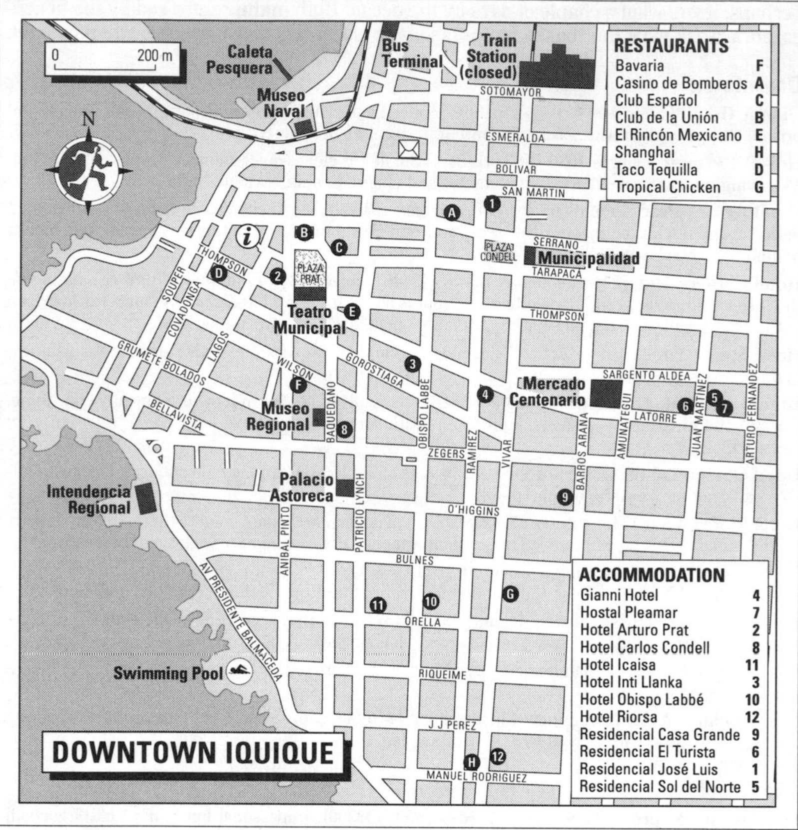

senting the four seasons. It was built in 1890 as an opera house, and was visited by some of the most distinguished divas of its time. These days productions aren't quite so grand, taking in anything from national ballet to local school concerts. If the programme doesn't appeal, it's still worth taking a look inside (daily 8am–7pm; CH$400) to admire the lavish, if slightly faded, furnishings, and grand proportions of the auditorium. Opposite the theatre, in the centre of the square, the **Torre Reloj** is a tall white clock tower with Moorish arches, adopted by Iquique as the city's symbol. On the northeast corner of the square, the **Club Español** – formerly a gentlemen's club, now a restaurant – features an extravagant Moorish-style interior with oil paintings depicting scenes from *Don Quijote* hanging from the walls, and is definitely worth a visit. Leading south from here, **calle Baquedano** is lined with an extraordinary collection of turn-of-the-century timber houses, all with porches and balconies and fine wooden balustrades. This is the showcase of Iquique's nitrate architecture, and has been designated a national monument. Two buildings on this street are open to the public: the **Museo Regional** at no. 951 (Mon–Fri 9.30am–1pm & 3–6.30pm; CH$400), which houses an eclectic collection of pre-Hispanic and natural history artefacts, including deformed skulls and a pickled two-headed shark, and the **Palacio Astoreca** (Tues–Fri

10am–1pm & 3–8pm, Sat & Sun 10am–1pm; CH$400; entrance at the corner of Lynch and O'Higgins), a glorious, though deteriorating, mansion featuring a massive wood-panelled entrance hall with a painted glass art nouveau ceiling. Further attractions include the **Museo Naval**, one block south (Tues–Sat 9.30am–12.30pm & 2.30–6pm, Sun 10am–1pm; free) displaying letters, maps and photos relating to Arturo Prat, hero of the War of the Pacific, and, just behind, the **Caleta Pesquera**, where the huge, yawning pelicans strutting around the pier make compelling viewing. You can take **boat tours** around the harbour from here, worth it for the views onto the steep desert mountains rising directly behind the city.

The beaches

There are two beaches within striking distance of the city centre: **Playa Cavancha**, the nearest and most popular, and **Playa Brava**, larger, less crowded and more windswept. You can just about walk to Playa Cavancha, which begins at the southern end of Amunategui, but it's far easier, and very cheap, to take one of the numerous taxis constantly plying between the plaza and the beach; many continue to Playa Brava, as well, for a slightly higher fare. Both beaches, particularly Cavancha, are lined with modern hotels and apartment blocks, but the construction is fairly low-level, and not too ugly. Further south, between Playa Brava and the airport, there's a series of attractive sandy beaches including **Playa Blanca**, 13km south of the centre, **Playa Lobito**, at km 22 and the fishing *caleta* of **Los Verdes**, at km 24. You can get to these on the airport bus or *colectivo*.

The Zofri

About 3km north of the centre, located in a large industrial compound, the duty-free shopping complex known as the **Zofri** (Mon–Fri 10am–1.30pm & 4.30–9pm, Sat 10am–2pm & 5–9pm) is widely touted as one of the great attractions of the north. Thousands of Chileans flock here from up and down the country to spend their money at what turns out, at close quarters, to be a big, ugly mall crammed full of small shops selling electronic items like cameras, watches and domestic gadgets. There's a curious mixture of the upmarket and the tacky, with the latter tending to dominate. The building itself is shabby and old-fashioned, and the bargains aren't really good enough to deserve a special trip. If you do want to check it out, take any *colectivo* marked "Zofri" heading north out of town – the east side of the Plaza or calle Armunategui are a good bet for catching one.

Eating, drinking and entertainment

While there's a reasonable choice of **restaurants** in the centre, it's worth coming out to have at least one evening meal by the beach, to see the ocean lit up with coloured lights projected from the promenade. As for entertainment, there are several **nightclubs** that get very crowded in summer and maintain a gentle buzz during low season. Iquique's **cinema** is at Serrano 206.

Downtown restaurants

Bavaria, Aníbal Pinto 926. Downstairs café and upstairs restaurant that are part of a nationwide chain specializing in mid-price meat dishes.

Casino de Bomberos, Serrano 520. Friendly firemen's canteen (open to the public), serving filling, tasty and inexpensive lunches.

Club de la Unión, Plaza Prat. Uninspired food (typical meat and fish dishes) but the building is spacious and rather grand, with views onto the Teatro Municipal. A good place for lunch.

Club Español, Plaza Prat 58. Huge, fabulous dining room decorated like a mock Moorish palace. The food is unexceptional, but this is a must-visit.

El Rincón Mexicano, Patricio Lynch 754. Cosy Mexican restaurant owned by football-mad Mario, with regular showings of Mexican football on the TV.

Mercado Centenario, Barros Arana, between Latorre and Sargento Aldea. Cheap fish lunches available upstairs at the ten or so bustling *marisquerías*.

Shanghai, Vivar 1583. Friendly Chinese restaurant offering decent, if unadventurous, Chinese food at very reasonable prices.

Taco Tequilla, Thompson 123. Funky, colourful decor, good Mexican food and great tequilas. Very lively at weekends, when they have live *mariachis*. Watch out for overcharging.

Tropical Chicken, Vivar 1254. Fast-food outlet with tables and chairs on the street, serving inexpensive chicken roasted on a spit.

Restaurants by the beach

Aloha, 11 de Septiembre opposite *Holiday Inn Express*. Excellent but very expensive food served in a faux-rustic hut overlooking the beach. Good service and lovely views.

Club Nautico, Los Rieles 110. First-rate, reasonably priced restaurant, run by a French guy from Toulouse, with great views from its outdoor terrace, especially at night.

El Sombrero, Los Rieles 704. Rather formal, expensive restaurant specializing in seafood – invariably served up in rich, roux-based sauces. It's right by the sea, with floor to ceiling windows giving great views.

Bar and discos

Barracuda, Gorostiago 601, at the corner with Ramírez. Very popular wood-panelled pub serving foreign beers, tea, coffee, milkshakes and delicious snacks. Soft jazz music and lovely mellow atmosphere.

Kamikaze, Playa Brava. Large pub-disco (Thurs–Sat) with a replica of a crashed aeroplane on its roof. Part of a successful chain, with identical versions in Santiago, Reñaca and La Serena.

Mascarrieles, just off Plaza Prat, by *Hotel Arturo Prat*. Friendly bar-restaurant with lots of dark, wood panelling; popular with locals at lunchtime or after work.

Timber House, Bolívar 553. New, *Barracuda*-style pub in an old timber building, serving beers, cocktails and Mediterranean snacks.

Listings

Airlines Air France, Libertad 738 (☎57/424774); Avant, Aníbal Pinto 257 (☎57/428800); Iberia, Vivar 632 (☎57/411878); Ladeco, San Martín 428 (☎57/413038); Lan Chile, Vivar 675 (☎57/414128); Lufthansa, San Martín 151 (☎57/412591); United Airlines, Ramírez 411 (☎57/428266).

Banks and exchange Iquique has numerous ATMs, including those at: Banco Santander, Plaza Prat; BCI, Tarapacá 404; Banco Sudamericano, Uribe 530; Corp-Banca, Serrano 343. There are fewer *casas de cambio*, but you could try Afex on the corner of Serrano and Lynch, downtown, or Fides Ltda at the Zofri Plaza de Servicios.

Car rental Best value may well be at Jofamar, Libertad 1156 (☎57/411639), or Stop, at Bulnes 168 (☎57/416382). You could also try: Budget, O'Higgins 1361 (☎57/422527); Continental, 18 de Septiembre 1054 (☎57/411426); Hertz, Souper 650 (☎57/420213); J. Reategui, Serrano 1058 (☎57/429490); Rocar, Cerro Dragón 2789 (☎57/435233); Senort, Souper 796 (☎57/413480).

Laundry Lavamatic, Orella 756, near corner with Barros Arana; Lavalindo, O'Higgins 618, between Vivar and Ramírez; Autoservicio, San Martín 490.

Post office The main office is at Bolívar 485, a few blocks northeast of Plaza Prat.

Swimming pool There's a fantastic outdoor pool (☎57/411573) overlooking the Pacific at Av Costanera with Riquelme, opposite the Copec station.

Taxis Taxi Aeropuerto (☎57/413368); Iquique (☎57/413848).

Telephone offices CTC, Serrano 620; Entel, Gorostiaga 287; Chilexpress, Tarapacá 580, plus many more around town.

MOVING ON FROM IQUIQUE

Most **long-distance buses** depart from the Terminal Rodoviario, at the north end of Lynch, but many bus companies also have offices around the Mercado Centenario, including: Buses Carmelita, Barros Arana 841 (☎57/412337); Flota Barrios, Sargento Aldea 987 (☎57/426941); Ramos Cholele, Barros Arana 851 (☎57/411650); Tramacá, Sargento Aldea 988 (☎57/412323); and Tur Bus, Barros Arana 825 (☎57/413028). There are regular daily buses to **Pica** (with stops at **Matilla** and **La Tirana**) with San Andres, on the corner of Barros Arana and Sargento Aldea (☎57/413953), and Buses Tamarugal, Sargento Aldea 781 (☎57/412981). The latter also has twice-daily services to **Mamiña** (Mon–Sat 8am & 4pm, Sun 8am only). Yellow *colectivos* for **Pozo Almonte** leave from the side of the market, and will drop passengers at Humberstone. Buses Geminis, Obispo Labbé 151 (☎57/413315), goes to Salta in Argentina, and Oruro and La Paz, in Bolivia, while Tramacá also goes to Salta. You can fly out of Iquique to all the main cities of the north, and to Santiago.

Travel agencies There are numerous travel agents in town, including Atlantic, at San Martín 421, or Aries 1, at Thompson 112. For tours into the cordillera, see the box below.

Inland from Iquique

Iquique lies within easy reach of many inland attractions. Just half an hour away, **Humberstone** and **Santa Laura** are perhaps the most haunting and atmospheric of all the nitrate ghost towns. South of here, close to the Panamericana, **Cerro Pintados** is the site of a dense collection of geoglyphs, among the most impressive in Chile. East of Pintados, **Pica** is a pretty oasis village home to a lovely thermal pool, while **Mamiña**, further north, is the Norte Grande's hot-springs town *par finesse*. You could also visit **La Tirana**, an important pilgrimage centre, famous for its colourful festival in July. Public transport around this area is sporadic but manageable.

Humberstone and Santa Laura

Some 45km inland from Iquique, sitting by Ruta 16 just before it meets the Panamericana, **HUMBERSTONE** is a former nitrate *oficina*, abandoned in 1960 and now the best-pre-

TOURS FROM IQUIQUE

A number of Iquique tour companies offer one-day circular tours – from around CH$13,000 per person – taking in the nitrate ghost towns of **Humberstone** and **Santa Laura** (see above), the geoglyphs of Pintados (see overleaf), the oases villages of **Matilla** and **Pica**, with a plunge in Pica's hot springs, (see p.212) and the basilica and nitrate museum of **La Tirana**, (see p.212). Another standard tour offered by some companies is the highly memorable route up into the cordillera, continuing north across the altiplano and descending in Arica – taking in the geysers of **Puchildiza** (see p.216), **Parque Nacional Volcán Isluga** (see p.216), the **Salar de Surire** (see p.231), and **Parque Nacional Lauca** (see p.228). The tour normally takes three days, with prices starting around CH$95,000 per person. Recommended companies include Andino Expediciones at Baquedano 982 (☎57/417546, fax 419144), Surire Tours at Baquedano 1035 (☎ & fax 57/411795), and – longest on the scene – Turismo Lirima, at Baquedano 1067 (☎57/414620). For the one-day tour, you could also try Turismo Mamiña at Latorre 779 (☎ & fax 57/420330).

served ghost town in Chile. It began life in 1862 as Oficina La Palma, but was renamed in 1925 in honour of its British manager, James Humberstone, an important nitrate entrepreneur famous for introducing the "Shanks" ore-refining system to the industry. In its time it was one of the busiest *oficinas* on the pampas; today it is an eerie, empty ghost town, slowly crumbling beneath the desert sun. What sets Humberstone apart from the other ghost towns is the fact that just about all of it is still standing – from the white, terraced workers' houses (now in total disrepair) and the plaza with its bandstand, to the theatre, church and company store. The **theatre**, in particular, is highly atmospheric with its rows of dusty seats staring at the stage. You should also seek out the hotel, and walk through to the back where you'll find a huge, empty **swimming pool** with a dive board. A short distance from the town are the sheds and workshops, with old tools and bits of machinery lying around, and invoices and order forms littering the floors. About 2km down the road, clearly visible from Humberstone, **SANTA LAURA** has only a couple of remaining houses but its processing plant is quite amazing, seeming to loom into the air like a rusty old dinosaur. As you walk around the site, listening to the endless clanging of machinery banging in the wind, the sense of abandonment is almost overwhelming.

Getting there from Iquique is easy: just take a yellow *colectivo* for Pozo Almonte from the stand by the Mercado Centenario, and ask to be dropped off en route. Getting back is trickier as all the *colectivos* that pass will be full, which means hitching a lift. There's a lot of passing traffic, but make sure you have a plenty of water and sunscreen to keep you going while you're waiting (drinks are also available in a kiosk across the road). Both sites have open access so you can visit them at any time. There's no entry charge, but you may be asked for a "voluntary contribution" by the occupants of the house at the entrance to Humberstone – these have nothing whatsoever to do with its upkeep and are simply making a bit of cash from unsuspecting tourists.

Pampa del Tamarugal and the geoglyphs of Pintados

About 20km south of the junction between Ruta 16 and the Panamericana, the latter passes through the **RESERVA NACIONAL PAMPA DEL TAMARUGAL**, an extensive plantation of wispy, bush-like tamarugo trees. These are native to the region, and are especially adapted to saline soils, with roots that are long enough to tap underground water supplies. There's a Conaf-run **campsite** here, exactly 24km south of Pozo Almonte, on the west side of the Panamericana. While the tamarugos aren't really interesting enough to merit a special trip, you can take a look at them on your way to the far more impressive **Cerro Pintados** (daily 9.30am–6.30pm; CH$1000), the site of the largest collection of **geoglyphs** in South America, situated within the reserve's boundaries. Extending 4km along a hillside, the site is composed of over four hundred images (not all of them visible from the ground) representing animals, birds, humans and geometric patterns. There's a picnic area near the biggest concentration of images, but it pays to explore the rest of the site as well. Cerro Pintados begins 5km west of the Panamericana, reached by a gravel road that branches off the highway 45km south of Pozo Almonte, almost opposite the turn-off to Pica. There's a Conaf control 2km along the road, where you pay your entrance fee. If it's shut when you arrive, you can continue with your car as far as the barrier, which is just a short walk from the geoglyphs. If you haven't got your own transport, you should be able to arrange a lift there and back with a *colectivo* from the stand outside Iquique's Mercado Centenario – it's probably not a good idea to hitch and try walking to the site from the Panamericana, due to the relentless heat and lack of shade.

Pica and Matilla

Driving across the vast, desert pampa, the neighbouring oases of Pica and Matilla first appear as an improbable green smudge on the hazy horizon. As you get nearer, it

THE NITRATE BOOM

Looking around the desert pampa, it's hard to believe that this scorched, lifeless wasteland was once so highly prized that a war was fought over it – and still more difficult to imagine it alive with smoking chimneys, grinding machinery, offices, houses and a massive workforce. But less than a century ago, the far north of Chile was the scene of a thriving industry built on its vast supplies of **nitrate deposits**, heavily in demand in Europe and North America as a fertilizer. Nitrates first began to be exploited in the Atacama desert in the 1860s, when the region still belonged to Bolivia (around Antofagasta) and Peru (around Iquique and Arica). From the early stages, however, the Chilean presence was very strong, both in terms of capital and labour – in the 1870s Chileans made up over fifty percent of the workforce in Iquique, and some eighty percent in Antofagasta, while the largest nitrate company, the Compañía de Salitres y Ferrocarril de Antofagasta, was a Chilean enterprise. When in 1878 the Bolivian government violated an official agreement by raising export taxes on nitrate (hitting Chilean shareholders, including several prominent politicians), Chile protested by sending troops into Antofagasta. Two weeks later, Chile and Bolivia were at war, with Peru joining in (on the Bolivian side) within a couple of months. The War of the Pacific (see p.453), as it was known, went on for five years, and resulted in Chile, the undisputed victor, extending its territory by 900km, taking in all of the nitrate grounds. With the return of political stability after the war, the nitrate industry began to boom in earnest, bringing in enormous export revenues for Chile. Foreign – particularly British – investors poured money into companies like the Liverpool Nitrate Company, and a trail of processing plants, known as *oficinas*, sprang up all over the pampa, connected to the seaports by an extensive railroad network.

Each *oficina* sat in the centre of its prescribed land, from where the raw nitrate ore – found just beneath the surface of the earth – was blasted using gunpowder. The chunks of ore, known as *caliche*, were then boiled in large copper vats, releasing a nitrate solution which was crystallized in the sun before being sent down to the ports to be shipped abroad. The plants themselves were grimy, noisy places. A British journalist, William Russell, who toured the pampa in 1889, wrote: "The external aspect of the *oficina* was not unlike that of a north country coal or iron mine – tall chimneys and machinery, corrugated iron buildings, offices and houses, the shanties of workmen, a high bank of refuse." It was a hard life for the labourers, who worked long hours in dangerous conditions, and were housed in squalid shacks, often without running water and sewerage. The (mostly British) managers, meanwhile, lived in grand residences, dined on imported delicacies and enjoyed a whirl of social activities – Russell wrote of "picnics, nightly dances and even balls to which the neighbours came from the *oficinas* around, from Iquique and Pisagua below by special train, which conveyed bands of music and armies of cooks, confectioners and waiters". Nitrate provided more than half of the Chilean government's revenues until 1920, by which time the boom was over and the industry in decline. It was World War I that dealt the first serious blow to the nitrate companies, when the suspension of sales to Germany – Chile's major European buyer – forced almost half the *oficinas* to close down. The final death knell was sounded when Germany, forced to seek alternative fertilizers, developed cheap synthetic nitrates which quickly displaced Chile's natural nitrates from their dominant role in the world market. Most of what was left of the industry was killed off by the World Depression in the 1930s, and today just two *oficinas* – Maria Elena and Pedro de Valdivia (see p.192) – remain in operation.

becomes apparent that this is not a mirage and you are, indeed, approaching cultivated fields and trees. It's a remarkable sight, and anyone who has not seen a desert oasis should make a special effort to visit. By far the larger of the two oases, **PICA** is a sleepy little town overflowing with lemon trees and flowers. It's the largest supplier of fruits to Iquique, and one of the treats of visiting is drinking the delicious *jugos naturales* – orange, mango, pear, guava and grapefruit – freshly squeezed in front of you in the little streetside kiosks. Its plaza, by the entrance to town, is neat and tidy, and is overlooked by a beautiful pale-coloured **church** with a grand Neoclassical facade, built in 1880. Pica's real selling point, however, is the **Cocha Resbaladero** (daily 8am–8pm; CH$800), a gorgeous **hot-springs pool** carved into a rocky hollow with two caves at one end. It's at the far end of calle Presidente Ibañez, quite a walk from the main part of town, but there are several places to stay up here if you want to be close to the waters.

About 5km away, **MATILLA** is a tiny, pretty village with another beautiful church, more humble than Pica's. It also has an eighteenth-century wine press, just off the plaza, used by the Spaniards to produce wine made from vines whose roots were brought over by the conquistadors. While you're here, you should also try the wonderful *jugos* in the café opposite the church.

Practicalities

Pica is 114km southeast of Iquique, connected to the Panamericana by two good roads. Daily **buses** leave from opposite Iquique's Mercado Centenario (see p.209); the journey takes two hours. The town has a rudimentary **Oficina de Turismo** in the Municipalidad on the main square (Mon–Fri 8.30am–1pm & 3–7pm), as well as several *centros de llamados* and a post office on the main street. The nicest **place to stay** in the centre is at *Hotel Los Emilios*, at Lord Cochrane 213 (☎57/741126; ③), which offers comfortable rooms with private bath in a handsome old house with a plunge pool in the back garden (first right from the plaza as you come into town). Up by the hot springs, you'll find basic but clean rooms in *Residencial El Tambo*, at Ibañez 68 (☎57/741041; ②), and a few attractive wooden *cabañas* overlooking the pool at Ibañez 57 (Sr Medina, ☎ & fax 57/741316; ④). There's a **campsite**, *Camping Miraflores* (☎57/741338; ②), just round the corner on calle Miraflores. As for **eating**, you could try *La Viña* at Ibañez 79, up by the hot springs, or the delightful *Mía Pappa* down in the centre, at Balmaceda 118, where food is served on a quiet patio under the shade of fragrant lemon trees. The best **fruit-juice stalls** are on Ibañez, towards the hot springs, and there's a wonderful **shop** selling home-made jams and conserves a little further along from the campsite.

La Tirana

Driving back to the Panamericana from Pica, if you take the right-hand (northbound) road, rather than the left-hand one, you'll pass through the little town of **LA TIRANA**, 10km before you get back to the highway. It's a rather cheerless place, made up of dusty streets and neglected adobe houses, which makes it all the more surprising when you come across its immense, paved square stretching out before the imposing **Santuario de la Tirana**. This curious church, at once grand and shabby, is made of wood covered in cream-coloured corrugated iron. It's the home of the **Virgen del Carmen**, a polychrome carving that is the object of a fervent cult of devotion. Every year, from July 12 to 18, up to eighty thousand pilgrims come to honour the Virgin and take part in the riotous **fiesta** in which dozens of masked, costumed dancers perform "*bailes religiosos*". These dances have their roots in pre-Spanish, pre-Christian times, and have an exuberant, carnival feel wholly out of keeping with traditional Catholic celebrations. If you're not around to see them in action, you should at least visit the small **museum** in a wing of the church (Sat & Sun 10am–8pm; CH$200) where many of the costumes and masks are displayed (try asking the caretaker to let you in if it's shut). Also worth a visit is the family-run **Museo del Salitre** (Mon–Sat 8am–1pm & 3–8pm; free), standing opposite the church (entrance through the store next door), which is bursting with oddments left over from the nitrate era. These include old ice-cream makers, a film projector (with a reel of Hitchcock inside), typewriters, workers' clothes and boots, sewing machines, photos and, most bizarrely, a stuffed condor. Unless you're

THE LEGEND OF LA TIRANA

La Tirana is named after an Inca princess whose story is vividly recorded in twelve large panels inside the town's church. It all began in 1535 when Diego de Almagro marched south from Cuzco to conquer Chile. He took with him some five hundred Spaniards and ten thousand Peruvians, including Paullo Tupac, an Inca prince, and Huillac Huma, high priest of the cult of the Sun God, who was accompanied by his beautiful 23-year-old daughter, *la ñusta*, or princess. The party also included, unknown to Almagro, a number of "Wilkas", or high-ranking warriors from the Inca Royal Army. When the party reached Atacama la Grande, the high priest took the opportunity to slip away from the group and flee to Charcas, where he planned to stir up rebellion against the Spaniards. Later, while the group was resting for several days in the oasis of Pica, the princess followed her father's lead and escaped from the Spaniards – this time, with 100 Wilkas and followers – and fled to the tamarugo forests which at that time covered much of the pampa. She lost no time in organizing her followers into a fierce and sophisticated army that, for the next four years, waged a relentless war against their oppressors, the Spaniards. Her mission was clear: death to all Spaniards, and to all Indians who had been baptized by them. Before long, this indomitable woman became known far and wide as La Tirana del Tamarugal – the Tyrant of the Tamarugal.

One day, in 1544, La Tirana's army attacked an enemy group and returned to their leader with a prisoner – a certain don Vasco de Almeyda, one of the Portuguese miners established in Huantajaya. Don Vasco was clearly a man of exceptional qualities for, according to the legend, "*Mirarle y enamorarse fue una sola cosa*" – simply to look at him was to fall in love with him. And so La Tirana, hitherto immovable, fell passionately in love with the foreigner. But according to everything she stood and fought for, he must be sentenced to death. In desperation, she devised a ruse to prolong the prisoner's life: she consulted the stars and her tribe's gods, and claimed that they had ordered her to keep him alive until four moons had passed. For the next four months, La Tirana and her prisoner spent day after day talking to one another in the shade of the tamarugos, and a tender love grew up between them. The princess neglected her people and her duties, arousing the suspicion of the Wilkas, who began to keep a secret watch on her. Finally, as the fourth month was coming to an end, La Tirana asked her loved one if they would be reunited for eternity in heaven if she too were a Christian. On his affirmative reply, she begged him to baptize her, and bent down on her knees with her arms crossed against her breast. Pouring water over her head, Almeyda began to do so but before he could finish, the couple were showered with arrows from the bows of the betrayed Wilkas. As she lay dying in the wood, the princess cried, "I am dying happy, sure as I am that my immortal soul will ascend to God's throne. All I ask is that after my death, you will bury me next to my lover and place a cross over our grave." Ten years later, when Padre Antonio Rondon arrived in these parts to evangelize the Indians, it was with astonishment and joy that he discovered a simple cross in a clearing of the wood. The priest erected a humble chapel on the site, which was later replaced by a larger building, and became, in time, the centre of worship in a town that took its name from the beautiful princess who had died there.

here at fiesta time, you're unlikely to want to stay in La Tirana, which in any case has only a rather barren **campsite** and no *residenciales*. **Buses** between Iquique and Pica make a stop in La Tirana (see p.209).

Mamiña

Back on the Panamericana, a paved road branches east at Pozo Almonte and climbs gently through the desert to **MAMIÑA**, 74km away. First impressions of Mamiña are not encouraging; huddled on a hillside overlooking a valley, its narrow streets and crumbling stone houses seem to belong to a forgotten town, left to the mercy of the heat and dust. Continue down the valley, however, and its charms become more apparent as you come upon the fertile terraces emerald with alfalfa, and the little stream running through the *quebrada*. The real reason to come here, though, is for the **hot springs** for which Mamiña is famous throughout Chile. Unlike Pica or Chusmiza, Mamiña doesn't have just one hot spring, but many, and their waters are piped to every house in the village. Furthermore, these waters are not merely hot, but are reputed to cure all manner of afflictions, from eczema and psoriasis to respiratory problems and anxiety. Whatever their medicinal value, there's no doubt that the waters are supremely relaxing to bathe in. This you can do in any of the village's hotels or *residenciales*, usually in your own private *tina*, or bathtub. There are also a number of public springs, including the **Baños Ipla** (9.30am–12.30pm & 3.30–7.30pm; CH$500), down in the valley, whose four large *tinas* are filled with hot sulphurous water (45°C) bubbling up from underground. Nearby, the **Vertiente del Radium** is a little fountain whose radioactive waters are supposed to cure eye infections and, according to legend, restored the sight of an Inca princess. A short walk from here, behind the water bottling plant, you'll find the famous mud baths of **Barros Chino** (daily 9am–3pm; CH$500) where you plaster yourself in mud (don't let the caretaker do it for you, if he tries), lie on a wooden rack while it dries, then wash it off in a small thermal pool.

When you're not wallowing in the waters, you can go walking in the outskirts of Mamiña. It's worth seeking out local sculptor, Giuliano Pavez (ask in *Residencial Inti Raimi*), who'll take you on guided walks into the nearby *cerros* and archeological sites – he always carries his flute with him, and listening to him play Andean melodies high up in the hills is a truly memorable experience. Up in the village, you should also take a look at the unusual two-towered church, built in 1632.

Practicalities

Mamiña is 125km and a two-and-a-half-hour drive from Iquique. It's reached by a good paved road branching east of Pozo Almonte, on the Panamericana, and is served by a twice-daily **bus** from Iquique (see p.209). **Accommodation** is centred in two quite separate areas, one on the ridge overlooking the valley, and the other down in the valley, by the Baños Ipla. All are run on a **full-board basis**. Of the first lot, you could try the *Refugio del Salitrero* (☎57/751203, fax 420330; ⑤), Mamiña's oldest spa hotel, offering upmarket rooms in its new section and fairly basic ones in the old building. Down in "sector Ipla", you'll find modest rooms at *Inti Raimi* (no phone; ③), run by a friendly young couple, and *El Tamarugal* (☎57/414663; ③), whose dining room has lovely views. If you can afford to pamper yourself, try Austrian-run *El Cardenal* (no phone; ⑤) which offers comfortable rooms in a large family house, fabulous *tinas* and a pool; or the *Llama Inn* (☎09/543 2106; ⑤), with a bright, sunny dining room, a pool and a beautiful lounge with floor to ceiling windows giving stunning views. For a small fee you can **camp** in the yard behind *El Bacian*, or in the land belonging to *Inti Raimi*; a better place, however, is by the pool on the track out to Cerro del Inca, about a thirty-minute walk from the Ipla baths.

Up to Parque Nacional Volcán Isluga

At the one-horse-town of **Huara**, 33km up the Panamericana from the turn-off to Iquique, a good road branches east into the desert, then climbs high into the mountains, continuing all the way to Oruro in Bolivia. It's paved as far as **Colchane**, on the Chilean side of the border, but the main appeal lies in getting off the tarmac once you're up into the cordillera and heading for the deserted wilderness in and around **Parque Nacional Volcán Isluga**. Here you'll find a remote, isolated landscape of wide plains,

LA RUTA ALTIPLÁNICA

In April 1998 regional municipalities from Chile, Bolivia and Peru got together to pledge their commitment to the proposed **Ruta Altiplánica de Integración** – a paved highway stretching 1500km across the altiplano, from San Pedro de Atacama in Chile to Cuzco, Peru. The "altiplano summit", as it dubbed itself, set the year 2000 as its goal for getting work started, but this is looking highly unlikely as the multimillion-dollar costs of the project haven't even been calculated, let alone raised. Nonetheless, with support from all three governments, the highway is a realistic prospect for the coming decade. The new road, if it's built, will certainly open up what's currently a remote and largely inaccessible area, and is likely to inject an economic boost to the whole altiplano region.

In the meantime, crossing the altiplano's pot-riddled dirt tracks by jeep is still the road adventure of a lifetime – and should be enjoyed to the full before the arrival of tarmac and increased traffic. Probably the best starting point is Iquique (the ascent in altitude is more gradual in this direction), heading into the cordillera as far as Parque Nacional Volcán Isluga, continuing north across the altiplano to Parque Nacional Lauca, and finally descending in Arica. It's a 700km journey, and takes about four to five days at an easy pace. Accommodation options include the hot-springs hotel at Chusmiza (see below) and the Conaf *refugíos* at Enquelga (see overleaf), the Salar de Surire (see p.231), Lago Chungará (see p.230) and Parinacota (see p.228). If you do the trip, remember that there's no petrol once you're off the Panamericana, which means taking it all with you in jerry cans (*bidones*, available in most ironmongers). Always take much more than you think you need. Another essential precaution is to take two spare tyres, not just one. For more on 4x4 driving, see Basics, p.25.

dramatic, snow-capped volcanoes and semi-abandoned villages, home to indigenous Aymara herding communities that have been a part of this windswept land for thousands of years. Unlike Parque Nacional Lauca, further north, this region hasn't yet been "discovered", and it's unlikely you'll come across many other tourists. There are a number of attractions on the way up, as well, in particular the weird desert geoglyph known as the **Gigante de Atacama**, in the pampa, and the hot-springs village of **Chusmiza**, in the lower slopes of the Andes. There's no public transport around this region, so to explore it you must either take an organized tour from Iquique (see p.209), or rent a high-clearance vehicle, preferably 4WD.

The Gigante de Atacama

The road starts out as a thin, solitary line trailing through the flat desert pampa – an endless expanse of dull yellow and brown. Thirteen kilometres from the turn-off at Huara, you pass an isolated hill, **Cerro Unita**, whose southern slope is adorned with the largest geoglyph in the world, the **Gigante de Atacama**. This stylized anthropomorphic image is a full 86m long and looks like a giant alien, its head, eyes, mouth and torso represented by thick rectangular images. Its arms are outstretched, bent at the elbows, and a dozen rays project from its head, further adding to its extraterrestrial appearance. Cerro Unita is set about 1km back from the road; the image is best viewed around 200m from the foot of the hill.

Chusmiza

As the road continues east it starts to climb, gently, into the foothills of the Andes. Before long, you're twisting up the brown, dry slopes, and the temperature drops noticeably as you leave the intense heat of the desert behind. Around 70km from Huara a steep, rough track branches off the main road and crawls 5km down to the tiny village of **CHUSMIZA**, set at the bottom of a narrow, rocky canyon. Follow the road through the village to the end of the canyon, and you'll find a large, unnamed, ramshackle **hotel** (no phone; ②). Despite its unprepossessing appearance, this is one of the most unusual and enjoyable places to stay in Chile – certainly not for its furnishings, which are spartan and basic, but for its location (the views down the canyon are wonderful) and for the enormous sunken baths in every room that are filled with thermal water piped directly from the **hot springs** outside the hotel. Set at 3650m above sea level, this is the perfect place to spend a night en route to the altiplano, allowing you to acclimatize before reaching more extreme heights. If the caretaker, Luisa, isn't there, pick up the key from her brother-in-law, Simón, in the village.

The Puchuldiza geysers

Back on the road to Colchane, you can make another highly recommended detour, this time to **Puchuldiza**, a geothermic field containing several geysers and dozens of bubbling water holes. Framed by a backdrop of distant volcanoes, the geysers shoot tall, strong jets of water high into the air, right next to a small lake tinged white with salt. In winter (May–Sept), the scene is particularly dramatic as the geysers' spray freezes, forming a giant, blue-white ice block, as big as a two-storey house, dripping all over with icicles. While nowhere near as numerous as their counterparts at El Tatio, near San Pedro de Atacama (see p.202), the geysers here have two big advantages: first, they spurt water 24 hours a day, so there's no need to get up at the crack of dawn to visit; second, no one seems to go there, so you'll probably have the spectacle all to yourself. Take great care when inspecting the water holes, as the crust around them is thin in parts, and some of them hold water as hot as 85°C. Puchuldiza is reached at the end of a signed nineteen-kilometre dirt road branching north of the paved road, some 60km beyond the turn-off to Chusmiza. After visiting the geysers you could come back to the paved road and continue to Colchane, but a far more interesting option is to retrace your route for part of the way then follow the signed turn-off to Mauque (a 20-house hamlet) and keep on going to Enquelga, about 15km away.

Parque Nacional Volcán Isluga

PARQUE NACIONAL VOLCÁN ISLUGA, lying in the heart of the altiplano, is named after the towering, snow-capped volcano whose 5500-metre peak dominates the park's landscape. Its administrative centre is in **ENQUELGA**, a dusty, tumbledown hamlet – 3850m above sea level – home to a small Aymara community. Many of its inhabitants, particularly the women, still dress in their traditional, brightly coloured clothes, and most live from tending llamas and cultivating potatoes and barley. There's a **Conaf refugio** in the village, with **accommodation** for five people (CH$5000 per person); it's supposed to be open year-round, but sometimes isn't. Two kilometres on from Enquelga, **Aguas Calientes** is a long, spring-fed pool containing warm (but not hot) waters, set in an idyllic location with terrific views of the volcano. The pool is surrounded by pea-green *bofedal* – a spongy grass, typical of the altiplano – and drains into a little stream, crossed every morning and evening by herds of llamas driven to and from the sierra by Aymara shepherdesses. There's a stone changing-hut next to it, and a few **camping** spaces and picnic areas, protected from the evening wind by thick stone walls.

Six kilometres east of Enquelga, still within the park's boundaries, **ISLUGA** is composed of a hundred or so stone and adobe houses huddled around one of the most beautiful churches of the altiplano. Built some time in the seventeenth century (it's not known when, exactly), it's a humble little church made of thick, whitewashed adobe that flashes like snow in the constant glare of the sun. The main building, containing a single nave, is enclosed by a low wall trimmed with delicate arches; just outside the wall sits the two-tier bell tower with steps leading up to the top, where you can sit and survey the scenery, or watch the hummingbirds that fly in and out to play. The church,

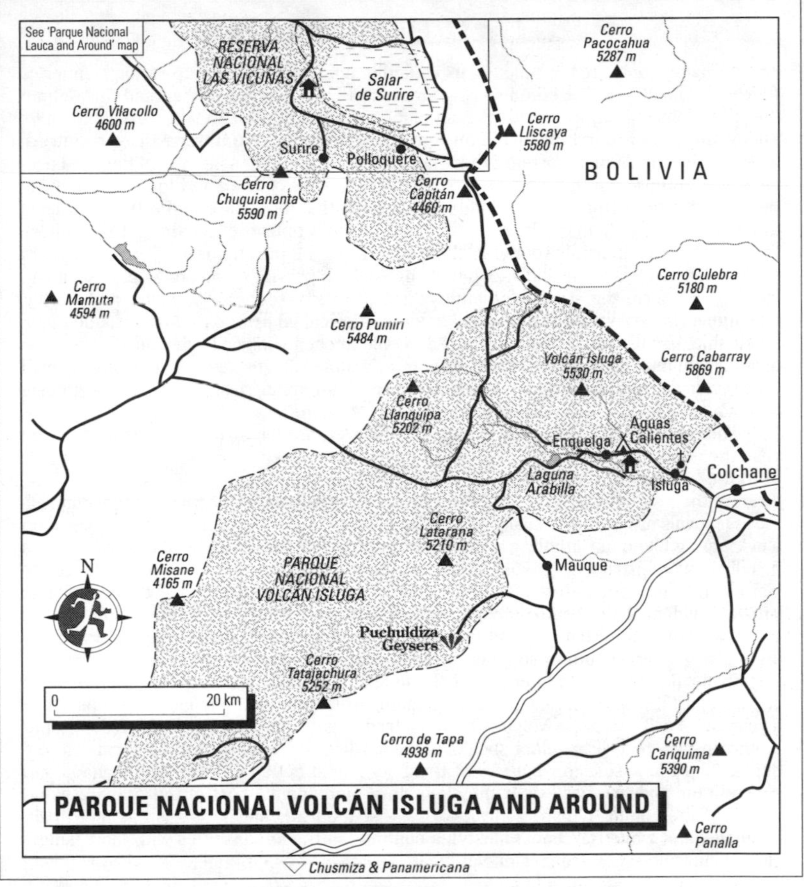

PARQUE NACIONAL VOLCÁN ISLUGA AND AROUND

along with the entire village, remains locked up and abandoned for most of the year – Isluga is a "**ceremonial village**", whose inhabitants come back only for festivals, important religious ceremonies and funerals; the principal fiestas are held on February 2–3, March 10, Easter week, and December 8, 12 and 21–25.

Colchane

Ten kilometres from Isluga, at the end of the paved road from Huara, **COLCHANE** is a small, unattractive border town of grid-laid streets and truckers' canteens. Most days, the only reason you might want to come here is for **accommodation** (basic rooms in *Pensión Challapas*, opposite the border post; ②); emergency **petrol** (*bencina verde* usually available in André García's back yard, in the street opposite the school); or to cross over into **Bolivia** (border control open daily 8am–1pm & 3–7pm). Twice a month, however, on alternate Saturdays, Colchane takes on a bit of life and colour as the neighbouring altiplano villagers bring their fresh produce, weavings and knitwear to sell at the **market**.

THE AYMARA OF CHILE

The Aymara people are the second largest indigenous linguistic group of South America (after the Quechua). The culture grew up around Lake Titicaca and spread throughout the high-plain region, known as the altiplano, of what is now Bolivia, Peru and Chile. Today, there are around three million Aymara scattered through these three countries, with the Chilean Aymara forming the smallest group, totalling some forty thousand people. Most of these now live and work in the coastal cities of Arica and Iquique, following the big migrations from the highlands to the coast that took place in the 1960s. At least thirteen thousand Aymara, however, remain in the altiplano of northern Chile where their lifestyle is still firmly rooted in the traditions of the past thousand years. The main economic activity is llama and sheep herding – which provides wool, milk, cheese, meat, leather and fertilizer – and the cultivation of crops such as potatoes and barley. Traditionally, the Aymara live in small communities called *ayllu* based on extended family kinship, usually with about a hundred people in each village. Their houses are made of stone and mud with rough thatched roofs, and most villages have a square and a small whitewashed church with a separate bell tower – often dating from the seventeenth century when Spanish missionaries evangelized the region.

Nowadays many of the smaller villages, like Isluga, are left abandoned for most of the year, the houses securely locked up while their owners make their living down in the city, or in the larger cordillera towns like Putre. Known as ceremonial villages, they're shaken from their slumber and burst into life when all their people return for important religious festivals or funerals, usually two or three times a year. Andean fiestas are based on a fascinating blend of Catholic and indigenous rites. For instance, the aim of the fiesta is usually to worship the Virgin, but sometimes a llama or lamb will be offered as a sacrificial victim – in some cases after the Virgin herself has put this request to the village *yatiri*, or elder. At the centre of Aymara belief is the respect of the life-giving mother earth, known as *pachamama*, and traditional ceremonies – involving singing and dancing – are still carried out in some communities at sowing and harvest time. Along with respect for the earth is the belief that the tallest mountains looming over their villages contain spirits, or *mallku*, that guard over them, protecting their animals and crops. Once a year, on May 3 – Cruz de Mayo – the most traditional communities climb up the sacred mountains where a village elder speaks to the *mallku*, which appears in the form of a condor. It's hard to assess to what extent these long-held beliefs survive only as habit and superstition, and to what extent they remain a fundamental part of the Aymara world view. Today's young Aymara go to local state schools and speak Spanish as their main language, and while traditional lifestyles continue in the altiplano, it's with increasingly closer links with mainstream Chilean life.

The Panamericana between Iquique and Arica

Some three hundred long, dusty kilometres spread out between Iquique and Arica in a continuous stretch of brown desert hills and dried-up rivers. Most people whizz up here in about four hours without stopping, but there are a couple of interesting places you could visit on the way: **Tiliviche**'s nineteenth-century graveyard and pre-Columbian geoglyphs can be explored in an hour or so, while **Pisagua** – a crumbling, atmospheric nitrate port about an hour's drive west to the coast – is more suitable as a night's stopover.

Pisagua

Eighty kilometres north of the turn-off to Iquique, a poorly paved side road leads 52km down to the once-important, now forgotten town of **PISAGUA**. The final stretch is very steep, giving dramatic views down to the little toy-town cowering by the ocean, the only sign of life on this barren desert coast. Pisagua is a funny sort of place, part scruffy, ramshackle fishing town, part fascinating relic of the past. It was one of the busiest and wealthiest ports of the nitrate era, and is still dotted with many grand nineteenth century buildings, some of them restored and repainted, others decaying at the same slow pace as the rest of the town (which has only 150 inhabitants today). Most striking is the handsome, white-and-blue timber **clock tower**, built in 1887 and still standing watch from the hillside. The other great monument to the nitrate era is the old **theatre**, a fine wooden building erected in 1892, with a typical nineteenth-century facade, featuring tall wooden pillars, a balcony and a balustrade. You can borrow the key from the *Carabineros* and wander inside to take a look at the large, empty stage, the rows of polished wooden seats, and the high ceiling, lavishly painted with cherubs dancing on clouds. The ghostliness of the place is made all the more intense by the monotonous sound of the waves crashing against the building's rear wall, which plunges directly down to the sea.

At the far end of town, next to the *Carabineros* station, the village's more recent history is the subject of a haunting **mural** dedicated to the memory of those executed here during the military dictatorship, when Pisagua was used as a concentration camp. A couple of kilometres north, on the edge of the cemetery, the former site of the mass graves is marked by an open pit bearing a simple cross, a scattering of wreaths and a block of stone inscribed with a single line by Pablo Neruda: "Even though a thousand years shall pass, this site will never be cleansed of the blood of those who fell here."

There's a free (and shadeless) **campsite** close to the *Carabineros* station, but to really soak up the nitrate-era atmosphere you should **stay** at *Hotel Pisagua* (☎57/731509; ④), located in what was once the town prison. The guest rooms are in a beautiful wooden building – originally the warders' residence – built around a large patio filled with tall, lush banana plants and squawking parrots. The prison cells, in the adjacent building, are now filled with snooker and ping-pong tables, for the use of guests. The hotel is also the best place **to eat** in Pisagua, serving excellent, fresh fish and good breakfasts. There is no public transport here.

Tiliviche

Ten kilometres north of the turn-off for Pisagua, just before the bridge across the Quebrada de Tiliviche, a short track branches left (west) to the **Hacienda de Tiliviche**. At the end of the track you'll find the old *casa patronal*, a charmingly dilapidated house overlooking a yard full of clucking chickens and lethargic dogs. It was built in 1855 for a British nitrate family, and remained in British hands until very recently; the current owners have plans to renovate it and turn it into a hotel, but lesser plans have gone to waste in the desert. Set within the hacienda grounds, on the other side of the stream, stands a nostalgic testimony to the nitrate era – the old **British Cemetery**, enclosed by tall iron railings and a huge, rusty gate, whose key you can borrow from the hacienda's caretaker. Inside, about a hundred lonely graves stand in the shade of a few tamarugo trees, at the foot of the desolate mountain that rises over the *quebrada*. This stark desert setting is strikingly at odds with the very English inscriptions on the tombstones, like "Thy will be done", and the graves read like a who's who of the erstwhile British business community, including people like Herbert Harrison, the manager of the Tarapaca Waterworks Company and, most famously, **James Humberstone**, the manager of several nitrate *oficinas* (see p.210).

The southern wall of the *quebrada* is also the site of some of the most impressive **geoglyphs** in Chile. They're best viewed from the pull-in just off the Panamericana, a few hundred metres up from the bridge on the northern side of the *quebrada*. From this vantage point, you can see the images in all their splendour – a large crowd of llamas covering the hillside. All of the llamas are moving in the same direction, towards the sea, and it's thought that the drawings were designed to guide caravans descending from the mountains on their journey towards the coast.

Arica

ARICA's favourite name for itself is "*la ciudad de la eterna primavera*" – "the city of eternal spring". Chile's northernmost city, 19km south of the Peruvian border, is certainly blessed with an agreeable climate, which, along with its sandy beaches makes it a popular holiday resort for Chileans and Bolivians. Its compact, tidy centre sits proudly at the foot of the Morro cliff, the site of a major Chilean victory in the War of the Pacific (and cherished as a symbol of national glory). It was this war that delivered Arica into Chilean hands, in 1883, and while the city is emphatically Chilean today, there's no denying the strong presence of mestizo and Quechua Peruvians on the streets, trading their fresh produce and *artesanía*. This, added to its role as Bolivia's main export centre, make Arica more colourful, more ethnically diverse and a good deal more vibrant than most northern Chilean cities. It would be stretching it a bit to describe Arica as beautiful, but it does boast some fine pieces of nineteenth-century architecture, several pretty squares filled with flowers and palm trees, and a young, lively atmosphere, making it, all in all, a pleasant place to spend a couple of days – or longer, if you feel like vegging by the beach. A short taxi ride out of town, in the Azapa Valley, the **Museo Arqueológico** certainly deserves a visit, while a few hours' east, up in the cordillera, **Parque Nacional Lauca** is one of the most popular attractions in the north of Chile.

Arrival and information

Coming in **by bus**, you'll arrive at Arica's Terminal Rodoviario, quite a distance from the centre on Avenida Diego Portales. From here, it's easy to get a *colectivo* or *micro* into the centre. Arica's **airport** is 18km north of the city and is connected to the centre by reasonably priced airport taxis. For tourist information, head for the very helpful **Sernatur** office (Mon–Fri 8.30am–1pm & 3–7pm; ☎58/254506) on the second floor of the same building used by the post office, at Prat 305. The regional **Conaf** office is at Sotomayor 216 (☎58/231559), where you can pick up basic maps and information on Parque Nacional Lauca and adjoining protected areas. You can also reserve beds at the Conaf *refugíos* in these areas, if you know exactly when you'll be arriving.

Accommodation

Unlike Iquique, Arica has very little seafront accommodation, and what there is tends to be upmarket and overpriced. In the centre, there's no shortage of *residenciales*, ranging from the dirt-cheap to the polished and comfortable. Typically for these parts, however, there's a lack of decent mid-range options. **Camping** options are limited to *El Refugio* (☎58/227545; CH$7000 per tent), a shady grassy campsite with a pool 1.5km up the Azapa valley, reached by frequent *colectivos* (see p.223).

Hostal Jardín del Sol, Sotomayor 848 (☎58/232795, fax 231854). Small, tidy rooms with private bath off a flower-filled courtyard with tables, chairs and a swing-sofa. Very friendly too – great for the price. ③.

Hostal Prat, Prat 555 (☎58/252138). Spartan but spotless little rooms with white walls, tiled floors and clean baths; a good bet in this price range. ③.

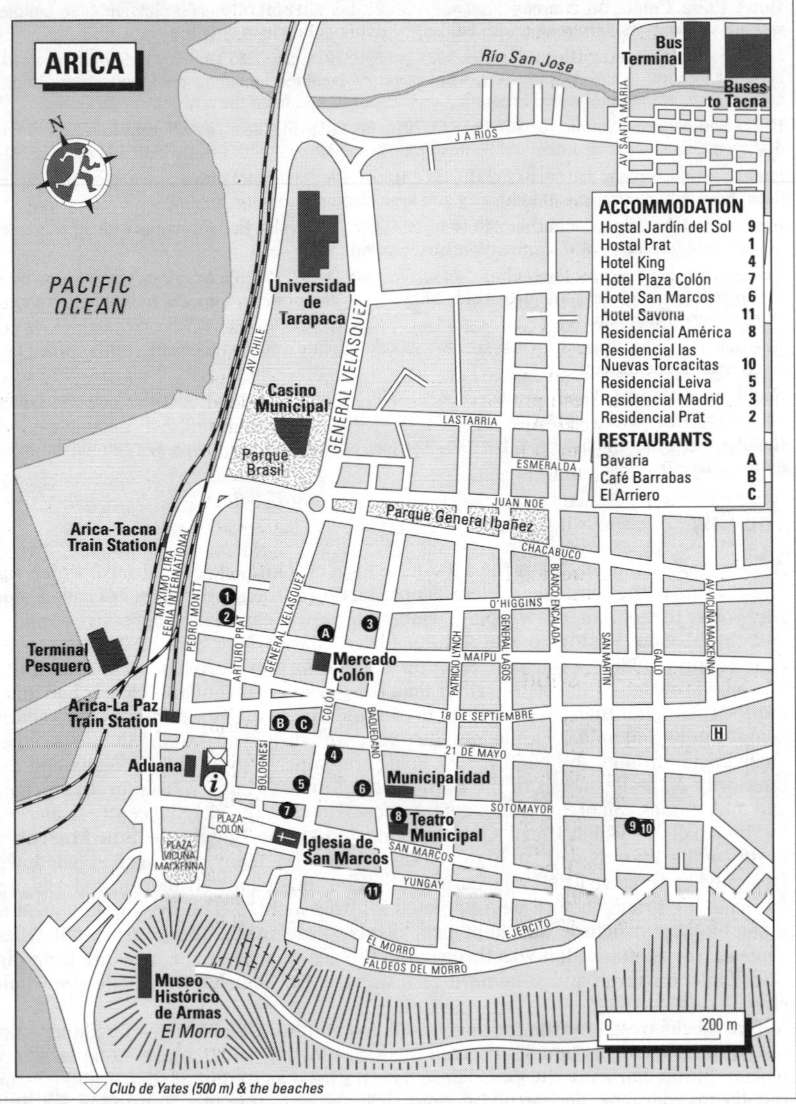

Hotel Arica, Av San Martín 599 (☎58/254540, fax 231133). Upmarket hotel overlooking the ocean, with smart rooms and *cabañas*, a beautifully located pool and an elegant dining room with great views out to sea. ⑥.

Hotel King, 21 de Mayo 373 (☎58/232094, fax 251124). Really dated feel here, with Fifties-style furnishings, but the rooms, all with bath, are spacious and well-maintained. Those at the back are quietest. ④.

Hotel Plaza Colón, San Marcos 261 (☎58/254424, fax 231244). Cheerful pink-and-blue building with small, clean, modern rooms with balconies, giving good views onto the plaza. ⑤.

Hotel Saint Georgette, Diego Portales 3221 (☎58/221914, fax 223830). Tidy little bungalows in a peaceful location in the Azapa valley, with excellent facilities including pool, squash and tennis courts, gym, jacuzzi and sauna. Free minibus transfer to and from the city centre. ⑥.

Hotel San Marcos, Sotomayor 367 (☎58/232970, fax 251815). Clean, airy Seventies-style rooms – disappointing after the beautiful old Spanish tiles in the lobby – with private bath and parking. ④.

Hotel Savona, Yungay 380 (☎58/232319, fax 231606). Pleasant hotel with a nice lounge and garden patio. Rooms fairly simple, but light, airy and very clean. ⑤.

Residencial América, Sotomayor 340 (☎58/254148). Good-value budget rooms with an encouraging odour of furniture polish. Some rooms have private bath. ②.

Residencial las Nuevas Torcacitas, Sotomayor 884 (☎58/253715). A curious place with a large corrugated iron roof and a mixture of old, dingy rooms and new, fresh rooms with private bath; the latter are good value. ③.

Residencial Leiva, Colón 347 (☎ & fax 58/232008). Slightly drab but adequate rooms, owned by a rarely seen Frenchman. ③.

Residencial Madrid, Baquedano 685 (☎58/231479). Humble little place offering clean rooms looking onto a flower-filled patio; a good budget choice. ②.

Residencial Prat, Prat 545 (☎58/251292). Thirteen spruce and tidy rooms, very simple but good for the price. ②.

The City

Arica's most visible feature is the 110-metre-high cliff known as **El Morro**, which signals the end of the coastal cordillera. Steps starting at the southern end of calle Colón lead you to the top, where sweeping, panoramic views (especially impressive at night) and the **Museo Histórico de Armas** (daily: March–Nov 8am–8.30pm; Dec–Feb 8am–10pm; CH$300) await you. Built on top of a former Peruvian fortification, this museum is owned by the army, rather than the government, and has clearly had more money spent on it than most Chilean museums. The exhibits – primarily nineteenth-century guns and military uniforms – are very well displayed, but the theme is rather chauvinistic in tone, the main thrust being the superiority of the Chileans and the inferiority of the Peruvians in the Battle of the Morro, when Chilean forces stormed and took possession of the hilltop defence post. Down in the city, the centre is marked by the small, tree-filled **Plaza Colón**, dominated by the **Iglesia de San Marcos**, a pretty white church with a high, Gothic spire and many tall, arched windows. Designed by Gustave Eiffel, this curious church is made entirely of iron, and was prefabricated in France before being erected in Arica in 1876. The riveting key used to assemble the structure was kept in a display case inside the church, but when Chilean troops attacked, it was thrown into the sea to prevent the invaders from dismantling the church and stealing it as a war trophy (instead, they stole the whole city).

Two blocks west, towards the port, you'll find another Eiffel-designed building – the old **Aduana** (customs house), erected in 1874, sporting an attractive stone facade of pink and white horizontal stripes. These days it's used as a cultural centre, and puts on regular photographic and art exhibitions. It looks onto **Parque Baquedano**, a little square full of tall palm trees and shady benches, flanked to the south by the coastal avenue, and on its northern side by the Arica–La Paz **train station**. Built in 1913, this large wooden building is worth a wander inside, where you'll find a couple of shiny black locomotives displayed in an interior patio, and a roomful of turn-of-the-century railway paraphernalia (ask a guard to let you in). There's another old locomotive in front of the station, a 1924 German model, formerly used on the Arica–La Paz line.

Other points of interest include **calle 21 de Mayo**, the always-lively main pedestrian street; the **artesanía stalls** on Bolognesi, just off 21 de Mayo; and the **Feria Internacional**, a street-long market on calle Máximo Lira, where you'll find a jumble of Peruvian and Bolivian products, including large boxes of coca-leaf tea bags and numerous alpaca sweaters. Right by the *feria*, and also worth a look-in, is the smelly but colourful **terminal pesquero** where inquisitive pelicans wander around the fish stalls. Out towards the Azapa valley, on calle Hualles, just south of the river, the **Poblado Artesenal** is a replica of an altiplano village, where twelve white houses serve as workshops for artisans selling handicrafts ranging from ceramics and glass to knitwear and leather items. To get here, take a *colectivo* from the corner of Lynch and Chacabuco, or Lynch and O'Higgins.

The beaches

The closest beach to the centre is the popular **Playa el Laucho**, a curved, sandy cove about a twenty-minute walk down Avenida San Martín, south of El Morro. You can also get *micros* down the avenue, which continue to several other beaches, including **Playa La Lisera** and **Playa Brava**, both attractive, and the usually deserted **Playa Arenillas Negras**, a wide expanse of dark sand backed by low sand dunes, with a fish-processing factory at its southern end. Two kilometres north of the centre, **Playa Chinchorro** is a large, clean beach where you can rent jet skis in high season (Dec–March; CH$12,000 for 30min). This is also where you'll find Arica's Olympic-size **swimming pool** (Tues–Sun: Jan & Feb 3–6.30pm; March–Dec 9am–2pm; CH$800), just back from the beach, enclosed by a large white wall. Further north, **Playa las Machas** is quieter but more exposed to the wind. To get to **Playa Chinchorros**, take bus #5-A from General Velásquez with Chacabuco.

Out to the Museo Arqueológico

Avenida Diego Portales extends out of the city centre into the green **Azapa valley**, to all intents and purposes a suburb of Arica, particularly the western end, which is crammed with hotels. Thirteen kilometres along the road, the **Museo Arqueológico** (daily: Jan & Feb 9am–8pm; March–Dec 10am–6pm; CH$1500), part of the University of Tarapacá, houses an excellent collection of regional pre-Columbian artefacts, including four extraordinary Chinchorro mummies – of a man, a woman and two children – buried over 4000 years ago. Other exhibits include finely decorated Tiwanaku ceramics, ancient Andean musical instruments and snuff trays, many beautifully-embroidered tapestries (look out for the one in case 11, decorated with motifs of smiling women), and displays on contemporary Aymara culture. All the pieces are well presented, and there are, unusually, explanatory leaflets available in English, French and German. The Azapa valley is also the site of several **geoglyphs**. The most impressive example is **Alto Ramírez**, a large, stylized human figure surrounded by geometric shapes; you can see it (from a distance) from the main road, on the way to the museum – ask your *colectivo* driver to point it out to you – or take a detour to get a closer look. *Colectivos* to the Museo Arqueológico and to the nearby geoglyphs leave from the corner of Lynch and O'Higgins in the city centre.

Eating, drinking and entertainment

You'll find the biggest concentration of **restaurants**, **cafés** and **bars** on the pedestrianized section of 21 de Mayo, the city's main thoroughfare. The choice of eating and

CHINCHORRO MUMMIES

In 1983, while laying a new pipeline near the foot of El Morro, the Arica water company came across a hoard of withered corpses buried a couple of metres beneath the sand. Work immediately ceased and archeologists from the University of Tarapacá were rushed in to assess the scene, which turned out to be a seven-thousand-year-old búrial site containing 96 bodies – the largest and best-preserved find, to date, of **Chinchorro mummies**. This ancient practice of mummification – the oldest known in the world – was first identified in 1917 when Max Uhle, a German archeologist working in Arica, discovered a series of highly unusual human remains. The Atacama had already yielded prehistoric bodies naturally mummified by the heat and dryness of the desert, but Uhle realized that these bodies were different – they were, in fact, the result of an elaborate, and highly skilled form of artificial mummification that had kept them intact for thousands of years. Further excavations revealed similar findings spread along the coast, concentrated between Arica and Camerones, 65km south, and it became apparent that they were relics of an ancient cultural group that archeologists have named the Chinchorro culture. Uhle originally estimated that the Chinchorro people started mummifying their dead some 2000 years ago, but modern radiocarbon dating has established that the practice was well under way by 5000 BC – more than two millennia before the Egyptians began practising mummification.

No one knows exactly where the Chinchorro people came from; some archeologists speculate that they moved down from the north, others that they came from the Andean highlands. What's clear, however, is that by 7000 BC scattered groups of people – possibly extended families – were spread along the coast of Chile's far north, where they lived on the abundant crabs, clams, mussels, seaweeds, pelicans, sea lions and other marine life of the region, supplementing their diet with guanaco and wild berries. The great simplicity of their hunter-gatherer lifestyle makes the sophisticated techniques they developed to preserve their dead all the more extraordinary. The practice involved removing the brain through a hole at the base of the skull, and removing all internal organs, which were probably discarded. After this, the cavaties were dried with hot stones or fire and then refilled with straw and ashes. The bones of the arms and legs were replaced with sticks bound into place with reeds, and the skeleton was given extra padding before the body was stitched up. The face was then coated in paste that dried into a hard mask with a sculpted nose and incisions marking the eyes and mouth. The finishing touch was provided by a wig made of human hair that was attached to the skull. One of the most curious aspects of the Chinchorro mummies is that they probably weren't buried immediately – signs of repeated "repair jobs" on many of them suggest they were kept on display and venerated before being wrapped in their reed shrouds and buried with their funerary offerings. Whether or not this was the case, there's no doubt that the cult of mummification was based on a complex approach to the dead and the afterlife. The Chinchorro culture performed this elaborate skill for over three thousand years until, for unknown reasons, the practice died out around 1500 BC, and the era of the oldest known form of artificial mummification came to an end.

drinking spots is marginally better than in most northern cities, and there are a couple of places nice enough to return to several times. It should be noted that Arica is the centre of the **roasted-chicken-on-a-spit** industry – you'll find a huge concentration of these low-cost places on Maipú, between Baquedano and Colón. The **disco** scene gets quite lively in high season, and even in low season there are a couple of locales where you'll always find a crowd on a Friday and Saturday night – *Bar Barrabas* is the most enduringly popular. For something quieter, you could try the **cinema** at 7 de Junio 190.

Restaurants

Bavaria, Colón 611. Always reliable (and predictable) German-style meat restaurant.

Caballito de Mar, Mercado Colón, local 22. One of many simple, great-value *marisquerías* in this chaotic covered market offering cheap, fresh fish and shellfish lunches.

Café Barrabas, 21 de Mayo, between Bolognesi and Colón. Great place with lots of swirling art-nouveau-type wrought iron and painted glass, funky music and an interesting menu featuring Mexican, Italian, Argentinian and Chilean dishes. Delicious juices, milkshakes and ice creams, too – highly recommended.

Club de Huasos, km 3.5, Azapa valley. One of several country restaurants offering hearty Sunday lunches in the green Azapa valley, very popular with families. Regular *colectivos* go here from the corner of O'Higgins and Lynch.

Club de Yates, Ex Isla Alacrán. Privileged location, on a spur (once an island) projecting into the ocean, with outdoor seating and great views (especially at night). Serves reasonably priced omelettes, salads and meat and fish dishes. Closed to non-members Sat & Sun.

El Arriero, 21 de Mayo 385. Mid-price grill house serving good fillet steaks and other meat dishes; often has live folk music at weekends.

El Fascinador, Av San Martín 1010, Playa La Lisera (☎58/231890). Good-value *parilladas* served right by the beach in a wacky, jungle-themed dining room with fake leopard-skin chairs and a bamboo roof. To get here, take any *colectivo* south down the coastal avenue; to get back, they'll call a taxi for you.

Hotel Arica, Av San Martín 599. Fairly imaginative "international" menu offered in this classy, beautifully located dining room looking right onto the ocean.

Bars

Puesta del Sol, Av Raul Pey 2492, Playa Chinchorro. Brightly painted wooden building with tables on the front terrace; a lively, pleasant place to sit and chat over a beer by the beach.

Bar Barrabas, 18 de Septiembre 520, corner with Lynch. Trendy, popular pub featuring the same kind of imaginative decor as its sister restaurant, with much wrought iron and odd architectural salvage pieces. Good music, good drinks, good atmosphere. Has a disco attached next door that fills up after midnight.

Schop 21, 21 de Mayo 201, corner with Colón. Popular gringo hangout, with lots of outside tables and chairs on this lively, pedestrian street.

Listings

Airlines Avant, 21 de Mayo 277 (☎58/232328); Iberia, Edificio Empressarial, 7th floor (☎58/232079); KLM, Colón 197 (☎58/231657); Ladeco, 21 de Mayo 443 (☎58/252021); Lan Chile,

MOVING ON FROM ARICA

Moving on from Arica, you have a lot of different options. To get up to the **altiplano**, you can take a bus to **Putre** with Buses La Paloma, Germán Riesco 2071 (☎58/222710); to **Parinacota** with Buses Humire, Pedro Montt 662 (☎58/253497); or to **Lago Chungará** on any bus to La Paz (see below; you may have to pay full fare to La Paz). From the main bus terminal there are plenty of **inter-city buses** heading south down the Panamericana, as far as Santiago. You can also catch buses from here to **La Paz**, in Bolivia, with Tas Choapa (☎58/222817) and Geminis (☎58/241647), or alternatively with Buses Litoral from Chacabuco 454 (☎58/254702), or Buses Trans Salvador, from Galería San José, Av Santa María 2010 (☎58/246064). La Paz can also be reached by **ferrobus** (a bus on rails), a really memorable 12hr journey across the altiplano, which runs twice a week from the station on Parque Baquedano, currently on Tues and Sat (plus Thurs in summer, but check on ☎58/232844), costing around US$60. **Tacna**, 55km north in Peru, can be reached by **train** (full of Peruvian *campesinos* – good atmosphere) from the station at Máximo Lira 889 (Mon, Wed & Fri; 1hr 30min; ☎58/231115), or, far more quickly, by **colectivo** from calle Chacabuco, between Baquedano and Colón. There are regular **flights** from Arica to Iquique, Antofagasta, La Serena and Santiago, as well as to La Paz in Bolivia, and Arequipa and Lima in Peru.

21 de Mayo 345 (☎58/251641); Lloyd Aereo Boliviano, Lynch 298 (☎58/251919); Lufthansa, 18 de Septiembre 112 (☎58/231126).

Banks and exchange Arica has many ATMs – mostly on 21 de Mayo – but only two *casas de cambio*: Yanulaque, at 21 de Mayo 175 will change most major currencies in cash, but only US dollar travellers' cheques; Marta Daguer, 18 de Septiembre 330, deals only in US dollars. There are also several moneychangers on the street, at the corner of 21 de Mayo and Colón.

Car rental American Rent-a-Car, General Lagos 559 (☎58/252234); Avis, Chacabuco 180 (☎58/232210); Budget, 21 de Mayo 650 (☎58/252978); Hertz, Velásquez 1109 (☎58/231487); Klasse, Velásquez 760 (☎58/254498); Reinco, Baquedano 999 (☎58/251121).

Laundry Good-value washing and ironing at Lavandería La Moderna, 18 de Septiembre 457.

Post office The main office is at Arturo Prat 305.

Taxis Radiotaxi Chacalluta, Prat 528 (☎58/250340); Taxi Turismo Pucarani (☎58/244997).

Telephone offices Entel, 21 de Mayo 388; CTC, Colón 476; Telex Chile, 21 de Mayo 372. Many more around town.

Travel agencies The numerous travel agencies in town include Mega Tour, Bolognesi 391 (☎58/254701); Tacora, 21 de Mayo 171 (☎58/232786); and Globo Tour, 21 de Mayo 260 (☎58/232909), all of these are good for air tickets, etc. For tours to Parque Nacional Lauca, see box opposite.

Up to Parque Nacional Lauca

Some 160km east of Arica, **Parque Nacional Lauca** is the perfect microcosm of the Chilean altiplano, offering snow-capped volcanoes, pristine lakes, whitewashed villages and wild vicuña – all conveniently located at the end of a paved highway, just four hours' drive from the city. The journey there takes you through some beautiful and varied scenery, ranging from deep-green vegetation to rippling desert hills. There are several opportunities for overnighting en route to the park, which is strongly recommended to avoid the risk of altitude sickness. Once you're up there, you can head south across the altiplano to neighbouring **Parque Nacional Las Vicuñas** and the **Salar de Surire**, and if you're feeling really adventurous, continue to **Parque Nacional Volcán Isluga**, descending in Iquique. Remember to take warm clothing with you, as temperatures can drop as low as -20°C at night.

Into the cordillera

The first stretch of the journey follows the saline río Lluta through the fertile **Lluta valley**, an astonishingly green strip of land threading its way through brown, sterile hills. As the road climbs up from the valley floor, the views down to the narrow cultivated belt are spectacular, especially when the early morning mist hovers over the hills, punctured by shafts of sunlight. As you climb higher, you leave all traces of greenery behind and the hillsides, now arid and dusty, are suddenly filled with hundreds of **candelabra cactus** plants – huge things up to 4m high, starkly silhouetted against the sky. About 90km up the road, you'll pass a brightly painted railway carriage and a wooden building by the roadside – this is **Posada Taki**, a café, inn, campsite and alternative tour agency run by a multilingual, hippie couple. At just over 3000m above sea level, it's a good place to stay to get acclimatized to the altitude, and the owners offer guided walks and jeep tours to local archeological sites, as well as home-made bread and *mate de coca*. About ten kilometres on from here, look out for the sign on the right pointing to the **Pukará de Copaquilla**, the ruins of an Inca fortress standing on a promontory just off the road. Here you'll find the remains of several large circular stone walls built between 1350 and 950 BC, and sweeping views down to a steep, narrow canyon backed by endless rolling hills.

TOURS FROM ARICA

There are many companies in Arica offering **tours** up to **Parque Nacional Lauca**. The problem, however, is that the cheapest, and most commonly available, take place in a single day, which means going from sea level to up to 4500m and down again in a short space of time – really not a good idea, and very likely to cause some ill effects, ranging from tiredness and mild headaches to acute dizziness and nausea. In very rare cases the effects can be more serious, and you should always check that the company carries a supply of oxygen and has a staff member trained to deal with emergencies. Altitude aside, the amount of time you spend inside a minibus is very tiring, which can spoil your experience of what is one of the most beautiful parts of Chile. In light of this, it's really worth paying extra and taking a tour that includes at least one overnight stop in Putre on the way up, an option being offered by more and more tour companies, some of which continue south to the Salar de Surire (see p.231). One-day trips start at around CH$12,000 per person, while you can expect to pay around CH$20,000–25,000 for a two-day tour, overnighting in Putre, and around CH$45,000–50,000 for a three-day tour, sleeping in Putre and the Salar de Surire.

Inka Tour, Thompson 251 (☎ & fax 58/253844; *turismo@hotmail.com*). Newly established company whose tours to Lauca and back focus on esoteric themes like "Andean cosmo-vision" – some also include a coca-leaf reading by an Aymara shaman, and a ritual cleansing of the body in a spring. Different, anyway.

Latinorizons, Thompson 236 (☎ & fax 58/250007; *latinor@entelchile.net*). Friendly Belgian-run company offering a wide range of altiplano tours with a more adventurous feel than most of the others on offer. Speaks French and English.

Parinacota Expediciones, Patricio Lynch 371 and Bolognesi 475 (☎ & fax 58/251309). Sixteen-year-old company offering several options for visiting Parque Nacional Lauca and around, including the usual day-trip, an overnight stop in Putre and a two-night tour taking in Guallatire and the Salar de Surire.

Transtours, Bolognesi 421 (☎58/253927, fax 251675). Slick, professional but fairly impersonal company offering one-day tours with English-speaking guides.

Turismo Lauca, Prat 430 (☎ & fax 58/252322). Reliable firm offering one- to three-day tours up to Lauca and the Salar de Surire.

Socoroma

Sixteen kilometres beyond the *pukará* a steep track branches left from the main road, leading treacherously down the hillside to the pre-Hispanic hamlet of **SOCOROMA**. It appears, from a distance, as a dark-green pocket of trees and fields lying at the bottom of a scrub-covered valley; close-up, it's a charming village with a jumble of cobbled streets and a restored sixteenth-century church. From behind the church you get fabulous, panoramic views onto the ancient green terraces staggered down the wall of the *quebrada* – they're used principally for growing oregano, and during harvest time the whole village is filled with its aroma. Socoroma, at 3060m above sea level, also makes a quieter alternative to Putre (see below) for acclimatizing overnight – basic **rooms** and **meals** are provided by the very friendly Emilia Humire (no phone; ②), who also runs a shop selling home-made jams and other products.

Putre

Twenty-four kilometres on from Socoroma, **PUTRE** is a busy little mountain town surrounded by a patchwork of green fields and Inca terraces. At 3500m above sea level, it's a popular overnight stop en route to the higher altitudes of Parque Nacional Lauca – climbers, in particular, like to spend a few days walking in the hills here before attempting the volcanoes in the park. Putre's rustic houses are clustered around a large, green square, overlooked by the Municipalidad, which provides basic **tourist information** (Mon–Fri 8.30am–12.30pm & 3–6pm). Nearby, off the northeast corner, you'll find the **church**, built in 1670 after an earthquake destroyed the original church, which, according to old Spanish chronicles, was clad in gold and silver. The current building, heavily restored in 1871, is considerably more modest, consisting of a small stone chapel and a whitewashed, straw-roofed bell tower.

There are several options for eating and sleeping in Putre. On calle Baquedano, you'll find small, tidy **rooms** off a sunny back yard at *Residencial Cali* (no phone; ②), and basic but reasonable rooms in a large, covered yard at *Residencial La Paloma* (no phone; ②) which also has a restaurant. Across the bridge and up the track, *Hostería Las Vicuñas* (☎58/228564; ⑥) is the smartest, and most expensive, place to stay, offering slightly faded-looking en-suite bungalow rooms. Putre's **restaurants** are all pretty similar, serving hearty mountain food like *picante de conejo* (a sort of rabbit curry) or llama steak; try *La Paloma*, in Baquedano, *Rosamel*, on the square, or *Oasis*, on Cochrane. There is one **tour agency** in Putre, Birding Alto Andino (☎58/300013, fax 222735), run by an Alaskan naturalist, who offers wildlife-viewing excursions around Putre, and to Parque Nacional Lauca and around; she also has a few simple, clean rooms (③), with cooking and laundry facilities. There are regular **buses** to Putre from Arica, with Buses La Paloma, Germán Riesco 2071 (☎58/222710).

Parque Nacional Lauca

Continuing up the main road, about 4km on from the turn-off to Putre, a little dirt road on the right leads 3km to the **Termas de Jurasi** – a beautifully situated tin shack containing two large baths you fill with hot thermal water by connecting the pipes at the back of the shack (don't forget to disconnect them when you've finished). Back on the paved road, seven steep kilometres up from the turn-off to Jurasi, you cross the boundary into **PARQUE NACIONAL LAUCA** located on a 4400-metre-high mountain pass. By now the air is thin and cold, and the road is flanked by light-green *bofedal* where herds of wild vicuña come to feed in the mornings. Ten kilometres into the park, you reach the Conaf hut at Las Cuevas, a good place to stop to check on weather and road conditions. From here the road continues through a wide, green plain filled with grazing llamas and alpacas, passing the turn-off for Parinacota, 19km on from the Conaf hut, and Lago Chungará, a further 18km along the road.

Parinacota

The park's headquarters are in **PARINACOTA**, an idyllic *pueblo altiplánico* composed of fifty or so crumbling, whitewashed houses huddled around a beautiful little **church**. Built in 1789, this is one of Chile's most assiduously maintained Andean churches, sporting brilliant white walls and a bright-blue wooden door, trimmed with yellow and green. Like most churches of the altiplano, it has thick stone and adobe walls and a sloping straw roof, and is enclosed within a little white wall incorporating the bell tower into one of its corners. It's usually open in the morning (if not, you can borrow the key from the caretaker – ask at the *artesanía* stalls). Inside, you'll find a series of faded, centuries-old friezes depicting the stations of the cross and vivid scenes of sinners suffering in hell. There's also a collection of skulls belonging to former priests, and a magical, "walking" table that's kept chained to the wall, for fear it will wander off in the night. Opposite the church, in the plaza, local women sell alpaca knitwear and other **artesanía** – a sign of life returning to Parinacota, which until recently was virtually depopulated. Many of its houses are still under lock and key for much of the year, their owners returning only for important fiestas and funerals (see box on p.218). The **Conaf** administration centre and **refugio** is a large, chalet-style building with several bunk

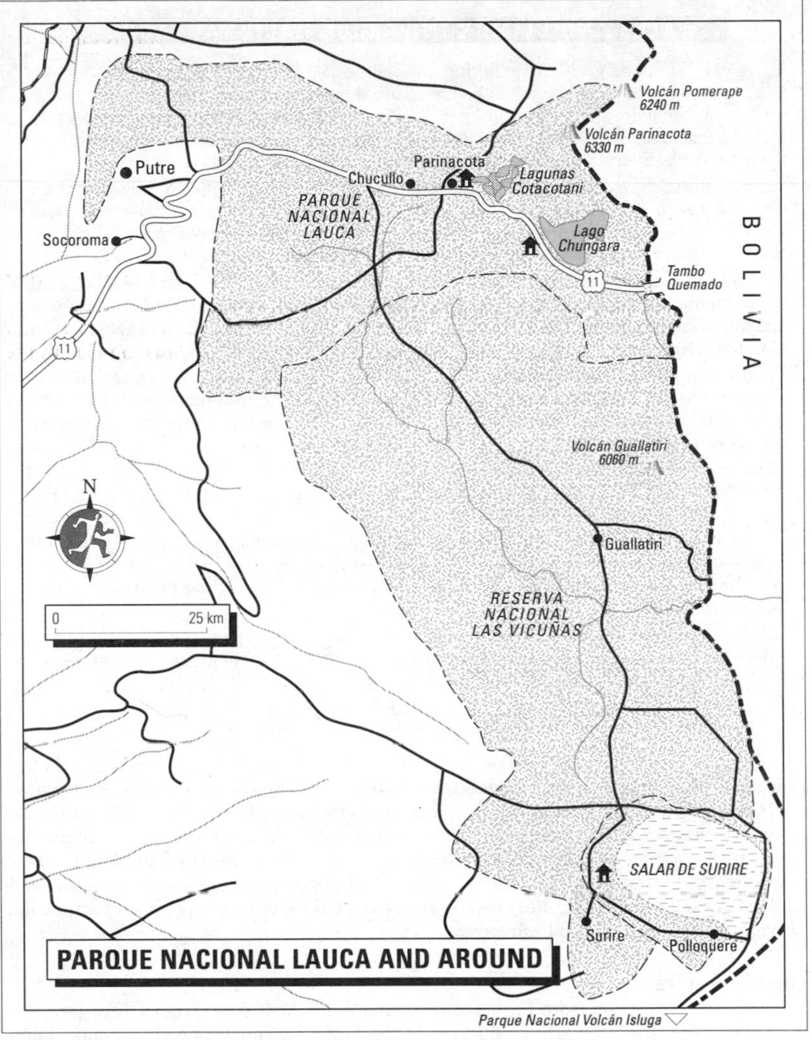

PARQUE NACIONAL LAUCA AND AROUND

dormitories (CH$5000 per person) and a kitchen, and space for **camping** out the back (CH$5000 per site). Parinacota can be reached by **bus** from Arica (Thurs & Sat) with Buses Martínez, Pedro Montt 620 (☎58/232265) and, a few doors along, Buses Humire, at no. 662 (☎58/253497).

Lagunas de Cotacotani

About 8km east of Parinacota, and clearly visible from the paved highway to Bolivia, the **Lagunas de Cotacotani** are a collection of small, interconnected lakes lying in a dark

WALKS AND CLIMBS IN PARQUE NACIONAL LAUCA

Lauca doesn't offer a great many hiking possibilities, and most people are content to just admire the scenery and the wildlife. There are, however, at least three half-day or day **walks** you could do, and many more possibilities for **climbing**. Remember to respect the altitude, and to allow yourself more time to cover distances that you could walk quite easily at lower elevations.

Cerro Choquelimpie As with Guane Guane, no technical experience or equipment are necessary to climb this 5288-metre-high peak, reached in about four hours from the *refugio* at Lago Chungará. From the top, you get views down to the gold mine behind the mountain, and onto Lago Chungará and Volcán Parinacota.

Cerro Guane Guane A slow but straightforward climb up this 5096-metre peak, rewarded by panoramic views over the park. It's suitable for any fit person used to hill-climbing, and takes around four hours to the top from the *refugio* at Parinacota, and two to three hours back down.

Lago Chungará to Parinacota (or reverse) It's an 18km walk from the *refugio* at Lago Chungará to Parinacota, taking about six hours. Follow the paved highway as far as the *mirador de Lagunas Cotacotani*, then climb down to the lakes, from where a jeep track continues to Parinacota.

Parinacota to Lagunas de Cotacotani A rewarding, not-too-difficult walk, taking about three hours (one way) from Parinacota; ask the *guardaparque* in the *refugio* to point you in the direction of the jeep track you need to follow.

Sendero de excursión de Parinacota An easy, 6km circular walk, marked by blue stones starting behind the *refugio*, taking you past the *bofedal de Parinacota*, where you can observe numerous grazing alpaca. Good views onto surrounding mountains. Allow two to three hours.

Volcán Parinacota Suitable only for experienced climbers carrying crampons and ropes (though it's not always necessary to use them). Allow two days to get up and down from the base camp (a day's hike from Parinacota), including one night camping on the volcano. Avoid this climb between mid-December and February, due to weather conditions.

lava field, filled with exquisite jade-green water. The lakes were formed by volcanic eruptions and are surrounded by fine dust and cinder cones, further adding to their lunar appearance. Their waters are filtered down from Lago Chungará, and then continue to the *bofedal de Parinacota*, which is the source of the río Lauca. On closer inspection the lakes aren't as lifeless as they first appear, and are home to many wild Andean geese. They're definitely worth exploring, either as a day hike from Parinacota, or from the *mirador* on the highway.

Lago Chungará

Eighteen kilometres on from Parinacota, at an altitude of 4600m, **Lago Chungará** is a wide blue lake, spectacularly positioned at the foot of a snow-capped volcano, rising over its rim like a giant Christmas pudding covered in cream. This is 6330-metre-high **Volcán Parinacota**, one of the highest peaks in Chile, and the park's most challenging climb. On the southern shore of the lake, right by the highway, there's a small stone **Conaf refugio** with five beds (CH$5000 per person), a kitchen, **camping** spaces (CH$5000 per site) and unbeatable views. This is unquestionably the best place to stay in the park, allowing you to observe the changing colours of the lake and volcano at different times of day, from the transparent pinks of early morning to the deep blues and gleaming whites of the afternoon. From the *refugio* you can clamber down to the shore (much further away than it looks) and get closer views of the pink flamingos, ducks and giant coots that live on the lake.

Reserva Nacional las Vicuñas and the Salar de Surire

Directly south of Parque Nacional Lauca, the **RESERVA NACIONAL LAS VICUNAS** stretches over 100km south across spectacular altiplano wilderness filled with wild vicuña, green *bofedales*, abandoned Aymara villages and a skyline of volcanoes. It's far less accessible than Lauca, with no public transport, which means hiring a high-clearance 4x4 vehicle, or taking an organized tour. Note that the drive into the reserve involves fording several streams, which are usually very low but can swell dangerously with heavy summer rains – check with Conaf before setting out. The reserve's administrative centre is about a ninety-minute drive from Lauca, in **Guallatire** (4428m altitude), a pretty hamlet with a traditional seventeenth-century Andean church. There's also an obligatory *Carabineros* checkpoint here, and a **Conaf refugio**, open year-round, with four beds (CH$5000 per person). Looming over the village, snow-capped **Volcán Guallatire** puffs wispy plumes of smoke from its 6060-metre peak, while a grassy-banked stream snakes at its foot.

Following the road south of Guallatire you'll be rewarded, about 40km on, with sudden, dramatic views of the **SALAR DE SURIRE**, a dazzling-white salt flat containing several lakes with nesting colonies of three species of flamingo. Originally part of Parque Nacional Lauca, its status was changed to that of national monument in 1983, to allow borax to be mined from its surface; this is still going on today, and you can see the mine's enormous trucks driving over the *salar*, dwarfed by its massive dimensions. On the west shore of the *salar* there's a comfortable Conaf **refugio** with four beds (CH$5000 per person), hot water and a kitchen – this is a wonderful place to stay, with terrific views onto the salt flat. Sixteen kilometres from here, skirting the southern edge of the salt flat, **Polloquere** (also known as Aguas Calientes) is the site of several pale-blue pools filled with hot thermal water, an absolutely stunning place to take a bath – though be sure to get there in the morning, before the bone-chilling afternoon wind picks up. There are a couple of picnic areas and **camping** spaces here, too, but it's a very exposed site.

travel details

Buses

Antofagasta to: Arica (4 daily; 10hr); Calama (every hour; 3hr); Caldera (every hour; 6hr); Chañaral (16 daily; 5hr); Chuquicamata (5 daily; 3hr); Copiapó (every hour; 7hr); La Serena (16 daily; 11hr); María Elena (2 daily; 3hr); Mejillones (every 30min; 40min); Santiago (every hour; 20hr); Tocopilla (2hr 40min).

Arica to: Antofagasta (4 daily; 10hr); Calama (6 daily; 10hr); Chañaral (5 daily; 15hr); Copiapó (18 daily; 16hr); Iquique (every 30min; 4hr 30min); La Serena (18 daily; 18hr); Putre (1 daily; 3hr); Santiago (18 daily; 29hr); Vallenar (18 daily; 20hr).

Calama to: Antofagasta (6 daily; 3hr); Arica (6 daily; 10hr); Chañaral (10 daily; 8hr); Chuquicamata (every 30min; 30min); Copiapó (12 daily; 9hr 30min); Iquique (4 daily; 7hr); La Serena (14 daily; 12hr 30min); Santiago (10 daily; 22hr 30min); Toconao (1 daily; 2hr 30min).

Chañaral to: Antofagasta (16 daily; 5hr); Arica (5 daily; 15hr); Calama (10 daily; 8hr); Chuquicamata (2 daily; 8hr 20min); Copiapó (10 daily; 2hr); Iquique (8 daily; 11hr); La Serena (11 daily; 7hr); Mejillones (2 daily; 5hr 40min); Ovalle (10 daily; 9hr); Santiago (16 daily; 14hr); Taltal (2 daily; 2hr 30min); Tocopilla (2 daily; 8hr); Vallenar (14 daily; 4hr).

Iquique to: Antofagasta (8 daily; 7hr); Arica (every 30min; 4hr 30min); Calama (4 daily; 7hr); Caldera (12 daily; 12hr); Chañaral (8 daily; 11hr); Chuquicamata (2 daily; 6hr 30min); Copiapó (12 daily; 13hr); La Serena (every hour; 16hr); La Tirana (7 daily; 1hr 40min); Mamiña (2 daily; 2hr 30min); María Elena (2 daily; 5hr); Mejillones (2 daily; 5hr); Pica (7 daily; 2hr); Santiago (every hour; 25hr); Tocopilla (7 daily; 3hr).

Flights

Antafagasta to: Arica (3 daily; 1hr 30min); Calama (3 daily; 35min); Copiapó (6 daily; 1hr 50min); Iquique (6 daily; 45min); La Serena (3 daily; 2hr 30min); Santiago (11 daily; 2hr).

Arica to: Antofagasta (3 daily; 1hr 30min); Calama (2 daily; 35min); Copiapó (3 daily; 1hr 20min); Iquique (5 daily; 35min); La Serena (1 daily; 1hr); Santiago (8 daily; 3hr 30min).

Calama to: Antofagasta (3 daily; 35min); Arica (2 daily; 35min); Copiapó (4 daily; 1hr 20min); Iquique (5 daily; 30min); La Serena (2 daily; 3hr); Santiago (5 daily; 2hr direct, 3hr via Antofagasta).

Copiapó to: Antofagasta (6 daily; 1hr 50min); Arica (3 daily; 1hr 20min); Calama (4 daily; 1hr 20min); Iquique (5 daily; 2hr 25min); La Serena (3 daily; 3hr 30min); Santiago (5 daily; 2hr).

Iquique to: Antofagasta (6 daily; 45min); Arica (5 daily; 35min); Calama (5 daily; 30min); La Serena (3 daily; 3hr 30min); Santiago (11 daily; 2hr 20min).

CHAPTER FIVE

THE CENTRAL VALLEY

Extending south from Santiago as far as the río Bío Bío, Chile's **CENTRAL VALLEY** is a long, narrow plain hemmed in by the Andes to the east and the coastal range to the west, with a series of gentle ridges and lateral river valleys running between the two. This is the most fertile land in Chile, and the immense orchards, vineyards and pastures that cover the valley floor form a dazzling patchwork of greenery. The kernel of the Central Valley lies between the capital and the city of **Chillán**, some 400km south – a region which for over two hundred years constituted the bulk of colonial Chile. It was here that the vast private estates known as *estancias*, or *haciendas*, grew up, and where the country's most powerful families exercised an almost feudal rule over the countryside, a situation that persisted well into the twentieth century. These days most of the land is controlled by commercial food producers rather than old, moneyed families, but signs of the colonial way of life are still very much in evidence, with grand *casas patronales* lurking behind the adobe walls of the region's back lanes, and endless rows of poplars still marking the divisions between the former estates. The people, too, have held on to many of their rural traditions: most farm workers still prefer to get around by horse, and the cult of the *huaso*, or "cowboy", is as strong as ever, as can be witnessed at the frequent rodeos held in stadiums known as *medialunas*. Even in urban zones, country ways hold sway, and the Central Valley is perhaps the only part of Chile where it is not uncommon to see horse-drawn carts plodding down the Panamericana Highway.

Further south, the busy city of **Concepción** guards the mouth of the **Bío Bío**, the mighty river that for over 300 years was the boundary between conquered, colonial Chile and unconquered **Mapuche territory**, whose occupants withstood Spanish domination until 1883. While today the river is more famous as a **white-water rafting** destination, and its rich soils have long been incorporated into the production belt of the Central Valley, traces of the frontier still linger, visible in the ruins of old forts, the proliferation of Mapuche place names and the tin-roof pioneer architecture. Beyond the Bío Bío, towards the Lake District, the landscape alters, too, the gently sloping plains giving way to verdant native forests and remote, primeval lakes.

Many visitors bypass the Central Valley altogether, whizzing south towards the more dramatic landscapes of the Lake District and beyond. Certainly the agricultural towns dotted along the highway – **Rancagua**, **San Fernando**, **Curicó**, **Talca**, **Chillán** and **Los Angeles** – are, on the whole, rather dull, offering little to tempt tourists off the bus or out of their car. But stray a few kilometres off the Panamericana and you'll catch a glimpse of an older Chile impossible to find elsewhere, abounding with pastoral charms. Chief among these are the splendid **haciendas**, the best of which are to be found near San Fernando. The region's small, **colonial villages** with their colourful adobe houses topped by overhanging, clay-tiled roofs are another Central Valley highlight – among the prettiest examples are **Vichuquén**, west of Curicó, and **Villa Alegre**, south of Talca in the Maule valley, where you can also visit a trail of lush, emerald **vineyards**.

Out of the valley floor, you'll find attractions of a very different nature. To the west, up in the coastal hills, a couple of lakes offer great **water sports** facilities, notably **Lago Rapel**, while further west, a number of inviting **beaches** and cheerful seaside towns are scattered down the coast, among them **Pichilemu**, **Curanipe** and **Dichato**.

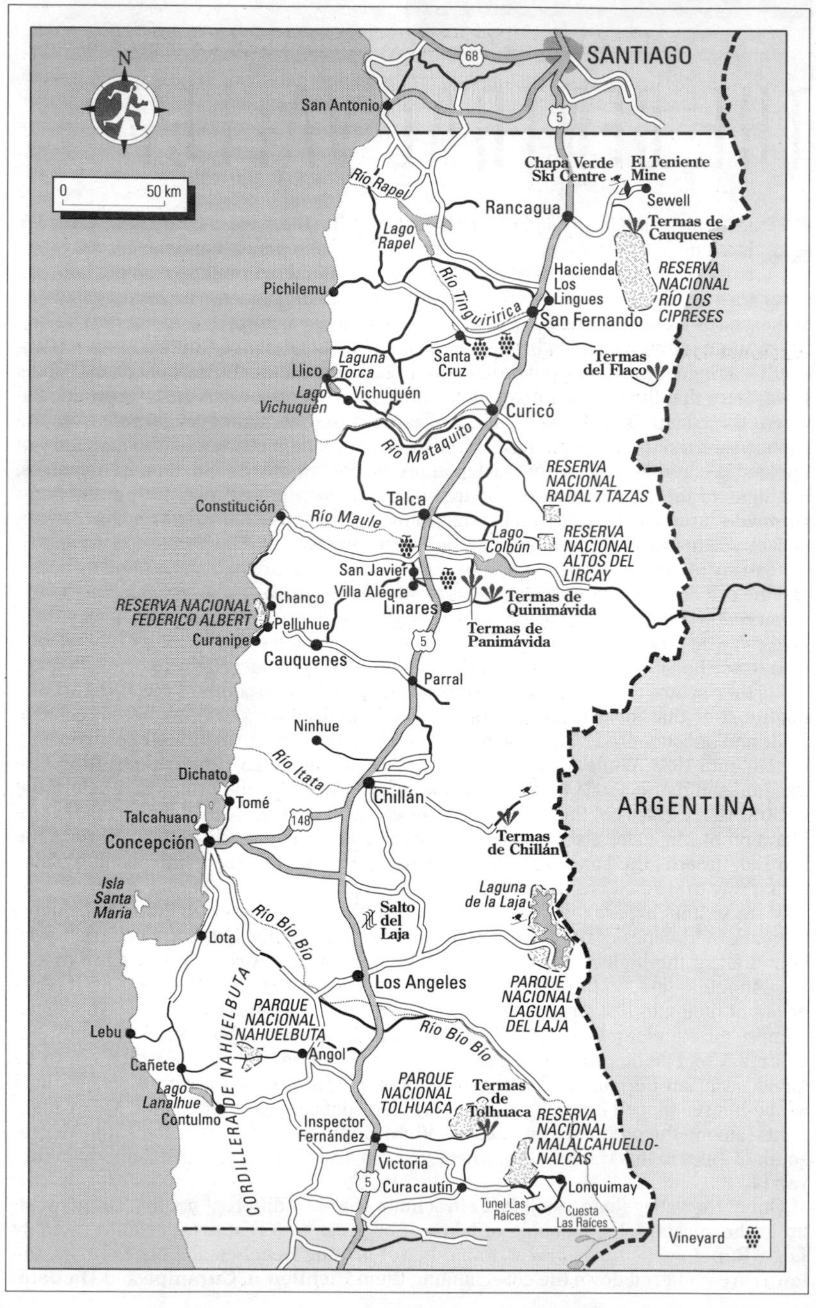
SANTIAGO
San Antonio
Chapa Verde Ski Centre
El Teniente Mine
Sewell
Rancagua
Termas de Cauquenes
Río Rapel
Lago Rapel
Hacienda Los Lingues
RESERVA NACIONAL RÍO LOS CIPRESES
Pichilemu
Río Tinguiririca
San Fernando
Santa Cruz
Termas del Flaco
Laguna Torca
Llico
Lago Vichuquén
Vichuquén
Curicó
Río Mataquito
RESERVA NACIONAL RADAL 7 TAZAS
Talca
Constitución
Río Maule
Lago Colbún
RESERVA NACIONAL ALTOS DEL LIRCAY
San Javier
Villa Alegre
Chanco
RESERVA NACIONAL FEDERICO ALBERT
Pelluhue
Curanipe
Linares
Termas de Quinimávida
Termas de Panimávida
Cauquenes
Parral
Ninhue
Río Itata
Dichato
Tomé
Talcahuano
Concepción
Chillán
Termas de Chillán
ARGENTINA
Isla Santa Maria
Laguna de la Laja
Salto del Laja
Río Bío Bío
Lota
Los Angeles
PARQUE NACIONAL LAGUNA DEL LAJA
PARQUE NACIONAL NAHUELBUTA
Lebu
Cañete
Angol
PARQUE NACIONAL TOLHUACA
Termas de Tolhuaca
Lago Lanalhue
Contulmo
CORDILLERA DE NAHUELBUTA
Inspector Fernández
RESERVA NACIONAL MALALCAHUELLO-NALCAS
Victoria
Curacautín
Longuimay
Tunel Las Raíces
Cuesta Las Raíces
Vineyard
0
50 km
N
68
5
148

ACCOMMODATION PRICE CODES

Prices are for the cheapest **double room** in high season. At the lower end of the scale, **single travellers** can expect to pay half this rate, but mid- and upper-range hotels usually charge the same for a single as for a double. For more information see p.27 in Basics.

① Less than US$10/CH$4800
② US$10–20/CH$4800–9600
③ US$20–30/CH$9600–10,080
④ US$30–50/CH$10,080–24,000
⑤ US$50–75/CH$24,000–36,000
⑥ US$75–100/CH$36,000–48,000
⑦ US$100–150/CH$48,000–72,000
⑧ over US$150/over CH$72,000

East of the valley, the dry, dusty slopes of the Andes offer excellent **horse riding** and **hiking** opportunities, particularly along the trails of protected areas like **Reserva Nacional Los Cipreses**, near Rancagua, and **Reserva Nacional Altos del Lircay**, near Talca. After a strenuous day in the mountains, there are plenty of **hot springs** at hand to relax in: the **Termas de Chillán** are among the most famous and visited in Chile, but more rewarding are the beautiful **Termas de Cauquenes**, near San Fernando, and the rustic **Termas de Tolhuaca**, southwest of Los Angeles. This last also enjoys a privileged site on the edge of the great forests of **Parque Nacional Tolhuaca**, as well as being handy for one of Chile's most unusual "sights": the **Tunnel de las Raices**, cutting 4.5km through the cordillera, and the longest tunnel in South America.

Getting down the Central Valley by **public transport** is easy, with hundreds of **buses** ploughing down the Panamericana. Branching off into the cordillera and to the coast normally requires catching a "rural bus" from one of the cities dotted down the highway, though some of the more remote places can only be reached with your own transport. Another option worth considering is the **train** from Santiago, which stops at Rancagua, San Fernando, Curicó, Talca, Chillán and Concepción – much slower than the buses, but more leisurely and scenic.

Rancagua and the Rapel Valley

Zipping down the Panamericana from Santiago, you can reach the prosperous agricultural town of **Rancagua**, 87km south, in less than an hour. With a little time and your own transport, however, the old road from Santiago (signed Alto Jahuel) makes a far more appealing route, winding its way past swaths of vines, fruit trees and old haciendas, half-hidden behind their great adobe walls. Once in town, you'll find little to hold your interest for more than a few hours – unless your arrival coincides with a **rodeo** – but Rancagua makes a useful jumping-off point for several attractions in the adjacent **Rapel Valley**: a paved highway known as the Carretera del Cobre heads up into the cordillera to the copper mine of **El Teniente** and the **Chapa Verde ski resort**, while a southern fork takes you to the charming **Termas de Cauquenes** and the nearby **Reserva Nacional Río de los Cipreses**. In the opposite direction, some 96km west of town, **Lago Rapel** is a popular weekend destination for Santiaguinos.

Rancagua

RANCAGUA presents a picture that is to repeat itself in most of the Central Valley towns – large, well-tended plaza; single-storey adobe houses; a few colonial buildings; sprawling, faceless outskirts. It is, however, a particularly affluent version of the model, reflected in the modern malls and department stores found in its centre, and in the care the munici-

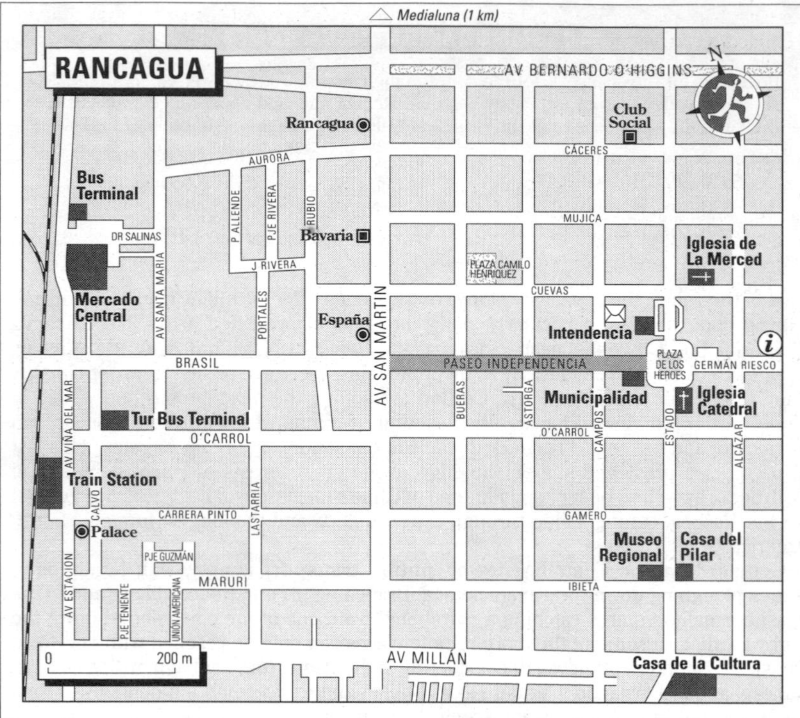

pality has lavished on the town's historic buildings. Unusually, its square is known not as the Plaza de Armas, but as the **Plaza de los Héroes**, in honour of the patriot soldiers, headed by Bernardo O'Higgins, who defended the city against Royalist forces in 1814, only to be crushed in what has gone down in Chilean history as the "Disaster of Rancagua". In the centre of the square, a rearing equestrian statue honours O'Higgins' triumphant return to the city, four years after he had left it in ruins, to present it with a coat of arms depicting a phoenix rising from the ashes. The square's other major monument is the towering, red-walled **Iglesia Catedral**; it dates originally from 1775 but, suffering heavy damages in the battle, was rebuilt in 1861 by an Italian architect who gave it its Doric columns and double tower. One block north of the square, at the corner of Cuevas and Estado, the **Iglesia de la Merced** suffered fewer battle scars, despite being used as O'Higgins' headquarters, and its plain white walls and tower are the same that stood when the church was first built in the mid-eighteenth century. Another well-preserved colonial building is the house occupied by the **Museo Regional** at Estado 685 (Tues–Fri 10am–6pm, Sat & Sun 9am–1pm; CH$500), dating from the late eighteenth century. Built of thick white adobe walls around a large interior patio, this handsome, single-storey house is typical of the urban colonial style. Inside, three of its rooms maintain the decor and furnishings of a colonial drawing room, bureau and dining room, while another is crammed with objects and documents relating to the independence movement. Opposite the museum, at Estado 682, the **Casa del Pilar de Esquina** is a splendid two-storey late colonial house, but is only rarely open to visitors. One block south, on the corner of Cachapoal and Millán, the **Casa de Cultura** is more accessible, hosting regular photographic and art exhibitions – though the main draw is its rural colonial architecture, including its thick foundations made of river boulders filled with mud. Finally, no account of Rancagua could fail to mention its fame as Chile's **rodeo** capital, hosting the national rodeo championships each March or April in its *medialuna* on the northern edge of town (on the corner of Avenida España and Germán Ibarra).

Practicalities

Arriving by **bus**, you'll be dropped at the terminal at Salinas 1165 (☎72/225452); a couple of blocks south, the **train station** (☎72/230361) is served by the fast *metrotrén* and slow train from Santiago. There's an extremely helpful **Sernatur** office one block east of the plaza at Germán Riesco 277 (Mon–Fri 8.30am–5pm; ☎72/230413, fax 232297), as well as a tourist information kiosk just off the plaza on the pedestrianized Paseo Independencia (Mon–Fri 10am–1pm & 4–7.30pm, Sat 10am–2pm). *Hotel España*, at San Martín 367 (☎72/230141; ④), has quiet, pleasant (if slightly neglected) **rooms** around an interior patio in an old, colonial-style building, while *Hotel Rancagua*, a few blocks north at San Martín 85 (☎72/232663; ④–⑤), has comfortable rooms upstairs in the main house, but tiny, dark rooms out the back. If you're looking for somewhere cheaper, your only option is *Hotel Palace* at Calvo 635 (☎72/224104; ②), near the Tur Bus terminal – the little hearts on its sign give it away as a "love hotel" (where rooms can be rented by the hour), but it's clean and tidy, and all rooms have private bath.

As for **eating**, you'll find good-value if unexciting food like *pollo asado* at the *Club Social*, an attractive cream-and-pink adobe building at Cáceres 486. Alternatively, there are plenty of cheap *fuentes de soda* on Paseo Independencia, plus the ubiquitous *Bavaria* at Av San Martín 255. Rancagua's sole **casa de cambio** is Transafex at Campos 363, and there are several ATMs on Paseo Independencia. **Car rental** is available at Weber Rentacar, Galería Membrillar 40, Oficina 2 (☎ & fax 72/226005); another

RODEOS

The Central Valley is the birthplace and heartland of Chilean **rodeo**, whose season kicks off on Independence Day, September 18. Over the following six months, regional competitions eliminate all but the finest horses and *huasos* in the country, who go on to take part in the national championships in Rancagua in March or April. Rodeos are performed in *medialunas* (literally "half moons"), which are circular arenas divided by a curved wall, forming a crescent-shaped stadium and a smaller oval pen called an *apiñadero*. The participants are **huasos** – Chilean "cowboys", or horsemen (see p.49) – who cut a dashing figure with their bright, finely woven ponchos, broad-rimmed hats and shining silver spurs. *Huasos* are normally inseparable from their horses, but the mounts they ride in the rodeo are specially bred and trained *corraleros* which are far too valuable for day-to-day work.

A rodeo begins with an inspection of the horses and their riders by judges who award points for appearance. This is followed by individual displays of horsemanship which make ordinary dressage look tame. In the main part of a rodeo, pairs of *huasos* have to drive a young cow or *novillo* round the edge of the arena and pin it up against a padded section of the wall. The teamwork between horses and riders is impressive to watch, with one riding as close to the rear of the *novillo* as possible while the other gallops sideways, keeping his horse's chest close to the cow's front shoulders. When they reach the cushion the object is to bring the cow to a sudden stop and hold it up against the wall until the judges have awarded points for style.

Rodeos are as much about eating and drinking as anything else and the canteen and foodstalls by a *medialuna* are a good place to sample **regional cooking**, wine and *chicha* (cider). Spread over a weekend, the rodeo ends with music and dancing, and this is where you can see the **cueca** (see p.48) being danced at its very best. For the dates of official rodeos, contact the **Federación de Rodeos** in Santiago (☎ & fax 2/699 0115).

alternative for getting into the hinterland would be to book a **tour** with Turismo Dakota (see below).

El Teniente copper mine and the Chapa Verde ski centre

Fifty-five kilometres east of Rancagua, up in the cordillera, **El Teniente** is the largest underground copper mine in the world. Local legend has it that its name – "the lieutenant" – refers to a disgraced Spanish lieutenant who, while heading to Argentina to escape his creditors, discovered enormous copper deposits, thus making his fortune and saving himself from bankruptcy. Today, the mine belongs to Codelco, the government-owned copper corporation, which also owns the famous Chuquicamata mine in the far north (see p.194).

You aren't allowed to just turn up and visit (a barrier blocks the access road) but Codelco organizes daily **tours** in conjunction with a couple of Rancagua travel agents: Turismo Dakota, Astorga 270 (☎72/228166, fax 228165; *tdakota@entelchile.net*), and Sewell 2000, Mujica 0269 (☎72/242144). The five-hour tours – which cost from CH$12,000, including transport from Rancagua and bilingual guides – kick off with a video display on the copper industry and the mine, followed by a visit to the now abandoned company town of **Sewell**, staggered in dramatic tiers up the mountainside. After this, you don protective overalls, boots and miner's lamp and go down the shafts to the gloomy underground tunnels, where you're shown all the different stages of the mining process. If you want to have a go at arranging a visit independently, contact Codelco's public relations office (☎72/292225, fax 292145).

A few kilometres north of the mine, the Codelco-owned **Chapa Verde ski centre** (☎ & fax 72/217651) is open (snow permitting) between June and September, with eight pistes, from beginners to advanced level, served by two lifts. You can rent all equipment up there, and with advance booking you can arrange ski lessons. There's no accommodation, but a simple **restaurant** offers reasonably priced snacks, drinks, meals and toilet facilities. You can't drive up in your own vehicle, but need to take Codelco's own bus from the Hipermercado Independencia at Av Miguel Ramírez 665, Rancagua (Mon–Fri 9am, Sat & Sun 8am; CH$4000; ☎72/217651). Lift tickets cost CH$9000, CH$12,000 at weekends, and full equipment rental costs CH$11,000.

Termas de Cauquenes

A couple of kilometres on from the turn-off to El Teniente, a southern fork branches off the road to the **Termas de Cauquenes**, 6km beyond. Sitting high above the río Cachapoal, surrounded by the rolling foothills of the Andes, this is one of the most beautiful hot springs resorts in Chile. The centrepiece is the nineteenth-century *sala de baños*, a huge, wooden hall with an extremely high ceiling, painted wooden beams, stained-glass windows and marble floor tiles. From the entrance, steps lead down to 24 cubicles containing the *tinas* – the original Carrara marble bathtubs that were installed in 1856, where guests take their hot thermal baths of between 42° and 48°C. The waters, which contain magnesium, potassium and lithium among other minerals, have been revered for their curative properties from the earliest days of the colony when, according to old chronicles, ailing Jesuits were sent here to be cured of their "gout, syphilis, anaemia and many other problems". Over the years, their fame increased and they were visited by a number of important figures, including Bernardo O'Higgins and the great Argentinian Liberator José de San Martín, who spent a month here before bringing his "Army of the Andes" across to liberate Chile from the Royalists – needless to say, locals are convinced that the uplifting effects of the waters played a decisive role in San Martín's victory.

As well as the *sala de baños* there's an old, colonial-style chapel, an outdoor swimming pool and comfortable but unremarkable **rooms** (☎ & fax 72/297226; ⑦), some arranged around a pleasant patio, others looking down to the river. The **food**, however – served in an immense dining room with fine river views – is exceptional, prepared by the Swiss chefs who own the resort. You can visit for the day, as well: non-guests are charged CH$3000 for half an hour in the marble *tinas,* but can't, however, use the outdoor pool. A **bus** for the *termas* leaves at 11am and 5pm from Rancagua's regional terminal, returning to Rancagua at 8.30am and 2pm (to confirm times, call the hotel).

Reserva Nacional Río de los Cipreses

Beyond the Termas de Cauquenes the road continues for a further 14km to the **Reserva Nacional Río de los Cipreses** (daily 8.30am–6pm; CH$1500; ☎72/297505) – a little-known gem of the Central Valley stretched along the narrow canyon of the Río de los Cipreses, and a great place to come **hiking** or **horse riding**. From the entrance, a jeep track leads 6km to **Sector El Ranchillo**, a camping and picnic area – take the left fork just before El Ranchillo and after another 6km you'll reach **Sector Maitenes**, which boasts a few camping areas and running water. This is the end of the jeep track, and all vehicles must be left here. Beyond, a trail follows the river along the canyon, passing through forests of towering cordillera cypress and other native trees, and with occasional views onto high Andean peaks like Cerro El Indio and Cerro El Cotón. Lateral ravines regularly branch out from the river, leading to waterfalls, lakes and "hanging" valleys carved out of the hills by glaciers. None of these is signed, however, so unless you're with an *arriero* (horseman), it's probably best to stick to the main path. Twenty kilometres on from Sector Maitenes, the path reaches **Sector Urriola** where there's a rustic *refugio* and a few camping areas; count on taking around six or seven hours to get here on foot from Maitenes, and about four or five on horseback. Beyond Urriola, the path continues for a further ten or so kilometres, giving great views onto the 4900-metre-high Volcán Palomo, looming ahead at the end of the valley. If you want to hire a **horse** (around CH$20,000 per day) call the reserve's administration number and ask to speak to Nelson Orellana. Failing that, there are usually horses for hire in the corral a couple of kilometres before the reserve entrance.

Lago Rapel

Forty-kilometre-long **Lago Rapel** nestles in the low coastal hills southwest of Rancagua. It is, in fact, an artificial lake, formed by the damming of the Cachapoal and Tinguirica rivers, whose waters drain from the western tip of the lake into the río Rapel. The massive, concrete wall of the dam makes an impressive sight, particularly when the floodgates are opened after heavy rain and the overflow spills out in a thunderous, foaming waterfall. The lake's main attraction, however, is its excellent **water sports facilities**, with speed boats, windsurfers and jet skis available for rent from several hotels and campsites. Of these, the *Club Nautico Rapel* (☎2/638 1680; ⑥), which also offers smart *cabañas* and very expensive camping (CH$16,000 per site), is easiest to reach by public transport, conveniently located near the village of **El Manzano**, on the lake's western shore. Other places offering water sports are the *Camping Alemán* (☎09/751 4427) with camping (CH$3000 per person) and rustic *cabañas* (④), 8km west of El Manzano along the lakeshore; *Camping Bosque Hermoso* (☎72/512179; CH$4000 per site), set amid pine and eucalyptus trees 3km north of the village, just across the bridge; and *Hotel Resort Marina Jardín del Lago* (☎72/232055, fax 232970; ⑤), a couple of kilometres further north, with smart accommodation. From Rancagua's regional terminal you can get to El Manzano **by bus** with Buses Galgo (☎72/230640) every twenty minutes, and Buses Sextur (☎72/231342) every hour.

San Fernando and the Colchagua valley

Fifty-five kilometres south of Rancagua, **San Fernando** is a busy little town sitting in the valley of the río Tinguiririca, known locally as the **Colchagua valley** after the province through which it runs. This is serious fruit production territory, as signalled by the numerous fruit stalls and large Del Monte factories lining the highway on the approach to San Fernando. The town itself is emphatically agricultural, and known throughout the region as *the* place to get your tractor repaired. Somewhat short on "sights", it is, however, a starting point for several popular excursions: 20km northeast of town, **Hacienda Los Lingues** is a splendid, privately owned hacienda, operated as a hotel and open for visits; while further east, high in the cordillera, the **Termas del Flaco** is an inexpensive option for soaking in hot springs; west of San Fernando, the so-called **Ruta del Vino** takes in a trail of local vineyards, as well as the excellent **Museo de Colchagua** and **Hacienda El Huique**, while if you continue to the coast, you'll get to the seaside town of **Pichilemu**, popular with surfers.

San Fernando

Surrounded by low, rippling hills washed golden in the sunlight, **SAN FERNANDO** enjoys an attractive setting and an hour or two's wander through its narrow streets can be quite enjoyable. The main commercial street is Manuel Rodríguez, lined by shops, snack bars and – on the corner with Valdivia – the huge bulk of the nineteenth-century **Iglesia de San Francisco**, a neo-Gothic church with a 32-metre-high tower. Clearly fond of its Gothic religious architecture, the town boasts another similar monument, the **Capilla San Juan de Dios**, eight blocks north of Manuel Rodríguez, on the corner of Negrete and Avenida Manso de Velasco. Built in 1884 as an attachment to the adjacent Hospital San Juan de Dios, it consists of a very high and narrow single nave, containing a massive baroque altar carved from dark, heavy wood. Close by, at the corner of Avenida Manso de Velasco and Jimenes, the **Casa de Lircunlauta** is a good deal less flamboyant – the oldest building in San Fernando, it was orginally the *casa patronal* of the eighteenth-century Hacienda Lircunlauta, whose owner donated 450 "blocks" of land for the foundation of San Fernando in 1742. It's a large, single-storey building resting on thick stone foundations, with white adobe walls, an imposing entrance, and a sloping roof still covered with its original handmade clay tiles and supported by oak rafters and pillars. The house belongs to the Municipalidad, and is occasionally used for art and photographic exhibitions; you can wander in to take a look inside during office hours (Mon–Fri 8.30am–1pm & 3–6pm).

Practicalities

Buses pull in at the **bus terminal** (☎72/713912) on the corner of Avenida Manso de Velasco and Rancagua. There's no Oficina de Turismo, but you could try the Municipalidad on the plaza at Carampangue and Argomedo for basic **information**. Of San Fernando's four **hotels**, three are on Manuel Rodríguez: at no. 770, friendly *Hotel Imperio* (☎72/714595; ④) has comfortable rooms and a pleasant dining area; a couple of blocks west at no. 968, *Hotel Marcano* (☎72/714759, fax 713943; ④) is darker and gloomier; while opposite, at no. 959, *Hotel Español* (☎72/711098; ⑤) offers bland, functional rooms with TV and phone. Slightly cheaper than the others, *Hotel Diego Portales*, one block north at Av Bernardo O'Higgins 701 (☎72/714696; ④), has comfortable enough rooms and a decent **restaurant**, popular with locals. Other places to eat include

the *Club Social*, Manuel Rodríguez 787, where you'll find typical, filling meat dishes like *pollo asado* and *lomo*, while nearby *Café Roma* at no. 815 serves sandwiches and other light snacks. **Car rental** can be arranged with Alvaro Asenjo at España 928 (☎ & fax 72/712105).

Hacienda Los Lingues

Twenty kilometres northeast of San Fernando, **Hacienda Los Lingues** (☎2/235 5446, fax 235 7604) is one of the oldest and best-preserved haciendas in Chile. Its history goes back to 1599 when King Felipe III of Spain presented it as a gift to the first mayor of Santiago. Since then, the hacienda has always remained in the same family, and is today presided over by the elderly and redoubtable don Germán. The main house dates from the seventeenth and early eighteenth century, and bears all the hallmarks of the colonial *casa patronal*, including thick adobe walls and an overhanging clay-tiled roof supported on oak pillars forming a "corridor", or covered veranda, around its interior patio. Inside, the European tastes of Chile's old moneyed families are reflected in the decoration and antique furniture of rooms such as the "salón francés" and the "salón inglés" – in the English room, look out for the framed letter from Buckingham Palace, confirming that don Germán's wife is, in all likelihood, a very distant relative of the Queen of England. Although it now functions as a hotel –

and is one of just four South American hotels to be a part of the exclusive Relais et Châteaux group – the hacienda is still, unquestionably, a family home: don Germán and his various relatives attend Mass in the hacienda's chapel every evening, and the grand drawing rooms and library are in regular use. Even the guest bedrooms bear little resemblance to hotel rooms, liberally decorated with family portraits, old pictures and religious iconography. Outside, the hacienda's grounds take in sumptuous, mature gardens, a *medialuna* and the stables where thoroughbred "Aculeo" horses are bred, reputed to be among the finest in South America. The high rates (⑧) deter most people from staying overnight, but you can visit the hacienda on a short tour, lasting about forty minutes (CH$5000) or for the day (CH$20,000), which includes lunch and the chance to watch a rodeo.

Termas del Flaco

Seventy-seven kilometres east of San Fernando, sitting high in the cordillera some 1700m above sea level, the **Termas del Flaco** (Dec–April; CH$500) are among the most visited thermal baths in the Central Valley. They're reached by a serpentine dirt road that follows the río Tinguiririca through a beautiful gorge, so narrow in parts that *Carabineros* allow traffic to go in only one direction at a time (up Mon–Sat 5.30pm–midnight, Sun 5am–noon; down Mon–Sat 6am–2pm, Sun 2pm–midnight); you'll need to stay overnight to visit during the week. On arriving, the wild beauty of the cordillera and the feeling of remoteness and solitude are suddenly interrupted with the appearance of numerous shack-like, tin-roofed houses – almost all of them *residenciales* – crowded around the thermal baths. Nor are these baths particularly attractive, consisting of several rectangular concrete, open-air pools. The waters, however – which reach up to 57°C in some pools – are blissful, and if you manage to escape the crowds and get here midweek, outside January and February, you can lie back, close your eyes and just relax – for a fraction of the price you have to pay in most other *termas*.

Accommodation is abundant, with little to distinguish one place from the next, and most operating on a **full-board** basis. *Posada Amistad* (☎72/452160; ③) is right next to the bus stop, and offers small, basic rooms around a garden patio; overlooking the baths, *Posada La Ponderosa* (☎72/262232; ③) has good views, though some of the partition walls are very thin. You'll find more comfort in the new wooden *cabañas* at *Hotel Las Vegas* (☎ & fax 72/222478; ⑤), which has a large dining room with floor-to-ceiling windows looking down to the valley and its own small thermal pool. **Transport** to the *termas* is provided by Buses Amistad, with one departure daily from Rancagua and three from San Fernando (check times on ☎72/817227 or 452007).

Ruta del Vino, Museo de Colchagua and Hacienda El Huique

West of San Fernando, the paved road running through the Colchagua valley to the coast takes you past a couple of glorious **haciendas**, converted into museums, as well as a trail of **wineries**. Six of these – Pueblo Antiguo, Viu Manent, La Posada, Santa Laura, Mont Gras and Bisquertt – have banded together to create a wine tour called **"La Ruta del Vino del Valle de Colchagua"**, which operates out of the small town of **Santa Cruz**, 40km down the road and reached by frequent buses from San Fernando (office at Plaza de Armas 140; ☎ & fax 72/823199; *www.chilevinos.cl/rutadelvino*). The tour visits two vineyards, with a guided explanation of the whole wine-making process, and includes lunch (accompanied by lots of wine) at one of them, followed by a visit to either the Museo de Colchagua or the Hacienda El Huique (see opposite). The best time to take the tour is in March, when the wineries organize their own Fiesta de la Vendima (grape-harvest festival), with demonstrations of the sorting, crushing and filtering processes, plus extra tastings.

On the edge of Santa Cruz, at Errázuriz 145, the **Museo de Colchagua** (Tues–Sun 10am–6pm; CH$1500) is housed in a splendid, plum-coloured colonial hacienda, flanked by ancient palm trees. Displayed inside is a large collection of quite diverse objects, ranging from fossils and pre-Columbian pottery to relics from the War of the Pacific and the Independence movement. Among the most evocative exhibits are the shiny black nineteenth-century carriages, steered by ghostly mannequins wearing Victorian capes, and the beautiful old saddles, carved wooden stirrups and silver spurs in the "*huaso*" display.

Another 14km along the road towards the coast, just past the Los Errázuriz bridge, the superb **Hacienda El Huique** (Wed–Sun 11am–5pm; CH$1000), is one of the Central Valley's most atmospheric haciendas, perfectly preserved along with all its furniture and outbuildings, and open to the public as a museum. The hacienda's history dates from the seventeenth century, in the colonial period, but the current *casa patronal* was built in the early years of independence, in 1829. The main house is built around a beautiful large patio, filled with palm trees, flowers and climbing, sweet-smelling jasmine. Standing alongside, and entered through a huge doorway, is the **chapel**, sporting a 23-metre-high bell tower. Arranged around a series of patios behind the house are the various outbuildings, including store rooms, the dairy, the wine shed, the stables and the tack room, giving a clear picture of how life was organized on these almost totally self-supporting haciendas. Inside, the rooms are crammed with old furniture and family heirlooms – dark old oil paintings, crucifixes, fans, sepia photographs and personal objects belonging to the Echenique family, who owned the hacienda for over 200 years before donating it to the army in 1976. Added to all this, the remoteness and tranquillity of its setting bolster the illusion of time standing still, with no intrusions from the outside world.

Pichilemu

Continuing west towards the coast you'll end up, 87km on from Santa Cruz, at the bustling seaside town of **PICHILEMU**, built around a wide, sandy bay at the foot of a steep hill. The town dates from the second half of the nineteenth century when Agustín Ross Edwards set out to create a European-style seaside resort, connected to San Fernando by railway, and today Pichilemu wears the charming, melancholy air of a faded Victorian seaside town. Elegant promenades and terraces overlook the bay, lined with distinctive balustrades painted cherry-pink and white; from the seafront, a broad flight of identically coloured steps sweeps up the hillside to the splendid **Parque Ross**, planted with century old Phoenix palms and extravagant topiary. On the edge of the park, jutting out over the hillside, the grand old **casino** – the first in Chile – is perhaps the most evocative of Ross's legacies, now in disuse, with its windows broken and its imposing nineteenth-century architecture in a sorry state of disrepair. In contrast to this faded elegance, Pichilemu's central streets are crammed with snack bars and *schoperías* catering to the crowds of young surfers who come to ride the waves of the local beaches – to join them, rent a board and wet suit at Surf Shop (☎72/841236) on the corner of Aníbal Pinto and Ortúzar. The most challenging surf is at Punta de Lobos, 6km south, where Chile's national surfing championships are held each summer.

Arriving in town by bus, you'll be dropped a couple of blocks north of the main street, calle Ortúzar. One block south, you'll find a small **Oficina de Turismo** in the Municipalidad at Angel Gaete 365 (Mon–Fri 8am–1pm & 2.30–6.30pm; ☎72/841017), where you can pick up a map of the town and a list of places to **stay**. The most atmospheric of these, without doubt, is the *Gran Hotel Ross* right opposite the Parque Ross at Av La Marina 130 (☎72/841038; ④) – a huge, colonial-style house with an immense dining room full of crumbling antiques and vast, somewhat down-at-heel rooms off a courtyard (don't let them fob you off with the modern bungalow rooms out the back).

Another good choice is the *Hotel Chile España* down towards the sea at Ortúzar 255 (☎72/841270, fax 841314; ③) where you'll find simple but neat rooms off a sunny glass-walled corridor dotted with plants and deck chairs. The best place to **eat** in town is the down-to-earth, always-popular *Hostería La Gloria* – it's a bit of a walk from the centre, ten blocks south of the seafront at Prieto 432, but worth it for the excellent fresh seafood, including wonderful *machas a la parmesana* and dressed crab. Frequent **bus services** to Pichilemu are provided by Buses Andimar (☎72/711817) and Buses Nilahue (☎72/711937) from San Fernando and Rancagua.

Curicó and the Mataquito valley

Back on the Panamericana, 54km south of San Fernando, the prosperous, manicured town of **Curicó** makes an appealing place to break your journey – en route, perhaps, to the nearby attractions of **Lago Vichuquén**, towards the coast, or the **Siete Tazas waterfalls**, southwest towards the mountains.

Curicó

The easy-going town of **CURICÓ** is built around one of the most beautiful central **plazas** in Chile, luxuriantly planted with sixty giant Canary Island palms. Standing in their shade, on the northern side of the square, is a highly ornate, dark-green wrought-iron **bandstand**, constructed in New Orleans in 1905, while close by, an elaborate fountain, featuring a cast iron replica of *The Three Graces*, spouts water into a small pond full of water lilies and black-necked swans. In contrast to these rather fanciful civic commissions, the memorial to **Toqui Lautaro** – the Mapuche chief at whose hands Pedro de Valdivia came to a grisly end – is a raw and powerful representation, carved out of an ancient tree trunk by the Mapuche sculptor, Heraelio "Kako" Calquín. Standing on the northwest corner of the square, the **Iglesia La Matriz** makes a curious sight, its grand Neoclassical facade giving onto an empty shell ever since the great 1985 earthquake. Next door, the dignified **Club de la Unión** escaped unscathed, its fine white pillars and balconies still perfectly intact. Beyond the plaza, there's little to do except wander around the town's lively streets (look out for the old cinema on the corner of Yungay and Merced, whose Art Deco facade features two malevolent-looking gargoyles) or climb **Cerro Carlos Condell**, the little hill on the eastern edge of town, and survey the scene from its 99-metre-high summit. While you're in town, you could also make an easy excursion 5km south to the **winery** of Miguel Torres (Mon–Fri 8.30am–5.30pm, Sat 10am–5pm; free), the innovative Spanish vintner who revolutionized the Chilean wine industry in the 1980s; you'll be given an informal tour, ending up, of course, at the *sala de ventas* (salesroom). To get there, take a bus heading to Molina from the terminal (every 10min) and ask to be set off outside the *bodega*, which is right next to the Panamericana.

Practicalities

Arriving in Curicó by bus, you'll pull in at the **terminal** (☎75/311818) on the corner of Avenida Camilo Henríquez and Carmen, three blocks north of the plaza. You can pick up a map of the town and other **tourist information** at the kiosk on the eastern side of the square (no fixed opening hours) or, failing that, in the Municipalidad right opposite. Reasonably priced **accommodation** is available at *Hotel Prat*, a large *residencial* at Peña 427 (☎75/311069; ③), offering dark but spotless rooms, and, opposite at no. 410, *Residencial Rahue* (☎75/312194; ②), with tiny, thin-walled rooms but cheerful communal areas abounding with flowers and ornaments. Alternatively, there's the more upmarket if rather drab *Hotel Comercio* on Yungay 730 (☎75/312443; ⑤). Options for **eating** include the unpretentious straw-roofed *El Fogón Chileno*, at Yungay 802, for good-value *parilladas*, and the handsome old *Club de la Unión* on the plaza, for filling Chilean staples. The *Centro Español*, at Prat 474, is a little more expensive and imaginative, with good fish and seafood on offer. Curicó has a single **casa de cambio**, Curicambio at Merced 255, oficina 106.

Lago Vichuquén and around

West of Curicó, a scenic road follows the northern bank of the río Mataquito through the fertile river valley, covered with wheat fields and fruit trees. Eighty-five kilometres along the paved road, just beyond the village of Hualañé, take the right fork and follow the signs for a further 25km along a dirt road to tiny **VICHUQUÉN**. This is one of the best-preserved villages in the Central Valley, its narrow streets packed with flowers and orange trees, and lined with brightly painted adobe houses. Most of these date from the mid-nineteenth century, but Vichuquén's history goes back much further: there was a settlement here long before the arrival of the Spaniards, and it was chosen by the Incas, during their expansion in the sixteenth century, as a site for one of their *mitimaes* – agricultural colonies populated by Quechua farmers brought down from Peru. You'll find relics of the Inca occupation in the village's little **Museo Histórico** (daily 10.30am–1.30pm & 4–6pm; CH$600) on calle Rodríguez, along with a 3000-year-old mummy, and displays on the conquest and the independence movement.

Four kilometres beyond you'll reach the southern tip of **Lago Vichuquén**, a long, narrow lake enclosed by deep-green pine-covered hills. Considerably more upmarket than Lago Rapel, further north, this is a popular holiday destination with Santiago's upper classes whose beautiful villas line the lakeshore, their lush, manicured gardens giving onto private beaches. There are several **places to stay and eat**, including – in the hamlet of Aquelarre, on the far southern shore – the unpretentious *Hostería Aquelarre* (③) and the luxurious *Marina Vichuquén* (☎75/400265, fax 400274; ⑥), which also has excellent **water sports facilities**, as well as mountain bikes and horse riding (all available for non-guests, too). Other options are dotted along the winding road that follows the lake's western shore: just beyond Aquelarre, *Camping Paula* is a small, inexpensive campsite (CH$6000 per site) near the tiny beach called Playa Paula; a few kilometres further on, *Cabañas Rincón Suizo* (☎75/400012; ④) has reasonably priced if past-their-best rooms and *cabañas*; while approaching the northern shore, poorly signed *Cabañas del Tío Omar* (☎75/400198; ⑤) has smart, secluded *cabañas* overlooking the lake.

Laguna Torca and Llico

Beyond the northern tip of the lake, the road comes to a junction. The right fork takes you across the rickety Puente de Llico to **Laguna Torca**, a marshy lake a couple of kilometres away, preserved by Conaf as a breeding sanctuary for hundreds of black-necked swans and other marine birds, which can be viewed from several wooden observation platforms. You can get more information from the Conaf office (just beyond the bridge, hiding behind the large house with the veranda), and there's a hard-to-find camping area (CH$4000 per site) in a eucalyptus grove (turn right immediately after the bridge, then first left). Back at the junction, the left fork leads to nearby **LLICO**, a rugged little seaside town perched on the edge of an exposed sandy beach whose turbulent waves attract many surfers. **Accommodation** here is much cheaper than along the Lago Vichuquén: you'll find simple rooms with private bath at the *Atlandtida 2000* (☎75/400264; ③) on the road into town and, right on the beachfront, at *Residencial Miramar* (☎75/400032; ③), whose cramped, en-suite rooms have balconies and good sea views. The *Miramar* also has an excellent seafood **restaurant** that pulls in a buzzing crowd in summer, when brisk, efficient waiters tear around with steaming bowls of *paila marina* or plates piled high with fresh crab, mussels or clams.

Reserva Nacional Radal Siete Tazas

Of all the natural phenomena in Chile, the **Siete Tazas**, 73km southwest of Curicó, must be one of the most extraordinary. In the depths of the native forest, a crystal-clear mountain river drops down a series of seven waterfalls, each of which has carved a sparkling pool out of the rock. The falls are set within the Conaf-administered **Reserva Nacional Radal Siete Tazas** (Dec–March 8.30am–8pm; April–Nov 8.30am–6pm; CH$500), reached by a poor dirt road from the village of Molina, 18km southwest of Curicó. Also within the reserve is the **Velo de Novia** ("Bride's Veil"), a 50m waterfall spilling out of a narrow gorge. Conaf has a small hut on the road towards the Siete Tazas, but for more information (about the geology of the area, and the native trees in the surrounding forest) you need to go to the administration at **Parque Inglés**, 9km further east, at the end of the dirt road. There's a rough **camping** area here, though you'll find more facilities, including freshly baked bread for sale, at the private campsite, *Valle de Las Catas* (CH$10,000 per site), halfway between Parque Inglés and the Siete Tazas, close to the Puente de Frutillar. You can get to the Siete Tazas on **public transport** from Curicó with Buses Hernández, which has two services daily throughout the year.

Talca and the Maule valley

Continuing south from Curicó, the next city you reach is **Talca**, 67km down the Panamericana. A fairly unmemorable place, its main use is as a jumping-off point for several rewarding excursions spread along the valley of the **río Maule**. Just east of town, the **Villa Cultural Huilquilemu** is a handsome nineteenth-century hacienda, open as a museum, while further east, high in the cordillera, the **Reserva Nacional Altos del Lircay** provides trails through dramatic mountain scenery. Further south, you'll find the neighbouring hot-springs resorts of **Termas de Panimávida** and **Quinimávida** and, down in the valley floor, a proliferation of **vineyards**, many of them conveniently located between the town of **Villa Alergre** and village of **San Javier** on a route served by plenty of local buses from Talca. West, the río Maule empties into the Pacific by the industrial port of **Constitución**, from where a coast road leads to the seaside villages of **Chanco**, **Pelluhue** and **Curanipe**.

Talca

As the capital of Region VII, **TALCA** boasts its fair share of services and commercial activity, most of it centred on the main shopping street, **calle 1 Sur**. Away from the frantic bustle of this thoroughfare, however, the rest of Talca seems to move at a snail's

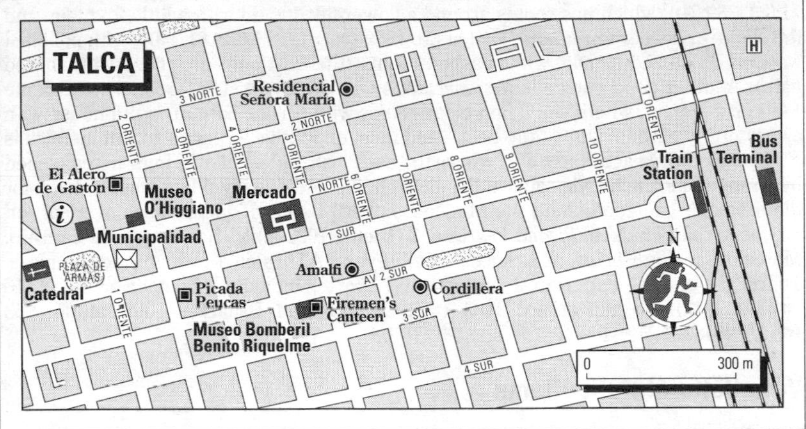

pace, not least the tranquil **Plaza de Armas**, shaded by graceful bougainvilleas, jacarandas and magnolias. Half-hidden beneath their foliage is a handsome iron bandstand, dating from 1904, and a number of stone statues plundered from Peru by the Talca Regiment in 1881, following their victories in the War of the Pacific. Standing on the northwest corner of the square, the neo-Gothic **Cathedral**, built in 1954, is a pale grey church with a long, thin spire and a series of turrets running along each side. It's worth popping inside to look at the delicately coloured stained-glass Belgian windows, and the sombre main altar under which a couple of long-dead bishops lie buried.

One block east of the square, on the corner of 1 Norte and 2 Oriente, the **Museo O'Higgiano** (Tues–Thurs 9.15am–1.45pm & 2.30–6.45pm, Fri 9.15am–1pm & 3–7pm, Sat & Sun 10am–1pm; CH$500) occupies a handsome colonial house that hosted some of the most important developments of the independence movement: here it was that Bernardo O'Higgins, future "Liberator" of Chile, lived as a nine-year-old; where the Carrera brothers established the first *Junta de Gobierno* in 1813; and where O'Higgins signed the final Act of Independence in 1818. Today, the museum houses copious (and rather dull) historical documents relating to Chilean independence, along with an eclectic assortment of oil paintings, sculpture, nineteenth-century furniture, pre-Columbian spearheads, old coins and more. A few blocks southwest at 2 Sur 1172 (near the corner with 5 Oriente), the **Museo Bomberil Benito Riquelme** (variable times) is crammed full of shiny red antique fire engines, hoses and other firefighting equipment, and makes an enjoyable browse.

Practicalities

Buses to Talca pull in at the **Terminal de Buses** (☎71/243270) on 2 Sur, ten blocks east of the Plaza de Armas. The **train station** (☎71/226254), served by trains from Santiago, Temuco and the nearby port of Constitución, is one block east of the bus terminal, on the other side of the tracks (while you're here, check out the funky murals on the walls of the ticket office). To get into the centre, take any *colectivo* or *micro* along 1 Sur (and to get back to the terminals, along 1 Norte). There's a friendly and helpful **Sernatur** office just north of the plaza at 1 Poniente 1281 (Mon–Fri 8.30am–5.30pm; ☎71/233669, fax 226940), while **Conaf** is on the corner of 2 Poniente and 3 Sur (☎71/228029). You'll find a cluster of **places to stay** on 2 Sur, a few blocks west of the bus terminal, of which the stand-outs are the cheerful *Hotel Amalfi* at no. 1265 (☎ & fax

71/233389; ④), which has rooms around a flower-filled patio with a little fountain, and the slightly cheaper *Cordillera Hotel* at no. 1360 (☎ & fax 71/221817; ④), with polished wooden floors and simple, whitewashed rooms (the best ones are those with shared bath). Another good choice is *Residencial Señora María* (☎71/225583; ③), 6 Oriente 1340 (at 2 Norte), where you'll find clean rooms with private bath in an old house with a very pretty garden. One of the best – and most expensive – **places to eat** in Talca is *El Alero de Gastón* at 2 Norte 858, where the usual fish and meat offerings are enlivened by a range of French-style sauces. For better-value and equally filling staples, head for the firemen's canteen behind the Museo Bomberil Benito Riquelme (see overleaf) or, for cheap roast chicken, *Picada Peucas* at 2 Oriente 1032. Talca has a **casa de cambio**, Marcelo Cancion Cortes, at 1 Sur 898, and several **ATMs** on 1 Sur, around the plaza. There are several **car rental** outlets on 1 Norte, including Comaba at no. 1516 (☎71/233242), Kovaks at no. 2183 (☎71/241868) and Ballart e Hijos at no. 953 (☎71/226489).

Villa Cultural Huilquilemu

Ten kilometres along the paved road heading east out of Talca towards the Argentinean border, **Villa Cultural Huilquilemu** (Tues–Fri 3–6.30pm, Sat 4–6.30pm, Sun 11am–2pm; CH$500) is a beautifully restored *casa patronal* built in 1850 and now open to the public as a museum, administered by the Universidad Católica del Maule. Inside, three long rooms off a series of colonnaded courtyards are devoted to religious art, housing paintings, statues, cassocks, furniture and two vivid, life-sized tableaux carved out of wood depicting the Last Supper and the appearance of the Angel Gabriel before the Virgin Mary. Another room displays examples of regional *artesanía*, including pottery, woven baskets, wooden carvings, textiles and delicately woven horsehair miniatures. Wander out the back and you'll find a machinery shed full of wonderful old nineteenth-century farming and wine-making contraptions, whose precise function can only be guessed at. There's also a *sala de vinos*, where several Maule valley wineries offer tastings of their products – which can also be bought to wash down a meal in the excellent **restaurant** attached. Finally, you can take a stroll around the mature gardens, where a collection of abstract sculptures by young local artists are dotted in the shade of century-old native and exotic trees. The Villa Cultural Huilquilemu is an easy, fifteen-minute **bus ride** from Talca on any *micro* heading to San Clemente from the terminal (every 10min).

Reserva Nacional Altos del Lircay

Continuing east along the road, some 30km on from Villa Huilquilemu, a left fork (along a poor dirt road) leads 25km to the mountain village of **VILCHES ALTO** and on to the entrance to the **Reserva Nacional Altos del Lircay** (daily: Dec–March 8.30am–8pm; April–Nov 8.30am–6pm; CH$500), 6km beyond. This is an extremely beautiful part of the central cordillera, with a covering of ancient native forest and fantastic views onto surrounding mountain peaks and volcanoes streaked with snow. Close to the entrance, an **information centre** has displays on the flora and fauna within the park, and on the area's pre-Columbian inhabitants, whose traces survive in the **piedras tacitas** (bowls used for grinding corn) carved out of a flat rock face a few hundred metres from the information centre along a signed path. Of the several **trails** inside the reserve, the most popular is to a hilltop viewpoint known as **El Enladrillado**. From the reserve entrance (get more detailed directions from the *guardaparque*), follow the steep track up the hillside for about 2.5km, then follow the signed turn-off, from where it's a stiff uphill walk of about four hours. The views from the top are exhilarating, down to the canopy of native coigues and lenga forests covering the valley beneath, and across to the towering Volcán Descabezado and surrounding peaks. You'll also find up here areas of exposed volcanic rock resembling giant crazy paving, giving the spot its name, which translates roughly as "brick paving".

Other paths in the reserve lead through forested ravines, past small lakes and up to *miradores* (viewpoints), but they're unsigned, and difficult to find with the rudimentary map available from Conaf. If you want to explore more, a highly enjoyable option is to do it on **horseback**. Posada Expediciones, based at 1 Norte 2280 in Talca (☎71/243833, fax 243822) offers three-day rides through the reserve, with good-quality horses, guides and camping equipment, for about US$250 per person (transport from and back to Talca, and all food included). You can make your own way with Buses Vilches (☎71/243366), who run two daily **buses** up to Vilches Alto, continuing to the reserve entrance in summer. There's no **accommodation** within the park, but you're allowed to camp wild, and you'll find a number of places to stay and eat down in Vilches Alto, including *Cabañas Campo Lindo* (☎71/226765; ④) and *Hostal Alto Vilches* (☎71/235442; ③).

Lago Colbún and the Termas de Panimávida and Quinimávida

Continuing along the international road to Argentina, 7km beyond the turn-off for Vilches Alto, the road skirts the northern shore of **Lago Colbún**, Chile's largest artificial lake, stretching 40km from east to west. It was created between 1980 and 1985 when the río Maule was dammed as part of a huge hydroelectricity project, and it wasn't long before its shores, framed by undulating hills, were dotted with holiday chalets and mini-markets. There are several **campsites**, too, though these are along the **southern shore** which can be a pain to get to – though two bridges span the lake, access to them is often barred by the hydroelectricity company, which means going back to the Panamericana and driving instead along the southern bank of the río Maule. This route provides access to **Colbún Alto**, a small village on the southwest shore of the lake, with a well-equipped campsite, *Marina del Cóndor* (☎73/211743); the village is served year-round by a couple of daily **buses** from Talca, with Buses Colbún (☎71/245478).

This road also leads to a couple of neighbouring hot-springs resorts a few kilometres south of the lake. The first one you reach is the **Termas de Panimávida** (☎73/211743; ⑤), a nineteenth-century hacienda-style building, arranged around numerous courtyards and patios. These are filled with immaculate gardens, overflowing with rose bushes, flowering trees and ornamental fountains, and form a sharp contrast to the rambling old building, which has rather gone to seed, its grand ballrooms no longer in use. It is, however, very atmospheric, especially the distinctly Victorian-looking wing housing the long row of cubicles where guests soak in the thermal waters (not especially hot at 33°C), mud baths and steam rooms. There are also a couple of outdoor pools, backed by lovely views onto the foothills of the cordillera. Five kilometres further south, the **Termas de Quinimávida** (☎73/213887; ⑤) is another labyrinthine hotel, this one featuring a huge indoor thermal pool (like a massive hot bath) in addition to the usual *tinas*, mud baths and Turkish baths. Attempts have been made to keep the building up-to-date, though not altogether successfully, leaving a curious mixture of smart modern wings and dated, 1970s areas. Moreover, the guests here all seem eighty if they're a day, and the set dinner is carefully chosen with dentures in mind. Both *termas* can be visited for the day, with use of the waters costing from CH$5000. You can get there from Talca on **public transport** with Buses Villa Prat (☎71/242120), which runs two services a day in both directions.

San Javier, Villa Alegre and the wineries

Twenty kilometres south of Talca, **SAN JAVIER** is a bustling little town sitting in the heart of the Maule valley's wine zone. It was clearly an important commercial centre in its day, as testified by the stately nineteenth-century mansions surrounding its wide plaza – which sports a finely carved statue of Bernardo O'Higgins in its centre. Today, the town's main interest lies in its proximity to many local **vineyards**, which the Municipalidad – eager to emulate the Colchagua valley's new "Ruta del Vino" (see p.242) – has banded together to form its own "Ruta del Vino San Javier-Villa Alegre". This is composed of 23 wineries spread between and around San Javier and the little village of **Villa Alegre**, 9km further south, all of which are marked on a map distributed by Sernatur in Talca. Most of these wineries, however, seem scarcely aware of the Ruta, and while none object to you having a look round, few offer formal tours and tastings. One notable exception is **Viña Balduzzi**, at Av Balmaceda 1189 in San Javier (☎73/322138), where tours of the *bodegas* (open Mon–Sat 9am–noon & 1.30–5pm) take you through the wine-making process, followed by free tastings and the chance to buy its wines, most of which are produced exclusively for export. Set in beautiful grounds, with an old *casa patronal*, a chapel and a *parque centenario* full of hundred-year-old trees, it's also a very picturesque example of a Central Valley vineyard. Further south towards Villa Alegre, a few hundred metres along the road to Constitución, **Viña San Clemente** (Mon–Fri 10am–1pm & 2–5pm; ☎73/381474) is a lot less polished, but is a good one to visit for its local, rustic atmosphere. Various pieces of rusting old machinery lie around the yards while inside, dozens of brick vaults are stacked full of dusty, unlabelled wine bottles, dappled with shafts of sunlight pouring in through the holes in the roof. There are no tastings here, but you can buy inexpensive wine (domestic market) in their *sala de ventas*, along with home-made cheeses and marmalades.

Continuing south, you approach **VILLA ALEGRE** through a stunning avenue of trees whose branches meet overhead to form a dense green canopy. This is one of the most beautifully preserved villages in the Central Valley, and a stroll down its main street, lined with fragrant orange trees, will take you past grand *casas patronales* set in luxuriant grounds, and an almost uninterrupted stretch of nineteenth-century adobe houses, topped by overhanging clay-tiled roofs leaning on thick wooden pillars. Vineyards here include **Viña El Aromo** (☎71/242438), just off the avenue of trees, whose modern, busy *bodegas* can be toured with a bit of advance notice, and **Viña Carta Vieja** (☎73/381612), on the access road to the Panamericana (right on the bus route), with impressive grounds and a lobby plastered with wine awards; they're mainly geared up to showing potential clients round, but will arrange a tour if you ring the day before.

This circuit makes an excellent day-trip from Talca, and is, moreover, very easy to do on **public transport**, with Interbus (☎71/242930) and Pullman del Sur (☎71/244039) providing frequent services down the Panamericana, into Villa Alegre, up to San Javier and back to Talca. There's nowhere **to stay** in Villa Alegre, but you'll find a couple of choices in San Javier – *Hotel Zapallar*, at Prat 2625 (☎71/321113; ③), has basic, neat rooms around a patio in a large old adobe house owned by an elderly lady, while the unsigned *Residencial Marta Silva* on Chorillos 1264 (☎71/321348; ③) has a few small rooms in a family house, run by a friendly *señora* who treats guests to a bear hug when they depart.

Constitución and the coast

Halfway between San Javier and Villa Alegre, a good, paved road branches west to the coast, ending up at the busy port of **CONSTITUCIÓN** at the mouth of the río Maule. With the foul stench of the local cellulose plant permeating every corner of town, this is unlikely to be a place you'll want to spend a lot of time in. While passing through, however, you could stop off for a drink and a snack at one of the cafés lining the shady Plaza de Armas, dominated by the rose-pink **Templo Parroquial**, built in 1860 and sporting a grand Palladian facade with three massive doors, topped by a long, pointy spire. Other possible diversions include a stroll along the wooded banks of the **río Maule**, where you can poke your head in the shipyards to see the traditional, twenty-metre-long wooden boats being built, or a walk out to the town's grey-sand **beaches**, where huge and weird rock formations loom out of the sea. Among these is the impressive **Piedra de la Iglesia**, which does indeed resemble a towering stone church, and the fancifully named **Arco de los Enamorados** ("Lovers' Arch") and **Piedra Calabocillos** ("the snail"). Otherwise, the main reason you might want to come here is to move on to the 60km of quiet beaches and small fishing towns stretching to the south.

From Talca, Constitución is served by plenty of **buses** and a daily **train**, which pull in opposite each other on the riverside, a few blocks northeast of the plaza. Should you need to **stay** here, the best place to head for is the unsigned *Hotel Avendaño* at O'Higgins 681 (☎71/672958; ④), whose rooms boast unfeasibly high ceilings and stately brass beds. You could also try good-value *Residencial Anita* (☎71/673700; ②), a small, clean, family house at Prieto 357, or the fairly smart *Hostería Constitución* (☎71/671450, fax 671480; ⑥), perched on the banks of the Maule, with good river views and a decent restaurant. There are also a couple of beachside **campsites** on the coast road out of town – *Calabocillos* (☎71/673988; CH$7000 per site) is 2km south, while the more attractive *Porterillos* (☎09/742 8275; CH$5000 per site) is another 2km beyond. Besides the *Hostería Constitución*, good places to **eat** include the string of rustic fish restaurants lining the beach, near the pier – though the fumes wafting over from the cellulose plant are enough to put many a diner off their food.

Chanco and the Reserva Nacional Federico Albert

From Constitución, a paved road follows the coast as far as the little seaside resort of **Curanipe**, 80km south. The first forty kilometres or so takes you past extensive pine plantations bordered by grey, empty beaches and sand dunes. Fifty-eight kilometres down the road, you reach **CHANCO**, a tiny village almost fossilized in the nineteenth century, populated by ageing farmers who transport their wheat, beans and potatoes to market on creaky, ox-drawn carts. Its narrow streets are lined by colourful old adobe houses, fronted by wooden verandas, large oak doors and long, thin windows, and it has a wonderful sky-blue **church**, with images of various saints covering its interior. On the northern edge of the village, the **Reserva Nacional Federico Albert** (daily 8am–6pm; CH$800) is a dense pine and eucalyptus forest planted in the late nineteenth century in an attempt to hold back the advance of the coastal sand dunes – which by then had already usurped much valuable farmland. Within the forest there's an attractive **camping** area (CH$6500 per site), while a three-kilometre **path** skirts the edge of the reserve, leading to an enormous sandy **beach** with small kiosks, picnic tables and running water. Amongst the large sand dunes, planted with tall reeds to stop them from drifting, you'll find vast stretches of sheltered sites to pitch a tent. Camping aside, the only place to **stay** in Chanco is the nameless *hospedaje* at Errázuriz 141 (☎71/551052; ②), one block from the reserve entrance. It also provides **meals**, although a better option is *Restaurante Yugo*, at Freire 292. Chanco is served by several daily **buses** from Constitución and Talca, run by Buses Contimar (☎71/244197).

Pellehue and Curanipe

Eleven kilometres south of Chanco, **PELLEHUE** is a popular summer seaside resort composed of an undisciplined collection of houses strung around a long, curving black-sand beach. There are stacks of places to **stay**, including *Hostería Longave* at Condell

819 (☎73/556066; ④), which has a good seafood **restaurant** and spacious rooms with floor-to-ceiling windows looking down to the ocean, and *Residencial Las Palmeras* at Condell 701 (☎73/541051; ②), an old and slightly run-down building with a small garden on the edge of a cliff and access to a secluded cove. The resort has an untidy, slightly ramshackle feel to it, however, that doesn't encourage you to stay long, and you'd be better off continuing a further 7km south to the prettier village of **CURANIPE**. With a backdrop of rolling hills, wheat fields and meadows, Curanipe's dark-sand **beach**, dotted with colourful wooden fishing boats pulled onto the sands, is a lovely place to hang out – though that's just about all there is do here. You'll find neat, simple **rooms** at the *Hostería Pacifico*, on Comercio 509 (☎73/556016; ③), and slightly smarter ones at the newly built *Residencial La Bahía* a few doors along at no. 438 (④). There's also an attractive **campsite**, *Los Pinos*, set in pine and eucalyptus woods right by the beach. For fresh, locally caught fish, try the **restaurant** in the *Hostería Pacifico*, or the two little beachside *picadas* down the track from the *Hostería*. Pelluhue and Curanipe can by reached **by bus** from Constitución and Chanco, with Buses Amigo (☎73/511992), and from Talca (along the southern route, via the town of Cauquenes) with Buses Pullman del Sur (☎71/243431) and Buses Bonanza (☎71/243210).

Chillán and the Itata valley

Back on the Panamericana, a hundred and fifty kilometres – punctuated by the nondescript towns of **Linares** and **Parral** – separate Talca from the busy city of **Chillán**, sitting in the middle of the **Itata valley**. Though lush and very beautiful, the valley is short on specific attractions, which amount to a **naval museum** in the village of Ninhue, 50km northwest of Chillán, and the hot-springs resort and ski centre of the **Termas de Chillán**, 80km east, high in the cordillera.

Chillán

The busy city of **CHILLÁN** is famous throughout Chile as the birthplace of Bernardo O'Higgins, the founding father of the republic. Unlike most of the towns staggered down the highway, it is, moreover, a place worth visiting in its own right – principally for its vast **handicrafts market** and fascinating **Mexican murals** – and not just as a staging post to arrange transport to neighbouring attractions.

Arrival and information

Many **long-distance buses** use the new Terminal María Teresa at Av O'Higgins 010, on the northern edge of town, but a few (including Buses Lit, Tas Choapa and Tur Bus) pull in at the old terminal on the corner of Avenida Brasíl and Constitución, five blocks west of the central plaza. **Local** and **regional buses** use the centrally located Terminal Rural, a few blocks southeast of the plaza. **Trains** from Santiago and Concepción pull in opposite the old bus terminal on Avenida Brasíl. You can pick up **tourist information** at **Sernatur**, at 18 de Septiembre 455 (☎71/223272) and at the **Oficina de Turismo** (Mon–Fri 8.30am–12.30pm & 3–6pm; ☎42/214117) in the Municipalidad on the Plaza de Armas.

Accommodation

Chillán has a wide range of accommodation, although the upper- and mid-range hotels cater primarily for business travellers and tend to be functional rather than intimate. Budget accommodation is plentiful, but not of a great standard.

Casa Pensión, Itata 288 (☎42/214879). A friendly, popular, family house offering excellent-value rooms and kitchen facilities. Note that solo travellers might have to share rooms when it gets busy. ②.

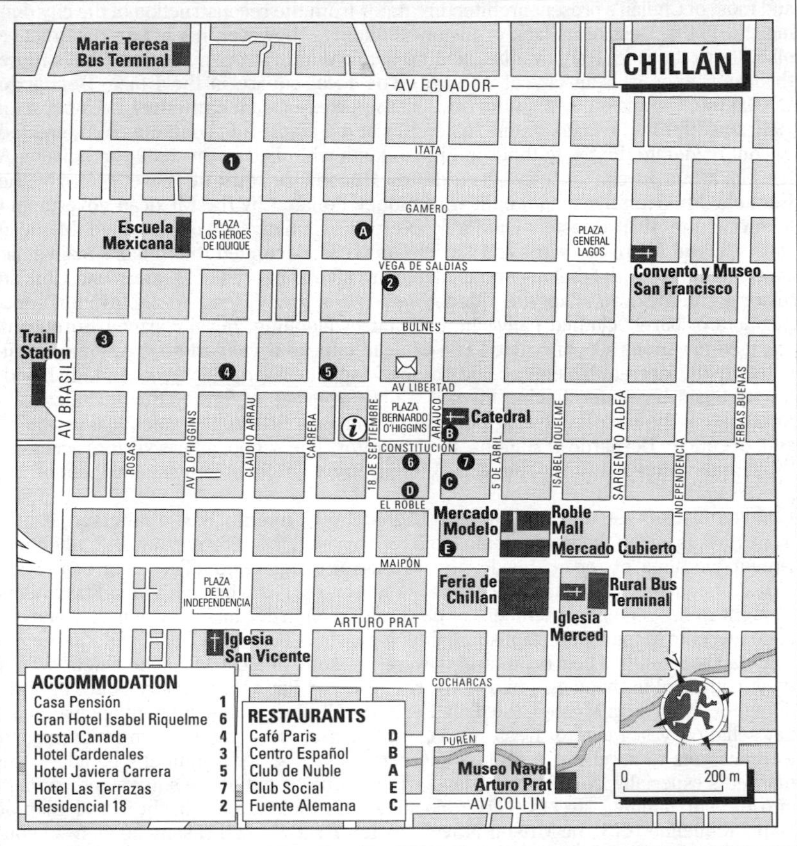

Gran Hotel Isabel Riquelme, Arauco 600 (☎42/213663, fax 211541). Old-fashioned hotel with large en-suite rooms and a restaurant with a good international menu and cheaper set meals. ⑥.

Hostal Canada, Libertad 269 (☎42/234515). Small and clean with bright, airy rooms and a rooftop terrace. A good budget choice. ②.

Hotel Cardenales, Bulnes 34 (☎42/224251). A spanking new place offering quiet, bright rooms with private bath, some of them boasting jacuzzis. ③–④.

Hotel Javiera Carrera, Carrera 481 (☎42/221175). Neat and comfortable with good facilities and fair-size rooms. ④.

Hotel Las Terrazas, Constitución 664 (☎42/227000, fax 227001). On the fifth floor of a modern office block, an attractively decorated hotel with bright, comfortable, well-equipped rooms. ⑤.

Residencial 18, 18 de Septiembre 317 (☎42/211102). An immaculate *residencial* complete with pool table and games room. Inexpensive meals are available. ②.

The Town

Thanks to periodic earthquakes and regular Mapuche attacks, Chillán has seen itself repeatedly rebuilt since its foundation in 1550. The last major earthquake was in 1939, and most of Chillán's present architecture dates from the reconstruction of the city during the 1940s. Despite its lack of historic buildings, however, it's not an unattractive place, with its wide, leafy avenues and no fewer than five open squares (that's more than any other Chilean city of its size). The focal square is the **Plaza Bernardo O'Higgins**, dominated by the futuristic, earthquake-resistant **cathedral**, built between 1941 and 1961 in the form of nine tall arches and a giant, 36m concrete cross, erected to commemorate the thirty thousand inhabitants who died in the 1939 earthquake. A few blocks northwest, the leafy **Plaza de los Héroes de Iquique** is overlooked by the **Escuela Mexicana**, a school built with money donated by the Mexican government following the 1939 disaster. On Pablo Neruda's initiative, two renowned Mexican artists, David Alfaro Siqueiros and Xavier Guerrero, decorated the school's main staircase and library with fabulous murals depicting pivotal figures of Mexican and Chilean history. The Mexican images, entitled *Muerte al Invaser* ("Death to the Invader"), feature lots of barely clothed native heroes and evil-looking, heavily armed Europeans engaged in various acts of cruelty. The Chilean tableau is even more gruesome, dominated by the lacerated, bleeding body of the Mapuche *toqui*, Galvarino, and his bloodthirsty Spanish captors. Joining them is a diverse group of figures that includes Luis Recabarren, the radical left-wing politician, Francisoc Bilbao, the polemical essaysist, and, of course, Bernardo O'Higgins, the Liberator. The school allows visitors access to the murals (Mon–Fri 10am–1pm & 3–6.30pm) in return for which small donations are appreciated.

Seven blocks east, on Plaza General Lagos, the **Convento San Francisco**, dating from 1906, is one of the few buildings to have survived the 1939 earthquake, albeit in a lamentable state of repair. Inside, the **Museo Franciscano** (Tues–Sun 9am–3pm; CH$200) contains a collection of colonial furniture, religious objects and military items brought to the region by members of the Franciscan order in 1585 when they arrived to convert the Mapuches, establishing fifteen missions between Chillán and Rió Bueno, some 500km south. Their main targets were the sons of local Mapuche chiefs, whom they instructed in theology, philosophy, rhetoric and Latin. Five blocks south of here, filling the Plaza de la Merced, the daily **Feria de Chillán** is an exuberant open-air market selling a vast range of fresh produce and *artesanía*, ranging from knitwear and leather items to jewellery, paintings and ceramics. A souvenir-hunter's paradise, the market is especially lively on Saturdays, when it bulges out of the square and spreads into the surrounding streets. Three blocks south, tucked away in the Naval Club at Isabel Riquelme 1173, the **Museo Naval Arturo Prat** (Mon–Fri 9am–noon; free) contains a small and rather disappointing collection of model ships (naval fans will be better off skipping this and heading straight for the museum at Ninhue – see opposite). Wrapping up Chillán's attractions, a short bus ride south along Avenida O'Higgins, is the **Parque Monumental Bernardo O'Higgins** (daily: Dec–March 8am–8pm; April–Nov 8am–6pm; free), a handsomely landscaped park featuring a 60m wall covered with a badly faded mosaic depicting the life of the city's most famous son. In a small chapel nearby, O Higgins' mother, Isabel Riquelme and his sister, Rosita, are both buried, not far from the site where Bernardo was born.

Eating

For a cheap bite and a great, buzzing atmosphere, head one block north of the Feria de Chillán to the hectic **Mercado Cubierto**, crammed with butchers' stands and boisterous food stalls, and the slightly more restrained **Mercado Modelo**, with its good-value restaurants and lines of communal tables. Next door, the **Roble Mall** has plenty of fast-food outlets that make another inexpensive option.

Arco Iris, Plaza de Armas. Good-value vegetarian lunches, including delicious omelettes and salads.

Café Paris, Arauco 666. Bustling café with outside tables, a snack-bar downstairs that stays open until 4am, and a smart upstairs restaurant with a balcony.

Centro Español, Arauco 555. A bright, cheerful restaurant serving all the usual Chilean staples plus a range of Spanish specialities, including paella.

Club de Nuble, 18 de Diciembre 224. With its exceptionally attentive staff and formal dining room, this place has the atmosphere of an old-fashioned gentlemen's club. The menu is good, specializing in meat dishes with a wide variety of sauces.

Club Social, Arauco 745. Down-to-earth, inexpensive restaurant with an airy dining room looking out onto a large patio.

Fuente Alemana, Arauco 661. The best place in Chillán for coffee, rich cakes and hot meat sandwiches.

Listings

Banks and exchange There are plenty of ATMs around the plaza on Arauco and Constitución, as well as a *casa de cambio* at Constitución 550.

Car rental First, 18 de Septiembre 380 (☎42/211218).

Laundry There's a reasonably priced *lavandería* on Arturo Prat, between Claudio Arrau and Carrera.

Post Office The main *correo* is on Av Libertad, on the Plaza de Armas.

Telephone offices Entel is at Arauco 623.

Termas de Chillán

Eighty kilometres east of Chillán, nestled at the foot of the 3122m **Volcán Chillán**, the all-season tourist complex of the **Termas de Chillán** is the most famous and most developed mountain resort south of Santiago (information from Chillán at Libertad 1042; ☎42/223887, fax 223576; and from Santiago at Av Providencia 2237, oficina P41; ☎2/233 1313, fax 231 5963; *ventanac@termachillan.cl*). Surrounded by glorious alpine scenery, it possesses nine open-air **thermal pools** (whose high content of sulphur and iron is alleged to cure numerous illnesses), **steam baths** inside dripping caves, hot **mud baths**, and a state-of-the-art **spa** centre, offering massages, facials, hydro-massages and a range of other treatments applied with frightening-looking contraptions. The hot baths and spa function year-round, but in winter the emphasis shifts to the resort's excellent **skiing** facilities, which include nine ski lifts and 28 runs, one of which is the longest in South America, at 2.5km. Added winter activities include heli-skiing, snow-biking, snowboarding and sleigh-rides pulled by Alaskan malamutes.

There are three types of **accommodation** within the resort itself, all of it top-range and very expensive: the large *Gran Hotel Termas de Chillán* (⑧) is the plushest, with new, first-class rooms, followed by the *Hotel Pirigallo* (⑦), which has both regular hotel rooms and condominium apartments. There are also five **restaurants** dotted around the complex, serving a range of food from simple snacks to fine cuisine. If you're put off by the high accommodation rates, you might consider visiting for the day: use of the hot sulphur pools costs CH$6000, while the steam baths cost CH$10,000; during the ski season (normally June–Sept), **lift tickets** cost from CH$20,000. On the way up you'll pass several **campsites** dotted along the road, as well as the excellent *Parador Jamón, Pan y Vino*, 73km from Chillán (☎ & fax 42/220018; ⑦), a mountain chalet with great home-cooking, making a worthwhile, though scarcely cheaper, alternative to the resort's own accommodation.

Santuario Cuna de Prat

Naval enthusiasts who were disappointed with Chillán's Museo Prat will not be failed by the **Santuario Cuna de Prat** (Tues–Sun 10am–6pm; CH$300), just outside the small village of **Ninhue**, 50km northwest of Chillán. Here, the Chilean navy has done a splendid job in preserving the fine colonial **Hacienda San Agustín de Puñal** (Tues–Sun 10am–6pm; CH$400) – where Arturo Prat was born in 1848 – as a shrine to the naval hero who died in 1879 in the Battle of Iquique while trying to capture a Peruvian ironclad gunship armed only with a sword. While the national obsession with the young officer – who has a thousand Chilean plazas and streets named after him – continues to mystify, the museum's collection of polished, lovingly-cared-for naval memorabilia and colonial furniture are worth a visit in their own right, and the building they're housed in is a beautiful example of colonial rural architecture, with its large interior patio and elegant verandas.

Concepción and the Bío Bío valley

South of Chillán and the Itata valley, Chile is intersected by the great **río Bío Bío**, generally considered to mark the southern limit of the Central Valley. One of Chile's longest rivers, it cuts a 380km diagonal slash across the country, emptying into the ocean by the large city of **Concepción**, over 200km north of its source in the Andean mountains. These days the river is best known as a world-class **white-water rafting** destination, but for more than three hundred years the Bío Bío was simply "La Frontera", forming the border beyond which Spanish colonization was unable to spread, fiercely repulsed by the native **Mapuche** population. Today, the Bío Bío valley still feels like a border, or transition zone, between the gentle pastures and meadows of central Chile, and the lakes and volcanoes of the south. While the valley floor is still covered in the characteristic blanket of cultivation, dotted with typical Central Valley towns like **Los Angeles** and **Angol**, the landscape either side is clearly different. To the west, the **coastal range** – little more than gentle hills further north – takes on the abrupt outlines of real mountains, covered in a dense layer of commercial pine forests and, further south, native araucaria trees in their hundreds, protected within the **Parque Nacional Nahuelbuta**. Cut off by these mountains, the towns strung down the coast road south of Concepción – such as **Lota**, **Arauco**, **Lebu** and **Cañete** – feel like isolated outposts, an impression enhanced by the ruins of old **forts** left over from the Spanish–Mapuche war. To the east, the Andes take on a different appearance, too: wetter and greener, with several outstandingly beautiful wilderness areas like **Parque Nacional Laguna del Laja**, with its volcanic landscape and stunning lake, and **Parque Nacional Tolhuaca**, which also boasts the beautiful araucaria trees.

Concepción

Sitting at the mouth of the Bío Bío, 112km southwest of Chillán along a fast motorway, the sprawling, fast-paced metropolis of **CONCEPCIÓN** is the region's administrative capital and economic powerhouse, and is Chile's third largest city after Santiago and Valparaíso. The commercial nucleus of local forestry, agricultural, hydroelectric and coal industries, it is surrounded by some of the ugliest industrial suburbs in the country. Nor can its centre be considered attractive, with its spread of dreary, anonymous buildings, few of them over sixty years old. This lack of civic splendour reflects the long series of catastrophes to have punctuated Concepción's growth – from the incessant Mapuche raids during the city's days as a Spanish garrison, guarding La Frontera, to the devastating earthquakes that have razed it to the ground over 200 times since its foundation in 1551. It does, however, have the energy and buzz of a thriving commercial centre, and the large number of students here gives the place a young, lively feel, and an excellent nightlife. By day, Concepción's chief attractions are its **Galería de la Historia**, depicting the city's turbulent history, and the striking Mexican mural inside the **Casa del Arte**. Sixteen kilometres north, moored in the harbour of neighbouring

Talcahuano, the historic ironclad **gunship** *Huáscar* is another popular tourist attraction, easily reached from Concepción.

Arrival and information

Most **buses** arrive at the Terminal Puchucay, northeast of the centre at Tegualda 860, just off the Autopista General Bonilla (☎41/311511); from here, plenty of *colectivos* and taxis will take you into town. If you arrive with Tur Bus, you'll be dropped either at the smaller Terminal Chillancito, also off the Autopista General Bonilla at Av Henríquez 2565 (☎41/315036), or at its downtown office at Tucapel 530. **Trains** from Santiago and Chillán arrive at the train station on Avenida Arturo Prat, six blocks west of the plaza (☎41/277777). If you're **flying** to Concepción, you'll land at Aeropuerto Carriel Sur, 5km northwest of town, from where you can get a taxi or minibus transfer directly to your hotel.

You can pick up maps, brochures and other tourist information at **Sernatur**'s office on the central square at Aníbal Pinto 460 (Dec–March Mon–Fri 8am–8pm, Sat 9am–2pm; April–Nov Mon–Fri 8.45am–1pm & 3–5.30pm; ☎41/227976). **Conaf** has an office at Serrano 529.

Accommodation

Concepción is well-endowed with upmarket, expensive hotels catering to business travellers, but budget accommodation is very thin on the ground, with no rock-bottom options at all.

El Araucano, Caupolicán 521 (☎41/230606, fax 230690). Top-notch luxury hotel with an indoor pool and a very good restaurant with a terrace over the Plaza de Armas. ⑦, weekends ⑥.

Holiday Inn Express, Av San Andrés 38 (☎41/489300). All the comforts of a North American chain hotel, including pool, jacuzzi, cable TV, immaculate rooms, fluffy white towels and your own coffee percolator. The downside is that it's way out of the centre. ⑦, weekends ⑥.

Hotel Bío Bío, Barros Arana 751 (☎41/228018, fax 242741). Bright and cheerful hotel with all the rooms looking onto a central lightwell. ④.

Hotel Maquehue, Barros Arana 786 (☎41/238348). A quiet hotel on the seventh floor with pleasant en-suite rooms, some of which command fine views over the city. ⑤.

Hotel San Sebastián, Rengo 463 (☎ & fax 41/243412). Small hotel with its own parking and bright, spotless if slightly old-fashioned rooms with private bath. ④.

Residencial Central, Rengo 673 (☎41/227309). An old building with lots of character and large rooms, a few with outside windows. ③.

Residencial O'Higgins, O'Higgins 457 (☎41/228303). A small B&B with basic but adequate rooms off a long corridor, among the cheapest in town. ③.

Residencial San Sebastián, Barros Arana 741, departamento 35 (☎41/242710, fax 243412). Good-value, simple rooms on the third floor of a modern commercial building. ③.

The Town

The focal point of Concepción is its busy **Plaza de la Independencia**, though there's little to detain you here once you've called into the Sernatur office. For a better introduction to the city, head for the **Galería de la Historia** (Tues–Fri 10am–1.30pm & 3–6.30pm, Sat & Sun 10am–2pm & 3–7pm; free) at the southern end of Lincoyán, in Parque Ecuador, where you'll find a series of impressive dioramas, some with sound and light effects, depicting the long and troubled history of Concepción. All the models and figures are beautifully made and give a good idea of the trials and tribulations suffered by the early inhabitants of this frontier town. If you walk up to the far end of the park and on to calle Larenas, you'll reach the **university**, set in splendid, landscaped gardens surrounded by thickly wooded hills. This is Chile's second largest university and has the curious distinction of being funded by the local lottery. It houses

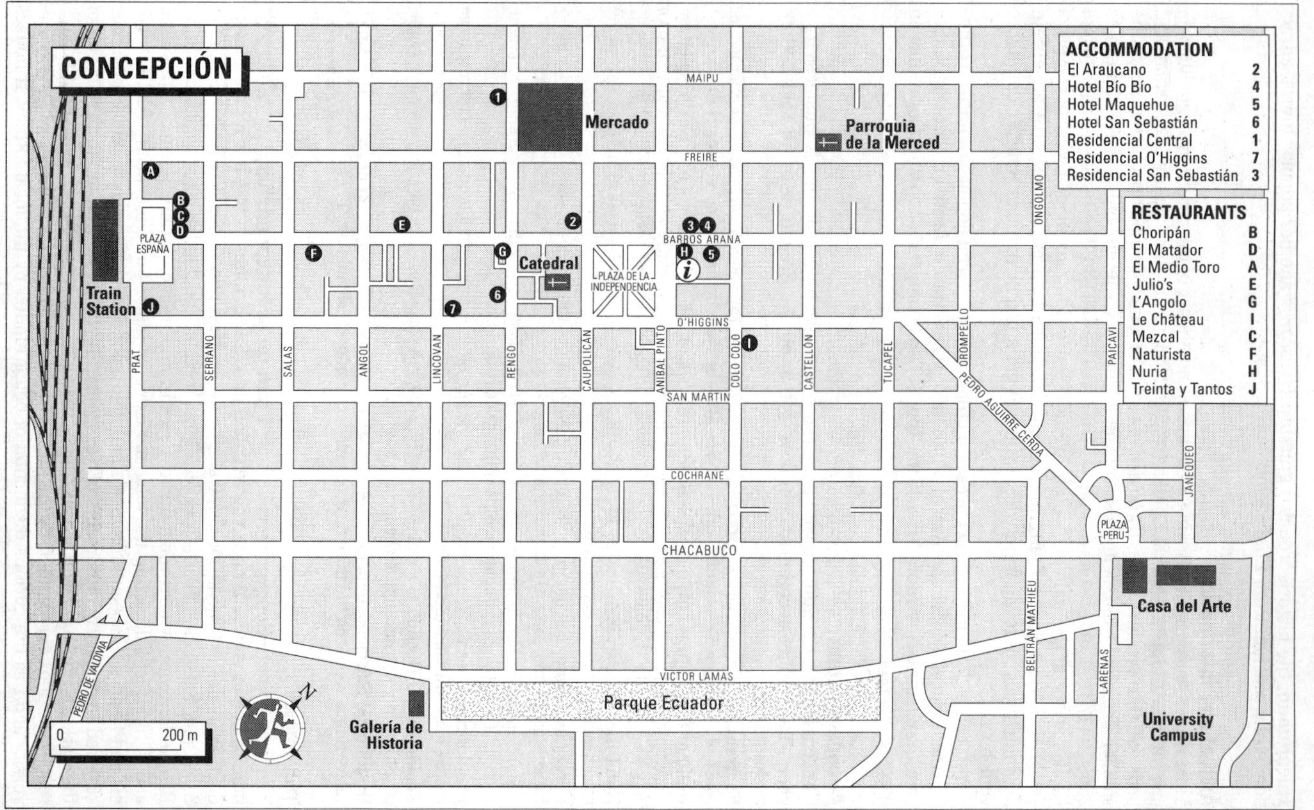
CONCEPCIÓN
ACCOMMODATION
El Araucano 2
Hotel Bío Bío 4
Hotel Maquehue 5
Hotel San Sebastián 6
Residencial Central 1
Residencial O'Higgins 7
Residencial San Sebastián 3
RESTAURANTS
Choripán B
El Matador D
El Medio Toro A
Julio's E
L'Angolo G
Le Château I
Mezcal C
Naturista F
Nuria H
Treinta y Tantos J
Mercado
Parroquia de la Merced
Catedral
PLAZA DE LA INDEPENDENCIA
PLAZA ESPAÑA
Train Station
Casa del Arte
University Campus
PLAZA PERU
Parque Ecuador
Galería de Historia
MAIPU
FREIRE
BARROS ARANA
O'HIGGINS
SAN MARTIN
COCHRANE
CHACABUCO
VICTOR LAMAS
PRAT
SERRANO
SALAS
ANGOL
LINCOVAN
RENGO
CAUPOLICAN
ANIBAL PINTO
COLO COLO
CASTELLÓN
TUCAPEL
OROMPELLO
ONGOLMO
PAICAVI
JANEQUEO
PEDRO AGUIRRE CERDA
BELTRÁN MATHIEU
LARENAS
PEDRO DE VALDIVIA
N
0
200 m

one of Chile's largest national art collections, displayed in the **Casa del Arte** (Tues–Fri 10am–6pm, Sat 10am–4pm, Sun 10am–2pm; free). The bulk of the collection consists of nineteenth-century landscapes and portraits by Chilean artists, but the showpiece is the magnificent mural in the entrance hall, *Presencia de América Latina*, painted by the Mexican artist Jorge González Camarena in 1964. Dominating the mural is the giant face of an *indígena*, representing all the indigenous peoples of the continent, while the many faces of different nationalities superimposed onto it indicate the intrusion of outside cultures and fusion of races that characterize Latin America. Woven into the densely packed images are the flags of every Latin American country, and several national icons like Chile's condor and the feathered serpent, Quetzalcoatl, the Mexican symbol of culture. You'll find another mural, though not quite in the same league, inside the railway station. Over 6m long and 4m tall, the massive *Historia de Concepción*, painted by the Chilean artist Gregorio de la Fuente in 1964, depicts Concepción's history from its pre-Spanish days of smiling, contented Mapuches, through the violent Arauco war, and into the modern era of economic strength.

At the western end of the Bío Bío estuary, a fifteen-minute taxi ride from the city centre, a large park with several kilometres of footpaths and an extensive collection of native and exotic trees surrounds the **Museo Hualpén** (Tues–Sun 10am–1pm & 2–6pm; CH$1500). The traditional single-storey hacienda building houses an eclectic collection of souvenirs from every corner of the globe, picked up by the millionaire industrialist Pedro del Río over three world trips in the nineteenth century. Oriental furniture, Egyptian art, a collection of smoking pipes, and Hindu and Mapuche silver body ornaments fill the rooms alongside fossils and mineral specimens.

Sixteen kilometres northeast of Concepción are the industrial suburbs and **Talcahuano** naval base where the historic ironclad gunship *Huáscar* is moored. From calle Chacabuco in Concepción, white buses marked "*Base Naval*" go right to the entrance of the base, where you need to ask the guard for permission to visit the ship (Tues–Sun 9.30am–noon & 2–6pm; CH$600). The *Huáscar* was built for the Peruvian navy at Birkenhead in 1866 and controlled the naval engagements during the War of the Pacific until 1879 when it was trapped off Cape Angamos, near Antofagasta, and forced to surrender. Kept in an immaculate state of preservation, the *Huáscar* is one of only two vessels of its type still afloat today. Note that you'll need to present your passport at the gate, and should take care not to photograph the base installations or naval ships.

Eating, drinking and nightlife

Concepción has a good range of **eating** places to suit all pockets, and boasts the liveliest **nightlife** in the Central Valley, fuelled by the large student population. Concentrated on calle Prat and Plaza España in the area known as the **Barrio Estación**, this revolves mainly around a string of small, intimate restaurants that double up as bars on Friday and Saturday night – if you want to go **clubbing**, head for the steamy *Hot House* at O'Higgins 20002, a short taxi ride out of town. Note that few of the places in the Barrio Estación are open for lunch, when a good, inexpensive choice would be the dozens of little *picadas* in the **Mercado Central**, on the corner of Freire and Caupolicán.

Choripán, Prat 546. Rustic little restaurant serving its speciality of bread and pork sausages until the early hours of the morning.

El Matador, Prat 528. Studiously rural decor, with a terracotta-roofed bar, and delicious, sizzling hamburgers.

El Medio Toro, Prat 594. A friendly *picada* serving authentic *criollo* food like *pastel de choclo* and *humitas*. A good place for a quiet drink and a chat.

Julio's, Barros Arana 337. Head here for excellent steaks and generous *parilladas* served by waiters wearing slightly comical Argentinean gaucho outfits.

L'Angolo, Rengo 494. Large and very popular café, full of young couples, families and frantic waiters serving delicious light meals and cocktails.

Le Château, Colo Colo 340 (☎41/229977). Easily the city's best restaurant, with a good atmosphere and an imaginative, French-based menu.

Mezcal, Prat 532. Colourfully decorated Mexican restaurant, serving tasty fajitas and burritos, accompanied by lots of raucous margarita- and tequila-drinking at the weekend.

Naturista, Barros Arana 244. An interesting health food shop-cum restaurant, owned by a dentist who speaks English and German and never puts sugar in his food. It's in a large old barn-like building and closes at 6pm.

Nuria, Barros Arana 736. Good-value, down-to-earth café-restaurant serving sandwiches and other staples amidst a bustling atmosphere. Also does takeaway food.

Treinta y Tantos, Prat 404. The longest-standing student haunt in the Barrio Estación, serving over 30 varieties of *empanadas* in a cosy restaurant with mellow music.

Listings

Airlines Aerolíneas Argentinas, O'Higgins 650, oficina 602 (☎41/242577); Air France, Barros Arana 492, oficina 137 (☎41/229821); American Airlines, O'Higgins 630, oficina 304 (☎41/227355); Avant, Barros Arana 455 (☎41/246710); Iberia, O'Higgins 770, second floor (☎41/244092); Ladeco, O'Higgins 533 (☎41/248824); Lan Chile, Barros Arana 451 (☎41/229138).

Banks and exchange There are many banks with ATMs, most of them on O'Higgins, by the plaza. You'll find four *casas de cambio* – Cambio Fides, Inter Santiago, Varex and Afex – inside the small shopping centre at Barros Arana 565.

Car rental Andes Rentacar, Tucapel 564, oficina 81 (☎41/230742); Avis, Chacabuco 726 (☎41/235837); Brasil Rentacar, Brasil 1205 (☎41/259571); Budget, Castellón 134 (☎41/225377); Diamond, Angol 659 (☎41/231776); Hertz, Prat 248 (☎41/230341).

Consulates Argentina, San Martín 472 (☎41/230257); Belgium, Orompello 61-A (☎41/230094); Denmark, Aníbal Pinto 222, oficina 11 (☎41/543864); France, Colo Colo 1 (☎41/254991); Germany, Chacabuco 856 (☎41/242591); Holland, Caupolicán 245 (☎41/368185); Italy, Barros Arana 243, second floor (☎41/229506).

Internet access *Cyberc@fé*, Caupolicán 553.

Laundry Laverap, Caupolicán 334, at O'Higgins; Lavanderá Santa Barbara, Barros Arana 565.

Post office On the corner of O'Higgins and Colo Colo.

Telephone centres Centro de Llamados Colo Colo, Colo Colo 487; Chilesat, O'Higgins 799; CTC, Caupolicán 649; Entel, Barros Arana 541.

Train information ☎41/277777 or 225286.

Travel agents There's a cluster of travel agents in an office block at O'Higgins 630, including Turismo Cocha, oficina 301, and Exportravel, oficina 503. Elsewhere, you could try Chile Travel, Rengo 465 (☎41/226112) or Gestur, Rengo 484.

MOVING ON FROM CONCEPCIÓN

There are direct **buses** to most towns and cities between Santiago and Puerto Montt, with the majority of companies leaving from the Terminal Puchucay. A notable exception is Tur Bus, whose downtown office is Tucapel 530 (☎41/316989), and which leaves from the Terminal Chillancito (see "Arrival and Information" p.257). If you're heading up the coast to **Tomé**, take a Costa Azul bus from Las Heras 530 (☎41/237562). The coastal route south of Concepción to **Cañete**, **Arauco**, **Lebu** and **Contulmo** is served by Los Alces (☎41/240855) and Buses J Ewart (☎41/229212), both companies leave from Prat, near to the train station. Moving on **by train**, there's a daily service to Santiago, and three per day to Chillán. There are regular **flights** from Concepción to most major cities between Arica and Punta Arenas. Several minibus companies offer inexpensive door-to-door transfers to the airport, including Turismo Ritz (☎41/237637), Airport Express (☎41/236444) and Taxivan (☎41/248748).

The northern beaches

North of Concepción, a series of small towns and golden, sandy bays is dotted up the coastline as far as the mouth of the río Itata, 60km beyond. The first 36km, as far as Dichato, is paved and served by regular **buses** and **colectivos**. Heading up the road, 12km out of the city centre you pass through the suburb of **PENCO** where the remains of a Spanish fort, **Fuerte La Planchada**, recall the area's turbulent history. Built in 1687, the fort was destroyed and rebuilt many times before becoming a prison to hold patriot soldiers during the War of Independence; today, it's been efficiently reconstructed, and retains the original long stone wall from where Spanish soldiers fired at raiding Mapuches and the occasional British pirate ship. A couple of gentle hills separate Penco from **LIRQUÉN**, a small industrial harbour used for exporting timber. Its beach is nothing special, but the nearby tangle of narrow streets known as the **Barrio Chino** is full of first-class, excellent-value seafood restaurants, famous throughout the region for their clam dishes. Beyond Lirquén, the road runs inland for 30km through tree plantations, and the only access to the ocean along here is the exclusive private beach, **Punta de Parra** (☎41/235507), which charges CH$6000 per vehicle for admittance to its powdery white sands. There's a restaurant here, too, and several upmarket *cabañas* (④), as well as a beautiful coastal walk along the old rail tracks that skirt this beach and several even more secluded ones.

Twenty-eight kilometres out of Concepción, the thriving timber and textile centre of **TOMÉ** is squeezed into a small flat-bottomed valley, its suburbs pushed up the slopes of surrounding hills. Hidden from the drab town by a rocky point is the long, white-sand **Playa El Morro**, with several places to **stay** including *Cabañas Broadway*, Av Werner 1210 (☎41/651117; ④), and *Hostal Villa Marina*, Sotomayor 669 (☎41/650807, fax 650947; ④). The beach, while very attractive, gets dreadfully crowded on summer weekends; a quieter alternative is **Playa Cocholgue**, a fine white beach studded with rocky outcrops, reached by taking the four-kilometre side road off the main coast road as you head out of Tomé. Eight kilometres north, **DICHATO** – free of factories and commercial wharves – is the most popular beach resort along this part of the coast, with a handful of **accommodation** options spread along the coastal avenue, Pedro Aguirre Cerda. Best value is *Hotel Cabañas Asturias* at no. 734 (☎41/683000; ③), which also has a seafood restaurant with excellent views; another good choice, at no. 760, is *Bahía Velero* (☎41/683014; ④), a small beachside hotel with a patio where the owners like to lay on barbecues, or let guests organize their own. At the southern end of the avenue, at no. 201, is the smart *Hotel Manantial* (☎ & fax 41/683027; ⑥), boasting bright rooms with balconies and good sea views, and a good, though expensive, **restaurant**. Other places to eat include *South Beach* at Vera 876, which by night turns into a lively drinking haunt. Five kilometres north of Dichato, on the dirt road that continues up to the río Itata, there's a **campsite**, *El Encanto* (CH$7000 per tent), with picnic tables and barbecue grills. Beyond here, the road passes through dense forests with tracks leading off to a series of isolated, yellow-sand **beaches**, pounded by strong waves. Among the most beautiful of these are **Playa Purda**, 8km north of Dichato, and tiny **Playa Merquiche**, a further 2km north.

The southern coast road and beyond

South of Concepción, a good road skirts the ocean for some 60km before straying inland and finally cutting across the densely forested coastal mountains – known here as the **cordillera de Nahuelbuta** – and heading down to the Central Valley floor and the Panamericana. The route takes in a series of drab towns which until as recently as 1963, when the road was built, could be reached only by sea or rail. Most were established as mining towns in the mid-nineteenth century when the Santiago industrialist

Matías Cousiño discovered the enormous submarine coal seam – the **Costa del Carbón** – running off the coast. The chief tourist attraction down here is the **Lota coal mine** and adjoining **Parque Cousiño**, as well as the charming **Isla Santa María**, reached by ferry from Lota. Further south, **Lebu** has great beaches, while nearby **Cañete**'s Mapuche museum is worth a visit en route to pretty **Lago Lanalhue**. Buses Los Alces and Buses J Ewart have regular **bus** services along this route from Concepción.

Lota

Squeezed into a small valley on the edge of the sea, the soot-streaked town of **LOTA** was the site of Chile's first and largest coal mine, opened by Matías Cousiño in 1849. Production finally ceased in 1997, and today the ex-colliery is turning its attention to tourism, with plans to install hotels, swimming pools and a casino. The town centre, in the lower part of town known as Lota Bajo, does not inspire enthusiasm, though while you're here you should check out the curious **statue of the Virgin**, carved out of coal, in the church on the plaza. Spread up the hillside west of the centre is Lota Alto, containing the former miners' residences and administrative buildings, as well as the impressive **Iglesia San Matías**, where the coal baron lies buried. From here it's a short walk to the attractive **Parque Lota** (daily: April–Oct 10am–6pm; Nov–March 10am–8pm; CH$1000), a formal garden laid out by an English landscape gardener in 1862 under the direction of Cousiño's wife, doña Isidora Goyenechea. An earthquake destroyed the Cousiño family palace in 1960 but the ponds, fountains and Neoclassical allegorical statues have survived, interlaced with a confusing maze of narrow footpaths, giving birds'-eye views down to the slag heaps and the entrances to the **coal mine**. You can visit the mine on **tours** (☎41/870682) guided by ex-miners, with the choice of going down the 820m shaft of the **Chiflón del Diablo** (6 tours daily; CH$2000) or the much deeper **Pique Carlos** (4 tours daily; CH$7000), 1500m below ground – a fascinating experience, involving a ride on a mine train through tunnels under the sea. Lota makes an easy day-trip from Concepción, with regular **bus services** provided by Buses J Ewart, leaving from Prat 535, near the train station.

Isla Santa María

From Lota's pier you can take a two-hour boat ride (Tues & Sat 10am; CH$3800; ☎43/876068) to **ISLA SANTA MARÍA**, a small, lush island with steep cliffs, rolling hills and a population of about 3000 farmers and fishermen. The island's mild climate and fertile soil have supported small Mapuche communities for hundreds of years. There are several secluded bays dotted around the island, with good beaches, sea lion colonies and excellent fishing for hake, bass and *congrio*. Other activities on offer include **horse rides** with René Guzman, **boat trips** to the sea lion colonies with Jorge Silva Chaparro, and, most unusually, **tractor rides** with Mario Muñoz. Basic accommodation and meals are provided by several family homes, including *Hospedaje Sra Vicky* (②) and *Hospedaje Roberto Ulloa* (②); there's also a **campsite** (CH$3000 per tent) with cold showers and a few rustic *cabañas* (③). None of these places has a phone, but there's a telephone message service on ☎43/885964. Boats **return** to Lota on Mondays and Fridays at 5.30pm.

Lebu

Seventy-six kilometres south of Lota, past a number of nondescript forestry and fishing towns, a 31-kilometre side road shoots off the highway to the small coastal town of **LEBU**, one of the few places still mining coal in this region. The main reason you might want to come here is for its huge, unspoilt **beaches**, including **Playa Millaneco**, 3km north, where you'll find several massive caves overgrown with ferns and lichen. Lebu's only other attraction is its pair of bronze cannons on display in the plaza, which were cast in Lima in 1778, and bear the Spanish coat of arms. No one is quite sure how they arrived in Lebu, but they were probably part of the booty brought back from Peru at the end of the War of the Pacific by Maximiliano Errázuriz, the owner of the local coal mines. The best place to **stay** is at *Hotel Central*, Pérez 183 (☎ & fax 41/511904; ④), a 110-year-old building with comfortable, excellently maintained rooms and a good **restaurant**.

Cañete

Back on the highway, 16km south of the turn-off for Lebu, **CAÑETE** is a busy agricultural town perched on a small rise above a bend in the río Tucapel. Just off the northern end of the main street, commanding fine views over the river valley, is the historic **Fuerte Tucapel**, founded by Pedro de Valdivia in 1552 and the site of his gruesome death at the hands of the Mapuche chief Lautaro two years later. The ruins – which amount to little more than a bit of stone terracing and four rusty cannons – actually date from the nineteenth-century reconstruction of the fort, when it was used in the later phases of the Arauco War. Just south of town, 1km down the highway, the **Museo Juan Antonio Ríos** (daily 9.30am–12.30pm & 2–6.30pm; CH$500) houses a fine collection of Mapuche artefacts, including textiles, silver jewellery, musical instruments and weapons. Perhaps the most striking exhibit is the *ruca* in the museum's garden – a traditional Mapuche dwelling made of wood and straw. In sedate contrast, the museum's upstairs room is given over to turn-of-the-century ceramics manufactured in Lota, giving a good example of middle-class tastes at the time. If you want to **stay** in Cañete, a good place to head for is the hundred-year-old *Hotel Gajardo* at Séptimo de Línea 817 (☎41/611218; ②), a family-run hotel in a charming building overlooking the valley. If you want a private bath, try the *Hotel Alonso de Ercilla* at Villágran 461 (☎41/611974; ③). The best place to **eat** is at the *Club Social* on the plaza, in an unprepossessing building but serving well-cooked meat and fish dishes. From Cañete, a dirt road climbs 46km to Parque Nacional Nahuelbuta (see p.266), while the highway curves south through a lower pass in the Cordillera de Nahuelbuta.

Lago Lanalhue

Ten kilometres out of Cañete, the road reaches the northern shore of **Lago Lanalhue**, nestling amongst dense pine forests on the western slopes of the coastal range. Its waters are crystal clear, and warmer than the Pacific, and its heavily indented shores form numerous peninsulas and bays, some of them containing fine white sand. There are several **campsites** and **hotels** dotted around the lake, including the *Posada Alemana* (☎41/618016; ⑤), a creaky old German farmhouse almost standing in the lake by the beach on its eastern shore. Close by is another fine old farmhouse, the *Hostal Licahue* (☎2/300 1086; ⑤), with a swimming pool, access to several forest walks, and good home cooking. Basic provisions can be bought in the village of **Contulmó**, about 5km along the highway – while you're here, carry on a couple of kilometres around the south shore of the lake to visit the **Molino Grollmus** (Jan–April Mon–Sat 10–11am & 6–7pm; free), an early twentieth-century wooden mill whose gardens contain one of the most impressive collections of *copihues* (Chile's national flower, the one featured on the boxes of the most common brand of matches) in the country. Some 44km east of Contulmó, the highway forks, with one branch heading to the town of Angol (see p.265), and the other continuing south to the Panamericana.

Down the Panamericana to the Salto del Laja and Los Angeles

From Concepción, the southern coastal route makes an interesting diversion but if you're in a hurry you'll want to take the direct 85-kilometre trunk road back to the Panamericana.

Heading south from here, the first major town you reach is **Los Angeles**, some 50km down the highway; halfway along this route, the Panamericana crosses the río Laja, giving excellent views down to the **Salto del Laja**, which rank among the most impressive waterfalls in Chile. Cascading almost 50m from two crescent-shaped cliffs down to a rocky canyon, they appear as a broad white curtain of foam, almost like a miniature Niagara Falls. There are parking spaces around the bridge (surrounded by tacky souvenir stalls), and a short path passes through the *Complejo Turístico Los Manatiales* (☎43/326365) to a closer viewpoint. The *complejo* has overpriced **rooms** (⑤) and **camping** areas (CH$8000), as do several similar establishments strewn around the highway and river, none of them attractive enough to make you want to stay. If you're relying on **public transport**, your best bet is to visit the falls on a short trip from Los Angeles on one of the frequent Buses Bío Bío services to Chillán – they run every fifteen minutes in both directions, so when you're ready to come back you can just flag one down without having to wait too long.

Los Angeles

LOS ANGELES itself is an easy-going agricultural town, pleasant enough with its leafy Plaza de Armas and bustling commercial core, but without any great attractions to grab your interest. Housed in the library on the southeast corner of the plaza is the town's single museum, the **Museo de la Alta Frontera** (Mon–Fri 8.30am–1pm & 2.30–8pm, Sat & Sun 10am–1pm & 5–8pm; free) where, amongst the stash of colonial rifles left over from the Arauco war, you'll find a collection of gleaming Mapuche silver ornaments and jewellery – best appreciated in January and February, when some of the items are displayed to stunning effect by a local Mapuche "model". While you're here, you could also wander up to the north end of Colón, eight blocks from the plaza, to take a look at the colonial **Parroquia Perpetu Socorro**, a church whose handsome colonnaded cloisters enclose a flower-filled garden. Otherwise, the town's main use is as a jumping off point for the beautiful scenery of the **Parque Nacional Laguna del Laja** (see below).

PRACTICALITIES

Arriving in Los Angeles by bus, you'll be dropped at the terminal on Avenida Sor Vicenta, the northern access road from the Panamericana; from here, plenty of *colectivos* go into the centre. You can get **tourist information** from the Oficina de Turismo (Mon–Fri 8.30am–12.30pm & 3–5.30pm) in the Municipalidad, on the southeast corner of the Plaza de Armas, as well as from Profo Turismo (Dec–March Mon–Fri 9am–1pm & 2.30–6pm; ☎43/322248), a private agency at Lautaro 252. Los Angeles is short on inexpensive **accommodation**, but you could try *Hotel Central* at Almagro 377 (☎43/323381; ②) for basic, adequate rooms off a courtyard, or *Residencial Almagro* (☎43/322782; ②), a family home with slightly gloomy rooms. Moving up the scale, *Hotel Winser*, at Rengo 138 (☎43/315140, fax 320348; ③–④), is a small, neat hotel with en-suite rooms, while *Hotel Mariscal Alcázar*, Lautaro 385 (☎43/311725; ⑥) is modern and well equipped. One of the best **restaurants** in town is the *Centro Español*, Colón 482, which, with twelve hours' advance notice, prepares huge, delicious paellas. Other good choices are *Julio's Pizza*, Colón 452, serving generously topped home-made pizzas, and *Donde Ramón* at Almagro 989, where the house speciality is *Pollona Angelina*, a great big stew of sausages and pork chops served in a clay pot. Los Angeles has two **laundries**: Lavajet Suprema at Valdivia 516 and Todo Lava at Colón 913, and **car rental** with First, Caupolicán 350 (☎43/313812), and Larma, Valdivia 158-B (☎43/320261).

Parque Nacional Laguna del Laja

Ninety-three kilometres east of Los Angeles, **Parque Nacional Laguna del Laja** (daily: Dec–March 8am–9pm; April–Nov 8am–6pm; CH$500; ☎43/237202) takes its name from the great green lake curling around the foot of 2985m **Volcán Antuco**, set in an otherworldly volcanic landscape of lava flows and honeycombed rock. The park boundary is 4km east of the village of **EL ABANICO**, reached by a mostly paved road from Los Angeles, but the Conaf hut, where you pay your entrance fee, is 12km on from the village (though they're thinking of moving it closer to the park boundary), and the **Centro de Informaciónes**, which offers talks and videos on the park, another kilometre beyond the hut. From here, an easy path leads a couple of kilometres to a pair of large, thundering waterfalls, **Saltos las Chilcas** and **Saltos del Torbellino**, fed by underground channels from the lake which emerge here to form the source of the río Laja. The road through the park continues east from the information centre towards the lake, passing a small **ski centre** (5km along the road) which operates from June to October on the slopes of the volcano. At this point, the road deteriorates into a terrible dirt track that skirts the southern shore of the lake for 22km, continuing to the Argentinean border. Few vehicles make it along here, and it provides an excellent walking trail through the sterile landscape with changing views of the lake and of the mountains of **Sierra Velluda**, in the southwest, which are studded with hanging glaciers.

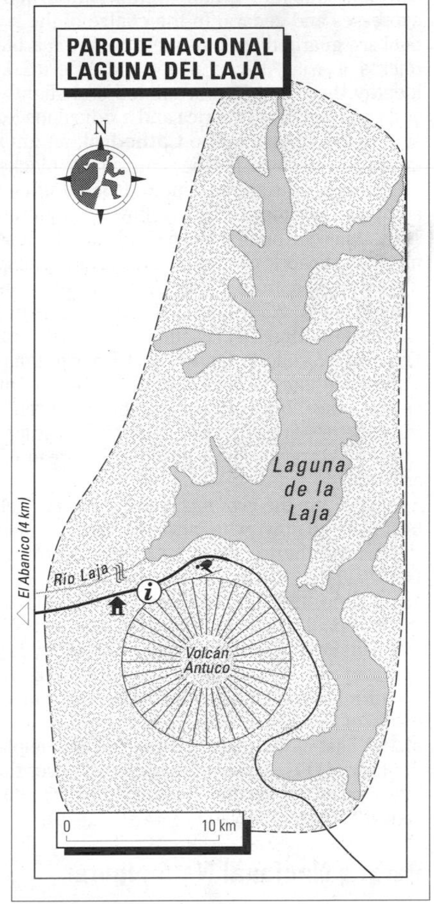

Getting to the park by **public transport** is difficult: from Los Angeles' Terminal Rural, at Villagrán 507, Buses ERS have three daily services to El Abanico, but from here it's a twelve-kilometre hike to the Conaf office, and another 5km to the lake. The only **accommodation** in the park is provided by the concessionaire *Cabañas y Camping Lagunillas* (☎43/323606), which has secluded camping areas (CH$6000 per site), four spacious *cabañas* (⑥) and a **restaurant**, by the banks of the río Laja, on the way to the Conaf administration.

Angol

Sixty-four kilometres southwest of Los Angeles, **ANGOL** is the final major town before Temuco, the gateway to the Lake District, and serves as a useful base for visiting the nearby **Parque Nacional Nahuelbuta**. The town's Plaza de Armas is one of the liveliest and most attractive in the region, full of kids on roller skates, toddlers on peddle cars and watchful grandparents sitting beneath the shade of the numerous elms, cypresses and cedars. In the centre of the square, the corners of a large, rectangular pool are guarded by four finely carved marble statues of women representing the continents of Asia, Africa, Europe and America. Dating from 1895, the stereotypes used to identify the continents are dated and slightly comical, including a feather headdress and skirt for Miss America and a ridiculous fez for Miss Asia. Standing on the southern side of the square is the **Cathedral**, an unexceptional red-brick church with a large tower. There's a far prettier church five blocks northwest, on the corner of Vergara and Covadonga – the adobe, square-fronted **Iglesia de San Buenaventura**, painted cream and pink, and topped by a yellow wooden tower. Founded by the Franciscan order in 1863, this was the first Spanish church built south of the Bío Bío, and was the centre of missionary work carried out by Franciscans amongst the Mapuches after the Jesuits were expelled from Chile. Angol's only museum, **Museo Dillman Bullock** (daily 10am–1pm & 2.30–6pm; CH$500) is out in the suburbs, 5km south down Avenida Bernardo O'Higgins, reached by *colectivo* from the Plaza de Armas. It's set within an agricultural college known as **El Vergel**, and contains a strange assortment of pre-Columbian funeral urns, a moth-eaten mummy, Mapuche artefacts, malformed foetuses and – most bizarrely – a number of cotton reels, all collected by Dr Dillman Bullock, the college's first director. It's worth visiting for the grounds alone, which are beautifully landscaped with an exuberant spread of flowers and shrubs, as well as sequoias and oaks.

Also within the grounds is the *Hostería El Angol* (☎45/712103 or 714741; ④), Angol's best place to **stay**, with large rooms in an old wooden house, and a good restaurant. In the centre, there's not a lot to choose from: *Residencial Olimpia*, at Caupolicán 625 (☎45/711162; ③) has reasonable rooms in a family home, while a couple of blocks along at no. 498, the *Club Social* (☎45/711103, fax 712269; ⑤) has light, airy rooms, an outdoor pool and a wood-panelled games room with fine old billiards tables. It also has a decent **restaurant**; another place to try is *Josánh Paecha* at Caupolicán 579, where you can eat in the attractive garden in fine weather. Angol's long-distance **bus terminal** is conveniently located on the corner of Caupolicán and Chorillos, one block north of the plaza, while rural services operate from the far end of Lautaro, three blocks east of the plaza. There's a very helpful **Oficina de Turismo** (☎43/711255) at the fork of O'Higgins and Bonilla, just over the river from the town centre. You can get information on Parque Nacional Nahuelbuta at **Conaf**'s office at Prat 191 (Mon–Fri 9am–12.30pm & 3–5.30pm; ☎43/711870).

Parque Nacional Nahuelbuta

From Angol, a dirt road (difficult to pass after rain) climbs 35km west to the entrance of **PARQUE NACIONAL NAHUELBUTA** (daily: Dec–March 8am–8pm; April–Nov 8am–5.30pm; CH$1800), spread over the highest part of the cordillera de Nahuelbuta. The park was created in 1939 to protect the only remaining araucaria trees in the coastal mountains, after the surrounding native forest had been wiped out and replaced with thousands of radiata pines for the pulp and paper industry. Today, it's a 68-square-kilometre enclave of mixed evergreen and deciduous forest, providing the coastal cordillera's only major refuge for wildlife such as foxes, pumas and *pudús* (pygmy deer). You're unlikely to catch sight of any of these shy animals, though if you look up amongst the tree trunks, you may well see large black woodpeckers hammering away. Of the park's trees, star billing goes to the towering araucarias, with their thick umbrellas of curved, overlapping branches covered in stiff pine needles. Some of these trees are over 40m high, and the most mature ones in the park are over a thousand years old. In addition to these are giant, 40m-high coigües, the smaller lenga, whose leaves turn dark red in autumn, and a dense undergrowth of ferns, shrubs and lichens.

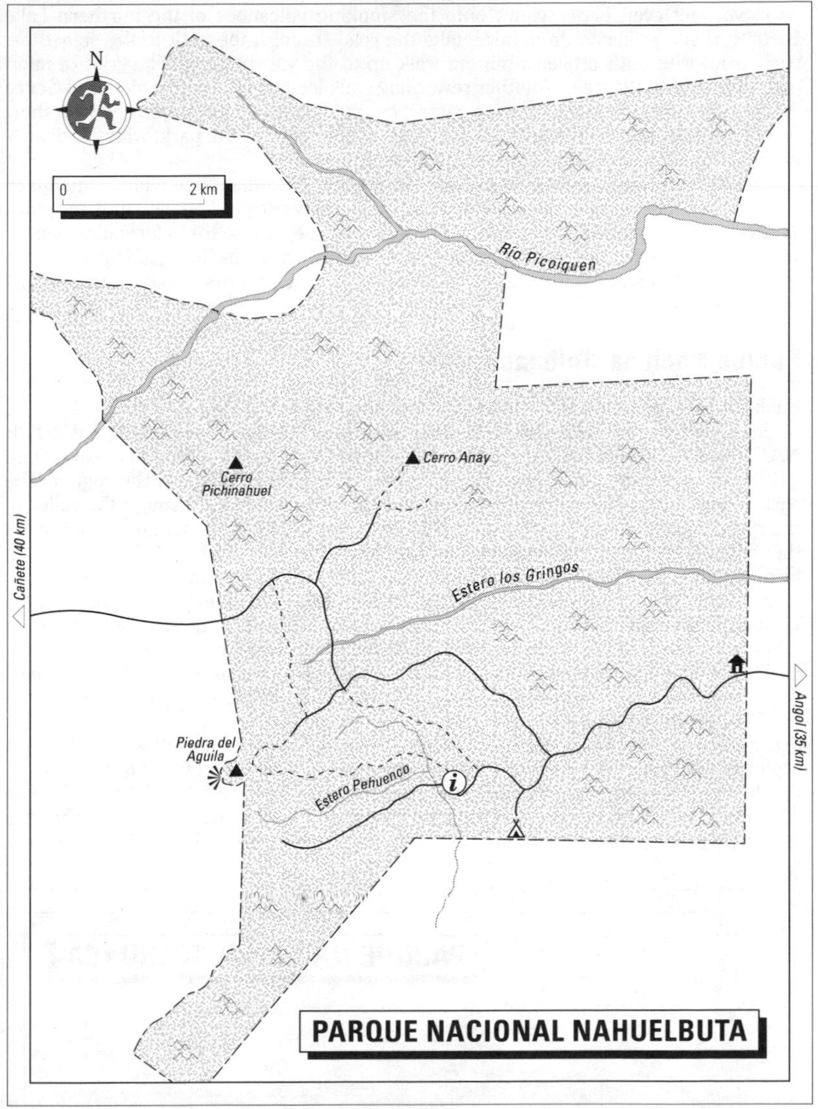

You can find out more about the park's flora and fauna at the **Centro de Informaciónes**, 5km west along the road from the entrance. From here, an easy four-kilometre footpath leads through the forest (look out for the giant araucaria about five minutes' walk along the path, estimated to be 1800 years old) up to the **Piedra de Aguila**, a craggy rock giving superb views which on clear days take in the whole width of Chile, from the Andes to the ocean. From a slightly lower, flatter rock a few metres west, you get even better views onto the smoking volcanoes of the northern Lake District. If you prefer to drive here, take the road through the park to the signed car park, from where it's a twenty-minute walk up to the viewpoint past a series of information panels on the trees. Another rewarding walk leads up the gentle slopes of **Cerro Anay**, 4km north of the information centre, reached by a jeep track followed by a short path. Its 1400m peak is the best place to take in the whole of the park, with the distribution of the different types of tree clearly standing out.

There's no regular **public transport** to Parque Nacional Nahuelbuta, though in January and February *micros* come here on Sundays from Angol's rural terminal. There are two **camping** areas (CH$5000 per site), one next to the information centre, with showers and toilets, and a more rustic one, with no facilities, about a twenty-minute walk away in Sector Coimallín. Bring all food, as there's nowhere to buy supplies in the park.

Parque Nacional Tolhuaca

Back on the Panamericana, 40km south of the turn-off to Angol, a detour into the Andean foothills will take you to another area of protected native forest, **PARQUE NACIONAL TOLHUACA** (daily: Dec–April 8am–9pm; May–Nov 8am–6pm; CH$1500), a pristine landscape offering some of the finest hiking in the region. The park covers a long and relatively narrow strip of land stretching through the valley of the río Malleco, hemmed in by steep, thickly wooded hills. Dominating the bottom of the valley is the wide and shallow **Laguna Malleco**, bordered by tall reeds rich in birdlife, while other attractions include waterfalls, small lakes and hundreds of araucaria trees. The best **approach** to the park is along the 57-kilometre dirt road (via the village of Inspector Fernández) branching east from the Panamericana, a couple of kilometres north of **Victoria** (a small, ramshackle town of no interest). This leads directly to the Conaf administration on the southeastern shore of Laguna Malleco, where you'll also find **camping** and picnic areas (CH$6000 per site). From here, a footpath follows the northern shore of the lake for about 3km through lush evergreen forest, leading to the **Salto Malleco**, where the lake's waters spill down into the río Malleco, forming a spectacular fifty-metre waterfall. About halfway along this path, another trail branches north, climbing steeply up the hillside before forking in two. The left fork follows the twelve-kilometre **Sendero Prados de Mesacura** across a gentle plain before climbing steeply again through dense forest. The right fork follows

the **Sendero Lagunillas** (also 12km), climbing moderately to a group of small lakes near the summit of Cerro Amarillo, from where you get fabulous panoramic views onto the surrounding peaks, including the 2800m Volcán Tolhuaca. Both of these are full-day hikes, requiring an early start. Following the flat path along the northern bank of the río Malleco eastwards, after about five kilometres you'll reach the trailhead of the eight-kilometre **Sendero Laguna Verde**, which climbs up and around a steep hill to the small, emerald-green Laguna Verde, 1300m above sea level and surrounded by soaring peaks. This makes a good camping spot, allowing you to spread the walk over two days.

Termas de Tolhuaca

From the Conaf administration, a terrible nine-kilometre dirt road (especially rough in the last few kilometres) leads to the **Termas de Tolhuaca** (☎45/881164, fax 881211), just outside the park's boundaries. The source of the *termas* is at the bottom of a narrow, rocky canyon, inside a large cave, where bubbling, sulphurous water seeps out of the rocks, and steam vents fill the cave with fumeroles, forming a kind of stone-age sauna. The small pools around the cave are too hot to paddle in, but a little further down the canyon, where the thermal water has mixed with cold stream water, there's a gorgeous natural pool that you can bathe in. The hot springs have been commercially exploited since 1898, shortly after they were discovered by a Russian surveyor who'd been hired to map the state's lands. The current administration operates two **hotels** (⑤–⑥), one down in the canyon, close to the cave, the other higher up, near a large swimming pool filled with thermal water. The rooms are very simple for the price, but the location (particularly of the lower hotel) is stunning. You can also visit the *termas* for the day, paying CH$5000 for access to the swimming pool, river and "cave sauna". It can get very busy here in January and February, especially at weekends, but outside these months the place is blissfully quiet. As well as the road from Parque Nacional Tolhuaca, the *termas* are also reached by a much better 33-kilometre road from Curacautín, 56km east of Victoria on the road to Lonquimay (see below). There's no public transport here.

The road to Lonquimay

At the dreary little town of **Victoria**, a good paved road branches west from the Panamericana to the small agricultural town of **Lonquimay**, 115km away, passing the entrance to the **Reserva Nacional Malcahuello-Nalcas** en route. There's nothing especially appealing about Lonquimay itself, but the road there – running through a narrow valley overlooked by towering volcanoes – is spectacular, particularly the stretch across the **Cuesta de las Raíces**. Fifty-six kilometres out of Victoria, the road passes through the logging town of **CURACAUTÍN**, from where a forty-kilometre dirt road branches south to Lago Conguillío, in **Parque Nacional Conguillío** (see p.280). As the northern gateway to the park, Curacautín has its fair share of hotels, including the staid but well-run *Hotel Plaza* (☎45/881256; ④) at Yungay 157 on the Plaza de Armas, and good-value *Hotel Turismo*, Tarapacá 140 (☎45/881513; ②), a clean, spacious old building offering good set meals. There's little to make you want to stay in town, however, and a better option is to carry on to the more dramatic scenery further along the road – including the 20m waterfall, **Salto del Indio**, just off the road, 14km out of Curacautín, and 8km beyond, the 50m **Saltos de la Princesa**.

Reserva Nacional Malalcahuelo-Nalcas

Some 30km west of Curacautín, you pass the entrance to the **Reserva Nacional Malalcahuelo-Nalcas** (daily: Dec–April 8am–8pm; May–Nov 8am–6pm; free), with the administration just a few hundred metres from the road. The Conaf staff are extremely helpful and friendly, and while there's no official **camping** in the reserve, they often let people camp for free in the gardens by the wardens' house. The main attraction here is a seven-kilometre trail, **Sendero Piedra Santa**, through different types of vegetation which, with an accompanying leaflet, illustrate the techniques used by Conaf to protect and manage native forest. The trail passes through quite separate areas of evergreen tepa (similar to the laurel, with strongly perfumed leaves), rauli (featuring a long, thin, cylindrical trunk), coigüe (up to 40m high, with branches only on the upper part of their trunks), lenga (home to the black woodpecker) and the famous araucaria. As well as being a good place to learn about Chile's native trees, parts of the path give excellent views onto 3125-metre-high **Volcán Llaima**, and 2890-metre-high **Volcán Lonquimay**. Count on taking around five hours to complete the trail.

Cuesta de Las Raíces

A couple of kilometres further along the main road from the administration, a gravel road (signed Volcán Lonquimay) branches north, and then forks in two. The left fork leads 4km to a small **ski centre** (☎45/881726) on the slopes of the volcano with bunk beds and a café, open year round. From here, the track continues up to a lookout point over **Cráter Navidad**, the gaping hole produced when the volcano last erupted, on Christmas Day, 1988. The right fork leads 26km to the village of Lonquimay across the **Cuesta de Las Raíces**, part of the volcanic chain that forms the highest peaks in this section of the Andes. This is a beautiful drive, through lush araucaria forests, with birds of prey swooping around the trees' branches. From the pass at the top, you get an extraordinary view down to the branches of the araucarias (which normally tower above you), spread out below like a vast green carpet.

An alternative route to Lonquimay is through the **Tunel de Las Raíces** (24hr; CH$1000 each way), reached by continuing along the paved road. Built in 1930 as a railway tunnel, in an abortive attempt to connect the Pacific and Atlantic by railroad, this four-and-a-half-kilometre tunnel is the longest in South America, but only wide enough for traffic to pass through in one direction at a time. Driving through is quite an adventure, as it's constantly dripping with water, and littered with potholes and puddles. In winter it's even more dramatic, when huge, metre-long icicles hang from the roof, transforming the tunnel into a sort of gothic, frozen cathedral. If there's no one behind you, it's worth pausing for a moment halfway through the tunnel and switching off your lights, just to experience the sensation of utter darkness.

Lonquimay

After the excitement of driving through the tunnel or crossing the Cuesta de Las Raíces, the rather sedate little town of **LONQUIMAY**, sitting at the end of the paved road, is something of a letdown. A quiet, bustle-free collection of small wooden houses and corner shops, the only interesting thing about the town is its bizarre street plan, laid out in the shape of a rugby ball with an elliptical Plaza de Armas. It is, however, beautifully located on a flat, fertile plain, to the east of the Andes – the only part of the country to cross the cordillera, claimed by Chile because the Bío Bío rises here, fed by numerous meandering rivers that flow through a hundred-kilometre stretch of pampa. There are several places to **stay** in Lonquimay, including the *Hotel de Turismo*, Caupolicán 915 (☎45/891111; ③), offering neat, sunny rooms with flowery curtains, and *Hostería El Pehuén*, O'Higgins 945 (☎45/891071; ④), with pleasant en-suite rooms and a good-value **restaurant**.

travel details

Buses

Chillán to: Concepción (every 20min; 1hr 15min); Curicó (11 daily; 2hr 30min); Los Angeles (every hour; 1hr 30min); Puerto Montt (7 daily; 7hr); Rancagua (10 daily; 3hr 30min); San Fernando (10 daily; 4hr); Santiago (14 daily; 5hr); Talca (12 daily; 1hr 45min); Temuco (8 daily; 3hr).

Concepción to: Cañete (every 40min; 2hr 20min); Chillán (every 20min; 1hr 15min); Contulmó (4 daily; 2hr 45min); Lebu (17 daily, 2hr 20min); Los Angeles (every 30min; 1hr 30min); Puerto Montt (15 daily; 7hr); Santiago (every hour; 6hr); Talca (11 daily; 3hr 45min); Temuco (every hour; 3hr 20min); Tomé (every 20min; 40min); Valdivia (11 daily; 5hr 20min).

Curicó to: Chillán (11 daily; 2hr 30min); San Fernando (every 15min; 40min).

Los Angeles to: Angol (every 30min; 45min); Chillán (every hour; 1hr 30min); Concepción (every half-hour; 1hr 30min); El Abanico (3 daily; 1hr 30min); Puerto Montt (9 daily; 5hr 45min); Rancagua (5 daily; 5hr); San Fernando (5 daily; 4hr 30min); Talca (15 daily; 3hr 20min); Temuco (16 daily; 2hr).

Rancagua to: Chillán (10 daily; 3hr 30min); Concepción (5 daily; 5hr); Lago Rapel-El Manzano (every 20min until 7.30pm; 1hr 40min); Los Angeles (5 daily; 5hr); Pichilemu (15 daily: 2hr 20min); Puerto Montt (10 daily; 11hr); San Fernando (every 15min; 40min); Santa Cruz (11 daily; 1hr 30min); Santiago (every 15min; 1hr); Talca (every 30min; 2hr); Temuco (10 daily; 7hr); Termas de Cauquenes (2 daily; 1hr 15min); Victoria (1 daily; 7hr).

San Fernando to: Angol (3 daily; 8hr); Chillán (10 daily; 4hr); Concepción (5 daily; 5hr 30min); Curicó (every 15min; 40min); Lago Rapel-El Manzano (every 15min; 2hr 20min); Los Angeles (5 daily; 4hr 30min); Pichilemu (every 45min; 1hr 40min); Puerto Montt (12 daily; 11hr 30min); Rancagua (every 15min; 40min); Santa Cruz (every hour; 45min); Santiago (every 15min; 1hr 30min); Talca (every 30min; 1hr 30min); Temuco (10 daily; 6hr 30min); Valdivia (7 daily; 8hr 30min).

Talca to: Chanco (3 daily; 2hr 20min); Chillán (12 daily; 1hr 45min); Colburn Alto (summer: 10 daily; winter: 3 daily; 2hr); Concepción (11 daily; 3hr 45min); Constitución (summer: every 30min, winter 4 daily; 1hr 20min); Curanipe (summer: every hour; winter: 3 daily; 1hr 30min); Los Angeles (15 daily; 3hr 20min); Panimávida (2 daily; 1hr 40min); Pelluhue (summer: every hour; winter 3 daily; 1hr 20min); Puerto Montt (9 daily; 9hr); Radal Siete Tazas (5 daily; 1hr 45min); Rancagua (every 30min; 2hr); San Fernando (1hr 30min); San Javier (every 15min; 30min); Santiago (17 daily; 3hr 20min); Temuco (15 daily; 5hr); Vilches Alto (summer: 8 daily; winter 2 daily; 1hr 30min); Villa Alegre (every 15min; 20min).

Trains

Chillán to: Concepción (1 daily; 2hr); Curicó (1 daily; 2hr 40min); Rancagua (1 daily; 4hr); San Fernando (1 daily; 3hr 15min); Santiago (3 daily; 5hr); Talca (1 daily; 1hr 40min).

Curicó to: Chillán (1 daily; 2hr 40min); Rancagua (1 daily; 1hr 20min); San Fernando (1 daily; 45min); Santiago (1 daily; 2hr 20min); Talca (1 daily; 1hr).

Rancagua to: Chillán (1 daily; 4hr); Curicó (1 daily; 1hr 20min); San Fernando (1 daily; 45min); Santiago (metrotrén, 11 daily; 40min); Talca (1 daily; 2hr 20min).

San Fernando to: Chillán (1 daily; 3hr 15min); Curicó (1 daily; 45min); Rancagua (1 daily; 45min); Santiago (1 daily; 1hr 45min); Talca (1 daily; 1hr 45min).

Talca to: Chillán (1 daily; 1hr 40min); Constitución (1 daily; 2hr); Curicó (1 daily; 1hr); Rancagua (1 daily; 2hr 20min); San Fernando (1 daily; 1hr 45min); Santiago (1 daily; 3hr 20min).

Flights

Concepción to: Puerto Montt (10 daily; 55min); Santiago (9 daily; 55min).

CHAPTER SIX

THE LAKE DISTRICT

The landscape gradually softens as you travel south along the Panamericana, and the road becomes bordered by undulating parkland where grazing herds of Aberdeen Angus ruminate under ancient oaks and beeches. This is the **LAKE DISTRICT**, a region that stretches from **Temuco** in the north to **Puerto Montt** in the south, 339km of lush farmland, dense forest, snow-capped volcanoes and deep, clear lakes, hidden for the most part in the mountains. As you drive, you can see far off to the east the occasional blue pyramid of a distant volcano, emitting clouds of ominous smoke, beneath which lie some of the twenty or so lakes from which the region gets its name.

For many years, the Lake District was covered with thick forests: to the north, the high, strange araucaria; on the coast, dense *selva valdiviana* and to the very south, thousand-year-old alerces. These forests were inhabited by the ferocious **Mapuche** (literally "people of the earth"), who fought off the Incas and resisted Spanish attempts at colonization for 350 years, before finally falling to the Chilean Army in the 1880s. This heritage is a badge of honour in today's Lake District, with at least half a million of the local population claiming Mapuche ancestry. Throughout the Lake District there are extensive Mapuche *reducciónes* (reservations), and many of the museums in the area have impressive displays on Mapuche history, the centrepieces of which are collections of beautiful **silverware**.

In little over a century since the subjugation of the Mapuche, the sweat of German, Austrian and Swiss settlers has transformed this region into some of the finest **dairy farmland** in Chile: much of the primeval forest has been grubbed up (though patches remain), pines and other non-native trees planted with a Prussian precision, and rolling meadowland laid out like a blanket. The imprint of the settlers is everywhere: Germanic churches in Valdivia, Germanic food in Futrono and, around Lago Llanquihue, third-generation immigrants who still speak only German at home.

The efforts of the European settlers opened the area up to travellers, and tourists have been coming here for a hundred years. The traditional centre of tourism is the adventure sports capital of **Pucón** on the shores of **Lago Villarrica**. Here you can climb the 2840-metre-high **Volcán Villarrica** (wearing a gas-mask as protection against the noxious fumes it emits), or descend into its bowels through long-cooled lava tubes, as well as hike, fish or swim in Lago Villarrica itself. Further south, the town of **Puerto Varas** on **Lago Llanquihue** is steadily mounting a challenge to Pucón, and offers the chance to climb the Mount Fuji-like **Volcán Osorno** (2652m), take a boat to Argentina across the serene **Lago Todos Los Santos**, or to hike in the wilderness of the **Parque Nacional Vicente Pérez Rosales**. The beautiful serenity of the sleeping volcanoes, and the blackened earth scorched by active ones characterize this unique corner of the world. In some places, such as **Parque Nacional Conguillío**, you can see the force of volcanic destruction where, in the space of a couple of miles a field of lava has torched a forest and buried it under molten rock. In other places you can feel a more benevolent side of this volcanic power, and in the **thermal springs** near **Puyehue** or **Liquiñe**, you can soak your bones in steaming hot mineral waters.

It isn't all mad tourist development, by any means: for those who have the time and energy to travel to more remote areas, the Lake District has places that are com-

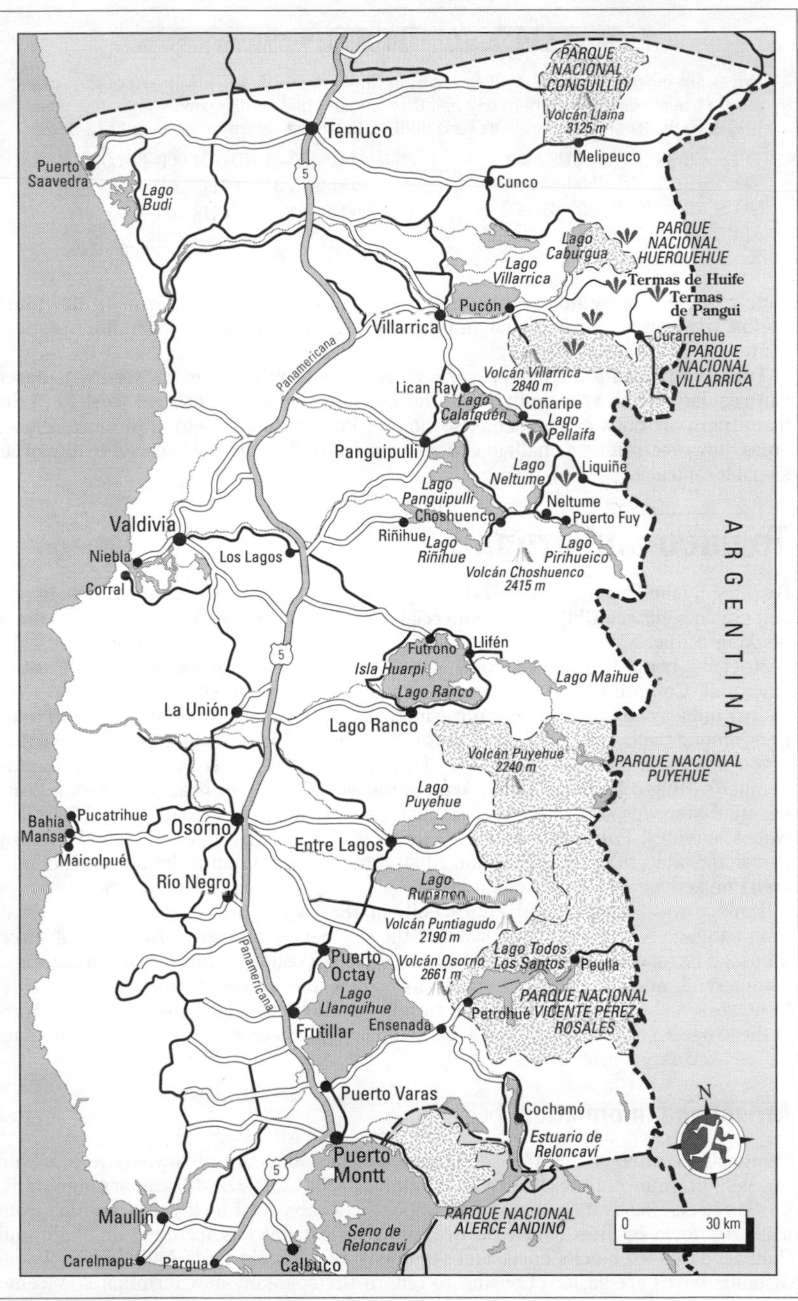

PARQUE NACIONAL CONGUILLIO
Volcán Llaina 3125 m
Temuco
Melipeuco
Puerto Saavedra
Lago Budi
Cunco
PARQUE NACIONAL HUERQUEHUE
Lago Caburgua
Lago Villarrica
Termas de Huife
Termas de Pangui
Pucón
Villarrica
Curarrehue
PARQUE NACIONAL VILLARRICA
Panamericana
Volcán Villarrica 2840 m
Lican Ray
Lago Calafquén
Coñaripe
Lago Pellaifa
Panguipulli
Lago Neltume
Liquiñe
Lago Panguipulli
Neltume
Choshuenco
Puerto Fuy
Valdivia
Riñihue
Lago Riñihue
Lago Pirihueico
Niebla
Los Lagos
Volcán Choshuenco 2415 m
Corral
ARGENTINA
Futrono
Llifén
Isla Huarpi
Lago Maihue
Lago Ranco
La Unión
Lago Ranco
Volcán Puyehue 2240 m
PARQUE NACIONAL PUYEHUE
Lago Puyehue
Bahia Mansa
Pucatrihue
Osorno
Maicolpué
Entre Lagos
Río Negro
Lago Rupanco
Volcán Puntiagudo 2190 m
Puerto Octay
Volcán Osorno 2661 m
Lago Todos Los Santos
Peulla
Lago Llanquihue
PARQUE NACIONAL VICENTE PÉREZ ROSALES
Petrohué
Frutillar
Ensenada
Puerto Varas
Cochamó
Estuario de Reloncaví
Puerto Montt
PARQUE NACIONAL ALERCE ANDINO
Maullín
Seno de Reloncaví
0
30 km
Carelmapu
Pargua
Calbuco
N
5

ACCOMMODATION PRICE CODES

Prices are for the cheapest **double room** in high season. At the lower end of the scale, **single travellers** can expect to pay half this rate, but mid- and upper-range hotels usually charge the same for a single as for a double. For more information see p.27 in Basics.

① Less than US$10/CH$4800
② US$10–20/CH$4800–9600
③ US$20–30/CH$9600–10,080
④ US$30–50/CH$10,080–24,000
⑤ US$50–75/CH$24,000–36,000
⑥ US$75–100/CH$36,000–48,000
⑦ US$100–150/CH$48,000–72,000
⑧ over US$150/over CH$72,000

pletely untouched by humanity like the hardly visited **Lago Riñihue** in the **Siete Lagos**, where you can simply sit and fish, or just relax and forget about the twentieth century.

Travelling around the main resorts of the Lake District is generally easy, as buses run regularly north and south along the Panamericana, and east and west from the main transport hubs of Temuco, Osorno and Puerto Montt. Getting to more remote areas, however, can be a challenge, as the roads are bad and only served by the occasional local truck.

Temuco and around

Bisected by the Panamericana, 677km south of Santiago, **TEMUCO** is the most important city in southern Chile – a commercial centre filled with jostling crowds and horn-honking traffic. Most visitors use it solely as a transport hub – gateway to the Lake District it's home to countless **bus services** – or as a base for exploring **Parque Nacional Conguillío** and the western mountains, but the city itself has a certain charm, not least its rich **Mapuche heritage**, evident in and around the colourful **markets**, among the best places in the country to hear the Mapuche language spoken. And if you don't visit another museum in the Lake District, you should at least pop into Temuco's **Museo Regional de la Araucanía**, where you'll see examples of some quite beautiful Mapuche silver treasure. Temuco's also proud of its connections with Chile's Nobel laureates, **Pablo Neruda** and **Gabriela Mistral** (Neruda was born in nearby Parral and went to school here, and Mistral taught here), but to be honest the links aren't milked as well as they could be.

Temuco was founded relatively recently in 1881, and it was only when the railway from Santiago reached here in 1893 that the city began to prosper. An influx of seven thousand European immigrants from seven different countries formed the farming and commercial nucleus which soon transformed the forested valleys and plains. Delicatessen shelves in the ultramodern supermarkets reflect the cosmopolitan origins of these people, where locally made camembert and cheddar are lined up behind dangling chorizos and *cotechini*.

Arrival and information

Temuco's **airport** (☎45/214896), Maquehue, lies 8km out of town. There are no buses to downtown, though Gira Tours (☎45/272041, fax 272042) can arrange transfers if you call in advance, and there are plenty of cabs outside. If you're coming from a nearby town by **bus**, you'll be dropped at the rural bus terminal on Pinto and Balmaceda, seven blocks north and seven east of the main Plaza Aníbal Pinto. Long-distance buses are so far choosing to ignore the spanking-new terminal at Vicente

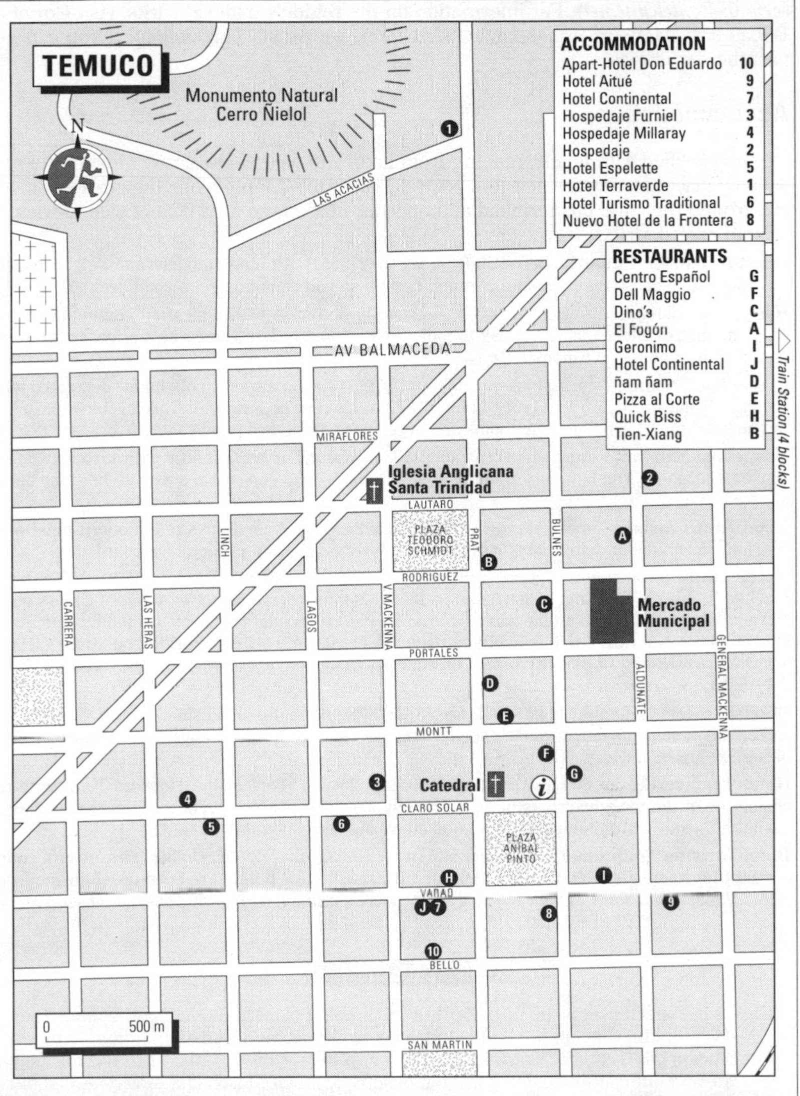

Pérez Rosales 01609, Sector Pueblo Nuevo (☎45/225005), instead pulling in at terminals all over the place – fortunately, most are within a seven-block radius of the plaza. The **train station** (☎45/233522) is eight blocks east of the town centre.

For general tourist information, visit the good **Sernatur** office on the north side of Plaza Aníbal Pinto (Jan & Feb Mon–Sat 8.30am–5.30pm, Sun 10am–2pm; Dec Mon–Fri 9am–5pm; rest of year Mon–Fri 9am–1pm & 3–5pm; ☎45/211969, fax 215509;

serna09@entelchile.net). For information on the region's national parks, visit **Conaf** at Bilbao 931 (Mon–Fri 9am–5pm; ☎45/211912), whose staff are helpful if you can get past the secretaries.

Accommodation

Temuco is filled with hotels, ranging from luxury to well below basic. Most of the reasonable places to stay are near the central Plaza Aníbal Pinto while the cheapest dives are around the rural bus terminal and open-air market, an area it's not safe to wander around after dark.

Apart-Hotel Don Eduardo, Bello 755 (☎ & fax 45/215554). Although modern and well-furnished, this apart-hotel doesn't seem to attract much custom so you can often get a good deal. ⑤.

Hospedaje, Aldunate 187 (☎45/270057). A clean, basic house with a pleasant communal sitting room and use of kitchen facilities. Ask to look at your room before you agree a price, as some are rather drab and have no windows. ②.

Hospedaje Furniel, Vicuña Mackenna 570 (☎45/237095). An attractive old house decorated with lashings of lilac paint. Run by a group of bubbly girls, it's very popular with Chilean students and so can be full during term time. The rooms are large, clean, basic and good value. ③.

Hospedaje Millaray, Claro Solar 471 (☎45/211384). A small, quiet first-floor flat with a jolly doll's-house atmosphere, run by a very friendly young landlady who appears to spend all her time painting the furniture. ②.

Hotel Aitué, Antonio Varas 1048 (☎45/211917, fax 212608). A medium-sized, modern hotel with tastefully decorated en-suite rooms – save for some very elaborate padded headboards. ⑤.

Hotel Continental, Antonio Varas 708 (☎45/238973, fax 233830). Hardly a cobweb has been touched in this old building, constructed in 1890. It's long been a favourite haunt of Chile's political and literary elite: room nine was favoured by Pablo Neruda, room ten (joined by a connecting door) by Gabriela Mistral, while presidents Cerda and Allende preferred room eleven. It's worth reserving one of the better en-suite rooms in advance although they cost an extra US$15. ④.

Hotel Espelette, Claro Solar 492 (☎ & fax 45/234805). After the initial shock of the kitsch green and cream sitting-cum-dining room, chock-a-block with colourful arts and crafts, the bedrooms are pleasantly bright and airy. ③.

Hotel Terraverde, Av Prat 220 (☎45/239999, fax 239455). Part of the Hotelera Panamericana chain, this is the most luxurious hotel in the city and is located in a quiet part of the outskirts. Facilities include a swimming pool and good international restaurant. ⑦.

Hotel Turismo Traditional, Claro Solar 636 (☎45/210583, fax 212932). Unlike at its modern counterpart (the *Nuevo Hotel Turismo* on Lynch), the rooms in this hotel have been tastefully modernized and still retain some of their old character. There's a small, uninspiring restaurant. ④.

COPIHUE

Chile's national flower is the rare **copihue**, a climbing plant found in the temperate rainforests of both the coastal and Andean cordilleras and most common between Concepción and Temuco. Reaching heights of up to four metres, the plant is extremely delicate and difficult to see. Only when it blooms between March and May does it stand out amongst other creepers, displaying conical, bell-shaped flowers five to ten centimetres long, ranging in colour from red and pink through to almost pure white. Don't confuse it with the coicopihue, a much more widespread plant that grows between Valdivia and the Magallanes. The coicopihue looks much more plastic, and has reddish flowers that bloom from November to April.

Traditionally, the Mapuche have used most of the copihue plant: the flowers are edible, tasting quite sweet, and the stems and roots are used for making fine baskets, as well as being ground up and used to treat gout, rheumatism and venereal disease.

Nuevo Hotel de la Frontera, Bulnes 726 (☎ & fax 45/200400). Facing each other across the street are two hotels, the *Clásico* and the *Nuevo*, that share many facilities. The *Nuevo* has the edge, as it's slightly more modern, and has a decent restaurant and piano bar. ⑤.

The Town

Temuco is divided by **Avenida Caupolicán** (the Panamericana): to the west are the city's quiet and exclusive residential districts, while to the east is an unattractive maze of shops and offices, rebuilt twice following a devastating fire in 1928 and a serious earthquake in 1960. The main commercial centre runs north from Plaza Aníbal Pinto along Bulnes and Prat – the cheaper shops and supermarkets are to be found on Portales between Bulnes and the train station.

Temuco's centre is the lush **Plaza Aníbal Pinto**, luxuriant with fine native and imported trees, set off by a large monument depicting the struggle between the Spanish and the Mapuche Indians. The square's a relaxing place to sit and watch the world go by, but there's not much of interest around it, save, at a push, for the **Cathedral** on the northwest corner, next to a tower block adorned with an enormous cross. A modern church, it's bright and airy inside, but the yellow stained glass casts a strangely discomforting light, and clashes terribly with the burgundy carpet.

A few blocks northeast of the Plaza, at the corner of Portales and Aldunate, the sprawling **Mercado Municipal** (Mon–Sat 8am–8pm & Sun 8.30am–3pm), built in 1929, is one of the best covered markets in the country. Festooned with strings of sausages and salamis, the stalls around the edge are all occupied by butchers and fishmongers, loud with the din of whirring bandsaws cutting through bones. In contrast, the centre of the market is a pleasant, peaceful retreat with benches and gurgling fountains, a choice of restaurants and countless craft stalls selling silver Mapuche jewellery, baskets, musical instruments, woven ponchos and more. At the entrance on Aldunate a traditional hat stall sells good-value sombreros.

Heading northwest of the market you come to **Plaza Teodoro Schmidt**, an attractive square planted with lime trees and European oaks, which in summer is filled with students selling their handiwork at small craft stalls. On the corner of the square by Lautaro and Mackenna, the clapboard **Iglesia Anglicana Santa Trinidad**, constructed in 1906, is one of the few remaining old buildings in the city centre.

Five blocks north of the Plaza Teodoro Schmidt is the **Monumento Natural Cerro Ñielol** (daily 8.30am–12.30pm & 2.30–6.00pm; CH$500), a densely forested hill with some enjoyable walking trails. From March to May, this a good place to see the red pendant **copihues** that are Chile's national flower (see box opposite), while on clear days the view from the hilltop **lookout point** is impressive: take a taxi or hike up, and relax in the café near the summit. It was on this hill in February 1881 that a treaty was signed between the Mapuche and the Chilean Army for the peaceful foundation of the future city, a fact commemorated by plaque on a Patagua tree.

Out to the east, opposite the train station, is Chile's liveliest and most colourful fruit and vegetable market, the **Feria Libre** (daily: Jan & Feb 8.30am–5pm; March–Dec 8.30am–4pm). Spread across the two blocks of Avenida Pinto between Barros Arana and Avenida Balmaceda, its every inch is crammed with fresh produce from all over Chile. This is a good place to savour typical local dishes in one of the numerous restaurants, or try one of the cold pig's trotters sold on every street corner. Star attraction for most visitors, though, has to be the Mapuche women in traditional dress, but be warned that they might well take offence at having their photographs taken.

Train buffs will want to walk the six blocks north to **Maestranza FFCC**, the old rail engine house, maintenance workshops and sidings (to visit, call ahead on ☎45/220984). Among the old rolling stock and machinery are a dozen steam engines built in the USA and Europe between 1915 and 1953. These were last rolled out and fired up in 1972 when Chile's road hauliers went on strike during Allende's presidency.

Museo Regional de la Araucanía

Ten blocks west of the centre (bus #1 or *colectivo* #11 from Manuel Montt) is the solid **Museo Regional de la Araucanía**, Av Alemána 84 (Mon–Fri 10am–5.30pm, Sat 11am–5.30pm, Sun 11am–noon; CH$500), in a fine 1920s house with a garden full of stately palms and totem poles of fat-faced people with buck teeth.

The most striking exhibit in the museum is the collection of silver **Mapuche jewellery**. Still worn by Mapuche women today, this ornamentation was originally an overt display of wealth, then a means of keeping treasure portable in times of crisis, and is now a distinct art form. The combination of functionality and exhibition is best represented in the *Punzón*, a cloak-fastening pin with an unfeasibly large orb or disc at one end. Also stunning are the *Trarilonko* (a necklace of discs and silver links) and a thick, three-stranded pendant called a *Prendedor Akuncha*. Sadly, the museum's display, while beautiful, is a bit short on detailed explanation.

Upstairs there's a room on the **war of Arauco** (the long, bitter and ultimately unsuccessful war the Spanish fought with the Mapuche in the three hundred years until the late nineteenth century), illustrated by reproductions of old engravings. There's also a display of arms, the Spanish breastplates and swords a stark contrast with the rocks and clubs of the Mapuche. The inequality of weapons makes you all the more impressed that the Mapuche held the Spanish off, a feat the mighty Incas in the north never achieved. In the light of this, the sad pictures of the nineteenth-century Mapuche forced into reservations (*reducciónes*) are all the more depressing.

The next room deals with the area's many colonizers. A picture of President Kruger, the Afrikaaner hero who stood up to the British in South Africa, is the whiskery testament to sixty Boers who made their way out here at the turn of the century to found the now defunct town of "Transvaal".

Eating and drinking

Temuco, as you might expect from a big town, is not short of good places to eat, but it *is* a bit short on things to do afterwards.

Centro Español, Bulnes 483. Enormous two-storey restaurant more suited to grand functions than quiet dining, though the downstairs bar has a charming, tiny garden. Ask for a plate of sliced *Jamon de Serrano*, a ham made locally. On Friday and Saturday, there's a special *Meson de Sancho*, a dinner-dance with *parilladas*.

Club Alemán, Senador Estebanez 772. Although a little way from the city centre, this twee Tyrolean chalet is a good place to come for typical German food.

MOVING ON FROM TEMUCO

Temuco is served by dozens of buses going up and down the Panamericana, and there's also a regular service to the coast at Puerto Saavedra and up into the mountains at Curacutín, Melipeuco and Parque Nacional Conguillío. There's also a frequent service to Pucón, Villarrica and the Siete Lagos. Most of the long-distance buses will leave from the new terminal (when the long-distance bus companies are persuaded to use it) and local buses use the rural bus terminal on Pinto and Balmaceda. Until the new terminal is used, long distance buses will leave from their own company's terminals – see the addresses in "Listings" opposite.

There's one train a day to Santiago, a journey which takes twelve hours, and six flights daily. Other flights leave Temuco's airport to most major cities.

Dell Maggio, Bulnes 536. The busiest café/restaurant in town, with an extensive menu, giant-size sandwiches and a good choice of cakes and ice creams. The large bar is open late, and has banquettes and intimate lighting.

Dino's, Bulnes 360. One of the best of a popular chain of restaurants in the south of the country with reasonably cheap set meals, and until 8.30pm on Thursdays and Fridays a self-service choice of seafood, fish and mixed meats, good value for the ravenous.

El Fogón, Aldunate 288. A lively, colourful restaurant with attention to detail right down to the jaunty hand-painted plates. Offal, meat and shellfish *parilladas* are a speciality and cost CH$10,000 for two. If you're brave, try the knockout Chuponao, a punch made with *aguardiente* (fire water).

Geronimo, Antonio Varas 983. Although the interior of this old wooden building has been deliberately "distressed" and a few "Wanted" posters stuck up, it's got little Wild West atmosphere. It's popular, though, especially in the evenings, and occasionally has live Country & Western music. Try the savoury pancakes.

Hotel Continental, Antonio Varas 708. Both the wall clock and time itself seem to have stopped in this traditional old hotel bar. At midday there is a clubby atmosphere with regulars sipping aperitifs and playing dice games underneath deer antlers on well-scarred wooden tables. A giant, rattling Kelvinator refrigerator adds to the charm.

ñam ñam, Portales on the corner of Prat. A lively and inexpensive sandwich bar which also serves basic and very cheap main meals.

Pizza al Corte, Cervecera Hungría, M. Montt 847. For real ale fans this bar is about as far as you are going to be able to get from the ubiquitous draught SCHOP. It is a basic, no-frills drinking establishment which serves its own home brew and cheap pizzas.

Quick Biss, Antonio Varas 755. Loud zebra stripes and soft natural woods are a unique combination for a fast-food restaurant and not typically Chilean. This is a great place for vegetarians, with a large self-service counter and salad bar.

Restaurant/bar del Cumbre, Cerro Ñielol. There is an excellent view over the city from the restaurant's terrace, and dinner-dances on Friday and Saturday nights. In the glare of daylight the restaurant does not look too inviting but it is worth a visit and a drink.

Tien-Xiang, Prat on the corner of Rodriguez. A comfortable, typically decorated Chinese restaurant with efficient service and good-value food.

Listings

Airlines AVANT, Prat 515, Local 24 (☎45/270670, fax 270843); Iberia-American Airlines, M. Bulnes 351 of 71 (☎45/215321); KLM, Claro Solar 727 (☎45/214807); Ladeco, A. Prat 565, Oficina 102 (☎45/213180); Lan Chile, Bulnes 655 (☎45/211339).

Banks and exchange Cambio Cautín, M Bulnes 743 (☎45/212840); Cambio Global, Bulnes 655, Oficina 1 (☎45/213699).

Buses Bío Bío, Lautaro 853 (☎45/210599); Erbuc, Miraflores 1149 (☎45/233958); Igi Llaima, on the corner of Bulnes 99/Miraflores (☎45/210241); JAC, Mackenna 798 (☎45/210313); Lit, San Martín 894 (☎45/211483); Nar Bus, Terminal de Buses Rurales, Of 4, Balmaceda (☎45/211611); Power, Bulnes 174 (☎45/236513); Tas Choapa, Antonio Varas 609; Tur Bus, Lagos 538 (☎45/234249); Turibus, Bus Norte, Cruz del Sur & 671 Vicuña Mackenna (☎45/210701).

Car rental Avis, V Mackenna 448 (☎45/238013); Christopher, Bulnes 667 (☎ & fax 45/211680); First, Antonio Varas 1036 (☎45/233890, fax 211828); Hertz, Las Heras 999 (☎45/235385); JM, Bello 755 (☎45/214133). Many companies also have kiosks at the airport.

Consulates France, Antonio Varas 708 (☎45/238973); Germany, Caupolicán 648 (☎45/211143); Holland, España 494 (☎45/247292); Italy, Trizano 411 (☎45/212658); Spain, M Montt 816, Oficina 31 (☎45/210976).

Hospital Hospital Regional, M Montt 115 (☎45/212525); Clinica Alemána, Senador Estébanez 645 (☎45/244244).

Laundry Marva, M Montt 415 (between Lynch and Lastteras).

Shopping For local crafts, try Casa de Arte Mapuche, Matta 25-A (☎45/213085). Also try the Plaza Teodoro Schmidt, and the Feria Libre.

Telephone centre Entel, Prat 505.

Travel agencies Gira, Andrés Bello 870, Oficina 5 (☎45/272041, fax 272042) is a highly respected local operator and can arrange tours to Mapuche *reducciónes*, the coast and the national parks, as can Christopher, Bulnes 667, Local 112 (☎45/211680), the Temuco office of a countrywide chain.

Parque Nacional Conguillío

Leaving the Panamericana and driving east out of Temuco, you'll see the grey peak of Volcán Llaima (3125m), about 90km away, looming up on the horizon. Wrapped around its neck is **PARQUE NACIONAL CONGUILLÍO** (8am–9pm but very variable; CH$2500), a park the volcano has been doing its best to destroy with belch after belch of foul black lava. It's a fascinating sight – the northern sector is lush, rich high forest, with steep cliffs covered in araucaria trees draped in furry lime-green moss. In the south, however, the volcano has wreaked havoc. The road passes over a wide lava flow, consisting of either rolling plains of thin dust or walls of recently congealed spiked rock, and across the valley you can see two isolated hillocks of green in a sea of black – all that was missed by the unstoppable burning rivers.

The volcano dominates the park, a malevolent smouldering presence, biding its time before its next eruption. It's one of the three most active volcanoes on the continent (Chile can claim another, in Villarrica near Pucón, see p.293); its last serious eruption was in 1957, though as recently as 1994 a lake, Lago Arco Iris, was formed by a lava flow blocking a river. You pass the new lake on the road to the administration from the south; it's now as clear as ice, pierced only by the silver trunks of massive dead trees.

The northern route into the park is through the village of **Curacautín** (97km from Temuco), entering the park at Sector Laguna Captren, while the southern road from **Melipeuco** enters at Sector Truful-Truful. The Park Administration sits midway between the two, to the northeast of Volcán Llaima, near the wide Lago Conguillío, where you'll also find an excellent visitor centre (daily 9am–1pm & 3–7pm).

Exploring the park

The park splits neatly into two main sectors – formed by the volcano's western and eastern slopes – each with its own seasonal appeal. The western slopes, otherwise known as Sector Los Paráguas, shine in winter, boasting a small ski centre with breathtaking views, two drag lifts and a refuge near the tree line, but there's no hiking here and in summer, the focus shifts to the **eastern slopes**, which form the bulk of the park and are further subdivided around the two entry points (see opposite).

Those with sufficient experience can make the difficult twelve-hour **ascent of Volcán Llaima**, but you need permission from Conaf (who will want evidence of your ability) and to be prepared to deal with crevasses and fumeroles. Aside from this, the best trek in the park is the three-hour **Sierra Nevada hike** which starts from Playa Linda on the eastern shore of Lago Conguillío, and heads up through the forest towards the mountains, before plummeting down to the sedimenting, evaporating Lago Captren, west of your starting point. The other long trail in the park, **Los Carpinteros**, is a pretty easy five-hour round-trip, the highlight of which is an araucaria that's estimated to be 1500 years old; this trek also starts from Lago Captren.

Less strenuous activities are available in summer, with details posted on the visitor notice board. These include guided hikes along the trails, excursions to other parts of the park, and talks on native birds and mammals. You can go boating on the lake – boats cost CH$1500 an hour from the shop which doubles as the reception for the *cabañas* (see opposite) – or take one of the hour-long self-guided nature rambles through the beautiful forest in Sector Truful-Truful. The visitor centre also has excellent displays – the best in Chile – on the geology, flora and fauna of the park. The exhibition on vulcanism is particularly fascinating, especially with the brooding presence of

Volcán Llaima looming the other side of the window: look out for the pyroclastic rock (a piece of material thrown out from the volcano when it erupted), a nugget of which has been sculpted by the air through which it flew into a smooth bomb-shape.

Park practicalities

Getting to the park without your own transport is difficult, though buses will take you as far as the gateway towns. The southern gateway to the eastern section is the tiny village of **MELIPEUCO**, 91km east of Temuco and 30km south of the Park Administration. Nar Bus (☎45/211611) runs eight **buses** a day from Temuco (4 on Sunday), often met in summer by Sr Desiderio Villeblanca Contreras, who'll ferry you to the park in his truck for CH$2000 if there's a full load. If he's not there, ask in the village shops for a lift or hitch. If you get stuck in Melipeuco, there's a surprisingly good *hostería* called *Hue Telen* (☎45/581005), which has wood-stove heated *cabañas* (④) and a basic double room (③).

The northern route into the park is through the village of **CURACAUTÍN** (see p.269), 97km from Temuco and 30km from the Administration; Buses Erbuc (☎45/233958) and Buses Bío Bío (☎45/210599) run about twenty services daily from Temuco. From Curacautín, you can get a taxi (CH$16,000) to the park.

Getting to the ski centre in the western section of the park is also tricky. Buses go the 106km from Temuco to the western ski slopes in winter, though off season rural buses stop 20km short at the village of **CHERQUENCO**.

There are plenty of **places to stay** in the park, all pretty pricey. On the edge of a dense wood, 6km in from the Melipeuco entrance, is a new complex of expensive five-person *cabañas* called *La Baita* (☎45/450161, fax 236037; *labaita@entelchile.net*; *www.labaita.co.cl*; ⑥); it's also an **activity centre**, co-ordinating trekking and ecotourism in the summer, and skiing and snow-walking in the winter, with other programmes run year-round. There are cheaper *cabañas* (☎45/214363; ⑤–⑥) near the Park Administration – ask in the well-stocked shop on the shores of Lago Conguillío; the lower-priced ones are circular huts strapped to trees and quite a novelty, though the bedding provided is useless. **Camping** in the park is extraordinarily expensive. There are about eighty sites, mainly at Lago Conguillío and Lago Captren, all run by concessionaires charging CH$12,000 a pitch. They're only open from November to April. Wild camping is not allowed.

West of Temuco to the coast

With two national parks in the cordillera east of Temuco, it's understandable that very few visitors turn their attention westwards towards the **coast**. However, if you've time to spare or you've had enough of mountains and lakes for the moment, the seaside here is a refreshing change, with some very pretty beaches and Lago Budi, Chile's only salt-water lake, rich in birdlife. The trip out here is interesting too, as the road passes through Mapuche communities where you'll see people living in traditional *rucas* (large communal thatched houses).

Puerto Saavedra

At the mouth of the Imperio River, 85km west of Temuco is **PUERTO SAAVEDRA**, dull as ditchwater but surrounded by very good beaches and an excellent place for both fishing and bird-watching. Once a thriving port, it was hit by a tidal wave in 1960 that not only flattened all its houses but also completely changed the course of the river near its mouth. Luckily, the inhabitants realized that a wave was coming and headed for higher ground in time.

Easily reached by bus from Temuco, the village boasts four good little restaurants, all of which have clean, basic **rooms**: the best are *El Viejo Roble*, Ejército 1134

(☎45/634048; ③) and *Hostería Vista Hermosa,* Villa Maule (☎45/235549; ③). Four kilometres south of Puerto Saavedra is the extremely popular *Hostería Boca Budi* (☎45/634044; ④), beautifully sited on the coast.

Lago Budi and the coast road south

Some 22km south of Puerto Saavedra, a little in from the coast, is **Lago Budi**. Chile's only saltwater lake, it's not that impressive to look at, but it's a rare treat for birdwatchers: the lake's an extremely important breeding ground for an estimated one hundred and thirty species and a haven for a multitude of birdlife, especially black-necked swans. The surrounding countryside of gently undulating farmland is interesting too, as it's part of a large Mapuche *reducción*.

It's difficult to get down here using public transport, but Temuco's tour operators organize day-trips which cost around CH$13,000 (minimum of 4 people). Those with a car should consider driving the hundred kilometres south to Valdivia, along a beautiful and almost unused road along a very remote, uninhabited coast.

Lago Villarrica and around

There's not much of interest on the central plain south of Temuco, and the next stop is tucked in the mountains some 86km to the city's southeast – **Lago Villarrica**, the most visited of all Chile's lakes. The reason for its popularity lies not in its size – at only 173 square kilometres, this isn't one of the Andes' biggest lakes – nor even in the beauty lent by the lush forests along its northern shore and the symmetrical cone of Volcán Villarrica (2840m) to the east. Rather, the draw is the presence of **Pucón**, 25km along its eastern shore, a town which has made full use of its natural bounty – including two national parks, thundering rivers and a clutch of accessible hot springs – to become one of Chile's prime outdoor adventure centres. At the other end of the lake to Pucón is **Villarrica**, a rather dreary, functional town but with a beautiful view.

The area around Lago Villarrica was first settled by the Spanish in the late sixteenth century, but they didn't have much time to enjoy their newly found territory, as their towns were sacked by the Mapuches in 1602. Recolonization didn't take place until the Mapuches were subdued 250 years later. With the arrival of the railroad from Santiago in 1933, the area's popularity as one of Chile's prime holiday destinations became secure.

Villarrica

Despite sitting on the southwestern edge of the lake with a beautiful view of the volcano, **VILLARRICA** the town has a distinct lack of holiday atmosphere and most people drive straight through it on the way to Pucón. It's pleasant enough, though, and it does have the merit of being cheaper and less crowded than its illustrious neighbour.

Those interested in the Mapuche will leap at Villarrica's sole tourist attraction, the municipal **Museo Histórico y Arqueológico**, on the main drag at Pedro de Valdivia 1050 (Mon–Fri 9am–1pm & 3–7.30pm; CH$100). It offers some good displays of silver jewellery and musical instruments, and an exclusive collection of unusual Mapuche masks, while in the garden, a traditional thatched *ruca* has been constructed employing thatching and wattling techniques unchanged for centuries. If you're here in season, you might witness further Mapuche celebrations in the annual **festival** (late Jan to early Feb), rich in traditional crafts, music and dance, while you can pick up other crafts year-round at the **Feria Artesenal**, around the corner from the museum on calle Acevedo.

And that's pretty much all there is to do, other than wander down General Körner – named after the architect of the Chilean Army, the man who introduced the goosestep

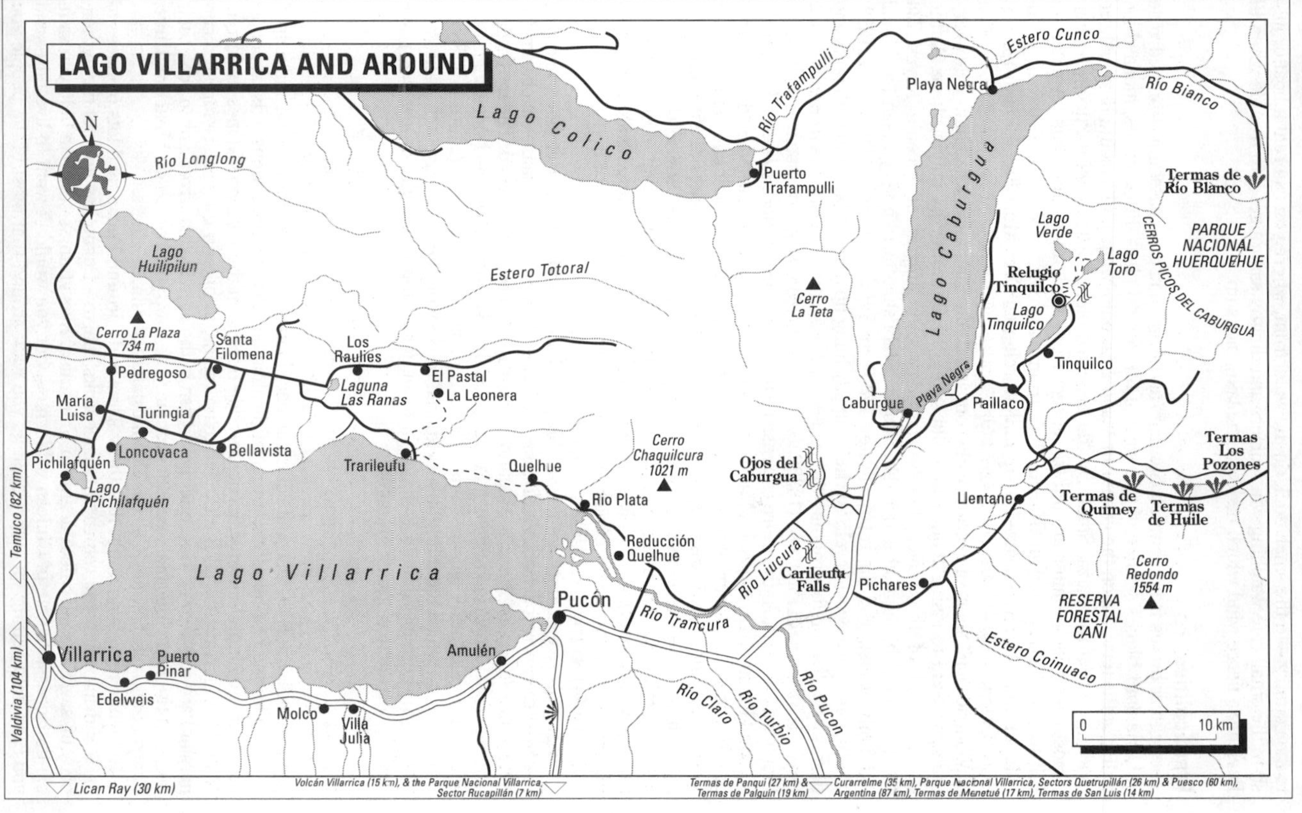
LAGO VILLARRICA AND AROUND
N
Lago Colico
Río Longlong
Río Trafampulli
Estero Cunco
Playa Negra
Río Blanco
Puerto Trafampulli
Termas de Río Blanco
Lago Huilipilun
Lago Caburgua
Lago Verde
Lago Toro
PARQUE NACIONAL HUERQUEHUE
CERROS PICOS DEL CABURGUA
Refugio Tinquilco
Lago Tinquilco
Tinquilco
Estero Totoral
Cerro La Teta
Cerro La Plaza 734 m
Santa Filomena
Los Raulies
El Pastal
La Leonera
Laguna Las Ranas
Pedregoso
María Luisa
Turingia
Loncovaca
Bellavista
Caburgua
Playa Negra
Paillaco
Pichilafquén
Lago Pichilafquén
Trarileufu
Quelhue
Cerro Chaquilcura 1021 m
Ojos del Caburgua
Termas Los Pozones
Llentane
Termas de Quimey
Termas de Huile
Río Plata
Reducción Quelhue
Río Liucura
Carileufu Falls
Pichares
Cerro Redondo 1554 m
Lago Villarrica
Pucón
Río Trancura
RESERVA FORESTAL CAÑI
Estero Coinuaco
Villarrica
Puerto Pinar
Amulén
Edelweis
Molco
Villa Julia
Río Claro
Río Turbio
Río Pucon
0
10 km
Temuco (82 km)
Valdivia (104 km)
Lican Ray (30 km)
Volcán Villarrica (15 km), & the Parque Nacional Villarrica, Sector Rucapillán (7 km)
Termas de Panqui (27 km) & Termas de Palguín (19 km)
Curarrelme (35 km), Parque Nacional Villarrica, Sectors Quetrupillán (26 km) & Puesco (60 km), Argentina (87 km), Termas de Menetué (17 km), Termas de San Luis (14 km)

to the country – to the small dock on the waterfront, where you can rent a boat or just sit in the small café watching windsurfers and dinghy sailors get into trouble when El Puelche, a fierce wind which bedevils the lake, picks up.

Practicalities

The regular **buses** from Temuco, Santiago and Argentina drop passengers on Pedro de Valdivia, four blocks south and one west of the central plaza. Rural buses, meanwhile, pull in at the terminal on the corner of Manuel Antonio Matta and Vicente Reyes, three blocks south of the plaza. Small shuttle buses connect the town with Pucón, leaving almost every five minutes around the corner from the long-distance bus terminal, on Bilbao. There's an excellent **Oficina de Turismo** at Pedro de Valdivia 1070 (daily: mid-Dec to mid-March 8.30am–11pm; mid-March–mid-Dec Mon–Fri 8.30am–1pm & 2.30–6.30pm; ☎45/411162, fax 414261; *turis@entelchile.com*).

Villarrica isn't short of **accommodation**, and if you don't mind a half-hour ride every time you want to visit Pucón, you could save a bit of money by staying here. At the cheaper end of the scale, there's *Hospedaje San Martín* at Vicente Reyes 734 (☎45/412043; ②), a good bed-and-breakfast establishment in a very clean traditional old family house, and the relatively new *La Torre Suiza*, Francisco 969 (☎45/411213; ①–②), run by two world cyclists who've finally hung up their pedals, and with tents and dorms as well as double rooms. Mid-range, try *Hospedaje & Cabañas Miranda*, Vicente Reyes 1037 (☎45/411309, fax 413332; ③), where the *cabañas* and upstairs rooms have their own kitchens. At the more expensive end of the market there's *Hotel El Ciervo* on General Körner 241 (☎45/411215; ⑤), a converted family house owned by descendants of early German immigrants, with an attractive garden, a swimming pool and a terrace overlooking the lake. **Camping**'s also an option, but both the lakeside sites on Playa Lopez near the eastern end of town are exposed to the wind. *Du Lac* (Dec–March; ☎45/412097; CH$8000) is the better option, planted with shrubs that offer some shelter, and with a good café in which to take refuge. There's more camping along the road to Pucón, but it's very expensive – *Eco-Camping Corentoso*, km 15 (Jan–Feb; ☎45/441061), costs CH$13,500 a site, for example.

Villarrica's **restaurants** are reasonably priced, many with far superior views to any in Pucón. A carnivore's delight, *Las Brasas*, Pedro de Valdivia 529, specializes in chargrilled meat, while *El Rey del Marisco*, Valentín Letelier 1030, is best for seafood. The most popular lunch spot in town is *Treffpunkt*, Pedro de Valdivia 640, which has good-value set meals, while for a quiet drink on rare calm sunny days visit *Parque Nautico*, Arturo Prat 880, a bar-restaurant which has a bright but exposed balcony right on the edge of the lake.

Though there are limited facilities in town, for all tourist services, however, you'll have a much better choice in Pucón.

Pucón

Nature smiled on **PUCÓN**, just 25km further along the lake from Villarrica, and helped turn it into one of Chile's great tourist destinations. Every year, thousands of people flock here to climb Volcán Villarrica, to ride horses on the volcano's slopes in Parque Nacional Villarrica, to raft the río Trancura rapids, to hike in the remote forested corners of Parque Nacional Huerquehue, to fish in the crystal-clear rivers, or to soak their bones in the many thermal spas surrounding the town: the *termas* de Menetué, Huife, Panqui, San Luis, Quimey-Co, Los Posones and Palguín.

But while there's no doubt that there's lots to do around Pucón, and lots of places to eat and drink when you return, the place lacks charm – Pucón has none of the authenticity of, say, San Pedro de Atacama or Valparaíso. Everything's set up to help you sample the accessible side of Chilean wilderness, but you wouldn't want to live here, and you can't help getting the impression as you walk around that most of the people you

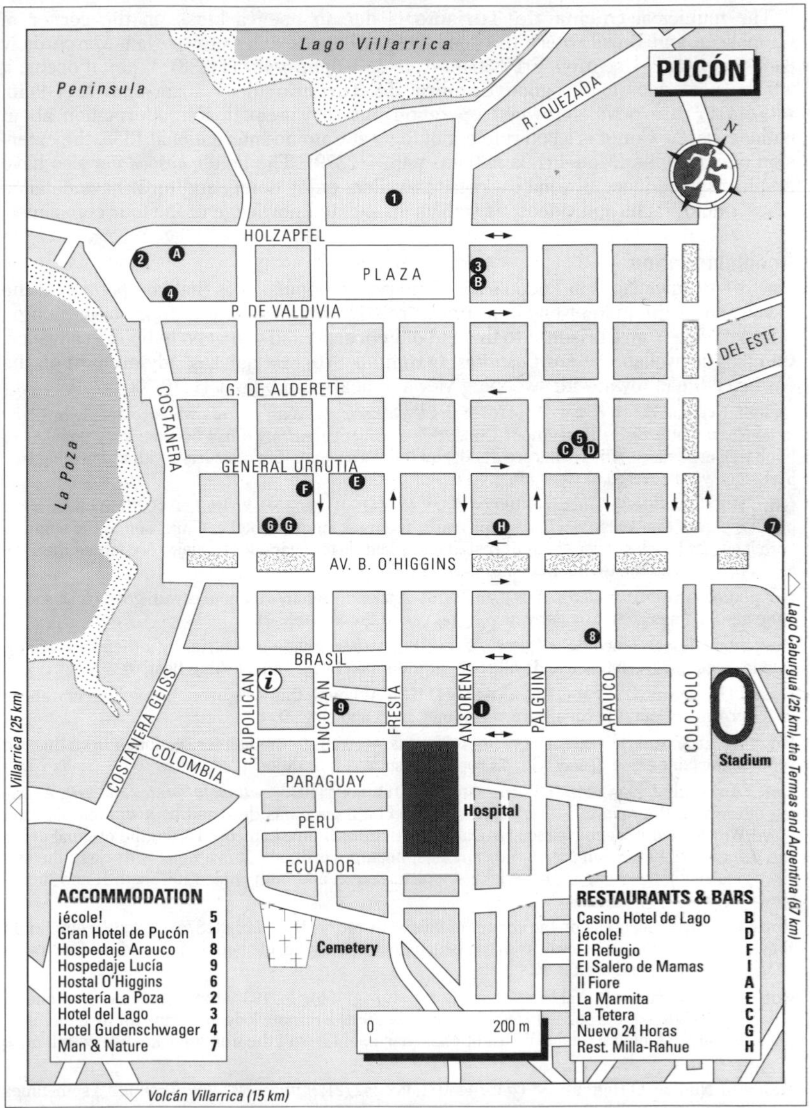

meet are only after your money, a feeling that's mercifully absent in much of the rest of Chile. Still, this probably won't stop you enjoying yourself.

Arrival and information

Pucón doesn't have a main bus terminal. Buses JAC and Tur Bus have their own purpose-built large terminals, the former at Palguín and Uruguay, the latter on O'Higgins on the outskirts of town. Other buses stop at a terminal on O'Higgins and Palguín.

The municipal **Oficina de Turismo** is due to open a kiosk on the corner of Caupolicán and Brasil where the road from Villarrica enters town (Jan–March daily 8am–9pm; April–Dec Mon–Fri 8.30am–1pm & 3–5pm; ☎45/443338). When it opens, it will be next door to the good **Camara de Turismo** (daily 10am–1pm & 4–9pm; ☎45/441671), a privately owned operation but very helpful. For information about national parks, **Conaf** is a taxi-ride out of town at Camino International 1355, the extension of O'Higgins (Mon–Fri 9am–6pm; ☎45/412379). The better *hospedajes* also have first-hand experience of what overseas travellers enjoy doing, and most have detailed maps, photographs and videos, as well as up-to-date knowledge of the tour companies.

Accommodation

One of the advantages in Pucón's meteoric rise in popularity is that competition at the lower end of the market has kept prices relatively stable. At the upper end, though, prices double from Christmas to the end of February, and you need to book in advance. Camping is available at *Los Castaños*, O'Higgins 870, in a quiet, shady orchard on the eastern edge of town, with sweeping views of fields and hills (CH$10,000).

¡école!, Urrutia 592 (☎ & fax 45/441675; *trek@ecole.mic.cl*). With owners who are deeply involved in conservation projects throughout Chile, this excellent *residencial* has become very popular, so book well in advance. The rooms are good, and there's a vegetarian restaurant with a charming trellised courtyard covered in vines. ③.

Gran Hotel de Pucón, Holzapfel 190 (☎ & fax 45/441001; *ghp-sk@entelchile.net*). Right on the most popular part of the beach, the *Gran* is probably the most famous hotel in Chile, and in the summer both it and its beach get very busy. It rested on its laurels for years until a major fire forced the owners to bring it into the twentieth century. ⑧.

Hospedaje Arauco, Arauco 272 (☎45/442223). A friendly family-run house, with good clean rooms – the garden ones are particularly nice – and use of the kitchen. ②.

Hospedaje Lucía, Lincoyán 565 (☎45/441721). Another private house run by a friendly landlady, who lets you use the kitchen and will rent out mountain bikes and a fishing boat. ②.

Hostal O'Higgins, O'Higgins 136-A (☎45/441153). Although this is right on the main avenue above an ice-cream parlour, the rooms are very quiet, light and airy. ④.

Hostería La Poza, Holzapfel 11 (☎45/441320, fax 441958). In the quieter section of town this is a very comfortable place to stay with all rooms en-suite in a traditional old house. ⑤.

Hotel Antumalal, 2km outside Pucón (☎45/441011, fax 441013; *antumalal@entelchile.net*). A little out of town on the road to Villarrica, this architectural gem was designed by a student of Frank Lloyd Wright, and it looks characteristically low-slung and unashamedly 1960s (the original decor and furnishings have been preserved) amongst beautiful grounds. It is a hotel with class: the service is excellent, the views over the lake are picturesque, and both Queen Elizabeth II and Jimmy Stewart have stayed here. ⑧.

Hotel del Lago, Ansorena on the corner of Valdivia (☎45/441873, fax 441875). A luxury hotel right above the casino one block away from the beach. Its facilities include both indoor and outdoor swimming pools, a gym and sauna. ⑧.

Hotel Gudenschwager, Valdivia 12 (☎ & fax 45/441156). In 1930, the descendants of one of Villarrica's 1880s settlers opened *Hotel Gudenschwager* as a remote lodge catering for fly-fishermen. The old wooden building retains its traditional charm, but it isn't the tranquil lake hideaway it once was. ⑥.

Man and Nature, O'Higgins 758 (☎45/443081, fax 442721; *nature_c@hotmail.com*). It's sometimes got a rather unfriendly atmosphere, but the dorm beds in this Israeli-owned hostel-cum-travel agency are the cheapest in town. Open in summer only. CH$200 per bed.

The Town

Your first sight of Pucón will probably be the bright paper flowers for sale, stuck into bushes by the side of the road – not real, but very pretty, rather like Pucón itself. And Pucón is very pretty, set in the shadow of the fuming volcano and by the shore of the deep-blue lake, whose waters are often cut by slashing lines of white foam

TOURS FROM PUCÓN

There are a multitude of **tour companies** in Pucón, mostly offering the same trips for similar prices. In many cases the larger ones help each other out and share punters, so there's little to choose between them, though there are some companies you should avoid. We've picked out a selection of the more established operators, and arranged them under the tours at which they are best.

Volcán Villarrica Including transport, climbing and descending, this is a full-day excursion, and prices start at CH$17,000 – if you feel lazy you can take the ski-lift up for part of the way for an extra CH$3,000. Note that climbing is not possible when the weather's bad. There are only four companies Conaf authorizes to climb the volcano: Politur, O'Higgins 635 (☎45/441373; *Politur@Politur.com*); Sol y Nieve, O'Higgins on the corner of Lincoyán (☎45/441070; *solnieve@enterlchile.net*); Trancura, O'Higgins 211-C (☎45/441189); and Apumanque, O'Higgins 323 (☎45/441085). In winter, the focus is on skiing, and companies such as Anden Sport, O'Higgins 535 (☎45/441048, fax 441236) rent equipment – mainly skis, but with snowboards becoming more common. Tours to the ski centre cost CH$12,000–15,000, and Politur offers cross-country skiing for CH$35,000, experienced skiers only.

Fishing Both fly-fishing and boat fishing trips can be arranged in the lakes and rivers surrounding the town. Prices for half-day's boat fishing on the río Liucura start at CH$42,000 per person, or CH$43,000 for fly-fishing, but there are substantial reductions for large groups. All fishing is catch and release, and the season's from November to April. The best company is Off Limits, Fresia 273 (☎45/441210, fax 441604; *offlimitspucon@hotmail.com*).

Horse-riding You can go for a full-day or half-day ride in the mountain wilderness of the Parque Nacional Villarrica. Prices start at about CH$13,500 for a half-day, CH$26,000 for a full day. Most agencies offer riding tours, or you can go directly to Rancho de Caballos (☎45/441575, fax 441604) a German-owned ranch 32km east of Pucón offering a range of treks from 3 hours to 9 days, or *¡école!* (see opposite).

Rafting There are three basic runs. The upper (alto) Trancura is a 14km run with 8 rapids, some grade 3 to 4; the lower (bajo) Trancura is tamer, though as it's a grade 2 to 3, its description in some of the flyers as a "family outing" is a misnomer. Both of these trips are half- or full-day excursions. The three-day trip to the mighty Bío Bío, a grade 4 to 5 river, includes food and accommodation in tents. Sol y Nieve and Trancura (see "Volcán Villarrica", above) have the latest equipment. Prices range from CH$4000 for the lower Trancura, CH$10,000 for the upper Trancura and US$250 for the Bío Bío. The season for rafting – depending on the amount of rainfall – is September/October (December for the upper Trancura) to March/April. Often the rafts all go down the river together, and the river can be very crowded in high season, so don't expect to experience the isolation of wilderness.

Tours of the area A sedate tour of the area in a minibus is run by every company in town, and will generally take in the Ojos de Caburgua (see p.289), some waterfalls (see p.294) and any or all of the thermal springs at Huife, Palguín, Menetué and Posones (see p.291). Prices range from around CH$8000 to CH$12,000. Going further afield, there are guided hiking trips in the Parque Nacional Huerquehue which take in the lakes Tinquilco, Toro, Verde and Chico (see p.290) and cost CH$12,000.

Two Pucón companies run slightly different tours from the ones listed above. **¡école!** (see opposite for contact details) is a great resource and very helpful. In association with a North American eco-charity it has set up a private araucaria forest sanctuary called Cañi about 30km east of Pucón, where it runs ecologically sensitive tours from around CH$10,000. The other company worth mentioning is **Man and Nature** (again, see opposite) which as well as the standard fare offers abseiling (CH$5000), but is only open in the summer.

churned up by waterskiers. The streets are wide and regular, and the whole town gives off a feeling of affluence and youth, bustling with tourist agencies, cafés and hotels.

The main street, Avenida O'Higgins, cuts the town in two, a wide boulevard lined with expensive cars and bustling shops. Its pavements throng with rich Argentinians on two-week breaks, or healthy bronzed Californians and multilingual Europeans passing out flyers to passers-by. Take a stroll to the sandy beach of **Playa Grande**, packed with oiled and sweating sunbathers lying in the shadow of the *Gran Hotel*, where in high season you can rent jet skis. Move on to **La Poza**, Pucón's other beach, and gaze at the boats in the marina. After this, there isn't much more to see, and you should make tracks for the travel agent or the car hire company.

But around Pucón there's plenty – the mighty river **Trancura** with its rapids, the iced pyramid of the volcano **Villarrica**, the deep-green of the **Parque Nacional Huerquehue** dotted with its forest lakes, and the steaming waters of the many **hot springs** that are scattered throughout the region's hills.

Eating

When metropolitan Chile decided to come to Pucón, the unfashionable *cazuelas* and plates of fried *empanadas* were cast out and replaced with crepes presented on wooden platters, among other novelties. An oasis of variety in a country which tends to lack a sense of culinary adventure, Pucón is a place to eat well.

Casino Hotel de Lago, Ansorena on the corner of Valdivia. Unless you are an inveterate gambler, the drawback of the *Casino*'s excellent restaurant is the sight and sound of people playing one-armed bandits outside its windows. The food, though, is French and Italian, and of the highest quality.

¡école!, Urrutia 592. Tasty and imaginative vegetarian dishes – moussaka, burritos and large, large salads – served in peace and quiet in a vine-covered courtyard.

El Refugio, Lincoyán 348. This small, comfortable restaurant has friendly staff and vegetarian, Arab or grilled set meals for $25. Crepes are a speciality and there is also a wide range of sandwiches.

El Salero de Mamas, Ansorena 555. This place specializes in *parilladas* with a difference, called "discos". They look a little like personal woks, and hold massive portions of meat, Oriental spiced chicken or fish.

Il Fiore, Holzapfel 83. There's a bewildering choice of home-made pastas and sauces on the menu, including three different types of lasagne, but if it's busy the service can be very slow.

La Marmita, Fresia 300. A rare example of a restaurant with candle-lit tables and atmosphere, specializing in two-person fondues: count on US$30 for two people. Indulge your sweet tooth and wallow in a chocolate one.

La Terera, Urrutia 580. A refreshing selection of teas, including the otherwise unobtainable lapsang souchong, properly made in a pot. They also make and serve fine cakes, not just confections of whipped cream.

Nuevo 24 hours, O'Higgins 192. A fast(ish)-food café for insomniacs, and one of the cheapest places to eat in Pucón.

Restaurant Milla-Rahue, O'Higgins 460. A popular fish and seafood restaurant on the main avenue with some interesting sauces.

Drinking

As you might expect from a town with so many young travellers, Pucón has a good nightlife scene, where the pisco flows and the music (a mixture of western and salsa) plays until the early hours.

Bar Bazul, 361 Lincoyán. It only really gets going here after 11pm, and has tables outside in the road so you can take a breather from the pulsating salsa and disco music.

Kamikaze, Camino International 2.5km. A cab ride out of town towards Argentina, this newly opened place is one of a chain of bars from the north, and has an aeroplane sticking out of the roof. Lively.

Mamas and Tapas, O'Higgins 597. In a wooden and glass building, a young, drinking crowd knock back seriously strong pisco sours.

Listings

Banks/money There are ATMs in O'Higgins (Banco Estado del Chile) and on Fresia between Gral Alderete and Gral Urrutia (Banco del Chile). There's a *cambio* in the travel agent Christopher at O'Higgins 335, opposite the enormous supermarket.

Book exchange La Tetera, Urrutia 580.

Buses Igi Llaima (☎45/441903); JAC, Terminal O'Higgins on Palguín (☎45/441923); LT (☎45/441055); Tur Bus (☎45/441965).

Camping and fishing equipment For camping equipment visit SCAI, Palguín 465, and for butane cylinders try R&M Alarcon, 590 O'Higgins, who also sell some fishing stuff, though there's a better choice at Off Limits, Fresia 273.

Car rental Hertz Alderete, on the corner of Fresia, 2nd floor (☎45/441664); *Man and Nature*, O'Higgins 758 (☎45/443081); Pucón Rent a Car, Camino International 1395-1510 (☎45/441922); SCAI, Palguín 465 (☎45/443449, fax 443436).

Flying and parachuting To go sightseeing in a Piper-Saratoga light aircraft, contact Daniel Achondo Bauzá (☎09/229 9610), who charges from CH$35,000 per hour. For tandem paragliding, contact Fabrice Pini, Coló Coló 830 (☎09/434 9888), US$55 for a half-hour. Tandem parachute jumps with Villarrica-based Peter Vermehren (☎45/411602 or 09/820 0194) cost CH$65,000.

Hospital San Francisco, Uruguay 325 (☎45/441177).

Internet access Cyber Bar Brink, Ansorena 243; SCAI, Palguín 465.

Laundry Elena, Gral Urrutia 520; Magala, Coló Coló 478.

Mountain bike rental Most of the travel agents also rent mountain bikes, and you can get a good deal if you shop around, though Off Limits, Fresia 273, generally come in cheap at CH$4000 a day.

Telephone centre Entel, Miguel Ansorena 299.

Water sports The small boat marina on La Poza will often rent out jet skis in summer, or contact one of the tour operators in the box on p287.

Lago Caburgua

If you want to escape at least some of the crowds, you could travel eight kilometres along the international road to Argentina, then turn left and head 17km along a good road to **Lago Caburgua**. After 11km, there's a turn to the left which leads to the **Ojos de Caburgua** (Eyes of Caburgua), a pair of waterfalls in the forest plunging into a deep pool of crystal-clear water. Thousands of years ago an eruption blocked this southern end of the valley, drowning it, and the water from the lake now flows out through subterranean streams and porous rock until it reappears here. Six kilometres further, the road arrives at the southern end of Lago Caburgua on a broad sandy beach, looking onto a long thin lake bordered by scrub- and forest-covered craggy peaks. The southern shore of the lake is densely developed with *cabañas* and campsites, but it's mostly hidden behind the trees. Just to the southwest is **Playa Blanca**, a beach composed of fine, pale rock crystals known locally as *ala de mosca* – literally, as thin as a fly's wing.

You can rent pedalos (CH$5000 per hour per person), or go for lake tours on what's proudly described as a "catamaran", but is actually a Heath-Robinson contraption made of chairs tied to a plank floor bolted onto inflatable pontoons with a motor strapped to the back: CH$25,000 (all day), or CH$1000 for a half-hour. There's no cheap **accommodation** here, and the nicest place to stay is *Hostería y Camping Parque Tierras Verdes* (☎45/411798; ⑥), but it gets a bit noisy outside. If you want to **camp**, the best spot is over at Playa Blanca at *Vergara Hnos* (☎45/441753; CH$10,000), a large park with plenty of isolated places to pitch a tent and private access to a small, secluded white-sand cove. It's a bit far back along the road to the restaurants and larger beaches, but it's possible to rock-hop or wade round the edge of the lake.

Many minibuses and *colectivos* come here from Pucón, leaving from both the rural bus terminal and the JAC terminal, though the service drops off somewhat in winter.

Parque Nacional Huerquehue

Rising up almost two thousand metres from the eastern shore of Lago Caburgua are forest-clad hills and peaks, which form the 125-square-kilometre **PARQUE NACIONAL HUERQUEHUE** (daily 8.30am–6pm; CH$2000). Crowned by araucaria forests, the horseshoe-shaped Cerros Picos de Caburgua (Caburgua Mountains) enclose a dozen breathtakingly beautiful lakes of which the largest – Tinquilco, Chico, Torro and Verde – are easily accessible.

Although volcanic in origin, Huerquehue's peaks have been dormant for thousands of years, and consequently it has a much richer biodiversity than neighbouring Parque Nacional Villarrica. At lower altitudes there are mixed forests of coigüe, one of the southern beeches, and the attractive conifer *mañío de hojas cortas*. Where areas of forest have been affected by fire there is often an impenetrable undergrowth of *colihue* and *quila*, types of native Chilean bamboo, incredibly irritating when you're trying to fight your way through.

Over eighty **bird** species have been sighted in the park, including two woodpeckers (the Magellanic and its smaller striped cousin), the delightful white-crested *diucon* or *fío-fío*, and the seldom seen but often heard red-chested *chucao*. Trout swim in the park's numerous lakes and rivers, introduced by European immigrants and now attract-

TERMAS AROUND PUCÓN

The combination of volcanic activity and a deep pool of tourist dollars means that there are more commercialized **hot springs** around Pucón than any other town in Chile. The facilities on offer are varied, ranging from the luxurious to very basic, but the alleged health-giving properties of the waters are just about the same: bathing in or drinking them can benefit arthritis, nervous ailments and mental fatigue. There are some more extravagant claims, however, and the waters at Palguín, for example, are apparently good for respiratory ailments, kidney problems, nerves, rheumatism, problems of the heart and the digestion, gastrointestinal disorders, joint problems, skin problems, ulcers, gout, sciatica, asthma and arthritis. Whether this is true or not, there's nothing quite as relaxing as lying in a pool of steaming, volcanically heated water, especially when it's cold, dark, raining or even snowing all around you.

The *termas* are mainly divided into two river valleys, the río Liucura and the río Trancura, and there's one on its own to the south, in the Parque Nacional Villarrica. We've arranged them in order of proximity to Pucón, with directions given to the nearest. Getting to the *termas* without your own car is difficult, though Colectivo Rínconada, at Miguel Ansorena 299, in Pucón, runs a local service to Huife for CH$1000, leaving at 12.30pm but turning around and coming straight back, so you'd have to spend the night there or hitch back. The other alternative is to charter a cab for the day, or a *colectivo*, which cost from CH$2000 per person each way (minimum of 4 people) and ask the driver to wait for you. Your hotel should be able to help with the arrangements (*¡école!* – see p.288 – has negotiated special rates with some taxi firms).

LIUCURA VALLEY

Termas Quimey-Co (☎45/441903 or 09/453 2671; CH$4000 a day). Two relatively simple but good swimming pools have been dug out of the rock right beside the río Liucura in an attractive spot with native forest coming right down to the river edge. From Pucón, drive towards Lago Caburgua and turn right at km 15, then continue for another 10km.

ing the large heron (*garza cuca*) and great grebes. The fascinating little Darwin's frog is also found here (see Contexts, p.462).

The park entrance is called **EL Nido del Aguila** (named after a nearby waterfall, the Eagle's Nest), 35km from Pucón, from where a trail leads into the forest: you can make it to the lakes Chico, Torro and Verde in two to three hours from here, but the path's a little steep. If you're going to hike further in, keep to the well-signed trails, as the forest can be dense and it's easy to lose your bearings: in 1997, two backpackers got so thoroughly lost that it took the Chilean Army two weeks to dig them out. You'll find the *JLM Pucón Trekking Map (No. 7)* very useful – it's readily available in Pucón. There's a two-day hike that continues on beyond the closer lakes, heading north of Lake Tinquilco towards the dense central forest and a Conaf campsite, *Renalue*, where you can spend the night. The trail then continues 8km (about 3hr) further, to the remote Termas Río Blanco, a thermal spring outside the park's northeastern boundaries, where you'll find a refuge (CH$2500) and a couple of houses.

Campsites fringe the park entrance: Conaf has its own site near the park entrance (CH$8000), or you could try *Olga's* or *El Rincon Tinquilco* (both CH$7000). However, the best **accommodation** option is the new *Tinquilco Lodge* (☎2/777 7673 or 09/822 7153, fax 2/735 1187; *tinquilco@lake.mic.cl*; ⑤), on the northeastern shores of Lake Tinquilco. Run by two of the authors of the *Insight Guide to Chile*, this airy, welcoming hostel offers both en-suite doubles and bunks without bedding (CH$4000 per bed), use of a kitchenette and meals. Squawking parrots swoop through the gardens,

---

Termas de Huife, 4km further on (☎ & fax 45/441222; CH$5500 a day). A well-designed complex with a tranquil atmosphere and a first-class swimming pool. It gets busy and entry is restricted, so you'll need to book in high season. There's a good restaurant, and luxurious double-bed *cabañas* (⑧) should you wish to stay.

Termas Los Posones, 2km beyond Huife (no phone; CH$3000 before 9pm, CH$4500 after). Simple, shallow pools dug out beside the river and dammed up with stones. It's open all night, though there is a three-hour time limit to stop the place being used as cheap accommodation.

RÍO TRANCURA VALLEY

Termas de Menetué (swimming pools open Dec–April, *termas* all year; ☎09/443 3710; CH$5000 a day). Set in beautiful gardens near the river, with naturally heated rock pools, a small restaurant and *cabañas*. To get here, head out of Pucón towards Argentina on the international road for 27km then turn left across the Puente (bridge) San Luis and continue west for 5km.

Termas de San Luis, 2km to the east of the San Luis bridge (☎45/412863, fax 411388; CH$5500 a day). Also known as the "Kerpen Centro Vacacional", this modern but sensitively built complex blends in well with the wooded surroundings, and has a covered thermal pool, an open-air swimming pool and a sauna.

Panqui, 15km further east of Termas de San Luis (☎45/442039, fax 442040; CH$4700 a day). A North American reinterpretation of the Andean forest, Panqui concentrates on the more mystical side of the hot springs, and calls itself a "Healing Retreat Centre". There are two thermal pools, a swimming pool, a mud bath and a medicine wheel. Accommodation can be arranged in tepees.

PARQUE NACIONAL VILLARRICA

Termas de Palguín. Most remote from Pucón, and deep in the Quetrupillán Sector of the Parque Nacional Villarrica. The gloriously rustic old hotel sadly burnt down in 1998, but the all-curing waters are still flowing. To get here by car, drive 18km along the Camino International towards Argentina, then turn right after a bridge near the village of Llafenco Alto, and drive 13km south down the dirt road.

and short trails lead through local woods – and, rather disturbingly, through the smallholding where tomorrow's dinner can be pointed out to you, still bleating or clucking.

There's no public **transport** to the park, but Buses JAC and Buses Cordillera (Ansorena 302 in Pucón) run from Pucón to a village called **Paillaco**, 7km down the road from El Nido del Aguila. From here it's a steep walk up a potholed track to the park entrance. If you're driving, take the road to Lago Caburgua and turn right at km 14, from where it's 16km to the park entrance.

Parque Nacional Villarrica

The centrepiece of the **PARQUE NACIONAL VILLARRICA** (daily: Jan–March 8.30am–8pm; April–Dec 8.30am–6pm; CH$1000) is, of course, the Volcán Villarrica, just 15km south of Pucón, in all its smoking, snow-capped beauty. But the park is much more than its most celebrated feature, and the vast majority of visitors do no more than trek up, have a look at the crater, then trek down again. It actually stretches 40km to the Argentinian border (74km by road), contains two more volcanoes, and is one of the

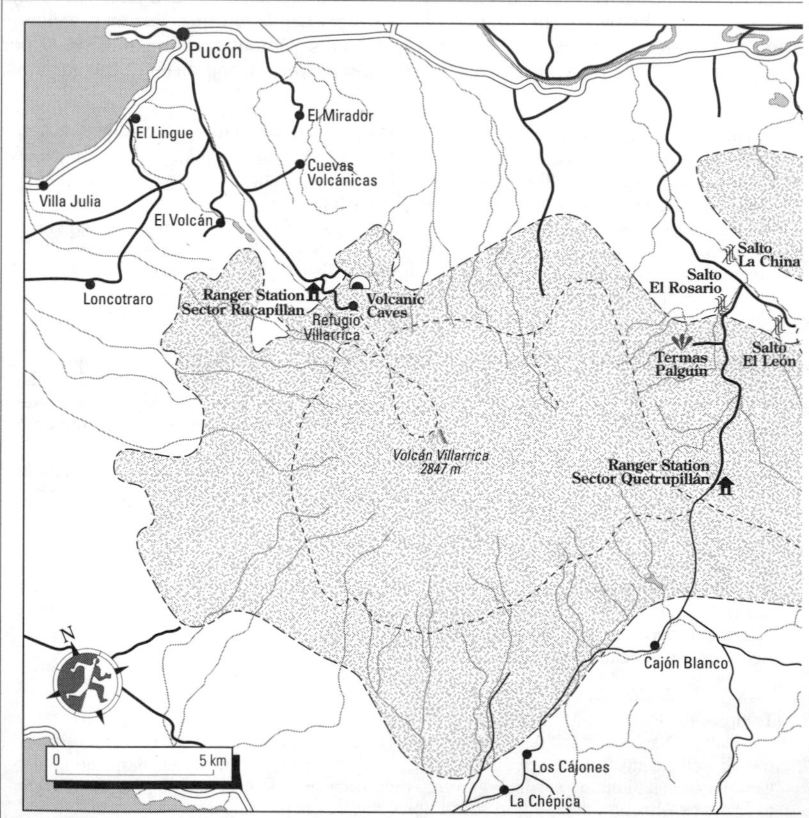

few national parks in the Lake District in which you can camp wild and hike for long-distances.

The park divides into three sections: **Rucapillán** is nearest Pucón, and contains Volcán Villarrica; **Quetrupillán**, next along, entered 9km beyond the turning to the Termas de Palguín on the dirt track that leads from the international road to Coñaripe, and **Puesco**, near the border with Argentina. It was inhabited long before the arrival of the Spanish, and the names of its peaks reflect this: Volcán Villarrica's original Mapuche name, Rucapillán, means house of the devil, because of its frequent eruptions, while Quetrupillán, the dormant volcano next-door, means mute devil. Another peak towards the border with Argentina is called Quinquili, meaning devil's fang.

Sector Rucapillán

Sector Rucapillán, home to the magnificent **Volcán Villarrica** (2840m), presents a visual contradiction: below the tree line it's a lush forest, home to a wide variety of bird and plant life; above it's a black waste of lava, dotted with snow and encrusted with an ice-cap. The volcano forms the obvious focal point, standing sentinel over the park, and it's very active – there have been sixteen recorded eruptions this century. It most

recently blew its top in 1984, though there were underground explosions in 1992, and part of the crater fell inside itself in 1996. Despite this, it's quite safe to visit, as considerable warning is given before serious activity.

A good road branches off the Pucón–Villarrica road, running up the northern slopes of the volcano. After 7km you reach the **park entrance**, and almost halfway up, 12km from Pucón, you reach the **ski centre**, a concession run by the *Gran Hotel de Pucón* (see p.286; Jun 28–Oct 12; ski pass CH$5000) with a café and restaurant. The volcano has four black runs, a complicated web of six red runs, four blue runs and a couple of green runs. All the ski lifts were destroyed by the 1984 eruption, and new chair- and T-bar-lifts are currently being built.

Just under a kilometre after the entrance, a signpost points you 4km left to the **Volcanic Caves** (daily: Dec to mid-March 9am–9pm; mid-March to Nov 10am–6pm; CH$5000). A large lava tube, the main cave is big enough at its opening to drive a tank into, and looks rather like a dragon's lair: the rock walls and ceiling could almost be made of scales. It's dank and wet, but there's a dry path, and electric bulbs, so you can see the multicoloured minerals on the walls. The tube hasn't been fully explored, and apparently continues for miles and miles.

Without a doubt, though, the main activity in this section of the park is **climbing the volcano**. The path leaves from the ski centre, and it's four hours up to a crater in which, if you're lucky and the gas clears, you'll see bubbling pits of molten rock. The route to the top passes over snow, and whilst it doesn't demand technical climbing skills you do need ropes, ice-axes, plastic mountaineering boots, crampons, and, rather bizarrely at first sight, a gas mask (to protect against the noxious gases the volcano emits). You'll also need a windproof jacket and trousers, but if you're taking a tour, all this equipment should be included. There are only four companies authorized by Conaf to guide up the volcano: Apumanque, Sol y Nieve, Trancura and Politur (see p.287 for details). These may change, as Conaf periodically reviews its approval. A maximum of nine climbers are allowed with one guide (fewer in winter), but Conaf will let up to four people a day climb without a guide if they've got the experience and equipment and can prove their ability. It all gets very crowded up there in high season.

Sectors Puesco and Quetrupillán

It's possible to walk for seven days through virgin forest, including the most southerly stands of araucaria in Chile, from Rupacillán to Puesco, longer if you're tempted by the numerous side-trails to waterfalls, precipices and springs. You need to carry lots of water, as the seasonal streams can't be relied on, and should take the *JLM Pucón Trekking Map (No. 7)*, widely available in Pucón. Wild camping is allowed.

Sector Quetrupillán, the middle section of the park, is dominated by the rarely visited majesty of Volcán Quetrupillán (2009m). It's a remote area of wilderness, tucked between two volcanoes, and accessible only on foot, by horse or down a rough side road which turns south from the Camino International 18km out of Pucón. Here you can find the gloriously rustic old **Termas de Palguín,** whose all-curing waters once flowed around an old hotel (which sadly burnt down in 1998). Here also are four **waterfalls** – Palguín, la China, El León and Turbina. La China, at 73m, is the highest, but El León is more spectacular; all are surrounded by native trees and lush vegetation, though this is actually private land and the owners sometimes charge for access. From the *termas*, a terrible track continues for 10km to the Conaf ranger post, and then on to Coñaripe (see p.297). It's often totally impassable, even for large 4WD vehicles and you're discouraged from using it.

East of Quetrupillán, close by the border with Argentina, the third part of the park, Sector **Puesco** is very beautiful, and rather like the Canadian Rockies, with pine forests and craggy mountainsides. The Conaf station is at the settlement of **PUESCO**, where there's nothing else except a customs post and a *hostería*. From here it's a seven-hour walk west to **Laguna Abutardes**, tucked in the side of dormant **Volcán Quetrupillán** (2360m), a haven for birds, and with ancient araucaria trees sweeping almost to its shore. On your way here from Pucón, 10km out of the village of Curarrehue, keep an eye out on the left (east) for the **Cordón de las Peinetas**, a rock formation that looks a little like a small version of the Torres del Paine, the famous rock towers in the south of Chile.

Right on the border with Argentina (the border runs right through the summit) is **Volcán Lanin**, the least-visited volcano in the park and with no trails. If you intend to trek or climb it, you'll need to get permission from Conaf and DIFROL (see p.53) and you must be *very* careful not to cross into Argentina.

Park practicalities

Now that the fabulous hotel at the Termas de Palguín has gone, there's no **accommodation** inside the park, but *Hostería Trancura* at Puesco, has *cabañas* (④) and a campsite (CH$2500). There are also **campsites** near the entrance to Rucapillán (CH$4000), but the only campsite actually in the park is near the Quetrupillán Conaf station (CH$8000).

There's no **public transport** to Sector Rucapillán, though there are dozens of tour buses, and a taxi will cost around CH$6000. In the winter, most tour agencies will take you there for CH$4000 per person, leaving Pucón at 9.30am and returning 4.30pm (see p.287 for companies). To get to Quetrupillán and Puesco, either take one of the local buses that ply the international road, or take an international bus heading to Junín de los Andes in Argentina and ask to be dropped off. Whilst you should be able to get off at the Puesco customs post and Conaf station, the nearest you'll get to Quetrupillán will be the hamlet of **Palguín Bajo**, 9km away down a dirt track. If you've got permission, take the same bus to get to Volcán Lanin.

The Siete Lagos

Overshadowed by the sexier resort of Pucón, the **SIETE LAGOS** – or region of seven lakes – are the next lakes south of Villarrica, six of them in Chile, one in Argentina, and all linked by rivers in one hydrological system. They offer a mixture of attractive small villages with good tourist facilities, and countless tracks that plunge deep into remote parts of the cordillera.

The reason for Siete Lagos' relative tranquillity is that it was largely ignored by the Spanish. Pedro de Valdivia became the first European to visit the area in 1551, but apart from a short-lived silver mining enterprise, the Spanish kept away. Its first settlement, Lican Ray, was a small trading post in the late nineteenth century, founded to serve the Pehuenche and Mapuche Indians driven from the pampas by Argentinian clearances.

Today, the busiest lakes are the largest ones, **Lago Calafquén**, 30km south of Villarrica along a good tarred road, and **Lago Panguipulli**, 17km on. The next valley down contains the slightly smaller **Lago Riñihue**, hardly visited and perfect for nature-lovers and fishermen. To the east of Calafquén, beside a little-used road into Argentina, lies **Lago Pellaifa**, near a concentration of good *termas*. To the east of lagos Panguipulli and Riñihue, nestling deep in the pre-cordillera and surrounded by two-thousand-metre peaks, are the most remote of the Siete Lagos, **Lago Neltume** and **Lago Pirihueico**, neither of which was accessible by road until thirty years ago and today could not be quieter or more unspoilt.

Lago Calafquén and around

Lago Calafquén is the most developed of the seven lakes, with a good tarred road for the 30km along its northern shore between the settlements of **Lican Ray** and **Coñaripe**, and a passable road around most of the rest. In a pattern that's typical of the lakes of the Lake District, the western end is surrounded by rich farmland which stretches all the way to the coastal mountains, while the northern and southern shores are steep forested hillsides with only occasional pockets of fertile land and isolated farmsteads. To the east is tiny **Lago Pellaifa**, created by an earthquake in 1960 that altered the water-flow in the region and bordered by an international road to Argentina that passes a clutch of thermal springs around the mountain hamlet of **Liquiñe**.

Lican Ray

Thirty kilometres south of Villarrica and sitting on the northernmost point of Lago Calafquén, **LICAN RAY** is a slightly scruffy holiday town, its shady plaza bordered by loud video-game arcades. Most of the town's roads are narrow dirt tracks which throw up dust in summer and become quagmires in the rain. The town has two pleasant beaches, Playa Chica with a small forested promontory, and Playa Grande, a strip of dark sand framed by the surrounding hills, and exposed to frequent freezing winds. In the summer you can rent boats at both beaches, but Playa Chica is cheaper at CH$1500 an hour.

In the winter the town is pretty much dead, but for the first weekend of January Lican Ray becomes famous. On that weekend, the whole length of the main street, Gral Urrutia, is transformed into a **world-record breaking outdoor barbecue** (*asado*) in which around three hundred lambs meet their bitter, spicy ends. The origins of the feast aren't clear, but the excuse given is that it's to celebrate the beginning of summer, and each year's is bigger than the last as the town attempts to break its own world record. That is, until 1999 when there was no barbecue because the town ran out of money.

The helpful and friendly **Oficina de Turismo** is on the plaza (Jan–March daily 9am–11pm; April–Dec Mon–Fri 9am–12.30pm & 2.30–6pm; ☎45/431201). There's no shortage of **places to stay** in Lican Ray. The best are *Hostería Inaltulafquén*, on Playa Grande at Cacique Punulef 510 (☎ & fax 45/431115; ⑤), an attractive house with good rooms, owned by a helpful Canadian couple who organize local tours; and *Hotel Becker*, Manquel 105 on Playa Chica (☎45/431156; ⑤), which has comfortable rooms with a view of the lake, and a wide veranda. Two kilometres out of town on the road to Coñaripe is *Cabañas and Camping Foresta* (☎ & fax 45/211954), an expensive shady campsite in a wood, with sites for six people (CH$18,000) and *cabañas* for four (CH$50,000).

Lican Ray is well connected to the rest of the Lake District, and beyond: Buses JAC regularly link it with Villarrica, Pucón, Valdivia, Temuco and Santiago, as well as with Lago Calafquén and Panguipulli. Buses Estrella del Sur and Igi Llaima go to Villarrica.

Coñaripe and Liquiñe

A 21km drive along the northern shore of Lago Calafquén takes you to the nine blocks that make up the village of **COÑARIPE**, just a couple of black-sand beaches and a sleepy air that's occasionally disturbed by erupting volcanoes. The small image of Christ, on the lake shore by the entrance to town, is a memorial to two lava-engulfed victims and a testament to the uncertainty of living in this volcanically unstable area.

The municipal **Oficina de Turismo** is in a kiosk on the main street, Avenida Guido Beck de Ramberga, at the entrance to town from Lican Ray (Dec–March daily 9am–9pm; no phone). There's some decent **accommodation** should you want to stay the night: try the *Hotel Entre Montañas* (☎63/317298; ④), a modern pine and plastic building with a cheerful restaurant and small en-suite rooms; or the cheaper *Hospedaje Calafquén*, Av Guido Beck de Ramberga 761 (☎63/317301; ②), a traditional wooden house with a patio and small garden, run by a friendly family who will provide good-value meals on request.

After Coñaripe there's a junction. The road to the right (south) follows the shore of Lago Calafquén to the town of Panguipulli (see overleaf), while the main road in front (east) climbs through native forest – with superb views of Lago Pellaifa, volcano Villarrica and Choshuenco – for 22km to the tiny village of **LIQUIÑE**. Overlooked by a church and on the banks of the deep, wide río Liquiñe, this pretty hamlet is surrounded by mountains and has a climate all of its own: in the summer the 2000m peaks trap the heat and it's difficult to believe that you're deep in the southern Andes. The hills around the village are riddled with **thermal springs** (see box overleaf). Many of these have been developed, and offer **accommodation**, but if you're looking for something cheaper, the *Residencial La Frontera* (messages: ☎63/311060; ②) has several plain rooms.

Coñaripe is served by frequent **buses** from Villarrica, operated by Buses JAC, Buses Estrella del Sur, and Igi Llaima, two of whose buses (departing Villarrica at 11.30am and 5.10pm) continue on to Liquiñe. There are also buses from both Coñaripe and Liquiñe to Panguipulli, operated by Buses San Pedro and Buses Pirehueico.

LIQUIÑE AND THE TERMAS

East of Coñaripe, deep in the mountainous forest either side of the little-used international road to Argentina, there are many **thermal springs**, less well-known than those around Pucón, but every bit as good. They are listed in order of proximity to Coñaripe.

Termas de Coñaripe, 13km from Lago Calafquén, (☎ & fax 45/411111 or 63/317330; ⑧). This is a popular holiday complex, built from glass and wood, with a good restaurant and first-class accommodation. The *termas* from which the place gets its name have been diverted into four swimming pools of varying temperatures, which cost CH$5000 a visit to use.

Termas Manquecura, 2km up a bad track marked with a painted condor at the entrance to Liquiñe (messages: ☎63/311060; ④). Here there are rustic open-air pools amongst the fields, private baths, mud baths, a small restaurant and some basic *cabañas*. Entry to the *termas* costs CH$1800, and they can become surprisingly busy with coach parties staying for several days.

Termas Río Liquiñe, on the river bank in the centre of the village (☎ & fax 63/317377; ⑤). The *cabañas* have thermal water piped into private baths, and there's a big, square swimming pool, access to which costs CH$4000.

Termas De Liquiñe, 100m from rio Liquiñe (messages: ☎63/311060; ④). Owned by the Chilean navy and slightly run-down, but at the foot of a steep, forested hill there's a peaceful, secluded swimming pool and good *cabañas*. Access costs CH$3000.

Termas Trafipan, just below the tree line. A simple pool and rustic private baths, fed by a spring 600m above. The water's pleasantly unsulphurous, and the place costs CH$1500 to use.

Termas Punulaf, a 15min walk away across open fields: local children will take you for a tip. A large open-air pool fringed by trees, mud baths and private tubs which cost CH$1500 to use. If you want to use the pools early in the morning or late at night you can camp here for CH$5000.

Termas Hipólito Muñoz, 8km towards Argentina. A campsite (CH$4700) and a few rustic *cabañas* in a beautiful, thickly forested riverside setting. There is a charge of CH$1500 to use the pools that have been dug out beside the river and there are mud baths too.

Lago Panguipulli and around

Ten kilometres south of Lago Calafquén is the northern snout of long, thin **Lago Panguipulli**, a lake which stretches 26km southeast into the cordillera. Its western edge is a shore of little bays and hills, its east is cleared forest, the trees long since felled and taken by boat to the neat little town of Panguipulli on the lake's northwesternmost tip. Thirty years ago, a road was built around the uninhabited eastern shore to the remote Lagos **Neltume** and **Pirehueico**. These beautiful lakes are hardly touched by humanity, save for a ferry that crosses Lago Pirehueico, carrying cars and passengers towards Argentina.

Panguipulli

The southern shore road from Coñaripe leads, after 37km, to **PANGUIPULLI**, a town more easily reached by one of two 50–60km spurs from the Panamericana. Set amongst rolling fields, forests and peaks of grey and purple, and florid with bright roses, dark copper beech trees and manicured lawns, it's an attractive place.

Founded in 1885, Panguipulli started life as a trading post for Pehuenche and Mapuche Indians driven off the Argentinian pampas. It grew beyond these humble origins in 1903 when a Capuchin mission was established here, and when the railway arrived in 1937, the town became an important timber centre. The trees are gone now, and the boom is over, but Panguipulli remains the administrative hub for the Siete Lagos, with good shops, services and accommodation. It's best known today as the **town of roses**, with an estimated 14,000 closely pruned roses lining the streets, and a crowd-pulling festival, *Semana de las Rosas*, every January.

There's not much to do in Panguipulli except sit on the beach, look at the view, smell the roses and check out the famous **church** around the corner from Plaza Arturo Prat (unpredictable opening hours): built by the Capuchins, and envied and copied throughout the Lake District. It's modelled on traditional chapels around Berne in Switzerland, and is an unexpected sight – a twin-towered latticed confection of yellow, red, brown and white, looking like a massive iced chocolate cake. Down on the lakefront are a group of **wooden statues** – two Indians, a missionary and a pioneer – each carved from a single block of wood.

Near the church, on Plaza Arturo Prat, is the unhelpful **Oficina de Turismo** (Dec–Feb daily 9am–9pm; ☎63/311311 ext 731), which has all the information you'll need but just doesn't want to give it to you. There's lots of accommodation here, dating back to the heyday of rail transport and lake steamers, and for the most part all wood and wobbly beds. Try the *hospedaje* at Freire 98 on the corner of Rozas (no phone; ②), a creaky old building lovingly cared for by its ageing owner, with large rooms and a colonial-era bathroom. Meals are available in the next-door neighbour's house. About the same standard is *Hospedaje Monserrat*, O'Higgins 1112 (no phone; ②) a very popular place with young Chileans who enjoy the lively atmosphere and don't seem to mind queueing for the solitary bathroom. If you want a bit more luxury, there's *Hotel España*, O'Higgins 790 (☎63/31116; ④), friendly, and more like a family house than a hotel with large, comfortable en-suite rooms. The nearest **campsite** is *El Bosque*, (mid-Nov to April; ☎63/311489; CH$6000) a five-minute walk up Padre Sigifredo from the Oficina de Turismo, hidden from the road in a small sheltered orchard.

Panguipulli's no town for gourmets, but it does have a **cookery school** – *Restaurant Didáctico*, Freire 394 – which, in January and February, sometimes opens its doors to the paying public. Apart from this, the only places to recommend are two cafés and neither because of the food: *Café Central*, Martínez de Rozas 880, because it's got a secluded patio and small garden, and *Café de la Plaza*, O'Higgins 816, because it has some tables on the plaza.

Panguipulli is very well connected to the rest of the Lake District. The **bus terminal** is on Diego Portales, two blocks from the main plaza, at the corner of Gabriela Mistral and there are good local and long-distance services, heading as far afield as Santiago. The major bus companies are Pirehueico (☎63/311497), Igi Llaima (☎63/311347), Tur Bus (☎63/311377) and Inter Sur (☎63/311309).

Southeast towards the border

Turning right from the shore road at the southern end of Lago Panguipulli, 42km from Panguipulli town, you pass along a magnificent avenue of trees which forms an incongruous entrance to tiny **CHOSHUENCO**. Once a steamer port in the days when boats plied the waters of Lago Panguipulli, Choshuenco is now a small village with just over five hundred human inhabitants, and the remains of an old dead steamer rusting on the beach. It's a base for fishermen in the summer, and for wild boar hunters in the winter, who tend to stay in *Hostería Pulmahue*, at the end of the beach just outside the village (Oct–April: ☎63/224402 ext 224; ④). The *hostería* has a commanding view of the lake, the atmosphere of a mountain hunting lodge, a roaring log fire and some hearty home cooking.

Fifteen kilometres along a dirt road southwest of Choshuenco is **Enco**, a tiny logging camp at the end of Lago Riñihue, the next lake south of Lago Panguipulli. From Enco, a nine-kilometre track leads up through the Reserva Nacional Mocho Choshuenco to a ski refuge, just above the tree line, which can be used as a base for climbing **Volcán**

Choshuenco (2415m). Another 30km logging track leads to the town of **Riñihue** on the northern shore of the lake, passing through thick forest and along the edges of high cliffs to reveal constantly changing views across the lake. Walkers or cyclists who use it are unlikely to meet another soul. Be warned, though, that temporary bridges cross countless streams which, after even moderate rainstorms, turn long sections of the track into one great sticky bog.

Lago Neltume and Lago Pirehueico

Back on what was the shore road, 5km after the turn for Choshuenco a gravel road branches left to smallish **Lago Neltume**, depositing you on its eastern shore. The other side of the lake is a mountain: the densely forested side of the impressive Cerro Paillahuinte (1435m rising straight up from the water). Heading once more towards Argentina, after another seven kilometres you'll reach the waterfalls **Saltos del Huilo Huilo**, a powerful torrent forced through a 10m-wide green cleft in the rock to deafening effect.

Six kilometres further on lies **Lago Pirehueico**. Pirehueico means "worm of water" in the local Mapuche language, and there couldn't be a better name for this curving, twisting, snake-like lake, bordered by forest-clad mountains. It's crossed by a **ferry**, from Puerto Fuy in the north to Puerto Pirehueico in the south (2 daily, except Sun April–Nov 1 daily; 2hr; CH$12,000 for cars, CH$700 foot passengers; information ☎63/311334). There isn't much in either village: **Puerto Fuy** has one general store and some basic accommodation, usually occupied by temporary workers; **Puerto Pirehueico** is just the one building, a *residencial* which serves lunch and snacks. Hardly anyone stops in either place, though because of their remoteness, the surrounding lakes and forests have more wildlife than most of the national parks. Eleven kilometres further is the **border**, where there is a café and a customs post, open 8am to 8pm, all year round.

If you haven't a car, getting to these lakes is a problem, as public transport doesn't go beyond Choshuenco and there isn't enough traffic to make hitching anything more certain than a long, boring wait.

Lago Riñihue

Lago Riñihue, the beautiful flooded valley to the south of Lago Panguipulli and the last of the Siete Lagos, has been almost completely untouched by tourism. There is no apparent reason why – the tiny village on the western shore of the lake was the first to be connected to the railway in 1910, there's a good tar road linking it with the Panamericana, 50km to the west, and the vast sweep of the morainic plain is well-known by Chileans for producing famous Swiss- and German-style hard cheeses.

This means, of course, that there are precious few tourist facilities, save for a very plush complex of luxury *cabañas* called *Centro Turística Huinca-Quiñay* (reservations Santiago ☎2/227 6337; ⑧), with stunning views and a first-class restaurant, a couple of kilometres down the road. Otherwise, **RIÑIHUE** itself is merely a collection of houses built on the slight rise pushed up by an old, long-melted glacier, with a small village store, a disco, a small bar, and two campsites, one permanent (☎63/461344; CH$9000 for 5 people), one temporary (Feb 21–March 15; CH$4700). Campers can **eat** at the complex restaurant – if they're deemed clean enough.

Valdivia and around

Apart from a very minor private road from Puerto Fuy round the far side of Volcán Choshuenco, the only way south from the Siete Lagos is to head back to the Panamericana, via Panguipulli (60km) or Riñihue (47km). Both routes end up at **Los Lagos**, a town that used to be an important river port, but these days is little more than

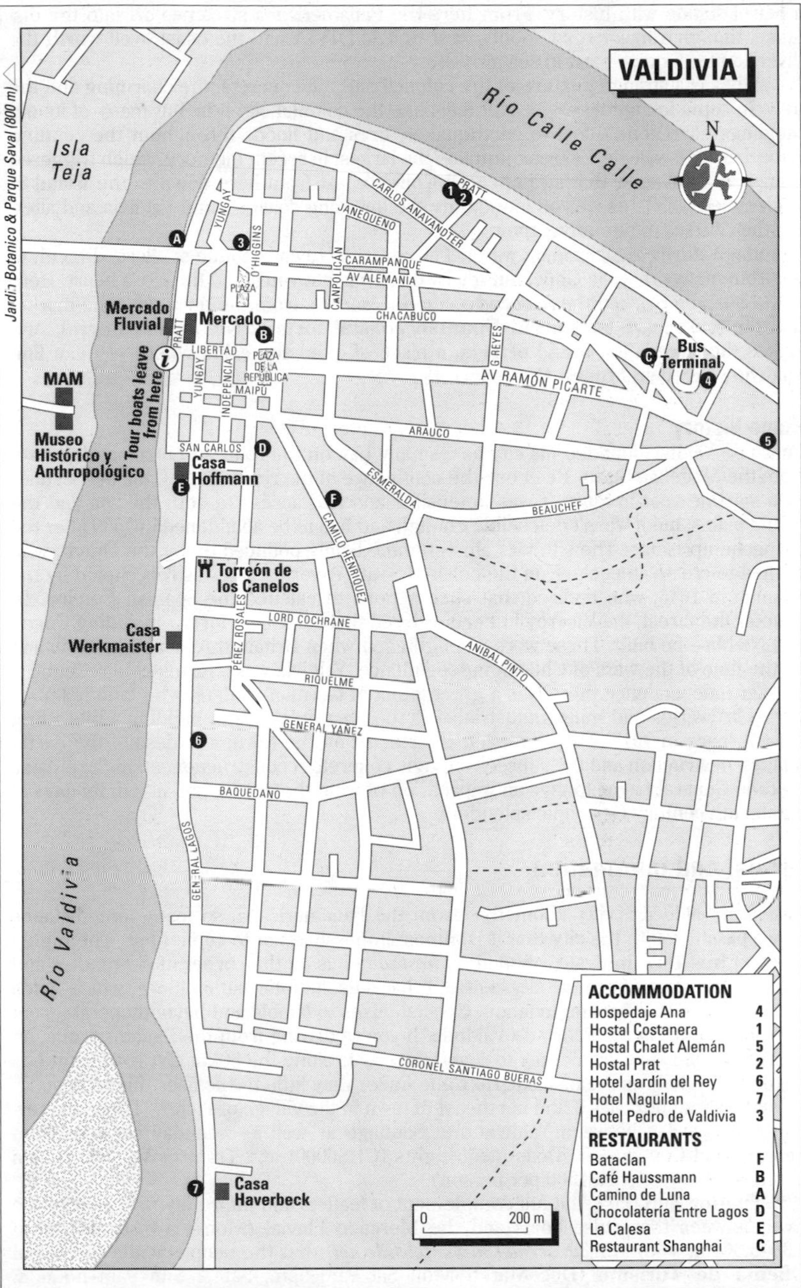
VALDIVIA
Río Calle Calle
N
Isla Teja
Jardín Botanico & Parque Saval (800 m)
Mercado Fluvial
Mercado
MAM
Museo Histórico y Anthropológico
Tour boats leave from here
Casa Hoffmann
Torreón de los Canelos
Casa Werkmaister
Bus Terminal
Casa Haverbeck
Río Valdivia
PRATT
CARLOS ANAVANDTER
JANEQUENO
YUNGAY
O'HIGGINS
CAMPOLICÁN
CARAMPANQUE
AV ALEMANIA
PLAZA
CHACABUCO
LIBERTAD
PLAZA DE LA REPÚBLICA
INDEPENCIA
MAIPÚ
G REYES
AV RAMÓN PICARTE
ARAUCO
SAN CARLOS
ESMERALDA
BEAUCHEF
CAMILO HENRIQUEZ
PÉREZ ROSALES
LORD COCHRANE
ANIBAL PINTO
RIQUELME
GENERAL YAÑEZ
BAQUEDANO
GENERAL LAGOS
CORONEL SANTIAGO BUERAS
0 200 m
ACCOMMODATION
Hospedaje Ana 4
Hostal Costanera 1
Hostal Chalet Alemán 5
Hostal Prat 2
Hotel Jardín del Rey 6
Hotel Naguilan 7
Hotel Pedro de Valdivia 3
RESTAURANTS
Bataclan F
Café Haussmann B
Camino de Luna A
Chocolatería Entre Lagos D
La Calesa E
Restaurant Shanghai C

a petrol station with history. From here the Panamericana stretches off into the distance, though a major road shoots west to **VALDIVIA** and the coast, well worth the diversion for a quick blast of sea air.

Valdivia is a strange mixture of the colonial and the concrete, the charming and the ugly. In some intangible way it still feels like the colonial city it is, but many of its old buildings have gone – lost to earthquakes, fires and floods throughout the century. Especially bad was the 1960 earthquake, the largest in recent memory, which triggered a massive tidal wave that swamped all Chile's coast from here down to the island of Chiloé (see p.333), as well as inundating the low-lying coast around Valdivia and altering the courses of numerous rivers.

Today Valdivia is focused on water. The centre of town is a little soulless, difficult to tell from many others in Chile, but it's by the river that you'll find the city's heart. Here is the bustling market, the **Mercado Fluvial**, and it's from the quay near the market that the tours leave for the **old Spanish coastal forts** of **Niebla** and **Corral**. And across the river is the island of **Teja**, a place of quiet and calm, where you can find Valdivia's excellent **Museo Histórico**.

Some history

Pedro de Valdivia founded his city as a supply halt on the route to Lima, six days' sail from the Magellan Strait. He chose the confluence of the rivers Calle Calle and Cruces as a suitable spot because it was defensible and had access to both the sea and the inland plains, but it wasn't defensible enough and had to be abandoned in 1599 after the Mapuche uprisings. The site was almost immediately pounced on by the Dutch, who wanted to create an enclave on the coast of South America, but was reoccupied by the Spanish in 1645, who realized that such actions threatened the Spanish Empire. To counter the threat, the Viceroy in Peru ordered that a string of forts – including Corral and Niebla – be built. These were strengthened when Britain threatened in 1770, and by the time of the wars of Chilean independence, Valdivia was a formidable redoubt.

After independence there was a great influx of German settlers, who founded shipyards, breweries and mills, industrializing the area quickly and building Chile's first blast furnace in 1913. They have left their mark on the town, and despite the earthquakes' destruction and the subsequent ugly concrete reconstruction, enough remains on calle General Lagos to give an impression of what the city looked like in its days of nineteenth-century Germanic splendour.

Arrival and information

Although Valdivia is fifty kilometres from the Panamericana, so many long-distance buses pass through the city that it is almost impossible not to come here. The highly efficient **bus terminal**, surrounded by *hospedajes*, is on the corner of Anwandter and Muñoz, five blocks from the city centre. It has a useful information kiosk, which holds details of approved accommodation. Coastal buses to Niebla and beyond operate from the city end of Puente Pedro de Valdivia. If you're driving from the Panamericana, an alternative and very scenic way to reach the city is along the 50km dirt road from Los Lagos which follows the majestic río Calle Calle. Very little traffic uses this route.

Valdivia's **airport** lies 32km northeast of town in the village of Pichoy. There are several flights a day between Valdivia and Santiago as well as weekday services from Temuco and Concepción. Taxis meet flights (CH$6000) and Transfer Valdivia runs a minibus into town (CH$1500 per person).

Sernatur, with the usual full complement of leaflets and information, is next to the river between the cruise boats and the Mercado Fluvial (Mon–Fri 8.30am–1pm & 2.30–6.30pm; ☎63/215739; *serna13a@entelchile.net*), but the people at the municipal **Oficina de Turismo** (Dec–March Mon–Sat 9am–9pm, Sat & Sun 9am–noon &

4–9pm; no phone), in the indoor market across from the Mercado Fluvial, are more motivated.

Accommodation

In January and February, when Valdivia's student population is on holiday the city has some of the cheapest accommodation in the country. In the mid-range there are some beautiful old private houses with very good facilities, and at the top end there are a couple of modern luxury hotels.

Hospedaje, Muñoz 345. A clean, cheap, no-frills and no-food place with use of the kitchen. ②.

Hospedaje Ana, José Marti 11 (☎63/222468). Very close to the bus station, this is a good place for small groups to stay, with well-equipped five-bed *cabañas* (④) as well as rooms, some of which have bunk beds. ②.

Hospedaje Anwandter, Anwandter 800 (☎63/217925). A student hostel during term time, it's down the end of a very quiet drive, and is owned by a friendly biology professor with an ear for loud music. ②.

Hostal Chalet Alemán, Picarte 1134 (☎ & fax 63/218810). A traditional old house with river views, an attractive garden and en-suite rooms. ⑤.

Hostal Costanera, Av Prat 579 (☎63/250042, fax 250038). A large house with a steeply pitched roof, good views, a large dining room, en-suite rooms and a restaurant which serves some German dishes. ③.

Hostal Prat, Av Prat 595 (☎63/222020). A bargain. Overlooking the river, this smart, newly refurbished hotel with en-suite rooms and cable TV is run by a small, energetic woman who's eager to please. ②.

Hotel Jardín del Rey, General Lagos 1190 (☎ & fax 63/218562). A building oozing colonial charm, and retaining the dignified bearing of a prosperous family home. The en-suite rooms are very large and comfortable. ⑤.

Hotel Naguilan, General Lagos 1927 (☎63/212851, fax 219130). Part of the Best Western chain and right on the edge of the río Valdivia, this is a modern hotel with a swimming pool. All the rooms overlook a reed-covered island and face the setting sun – which gives the place its Mapuche name. ⑥.

Hotel Pedro de Valdivia, Carampangue 190 (☎63/212931, fax 203888). Right in the centre of the city, this large traditional old hotel prides itself on having the best location in Valdivia. It's a well-run place with a very good international restaurant, attractive gardens and a pool. ⑦.

The Town

Unlike most Chilean towns, Valdivia's heart is not its plaza but its bustling waterfront, where the río Calle Calle and the río Cau Cau meet the río Valdivia. The rivers bend sharply to form a "U" shape, and it's along the south and east banks that the *costanera*, the bankside road, runs. Inland from the rivers, to the east, lies the modern concrete town centre. The main east-to-west street is Avenida Ramón Picarte, and the main north-to-south street is Yungay, which changes its name to General Lagos three blocks south of the indoor market. Opposite the town centre, across the new Pedro de Valdivia bridge, is **Isla Teja** a haven of tranquillity, home to the **Museo Histórico**, and has beautiful views back across the river to the Mercado Fluvial.

Just south of the bridge to Isla Teja, the **Mercado Fluvial** is where you'll find Valdivia's fish quay on the riverfront, with wizened fishermen gutting and selling rows of slimy *congrio* and *merluza*, and setting out battalions of monstrous red spider crabs, some the size of a small child, on concrete slabs covered with striped awnings. Opposite, on the other side of the path, are stalls selling all types of bright fruit, vegetables and strings of smoked shellfish. Across the road there's the **indoor market**, not much in comparison, just a couple of butcher's shops and some *marisquerías* (seafood restaurants) inside a modern arcade. Just to the south of the Mercado Fluvial are the touts offering ferry tours (see box overleaf).

FERRY TOURS

Just down from the Mercado Fluvial there are the kiosks and touts of the ferry tour companies, offering to take you down to the coastal forts, or upriver to the wetlands. The tours on offer vary greatly. One of the most important factors in choosing a boat is the weather – the amount of deckspace varies considerably from one vessel to another and you don't want to be sitting out in the rain all afternoon. Lunch is an optional extra on several boats and policy varies as to whether you can consume your own food and drink on board. Above all it is worth checking what languages the running commentary is going to be in, if there is one, and if you can escape it by going out on deck. Remember to shop around, as one tout may be offering a trip at twice the price of his neighbour.

The cheapest boat to the coast is the *Tatiana* (no phone; CH$1000), leaving 1pm, returning at 6pm, and the most expensive is VIP class on the catamaran *Extasis* (☎ & fax 63/212464; CH$28,000, including lunch, wine and liqueurs), which leaves at 1.30pm and returns at 6.30pm. For trips to the Santuario de la Naturaleza, the best option is *Isla del Río* (☎63/225244; CH$15,500 including lunch), leaving 1.30pm and returning 7.30pm.

The centre of town holds fewer attractions. Valdivia is proud of a couple of squat, grubby defensive towers that date from 1774 – **Torreón del Barro** on Avenida Picarte and **Torreón de los Canelos** on the corner of Yerbas Buenas and General Lagos. However most visitors head for **calle General Lagos**, which heads south out of town parallel with the river. This old street is filled with Valdivia's gems, a series of nobly proportioned nineteenth-century buildings. Take a stroll down the road, and peek through the railings at the austere, double-staircased **Casa Werkmaister** (between Cochrane and Riquelme), or at the crinkly gabled **Conjunto Haverbeck** on the way out of town, or at many others between the two. The only one you can actually visit is **Casa Hoffmann** at Yungay 733 (daily except Mon 10am–1pm & 4–7pm; free), also known as the Centro Cultural "El Austral". It was constructed in 1870 as a private residence by Alberto Thater, a German who came to Valdivia in 1857, and has been lovingly restored and furnished in the popular style favoured by successful merchants during Valdivia's golden years: bright, strong decoration which looks almost Regency, with trompe l'oeil wall hangings and mismatched, passed-down furniture. Temporary art exhibitions are mounted in the upstairs rooms.

Isla Teja

Your first sight of **Isla Teja** will probably be from the Mercado Fluvial, as you look beyond the fishmongers' stalls at the banks across the river. Only the easternmost part of the island is urban, the rest is low-lying reed beds and wetland. It's a quiet place, and the part of Isla Teja that Valdivia has stretched onto has a quiet, suburban atmosphere.

The island is reached via the concrete bridge to the north of the Mercado Fluvial. Heading south from the bridge is Isla Teja's main attraction, the splendidly sited **Museo Histórico y Antropológico Maurico van de Maele** (Dec–March daily 10am–1pm & 2–8pm; April–Nov Tues–Sun 10am–1pm & 2–6pm; CH$700), in an old colonial house surrounded by a veranda. It was once owned by Karl Anwandter, founder of Chile's first brewery, and like the Casa Hoffman (see above), is still furnished with the trappings of nineteenth-century European society, such as a double piano, an ornate red-marble fireplace and a magic lantern, and has a fascinating collection of old sepia prints of the first German settlers.

The highlight of the museum is the collection of **Mapuche artefacts**, mainly silverwork and cloth. The cloth resembles the patterns of the Aymara and Quechua, indigenous peoples from the north of Chile and Peru. The display of Mapuche silver is good too, and if you haven't visited a museum in the Lake District yet you should come and see examples of their heavy, intricate yet strangely contemporary treasure. There's a collection of reproductions of old photographs which show the silver's original owners and how it would have been worn. The museum contains other bits and bobs: some lovely old maps of South America on the wall of the stairway, and a room of memorabilia pertaining to Lord Cochrane (see box below) including his staff.

Next door to the Museo Histórico, housed in Valdivia's old brewery, is the **Museo de Arte Contemporaneo** or "MAC" as it's known (Tues–Sun 10am–1pm & 3–6pm; CH$1000). An attractive modern building, it is bare inside with white partition walls and a rough concrete ceiling – a space with a raw, unfinished feel for installations as well as

LORD COCHRANE

South America's struggle for independence is a colourful blend of farce and heroism, performed by a polyglot band of brigands and adventurers, most of whom were seasoned veterans of the Peninsular War and knew little but the art of warfare. **Lord Thomas Cochrane**, tenth Earl of Dundonald, GCB, was one such man.

Cochrane was born into an impoverished family in Annsfield, Lanarkshire, in 1775. At the age of seventeen he entered the Royal Navy as a midshipman, and over the next twelve years wreaked more havoc on the Spanish and French forces than Nelson, prompting Napoleon to dub him Le Loup de Mer (the Seawolf). By 1818, however, when he was approached by Chile's political agent in Britain to be the first Vice Admiral of Chile's three-ship navy, Cochrane was in trouble: he'd just been imprisoned for taking part in a successful ruse to defraud the London Stock Exchange of half a million pounds. Cochrane accepted the Chileans' offer with alacrity – he needed the money. For their part, the Chileans – desperate for a naval commander with bravado to take on the Spanish navy, the key to the ultimate defeat of the Spanish in South America – were happy to overlook his shady past. José de San Martín, commander-in-chief of the Chilean Army, described him as "a great child who will give a lot of trouble but his services may prove invaluable".

Valdivia was the key to the Spanish supply routes, and was so well-fortified by the Spanish that it was called the "Gibraltar of South America". General Ramón Freire, the Chilean general waging a bitter war against the Spanish-backed Mapuche Indians, considered that "cold calculation would make it appear that the attempt to take Valdivia is madness". However, late one summer evening in 1820, Cochrane sailed into the mouth of the río Valdivia on board a captured fifty-gun barque, right under the noses of the Spaniards and of their 118 bronze cannons. There he broke out the Spanish colours and requested a pilot, who he promptly clapped in irons, then sailed back out to sea. Convinced that such a ruse could work again he went north to Concepción, and persuaded a reluctant General Freire to lend him men and ships to undertake a seemingly impossible attack on Spain's most impregnable Pacific port. Freire offered Cochrane as much as he could because, he said, "the Spaniards will hardly believe us in earnest even when we commence".

Cochrane sailed south and anchored under the guns of Fuerte Aguada del Inglés, and attempted, once more, to pass off his ships as Spanish. The attempt failed, and the garrison opened fire on the ships' landing party of forty marines. But with the defenders distracted, a small group of soldiers led by a young Chilean ensign called Vidal were able to storm the fort from the rear. The Spaniards retreated in utter confusion, and the main Chilean force drove them out of one fort after another before finally taking Corral. The remaining forts were cleared of Spanish, and Valdivia was taken. Over seven hundred Spaniards had been defeated with the loss of seven Chileans.

When Cochrane left South America seven years later, he had played a decisive role in securing independence for not only Chile, but Peru and Brazil as well, and at the ripe old age of seventy he was helping drive the Turks from Greece. After his peaceful death in 1860 he was buried in London's Westminster Abbey, and *The London Times* wrote: "there have been greater heroes because there have been heroes with greater opportunities". On the corners of his tombstone are the coats-of-arms of Chile, Peru, Brazil and Greece.

more standard works. Its a museum for modern art, and doesn't have a permanent collection, filled instead with changing displays of visiting exhibitions.

North of the MAC and the Museo Histórico, at the end of Avenida Los Lingues, are two parks. The **Jardín Botánico** (daily: Dec–March 8am–8pm; April–Nov 8am–7pm; CH$300), east of the road in the grounds of the Universidad Austral de Chile, is peacefully located on the banks of ríos Cau Cau and Calle Calle, with a large collection of trees and shrubs from around the world. The much larger **Parque Saval** (daily: Dec–Feb 8am–8pm; March–Nov 8am–9pm; CH$150), on the other side of Avenida Los Lingues, to the west of the university campus, has waterfowl thriving on the attractive Laguna de los Lotus.

Eating and drinking

Valdivia has a couple of excellent restaurants, serving Chilean food with a Germanic twist, as well as the usual *lomo con papas fritas* outlets. Like most university towns, it also has a number of lively bars that thrive during term time.

Bataclan, Henriquez 326. Open from midnight until 5am, this music bar has live bands at weekends and its dance floor is inky dark and intimate.

Café Haussmann, O'Higgins 394. A small, old-fashioned bar where businessmen chat over a beer and plates of raw mince tartar on toast, or sip coffee and savour the excellent home-made cake.

Camino de Luna, Costanera Arturo Prat. Moored on a boat just upstream from the bridge to Isla Teja is the best restaurant in Valdivia. It's expensive, but worth it: try the German-Chilean hybrid *strudel de mariscos*.

Chester's, Henriquez 314. A small, cheerful café with good-value fast food.

Chocolatería Entre Lagos, Pérez Rosales 622. A famous chocolate shop, connected to a *salón de té* which sells giant veggie sandwiches, a wide range of ice creams and freshly made natural fruit juices.

La Calesa, Yungay 735 (☎63/225467; closed Sat evenings & Sun). Peruvian-owned, expensive international restaurant in a well-preserved colonial building. The menu includes steak Diane and chocolate fudge cake, and while some of the foreign dishes work well, the best ones are Peruvian.

Pub, Henriquez 326. A very popular evening haunt with live music and a good atmosphere.

Restaurant Shanghai, Carlos Anwandter 898. A comfortable, reasonably priced Chinese restaurant very close to the bus station.

Listings

Airlines Avant, Chacabuco 408, Local 27 (☎63/251431); Ladeco, Caupolicán 364, Local 7 y 8 (☎63/213392); Lan Chile, O'Higgins 386 (☎63/218841).

Banks and exchange There are quite a few banks with ATMs in the centre of town, such as Banco Santander at Pérez Rosales 585 (☎63/213066). For *cambios* try Arauco, Galería Arauco 331, Local 24; La Reconquista, Carampangue 325.

Car rental Assef v Méndez, General Lagos 1335 (☎63/213205, fax 215966); Autovald, Camilo Henríquez 610 (☎63/212786); Hertz, Ramón Picarte 640 (☎63/218316).

Internet access Letelier 236, Oficina 202, by the Prat Pharmacy; US$5 an hour.

Laundry There are many on Camino Henriquez, for example Lavasolo, at no. 656.

Telephone Centre Entel, Pérez Rosales 601, Oficina 1.

Travel agency Excursiones Turisticas "Los Notros", O'Higgins 189 (☎63/211030).

Niebla and Corral

At the mouth of the Río Valdivia, 18km from Valdivia by boat or car, is **NIEBLA** and its fort (Dec–March daily 10am–7pm; April–Nov Tues–Sun 10am–5pm; CH$500). Niebla

CHRISTOPHER SAINSBURY

Traditional wooden church, Tenaún, Chiloé

CHRISTOPHER SAINSBURY

Araucarias, Parque Nacional Conguillío

CHARLES BOWMAN

View across Lago Llanquihue to Volcán Osorno

CHRISTOPHER SAINSBURY

Palafitos, Castro, Chiloé

CHRISTOPHER SAINSBURY

Germanic house, Frutillar Bajo

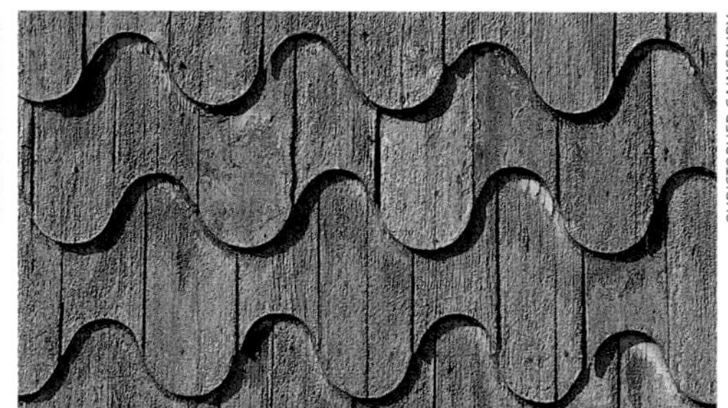

CHRISTOPHER SAINSBURY

Tejuelas (wooden tiles), Chiloé

CHRISTOPHER SAINSBURY

A truck on the Carretera Austral

CHRISTOPHER SAINSBURY

Confluence of the Nef and Baker rivers, Carretera Austral

B. GADSBY, TRIP

Wind-sculpted trees, Tierra del Fuego

CHRISTOPHER SAINSBURY

Estancia San Gregorio, Chilean Patagonia

A. GASSON, TRIP

Below the Laguna San Rafael glacier

CHRISTOPHER SAINSBURY

Guanacos in Parque Nacional Torres del Paine

ANDREW BENSON

Ahu Tongariki, Easter Island

itself is a motley string of *cabañas* and restaurants half-hidden from the road, often grey with mist or rain (*niebla* means fog in Spanish) but the fort is a little jewel. The **Fuerte de Niebla** (or Castillo de la Pura y Limpia Concepción de Montfort de Lemus, to give it its full name), was originally built by the Spanish from 1667 to 1672 as part of an extensive line of defences of this key position in their empire, and massively enlarged in the eighteenth century according to the design of the Royal Engineers in Madrid. Today it's been restored and houses a small museum, but the most interesting things remain the old features: the powder room, double-walled and well below ground level, the crenellated curtain wall hacked out of the bare rock, and the twelve slightly rusting cannons. The view from up here, high above the sea, is inspiring, and you can see how the fort dominated the mouth of the river far below. You can get here by boat from Valdivia (see p.304), or by one of the *colectivos* which run regularly from near the Mercado Fluvial and cost CH$400.

On the other side of the estuary lies the little village of **CORRAL**, a place with more substance than Niebla – it used to be a thriving port until it was flattened by the 1960 tidal wave – and another Spanish fort, **Castillo de San Luis de Alba de Almargos** (daily: mid-Dec to Feb 9am–7pm; March to mid-Dec 9am–11pm; CH$500). The only way across the river is by a half-hour ferry ride – boats leave from the pier at the entrance to town and the crossing costs CH$400 – keep an eye open for seals on the way over. For those who want to drive and have time to spare, there's an attractive 75km road from Niebla to Corral via Valdivia, which passes through thick forest along the banks of the rivers Valdivia, Angachilla, Futa and Tornagaleones.

The fort is just above the waterline and was built to complement Niebla's height. It's more ornate than Niebla, with little, stone-roofed towers to protect those unfortunates who had to spot the fall of the shells. From December 15 until the end of February, there's a twice daily re-enactment of an attack by corsairs at 3pm and 5pm, which ranges from an impressive display of period uniforms and weapons to a wet, miserable show by two men, a musket and a tired donkey.

Santuario de la Naturaleza Río Cruces

After the 1960 earthquake, the fifty kilometres of low-lying land around the río Cruces north of Valdivia was flooded, forming an extensive delta which has been called the **Santuario de la Naturaleza Río Cruces**. This marsh now forms an important breeding ground and resting place for over ninety species of migrating birds. The importance of this wetland area was officially recognized by UNESCO in 1981, and forty-eight square kilometres became a protected nature reserve in 1982. You can catch glimpses of the area travelling along the road between Temuco and Valdivia, but to fully appreciate it you need to take a boat tour from Valdivia (see p.304).

Lago Ranco

Back on the Panamericana and heading south, the next temptation off the highway is pretty **Lago Ranco** 91km east of Valdivia, surrounded by dozens of distant mountains on a high and rugged skyline. The lake is big – the second largest in the region, covering over four hundred square kilometres – and is bordered to the east by flat land, and to the west by the rising Andes. Around the lake's edge is a 121-kilometre dirt road, passing the village of **Futrono** – small and tidy but boring – and leading to **Llifén** on the eastern shore, a small village with good fishing. Beyond Llifén, hidden away in the mountains, is **Lago Maihue**, untouched and almost unvisited, while on the southeast shore is the village of **Lago Ranco**, undeveloped and shabby. In the middle of the lake is **Isla Huapi**, a Mapuche *reducción*, which you can visit from Futrono.

Because of its great size, in any other country Lago Ranco would be a major tourist attraction, but in Chile's Lake District it suffers from the competition: it's not as rustic as the Siete Lagos to the north, nor as fashionable as Lago Llanquihue to the south, and there's no way it can compare with Pucón's Lago Villarrica. Despite this, it's a pleasant place, somewhere to come and fish, or look at the scenery, or simply relax.

Futrono and Isla Huapi

FUTRONO, the village on the northern shore of Lago Ranco, is a one-street town with a good **Oficina de Turismo** (Mon–Fri: mid-Dec to mid-March 9am–9pm; mid-March to mid-Dec 8am–1pm & 2–6pm; ☎63/481389) but nothing much to offer. It's a ten-minute walk from the lake, has no decent beach, and as a result has seen minimal tourist development. The only thing to draw you is the fact that the **boats for Isla Huapi**, the Mapuche reserve, leave from here on Mondays, Wednesdays and Fridays at 7am, returning at 5pm. The crossing costs CH$500.

Futrono has a couple of **places to stay**: *Posada del Lago*, Juan Luis Sanfuentes (☎ & fax 63/481660; ④), right on the edge of the lake and built like a Swiss chalet, is comfortable and has a terrace above the stony beach. Nearer the centre of the village *Hostería El Rincon Arabe*, Manuel Montt (☎63/481406; ③) is set in a small quiet garden with a swimming pool and has a restaurant specializing in Arab food. There's a **campground** ten kilometres west of Futrono called *Camping Bahía Coigüe* (☎63/481264) with a good beach and supervized activities. It's expensive – sites cost CH$28,000 in January and February, and CH$14,000 during the rest of the year – but good for a splurge if you've got a car.

Futrono's connected to Valdivia by one bus an hour, run by Buses Futrono (☎63/202225).

Isla Huapi, the largest island in the middle of Lago Ranco, is a Mapuche *reducción* and a haven of peace and quiet, with pocket-sized fields, scattered huts, and winding tracks just wide enough for the teams of oxen that pull water carts up from the lakeshore. Visitors are made very welcome but you should be sensitive, especially with your camera. There are two separate communities on the island and at the full moon between January and February they both meet for a great council, **trapëmuwn**, which lasts for twenty-four hours. With its origins in the ancient Mapuche harvest ceremony, *lepún*, this gathering decides all matters affecting the island's two communities. Held in the open, the proceedings are shrouded from the view of outside observers by a thick stockade of branches which also serve to protect the participants from the elements, but there is enough to see and hear, with the seemingly interminable debates being broken by the beating of drums, *kultrún*, and blowing of pipes, *trutruca*. Take food and drink because this can be quite a long day. There's no accommodation on the island.

Llifén and Lago Maihue

LLIFÉN, 22km along the northern shore from Futrono, is a remote little place, tucked on a ledge between the forest and the lake, but it's been a famous **fishing destination** since the 1930s, when the logging companies moved in and discovered that its rivers and lakes were teeming with fish. There's plenty of **accommodation** here, most of it oriented towards fishermen, and quite expensive. Just outside the village on its own private beach is *Hostería Huequecura* (Nov–April; ☎09/653 5450; ⑤), which has excellent views across the lake and an agreeable run-down air. Cheaper is *Hostal Llifén* (☎63/481669; ③), an old family house with newly modernized en-suite rooms and a large garden. Twelve kilometres east is the *Cumilahue Lodge* (reservations: ☎ & fax 2/231 1027; ⑦), Chile's best-known fly-fishing lodge, set in native forest with exclusive river access.

Even more remote than Llifén, and hardly known about, is **Lago Maihue**, 12km to the east as the crow flies, but 33km by road. It's a beautiful, lonely lake, surrounded by forest and with the jagged ice of the high Andes on the horizon. There's no accommodation here, not even a village, just the occasional farmer, so wild **camping** is the only option. There's no public transport either, so to get here you have to hitch or drive.

Lago Ranco village

A passable but rough dirt road, dotted with the occasional campsite and *hostería*, follows the southern edge of the lake 47km from Llifén to **LAGO RANCO** village – a scruffy place, its streets lined with dogs dozing against the peeling weatherboard and the lakefront hidden by a jungle of trees, but with a neglected charm. There's a good beach, and a two-minute swim into the lake offers beautiful views of the cordillera. On the lakefront are a couple of passable neighbouring *residenciales*: *Casona Italiana*, Viña del Mar 145 (☎63/491225; ③), with *cabañas* that look like oversized dolls' houses; and *Hostería Phoenix*, Viña del Mar 141 (☎63/491226; ④), a little hotel with a restaurant. The best place to **eat** is *Ruca Ranco*, near the jetty, which serves good, standard Chilean set meals. The **tourist office** (Dec–March Mon–Fri 10am–9pm; no phone) is on the western edge of town, run by very helpful, friendly volunteers.

Lago Ranco is well served by **buses**: Inter Sur, Tur Bus, Buses Cayumapu, Pirehueico and Expresso Panguipulli all come here from Valdivia every half- hour, and there are also regular services from Santiago and Osorno.

Osorno and around

As with the Siete Lagos, the only way of getting south from Lago Ranco is to head back to the Panamericana. The 50km road west from Lago Ranco village joins the highway at the unremarkable town of **Río Bueno**, and 30km south is **OSORNO**.

Despite being founded in one of the best defensive positions of all the Spaniards' frontier forts, Osorno was regularly sacked by Mapuche Indians between 1553 and 1796 when Chile's governor, Ambrosio O'Higgins, ordered it to be resettled. From tentative beginnings it has grown into a thriving city mainly due to the industry of European settlers who felled the forests and began to develop the great dairy herds that form the backbone of the economy today.

Today, Osorno is an agricultural city: it's almost easier to buy a tractor here than to cash a traveller's cheque, and it has little for the tourist – except **buses**, which as transport hub for the southern Lake District and starting point for the region's main road into Argentina, it has aplenty. This abundance of public transport makes it easy to visit Osorno's surrounding attractions – **Lago Puyehue** in the cordillera; **Parque Nacional Puyehue**, one of Chile's most-visited national parks, **Volcán Antillanca**, which boasts some of the best skiing south of Santiago; and quiet, little-visited **Lago**

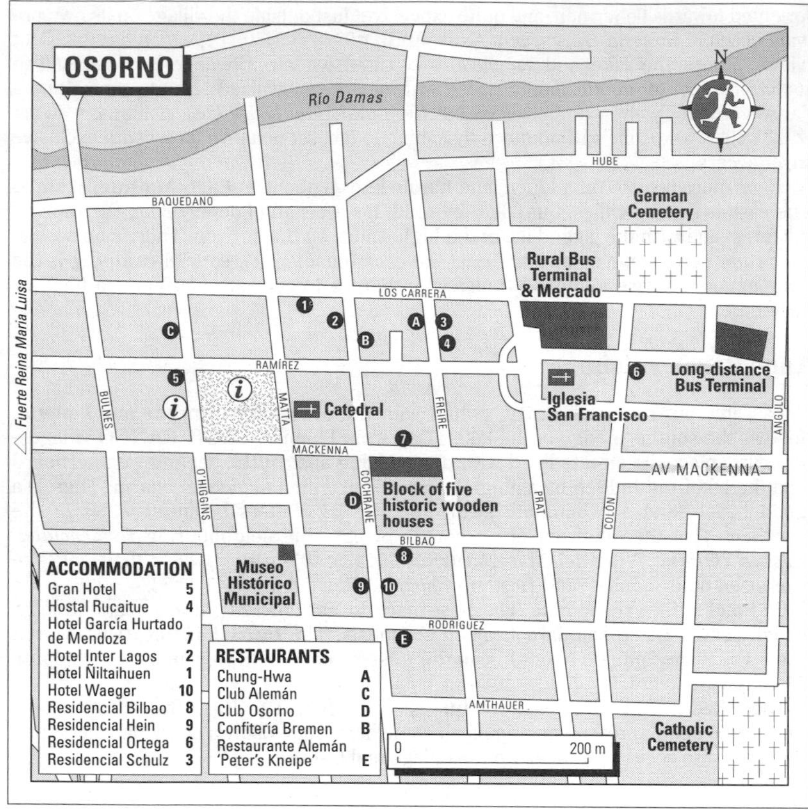

Rupanco. And if you've had enough of mountains and lakes for the moment, to the west there are the long sandy beaches on the coast around **Bahía Mansa**.

Arrival and information

Both of Osorno's **bus terminals** are less than a block from each other on calle Errázuriz and very close to the city centre. The long distance terminal is at Errázuriz 1400 (☎64/234149), and the rural terminal is at Mercado Municipal, Errázuriz 1300 ☎64/232073. Rail services no longer run to Osorno.

Seven kilometres from the city Osorno's **airport**, known as Carlos Hott Siebert or Cañal Bajo, is served by daily flights from Temuco and Santiago.Taxis wait for incoming flights.

Sernatur's **information office** (Mon–Fri 8.30am–1pm & 2.30–6.30pm; ☎64/237575, fax 234104) is in the Gobernación building on the west side of the Plaza de Armas, and is filled with maps and leaflets. Rather better, though, is the municipal Oficina de Turismo in the Municipalidad building, on the south of the plaza (same hours as Sernatur; ☎64/232523, fax 232073). There's also an information kiosk on the plaza in summer, and another in the long-distance bus terminal. Conaf is at Martínez de Rozas 430 (☎ & fax 64/234393).

Accommodation

Osorno's **accommodation** is largely aimed at travelling salesmen and businessmen, so the mid-range is good but the low end's a bit thin on the ground. The cheapest option is to pitch a tent at the municipal **campsite**, *Olegario Mohr* (CH$2000), which is a taxi ride from town, by the río Damas near the Panamericana.

Gran Hotel, O'Higgins 615 (☎64/232171, fax 239311). A large 1950s building, with small, spartan rooms, but those overlooking the Plaza de Armas make up for it with a good view. ⑤.

Hostal Rucaitue, Freire 546 (☎64/239922, fax 310617). Bright and cheerful, with en-suite rooms and a good café/bar. ④.

Hotel García Hurtado de Mendoza, Juan Mackenna 1040 (☎64/237111, fax 237113). A modern hotel with a sauna, gymnasium, a good restaurant and bar with outside tables. ⑥.

Hotel Inter Lagos, Cochrane 515 (☎64/234695, fax 232581). Of all the similar hotels aimed at businessmen, the *Inter Lagos*' is the most characterful, and the staff are very friendly. ⑤.

Hotel Ñiltaihuen, Carrera 951 (☎64/232356, fax 238772). An old colonial house that's been converted into double and triple suites with cooking facilities. ④.

Hotel Waeger, Cochrane 816 (☎64/233721, fax 237080). A relaxing hotel, mainly due to the muted colour scheme and subtle lighting from intriguing junk metal wall lamps. The rooms are modern and good. ⑥.

Residencial Bilbao, Bilbao 1019 (☎64/236755, fax 231111). Jolly, welcoming and well-equipped for the price, with snug rooms. There's a small dining room in which set meals are available. ④.

Residencial Hein, Cochrane 843 (☎64/234116). Almost as old as its chatty owner, this traditional little house has clean rooms and a welcoming little bar-cum-dining room. ③.

Residencial Ortega, Colon 602 (☎64/232592). Close to the bus terminal a small, clean bed and breakfast with a sunny conservatory to sit in: whilst you're having your breakfast you can watch all the travelling salesmen cleaning their cars. ③.

Residencial Schulz, Freire 530 (☎64/237211, fax 246466). Once past the overwhelming log cabin of a lobby, the rooms in this establishment are clean and cheerful. ③.

The City

What strikes you first about Osorno is its ghastly **churches**, the most obvious being the **cathedral** on the Plaza de Armas. Topped with a large concrete lattice shaped like a two-dimensional, five-storey abstract of a bishop's mitre, this grim ferro-cement facade stamps an impression of uncompromising ugly modernity on all around. There's another horrible church, **Iglesia San Francisco**, three blocks east.

The southern side of the Plaza is calle Juan Mackenna, the east–west road on which the Municipalidad stands. If you walk two blocks east, you'll see a row of **wooden houses**, built between 1876 and 1923, that have miraculously survived earthquake, fire and ruthless property developers and have been declared national monuments. The prettiest is the two-storey clapboard **Casa Schüller**, painted pink, with a grey roof and lime green borders, an ornate porch, and a hexagonal side tower that sports a weather vane. Unfortunately, you can't go inside most of them, except for **Casa Stuckrate**, at no. 1069, which is also a shop.

One block southwest of Juan Mackenna is the **Museo Histórico Municipal**, Matta 809 on the corner of Bilbao (Mon–Fri 9am–12.30pm & 2.30–6pm, Sat 10am–1pm & 3–6pm; Jan–March also Sun 3–6pm; free), housed in one of Osorno's earliest stone buildings, constructed in 1929, and a little disappointing. Osorno's history is depicted mainly in some old photographs, with a collection of daggers and swords from the colonial era, as well as the odd piece of Mapuche pottery and cloth. The gloomy ground floor rooms grab the attention the most, containing the bones, teeth and tusks of a mastodon, one of the giant herbivores that roamed the central plain between the coastal range and the Andes, twenty thousand years ago. Also here are artefacts belonging to the Atacameña culture, which thrived around Azapa near Arica in the far north, including fragments of textiles, pottery shards and a mummified body thousands of years old.

The ancient world is also in evidence five blocks or so west of the plaza, south of the bridge over the río Rahue. The **Fuerte Reina María Luisa** is a reconstructed fort on the site of the town's original foundations. From the low stone battlements there is a good view down onto the river, lined with tall Lombardy poplars and weeping willows.

Eating and drinking

The food in Osorno has a strong Germanic flavour, a legacy of the nineteenth-century settlers – don't miss out on the Germanic cakes (*küchen*), tarts (*tortas*) and chocolates.

Chung-Hwa, Matta 517. One of the oldest Chinese restaurants in the south, which has a friendly family atmosphere but average food.

Club Alemán, O'Higgins 563. Old-fashioned place, with a menu of local specialities based on trout, pork and venison dishes, and a cosy separate bar with wood panelling and incongruous tartan decor.

Club Osorno, Cochrane 759 (closed Sun). From the outside this club looks very uninviting, more like a Methodist meeting hall than a gaming den. Inside, there's a bar serving a wide range of appetizing nibbles (*picoteos*) to keep the local businessmen going during their games of *dudo* (liar dice). Set lunches for CH$3500 are served all afternoon during the week.

Confitería Bremen, Cochrane 588. A very popular café with a huge selection of *küchen* and an unhurried atmosphere.

La Paisana, O'Higgins 827. Impossible to guess from the name, but this is predominately an Arab restaurant. Try the mouthwatering set meal of stuffed aubergines, sweet peppers, vine leaves and meatballs for CH$4500.

Restaurante Alemán "Peter's Kneipe", Manuel Rodríguez 1039. Dishes from the Vaterland: huge meat platters, *chucrut* (sauerkraut) and strudel.

Listings

Airlines Air France, Bilbao 943, Oficina 1 (☎64/234850); Alitalia, Cochrane 651, Oficina 101 (☎64/237878); Iberia, Freire 602, Oficina 311 (☎64/246666); KLM, Bilbao 717 (☎64/237878); Ladeco, Mackenna 1098 (☎ & fax 64/234355); Lan Chile, Matta 862 (☎64/236688).

Banks and exchange There are banks and ATMs around the plaza. For *cambios*, try Cambio Tour, on Mackenna at 1004, or Turismo Frontera, Ramírez 959, Oficina 11.

Bus companies International buses: Andesmar (☎64/233050); Bus Norte International (☎64/233319); Cruz del Sur (☎64/232777); Rio de la Plata (☎64/233633); Tas Choapa (☎64/233933). Regional buses: Buses Pirehueico (☎64/233050); Igi Llaima (☎64/234371); Lit (☎64/237048); Pullman Sur (☎64/232777); Varmontt (☎64/232732); Via Tur (☎64/230118). Local for the coast: Buses Maicolpue (☎64/230402); Buses Mar (☎64/236166); for Puyehue: Expresos Puyehue (☎64/243919); Geo Sur Mercado (☎64/243927).

Car rental Budget, Freire 848 (☎64/235303); First, Mackenna 959 (☎64/233861); Osorno Rent a Car, Ejército 448 (☎64/245488).

Consulates France, O'Higgins 517 (☎64/232647); Germany, Mackenna 967, Oficina 4 (☎64/232151).

Hospital Hospital Regional, off Buhler in the suburb of La Cantera (☎64/235572).

Internet access *Satanca Pub*, Patio Freire 542.

Shopping Alta Artesanía, Juan Mackenna 1069, is crammed with every conceivable type of gift, from replica Mapuche jewellery to flying ducks. You can pick up very good leatherwork in the Mercado Municipal, Errázuriz s/n.

Telephone centre Entel, Eleuterio Ramírez 1107 L 9.

Travel agencies Tours to Parque Nacional Puyehue cost CH$25,000 for a half-day and CH$35,000 for a full day. Turismo Reina Luisa (the name might be changing), O'Higgins 580, Oficina 43 (☎ & fax 64/243855) is run by the woman who also manages the municipal tourist office, while Osorno Tour, Ramírez 949, Oficina 5 (☎ & fax 64/238034), and Agencia Aventur, Patio Freire, Oficina 8 (☎64/243036), are well-respected local operators.

The coast

Until recently, the only occupant of **BAHÍA MANSA** and its neighbouring beaches was a small fishing fleet. The building of a good 64-kilometre tarred road west from Osorno changed that, and this small, sandy stretch of coast is now an increasingly popular summer holiday area. It's all a bit basic, though, and small chalets are springing up all over the vertiginous hillsides without proper services.

There's not much at Bahía Mansa itself, just a fish dock surrounded by high cliffs, but 2km further south, **Maicolpué** is a large, beautiful bay, and has bars, discos, very good-value seafood restaurants and a couple of rustic but comfortable **places to stay**. The German/Chilean-owned *Hostería Miller* (Dec–April; ☎64/233087; ④) has *cabañas* and rooms with good views, while *Hostería Maicolpue* (no phone; ③) has small, clean rooms and a good restaurant with a terrace overlooking the beach. There is a poor **campsite** by the beach, which costs CH$3000 (cold showers are extra), but there are some small secluded bays where wild camping is possible.

North of Bahía Mansa, a 4km road follows the very beautiful río Tarahuín to the attractive beach of **Pucatrihue**. There, sand dunes have formed a lagoon rich in birdlife, above which is perched *Hostería Las Dunas* (Dec–April; no phone; ③). Very exposed on top of its dune, the wind can really whistle through this old wooden building, but it has reasonable small rooms and a large restaurant.

You can visit the coast on a day-trip from Osorno: Buses Mar and Maicolpue, come here twice daily, departing from the Mercado Municipal in the suburb of Rahue.

Lago Puyehue and the thermal springs

The 47km road which shoots east from Osorno to **Lago Puyehue** passes through some rich and fertile farmland. Every hundred metres or so you see roadside signs advertising *miel* (honey), *tomates* (tomatoes), *frambuesas* (raspberries), *frutillas* (strawberries) and, just occasionally, *torros* (bulls). It's a land of flat, lush meadows and trees, of battered aluminium milk churns left by the road for collection. As the road nears the lake, you see rugged hills and mountains on the horizon, including the spiked pyramid of **Volcán Puntiagudo** (2490m). Reaching the village of **ENTRE LAGOS**, you glimpse the water of Lago Puyehue stretching away into the distance, enclosed in deep-green hills.

Entre Lagos is pleasant enough and makes a base from which to explore the thermal springs further up the road, but it has no real tourist facilities, save for a clutch of *residenciales*. The priciest night's sleep is at *Hostería Entre Lagos*, Ramírez 65 (☎ & fax 64/371225; ⑤), right on the edge of the lake, with modern en-suite rooms and a reasonable restaurant, but *Hostal Millaray*, Ramírez 333 (☎64/371251; ③), is better: an excellent B&B, with a secluded balcony overlooking the water. The cheapest option is *Hospedaje y Camping Panorama*, General Lagos 687 (☎64/371398; ②), with a lakeside garden where you can camp (CH$3750), run by a friendly family who will let you use the kitchen. *La Chacrita*, on the edge of town by the main road, is a good place to **eat**, with enormous portions of meat.

As you drive east of Entre Lagos the lake appears and disappears through the trees on your left, and the lakeshore is dotted with campsites, *hospedajes* and hotels. There's a fork after 32km: the left-hand road heads on to the Anticura section of the Parque

Nacional Puyehue and the Argentine border, while the right-hand one leads to the Aguas Calientes section and the Antillanca skiing resort, passing the thermal springs of one of Chile's most famous and fashionable hotels.

The thermal springs

For many years, the **Gran Hotel Termas de Puyehue** (☎2/293 6000, fax 283 1010; *puyehue@ctcreuna.cl*; ⑥), 1km beyond the fork, was considered to be one of Chile's best hotels, and the rich, famous and powerful passed through its massive entrance tower. Like many other Chilean hotels, however, it rested on its laurels and let a couple of decades of interior design pass it by, but now it's beginning to wake up and is currently being renovated. Although the rooms show their age a little and the vast halls are empty and echoing, it's still a beautiful place, with idyllic woods, rolling lawns and a sweeping view over Lago Puyehue.

Its *raison d'être*, though, are the **hot springs** that flow in its grounds. A new, beautiful spa has been built, and the volcanic waters now trickle into kidney-shaped pools under a pitched roof of local honey-coloured woods. There are hot, warm and cool pools, as well as mud baths, water massage, mountain bikes for rent and horse-riding. A day spent here will relax even the most stressed, and all-day use for non-residents costs from CH$7000.

Two kilometres down the road, there's another set of hot springs at *Aguas Calientes* (☎64/232881; Jan to mid-March ⑤; mid-March to Dec; ③), right at the entrance to the Parque Nacional Puyehue. It's run by the same company as the *Gran Hotel*, and offers much the same thing as its distinguished neighbour, but in less plush surroundings. It has *tinas* (personal bathtubs), double *tinas* (so you can bathe with a friend), and indoor and outdoor pools. Use of the pools is CH$3000, a cost that's included in the price of a *cabaña* in summer. These *cabañas* are well-equipped (modern fridges, cookers, wood stoves and so on), but they are arranged in a military-style row that gives little privacy. For those who want somewhere more private, there are two **campsites** which charge upwards of CH$7000 a site.

Geo Sur Mercado and Expresos Puyehue **buses** leave twice daily from Osorno and travel up to the *termas*.

Parque Nacional Puyehue

PARQUE NACIONAL PUYEHUE (daily 8.30am–6.30pm; CH$800), 81km from Osorno, is one of Chile's busiest national parks, largely because of the traffic on the international road that runs through its middle. It's part of a massive, fifteen-thousand-square-kilometre area of protected wilderness, one of the largest in the Andes: it borders the Parque Nacional Vicente Pérez Rosales to the south, and some Argentinian parks which stretch all the way to Pucón's Parque Nacional Villarrica in the north. The land is high temperate rainforest spread over two volcanoes, Volcán Puyehue (2240m) and Volcán Casablanca (1990m), on the west slope of which is the Antillanca ski resort.

The park's divided into three sectors: **Aguas Calientes** where the *termas* are (see above), **Antillanca** and **Anticura**, which straddles the international road.

The Conaf station and information centre is at Aguas Calientes, where there's a large, detailed **map of the park** on the wall, invaluable for orienting yourself. There are several **walks** in the area, mainly short, self-guided nature trails, but also a couple of longer hikes. El Pinero (3600m return), for example, is a ninety-minute walk up a nearby hill, from where there's a good view of Volcán Casablanca, the río Chanleufu and part of Lago Puyehue. A two-day trip Lago Bertín y Antillanca (17km), follows the old road to Antillanca Sector, through the dense forest along the banks of the río Chanleufu. There's a six-bed **refugio** around the halfway point at Lago Bertín, deep in the heart of the park, and the next day you can continue on to Antillanca, 9km further

on, returning to Aguas Calientes along the road (there's usually enough traffic to hitch).

The **ski centre** at Antillanca, the *Centro Turistico Deportivo Antillanca* (☎64/235114, fax 238877; ⑥), is 18km from Aguas Calientes by road. The centre's open all year, and has a restaurant, open-air swimming pool, gymnasium, ski-rental shop and some apartments which book up quickly in season, as well as plenty of good runs. In summer it's quiet with excellent views along the cordillera and right across the central plain to the Pacific Ocean, but in winter (June–Oct) it gets so busy that traffic here is subject to time restrictions (Mon–Fri up 8.30am–2pm & 3–5pm, down 2.20–4.20pm & 5.30–7.30pm, Sat & Sun up 8.30am–4pm, down 1.20–8pm).

Anticura is 22km from Aguas Calientes, back to the junction by the *Gran Hotel Termas de Puyehue* and along the international road to Argentina, a very pretty length of road with lakes dotted either side. There are a number of short **hikes** around the Conaf station, mostly designed for car drivers who just want a quick amble, and the prettiest is the walk to El Salto del Indio (CH$800) a half-hour stroll through a forest of ancient coigüe to a broad waterfall. More adventurous is the trail to Volcán Puyehue, which starts 2km west of Anticura, opposite a church, where there's a small Conaf office. The beginning of the path passes over some private property, where you can organize a guide and horses (though you don't need either), and after three hours reaches a refuge near the end of the forest. Shortly past here, the path forks: the right-hand route goes up the volcano (2hr; no special equipment needed) and from the crater there are views over Lagos Puyehue and Rupanco. The left-hand path leads to a thermal spring next to an icy stream, half a day's walk from the refuge. You can mix the waters and bathe – an amazing experience at night, cooking yourself gently in the waters underneath the stars.

Park practicalities

Apart from the ski centre, the refuges and the Aguas Calientes complex, there's nowhere to stay or eat in the park. There are a couple of **buses** a day to Aguas Calientes from Osorno, run by Geo Sur Mercado and Expresos Puyehue. There aren't any buses to Antillanca, but Agencia Aventur in Osorno (see p.313) arranges transport on request. To get to Anticura, take one of the many international buses heading to Bariloche in Argentina and ask to be let off when the bus passes the Conaf station. The Chilean customs post (daily: Nov–March 8am–9pm; April–Oct 9am–7pm) is 4km down the road from Anticura, and the Argentine border post is 44km beyond it.

Lago Rupanco

Lago Rupanco, 13km south of Lago Puyehue, is a very pretty flat blue lake, delved into by fingers of pine-covered spurs and ringed by five volcanoes. In the west the land is flat pasture, lined with hedgerows and rows of stately poplars, and in the east it rises into forest, volcanoes and towering rock ridges. With no tar road it's still rural and undeveloped, and much of the traffic is made up of *huasos* and their dogs, driving herds of cattle in clouds of dust.

The eastern end of the lake is just about completely owned by *Hacienda Rupanco* (☎ & fax 64/203000; ⑧), one of the largest dairy farms in Chile. It has recently diversified into upmarket tourism (ambassadors spend their holidays here), and offers a couple of well-furnished houses and a wide range of activities on its vast lands: horse-riding (from CH$9400 for a half-day), fishing (from CH$47,000 for a day), and "agro-tourism" – generally helping out with the livestock and seeing how the farm works (CH$11,750 a day). If this is too rich for your blood, then head 23km along the south bank of the lake where you'll hit the other end of the scale. The *Hostería Piedra Negra Rupanco* (no phone; ②) looks like it's shut – dogs bark as you come in, the main building is locked and the locks are rusted – but up a hill by the chicken coop there's a man in a string vest who will let you use the musty old *cabañas*.

At the far east of the lake, 23km beyond the *hostería*, there's one of the most beautifully sited fishing lodges in the whole Lake District. *Bahía Escocia Fly Fishing* (☎64/371515 – a temperamental radio phone; ⑥), 2km beyond the bus stop in the village of **Puerto Rico**, looks out over the rugged hills and down the lake towards the pastoral west. The lodge has all the atmosphere of a family home, and it's run by a Chilean-American couple, he a fly-fishing guide, and she a chef from Seattle. It's more a centre for fishing (weekend's angling trip with full board CH$185,650) and horse-trips than a backpacker's lodge, but even if you don't want to fish and hate horses it's worth staying here because it's so gorgeous.

Igi Llaima runs one **bus** a day (2hr) from Osorno to Puerto Rico, the village 2km west of the *Bahia Escocia* lodge. A boat often meets it and transfers passengers off to the trail-head of the Los Todos Santos hike (see p.322), charging CH$20,000 per boatload.

Lago Llanquihue and around

Lago Rupanco isn't well served with roads, and although you can head south along some scenic dirt tracks, most people travel back to Osorno and down the Panamericana. From Osorno this venerable road at first passes through some unremarkable scenery, but after about 55km you catch sight of a large body of water. This is **Lago Llanquihue**, the only one of the region's lakes that's visible from Ruta 5, and an immense inland sea of 870 square kilometres. Far across the lake is one of the icons of the Lake District, the symmetrical perfection of the Mount Fuji-like **Volcán Osorno** (2661m). It's a stunning sight, all the more extraordinary because the lake is not surrounded by the extreme country you normally associate with volcanoes, but by gently rolling pastures, dotted with black and white Friesian cows, and stalls selling fresh and smoked trout.

The little villages around Lago Llanquihue differ greatly. **Frutillar Bajo** on the west is a summer holiday resort beloved by Chileans, **Puerto Octay** to the north is a neat little Bavarian-looking town, and bustling **Puerto Varas** in the south is fast challenging Pucón as the Lake District's adventure tourism centre. One thing that unites them is their shared German heritage, a result of an influx of German and Swiss settlers in the mid-nineteenth century. Some people still speak German rather than Spanish at home, and live in houses filled with portraits of flaxen-haired, pale-eyed European men in high-collared Victorian apparel.

By the time you come to the village of **Ensenada** on the far east of the lake, forest has overtaken dairy fields and the land begins to rise as you enter the foothills of the Andes. This forest extends to the border, and is protected by the **Parque Nacional Vicente Pérez Rosales**. The national park is a favourite scenic route into Argentina, as it contains the long, sinuous **Lago Todos Los Santos** across which ferries run towards the border.

South of Ensenada the road winds its way down through isolated country down to the placid calm of Chile's northernmost **fjord**, a branch of the Estuario de Reloncaví. Here, a hundred kilometres inland from the open sea you can taste the salt air, and eat fresh shellfish in the tiny villages of **Ralún** and **Cochamó**.

Frutillar Bajo

The Panamericana first approaches Lago Llanquihue at Frutillar Alto, a low-cost housing suburb 4km west of **FRUTILLAR BAJO**, the little village that for many Chileans is synonymous with summer holidays. Frutillar Bajo is a village of black-sand beaches, fastidiously tended grass verges and a magical view of Volcán Osorno, soaring above the shimmering surface of the lake. Because it's so popular it gets very crowded here in summer, especially in the second week of February when the town hosts an **international music festival**.

There are only two main streets to Frutillar Bajo: Vicente Pérez Rosales and Avenida Phillippi, which both run parallel with the coast. At the bottom of the hill leading from Frutillar Alto, near the junction with Vicente Pérez Rosales, is a beautifully tended garden, an old water mill and several other traditional wooden buildings which make up the **Museo Colonial Alemán** (daily: mid-Dec to mid-March 10am–2pm & 3–8pm; mid-March to mid-Dec 10am–2pm & 3–6pm; CH$1000). The museum houses a wide variety of household objects and farm machinery used by the earliest emigrants to Llanquihue, but most interesting is the barn outside. Circular barns, *campanarios*, like the one which now houses a collection of early agricultural machinery, were once a common sight in the coastal mountains but have now completely vanished. Inside, pairs of horses were tethered to the central pillar and driven round in circles, threshing sheaves of corn with their hoofs. Further up the hill in the **Casa del Herrero**, the blacksmith's house, you can buy horseshoes with your name stamped on them, and higher up still is the reconstruction of a typical early farmhouse filled with period furniture.

Crossing over the main road by the museum and turning left at the end of Vicente Pérez Rosales, a dirt road leads to the **Reserva Forestal Edmundo Winkler** (daily 10am–7pm; CH$400). Hemmed in by low hills, in an area of perfectly preserved native forest, the Universidad Austral de Chile has set up an experimental forestry station. In January and February students and staff conduct guided walks and help visitors to identify the sixty species of trees, flowers and shrubs that grow here, and the station sells native and exotic saplings.

Practicalities

You'll **arrive** in Frutillar Alto, not Frutillar Bajo, unless you've caught one of the summer minibuses that run directly there from Puerto Montt and Puerto Varas. From Frutillar Alto, you can walk the 4km down to the lakeshore, or catch one of the *colectivos* which run shuttle services from the Varmontt stop (at the Panamericana end of the main street Carlos Richter). In Frutillar Bajo there's a lakefront **tourist information office**, on Avenida Phillippi and O'Higgins (Jan & Feb daily 8.30am–1pm & 2–9pm; April–Dec Mon–Fri 8.30am–1pm & 2–5.45pm; ☎65/421080).

Apart from the bank and town hall, every building in Frutillar seems to offer **accommodation** during the summer. Anywhere on Avenida Phillippi with rooms facing the lake charges a premium and gets booked up well in advance, though if you *must* have a lakeshore bed there are some excellent farmhouse B&Bs outside the village. In the centre the cheapest option is *Hospedaje Alemán*, Phillippi 231 (☎65/421324, fax 421224; Jan–Feb ③, Aug–Dec ②; closed March–Sept), with its entrance behind the school. The rooms are good, there are private bathrooms, a communal kitchen and breakfast is included. More expensive is *Hotel Klein Salzburg*, Phillippi 663 (☎65/421201, fax 421201; ⑥), with gingerbread eaves and an authentically decorated dining room. Between the two prices is *Hospedaje Melita von Bischoffshausen*, Phillippi 1379 (☎65/421416; closed April–Dec; ③), a small bed and breakfast in an attractive house crammed with German books. One kilometre south of the village there's *Hostal Parque del Lago* (☎65/421235; ③), a working farm owned by a friendly young couple, who have horses you can ride.

As you might expect, there's no shortage of places to **eat** in Frutillar and *onces* (afternoon tea) is almost an obligatory ritual. There are several cafés along Phillippi where you can partake of the ritual, all of which have home-made *küchen*, but because of its large picture windows *Salón de Té Trayén*, Phillippi 963, is the best place to sit and soak up the calories. For good-value set lunches the only place to go is *Club Bomberos*, Phillippi 1065, in the old fire station. Upstairs in the quiet club room there is a good view over the lake and an impressive mural of a fire, with caricatures of the local firemen. By the square, halfway along Avenida Phillippi, Frutillar's *Club Alemán* has excellent service and good set lunches as well as a traditional à la carte menu.

There's not much in the way of services in Frutillar, and you're better off making the trip down to Puerto Varas for changing money and the like, but there is a *casa de cambio* at Phillippi 883. **Buses** leave Frutillar for Puerto Montt every ten minutes, operated by Thae Bus, Varmontt, Full Express and Expressos Puerto Varas.

Puerto Octay and Lago Llanquihue's northern shore

From Frutillar there's a dirt road that follows the shore of the lake, passing some attractive farmhouses and churches set in rolling meadowland punctuated with stately lines of tall poplars. This is a restrained countryside, contrasting with the dark shoulders of the plutonic Volcán Osorno further down the road. Thirty kilometres after Frutillar you arrive at **PUERTO OCTAY**, a friendly little town by the lake shore, nestling in the crook of some hills. It looks like it's been transplanted to Chile from the Alps, with its needle-steepled church and balconeyed houses with ornate eaves.

Puerto Octay was the first settlement on Lago Llanquihue and dates from 1852. The name (so the story goes) arose because of a village store that was opened here by one Cristino Ochs. It was the only shop for miles around, and people often used to ask each other "what's Ochs got?", which in Spanish became "¿Ochs hay?", hence Octay. The town developed into an important port in the days of the lake steamer, and today it's the municipal centre for a vast territory stretching up to Lago Rupanco in the north. It's proud of its long history, and a little envious of Frutillar's success with the tourists.

The **Oficina de Turismo** (Dec–March Mon–Fri 9am–9pm; ☎65/391491 ext 727) is next door to the Municipalidad on the Plaza de Armas, and staffed by garrulous volunteers. If you're interested in the history of the village, then you should visit the small museum of German colonization at Independencia 591 (Jan & Feb Mon–Sat 9.30am–1pm & 3–7pm, Sun 11am–1pm & 3–7pm; CH$500), which is filled with musical instruments, tableware and old photographs (the larger exhibits are in a barn on Andrés Schmoelz). You can also visit some of the old buildings, such as the **house at Pedro Montt 344**, built in 1894. This house is one of the village's oldest, and the elderly owner will sometimes show visitors (especially if you're German) the interior, which still has the original hand-stencilled decorations. The town's not all history, though, and there are a couple of nice **beaches** nearby: the grey sand **La Baja** is only 3km from Puerto Octay on Península Centinela (the headland to the south of the village), but **Maitén**, 9km to the east along the shore is better.

As for **accommodation**, Puerto Octay has a couple of little *residenciales* and one posh hotel. *Hospedaje Maria Yañez*, Pedro Montt 306 (☎64/391329; ③), is about the nicest *residencial*, a small family B&B with modern bedrooms, or you can **camp** at *Camping El Molino* (Dec–Feb; ☎65/391375), on the *costanera* for CH$5000 a tent (up to five people). The posh hotel is the *Hotel Centinela* (☎ & fax 64/391326; ⑤) on the end of Península Centinela, 5km from Octay. It is decorated in its original 1913 "High Bavarian" style, and looks like it hasn't changed since King Edward VIII stayed here in 1931 when he was still the Prince of Wales. You can reach Puerto Octay from Osorno on Buses Vía Octay, which runs two services an hour. There are five buses a day from Frutillar and Puerto Montt.

The road continues around Lago Llanquihue, passing beaches, fields and the villages of **Puerto Fonk** (20km) and **Puerto Klocker** (29km). This was the area of first settlement, and it was here in 1852 that 21 German families were allocated plots to farm – there's a plaque on the simple church at Playa Maitén commemorating the centenary of their arrival (look out for the weather vane of an angel blowing a trumpet on the top of the church steeple). Shortly after Puerto Klocker there's a turning to the east that leads 20km up the northern slope of Volcán Osorno to an unserviced **refuge** called *La Picada*, but the main road continues around the lake for 36km to **Las Cascadas,** a quiet hamlet with a beach, a couple of houses, a *hospedaje* and a *Carabineros* checkpoint. Beyond here the scenery changes as the road – by now unpaved – narrows and ploughs into dense scrub and forest. The fields have gone, and through the trees you catch glimpses of the volcano towering above you, looking no longer picturesque but menacing.

Volcán Osorno and Ensenada

Nineteen kilometres after Las Cascadas, deep in the forest, there's a turning to the east heading up the slopes of **Volcán Osorno**. It's 14km up to the *La Burbuja* refuge and Conaf station, from where there's a spectacular view. To the west you can see across Lago

Llanquihue, the central plain and across to the sea, and dominating the skyline to the south are the jagged peaks of Volcán Calbuco, which erupted spectacularly in 1893 ripping its summit apart and hurling rocks all the way to the coast. Up here keeping Conaf company there's the concrete pill-box of the Centro de Esquí La Burbuja, owned by the *Hotel Vicente Pérez Rosales* in Puerto Montt (information: ☎65/252571 fax 255473) and the *Refugio Teski Ski Club* (☎65/336490; ②), a rustic hut pegged out with wires to prevent it from taking off. *The Teski Ski Club*'s the nicer place, and inside there are bunkrooms and a cosy little café with interesting photographs of Volcán Osorno's deep-blue ice caves.

You can climb the volcano from *La Burbuja*. It's about five hours to the summit (two to the snowline, three more to the top), and there are many crevasses, so ice equipment is needed and a guide recommended. Conaf authorizes three companies to guide people up: Aqua Motion, Al Sur and Tranco Expediciones (see Puerto Varas, p.324). In the Conaf station is a maudlin display of obituary photographs and emotional letters from friends and relatives of tourists who have died or vanished in the crevasses on this seemingly innocuous hillside. In Mapuche mythology, a spirit called *hueñauca* lives on the volcano and preys on humans.

Back down on Llanquihue's shore road, 2km further, is a local beauty spot. From a car park, a signpost points out a ten-minute walk through the trees to **Laguna Verde**, an attractive pond near the edge of a lake. Almost immediately after the Laguna Verde car park the road breaks clear of the forest and you arrive in **ENSENADA**, a small village with basic services in a lovely location on the shores of the lake, and a good base from which to make excursions as it's at a staggered crossroads. There's a bit of **accommodation** here, starting with the campsite on the lakeshore, *Caleta Trauco* (also signed as *Playa Parque*; ☎65/212033), with a private beach and good facilities including tours and bike and boat rental – sites cost from CH$10,000. Also worth looking at is *Hospedaje Ensenada* (Dec–March; ☎65/212050; ④) a B&B lost in a 1940s time warp, with an attractive old garden by the edge of the lake. The most expensive accommodation is the *Hotel Ensenada* (Nov–March; ☎65/212017, fax 212028; ⑥) also lost in time and crammed with colonial memorabilia. To get to Ensenada, take a **bus** to Petrohué from Puerto Montt via Puerto Varas.

Lago Todos Los Santos and Parque Nacional Vicente Pérez Rosales

From Ensenada, a road heads 16km east through increasingly dense forest towards Lago Todos Los Santos. At the 10km mark are the **Saltos de Petrohué** (CH$1500), a series of rapids formed by an extremely hard layer of lava which has been eroded into small channels. Wild flowers thrive in the humid conditions around the falls, and there are marked nature trails along the river bank. Unfortunately this area is plagued during hot, dry summers by two biting flies, the *petros* and *távanos*, whose persistent pestering has to be experienced to be believed. About the only advice local people can offer in dealing with these silent monsters is not to wear dark clothing, particularly blue. According to local legend these rapids are the home of another monster, *cuchivilu*, which resembles a giant puma with a claw on the end of its tail.

The volcanic rock was part of a tongue of lava sent this way by Volcán Osorno in 1850, an eruption that diverted the Petrohué river from its old course into Lago Llanquihue. Driving alongside the river, areas of regenerating forest are clearly visible, and every spring sections of the road are washed away when rain and snow-melt pour down the flanks of the volcano. At the end of the road you reach **Lago Todos Los Santos**, deep-green and unfeasibly clear, one of the most beautiful in the Lake District – it's also known as Lago Esmeralda (Emerald Lake) because of the intense colour of its water. The lake and the forests that crowd its shores are protected by the Parque Nacional Vicente Pérez Rosales (see p.322). On the other side of the lake is a road that leads to the Argentine border. This route was first used as a border crossing by Jesuit

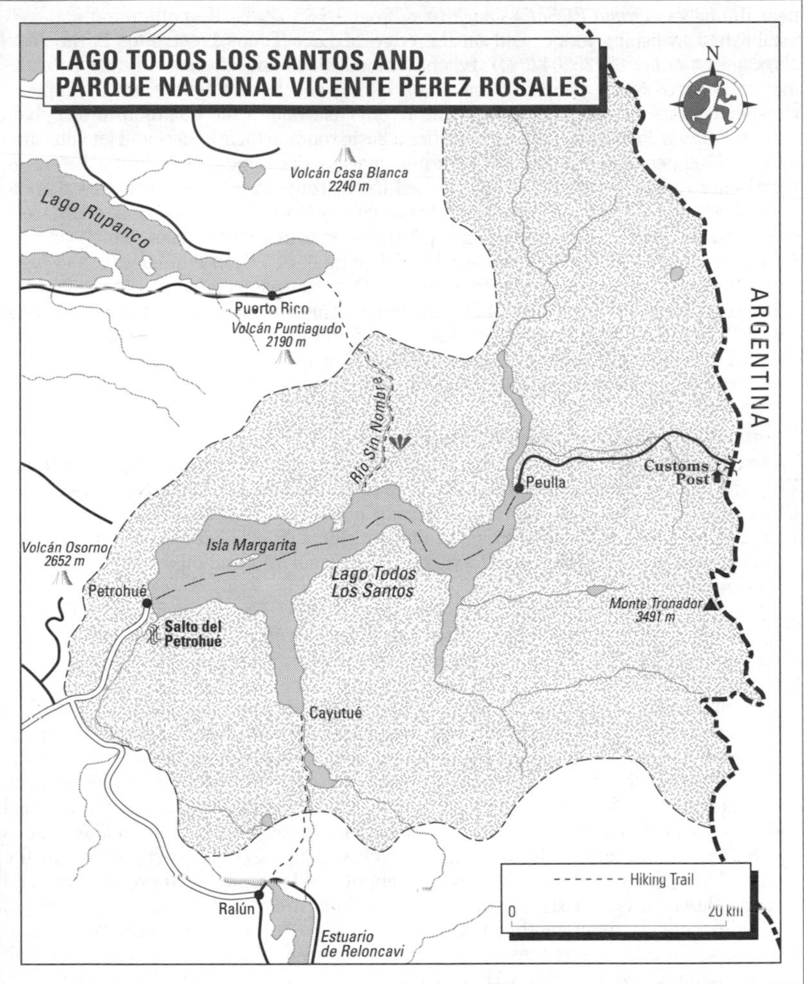

missionaries in the seventeenth century, in their attempts to convert the Tehuelche Indians on the pampas. The lake's now a twisting, turning, flooded valley, with forested banks and a sense of isolation in the jagged, pine-forested hills.

The road from Ensenada arrives at the hamlet of **PETROHUÉ** on the western shore of the lake. This settlement dates from the early twentieth century, when one Ricardo Roth began taking tourists across the lakes between Puerto Varas and Bariloche, a venture that led to the construction of two hotels – *Petrohué* and *Peulla* (see overleaf) and the foundation of Andina del Sud tour company. Roth is buried on the lake's Isla Margarita, and when tour boats pass they blow their horns in memory of him.

These days Petrohué is a bit of a hole, cursed in the summer by persistent biting insects, shouting children and libidinous adolescents. There's a post office here, some boats for rent on the lake and a couple of very expensive **places to stay**. In the forest near the falls is *Fundo El Salto Lodge* (☎ & fax 09/653 7233; ⑧), a charming and well-established fly-fishing lodge, and on the edge of Lago Todos Los Santos is the *Hotel Petrohué* (☎ & fax 65/258042; ⑥), recently modernized and offering outdoor activities including windsurfing, canoeing, mountain biking and fishing. There are a couple of cheaper options on the other side of the river – ask one of the boatmen to ferry you across: *Familia Kuschel* (no phone; ②) offer a basic room in their house, and let you camp for CH$2500 per tent, and Sra Rosa Burgos charges the same to stay in her house, *El Umakudau* (no phone; ②). Both places sell fresh trout. There are five **buses** daily to Petrohué from Puerto Montt via Puerto Varas, run by Buses Fierro and Buses Adriazola.

Andina del Sud (see Puerto Montt, p.331) offer **tours** on the lake, which provide unsurpassed views of Volcán Osorno, the spiked peak of Volcán Puntiagudo, and highest of all, the glacier-covered Monte Tronador. Day excursions to Peulla (at the far end) leave at 10.30am and cost CH$14,500. At Peulla, there's little except the border post (daily: Jan–March 8am–9pm; April–Dec 8am–8pm) and the *Hotel Peulla* (☎ & fax 65/257797; ⑥), a large old wooden building which is functional rather than comfortable. Argentinian customs is 30km east, on the shore of another lake, Nahuelhuapi.

Parque Nacional Vicente Pérez Rosales

The whole forest around Lago Todos Los Santos is protected by the **Parque Nacional Vicente Pérez Rosales** (daily: Dec–March 9am–8pm; April–Nov 9am–6pm; CH$1000). It is covered by an excellent **map** published by JLM, *Ruta de los Jesuitas (No. 15)*, available in Puerto Varas and Puerto Montt. You'll also find trail maps and a model on which you can pick out the hikes in the Conaf information centre by the hotel in Petrohué.

There are some short **trails**, and two longer ones. The best shorter trail, Paso Desolación, a seven-hour forest walk, leaves from Petrohué, and passes two *refugios*, *Winttner* and *Los Curas*. You can make a detour down to the lake, to Playa Larga, a three-hour trek through woods to a quiet little beach.

For the longer trails, you'll need to rent a **boat** from the dock at Petrohué (CH$25,000 for up to 6 people) to get to the starting point. The first trail, Termas de Callao, starts from the northern shores of the lake by the río Sin Nombre (No-Name River). Head up the river – the path's reasonably clear but be sure to always head upwards to the source – and after about three hours' climb you reach some thermal springs and a basic refuge. From here you can either come back down to Lago Todos Los Santos, having asked the boatman to pick you up again, or carry on up to the Laguna Los Quetros and over the pass: it's about two hours. From there you descend to Lago Rupanco (see p.316), which takes another three hours. From the shores of Lago Rupanco, it's about another hour to Puerto Rico, from where there are buses to Osorno (see p.309). Sometimes there's a boat-taxi waiting at the point where the trail reaches Lago Ranco, charging CH$20,000 per load to take you to the bus stop.

The second hike leaves from **Caytué**, a village on the south shore of the lake, and follows an old missionaries' route down to Ralún on the Estuario de Reloncaví (see below). It's only about a five-hour hike, and is a pretty easy walk through patches of farmland.

You should avoid wearing dark clothing when hiking, because you'll attract the local biting flies (*tavanos*).

The Estuario de Reloncaví

Returning towards Ensenada and taking a southern fork will take you along a good 33km road, fringed with large bushes of wild fuchsia and giant rhubarb plants, which leads to the **Estuario de Reloncaví**, a tranquil fjord, where you can come to escape, unwind and perhaps do a little fishing. Your first view of the sea – which is what this is – comes as you descend to **Ralún**, a hamlet with a couple of shops. The water's an amazing colour: bright green from one angle, deepest blue from another, and at the far end, standing sentinel over the fjord's exit, is Volcán Yate (2111m).

Ralún sits on a junction of two roads. The road down the west of the fjord leads to a hydroelectric project, and passes a couple of small farms on the edge of the Parque Nacional Alerce Andino (see p.358). The other road, along the east side of the fjord, goes through wild, dramatic scenery, with waterfalls crashing underneath snow-capped mountains. This is the beginning of the landscape of the Careterra Austral (see p.354), and there are unmapped trails through virgin forests in these mountains ready to be explored by the adventurous. Many of these trails lead to Argentina, and throughout history the low passes in this area have been used to cross the Andes. One of the most frequently trodden trails into Argentina starts at Puelo, the village at the end of this road, and eventually leads to El Bolsón on the other side of the cordillera.

After 14km, the road reaches **COCHAMÓ**, a beautiful little fishing village flanked with pine-clad hills. Sra Edita Moreno Paillan runs a *hospedaje* (☎65/250183 ext 256; ②) in the top floor of the general store on the seafront. It's a bargain of a place, new varnished wood everywhere, a balcony (if you can brave the fierce wind that blows down the fjord) and a communal lounge with a television. There's also the small and rustic *Hotel Cochamó* (☎65/250183 ext 212; ③), which is often full of salmon farmers, and 4km north there's *Campo Aventura* (Oct–April; ☎65/232910; ③), an adventure tourism complex run by Outsider Adventure Travel in Puerto Varas (see overleaf) who specialize in horse-trekking. They sometimes have a spare *cabaña*.

You can get down here from Puerto Montt by Buses Fierro, which has two services daily, leaving Puerto Montt at noon and 5pm, returning from Río Puelo (31km down the road) at 7am and 4pm.

Puerto Varas

Returning to Ensenada and taking the road to the west, you pass along an excellent tarred road along Lago Llanquihue's southern shore, and the land once again becomes tamed, lush and pastoral. After 47km you reach **PUERTO VARAS**, a spruce little town with wide streets, grassy lawns and exquisite views over two volcanoes, Osorno and Calbuco. It's a bit like Pucón, and like Pucón there's not much to see in the town itself – the reason you come to Puerto Varas is for its tourist facilities. However, it does have some old buildings because, despite recent rapid growth, it's not a new settlement – tourism took off in Puerto Varas as long ago as 1903, when the trail between Lago Todos Los Santos and Argentina was first opened. The historical buildings are to the northwest, around the curve of the old railway line. Some, like Casa Jüpner on Nuestra Señora del Carmen, are little more than wooden sheds, but Casa Kuschel, near the train station on Turismo, sports a wonderful wooden onion-dome.

Puerto Varas is built on a long bay that curves from southeast to northwest, and the heart of town is clustered around a small pier to the northwest. Here you'll find the Plaza de Armas, an attractive little square, but you'll be tempted down to the waterfront to view Volcán Osorno's perfection glimmering above the waves. The Plaza holds some interest, though, as there's often a **crafts market** here selling woollens, lapis lazuli, imitation Mapuche jewellery and ceramics. The town's other attraction is the thin strip of sandy beach at **Puerto Chico**, at the other end of Puerto Varas' long bay, down to the southeast.

Practicalities

The only way of arriving in Puerto Varas these day is by **bus**, as the train no longer runs. Only Varmontt has a proper terminal (San Francisco 666), and the other bus companies are scattered around town: many of the efficient minibuses that connect Puerto Varas to Ensenada and Petrohué stop at a bus shelter on San Bernardo opposite the Esso petrol station, and others use a shelter in Del Salvador between Santa Rosas and San Francisco. The **Oficina de Turismo** (Jan–March daily 8am–11pm; April–Dec Mon–Sat 9am–2pm & 4–8pm; ☎65/338542) is on the Plaza de Armas, on the corner of San José and Santa Rosa. It's very useful, and run by two enthusiastic women. Otherwise, you'll find a good selection of books on the area at Books El Libro del Capitan, Walker Martinez 417.

There are a number of private houses which let **rooms** during the summer, particularly along San Francisco, and the tourist office will have an up-to-date list of them – Sra Neile Adel de Berner, at Santa Rosa 756 (☎65/232504; ③) is a good example. They are often better value than some of the central *hospedajes* which are severely overpriced, charging up to CH$18,000 for bed and breakfast, a situation that gets worse in summer, when the town fills with people making the Todos Los Santos lake crossing to Argentina. A firm favourite, though, is *Colores del Sur*, Santa Rosa 318 (☎65/338588; ②), a multicoloured hostel, glossy, central, welcoming and run by Norwegians. The name's easily confused with *Colonos del Sur*, Del Salvador (☎65/233369, fax 232080; ⑦), an exclusive beachfront hotel with lots of polished wood, an indoor swimming pool and a sauna. Two other budget options are *Casa Azul*, Mirador 18 (☎65/232904; ③), freshly opened and painted, with a reading room, kitchen and garden, and *Hospedaje Ellenhaus*, Walker Martínez 239, Depto 1 (☎ & fax 65/233577; ②), run by Ellen, a very tall German, who rents out a small, clean, quiet upstairs apartment. Slightly more expensive is *Outsider*, San Bernardo 318 (☎ & fax 65/232910; ④), with warm, comfortable rooms, run by the German Outsider Adventure Travel, while a lot more expensive is *Hotel Licanrayen*, San José 114 (☎65/232305, fax 232955; ⑦), an oversized Swiss chalet overlooking the lake with excellent service. Another accommodation option is the increasing number of **farms** which offer "agrotourism" packages: a mixture of bed, breakfast and mucking out the horses: an organization called AGRHOSA, San José on the corner of Santa Rosa, (☎65/338542) has the details.

TOURS FROM PUERTO VARAS

The main tours offered by the many companies in Puerto Varas are rafting on the Petrohué river (grade 3 and 4; from CH$17,000 for a half-day), canyoning (climbing down precipices and waterfalls; CH$30,000 for a half-day), climbing Volcán Osorno (from CH$80,000), hiking in the Parque Nacional Vicente Pérez Rosales (from CH$94,000 for 2 days on the Termas de Callao trail – see p.322), and horseback riding, generally on the slopes of Volcán Calbuco, through old coigüe forest (from CH$33,000 for a half-day).

Al Sur Expediciones, Del Salvador 100 (☎ & fax 65/232300; *alsur@telsur.cl*) A good company – one of those authorized by Conaf as guides on Volcán Osorno – which, as well as the standard tours above, offers sea-kayaking to Parque Pumalín on the Careterra Austral (see p.361): CH$329,000 for a six-day trip. Also has a branch in Puerto Montt.

Andina del Sud, Del Salvador 72 (☎65/232811, fax 232511). Distinguished Lake District war-horse of a tour company, owning a monopoly on crossings on Lago Todos Los Santos. Also has a branch in Puerto Montt.

Aqua Motion, Imperial 0699 (☎65/232747; *aquamotion@enter-chile.com*). A well-respected agent with German- and English-speaking guides, authorized by Conaf to guide up Volcán Osorno. Also has a branch in Puerto Montt.

Campo Aventura, San Bernardo 318 (☎ & fax 65/232910; *outsider@telsur.cl*). The place to go for horse-trekking, from one day to ten days on the trails around the Estuario de Reloncaví (see p.322). Run by a German, Clark Stede, who not only has a name like a film star, but looks like one too.

Tranco Expediciones, Santa Rosa 580 (☎65/311311). An agency authorized to guide up Volcán Osorno.

The food's good in Puerto Varas, and while most of the **restaurants** are in the centre there are others out towards Puerto Chico and beyond. *Club Alemán*, San José 415, has a suitably subdued atmosphere for one of the oldest German clubs in the country with a traditional menu to match. *Aníbal Pizzas*, Del Salvador on the corner of the Plaza de Armas, is at the opposite end of the culinary spectrum, a cheerful fast-food café. The best place to go for fish are the two restaurants in the market, *Donde El Gordito*, and *Restaurant El Mercado* (above the market on San Bernardo), and if you're just after cakes and bread, then *Café Mamusia*, San José 316, is the place you want. Further out, there's an excellent café at *Cabañas Bellavista*, 34km along the road to Ensenada, which is famous not only for its *onces* (afternoon tea), but also because a female puma lives here as a pet.

There are many **banks** with ATMs around the Plaza de Armas, and along Del Salvador. For a *cambio*, try Del Salvador 257, Local 11 (in the Galería Real).

Puerto Montt and around

After passing Puerto Varas, the Panamericana begins to run out of land. It approaches a large bay where the central plain, the valley which has run for thousands of miles down Chile between the Andes and the coast, slips gently under the sea. This is the Seno de Reloncaví, and on its edge is the city of **PUERTO MONTT**, 17km from Puerto Varas.

Puerto Montt looks like a city at the end of a road. It was exactly that for many years, when both the Panamericana and the railway from Santiago ended here. The Panamericana now carries on south onto the island of Chiloé, and the railway has retreated north to Temuco, but the place still feels the same: houses are built from shingle-covered wood, and the weather's usually cloudy and chill. That doesn't mean that Puerto Montt is sleepy, as in fact it's a busy port, with a thriving fishing and fish-canning industry and, for tourists, an important launchpad: gateway to the rugged isolation of the Careterra Austral, and embarkation point for the long-distance ferry trips to the famous Laguna San Rafael (see p.374), with its floating glacier, or through the fjords to Puerto Natales in the far south (see p.400).

Arrival and information

If you're arriving by **bus**, you'll pitch up at the bus terminal, which is on the seafront, six blocks to the west of the town centre. It's a short walk to downtown, or you could take one of the many cabs or *colectivos* that run towards town. The **ferry terminal** is a further half-kilometre out of town, southwest towards the suburb of Angelmó. Again, taxis and *colectivos* run frequently into town. The airport (☎65/252019) is 16km northwest of Puerto Montt; flights are met by the ETM bus company, which will take you to the bus terminal for CH$750.

Puerto Montt has no less than five **tourist information offices**. The most brusque is the Oficina de Turismo, on the eastern side of the Plaza de Armas in a seafront park (mid-Dec to mid-March daily 9am–9pm; mid-March to mid-Dec Mon–Fri 9am–1.30pm & 3–6.30pm, Sat 9am–1pm; ☎65/261700), though there's a friendlier kiosk in the bus station (Mon–Sat 9am–1pm & 3–6.30pm; no phone) and another at the point where the Panamericana enters the city's northern outskirts (same hours as kiosk; no phone). Sernatur's main kiosk is also on the Plaza de Armas, in the foyer of the Gobernación building, and is by far the best choice in town, with its scores of maps and leaflets (Mon–Fri 8.30am–1pm & 2–6pm; no phone). Sernatur's regional administration office is up the hill in the Edificio Intendencia Regional, O'Higgins 480 (☎65/254580; *sernatur_pmontt@entelchile.net*).

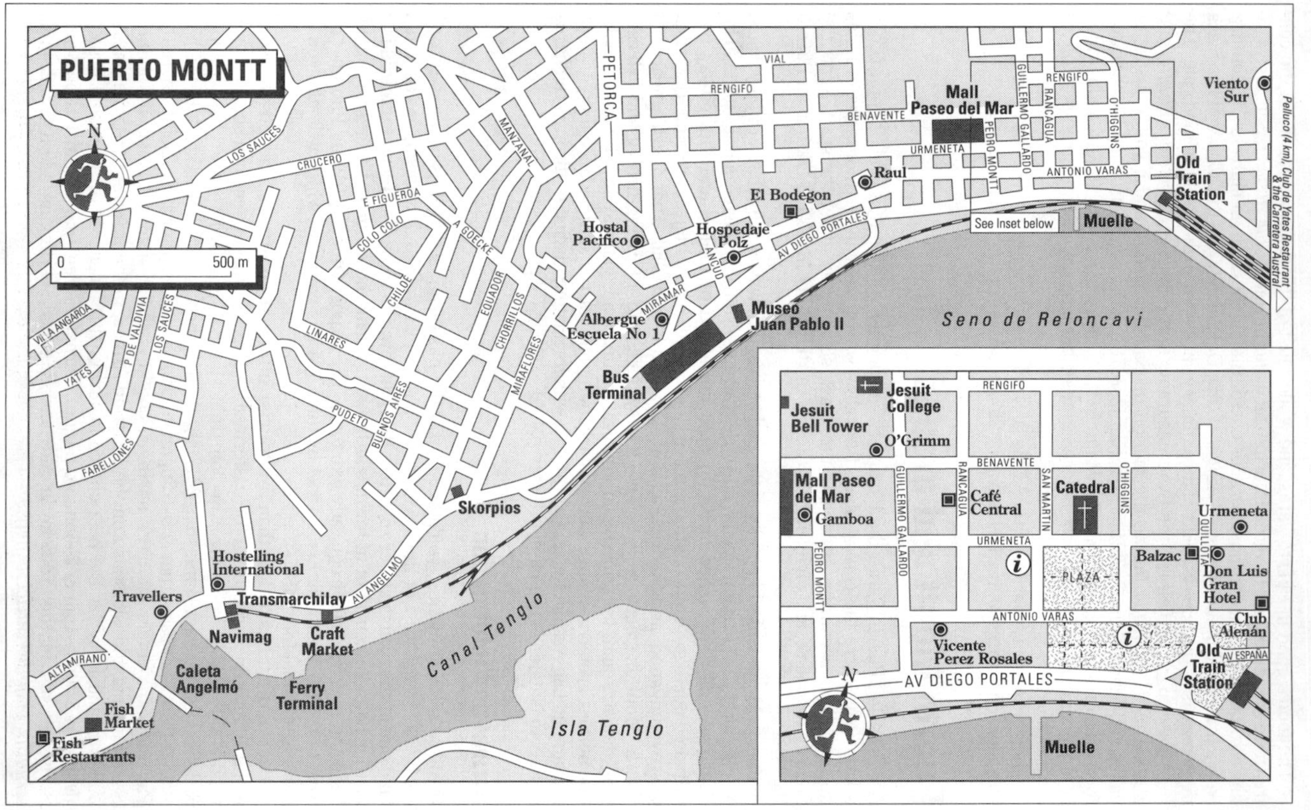
PUERTO MONTT
N
0
500 m
LOS SAUCES
CRUCERO
E FIGUEROA
COLO COLO
CHILOE
A GOECKE
MANZANAL
EQUADOR
CHORRILLOS
MIRAFLORES
LINARES
PUDETO
BUENOS AIRES
LOS SAUCES
P DE VALDIVIA
YATES
FARELLONES
PETORCA
VIAL
RENGIFO
BENAVENTE
URMENETA
Mall Paseo del Mar
PEDRO MONTT
GUILLERMO GALLARDO
RANCAGUA
RENGIFO
O'HIGGINS
ANTONIO VARAS
Viento Sur
Old Train Station
Pelluco (4 km), Club de Yates Restaurant & the Carretera Austral
Raul
El Bodegon
Hostal Pacifico
Hospedaje Polz
ANCUD
AV DIEGO PORTALES
See Inset below
Muelle
MIRAMAR
Albergue Escuela No 1
Museo Juan Pablo II
Seno de Reloncavi
Bus Terminal
Skorpios
Hostelling International
Travellers
Transmarchilay
AV ANGELMO
Navimag
Craft Market
Canal Tenglo
ALTAMIRANO
Caleta Angelmó
Ferry Terminal
Isla Tenglo
Fish Market
Fish Restaurants
Jesuit College
Jesuit Bell Tower
O'Grimm
RENGIFO
BENAVENTE
Mall Paseo del Mar
Gamboa
GUILLERMO GALLARDO
RANCAGUA
Café Central
SAN MARTIN
Catedral
O'HIGGINS
Urmeneta
QUILLOTA
URMENETA
PEDRO MONTT
PLAZA
Balzac
Don Luis Gran Hotel
ANTONIO VARAS
Club Alenán
Vicente Perez Rosales
AV ESPAÑA
Old Train Station
N
AV DIEGO PORTALES
Muelle

Accommodation

There's no shortage of cheap **accommodation** in Puerto Montt, and it's generally a buyer's market. Nor is it difficult to find, for although touting for accommodation is now illegal at Puerto Montt's bus station, you'll still get a couple of people sidle up to you and whisper an offer of somewhere to stay. At the top end, there are a couple of good hotels, but prices rise dramatically in the summer. Camping's intermittently available at the municipal site, *El Ciervo*, 1km west of Angelmó on the road to Chinquihue, and more regularly at *Paredes*, 4km west of Angelmó on the same road, a site with electricity and hot water charging from CH$1500 a tent. Buses and *colectivos* run here from the terminal.

Hostels and hospedajes

Albergue Escuela No 1, Eusebio Lillo s/n (Jan 12– Feb 14; no phone). The school opposite the bus terminal turns into a hostel in the holidays, and becomes the cheapest place in town. There are about a hundred beds, living is communal, and you have to supply your own sleeping bag. ①.

Hospedaje Polz, José Mira 1002 (☎65/252851). A yappy dog and a spiral staircase, but good-value rooms and a reasonable location. ②.

Hostelling International, Av Angelmó 2196 (☎65/257938). Bang opposite the ferry terminal, the youth hostel is a little spartan, but the owner's friendly and helpful and there's a communal kitchen. ③.

Raul, Concepción 136 (☎65/274143). Raul runs the cheapest year-round *hospedaje* in town – shabby, tucked away up a quiet cul-de-sac but enormously hospitable. ②.

Residencial Ancud, Ancud 116 (☎65/255623). Close to the bus station this house has clean, basic rooms with use of the kitchen. ②.

Hotels

Hostal Pacifico, J J Mira 1088 (☎ & fax 65/256229) Spanking new modern rooms with cable TV and private bath, friendly staff and parking. Up a little hill from the bus terminal. ④.

Hotel Don Luis, Quillota 146 on the corner of Urmeneta (☎65/259001, fax 259005). Now owned by the Best Western chain, a hotel in a tall building, with treacherous marble tiles on the foyer floor. Meals in the comfortable restaurant are limited to a daily US$10 fixed menu. ⑦.

Hotel Gamboa, Pedro Montt 157 (☎65/252741). Lovely old place with creaking floorboards and the smell of fresh furniture polish. The showers can be weak, but it's very central. ④.

Hotel O'Grimm, Guillermo Gallardo 211 on the corner with Benavente (☎65/252845, fax 258600). The stone-clad entrance might put some off, but this is a comfortable modern hotel with decent rooms and a good restaurant. ⑦.

Hotel Viento Sur, Ejército 200 (☎65/258701, fax 258700). The best positioned hotel in the city, on the hill overlooking the bay, beautifully decorated with native woods. There's a small restaurant which specializes in fish and home-made pasta. ⑦.

Residencial Urmeneta, Urmeneta 290 (☎65/253262). The heart of this old building is the kitchen, and you have breakfast sitting amongst piles of clean laundry, whilst an endless array of women bustle around vast cauldrons that bubble away on an enormous old hob. ③.

The City

Puerto Montt is strung out along the bay. To the east, around a headland, is the beach and slightly upmarket district of Pelluco, and to the west, down past the port and opposite Isla Tenglo, is the fishing district of Angelmó. Off to the south are the hills and fjords of the Careterra Austral, often obscured by clouds and occasionally temptingly visible. To the north you can sometimes see Volcán Calbuco, and even Volcán Osorno.

Puerto Montt was founded by the same influx of German colonizers that settled Lago Llanquihue to the north, but very little is left of the old city. The **cathedral**, for example, on the Plaza de Armas, was flattened in the 1960 earthquake, and the building you see today doesn't bear much resemblance to the original. It's based on the Parthenon in Athens, not entirely successfully, but the inside is peaceful and lined with Grecian columns. Three blocks away on Guillermo Gallardo, a much better job's been done in restoring the **Jesuit College**, which dates back to 1872.

Ten blocks west of the Plaza is Puerto Montt's museum, named **Museo Juan Pablo II** (daily: Jan & Feb 9am–7pm; March–Dec 9am–noon & 2–6pm; CH$250) to commemorate the pope's visit in 1987. It's not the greatest museum in the country. By the entrance there's a display of money from various countries throughout the ages, and around the corner there's the usual collection of stuffed animals – the pelican's rather good, though the others look a bit mangy. There are some colonial artefacts – musical instruments, pots, pans and irons and some photographs – but the star exhibits are contained in the bay to the left of the entrance: the pope's cruet and egg-cup from his Lan Chile flight, complete with his monogram.

Angelmó

A kilometre further west is **Angelmó**. This is the most attractive side of Puerto Montt, where the *costanera* is lined with a **feria artesanal**, or crafts market, its stalls crammed with woollen sweaters, socks, gloves, hats and ponchos; wooden and copper souvenirs; woven baskets and furniture and fleece rugs. Jewellery stalls sell rings and bracelets made out of Chilean silver and semi-precious stones, particularly lapis lazuli, while other stalls have fine leather saddles and tack for horses, and glistening spurs for *huasos*. On the opposite side of the road are stalls selling country cheeses, honey, bottles of powerful *licor de oro*, and dried sea produce: square bundles of tightly wrapped seaweed that looks like dried intestines, and smoked shellfish in long strings of red and grey, that hang from doorways, tempting scrawny cats onto their hind legs.

Angelmó was once a thriving small harbour, and the canal between it and the island offshore, **Isla Tenglo**, was filled with black-hulled sailing boats, then the only means of transport to the islands south of Puerto Montt and isolated communities now reached by road. Launches still go to the islands, and horse-drawn carts are used to unload cargoes of charcoal, seaweed and shellfish. These fleets are a common sight, particularly near the bus terminal, with small, skeleton-thin nags hauling their loads up Puerto Montt's steep hills.

Fresh **seafood** in Chile means Angelmó. At the end of the road, the **fish market** is filled with tiny stalls run by ebullient mothers and daughters, who crowd around the cauldrons, tempting punters by lifting the lids off steaming vats of *curanto* (a seafood dish with a sausage on top). Apart from in Chiloé, no other stallholders in Chile can match the pure drama of these women. After a recent fire burned down the covered fish market and food stalls, the local government decided to clean up the area. There was a nationwide outcry. New stalls in *palafitos* (houses on stilts) were built, overlooking the sea, but within days the old stalls were re-established and have proved as popular as ever.

Eating and drinking

As well as Angelmó for seafood (which isn't cheap), other districts around Puerto Montt have become famous for their food. **Chinquihue**, seven kilometres west, has some good restaurants, as has **Pelluco** to the east. Western-style fast-food restaurants can be found on the top floor of the Paseo del Mar, the mall on Urmeneta between Pedro Montt and Cauquenes.

Al Paso, Antonio Varas 625. A bar downstairs and a café upstairs, with black plastic 1970s-style armchairs and enormous lunchtime sandwiches.

Asturias, Av Angelmó 2448. Close to the fish market, but cheaper, this family-run restaurant is a quiet alternative to the hard sell of the fishwives.

Azzurro, Pelluco. Italian food made with fresh local ingredients. Try the smoked trout ravioli.

Balzac, Urmeneta 305. You'll recognize this restaurant from its advertising material: a chef in whites rowing out to sea. The dining room is painted attractive primary colours, and the crab is excellent, but the waiter is overworked.

Café Central, Rancagua 117. A good meeting place, full of bustle.

Club Alemán, Antonio Varas 264. An excellent restaurant, with starched tablecloths and attentive waiters, serving good food. Try the enormous seafood platter for two.

Club de Yates (☎65/263606). On a pier sticking out into the ocean, with a bright neon light on top, you can hardly miss the *Club de Yates*. It's less ostentatious on the inside, and is one of the best seafood restaurants in Puerto Montt – but it's expensive. Booking's advisable.

El Bodegon, Antonio Varas 931. An old-fashioned, workers' restaurant where set lunches cost CH$1500.

Fogón de Cotelé, Pelluco (☎65/278000). A good view over the sea, and the best steak in Puerto Montt: the meat's charcoal-grilled in front of you. Booking's essential, and the owner's been known to turn away tourists he didn't like the look of.

La Casona, Chinquihue km 8 (☎65/255044). Facing the sea is this first-class restaurant, serving fresh seafood with fine wines. It can get busy, so it's a good idea to book.

Super Yoco, Quillota 259. The decor, particularly an entire wall covered with a poster of alpine scenery, isn't wonderful, and the service can be slow, but this is the best place for traditional and reasonably priced Chilean meat dishes such as *parilladas*, huge mixed grills, and *pichangas*, mountains of chips with spicy sausages, pickles and hard-boiled eggs. Closed Sun.

Travellers, Av Angelmó 2456. Above the travel agent, a quiet café with a view of Isla Tenglo. They've got filter coffee and they know how to make tea.

Listings

Airlines Aerosur, Quillota 127 (☎65/252523); Ladeco, Benavente 350 (☎65/253002); Lan Chile, O'Higgins 167, on the Plaza (☎65/253141 or 253002, fax 278172).

Banks and exchange AFEX, Av Diego Portales 516; Exchange, Av Antonio Varas 595, Local 3 (Galería Cristal); La Moneda de Oro, Bus Terminal office 37. There are many banks with ATMs along Antonio Varas and Urmeneta.

Boat trips Infotel Turismo, Urmeneta 300, Local 2 and 3 (☎65/312169, fax 250168) offers nine-hour tours of the Seno de Reloncaví for CH$16,000 per person.

Book exchange Travellers, Av Angelmó 2456.

Bus companies Bus Norte (☎65/252783); Cruz del Sur (☎65/254731); Queilén Bus (☎65/253468); Rio de la Plata (☎65/253841); Tas Choapa (☎65/254826); Varmontt (☎65/254766).

Car rental Autovald, Diego Portales 504 (☎65/254306) & no. 1330 (☎65/256355); Fama's Rent a Car, Diego Portales 506 (☎65/259840); Travi Rent a Car, Cauquenes 60 (☎65/257137), Salfa Sur Pilpico 800 (☎65/290201).

Consulates Argentina, Cauquenes 94 (☎65/253996); Germany, Oficina 306, Antonio Varas 525 (☎65/252828); Netherlands, Chorrillos 1582 (☎65/253003); Spain, Rancagua 113 (☎65/252729); Uruguay, Mardre Paulina 337 (☎65/252153).

Hospital Clinica Los Andes, Río Mañiheico 123, Pichi Pelluco (☎65/282020).

Internet access Travellers, Av Angelmó 2456.

Laundry Narly Los Esperamos, San Martín 167, Galería Doggenweiler, Local 6.

Left luggage There's a *custodia* at each end of the bus terminal.

Maps Travellers, Av Angelmó 2456.

Shopping As well as the one in Angelmó, there are craft markets across the road from the bus terminal and to the west of the large Mundial supermarket across from the bus terminal, called Pueblito de Melipulli. Patagonia outdoor equipment is sold at Niklitschek y Morgado ltda, Antonio Varas 445.

Taxi Settur (☎65/251515); Traslados (☎65/274699).

Telephone centre Entel, Antonio Varas 567, Local 2.

FERRIES FROM PUERTO MONTT

One of the main reasons people travel to Puerto Montt is to catch a **ferry** south. From Puerto Montt you can sail to Chaitén on the Carretera Austral, Quellón on the island of Chiloé, Puerto Chacabuco on the Carretera Austral, the Laguna San Rafael far south in the fjords of the southern coast, and Puerto Natales in Magallanes. These ferry trips are almost always fully booked in summer, and you must **reserve ahead** if you want to be certain of travelling.

The seas on these ferry rides are usually flat calm, as for most of the time the ferries are sailing in fjords that protect them from bad weather. The exception is the trip to Puerto Natales, when the *Puerto Eden* heads out to the Pacific across the Golfo de Penas, where even travellers with the sturdiest sea-legs have been known to lose their lunch. The trips are long and can be boring, but the scenery is spectacular: wild forests, steep mountains and placid fjords. There are cafés and restaurants on most boats, but you should bring some extra food and alcohol, as the prices on board can be extortionate.

There are three main companies operating ferries. Each has a range of accommodation, and a range of prices, which are cheaper by half in low season. The prices we give below refer to the cheapest accommodation for a single passenger in high season.

• **Navimag**, Av Angelmó 2187 (☎65/253318, fax 258540; *www.australis.com*). The busiest of Puerto Montt's ferry companies, and it's recommended that you book ahead at least a month before travel. It holds reservations for up to 15 days before the boat leaves, after which you must pay or lose your berth. Within two weeks before travel, you can't make a provisional reservation and must pay up front to secure a ticket. Students with ID get ten percent discount.
– The short-distance *Alejandrina* serves Chaitén and Quellón; it costs CH$10,000 from Puerto Montt to Chaitén (9hr). For the Chaitén to Quellón leg, see p.364. It sails from Puerto Montt on Thursdays, Fridays, Saturdays and Sundays, returning on Fridays, Saturdays, Sundays and Mondays.
– The middle-distance *Evangelista* serves Puerto Chacabuco and the Laguna San Rafael; it costs CH$135,000 for a round trip from Puerto Montt to Laguna San Rafael (5 days, 4 nights), and CH$18,000 for a one-way to Puerto Chacabuco (24hr). For details of the trip from Puerto Chacabuco to the Laguna, see p.375. It sails from Puerto Montt every four days in summer.
– The long-distance *Puerto Edén* heads all the way down to Puerto Natales; it costs from CH$140,000 to Puerto Natales (3 days, price includes food), sailing from Puerto Montt about once a week.

• **TransMarChilay**, Av Angelmó 2187 (☎65/270416, fax 270415). Generally less busy than Navimag, but again for the trip down to the Laguna you have to reserve in advance and pay up front to be sure of a ticket.
– The short-distance boat *Barcaza Pincoya* travels to Chaitén and Quellón; it costs from CH$10,000 for the Chaitén trip (10hr). For the Chaitén to Quellón leg, see p.364. It sails from Puerto Montt to Chaitén on Fridays, and from Chaitén to Puerto Montt on Wednesdays.
– The middle-distance *El Colono* serves Puerto Chacabuco and the Laguna San Rafael; it costs from CH$13,500 to Puerto Chacabuco (26hr one-way), and CH$133,000 for the round trip to Laguna San Rafael (5 days, 4 nights). It sails from Puerto Montt on Fridays, and from Chacabuco on Saturdays. Sailings in summer only.

• **Skorpios**, Av Angelmó 1660 (☎65/252619, fax 258315). Upmarket company running expensive, luxury six-day cruises to the San Rafael Glacier in three different boats, the *Skorpios I, II* and *III*. Prices start at US$1838 for a single berth on the *Skorpios I*. The cruise lasts six days, and the boats sail every Saturday from September to May.

Tour agencies Tours offered from Puerto Montt are basically the same as those offered from Puerto Varas (see p.324), and Al Sur, Antonio Varas 445 (☎65/287628), Andina del Sud, Antonio Varas 437 (☎65/257797), and Aqua Motion, San Pedro 422, also have branches in Puerto Varas. The Pucón *hostería*-cum-travel agent *¡école!* has opened a Puerto Montt branch in the Melipulli crafts centre (contact via ☎45/441675) and offers, as well as the standard tours, sea kayak trips to the Parque Pumalín and classes. Travellers, Av Angelmó 2456 (☎65/262099, fax 258555; *travlers@chilesat.net*) is a thoroughly helpful company, owned by an Englishman who's become a fixture in the south of Chile, and provides general information as well as booking tours.

The road to Chiloé

After Puerto Montt, the Panamericana heads off to the southwest, the only direction left to go. The road is at first full of pretty *cabañas*, then fish-canning factories which give off faint smells, and then rolling hills and greenery. After 27km there's a turning to the left, which leads after 17km to the estuary town of **CALBUCO**, an attractive place, sitting on the mud flats with views onto small islands, and reached by a causeway which links it to the mainland.

Built on an island hillock, Calbuco was originally a Spanish fort, Real Fuerte de San Miguel, founded in 1602, but grew during the days of the Mapuche revolt as Spaniards fled here, abandoning their farms and settlements. Ironically enough, it was close to this retreat that the Spaniards' Pacific Fleet suffered its final defeat in 1866 at the hands of Chilean and Peruvian ships commanded by Admirals Prat and Grau. Today it's a town with steep streets and a flaking-paint charm. Its central plaza is hemmed in by the sea on one side, and on the other by a yellow, German-style **church** with steeple, inside which is an image of the Archangel Michael, brought here by the Spanish.

There are a couple of **places to stay**. The *Gran Hotel Calbuco*, Av Los Héroes 502 (☎ & fax 65/461833; ④), is above a popular restaurant on the seafront at the entrance to town and has good views. Just around the corner *Hotel Colonial*, Eulogio Goycolea 12 (☎ & fax 65/461546; ③) is in a quiet street and has attractive en-suite rooms. There's good seafood in this fishing community, and a fine place to **eat** it is *Costa Azul*, Av Vicuñia Mackenna 202. These hotels and restaurants operate **tours** to the islands where the way of life remains little changed since the departure of the Spaniards. Intersur, Bohle, Full Express and Fierro run buses to Calbuco from Puerto Montt, every ten minutes.

Back on the Panamericana, and 21km further southwest, there's another interesting diversion off to the right. **MAULLÍN** 16km away on the Pacific Coast, is a weather-beaten town, largely made of rusted corrugated iron and wood-tiled walls, the sort of place that has dogs too lazy to get out of the way of an approaching car. This village was founded at an important crossing point of a sprawling estuary, on which shellfish are cultivated and sole thrive. Ferries still cross the river as they did in colonial times, but Maullín is no longer the gateway to Chiloé that it was a century ago.

Sixteen kilometres further is **CARELAMPU**, another dying port town, and a favourite target for Dutch corsairs in the seventeenth century. The sleepy village comes alive on February 2, when on the day of the **Fiesta de la Candelaria** brightly coloured boats pack the bay, and the single street is lined with food stalls selling every type of traditional dish. The fields around Carelampu are all turned over to car parking, and the air fills with smoke from hundreds of cooking fires. There's a *hospedaje* (☎65/258461 ext 259; ②) right in front of Carelampu's church overlooking the bay. Buses ETM run a half-hourly service from Puerto Montt to Maullín and Carelampu on weekdays, and an hourly one at weekends.

The modern port for Chiloé is **PARGUA**, opposite the Chilote village of Chacao, 11km southwest of the turn-off to Maullín. There's nothing much here except the ferries, which are flat landing crafts that run in relays across the straits. During daylight, the most you'll have to wait is half an hour, and the crossing takes another half-hour. It costs CH$4800 for a car, and is free for foot passengers.

travel details

Buses

Osorno to: Aguas Calientes, Puyehue (9 daily; 1hr); Bahía Mansa (4 daily; 2hr); Bariloche, Argentina (every 2hr; 5hr plus border formalities); Entre Lagos (every hour; 40min); Panguipulli (2 daily; 2hr 30min); Puerto Montt (every hour; 1hr 30min); Puerto Octay (every 30min; 1hr); Puerto Varas (every hour; 1hr); Santiago (every hour; 13hr); Temuco (every 45min; 3hr); Valdivia (every hour; 1hr 30min).

Puerto Montt to: Bariloche, Argentina (1 daily; 7hr 30min plus border formalities); Calbuco (every 10min; 1hr 30min); Frutillar (every 10min; 1hr); Maullín (every 30min; 1hr 40min); Osorno (every 30min; 1hr 30min); Pargua (every 30min; 1hr); Panguipulli (2 daily; 4hr); Puerto Varas (every 15min; 30min); Santiago (every hour; 14hr); Temuco (every hour; 6hr); Valdivia (every 30min; 3hr 30min).

Temuco to: Melipeuco (8 daily; 2hr 30min); Osorno (every 45min; 3hr); Panguipulli (every 40min; 2hr 30min); Pucón (every 20min; 2hr 15min); Puerto Montt (every hour; 6hr); Puerto Saavedra (10 daily; 1hr 30min); Puerto Varas (every hour; 5hr 30min); Santiago (every hour; 9hr 30min); Valdivia (every hour; 2hr 30min); Villarrica (every 20min; 1hr 45min).

Valdivia to: Futrono (10 daily; 2hr 30min); Lago Ranco (every 20min; 3hr); Niebla (every 15min; 30min); Osorno (every 40min; 1hr 30min); Panguipulli (every 40min; 2hr); Puerto Montt (every 30min; 3hr 30min); Puerto Varas (every 30min; 3hr); Santiago (every hour; 11hr); Temuco (every hour; 2hr 30min).

Ferries

Puerto Montt to: Chacabuco (2 weekly; 24hr); Chaitén (1–4 weekly; 10hr); Laguna San Rafael (1 or 2 weekly; Dec–March; 4–5 days return); Puerto Natales (1 or 2 weekly; 4 days).

Flights

Osorno to: Concepción (3 daily; 1hr); Puerto Montt (3 daily; 1hr 30min); Santiago (4 daily; 2hr); Temuco (4 daily; 35min); Valdivia (4 daily; 1hr 45min).

Puerto Montt to: Balmaceda (4 daily; 1hr); Concepción (6 daily; 1hr); Osorno (3 daily; 1hr 30min); Punta Arenas (4 daily; 2hr 10min); Santiago (6 daily; 1hr 35min); Temuco (4 daily; 1hr); Valdivia (2 daily; 1hr 40min).

Temuco to: Balmaceda (3 daily; 1hr); Osorno (4 daily; 35min); Puerto Montt (4 daily; 1hr); Punta Arenas (2 daily; 1hr); Santiago (4 daily; 1hr 10min).

Valdivia to: Osorno (4 daily; 1hr 45min); Puerto Montt (2 daily; 2hr 40min); Santiago (2 daily; 2hr).

CHAPTER SEVEN

CHILOÉ

Just to the south of the Lake District, and across the Golfo de Ancud from the Careterra Austral, is **CHILOÉ**, a quiet rural archipelago famous throughout Chile for its myths and legends, missionaries and churches, bumpkins and farmers. It's a fascinating place, a land where the pace of life is slow and little substantial has changed in the 450 years since the arrival of the Spaniards: small fishing villages still glean a slender living from the sea, and **ancient wooden churches** still dot the land, built with their characteristic arched porticoes and towers. This is one of the few places in the country where you can still see **palafitos**, the houses built on stilts out above the sea, that were once the traditional dwellings of most of the fisherfolk of southern Chile.

Things *have* moved on, of course. The locals no longer farm their animals in rude woven-branch corrals, iron and horses have replaced the primitive tools that were once used to till the ground, and people no longer live in shelters of thatch, hide or sealskin called *rucas*. Nor do canoes ply the ocean in the search for fish, and the people are no longer governed in small tribal groups. But much of the old culture has been preserved, assimilated into Hispanic tradition by a profound mixing of the Spanish and Chilote that occurred here more than in other parts of South America; the settlers lived cheek by jowl with the Chilotes – everyone wore the same clothes, lived in the same villages and relied on the same subsistence crops for survival. This mixing of traditions has made today's Chiloé more pagan Catholic than Roman Catholic, and all sorts of **supernatural beings** are still believed to inhabit the archipelago. It wasn't only in a geographical sense that Chiloé was described by the visiting Charles Darwin in 1835 as "*el fin de la Cristiandad*" (the end of Christendom).

Chiloé is basically one big island, 200km long by 70km wide, cut in two by the Panamericana, which tears down the archipelago's main island, **Isla Grande**, past its two main towns, **Ancud** and **Castro**. Regular buses trundle up and down the highway, and the lesser roads are generally served by at least one bus a day. However, the best way to explore is to drive the islands' minor roads, which hold surprises at almost every turn, and it's well worth heading west into the densely forested **Parque Nacional Chiloé**, the most accessible part of the almost pristine wilderness of the coastal rainforest. To Isla Grande's east are hundreds of tiny islands, mostly uninhabited and practically unreachable. The two largest and easiest to visit are the inhabited **Isla Quinchao** and **Isla Lemuy**, both easily accessible by bus and car. On these remote outposts, winding dirt roads are filled with *huasos* driving cattle, ox-carts piled high with firewood or barrels of *chicha* (cider), and

ACCOMMODATION PRICE CODES

Prices are for the cheapest **double room** in high season. At the lower end of the scale, **single travellers** can expect to pay half this rate, but mid- and upper-range hotels usually charge the same for a single as for a double. For more information see p.27 in Basics.

① Less than US$10/CH$4800
② US$10–20/CH$4800–9600
③ US$20–30/CH$9600–10,080
④ US$30–50/CH$10,080–24,000
⑤ US$50–75/CH$24,000–36,000
⑥ US$75–100/CH$36,000–48,000
⑦ US$100–150/CH$48,000–72,000
⑧ over US$150/over CH$72,000

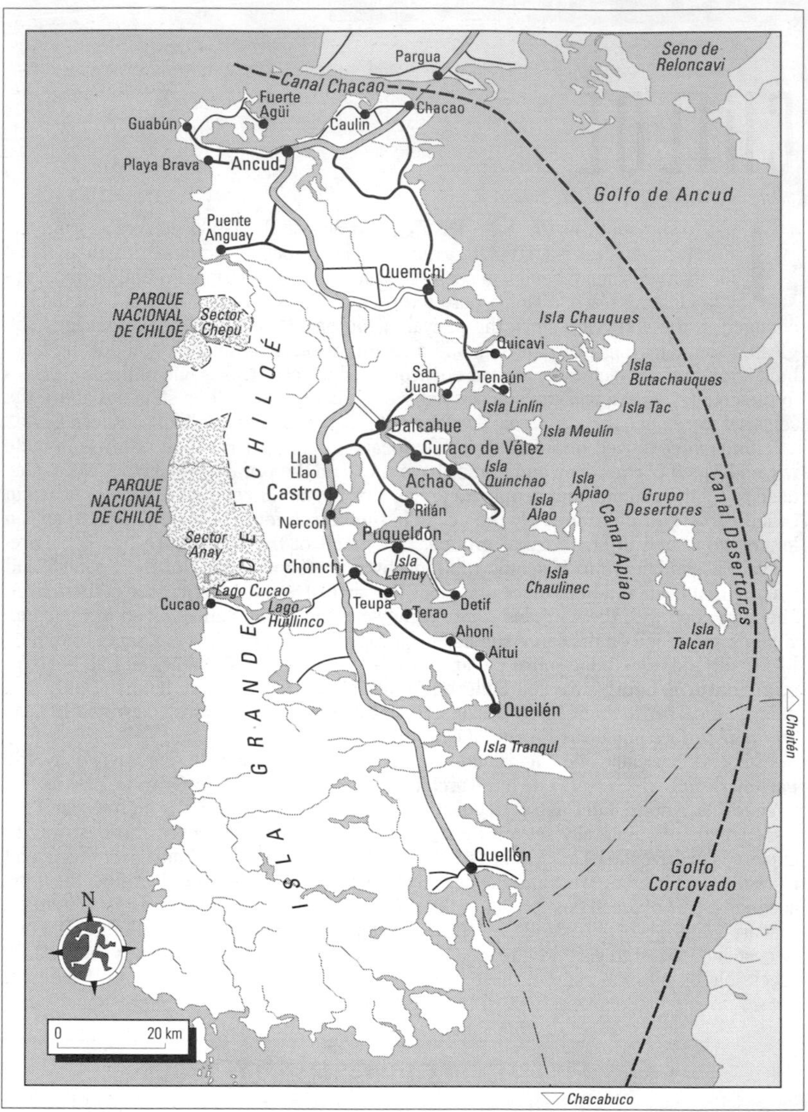

apparently ambulant hay-stacks which seem to move on a cushion of air, until you take a closer look and see they are being pulled on the Chilote *birloches* (sledges).

Arriving in Chiloé

The **ferry** from Pargua, 59km southwest of Puerto Montt on the mainland (daily every 30min; 30min; cars CH$4800, foot passengers free) arrives at **Chacao** on the Isla

Grande's northern shore. There's not much here to detain you, except perhaps the excellent **tourist kiosk** half a kilometre along the road to Ancud (Jan–March daily 9am–9pm; ☎65/262811 ext 237). If you've no transport you can pick up one of the **buses** coming off the ferry that run every fifteen minutes to Ancud (CH$700) or Castro (CH$1300).

Ancud and around

The Panamericana shoots west from Chacao 33km to Ancud, Chiloé's main northern settlement. After nine kilometres, though, a turn-off to the right leads to the little village of **CAULÍN**, a handful of exposed houses on the edge of a windswept, kilometre-wide sandy beach. When the tide's in, the water comes right up to the houses' doorsteps and covers the road – the distance between high and low tide here is one of the largest in the world. These tides make collecting shellfish easy, and the village has become famous for the **oyster beds** that lie just offshore. You can sample the delicacies at the fine *Ostras Caulín* restaurant (mobile ☎09/643 7005) and stay at the *Hotel Caulín* (☎65/267150; ④–⑥), with cosy rooms and five-person *cabañas*. It can be idyllic here if the weather's good, but it can also be a rain-lashed nightmare, in which case you're better off taking a bus (Buses Lorca; 4 daily) 28km down to Ancud.

Often overlooked by travellers on their way to Castro, **ANCUD** is a pretty little seaside town and a lively fishing port, with an excellent **museum**. Founded in 1769 as a Spanish stronghold, after Peruvian independence in 1824 it became the Spanish crown's last possession in South America – the pathetic remains of a once proud empire. Its forts resisted one attempt at capture, but finally fell in January 1826 when the lonely and demoralized Spanish garrison fled into the forest in the face of a small Chilean attack. The remains of these Spanish forts – **Fuerte San Antonio** in the town and **Fuerte Agüi** on a peninsula to the northwest – can still be visited today, and command wonderful views out over the bay.

Arrival and information

Long-distance buses **arrive** in the terminal on calle Aníbal Pinto, a five-minute taxi ride from the Plaza de Armas towards Ruta 5. The local bus terminal is on Pedro Montt, opposite Dieciocho. Ancud's tourist information office is **Sernatur** on the Plaza de Armas at Libertad 665 (Jan–March Mon–Fri 8.30am–8pm, Sat & Sun 10.30am–1.30pm & 3–7.30pm; April–Dec Mon–Fri 8.30am–1pm & 2.30–6pm; ☎65/622800). It has information on the entire archipelago, and is better than the information hut in Castro (see p.344).

Accommodation

There's much more accommodation in Ancud in the summer, when many private houses open their doors to offer bed and breakfast, but there's enough to go around even in winter.

Hospedaje, Dieciocho 191 (☎65/625539). A *hospedaje* with basic rooms run by a friendly family. It's central, but because it's near the market it can be noisy. ③.

Hospedaje, O'Higgins 6 (☎65/622266). From the almost life-size bronze statue facing the front door to the well-proportioned, pale-wood-panelled bright rooms with views over the bay, this is the best budget accommodation in Ancud. Closed April–Dec. ②.

Hostal Lluhay, Cochrane 458 (☎ & fax 65/622656). The hotel looks pre-fabricated from the outside, but inside you'll discover a 200-year-old French rosewood piano, a collection of antique gramophones and one of the best-stocked bars in Ancud. The owners are friendly and arrange private tours. ④.

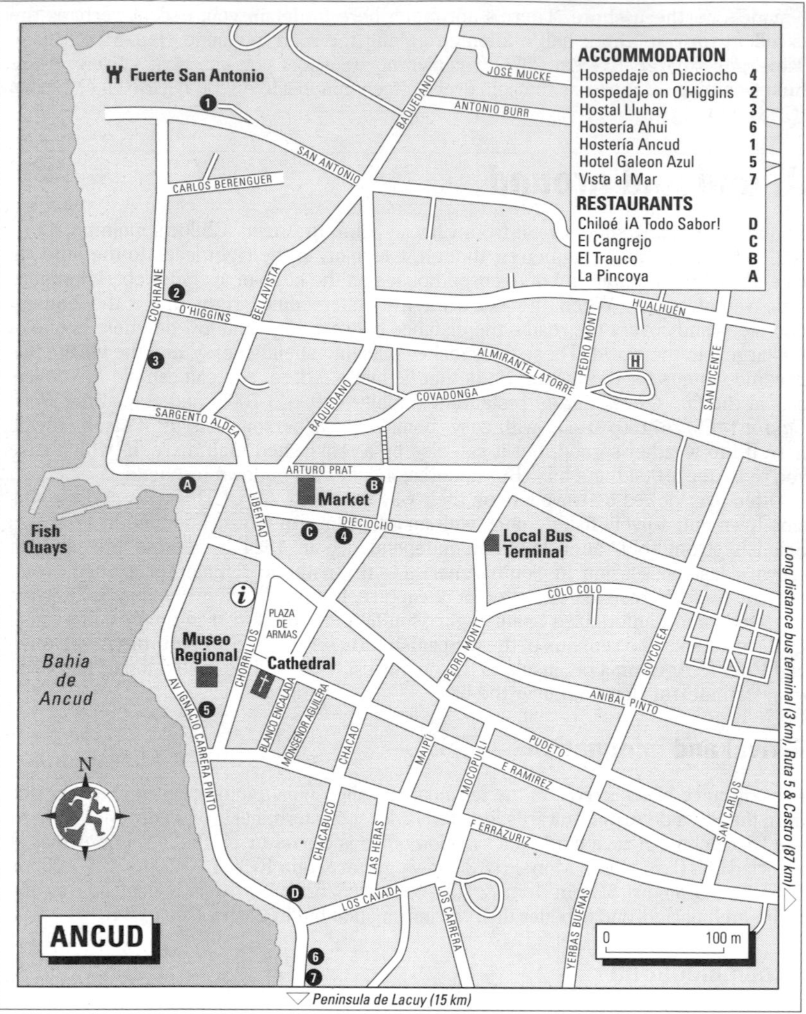

Hostería Ahui, Av Costanera 906 (☎65/622415). A two-storey beachfront building, with good views from the comfortable en-suite rooms, all of which makes it a popular mid-range choice. ④.

Hostería Ancud, San Antonio 30 (☎65/622340, fax 622350). Built up on the peninsula just to the north, this is the best hotel in town, with a luxurious log-cabin feel and large picture windows overlooking the sea. ⑦.

Hotel Galeon Azul, Libertad 75 (☎ & fax 65/622567). The views across the Golfo de Quetalmahue from this hotel are staggering but despite high-quality, modern rooms, its exposed position and clapboard feel give it all a slightly desolate air. ⑥.

Vista al Mar, Av Costanera 918 (☎ & fax 65/622617). Both a hotel and a youth hostel, this place is clean and newly refurbished. If you're the only people in the hostel (three rooms on the top floor), you'll get the cheapest apartment with the best views. ②.

The Town

Ancud is built on a small, square promontory jutting into the Canal de Chacao and the Golfo de Quetalmahue (often called the Bahía de Ancud). The town's spread along two sides of an old river bed, and – unlike most Chilean cities – isn't laid out on a grid pattern, but is a confusing mass of streets and one-way systems. The centre is the **Plaza de Armas**, a pretty little square which, in summer, is filled by the temporary craft stalls that spill out of the colourful **Mercado Municipal**, one block to the north.

There are some more stalls a block to the west, down near the hectic little **fishing harbour**. They're there because the harbour is a great place to hang around and watch the catch being landed, before it's transferred to the large shed where it's sold to dealers, with whole families deftly baiting enormous coils of deep-water fishing lines. Just south, a crushed-shell promenade leads past four or five intriguing pieces of **sculpture**, including a Henry Moore-style woman giving birth.

The Museo Regional

Looking left from the promenade, high up on a steep hill a full thirty metres above the sea, you'll see a **boat** familiar from posters throughout Chile: a schooner with white sails hanging motionless in the still air, which in the posters looks, because of a trick of perspective, as if it's floating on a calm blue sea. Named *La Goleta Ancud*, the boat is revered throughout Chile because in 1843 it carried the first Chilean settlers down to the Magellan Strait (see p.385). It is the culmination of a great tradition of Chilote boat-building, which started off with boats made from rude planks lashed together with vines and caulked with alerce bark.

The boat sits in the forecourt of the **Museo Regional**, a fort-like building on Libertad, one block south of the Plaza de Armas (Jan–March Mon–Fri 10.30am–7.30pm, Sat & Sun 10am–7pm; April–Dec Mon–Fri 10am–1pm & 3–6pm; CH$500). Also outside, incongruous beside the boat, is a traditional **fogón**, a type of hut introduced into Chiloé by the first Spanish missionaries three hundred years ago. A fire would burn in the middle of the floor, filling the roof space with smoke and curing the fish and potatoes hanging there. These were the staple of Chilote food, but during festivals pigs would be slaughtered and Chilotes would eat hams (*jamones*), smoked ribs (*costillares*), crackling (*chicharrones*), blood sausages (*longanizas*) and head cheese (*queso de cabeza*). Whilst the slaughtered pigs were being processed, Chilotes would quench their thirst with large quantities of apple cider (*chicha de manzana*) – you can see here the hollowed-out tree trunk where apples were pulped with long sticks. You can also see the flexible woven baskets where the pulp was strained, and an old wooden corkscrew where it was pressed.

Inside the museum you can see other examples of Chilote basket weaving: flat circular trays used for husking grain; lightweight ones with a coarse weave for collecting shellfish and fine-meshed liquid strainers. You'll also find a collection of **sledges**, a form of transport which evolved to deal with Chiloé's muddy tracks and small, steep fields. Finally, don't miss the collection of rustic carved demons from Chilote mythology outside on the museum's patio. They may look funny, but the locals take them so seriously that the figure of a demon called the *Trauco* – a desperately ugly woodland troll still blamed in Chiloé for unwanted pregnancies – has been chained up.

North of the Plaza de Armas

Walking back down to the fishing harbour from the museum, you'll find yourself at the end of calle Cochrane, a road that follows the coast to the north and heads uphill. Following it, you'll come to the reconstructed walls of the Spanish **Fuerte de San Antonio**,which affords a sweeping view over the Golfo de Quetalmahue and out to the

Pacific Ocean. By 1786 the Spanish had built an impressive chain of twelve such forts and gun batteries to control the passage of ships through the Canal de Chacao and protect the anchorage in Bahía Ancud, and the sixteen cannons in the Fuerte de San Antonio combined with the fifteen in Castillo de San Miguel de Agüi (on the peninsula across the water, see opposite) could sink any ship entering the bay. Further round this windswept headland, past the *Hostería de Ancud*, is the **Balneario Arena Gruesa**, a popular swimming beach sheltered by high cliffs. Further still is the **Mirador Cerro Eluaihue**, from which there's a bird's-eye view of the great río Pudeto estuary stretching away to the southwest, speckled with hundreds of tiny fishing boats lying at anchor.

Eating and drinking

Ancud is a fishing town and consequently has a collection of good **seafood restaurants**, all with the same menus. Most are collected around the sheltered courtyard in the Mercado Municipal, where it can get so busy that at times it's difficult to tell who's supposed to be serving you.

Chiloé ¡A Todo Sabor!, Costanera on the corner of Los Cavada. A German-run restaurant offering an unlimited buffet and *parillada* for CH$4000, this is a good place to go if you're very hungry.

El Cangrejo, Dieciocho 155. Basic café food, but with a particularly fine *empanada de mariscos*.

El Trauco, Blanco 515, corner of Prat. A more tourist-oriented seafood restaurant near the market, with friendly, garrulous waiters and decent food.

Hostería Ancud, San Antonio 30. The *hostería* has a good but expensive restaurant serving international food, and is the best place for a blowout meal.

La Pincoya, Prat 61. One of the best places to eat *curanto*, with a family-run atmosphere and excellent service.

Listings

Banks and exchange There are ATMs in Ramírez, one block away from the inland side of the Plaza. There aren't any *cambios*, so you should change money before you come here.

Car rental Alarcón Autos, Pudeto Bajo 1150 (☎65/622700), though you get a better deal in Castro.

Hospital Almirante Latore 301 (☎65/622355).

Internet access Centro Internet (no sign), Salvador Allende (also called the Costanera) 740, costing CH$2500 an hour.

Laundry Pudeto 45, around the corner from Sernatur.

Telephone centre Entel, Av Pudeto 219.

Travel agents Travel agents operate only in summer, and offer tours all over the island. The most popular run is to the Peninsula de Lacuy (see opposite). MB, Plaza de Armas (☎65/624349) offers the tour by land, charging CH$12,000 for the day. L/M Amadeus I, Blanco Encalada (☎65/623334) runs a trip by boat, and charges CH$3000. Also worth a visit are Turismo Huaihuén, Pudeto 135, second floor (☎65/623800).

MOVING ON FROM ANCUD

There are buses from Ancud to the south of the island every fifteen minutes, from both the local and long-distance terminals, costing CH$1100. Buses to Puerto Montt leave every half-hour, only from the long-distance terminal, and cost CH$1700 (the ferry to the mainland is included in the ticket). From the local terminal, there are daily buses west of Ancud, to the Peninsula de Lacuy (see opposite) and around.

Around Ancud

The road soon runs out of tar as you head **west** out of Ancud towards the Pacific Ocean. On the way you'll pass people laying out a stinking grey seaweed substance called *pelillo* – which resembles human hair – by the side of the road to dry, when they'll make it into a fibre. After 15km you reach the edge of the **Península de Lacuy**, a long arm of land that reaches out into the Pacific then bends back inland. Shortly afterwards, the road forks, with the left branch leading to the quiet beaches of **Playa Brava** and **Playa Guabún**, and ultimately to the northern tip of the peninsula and **Faro Corona**, an isolated lighthouse on a remote promontory. The right fork deposits you, after 21km, below **Fuerte Agüi** (always open; free) at the peninsula's easternmost edge, directly across the water from Ancud. The road worsens as you approach the fort, eventually petering out by a pleasant sandy beach, and you have to walk the final kilometre through a quiet forest, disturbed only by the sound of your feet, the buzzing of insects and the occasional put-put of a distant fishing boat. The fort was the last toehold of the Spanish Empire in South America, but today all that's left is a tranquil grassy lawn around a battery of rusting cannons. Standing on its ancient walls you can see right over the bay to Ancud, and on a clear day, all the way to Volcán Calbuco above Puerto Montt (see p.320).

You can get here by boat or bus. The boat is the *Amadeus I*, Blanco Encalada 587 (☎65/623334), which leaves daily from Ancud's port and costs CH$3000: watch out for seals and dolphins as you cross the bay. The buses are run by Buses Mar, and leave from Ancud's local bus terminal up to four times daily depending on the time of year, costing CH$900.

Thirty kilometres **south** of Ancud is the northern section of the **Parque Nacional Chiloé**, called **Sector Chepu** (Dec–March daylight hours; CH$800), whose main attraction are the **wetlands** that were created by the flooding following the 1960 earthquake, now rich in birdlife. It's remote and very difficult to get to, and unless you're a dedicated hiker with time to spare you'd be better off visiting the southern sector, **Sector Anay**, accessible by public transport from Castro (see p.346). Still, if you're determined, head south along the Panamericana then turn right (west) 22km out of Ancud to the tiny settlement of **Puerto Anguay**. From here, hike west for ninety minutes along the río Chepu, cross the estuary – you can usually rent a fisherman's boat – and finally, hike south, and after four hours you'll reach the Conaf station at Río Lar.

Ancud to Castro

The Panamericana heads southward, through trees, rolling hills and farmland until, after 66km, it reaches **Castro**. It's a fast but boring road, and if you have your own vehicle or a bit of time, it's worth taking things at a slower pace and travelling along the coast instead: turn east off the highway after 41km, and drive the 22km to **Quemchi**, before turning south. Here you'll get a much richer flavour of Chiloé, passing through small maritime villages with their characteristic wooden churches, and travelling through the centres of some of the islands' myths.

Quemchi and the coast

QUEMCHI is an attractive little town 65km south of Ancud, with narrow irregular streets sloping down to the water's edge. Beyond the fishing boats that lie beached on the sand is a wooded, field-strewn island across a choppy sea. Quemchi's a quiet place – once the centre of an important timber industry, now relying on salmon and shellfish farms for its existence. There's a helpful **tourist information** hut in the Plaza (Jan–March 10am–6pm), and two **places to stay**: the very central, friendly *Residencial Yungay*, almost overhanging the sea at Yungay 40 (☎65/691250; ③), with clean, bare rooms and a picturesque view; and, 5km north of town, an attractive farmhouse B&B (☎65/691250; ③), run by one Sr Juan Dougnac, with a garden and sea views. You can get to Quemchi on one of five daily **buses** from Ancud, operated by Buses el Rio and Queilen Bus (☎65/253468).

The coast south of Quemchi

A couple of kilometres further south there's a tiny wooded island, **Isla Aucar**, only accessible by a 500m-long footbridge, and, nestling within, a small wooden **church** with a duck-egg blue roof and white walls. Ten kilometres on, a turn to the east leads, after 7km, to the scattered houses that make up the seafront village of **QUICAVÍ**, whose ostensible sleepiness belies its importance in Chilote mythology. It's said that the coast between here and the next settlement south, Tenaún, is pitted with **caves** inhabited by witches, wizards, *peúchos* (who transmit mysterious untreatable diseases) and beautiful sirens, who tempt fishermen to their deaths with stories of a wonderful underwater paradise (those who succumb are never seen again, except on the ghostly sailing ship of lost souls, *El Caleuche*). Perhaps because of this wealth of superstition, the missionaries built a larger than usual **church** in Quicaví. One of the most important in Chiloé, it's an imposing brown barn of a place with a graceful arched entrance, but as it's almost permanently locked it's difficult to get a look inside. There's a daily **bus** to Quicaví from Castro (see p.342), leaving at about 4 to 4.30pm. There's no **accommodation** here, but you can ask one of the locals to camp on the beach.

Twelve kilometres further along the main road, another easterly turning heads to the somnolent village of **TENAÚN**, nothing more than two rows of houses facing each other across a kind of elongated plaza. The buildings are perfect examples of the island's vernacular architecture, a mixture of grand two-storey and quaint little fishermen's cottages. Smiling down between them is Chiloé's most extraordinary **church**, painted pale blue with two huge yellow stars daubed onto the wall. There's been a church in the village since 1734, but the present structure dates from 1861. It originally had twin towers at either side, but these were so poorly constructed that they had to be torn down two years later and replaced with the main tower and two small lateral ones you can see today. There's no public transport here, nor any accommodation.

The road and the coast now turn westward towards the town of Dalcahue. On your way, 16km from Tenaún, keep an eye out for the tiny village of **San Juan**, the island's most famous **boat-building** centre. Also look closely at its reed beds, which are home to one of the highest concentrations of black-necked swans in Chiloé, and check out the centuries-old stone corrals, artificial stone pools which the Chilotes used to trap fish when the tide went out. Once San Juan also had a graveyard, but when the 1960 tidal wave hit the village all the miniature wooden grave shelters floated out to sea.

Dalcahue

The coast road becomes tarred again at the bustling little town of **DALCAHUE**, 33km from the turn-off to Tenaún and 68km from Ancud. Along the busy waterfront there's a thriving traditional boat-building industry, and a constant stream of landing craft loading and unloading supplies for salmon farms, including live fish brought here for processing. A small car-ferry (see opposite) provides the only link with nearby **Isla Quinchao**, the largest in the Chiloé archipelago.

Until 1960 most of Dalcahue's inhabitants lived in *palafitos* (houses on stilts) along the edge of the sea, but that year's earthquake destroyed them all. The town was rebuilt, and the *palafitos* were replaced by a coast road and an attractive little square that's very much the heart of the place these days. On one side of the square there's an open-sided market building, constructed in the hope of retaining Dalcahue as the centre of Chiloé's handmade knitwear industry. Tour buses still come here from miles away on Sundays, but for the rest of the week the town's been eclipsed by Castro. On the opposite corner of the square is an Aladdin's cave of a **museum** (Mon–Fri 8am–1pm & 2–6pm; free), filled with a chaotic mess of pre-Hispanic and colonial artefacts and stuffed birds. Also on the square is an imposing church with a unique nine-arched portico, built in 1893.

Dalcahue straddles a river, and is dominated by two east–west roads, Ramón Freire and the *costanera* Montt (also called Ana Wagner), joined by a north–south O'Higgins. Buses and *colectivos* to Castro pull in at the little square where Ramón Freire meets O'Higgins, and the ferry for Isla Quinchao leaves from the western end of town. There's some reasonable **accommodation**, including a slew of *residenciales* clustered near the church. Right in the centre of town is *Pension Putemun*, calle Freire 305 (☎65/641330; ②), with comfortable rooms above a large busy restaurant. Alternatively, try *Residencial La Feria*, Rodriguez 17 (☎65/641293; ③), which also has good rooms. The line of small shops in the square includes some colourful fishermen's bars which do cheap **meals**, though for something a little more upmarket, there's the *Restaurant Brisas* overlooking the sea to the east of Pedro Montt, which has a good seafood menu and serves excellent squid.

Isla Quinchao

For some **Isla Quinchao**, a thin strip of land 30km long and for the most part not wider than 5km, is the cultural heart of the whole of Chiloé. This island, rich in traditional wooden architecture and pastoral calm, is just a fifteen-minute ferry ride from Dalcahue (services every half-hour during daylight; foot passengers free, cars Jan–March CH$3000 return, April–Dec CH$1000 return). The ferry arrives at a tiny quay, at the end of a dirt road that bisects the island.

Isla Quinchao only has two towns of any size, **Curaco de Vélez** and **Achao**, neither of which has more than a handful of buildings, but you'll get a better taste of traditional Chilote life from visiting either than you would from any museum.

Curaco de Vélez

Twelve kilometres from the ferry terminal, **CURACO DE VÉLEZ** comprises a couple of streets of weather-beaten shingled houses set around a beautiful bay, and bordered by gently rolling hills. Unusually, the Plaza de Armas features some decapitated **church steeples**, docked from the top of old churches, and a bust of local hero Almirante Riveros, who commanded the fleet that captured the Peruvian ironclad *Huáscar* during the War of the Pacific (see p.453). He's not the only Chilean notable to be born here, and the town also boasts of its sons Contralmirante Manuel Oyarzun, who also took part in the *Huáscar* engagement, and Piloto Carlos Miller Norton, who navigated the *Goleta Ancud* during its voyage to the Magellan Strait. The locals are very proud of this history – one of the town's names is *Cuna de Héroes* (Birthplace of Heroes) – and celebrate it on October 8 every year, when hordes of smartly dressed schoolchildren march round the Plaza de Armas, accompanied by the discordant tones of the fire brigade band, decked out in tarnished old Kaiser helmets and ill-fitting uniforms. The parade was first held rather more impressively in 1931, when six thousand people watched the President of the Republic arrive on a battleship, accompanied by submarines and flying boats.

Nearly all visitors to the island call at Curaco de Vélez, but there are few places offering **accommodation**, the best being *Central*, Errazuriz 9 (☎65/667238; ②). There are two places to **eat**, *Bahía* on the *costanera*, an upmarket shellfish restaurant, and *Nido del Jabalí*, Riveros 11, a downmarket café.

Achao

Coming over the hill and getting your first view of **Achao** resting in a fertile valley by the sea, 13km southeast of Curaco de Vélez, you could be forgiven for thinking you were arriving at an English seaside village. But the sight of the Chilote church, the distant mountains across a wide sea and the rows of single storey houses faced with wooden shingles soon puts you straight. Just about every building is clad in these alerce tiles (*tejuelas*), which are coloured in shades of soft pastels and silver, not caused by faded paint but by colonies of yellow and green lichens.

Achao is a living museum of Chiloé's *cultura de madera* (woodworking culture). The **church** is a good example, made up as it is of many different types of wood. A typical Chilote church, it's a great solid, squat structure built in 1862, more than forty metres long and totally devoid of exterior embellishment. The main framework is made from *ciprés de las Guaitecas*, a conifer that was once the most common tree species of the Chiloé archipelago, and *mañío*, a tree still common to southern Chile. Originally all the exterior was clad with alerce shingles but most of these have been replaced with *ciprés* boarding. In contrast to the plain outer shell the interior is a riot of colour and architectural styles with an intricately vaulted ceiling running the length of a broad central nave. Restoration work is a constant and expensive necessity – if you look around the *luma* floorboards you can see the church's foundations, a rare glimpse into the way these old buildings were constructed. All the joints are fixed with wooden plugs and dowels, even the dozens of shingles on the building's outside, which had to be laboriously drilled and fixed in place with plugs made from *canelo* (another type of Chilean wood).

Achao's other defining feature is its hectic **boat ramp** at the end of calle Serrano, one of the few places you can still see traditional sailing boats with whole families sleeping in large open cockpits and cooking on naked flames. All sorts of cargo is loaded and unloaded here and there is a small market at the top of the ramp selling island produce. Launches go to the islands of the Chilote archipelago, and you might be able to hire a fisherman to take you out to visit one of them.

The town's not short of places to **stay**, including the stand-out *Hostería La Nave*, one block north of the boat ramp at calle Prat on the corner of calle Aldea (☎ & fax 65/661219; ③), built on stilts over the beach with plenty of bright, cheery natural wood. On the north side of the Plaza de Armas is *Hostal Plaza* (☎65/661219; ③), a rather grand bed and breakfast in a very comfortable family house. The best **restaurant** is in the *Hostería La Nave* but *Mar y Velas*, overlooking the busy boat ramp, is better for people-watching – at lunchtime, half of Achao's population passes by.

Regular buses come to Achao each day from Castro via Dalcahue, run by San Cristóbal.

Ten kilometres south of Achao is Chiloé's **largest church**, the Iglesia de Nuestra Señora de Gracia de Quinchao, sitting rather incongruously near the edge of the sea, surrounded by half a dozen fishermen's cottages. There's been a church here since 1605, and ever since construction on the existing sixty-metre building was begun in 1869 its upkeep has sapped church funds, and on several occasions it's come close to collapsing on the congregation. Apart from its size, the church is unremarkable, save for an interesting religious festival on December 7 and 8, when pilgrims – and their sick horses – come to be healed by the Señora.

Castro and around

Built on a small promontory at the head of a twenty-kilometre fjord, **CASTRO**, 19km southwest of Dalcahue, occupies an unusual position both physically and historically. Founded in 1567, it's the third-oldest city in Chile, but it never became strategically important because it's a terrible harbour for sailing ships. It only flowered because the

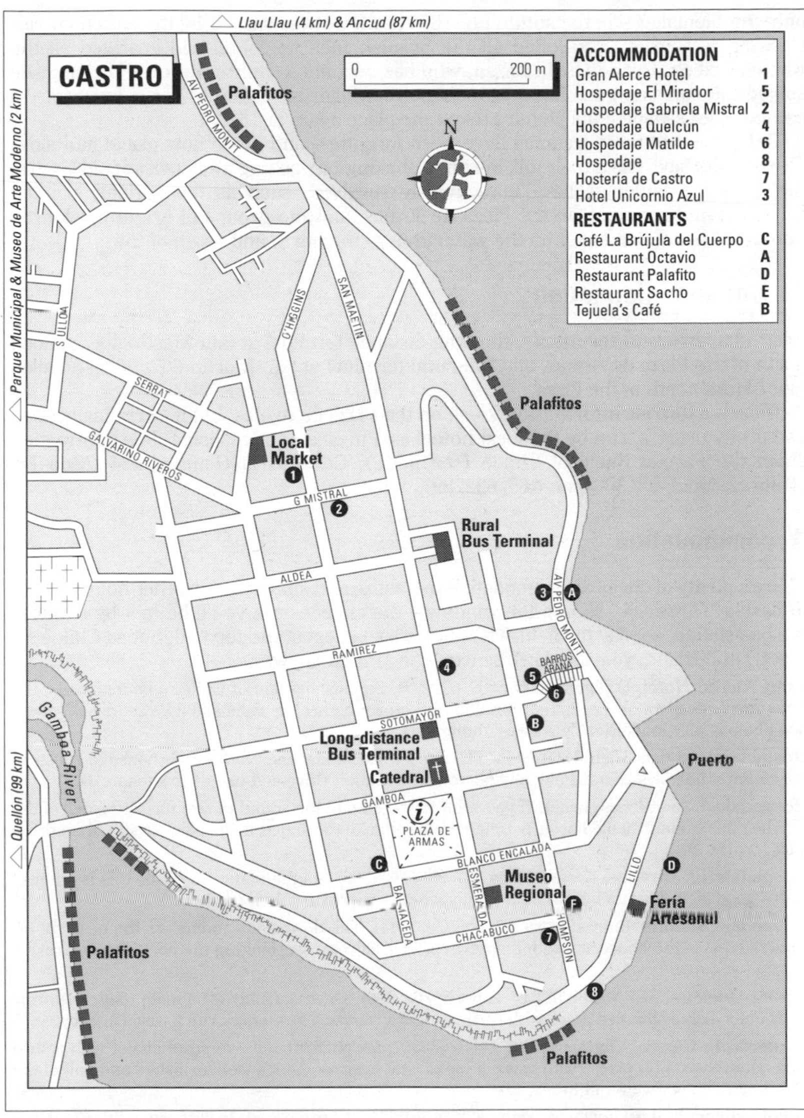

Jesuits chose to base their mission here, and because of their efforts it became a centre of evangelism, education and commerce.

It's had its fair share of difficulties. It was destroyed by earthquake in 1646, by fire in 1729, by earthquake again in 1739, by fire again in 1890, by fire once more in 1936, and most recently by earthquake and tidal wave in 1960. Anyone else would have given up and moved long ago, but the Chilotes keep hanging on. Nor has nature been the only troublemaker – in the autumn of 1600 the town was sacked by the Dutch corsair Baltazar de Cordes, who killed all the Spanish men he found and enslaved all the women (except Doña Ines de Bazan, who has become a Chilean heroine because she spiked the corsairs' guns and wet their powder, allowing some of her compatriots to escape). Not satisfied, the Dutch sacked the place again in 1643.

Today most of these traumas have been forgotten, and life is now placid and slow. The tumults have taken their toll, burning, shaking or washing away most of old Castro, though some buildings have miraculously survived, such as the garishly painted **Iglesia San Francisco** on the Plaza de Armas, and the groups of brightly coloured **palafitos** (houses on stilts) on the waterfront to the north and south of town.

Arrival and information

Castro has two **bus terminals**, the long-distance terminal at San Martín 486, a block north of the Plaza de Armas, and the rural terminal at San Martín 667, down an alley four blocks north of the Plaza.

There's a **tourist information** kiosk on the Plaza de Armas, but it's erratically open and pretty useless, run by the local hotels as a means of advertising. For information about the Parque Nacional Chiloé (see p.348), Conaf is at Gamboa 424 (Mon–Fri 10am–12.30pm & 2.30–4pm; ☎65/632289).

Accommodation

There's plenty of cheap accommodation in Castro, and almost every other house seems to have a "*Hospedaje*" sign in the window – the chances are you'll be met by a tout at the bus station, so play the field. The choice isn't great at the top end, but as Chiloé's a quiet, rural island, you shouldn't be expecting much anyway.

Gran Alerce Hotel, O'Higgins 808 (☎65/632267). Supposedly one of Chiloé's better hotels, the *Gran Alerce* desperately needs redecoration: the brown bathroom walls and fake zebra-skin doors don't help at all. Good, friendly service, though. ⑤.

Hospedaje, Gabriela Mistral 369 (☎65/632759). Two schoolteachers open their house to guests in the summer holidays (Jan & Feb), and let you park in their drive and use their kitchen. ②.

Hospedaje, Lillo 204 (no phone). If you want to wake up to the sound of seagulls and smell of the sea then this traditional old house, perched on the edge of the shore, is the place to stay, though it's a bit scruffy. ②.

Hospedaje El Mirador, Barros Arana 127 (☎65/633795). As the name suggests, this is a house with a good view. It's run by a friendly family who let guests use their kitchen. ③.

Hospedaje Matilde, Barros Arana 146 (☎65/633614). The downstairs rooms are the best, cut off from the rest of the house and with their own private balcony overlooking the port. The beds sag a bit. ②.

Hostal Quelcun, San Martin 581 (☎ & fax 65/632396). Down an alley off a main road, a surprisingly quiet alerce-shingled hotel, with clean, modern rooms. The owners run a travel agency. ④.

Hostería de Castro, Chacabuco 202 (☎65/632301, fax 635688). An oversized chalet with a strip torn out of the roof replaced with glass. It looks a bit bizarre, but it's well-furnished and half of the rooms have a good view out to sea. ⑥.

Hotel Unicornio Azul, Av Pedro Montt 228 (☎65/632359, fax 632808). In stiff competition with the Iglesia San Francisco for the virulence of its exterior colour scheme, this unmissable hotel down by the port is the most luxurious place to stay in town. ⑥.

The Town

A bit on the scruffy side, but charming nonetheless, Castro has the feel of an isolated town on the edge of the twentieth-century mainstream, like the west coast of

Ireland or the maritime provinces of Canada. The promontory on which it's centred is small, only five blocks wide and nine blocks long, and is fringed on the north and south by the town's **palafitos**, rickety shacks on stilts which the local government is torn between preserving as national monuments and condemning as unsanitary slums.

The centre of town is the **Plaza de Armas**, a block and a half from the southern tip of the promontory. On the northeastern corner is Castro's church, the **Iglesia San Francisco**, painted bright orangey-pink and purple, looking almost luminescent from afar and painted this colour for the pope's visit in 1987. It was designed in 1906 by an Italian, who originally wanted to build it using concrete, and it's just as well he didn't, because it's unlikely that concrete would have survived the 1960 earthquake. As it is, the box-frame survived well, and is sheathed in sheets of beaten tin, moulded to resemble the wooden shingles so characteristic of Chilote architecture. The impressive interior is a harmonious blend of the island's native hardwoods, lit with a soft light that brings out their warm hues.

Just off the southeast corner of the Plaza de Armas in calle Esmeralda is the **Museo Regional** (Jan–Feb Mon–Sat 9.30am–1pm & 3–6.30pm, Sun 10.30am–1pm; March–Dec Mon–Sat 9.30am–noon, Sun 10.30am–noon; free), a small but well laid-out museum containing artefacts from the various aboriginal tribes that inhabited the Chiloé archipelago before the arrival of the Spanish. Here you can find their stone tools, fish hooks and spear heads. Contemporary times are documented in a large collection of photographs, mostly taken before the earthquake, and there's also a bicycle made out of wood, a wonderful emblem of Chiloé's *cultura de madera*.

The road that runs south of the Plaza is **Blanco Encalada**. A few days before the catastrophic 1936 fire that just about razed Castro to the ground, several people living here reported seeing a giant sea-lion come out of the water and waddle up the street. In a community where superstition is second nature, this apparition was widely accepted as an evil omen. Perhaps it was, though you didn't really need an omen to foresee the danger, as 1930s Castro was a fire waiting to happen, built almost entirely of back-to-back wooden buildings. When the fire struck, the only thing the inhabitants could do was head for the sea, the only sanctuary available. They took to their boats and watched their homes burn from the waters of the icy fjord.

Two blocks east of the Plaza, down by the water, is the **feria artesanal**, a large covered market building where hand-knitted woollens vie for space with home-grown vegetables. Despite the day-trippers from continental Chile, there is an almost religious peace inside the market, broken only by the clicking of sturdy women knitting pullovers. Next to the market there's a line of *palafitos* on the sea, used today as restaurants. They're a great place to come and eat, but they get packed at lunchtime with visitors, so it's much more relaxed to wait until the afternoon.

Beyond the promontory the town stretches out to the northwest, where modern low-cost houses have been erected for a rural population who don't have much hope of finding work in the fields. Out here is the **Parque Municipal**, accessible by buses and taxis from the centre of town, from where you've got excellent views over Castro, across the archipelago and out towards the Andes. Nearby is the **Museo Arte Moderno**, or **MAM** (daily: Jan–March 10am–6pm; April–Dec Mon–Fri 11am–2pm; free), a collection of restored wooden barns home to a collection of modern art. Every February the park is the setting for an enormous feast, the culmination of the **Festival Costumbrista**, a celebration of traditional Chilote life, when *curantos* (meat and seafood stews) are cooked in great cauldrons, meat is roasted over open fires, and balls of grated potato – *tropon* – are baked on hot embers. When the outer part is cooked, the *tropon* is removed from the fire and the crisp shell peeled off and eaten – the inevitable burnt fingers and resultant hot-potato juggling and hopping are known as *bailar el tropon* (dancing the *tropon*).

Eating and drinking

Seafood dominates Castro's menus, plucked fresh from the Fiordo de Castro by the town's fleet of fishermen.

Café La Brújula del Cuerpo, O'Higgins 308. A bright café on the corner of the Plaza attached to the fire station. The menu's a bit laboured, relating everything to fire, but it's the best place in town for a quiet drink and a sandwich.

Restaurant Octavio, Av Pedro Montt 261. A family-run waterfront restaurant with a fine view over the sea, typical Chilean food and good service.

Restaurant Palafito, Lillo 30. One of the *palafito* restaurants by the market, serving standard Chilean seafood in a beautiful setting over the placid waters of Castro's fjord.

Restaurant Sacho, Thompson 213 (☎65/632079). The best restaurant in Castro, with a slightly dingy downstairs but an upstairs with views across the fjord. The owner almost spoils everything by playing Richard Clayderman on the stereo, but even this can't detract from the heavenly *carapaccio* (crab baked in cream). It's worth booking an upstairs table in the evening.

Tejuela's Café, Serrano 489. Basic tourist food (burgers and hot dogs) with local colour (smoked salmon).

Listings

Airlines Lan Chile and Ladeco, Blanco Encalada 299 (☎65/635254).

Banks and exchange There are ATMs around the Plaza de Armas, and Sr Julio Barrientos at Chacabuco 286 exchanges money.

Bookshop El Tren Libros, Thompson 229, has a small amount of secondhand books in English, German and French as well as a good selection of Spanish books.

Car rental Automotriz del Sur, Esmeralda 260 (☎65/637777, fax 637373), and Salfa Sur, Gabriela Mistral 499 (☎65/632704), are both cheaper than outfits in Puerto Montt.

Ferry TransMarChilay has an office on Thompson 241 (☎65/632629).

Internet access Gamboa 447, second floor.

Laundry Clean Centre, Serrano 490.

Post office The Correo is on the Plaza de Armas, at O'Higgins 326.

Telephone centres Chilesat, 171 San Martín; Entel, O'Higgins 480.

Travel agencies Pehuén Expediciones, Thompson 229 (☎65/632484, fax 635254), runs boat trips in summer to the small, uninhabited islands of the Chilote archipelago, lasting from a day to a week. It also runs city tours (CH$7000), trips to Isla Quinchao (CH$18,000) and the Parque Nacional Chiloé (CH$18,500). Turismo Quelcun, San Martín 581 (☎65/632396), is associated with the hotel (see "Accommodation", p.344) and has plans to run tours of the Chilote archipelago. Alerce Andino Expediciones, Gamboa 387, Local 116 (☎09/752 4073), runs day-trips and mountain biking and trekking in the Parque Nacional Chiloé (from CH$19,000).

MOVING ON FROM CASTRO

Regular buses run from the long-distance terminal via Ancud (1hr 30min) to Puerto Montt (3hr) every fifteen minutes. There are even a couple of buses every week to Punta Arenas down in Patagonia (32hr, via Argentina). Local buses leave from the local terminal to most points on the island: every hour on weekdays (every 2 hours at weekends) to Dalcahue (30min), Curaco de Vélez (1hr) and Achao (1hr 45min); hourly to Quellón and Queilen (both 1hr 30min); and four times daily to Cucao and the Parque Nacional Chiloé (1hr).

Around Castro

Chiloé is famous for its **churches**, and the small villages around Castro boast a wide variety of them, making for a diverting day out.

Four kilometres to the north of Castro on the way to Ancud, a badly signed turn to the east leads to the small village of **LLAU LLAO** (named after a golf-ball-sized fungi once made into a type of moonshine). There's not much to the village, just a couple of streets on a hillock dominated by a pretty, typically Chilote **church**, a long squat building with a tower and portico. The locals are very proud of the church because it's been declared a national monument. Anyone inside when you visit will often offer to show you around, and you can climb up into the tower to inspect the deep-blue barrelled roof. *Micros* and *colectivos* run here from Castro, or you can take any bus to Ancud and asked to be dropped at the crossroads.

Across the fjord from Castro, a nineteen-kilometre road runs southeast along a peninsula of gently undulating farmland, ending at **RILÁN**, a small village that dates from 1658. Facing a plaza near the edge of a small bay is a large church, **Iglesia Santa Maria**, with a five-arched portico and three-storey bell tower, extensively renovated after it was badly damaged in a fierce 1990 storm. There's nowhere to stay in Rilán, but you can always **camp** on the beach. Three buses call in every weekday from Castro's local bus terminal.

Four kilometres south of Castro, the church in the village of **NERCON** is a variation on the theme. The **Iglesia de Nuestra Señora de Gracia de Nercon** dates from

CHILOTE CHURCHES

It is impossible to visit Chiloé and not be struck by the sight of the archipelago's **wooden churches**. Two hundred years ago these impressively large buildings would have been the heart of a Chilote village, whereas nowadays many only have a couple of buildings nearby, and Mass may be held only once a year.

The churches generally face the sea, and are built near a beach or safe landing place with an open area, plaza or *explanada* in front of them. The outside of the churches is almost always bare, and the only thing that expresses anything but functionality is the three-tiered, hexagonal bell tower that rises up directly above an open-fronted portico. The facades, doors and windows are brightly painted, and the walls are clad with plain clapboard or wooden tiles, *tejuelas* (tiles or shingles). Inside, the double-pitched roof creates a feeling of space and tranquillity, and all churches have three naves separated by columns, which in the larger buildings are often highly decorated, supporting barrel-vaulted ceilings. The ceilings are often painted too, sometimes with allegorical panels, and sometimes with golden constellations of stars painted on an electric blue background.

Only the *pueblos* which had a priest had a main church, an *Iglesia parroquial*. If there was no church, the missionaries used to visit once a year, a visit called the *mission circular*. Using only native canoes, they carried everything required to hold a Mass with them, such as tables, sacraments and religious images carved out of wood. When the priest arrived one of the eldest Chilotes would lead a procession carrying an image of Jesus, and behind him two youths would follow with the most important images, San Juan and the Virgin, followed by married men carrying San Isidro and married women carrying Santa Neoburga. If the *pueblo* was important enough there would be a small *capilla* (bell tower) with altars to receive the statues. The building where the missionaries stayed when they came was known as a *residencia, villa, casa ermita* or *catecera*, and was looked after by a local trusty called a *Fiscal*, whose function was somewhere between that of a verger and lay preacher. This honorary position still exists, and in Chiloé's more remote areas, the *Fiscal* commands great respect in his community.

1734, and, a rarity on the island, has a little churchyard. The interior is highly decorated with imitation marbling, and on September 29 it's further decorated by foliage when the village celebrates the festival of San Miguel.

Parque Nacional Chiloé, Sector Anay

Every summer, hordes of Chilean backpackers descend on **PARQUE NACIONAL CHILOÉ, SECTOR ANAY** (daily 9am–7pm; CH$1000), 45km southwest of Castro, keen to camp on its twenty kilometres of white-sand beach and to explore its dense forest. This section of the national park (the other is Sector Chepu – see p.339) covers 350 square kilometres of the Cordillera de Piuchen (Piuchen Mountains), rising up to 800m above sea level. It's reached by a 25-kilometre road which shoots west from a junction on the Panamericana, 20km south of Castro.

At the end of the road is the gateway to the park, the picturesque but ramshackle village of **CUCAO**. Near to the sea, straddling a sluggish, murky river and with two lakes, Lago Cucao and Lago Huillinco, that almost bisect the island at this point, the village is dominated by water, and its few streets of tumbledown wooden huts are littered with whalebones, fishing floats and flotsam and jetsam from the Pacific. Clam-fishing and seaweed-gathering are big business, with wet-suited divers swimming out to sea to set their nets.

For many years a traditional Chilote community of Huilliches lived off this narrow coastal plain, collecting shellfish and growing potatoes, *quinoa* (a South American grain) and strawberries. With the arrival of missionaries in 1734, gold was found, and from then on the area was inhabited by a couple of hundred prospectors who scratched a bare living from the small streams that flowed from the impenetrable forest. This all changed on May 21, 1960, when a tidal wave swept two kilometres inland, and then retreated, taking with it the church, the houses and an unlucky gold panner called Abraham Lincoln. The geography of the coast changed forever, as Lago Cucao became flooded and forced its way out to the sea, cutting a new river as it went. The fragile vegetation along the beach was torn away, and sand dunes quickly buried fields and farms.

Cucao has since recovered, although it's still a remote community: the village has only been reachable by road since 1983. Today, buses drive along a new road carved out of the southern shore of the two lakes, and stop on the village football field by a suspension bridge which leads to the national park. Cucao's basic **accommodation** is in houses near the bridge: *La Paloma* (no phone; ①) has floor space, a garden in which you can camp, hot showers and a communal kitchen. Just across the river is the German-owned *Posada Darwin* (closed June & July; messages ☎65/6333040; ③) with small *cabaña* rooms and a small restaurant serving pizzas, *gulasch*, cakes, fish and clams. Out of season, the best place to stay is *Hospedaje Paraiso* (no phone; ②), when the snug little kitchen provides respite from the wind and rain. A converted barn next door serves fried fish and boiled potatoes. You can camp in the gardens of most of these places, and there's also a spot for wild camping by the river mouth, with a freshwater spring nearby.

One of the best ways of getting around is by **horse**, and there are dozens that can be hired from the villagers, either with guides or without. On the whole they are scrawny, plodding old nags, well-used to carrying novice passengers, though they don't come cheap – *Posada Darwin*, for example, charges CH$2000 for an hour or CH$10,500 a day.

Exploring the park

Across Cucao's suspension bridge and at the northern end of the wide, sandy beach is the Conaf **Cucao Ranger Post** (also known as the Chanquin Ranger Post). There's a

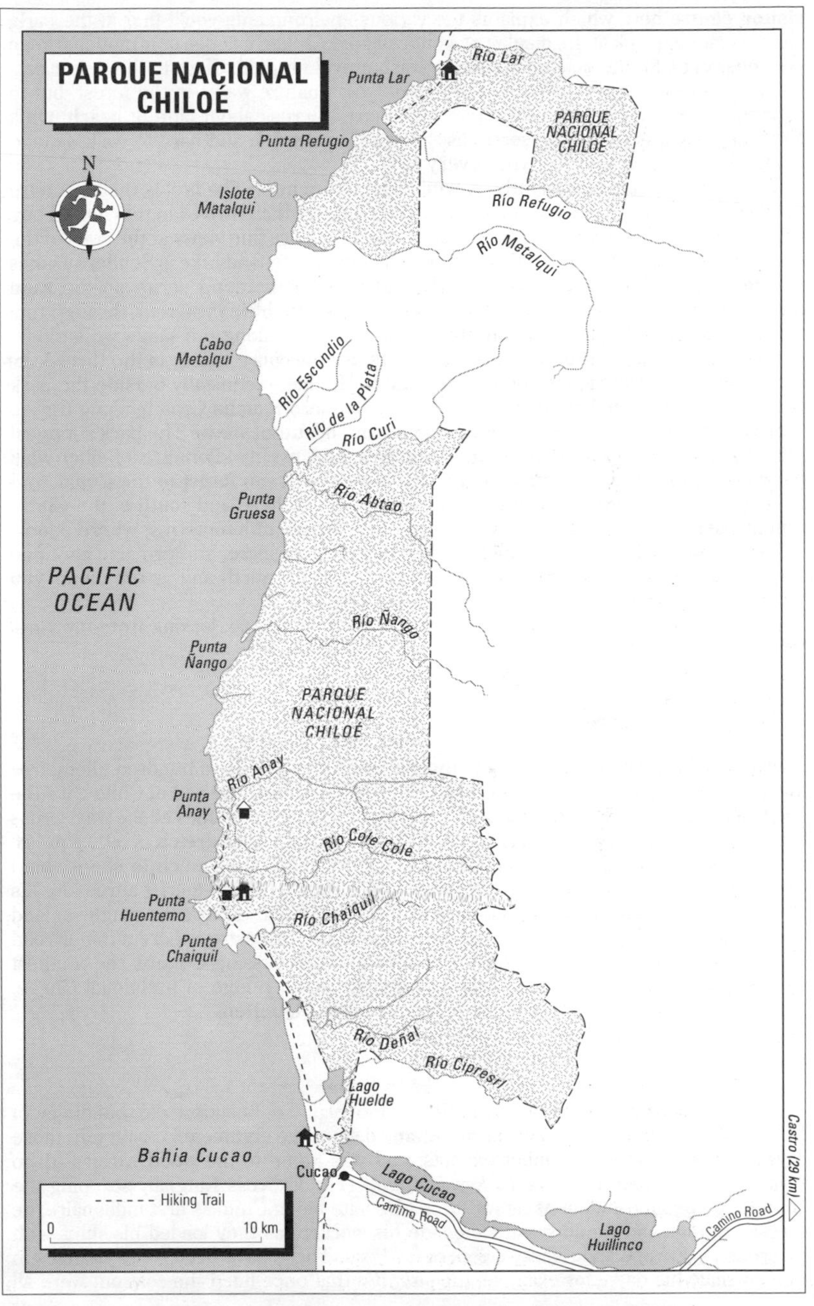
PARQUE NACIONAL CHILOÉ
N
Río Lar
Punta Lar
PARQUE NACIONAL CHILOÉ
Punta Refugio
Islote Matalqui
Río Refugio
Río Metalqui
Cabo Metalqui
Río Escondio
Río de la Plata
Río Curi
Punta Gruesa
Río Abtao
PACIFIC OCEAN
Río Ñango
Punta Ñango
PARQUE NACIONAL CHILOÉ
Río Anay
Punta Anay
Río Cole Cole
Punta Huentemo
Río Chaiquil
Punta Chaiquil
Río Deñal
Río Cipresrl
Lago Huelde
Bahia Cucao
Cucao
Lago Cucao
Camino Road
Lago Huillinco
Camino Road
Castro (29 km)
Hiking Trail
0
10 km

visitor centre here which explains the various environments you'll find in the park, and you can also look at the display of wonderful old Chilote wooden contraptions: keep your eyes open for the machines used to wash gravel for gold. Close to the visitor centre (ask there for directions) there are some short nature walks in the forest, but to experience fully the beauty of the park, you have to cross about 5km of beach. On a summer's day this can be tiresome, as the sand is very fine and hard to walk on, and biting flies called *tavanos* dog your every step.

There are a couple of short **hikes** which start from here. The first is the 770-metre Sendero el Tepual through an area of the Tepu forest which thrives in this humid bog land, with walkways across the wetter sections. There are fine views at the start of the walk, over the lake, the mountains and the village. The second hike is Sendero Dunas de Cucao, just short of a kilometre, through the regenerating scrub on the sand dunes. On parts of this walk you have to bend almost double as you walk through tunnels of dense vegetation, while on others you can stroll along the sands whilst looking out for the giant rhubarb-like *nalca* plants. A little more taxing is the three-kilometre (one-way) walk along the beach to Lago Huelde, technically outside the park boundary, where you pick up a trail known as Sendero Rancho Grande along the río Cipresal up to the edge of the tree line, revealing beautiful views. The park's longest hike, though, and its most popular, is the beautiful twenty-kilometre (4–6hr) walk north along the coast and through dense, native evergreen forest to the Conaf *refugio* at **Cole Cole**, just by Punta Huentemo, the second headland south of the Cucao ranger post. Call in at the houses along the first couple of kilometres, where people will sell bread, fish, clams and meat if they have any to spare. You can also continue another 5km north to the *Refugio Anay*, which is as far north and as remote as you can go.

There are at least three **buses** a day to Cucao from Castro, leaving from the rural bus station.

South of Castro

South of Castro, the Panamericana plunges down for just under a hundred kilometres to Chiloé's southernmost town, **QUELLÓN**. This is not only the end of Chiloé, it's the end of a road which – save for the Darién gap in Colombia – stretches all the way across two continents. Despite this romance, the Panamericana's final stretch is rather prosaic – the scenery down here is not dramatic, and Quellón isn't much to shout about either, being a commercial centre and fishing port rather than a tourist attraction. It's more rewarding to turn your attention away from Ruta 5 and explore the tongue of land that stretches to the southeast, beginning 17km south of Castro, where a minor road branches east off the Panamericana to follow the coast, passing **Conchi**, the prettiest town in Chiloé, and the ferry to **Isla Lemuy**, an island refuge of traditional Chiloé, before winding up, after 46km, at the fishing village of **Queilén**.

Conchi

Lined around the best harbour on the island are the beautiful old buildings of **CONCHI**, buildings which have hardly changed since the eighteenth century. In those days the town thrived on timber exports, and was home to the wood baron Ciriaco Alvarez, who earned the name *El Rey de Ciprés* (The Cypress King) by stripping the archipelago of almost all of its native forest. Despite being Chiloé's first millionaire, he dressed in rags and would sweat alongside his workers as they loaded his ships with pit props for Europe and railway sleepers for Peru. There have been some changes in Conchi since his day – for example, the *palafitos* that once lined the seafront were all destroyed by the 1960 earthquake – but Conchi's steeply curving main street, calle Centenario, still retains its beauty.

The town's cheerfully painted **church** repays a visit. It's not original, and has been rebuilt several times over the years, but it's recently been restored to its full glory, and the Neoclassical facade is one of the island's finest. It houses an image of the Virgin Mary, *La Virgin de la Candelaria*, which the locals believe saved them from the marauding corsairs that sacked Castro; the image is noisily celebrated at a festival every February 2, when townspeople fire guns into the air to symbolize a pirate attack. A short way down the main street from the church is the **Museo de las Tradiciones Conchinas**, Centenario 116, (Mon–Fri 9am–7pm; free), a beautifully restored old traditional house, filled with furniture, fittings and a large collection of photographs from the tree-felling heyday of *El Rey de Ciprés*.

A couple of doors along from the museum at Centenario 102 is one of Conchi's best **places to stay**, *Hotel Huildin* (☎65/671388; ③), quite a museum piece in itself. As is typical in large old Chilote houses, the upstairs bedrooms are large and high-ceilinged and face onto an enclosed veranda which runs around two sides of the building. Slightly tucked away on the eastern end of the seafront, *Esmeralda by the Sea* (☎ & fax 65/671328; ②) is a small *hospedaje* with a helpful English-speaking owner who organizes land and sea tours; it offers a book exchange, email facilities, a laundry and evening meals. Camping in the sheltered garden costs CH$2000 per person. You could also try *El Antiguo Chalet*, on the western edge of town, just uphill from the harbour (☎65/671221; ④) a beautiful, natural-wood house built in 1934 by one of the timber kings and set in large, well-kept grounds. **Eating** well in Conchi is a problem – for some reason, restaurants here come and go as quickly as the tides – but *El Trebol* at the southern end of the waterfront above the local market has good enough seafood dishes and seems to be standing the test of time. There are **buses**, run by such operators as Buses Regional Sur and Queilén Bus (☎65/253468), every hour from Castro to Conchi.

Isla Lemuy

On the coast 3km south of Conchi at **Huicha**, a ferry (daily 8am–9pm; Mon–Sat every 30min, Sun every 1hr; 20min; CH$3000) heads to the second-largest island in the Chiloé archipelago, **ISLA LEMUY**. At 120 square kilometres, it's only slightly smaller than Isla Quinchao, but it's a paradise of peace and quiet, seldom visited by tourists. If you're looking for bright lights and sophistication then pass this island by, as there's nothing in the way of even moderately sophisticated facilities for visitors. But if you're searching for traditional rural Chiloé, then you'll find it in the tiny little villages that dot the island, like **Ichuac**, 4km from the ferry terminal at Chulchuy, **Puqueldón**, the island's main settlement 5km to Ichuac's east, and **Aldachido**, 9km from Puqueldón on the tip of the northern coast, each of which boasts just a few houses and maybe a fine old church. Perhaps the most remote is **Detif**, on an isolated, bleak headland at the far eastern end of the island, about 20km from Puqueldón. Here, there's not much more than a chapel, inside which fishermen hang model boats. On a clear day you can sit on the grass outside the chapel and stare at a view that hasn't changed for thousands of years, across the flat calm of the gulf of Corovado, studded with islands, and over to the mainland and the brooding Volcán Michinmahuida.

The only **place to stay** on the island is near the village of **Puchilco**, 4km northeast of the main road from Puqueldón to Detif. Here there's a green and orange farmhouse where the Perez family takes in guests (no phone; ③) – don't be surprised to see the occasional sheep wandering around their front garden. There's one **bus** daily, run by Dalcahue Expresso, to Isla Lemuy from Castro, which crosses to the island on the ferry.

The road from Conchi to Queilén

Back on the mainland, the dirt road to Queilén runs above a string of pretty little villages down by the sea – Tepua, Terao, Ahoni and Aituy. The roads down to these villages are steep, and old or weak cars can't make the gradient. You'll notice around some of these villages, **Tepua**, for example, graveyards filled with strange huts. These are *mausoleos*, traditional structures in this part of Chiloé, shelters that protect mourners from the elements when they visit the graves of the dead. Some can be simple and basic, but some can be wonderfully ornate affairs, the outsides clad in alerce shingle and the insides beautifully vaulted and protected by delicate screens. They stand in contrast to the stark graves themselves, normally just plain crosses painted with the family name.

Forty-six kilometres from Conchi, the road pulls into **QUEILÉN**, a little fishing town whose one main street, Alessandri, bisects the neck of a long, sandy peninsula. The western end of town is very pretty, lined with fishermen's houses built on a long beach, sheltered by **Isla Tranqui** which lies just off the coast. There's nothing to do here except relax, although in February the town hosts a craft fair in which all types of local products are sold, from handicrafts and farming equipment to traditional medicines. The town's short on **places to stay**, but try the *Hospedaje Laura Gonzalez*, O'Higgins 93 (☎65/258271 ext 305; ②), or the church-run *Albergue Parroquial* 49, calle 21 de Mayo (☎65/258271 ext 237; ② but variable) with beds and floor space – they don't have a fixed charge but ask you to pay what you can afford. You can **eat** at *Restaurant Melinka*, upstairs at Alessandri 56, where there's friendly service, pleasant surroundings and fish, fish and more fish. Queilén Bus (☎65/253468) run seven **buses** a day to Queilén from Castro.

Quellón

If, at the junction where the coast road heads southeast to Conchi and Queilén, you stick on the Panamericana heading south, you'll speed along the last 79km of road on Chiloé which ends up at **QUELLÓN**, a commercial fishing port. The only reason to come here is if you're catching one of the ferries that run across to Chaiten on the Carretera Austral (see p.363). It's never been an attractive place, and was by turns a Jesuit mission, a coaling depot for the Chilean navy, a meteorological centre and a messenger-pigeon station. This changed in 1906 when the Patagonian logging companies arrived and drove roads and narrow-gauge railways into the **Cordillera de Pirulil**, an otherwise uninhabited and unexplored mountain range to the west. There they stripped the mountains, and by 1950 when the plant closed and the company's employees returned to Patagonia, a forest that once covered a third of Chiloé had been chopped down.

Today Quellón is a small place, based around three streets that run east–west parallel to the coast: the Costanera (also called Miramar and Pedro Montt) which runs along the seafront, Ercilla which runs north of the Costanera, and Ladrilleros which runs north of Ercilla. The central **Plaza de Armas**, is on two small streets sandwiched between the Costanera and Ercilla. Whilst waiting for your ferry, you can while away a couple of interesting hours in the small **Museo Inchin Cuivi Ant** on Ladrilleros (Mon–Fri 10am–8pm; CH$500), where a Chilote woman sits in a *fogón* (cooking hut) making *empenadas* and traditional potato cakes over an open fire. Ebullient and informative, she will tell you about the town's history and local mythology and show you how to work a traditional loom.

Hourly **buses** from Castro deposit you at the terminal a block west of the Plaza on calle Cerda, while **ferries** from Puerto Chacabuco and Chaiten – operated by TransMarChilay, Costanera s/n (☎65/680511, fax 680513) – call at the harbour a block south. There's a good **Oficina de Turismo** (daily 9am–1pm & 2–6pm; no phone) on the corner of Gomez García and Santos Vargas, a block north of the Plaza de Armas. While there's a wide choice of **places to stay** along the Costanera, none is particularly luxurious. Plushest is the *Hostería Quellón*, Costanera 369 (☎65/681310, fax 681250; ④) with good en-suite rooms and a restaurant that looks across the bay. More basic but clean are *Hotel Playa*, Costanera 427 (☎65/681278; ②), and the comparable *Hotel Chico Leo*, Costanera 325 and 445 (☎65/681567; ②). The *Albergue Torino*, La Paz 24 (no phone; ①) will let you lay your sleeping bag on the floor. Not surprisingly, the best place to **eat** is the restaurant at the *Hostería Quellón*, specializing in all forms of crab, closely rivalled by the *Restaurant Los Suizos*, at the corner of Ladrilleros and La Paz, which does a passable attempt at a Swiss fondue.

Ferries for Chaiten leave on Wednesdays at 3pm (5hr), and for Puerto Chacabuco on Saturdays. The only **tour company** in town is Turismo Millaguén, Gomez García s/n (☎65/681431), offering two-hour boat trips around the harbour in January and February for CH$5750.

travel details

Buses

Ancud to: Castro (every 15min; 1hr 15min); Caulín (4 daily; 30min); Chacao (every 15min; 30min); Peninsula de Lacuy (1 daily; 45min); Quemchi (6 daily; 1hr).

Castro to: Achao (3 daily; 1hr 50min); Ancud (every 15min; 1hr 15min); Conchi (every 30min; 30min); Cucao and the Parque Nacional Chiloé, Sector Anay (4 daily; 1hr 45min); Curaco de Vélez (3 daily; 1hr 30min); Dalcahue (every 30min; 30min); Llau Llao (every 15min; 15min); Puqueldón (at least 2 daily; 1hr 15min); Queilén (7daily; 1hr 30min); Quellón (hourly; 2hr 15min); Quemchi (2 daily; 1hr); Quicaví (1 daily; 1hr); Rilán (3 daily; 30min).

CHAPTER EIGHT

THE CARRETERA AUSTRAL

From Puerto Montt, the **Carretera Austral**, or "Southern Highway", stretches over 1000km south through the wettest, greenest and wildest part of Chile, ending its mammoth journey at the tiny settlement of **Puerto Yungay**, hundreds of miles from anywhere. Carving its way through tracts of untouched wilderness, the route takes in soaring, snow-capped mountains, Ice-Age glaciers, narrow fjords, jade-green rivers, and one of the world's largest swaths of temperate rainforest. Most of it falls into the region of **Aisén**, Chile's "last frontier", the final region to be opened up in the early twentieth century. Almost a hundred years on, Aisén remains very sparsely populated, and still has the cut-off, marginal feel of a pioneer zone. The original inhabitants of this rainswept land were the nomadic, hunter-gatherer **Tehuelches** of the interior, and the canoe-faring **Alcalufes** who fished the fjords and channels of the coast, but both peoples had become extinct by the late nineteenth century. In 1903, the government initiated a colonization programme which ultimately involved giving thousands of hectares of land to three large livestock companies, on the condition that they promote settlement, and export their produce from Chilean ports. Only one of them managed to meet the latter requirement, the other two depending entirely on Argentina for communications and transportation. At the same time, a wave of individual pioneers – known as *colonos* – came down to try their luck. Some arrived by sea, settling on the shores of rivers and fjords where they chopped down trees, built sawmills and shipped their produce up the coast. Others crossed over from Argentina and farmed land near the border on the edge of the concessionaires' *estancias*, forming a handful of permanent settlements. Like the livestock companies, these were totally dependent on Argentina for trade and communications.

Faced with the encroaching influence of its bigger and more powerful neighbour, and mindful of Argentina's hankering for a foothold on the Pacific, the Chilean government set out to actively "Chileanize" this new zone, organizing rodeos, for instance, and funding patriotic fiestas. Over the years, the population grew, communities expanded and communications improved, but the perceived need for state control of the region did not diminish, and explains the rationale behind the construction of the Carretera Austral, initiated by General Pinochet in 1976. Building the road – officially called the Carretera Longitudinal Austral Presidente Pinochet – was a colossal undertaking, swallowing up over US$300 million. The first section was completed in 1983, followed by two more stretches in 1988. Engineers are currently working on the final 100km leg from tiny Puerto Yungay to the frontier outpost of Villa O'Higgins, sitting by the Argentinian border. Further south, the mainland gives way to an impenetrable ice field bordered by a shredded mass of islets that defy even the most ambitious of road-building schemes. And so, from the end of this road, the only option to go is back the way you came.

Whatever political agenda was behind it, the Carretera Austral has provided access to an area of outstanding natural beauty, enjoyed by increasing – but still small – numbers of Chilean and foreign visitors. The attractions kick in from the very beginning: less than 50km down the road from Puerto Montt, you're at the first national park – **Parque Nacional Alerce Andino**, home to stands of ancient alerce trees – followed, some 70km beyond, by **Parque Nacional Hornopirén**, with its perfect, conical vol-

PACIFIC OCEAN
MAR CHILENO
Puerto Varas
Puerto Montt
PARQUE NACIONAL ALERCE ANDINO
Ralún
Cochamo
Villa Mascardi
Caleta Puelche
La Arena
PARQUE NACIONAL HORNOPIRÉN
Hornopirén
Ancud
Isla Llancahué
Cholgo
PARQUE PUMALÍN
Caleta Gonzálo
Isla de Chiloé
Santa Barbara
Chaitén
ARGENTINA
El Amarillo
Futaleufú
Trevelin
Lago Yelcho
Villa Santa Lucia
Puerto Ramírez
Corcovado
Tecka
Carretera Austral
Palena
Lago Palena
Melinka
Lago Gen. Paz (Lago Gen. Vinttner)
La Junta
Lago Verde
Lago Risopatrón
Puyuhuapi
Termas de Puyuhuapi
PARQUE NACIONAL QUEULAT
Puerto Cisnes
Villa Amengual
La Tapera
Lago Las Torres
RESERVA NACIONAL RÍO SIMPSON
Puerto Aisén
Chacabuco
RESERVA NACIONAL COYHAIQUE
Coyhaique
Río Mayo
Balmaceda
RESERVA NACIONAL CERRO CASTILLO
Villa Cerro Castillo
Puerto Ibañez
Puerto Murta
Lago Buenos Aires
Lago General Carrera
Laguna San Rafael
Puerto Tranquilo
Chile Chico
PARQUE NACIONAL LAGUNA SAN RAFAEL
Puerto Guadal
RESERVA NACIONAL LAGO JEINIMINI
Puerto Bertrand
Lago Bertrand
Lago Cochrane
Campo de Hielo Norte
Cochrane
Golfo de Penas
ARGENTINA
Puerto Yungay
Campo de Hielo Sur
Lago O'Higgins
Villa O'Higgins
0
100 km

ACCOMMODATION PRICE CODES

Prices are for the cheapest **double room** in high season. At the lower end of the scale, **single travellers** can expect to pay half this rate, but mid- and upper-range hotels usually charge the same for a single as for a double. For more information see p.27 in Basics.

① Less than US$10/CH$4800
② US$10–20/CH$4800–9600
③ US$20–30/CH$9600–10,080
④ US$30–50/CH$10,080–24,000
⑤ US$50–75/CH$24,000–36,000
⑥ US$75–100/CH$36,000–48,000
⑦ US$100–150/CH$48,000–72,000
⑧ over US$150/over CH$72,000

cano. The next stop is privately owned **Parque Pumalín**, where the Carretera cuts a passage through virgin temperate rainforest, on one of the loveliest stretches of the entire road. Further south, a couple of hours' drive beyond the small town and ferry terminal of **Chaitén**, a side-road branches east to the border village of **Futaleufú**, a growing centre for **white-water rafting** and other activities. Continuing down the Carretera Austral, you come to **Parque Nacional Queulat** whose extraordinary hanging glacier and excellent trails make this one of the most rewarding places to get off the road and into the hinterland. After a couple of days' hiking and camping, don't miss the chance to soak your bones in the secluded hot pools of the nearby **Termas de Puyuhuapi**, the finest thermal resort in Chile. As you push further south, the effects of settlement and land clearance become more apparent the nearer you get to the regional capital of **Coyhaique**, a thriving city of 40,000 inhabitants, with a wide range of useful services. West of here, the little port of **Chacabuco** is the starting point for boat excursions to the sensational **Laguna San Rafael glacier**, a 15km tongue of ice spilling into a lagoon. South of Coyhaique, the road loops around South America's second largest lake, **Lago General Carrera**, blessed by a balmy microclimate supporting several lakeside farming villages, such as **Chile Chico**. The final stretch of the Carretera connects the little town of **Cochrane** to **Puerto Yungay**, a remote port huddled on the edge of a fjord between the northern and southern icefields.

Getting around

"Doing" the Carretera Austral requires a certain amount of forward-planning, and time should always be allowed for unexpected delays. A limited **bus** service does exist between the few main towns along the road (see box opposite), but it's very sporadic and, more importantly, provides little opportunity for getting off along the way and exploring the backcountry. To really get the most out of the region, you'll need your own transport, which for a growing number of visitors means a **mountain bike**, but for most people means a rented **vehicle**. The road has a hard dirt covering which even in heavy rainfall rarely turns muddy. The layer of loose gravel on top, however, can make the surface very slippery, and by the far the best option is a sturdy pick-up truck which will hold the road well; 4WD is a bonus, but not essential. There are sufficient **petrol** stations along the way to get by without carrying your own fuel, but it's always worth keeping a spare supply in case you get caught out. Looking at a map, the choice of **route** options seems quite straightforward – down, and back up again – but a number of **ferry** services create extra possibilities and certain restrictions. Crucially, the first part of the road, between Puerto Montt and Chaitén, is "bridged" by two ferry crossings, one of which (the five-hour crossing between Hornopirén and Caleta Gonzalo) operates only in January and February. Outside these months you can still take the ferry to Chaitén, 200km down the Carretera Austral, and Chacabuco, a further 420km south, on year-round services from Puerto Montt and Quellón. Alternatively, if you manage to get the paperwork sorted out, you could start or end the journey on the

CARRETERA AUSTRAL: PRACTICALITIES OVERVIEW

FERRIES

It's always a good idea to book your ticket at least a week in advance, particularly in January and February. For details on services to the Laguna San Rafael, see p.375, and for more information on the ferry companies, see p.26 in Basics.

La Arena–Caleta Puelche (see p.359): Thirty minutes. Seven to ten crossings per day in each direction, operated year-round by TransMarChilay; CH$4500 per car, passengers free.

Hornopirén–Caleta Gonzalo (see p.359): Five hours. One daily in each direction, operated only in January and February by TransMarChilay; cars CH$32,500, passengers CH$5500.

Puerto Montt–Chaitén: Ten hours. TransMarChilay departs from Puerto Montt on Fridays, and from Chaitén on Wednesdays. Between December and March Navimag runs three to four crossings per week in each direction. Fares are from CH$10,000 per person, plus CH$45,000 for a vehicle.

Quellón–Chaitén: Five hours. TransMarChilay departs from Quellón on Wednesdays and from Chaitén on Saturdays; Navimag does four crossings per week in each direction between December and March. Fares are from CH$8000 per person and CH$40,000 per vehicle.

Puerto Montt–Chacabuco: Twenty-four hours. Three or four crossings per week in each direction with TransMarChilay and Navimag. Fares are around CH$18,000 for passengers and CH$65,000 for vehicles.

Quellón–Chacabuco: TransMarChilay departs from Quellón on Saturdays and from Chacabuco on Mondays; fares are around CH$9000 per passenger and CH$50,000 per vehicle.

BUS SERVICES

The following is an outline of bus links down the Carretera Austral; fuller details are given in the chapter and in "Travel Details", p.384.

Puerto Montt–Hornopirén: 3 daily; 5hr (Buses Fierro ☎65/253600).

Caleta Gonzalo–Chaitén: buses meet ferry arrivals.

Chaitén–Futaleufú: 6 or 7 per week; 4hr.

Chaitén–Coyhaique: 2–4 per week; 12hr.

Coyhaique–Cochrane: 4 per week; 10hr.

DRIVING TIMES

Expect to drive slowly along most of the road, somewhere between 40kph and 55kph, rarely faster. The following times are a rough guide only; always give yourself plenty of leeway, and allow for delays.

Puerto Montt–La Arena: 2hr

Caleta Puelche–Hornopirén: 1hr

Caleta Gonzalo–Chaitén: 1hr 30min

Chaitén–Puyuhuapi: 4hr 30min

Villa Santa Lucía–Futaleufú: 2hr

Puyuhuapi–Coyhaique: 5hr

Coyhaique–Cochrane: 8hr

PETROL STATIONS

Petrol stations are positioned at adequate intervals down the road, with reliable Shell or Copec stations at: Hornopirén; Chaitén; La Junta; Puyuhuapi; Puerto Cisnes; Puerto Aisén; Chacabuco; Coyhaique; Chile Chico; and Cochrane. In addition, you can sometimes buy petrol over the counter in small stores, but you can't rely on this. Many travellers choose to carry a spare canister of petrol to avoid the risk of being caught short.

largely paved roads on the Argentine side of the border, with convenient border crossings at Futaleufú and Chile Chico. Another option would be to **fly** to Coyhaique and use it as a base for exploring the southern part of the Carretera Austral, either in a rented vehicle or by public transport.

Parque Nacional Alerce Andino and around

Heading out of Puerto Montt, the Carretera Austral hugs the shore of the Reloncaví fjord, skirting wide mud flats and empty beaches. Some 40km down the road – just beyond the Puente de Lenca – a signed track branches left and leads 7km to the southern entrance of **PARQUE NACIONAL ALERCE ANDINO** (daily 9am–noon & 1–5pm; CH$1000), where you'll find a small Conaf hut, a ranger station and a **camping** area. The park was created in 1982 to protect what was left of the region's ancient, and rapidly depleting alerce forests, threatened with extinction by intense logging activity. Almost 20,000 hectares – half the park's land area – are covered by the massive alerces, mixed in with other native species like coigüe and lenga. This dense covering is spread over a landscape of steep hills and narrow glacial valleys dotted with dozens of lakes.

Unfortunately, very little of this wilderness is accessible, as the badly underfunded park lacks the resources to maintain its footpaths. Maps still show what was once a fabulous three-day hiking trail from the park's southern entrance, off the Carretera Austral, to the northern entrance at Correntoso (connected to Puerto Montt by a 46km dirt road), but the central portion has become impenetrable. What's left still makes a good, long **day-hike**, though – from the Conaf hut (in the southern entrance), the path follows the río Chaica for 5km as far as the pretty **Laguna Chaiquenes**, surrounded by steep, forested hills. On the way, about an hour from the hut, you pass some impressive waterfalls, and twenty minutes later, a huge, 3000-year-old alerce tree. From Laguna Chaiquenes, the now deteriorating path heads north for a further 4km, as far as the long, thin **Laguna Triángulo**, where it peters out. Count on taking around two and a half hours to get to Laguna Chaiquenes, and another three hours to get to Laguna Triángulo.

Parque Los Alerces de Lenca

Branching north from the access track to the national park, a steep and extremely rough jeep track (signed "Lodge") zigzags up through the adjoining, privately owned **Parque Los Alerces de Lenca**, spread over 2000 hectares of land. As you climb higher, you enter a dense covering of old-growth alerces, many of them looking grey and lifeless, towering like decrepit, elderly giants over the younger and greener coigües, lengas, and ñirres. Some 7km up the track, look out for the small sign pointing to *El Tata* ("The Daddy") – a gnarled colossus, estimated to be a staggering 4000 years old. Five kilometres beyond, the track comes to a halt at the park's centrepiece, the **Alerce Mountain Lodge** (☎ & fax 65/286969; *www.telsur.cl/alerce/*; ⑨), a sensitively designed timber lodge built around the alerces, with a 2000-year-old tree growing through the veranda. Set in a small depression by a lake, this is one of the most peaceful, beautiful and isolated places to stay in Chile, and if you can afford it – it's not cheap – makes a great way to experience the country's wilderness without roughing it. The price of a stay includes all meals (which are excellent) and various excursions led by friendly, English-speaking guides, including short or long hikes through the forests, a stiff climb up to a panoramic viewpoint, and horseback treks. Although the "park" operates more like a private estate, geared towards staying guests, you can book a day-visit, including lunch and guided excursions, for US$95 per person. If you don't have your own transport, the lodge's staff will pick you up and take you back to Puerto Montt.

ALERCE TREES

Native to southern Chile and Argentina, the **alerce** tree was given national monument status by the Chilean government in 1976, to protect old-growth forests from threatened extinction. The most mature alerces are between 3000 and 4000 years old, and are among the oldest and largest trees in the world. Found on high, soggy soil, usually on mountainsides between 600m and 800m above sea level, they can grow to a height of 45m, with a trunk diameter of up to 4m. After shooting up rapidly during their first hundred years, they slow down dramatically, their diameter increasing just 1mm every three years. As they grow, they lose their lower branches, keeping only their top crown of dark-green, broccoli-like leaves. The lighter, lower leaves belong to parasite trees, which often prove useful to the ancient alerces, supporting them when they topple and keeping them alive. When the surrounding forest – made up principally of coigüe, mañío and canelo – is cut down, the exposed alerces often have their tops blown off by the wind, leaving them shattered and dead-looking, with mangy side branches. The very old ones start rotting from the inside out, and it's not uncommon to find them lying on the forest floor, chopped down for their wood only to be abandoned when it was discovered that their insides had decayed.

The trees' grey, papery bark conceals a beautiful, reddish-brown and extremely valuable wood, with a large tree worth around US$30,000. In the late-nineteenth and early-twentieth centuries, the trees were chopped down willy nilly by early colonizers – sometimes to be used for telegraph poles or shingles, but often just to clear land which was later found to be useless for agriculture. Today, it's illegal to chop down an alerce, but it's not illegal to sell the wood of dead trees. This leaves a lot of room for getting round the protection laws, as landowners have been known to find clever ways of causing premature death to their trees.

Hornopirén and around

Thirteen kilometres south of the turn-off to Parque Nacional Alerce Andino – along an extremely narrow stretch of the road, blasted out of a cliff – you reach the sheltered, sandy cove of **LA ARENA**, the departure point of the **first ferry** ride (7–10 per day; CH$4500 per car, passengers free), which operates on a first-come, first-served basis. After the thirty-minute crossing, the ferry lands at tiny **Caleta Puelche**, from where the road winds through 58km of thickly forested hills, before arriving at the village of **HORNOPIRÉN** (also known as Río Negro), where you catch the **second ferry** plugging the gaps between the road (Jan & Feb; 1 daily; 5hr). Perched on the northern shore of a wide fjord, at the foot of **Volcán Hornopirén**, the village enjoys a spectacular location, though the view is frequently obscured by low, grey clouds and mist. An important timber centre in the nineteenth century, hit hard by the decline of the industry, Hornopirén has been recently stirred back to life by an invasion of salmon farmers, who plod the streets in their distinctive white rubber boots. The village's new prosperity is reflected in the shiny, mock-Victorian street lamps on the plaza, and immaculate, newly built church, sporting bright-red alerce shingles and a green roof.

Thanks to the steady flow of summer visitors passing through to catch the ferry, there's no shortage of places to **stay** in Hornopirén. The most charming is *Hotel Hornopirén* at Ignacio Carrera Pinto 388 (☎65/217256; ③), an old wooden building on the edge of the sea, boasting an ancient Heath Robinson sauna. The cheapest option is probably friendly *Hospedaje Chuchito* on O'Higgins (☎65/217210; ②), while *Central Plaza*'s timber *cabañas*, down from the square on Lago Pinto Concha (☎65/217247; ④–⑤), make a good deal for groups. The attached **restaurant** is one of Hornopirén's best, with a huge *quincho* (a cement base topped with a grill), over which meat and fish are barbecued on skewers. You could also try *Monteverde*, on O'Higgins, an inexpen sive choice, popular with locals, serving typical fried fish and meat.

Around Hornopirén

Because Hornopirén is so near the beginning of the Carretera Austral, most visitors are eager to just catch the ferry and push on down the road – which is a shame, because the village's surroundings really deserve a bit of exploration. It's worth setting aside a day to do the excellent hike along the río Blanco in **Parque Nacional Vocán Hornopirén**, or to visit the hot springs on **Isla Llancahué**. If you've only got a morning to spare, you could spend a couple of hours driving along the scenic **road to Cholgo** before getting back with plenty of time to catch the afternoon ferry.

Parque Nacional Volcán Hornopirén

Hornopirén is neighboured, to the east, by the five hundred square kilometres of protected wilderness that make up **Parque Nacional Volcán Hornopirén** (daily; 24hr; free). The park's centrepiece – 16km along a muddy track from the village – is the perfectly conical **Volcán Hornopirén**, whose steep slopes are densely forested, discouraging all but the most determined of hikers from reaching the 1500-metre summit. Five kilometres further along the track is the seldom-visited **Lago General Pinto Concha**, with excellent fishing and stunning views onto the 2111-metre **Volcán Yate**.

Back towards the village, a turn-off from the track leads south around the end of the fjord to a modern bridge over the turbulent **río Blanco**, filled with milky-white, freezing-cold water. A well-defined, 8km path follows the river upstream, passing through alternating patches of pastureland and forest before reaching a small farm. Although years of logging have stripped much of the native forest, there are still great swaths of alerce, coigüe, tepa and lenga around here, and if you continue on above the tree line, you'll enter a landscape of ice-covered peaks and glaciers. This makes a great **day-hike**, and you're unlikely to see another soul all day.

Isla Llancahué

One of the best excursions from Hornopirén is a boat trip to **Isla Llancahué**, a small, forested island sitting at the head of the fjord, famous for its 50°C **natural hot springs**. There's an old, timber-built **hotel** here, the *Termas de Llancahué* (☎09/653 8345; ④), where for CH$2500 you can wallow in single or communal hot tubs or in an open-air swimming pool overlooking a rocky bay. Even more romantic are the jets of hot water that emerge on the beach, cooled down by sea water but still hot enough for a good soaking, even in the grey, drizzly weather that so often plagues the area. It's a fifty-minute boat ride to the island from Hornopirén, costing around CH$35,000 return, per boat; the hotel can send one to pick you up and take you back, or you can arrange a ride in the village with Jorge Espinoda (☎65/217263). It's normally possible to get a cheaper ride from the village of Cholgo (see below), which is closer to the island. Most boatmen also offer rides to the remote, isolated thermal springs known as the **Termas de Cahuelmó** (described on p.363, under Parque Pumalín), but at around CH$80,000 return, this is a very expensive trip.

The road to Cholgo

The Carretera Austral doesn't actually stop at Hornopirén, but continues south for a further 28km to the tiny hamlet of **CHOLGO**, running partly through Parque Nacional Volcán Hornopirén, and then through land belonging to the Pumalín Project (see box on p.362). The route is quite breathtaking, as the road crosses glacier-fed rivers framed by soaring, snow-capped peaks, before tracing its way along the edge of a cliff, squeezed between the ocean and the overhanging forest. Heading even a small way down is highly memorable, and the numerous ravines that branch off the road, cutting through the forest, make for great, scrambly hiking. Cholgo itself is nothing special – just a cluster of houses and a load of black salmon-farming rafts bobbing in the bay. For the moment there's nowhere to stay here, but there are plans to install a visitor centre and camping areas as part of the northern section of Parque Pumalín, which currently has no access other than this road.

Parque Pumalín

After five hours of sailing through the island-studded channel between Chiloé and the mainland, the ferry from Hornopirén enters the steep-sided Reñihué fjord and unloads its passengers at **Caleta Gonzalo**, where the Carretera Austral resumes its course. Getting off the boat, you'll find yourself at the main arrival point of **PARQUE PUMALÍN**, the world's largest privately owned conservation area, covering 300,000 hectares of land. The Pumalín Project, founded by North American millionaire Douglas Tomkins to protect one of the world's last strongholds of temperate rainforest, has generated a considerable amount of controversy over the past five years (see box overleaf). But, standing at Caleta Gonzalo, faced with the jungle-like vegetation covering every inch of visible land, few would deny that the park represents a magnificent environmental achievement. It's a place of overwhelming natural beauty, and you'd do well to set aside at least a day to explore. If you've no time to hang around, you can still enjoy the landscape as you follow the Carretera Austral through the park – squeezed between steep-sided hills covered in dense, dripping foliage, with wispy clouds hovering over the mountains.

Arrival, information and accommodation

Just beyond the ferry ramp, where you **arrive**, is the park's **information centre** (daily 8am–8pm) – a rotunda-shaped timber building with a high, beamed roof and a huge copper-covered stove in its centre. Here, English-speaking staff hand out leaflets explaining the project's aims and detailing the trails in the park, and there's a range of locally produced *artesanía* for sale, including hand-knitted sweaters and hats. Opposite the information centre is a **café** (daily 7.30am–11pm), whose stylish interior features a large open fire, lots of pale, polished wood, and black-and-white prints of alerce trees. It serves simple but delicious organic food, including home-made bread, locally caught fish and succulent roast lamb – if you plan to camp and cook your own stuff, call in here for a supply of firewood, fresh bread, vegetables and herbs. The café is also the place to enquire about available **accommodation** in the seven nearby *cabañas* (⑤) lining the edge of the shore. Designed by Tomkins himself, they're impeccably tasteful inside, with waxed wooden floors, quality bed linen made of natural fabrics, and bed frames made out of reclaimed alerce wood.

There are also several **camping** areas, the main one just a few hundred metres from the information centre, with basic sites (CH$500 per person), covered areas with picnic

ADVANCE INFORMATION

To book accommodation or order a lamb in advance of your arrival – or for any other information – contact the Park's Puerto Montt office at Buín 356 (☎65/250079, fax 255145; *www.pumalinproject.com*). Information about the Pumalín Project is also available from its USA office at 1555 Pacifica Ave, San Francisco, CA 94109 (☎415/771-1102, fax 771-1121; *www.pumalinproject.com*).

DOUGLAS TOMKINS AND THE PUMALÍN PROJECT

In 1995 it was publicly announced that a North American millionaire, **Douglas Tomkins**, had used intermediaries to buy a three-thousand-square-kilometre chunk of southern Chile – marking the beginning of a five-year national soap opera that transformed Tomkins into one of the most controversial public figures in the country. The beginning of the saga dates back to 1991 when the 49-year-old Californian, deeply disillusioned with the corporate, industrial world, and becoming increasingly committed to environmental issues, sold up his fifty percent share in the Esprit clothing empire, bought an abandoned ranch in Chile, and moved there with his wife and kids. Their new home was stranded on the edge of the Reñihué fjord, 130km south of Puerto Montt, surrounded by one of the world's largest remaining tracts of virgin temperate rainforest. Inspired by the "deep ecology" movement pioneered by the Norwegian environmentalist Arne Naess, Tomkins set out to acquire more of the surrounding wilderness, with the aim of protecting it from the threat of commercial exploitation. As he did so, he was siezed with the idea of creating a massive, privately funded national park, which would ensure permanent protection of the ancient forest while providing low-impact facilities for visitors.

Over the next four years Tomkins spent more than US$14 million buying up adjoining tracts of land, in most cases keeping his identity secret to prevent prices from shooting up. His initial secrecy was to have damaging repercussions, however, for once his land acquisitions became public knowledge, he was engulfed by a wave of suspicion and hostility, fuelled by several right-wing politicians and the press. The biggest cause for alarm, it seemed, was the fact that Tomkins' land stretched from the Argentinian border to the Pacific Ocean, effectively "cutting Chile in two". His motives were questioned by everyone, with all sorts of wild accusations and conspiracy theories flying around: some claimed he planned to set up a new Jewish state, others that he would use the land as a dumping ground for North American nuclear waste, while others were simply unhappy with the way he was applying his corporate drive for acquisition and expansion to their home territory.

Tomkins attempted to quell the paranoia by appearing on national television, explaining his intentions to create **Parque Pumalín**, a nature sanctuary with free public access. Slowly, the public – or some of it – was won over. But the long struggle to have his lands declared a Santuario de la Naturaleza by the government – a status frequently given to private land, and the first step that would enable Tomkins to transfer ownership to a conservation foundation – were continually thwarted. Another problem was Huinay, a 30,000-hectare property owned by the Catholic University of Valparaíso, separating the two separate chunks of Tomkins' land. When the university announced its intentions to sell Huinay, it was natural that Tomkins should attempt to buy it, to join up the gap in his proposed park. Obstructions came from all directions, including church leaders who protested that Tomkins' belief in family planning was an affront to Catholicism. Eventually, the government agreed to support Tomkins' aims to establish Parque Pumalín – on the condition that for one year he would not buy more than 7000 contiguous hectares of land in the south of Chile. Left with little choice other than to accept this deal, Tomkins looked on as Huinay was sold to Endesa, Chile's largest energy corporation.

So, the park that caused so much fear by cutting through the width of Chile is itself severed through its middle. Ownership of Parque Pumalín has been transferred to the US-based Conservation Land Trust, and will soon be donated to the Chilean Fundación Pumalín, whose board will include Tomkins and his wife. In the meantime, Endesa has released no details of its plans for Huinay.

tables (CH$1000 per person) and an octagonal wooden hut with bunk beds and a log fire. There are barbecue facilities here as well, and if you phone in advance, the park staff will slaughter a lamb for your arrival, which you roast on skewers over the *fogón*. The two other camping areas in the park are 12km and 14km down the road.

Exploring the park

Parque Pumalín falls into two sections, cut in half by a large chunk of land owned by Endesa, the energy corporation. The **northern section** boasts the gloriously isolated **Termas de Cahuelmó**: a series of natural hot pools, carved out of the rock at the end of a steep, narrow fjord, accessible only by boat. There's a rustic camping area nearby, from where a 5km trail leads to the crystal-clear **Lago Abascal**. This is a dramatically beautiful area, but getting here is expensive, at around CH$80,000 per boat trip, which is best arranged in Hornopirén (see p.359) or Cholgo (see p.360).

The **southern section** has more infrastructure geared towards visitors. At Caleta Gonzalo, a wooden bridge across the river leads to a "**demonstration farm**", where visitors can get a close-up view of the kind of small-scale, ecologically friendly farming and animal husbandry that the project is promoting in the local community, with tours through the organic gardens, and demonstrations of cheese-, jam- and honey-making. Nearby, close to the ferry ramp, the **Sendero Cascadas** is a steep trail through a canopy of overhanging foliage up to a 15m waterfall (3hr round trip).

Three other trails have been carved out of the forest, branching off from the Carretera Austral as it heads south through the park. Twelve kilometres down the road, **Sendero Tronador** is probably the most exciting, crossing a narrow gorge filled with a rushing, white-water stream, climbing up to a look-out point with fabulous views onto Volcán Michimhuida, and ending at a pristine lake with a camping area alongside (1hr 30min to get there). One kilometre south, **Sendero Los Alerces** is a twenty-minute stroll, dotted with information panels, through a grove of ancient, colossal alerces. Another kilometre down the road, the **Sendero Cascadas Escondidas** (also with a camping area) is an easy, half-hour walk through the forest to several high, slender waterfalls. Exactly 15km down the road, right by the wooden distance marker, is a small, muddy **hot springs** pool, almost hidden by foliage, by the side of the road – a great place just to dip your feet in before moving on from the park.

Chaitén to Villa Santa Lucía

Just beyond the southern limit of Parque Pumalín, 25km south of Caleta Gonzalo, the Carretera Austral skirts the pale, calm expanse of **Lago Blanco** before turning west towards the coast. Twenty kilometres beyond, it reaches the ocean at the tiny hamlet of **Santa Barbara**, where a short track leads to a gorgeous, crescent-shaped **beach** dominated by Cerro Vilcún, a sugarloaf mountain looming over the bay. The beach is filled with dark, volcanic sand fringed by deep-green forest, and makes a great place to camp, though there are no facilities – for these, continue 7km down the road to *Camping Los Arrayanes* (☎65/218242; CH$4000 per site), equipped with showers and picnic areas. A further 4km south, you'll reach the self-important little town of **CHAITÉN**, whose ferry terminal is the starting point for journeys down the Carretera Austral outside January and February, when the Hornopirén–Caleta Gonzalo ferry doesn't function. Built on a flat stretch of land at the mouth of the Blanco and Yelcho rivers, and surrounded by densely forested mountains, Chaitén is a beautifully located but rather charmless town, made up of squat, modern houses and wide, grid-laid streets indented with potholes that are invariably filled with water. As the provincial capital and only commercial centre between Puerto Montt and Coyhaique, 420km south, it does, however, offer a number of useful services, including supermarkets, a petrol station, car mechanics, a public telephone, a *casa de cambio*, tour companies, a pharmacy and plenty of places to stay and eat, prompting most people travelling down the Carretera to spend a night here.

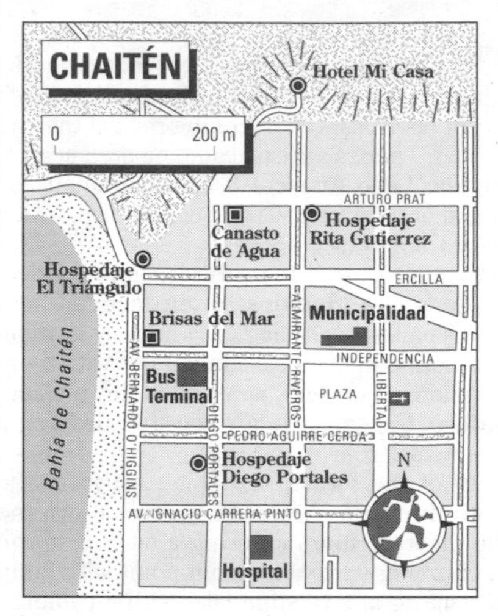

The cheapest **accommodation** option is probably *Hospedaje Rita Gutierrez* (☎65/731502; ②) on the corner of Almirante Riveros and Prat, where the jovial and eccentric Rita offers basic shared rooms and a large garden in which to pitch tents. *Hospedaje Diego Portales*, at Diego Portales 456 (☎65/731464; ③), is a modern family home with a few simple, spotless rooms and shared bath, while appealingly rustic *Hospedaje El Triángulo*, at Juan Todesco 2 (☎65/731312; ③), is a traditional old building with squeaking floorboards, a pervading smell of polish and a decent restaurant. Perched on top of the hill north of town, commanding fine views over the bay, *Hotel Mi Casa*, Av Norte 206 (☎65/731285; ⑤), offers comfortable, good-quality rooms in a bungalow-style building, and is the best choice in this price range. Places to **eat** include the good-value *Brisas del Mar* at Av Corcovado 278, with a sea view and basic fish and meat dishes, and the smarter *Canasto de Agua* at Prat 65, which does hearty *parilladas*.

The best supermarket is on the seafront, Avenida Corcovado, along with the telephone office and petrol station. Chaitén's single **casa de cambio**, changing US dollars and Argentinian pesos, is Turismo Carretera Austral, Almirante Riveros 491.

TOURS AND TRANSPORT OUT OF CHAITÉN

Run by a friendly young Chilean who speaks perfect English, Chaitur Excursiones (☎65/731429; *nchaitur@hotmail.com*), on Independencia, near the corner with Diego Portales, offers a range of good-value **tours** around Chaitén, taking you north to Parque Pumalín, south to glaciers and lakes along the Carretera Austral, and to the Termas del Amarillo (see opposite). Its office also serves as the unofficial **bus terminal**, where you can buy tickets and catch buses to Coyhaique (2–4 per week), La Junta (3 per week) and Futaleufú (6 or 7 per week). There are regular **ferries** to Puerto Montt and Quellón with TransMarChilay, Corcovado 266 (☎65/731272), and Navimag, Pinto 108 (☎65/731570). **Flights** to Puerto Montt, Balmaceda and Chile Chico are offered by a number of small airline companies which seem to come and go with bewildering regularity. Currently operating are Aero Sur, on the corner of Pinto and Riveros (☎65/731288); Aeromet, Todesco 55 (☎65/731340); and Aero VIP, Riveros 453 (☎65/731401).

South to Villa Santa Lucía

The stretch of road south of Chaitén reveals a series of heart-stopping views – as you cross the bridge into the village of **EL AMARILLO**, for example, 25km down the road, look left and you'll see a massive, gravity-defying glacier hanging implausibly off the edge of **Volcán Michimahuida**, 9km north. There are several places to stay in El Amarillo, including simple *Hospedaje Marcela* (☎65/264422; ③), which organizes horse rides to the volcano, the smarter *Cabañas Los Galpones, del Volcán* (☎65/731453; ⑤), with sweeping views and a friendly owner who can advise on local trekking paths. The best of these is the challenging, three-day hike south through the Sierranias Nevadas (or "Snowy Mountains") to Futaleufú (see below), along an unfinished track built in 1956 in a failed attempt to connect the two towns by road. Just beyond the bridge, a side road winds 5km up a wooded hillside to the **Termas del Amarillo** (daily: Jan & Feb 9am–9pm; March–Dec 9am–6pm; CH$2000), a couple of rustic open-air pools filled with thermal water, set in a clearing in the wood. There are also mud baths and private tubs, as well as cold showers to cool off in and a few camping areas (CH$3000 per site). The place is currently run by the Municipalidad, but there's been talk of selling it to a private company, so development may well be stepped up and prices increased in the near future.

Continuing down the Carretera Austral, about 20km south, you cross the río Yelcho on a modern suspension bridge that looks startlingly out of place amidst the wilderness. Just across it the road meets the northern tip of **Lago Yelcho**, a large, glacial lake famed for its abundant salmon and trout. Several places along the lakeshore offer accommodation and fishing excursions, including the upmarket *Centro Turístico Caví* (reservations in Santiago ☎2/334 1309, fax 334 1328; ⑤), with *cabañas*, camping areas and a decent restaurant. At the next bridge south, Puente Ventisquero, there's a parking area from where a well-trodden muddy path leads uphill for about an hour and a half to **Ventisquero Yelcho**, a small but impressive glacier feeding a number of high waterfalls that tumble down the mountainside. Twenty kilometres south you reach **Villa Santa Lucía**, a dull, modern settlement established in 1982, made up of regimented rows of prefabricated houses. There's a military base here, along with telephone services, shops selling basic provisions and a couple of *hospedajes*, though few people stop here, preferring to head east towards the mountain village of Futaleufú – up the first major side road off the Carretera Austral – or south to Puerto Puyuhuapi.

East to Futaleufú

The eighty-kilometre side trip up the Futaleufú river valley is one of the most enjoyable diversions off the Carretera Austral. Heading east from Villa Santa Lucía, you first skirt the southern shore of Lago Yelcho before coming to a fork, 30km along the road. The right turn goes to the quiet border village of **Palena**, while the left branch follows the turquoise **río Futaleufú** for 17km through towering gorges, lush forests and snow-streaked mountain peaks. With its big explosion waves and massive rodeo holes, the Futaleufú is regarded by many professional rafters and kayakers as the most challenging white-water river in the world. Though it's relatively undiscovered compared to big crowd-pullers like the Zambezi and the Colorado, a growing number of Chilean and US operators offer **rafting** trips down the river, which boasts over forty class IV–V rapids with alarming names like *Purgatorio*, *Infierno* and *Terminador*; for details of operators, see Basics on p.54.

Drifting away from the river, the road winds through forest and pastureland before skirting the edge of **Lago Lonconao**, a chocolate-box-pretty alpine lake whose deep-blue waters reflect the perfect symmetry of the surrounding mountains. Six kilometres beyond, a short track branches left to another beautiful lake, **Lago Espolón**, teeming with salmon and trout and bordered by sandy beaches.

Futaleufú

Continuing up the road, 8km on from Lago Espolón you'll arrive at the pretty village of **FUTALEUFÚ**, until recently a remote frontier outpost and now an increasingly popular summer base for rafting, kayaking, fishing and hiking. Sitting by the confluence of the Futaleufú and Espolón rivers, surrounded by forested, snowy peaks, Futaleufú more than earns the grandiose slogan – "A landscape painted by God" – coined by its inhabitants. Originally settled in the 1920s, it was completely dependent on Argentina until a horse track was built to connect it with the Chilean coast in the 1930s. Communications with the rest of Chile increased slightly in the 1950s when an aerodrome was built and light plane services introduced. Notoriously changeable weather, however, made flying an unreliable form of transport and in 1952 one plane was forced to make an emergency landing on one of the village's streets, which now bears the name of "Piloto Carmon" in honour of the unlucky pilot. Following the completion of the nearby stretch of the Carretera Austral in 1988, Futaleufú finally became connected to the rest of Chile by road – though it's easier to travel north and south by crossing the border into Argentina than plod along the bumpy Carretera. There's not much to do in the village itself, but most people are here for the **outdoor activities**. The best place to organize these is Futaleufú Expediciones, operating out of the *Hostería Río Grande* (see below), where Chilean and international guides offer hiking, horse trekking, mountain biking, fly-fishing, "floating" (drifting down a river on an inner tube), "canyoning" (abseiling down canyons) and canoeing, in addition to the obligatory rafting and kayaking trips.

Accommodation and camping in the Futaleufú valley

A string of **campsites** and **hosterías** has sprung up along the road to Futaleufú in the past five years, many of them in beautiful spots overlooking the river, or on the shores of neighbouring lakes. We've given a selection below, including their distance from the Carretera Austral as a reference.

Camping Cara del Indio, km 54. One of the best campsites in the valley, on the side of a cliff overlooking the river. The price includes firewood and use of a sauna. CH$5000 per site.

Camping La Vega, km 77. Attractive campsite right by the río Espolón, with shady sites under native coigüe trees and clean, modern sanitary facilities. CH$3000 per site.

Hostal Alexis, Puerto Piedra, km 25 (☎65/731505). Built on a wooden promontory on the shores of Lago Yelcho, this colonial farmhouse offers comfortable rooms, peace and quiet and well-priced fishing excursions. ④.

Hostería Verónica, Puerto Ramírez, km 30 (☎65/264431). A small, clean and friendly place to stay, with simple rooms and fishing boats for rent. ③.

La Casa del Campo, Lago Espolón, km 70 (☎65/314658). A small lakeside farmhouse owned by a welcoming couple, who give guests the run of the kitchen, let campers pitch tents in their garden, and offer meals, *asados*, horse rides and fishing excursions. ③.

Accommodation in Futaleufú

For what was until recently a sleepy backwater, lost in the mountains, Futaleufú boasts a surprisingly good bunch of **places to stay**. To contact them by telephone, you have to ring the telephone exchange – ☎65/258633 or 258634 – and ask for the appropriate extension number (*anexo*).

Cabañas Río Espolón (☎ anexo 216). A couple of new, six-bed *cabañas*, attractively located in a wood near the río Espolón, on the northeast edge of town. A good place for fishing enthusiasts, as the owner can organize a boat, transport and guide. ⑦.

Hospedaje Calipso, Lautaro 369 (☎ anexo 271). On the edge of town, this small, inexpensive *hospedaje* is a good bet for singles, but has just one double room. ②.

Hospedaje Familiar, cnr of Balmaceda and Aldea (☎ anexo 205). Neat and tidy family-run bed and breakfast; a good budget choice. ②.

Hostería Río Grande, O'Higgins 397 (☎ anexo 320). This modern, timber-built hotel is one of the best places to stay for miles around, with its chic-rustic decor, quality en-suite rooms, and fine restaurant and bar. The owners speak English, Dutch and German, and operate a tour company, Futaleufú Expediciones (see above), from the hotel. ⑥.

Hotel Continental, Balmaceda 597 (☎ anexo 222). One of the oldest hotels in the village, in a large, traditional family house with highly polished wooden floors, creaking beds, shared bathrooms, and hearty meals. ③.

Posada Campesina La Gringa, cnr of Aldea and Carrera (☎ anexo 260). Sitting in a beautiful garden on the edge of town, this charming house has the best view of the surrounding countryside. "La Gringa", one Lucia Harismendy de Witt, was the first person in Futaleufú to provide accommodation to visitors. ⑥.

Eating and drinking

Most hotels and *hospedajes* also offer **meals**; the best choice is cosmopolitan *Hostería Río Grande*, with its European-influenced menu, stylish decor and young crowd. On the corner of Cerda and Sargento Aldea, bright and airy *Restaurant Futaleufú* makes an inexpensive alternative, serving hearty meat and fish dishes, while *Restaurant Encuentro* at O'Higgins 651, does cheap, basic lunches and all-day sandwiches. As for **drinking**, the most popular place with gringos is, again, *Hostería Río Grande* – for something a bit more local, with cheaper beer, try *El Campesino* on the corner of Balmaceda and Prat.

South to Puyuhuapi, Parque Nacional Queulat and Puerto Cisnes

Back on the Carretera Austral, heading south, the road follows the gleaming, jade-green waters of the río Frío, whose banks make a great spot for a picnic. Some 70km south of Villa Santa Lucía you reach **LA JUNTA**, a depressing collection of tin houses established in 1983 as one of General Pinochet's "new towns". La Junta is not a place to linger in, but it has a grocery shop, a petrol station, a phone and a few places to **stay** – if you're in need of emergency accommodation, try *Hostería Valdera* (☎67/314105; ③) or *Residencial Copihué* (☎67/314140; ②), both on calle Varas. Your best bet, however, is to press on for 45km to the charming village of **Puyuhuapi**, the departure point for excursions to the **Termas de Puyuhuapi**, and a convenient base for exploring **Parque Nacional Queulat**. Driving down to the village, the road enters the northern sector of the park, where you'll see a dramatic change in the landscape as the towering hills close in, forming a narrow valley streaked with waterfalls. The southwest edge of the park, some 90km on from Puyuhuapi, is bordered by the little town of **Puerto Cisnes**, a low-key but pleasant detour from the Carretera Austral.

Puyuhuapi

Squatting at the head of the narrow Ventisquero fjord, the quaint little village of **PUYUHUAPI** is a good place to break your journey – not only for the wild beauty of its setting, but also for its proximity to a couple of the most compelling attractions along the Carretera Austral. Puyuhuapi's rambling streets and old timber houses make a pleasing contrast to the utilitarian "villages" installed along the Carretera in the 1980s, after the completion of the road, and you could easily while away an enjoyable hour just strolling around, or hanging out by the old jetty, looking for dolphins in the water. The village's history goes back to the 1940s when four young German brothers, the Hopperdietzels, settled here with their wives and children – fuelling dark rumours that they were setting up a supply base for German submarines. In fact, their activities were of a more commercial nature, and out of this tiny colony in the middle of nowhere was created a carpet manufacturing business which somehow flourished and acquired a fame throughout the south of Chile. The **carpet factory** – towards the shore, opposite the petrol station – is still going strong, and can be visited on guided **tours** (every 30min, Mon–Fri 8.30am–1pm & 3–7pm; CH$1000), where you can watch the dexterous women weavers, working in pairs, clunk away at ancient wooden looms in an old shed, while their husbands shave and beat the carpets into finished articles across the road.

The best place to **stay** in Puyuhuapi is the *Hostería Alemana* at Av Otto Uebel 450 (☎ & fax 67/325118; ⑤), a large, elegant timber house set in a mature garden. Opposite, *Hospedaje Marily* (☎67/325102; ②) provides a cheaper alternative, with small, neat rooms, pastel-coloured walls and a stuffed puma standing in the hall. Another good budget choice is *Residencial Elizabeth*, Circunvalación s/n (☎67/325106; ②), which offers simple rooms and filling home-cooking. You could also **eat** at the excellent *Café Rossbach* next door to the carpet factory, run by the Kroschewskis family who hunt high and low for wild berries which they turn into mouthwatering *küchen*.

Termas de Puyuhuapi

The **TERMAS DE PUYUHUAPI** (Santiago: ☎2/225 6489, fax 274 8111; lodge: ☎67/325129; *www.chilnet.cl/patagogonia*; ⑦) – thermal baths, lodge and spa – is a very special place. Marooned on the edge of a peninsula in front of a steep jungle of rainforest,

FLY-FISHING IN CHILE

Chile has an international, and well-deserved, reputation as one of the finest **fly-fishing** destinations in the world, counting Robert Redford, Jane Fonda, Ted Turner, Michael Douglas, Jimmy Carter and George Bush among those to have fished its pristine waters. Only a century ago it was home to few, if any, salmonids, but all that changed when Isidora Goyenechea introduced large numbers of salmon and trout in 1893. The fish thrived, more were imported, and today numerous rainbow, brown and brook trout, as well as Atlantic and some king salmon, pack the rivers, streams, creeks, lagoons and lakes spread throughout the south of the country.

Traditionally, it was the waters between the cities of Temuco and Puerto Montt – known as the Lake District – that attracted most anglers. However, while there's still some great fishing to be had there, the growth in the region's population, and ease of access to the lakes and rivers have increased fishing pressure and prompted enthusiasts to turn their attention to the fjordlands south of Puerto Montt – now considered to be the most exciting fly-fishing region in Chile. Here, local boatmen whisk fishermen through the bewildering maze of channels and islets to remote, hidden rivers, as clear as glass and teeming with fish. Acrobatic dolphins, sea lion colonies, snow-capped volcanoes and virgin forest all add to the magic of the scene.

The Carretera Austral has opened up the area to increasing opportunities for anglers, and a number of first-class fishing lodges have sprung up around the region. If you plan to do some serious fishing, bring a 6 or 7 weight **rod** with a reliable reel capable of carrying at least 90m of 9kg backing. You'll need a forward floating line, as well as a fast sink-tip line or shooting head. Your fly box should include a wide range of brightly coloured streamers and a selection of nymphs and dry flies. As for clothing, both neoprene and breatheable waders work here, and a breatheable rain jacket is a must. The **season** varies slightly according to the area, but in general lasts from October or November to May. You need a **licence** to be able to fish, which costs around CH$6500 and is widely available in town halls and sport fishing shops. To find out more about fly-fishing in Chile, contact the **Servicio Nacional de Pesca** (a government agency) at Yungay 1737, piso 4, Valparaíso, Chile (☎32/214371, fax 259564).

A FEW LODGES AND OPERATORS ALONG THE CARRETERA AUSTRAL

Outlined below are a few of the more established lodges and operators, all of which have guides fluent in English and Spanish. A fuller list can be obtained from Sernatur in

it is inaccessible by land, and can only be reached by boat. Three times a day in summer (10am, 12.30pm & 7pm) a motor launch collects passengers from the wooden jetty by Puyuhuapi's air strip, 10km south of the village, and whisks them off on a twenty-minute ride to the lodge. It's hard to imagine a more romantic form of arrival – particularly in one of the frequent downpours that plague the region, when guests are escorted to shelter beneath enormous white umbrellas carried by dapper young men. For many years, the *Termas de Puyuhuapi* was a handful of ramshackle cabins that no one had heard of. Today, it's a small luxury resort made up of low-lying, beautifully designed buildings made out of reddish-brown alerce and lots of glass. The transformation was brought about some ten years ago by its new owner, Eberhard Kossman, an East German who in his youth swam to the West in a wet suit made out of inner tubes. Apart from its remote and spectacular location, the main reason to come here is to soak in the steaming **hot springs**, channelled into three outdoor pools reached by a short walk through the forest. Two of the pools are large enough to swim in, and are located right on the edge of the fjord, while the third one, containing the hottest water, is a small pond enclosed by overhanging ferns and native trees. There's a large indoor pool, as well, that's part of the new state-of-the-art **spa** centre specializing in "thalasotherapy" (treatments involving heated seawater and seaweed).

Coyhaique, at Bulnes 35 (☎ & fax 67/231752; *sernatur_coyhai@entelchile.net*). Most lodges are of an extremely high standard, and charge around US$3000 per person for a seven-night package including accommodation, fishing guide, all food and an open bar.

El Saltamontes Lodge, Casilla 565, Coyhaique (☎ & fax 67/232779). Charming lodge on the banks of the río Nireguao, about 100km northeast of Coyhaique, offering dry fly-fishing (strictly catch and release) for brown trout.

Futaleufú Lodge, near Futaleufú; information from Casilla 1238, Viña del Mar (☎ & fax 32/812659). North American Jim Repine spent many years guiding in Alaska before coming down to the Futaleufú river valley. With just four guests per week, and excellent food and wine, this is an intimate, relaxing lodge, especially geared up towards couples. Rainbow and brown trout are most prevalent, with wading right at the front door.

Heart of Patagonia Lodge, Casilla 324, Coyhaique (☎ & fax 67/233701). One of the more easily reached lodges, on the banks of the río Simpson connected to the city of Coyhaique by paved road.

Isla Monita Lodge, information from Casilla 3390, Santiago (☎ & fax 2/273 2198). A remote, de luxe lodge sitting on a tiny island in the middle of Lago Yelcho, reached by a short flight from Chaitén, offering dry and wet fly-fishing from wooden boats. The lake has abundant salmon and trout, and was where the national fly-fishing record was set with a salmon of 17kg.

Patagonia Tours Service, Colón 203 (☎ & fax 67/232522). Long-established operator offering a range of camp-based fishing trips, including adventurous four-day excursions to Villa O'Higgins, beyond the end of the Carretera Austral. The cost of US$1600 per person includes return flights from Santiago as well as food, accommodation and guides.

Río Palena Lodge, information in the US: ☎1-888/891-3474, fax 860/434-8605. Timber lodge sitting in a forest on the banks of the río Palena, about 20km west of the border village of Palena. The lodge provides accommodation for around eight anglers and prices include transport from and to Puerto Montt.

Termas de Puyuhuapi, Puyuhuapi (☎67/325129; *patagonia@chilnet.cl*). Luxury lodge, combining a spectacular location and sensational thermal baths with top-notch guides and an intricate knowledge of the area's most hidden rivers and channels.

With assistance from Pablo Negri, head guide of the Termas de Puyuhuapi.

You don't need to be a staying guest to visit, though numbers are limited in high season, so you should phone ahead to book: the cost for **day-visits** is CH$10,000 for the outdoor pools, and CH$5000 for the return boat ride (free to guests). If you're considering a splurge, however, there's no better place to do it, and **staying** at the lodge allows you to indulge in the magical experience of lying in the hot pools in the middle of the night, gazing at the millions of stars overhead. If you do stay, try to get one of the shore-side rooms, with floor-to-ceiling windows giving fabulous views across the fjord. The resort can also be visited in conjunction with a cruise to the Laguna San Rafael glacier on board the company's catamaran – for more details, see box p.375. As befits its name (Puyuhuapi means "place of fish" in the native language of the region), it also offers upmarket **fly-fishing** excursions up the maze of scarcely-visited channels and rivers to the west, led by top-of-the-range guides.

Parque Nacional Queulat

As well as being a jumping-off point for visits to the *termas*, Puyuhuapi conveniently sits right on the doorstep of **PARQUE NACIONAL QUEULAT**, a vast expanse of virgin forest, towering granite peaks, and rumbling glaciers. The Carretera Austral runs through or along the edge of the park for 70km, entering the northern boundary 15km north of Puyuhuapi and crossing the southern limit 55km south of the village. Along the way, a number of trails lead off from the road into the park, while – for those not keen to stray far from their car – several scenic highlights can easily be reached from parking areas just off the Carretera. Twelve kilometres north of Puyuhuapi, a track pulls off the road to the Conaf *Guardería* of Sector Angostura (daily 24hr; free), on the shores of the long, thin **Lago Risopatrón**. The lake, flanked by steep mountains jutting abruptly out of its deep-blue waters, is a lovely spot, and the **camping** area (CH$7000 per site) near the Conaf hut is one of the prettiest along the whole road.

By far the most popular attraction, however, and the only port of call for the majority of the park's visitors, is the incredible **Ventisquero Colgante**, or "hanging glacier", 36km south. Wedged between two peaks, forming a V-shaped mass of blue-white ice, the glacier indeed seems to hang suspended over a sheer rock face. Long fingers of ice feed two thundering waterfalls that plummet 150m down to Laguna Los Témpanos, below. Adding to the spectacle, large blocks of ice periodically calve off the glacier and crash down the rocks to the lake. The easiest way to get a look at the glacier is from the **viewpoint** at the end of a signed 2km road branching off the Carretera Austral, about 24km south of Puyuhuapi; Conaf charges a CH$1500 fee to visit this sector of the park (daily: Dec–March 8.30am–9.30pm; April–Nov 8.30am–6.30pm), which you pay at the hut en route to the parking area. For views onto **Laguna Los Témpanos**, which isn't visible from the viewpoint, cross the bridge over the river and follow the 700-metre footpath to the edge of the lake. Its name – literally "Iceberg Lagoon" – refers to the large icebergs that floated on its surface until as recently as twenty years ago. Today, the Ventisquero Colgante has retreated too far to discharge icebergs, and the lake's emerald waters are covered with just a few bobbing blocks of ice. Besides these two easy targets, there are a couple of more demanding **trails** through this sector, described in the box opposite – you can get more information from the Conaf hut, or the adjacent wardens' houses. There's also a **camping** area (CH$7000 per site) by the river, on a fairly hard ground with toilets and cold showers.

Continuing along the Carretera Austral, some 20km south of the Ventisquero Colgante, you pass another short, easy footpath (signed Sendero Padre García) leading 200m down to a viewpoint over the **Saltos Padre García**, a powerful waterfall dropping 30m into the río Queulat. It's named after the Jesuit priest who, in 1766, was the first Spaniard to explore the Queulat river, while searching for the mythical "City of the Ceasars" (a Chilean El Dorado) after hearing what he though were church bells ring-

HIKING IN PARQUE NACIONAL QUEULAT

There are no long-distance hikes in the park, and no scope for getting off the trails, due to the density of the forest. That said, the day or half-day hikes listed below are among the finest in Chile, taking you through pristine, seldom-visited wilderness and rewarding you with superb views. The best times to hike here are from mid-November to February, when the forests are littered with wild flowers, or in late-March to early-May, when the leaves of the ñirre and lenga trees turn bright red and orange.

Sendero Laguna Los Pumos. Starting at the *Guardería* by Lago Risopatrón, this 7km trail (one-way) starts with a steep ascent, climbing from just above sea level to 1100m. From the plateau at the top, you get sweeping views onto surrounding mountains and out to the fjord. The trail then descends through a pass, leading to the shimmering Laguna Los Pumos, bordered by a sandy beach. Allow around 3hr up and 2hr down.

Sendero Mirador Ventisquero Colgante. Across the bridge from the car park in Sector Ventisquero, a clearly marked path leads just over 3km through forest around the moraine valley carved out of the mountain by glaciers, through which the río Ventisquero now flows. After a fairly stiff short climb, the path evens out and ends up at a lookout point giving breathtaking views onto the hanging glacier, and down to Laguna Los Témpanos. Allow 3–4hr round trip.

Sendero Río Cascada. An easy but exhilarating hike, branching off from the Carretera Austral on the southern edge of the park, just beyond the Portezuelo de Queulat (look out for the sign on the right-hand side of the road as you travel south). The trail leads 1.7km through ancient trees covered in moss and threads of lichen, and ends at the río Cascadas. From here, follow the river up the hill for another 800m, and you'll arrive at its source – a jade-green lake at the foot of a granite cliff, topped by a glacier and streaked by waterfalls. It takes around 1hr 30min–2hr to get up, a little less to get back.

Sendero Río Ventisquero. Starting close to the car park in Sector Ventisquero, this 6km trail follows the southern bank of the río Ventisquero valley, first climbing steeply through woods, then flattening out over open land, close to the river. The views over the valley are magnificent, and you see several glaciers along the way (though *not* the Ventisquero Colgante). It's currently about a 5–6hr round trip, though Conaf has plans to extend the trail for a further 12km, leading to the foot of a glacier – check how far they've got before you set off.

ing from within the forest. Just beyond, the road narrows and starts zigzagging up the steep **Cuesta de Queulat**, by sheer-sided mountains crowned with glaciers. At the top, as you drive through the pass (known as the Portezuelo de Queulat), you're met with a fabulous view onto a massive glacier, directly ahead. Five kilometres beyond, as the road heads down again, you get a glimpse of another mighty waterfall, forty-metre-high **Saltos del Cóndor**, which you can make out through the forest on your right. Just beyond is the southern boundary of the park.

Puerto Cisnes

Just beyond the southern limit of Parque Nacional Queulat, a 35-kilometre side road branches west from the Carretera Austral to **PUERTO CISNES**, a small fishing village in a dramatic setting near the entrance to the Puyuhuapi fjord. Colourful fishing boats in every state of disrepair line the beach in front of higgledy-piggledy wooden houses that seem to fight for a foothold on the tiny patch of land, overshadowed by brooding, vertical mountains. Though there's little to actually *do* in Puerto Cisnes, this detour is worth making if only to witness the incredible feats of engineering it took to build the road, blasted out of a cliff along the edge of the fjord. You'd be wise to drive cautiously, however, as there are few passing places and numerous blind corners where many cars have gone over the edge into very deep water.

Puerto Cisnes began life as a solitary sawmill, set up by a German pioneer back in 1929. A few other settlers followed, and eventually a small community sprang up. The most influential player in Puerto Cisnes' fortunes was Eugenia Pircio-Biroli, a remarkable Italian woman who arrived in 1957 and devoted all her energies to improving conditions in the village. While construction of the Carretera Austral was underway, there were no plans to connect it to Puerto Cisnes – so the feisty doña Eugenia, who by then had been elected mayor, decamped to Santiago and so persistently and successfully pestered General Pinochet to give her village road access that she became a household name throughout the country.

Accommodation in the village is quite expensive, though you should be able to haggle prices right down outside January and February. *Hostal Michay*, Gabriela Mistral 112 (☎67/346462; ⑤), is an attractive old family house with good rooms and excellent breakfasts, while *Hostería Gaucho*, perched on the edge of a stream at Holmberg 140 (☎67/346514; ⑤), offers more facilities, with a restaurant and bar. *Cabañas Manzur*, by the entrance to the village at Ethel Dunn 75 (☎67/346453; ⑤) has a few modern self-catering *cabañas* with a good view across the Puyuhuapi fjord; backpackers are welcome to camp in the garden for around CH$5000 per tent. As well as the *Hostería Gaucho*'s **restaurant**, you could try *Guairao*, near the bridge at Piloto Pardo 58, and the small, atmospheric fishermen's bars along the road by the sea. While you're here, you should try out the local speciality of *puyes*, similar to whitebait and absolutely delicious.

Puerto Aisén, Chacabuco and the Laguna San Rafael glacier

Back on the Carretera Austral, heading south, the road follows the río Cisnes along the foot of a massive granite outcrop known as the **Piedra del Gato**, where several simple crosses honour the workmen killed while blasting through the rock. Some 25km on from here, you pass **Villa Amengual**, another of Pinochet's tin towns, and, a few kilometres beyond, pretty **Lago las Torres**, backed by craggy, pyramidal mountains. Gradually, the dense forest is replaced by rolling farmland and wide-open pastures, cleared by settlers in the 1940s. Their main clearance method was fire, which frequently got out of control and whose legacy can be seen in the hundreds of burned-out black and silver tree stumps that poke out of the hillsides. Just over 100km south of the turn-off to Puerto Cisnes, you reach a fork in the road: to the left, the Carretera Austral continues to the regional capital of **Coyhaique**; to the right, a paved side road branches west to the small town of **Puerto Aisén**, providing an oasis of tarmac after the constant jolting of the Carretera. From Puerto Aisén, more paved roads link up with Coyhaique, and with the port and ferry terminal of **Chacabuco**, the departure point for day-cruises to the **Laguna San Rafael glacier**.

Puerto Aisén

Founded in 1914 as a port for shipping out cattle, **PUERTO AISÉN** literally became a backwater when its harbour silted up, forcing commercial vessels to use nearby Puerto Chacabuco from 1960. Most of its shops, houses and residents stayed put, however, and Puerto Aisén is still an important service centre and residential nucleus, with a long main street lined with supermarkets, bars and restaurants. Its main use to travellers is as a base for stocking up on supplies or booking ferry tickets, as – services aside – it has little to offer in the way of tourist attractions. That said, there are a couple of rewarding excursions you could do from the town, of which the best is a boat ride down the narrow and spectacular **Aisén fjord**, taking in the natural hot springs of the **Termas del Chilconal**, about two hours downstream. This can be arranged for around CH$15,000 per person with Turismo Rucaray, a very efficient travel agency on the plaza at Teniente Marino 668 (☎67/332862, fax 332725; *rucarary@entelchile.net*) – it also offers a range of **fishing excursions** to the surrounding lakes, and can book cruise or ferry tickets for the Laguna San Rafael glacier. You could also drive up the twelve-kilometre gravel road north of town to **Lago Los Palos** – a small, glass-like lake set in a wide valley – or along the 26-kilometre dirt road south to the more dramatic **Lago Riesgo**, enclosed by abundant vegetation. For other suggestions or more information, visit the **Oficina de Turismo** in the Municipalidad, on the plaza (Mon–Fri 9am–12.30pm & 3.30–6pm).

The best-value place to **stay** in Puerto Aisén is the unnamed *hospedaje* at Serrano Montaner 471 (☎67/332574; ③), offering simple, clean rooms with shared bath. Other choices include *Hotel Caicahues* at Michimalonco 660 (☎67/332888; ⑤), a modern hotel with en-suite rooms, a restaurant and bar, and the pricier *Hotel Roxy* at Sargento Aldea 972 (☎67/332704; ⑤), a comfortable enough but bland hotel. The best place to **eat** in town is *Gastronomía Carrera*, a down-to-earth restaurant at Cochrane 465, specializing in fish and seafood. Sandwiches, pizzas and other snacks are available in the many cafés that line the main street, Sargento Aldea, including *Café Irlandés* at no. 1077, *Dinas* at no. 382, and *Rincón Chilote* at no. 353. **Buses** for neighbouring Chacabuco leave every ten minutes from all along Sargento Aldea, and for Coyhaique every hour from no. 1090 of the same street.

Chacabuco

Fifteen kilometres west of Puerto Aisén, the busy port of **CHACABUCO** is dramatically set on a natural harbour enclosed by craggy, jagged peaks brushed with snow. Scanning this panorama, it's almost impossible to make out any outlet to the sea, and you'd be forgiven for thinking you were standing before a lake. Turn away from the ocean and you're greeted with a very different sight: rows of ugly fish processing factories stagger down the road to the shore, and the jetty is flanked by large, grim-looking warehouses. As you take in the scene, your thoughts may turn to the nauseating smell of fish wafting over from the warehouses, seeping into your clothes and hair, which it will cling to for days afterwards. All in all, Chacabuco is not a place to linger in.

It is, however, the embarkation point for day-trips to one of the most spectacular sights in Chile, the **Laguna San Rafael glacier** (see overleaf), a five- to sixteen-hour (200km) boat ride out to sea. And as the boats set out early in the morning, and get back late at night, you'll probably want to spend a night here before and after the trip. A cluster of basic *residenciales* has sprung up on the road down towards the ferry terminal, opposite the blue-and-white Pesca Chile warehouse: *Residencial Morales* (☎67/351155; ③) is the best of a motley bunch, with neat, spartan **rooms**, whitewashed wooden walls, decent showers and a **restaurant** downstairs. The *Ofqui* (☎67/351150; ③), just round the corner, has a cosy dining room with a huge open fire, but many of its rooms are in the dark, cramped basement. Both of these places are a two-minute walk from the ferry ramp. Up on the hill, a ten-minute walk away at calle José Miguel 50, is the far more attractive, and more expensive, *Hotel Loberías de Aisén* (☎ & fax 67/351115; ⑥), with well-furnished, en-suite rooms in a bungalow-style building with a smart fish restaurant attached.

Besides being the jumping-off point for visits to the glacier, Chacabuco is also the terminal for ferries to and from Puerto Montt and Quellón, operated by TransMarChilay

(☎ & fax 67/351144) whose office is on the road down to the ferry ramp, and Navimag. If you've just **landed** from one of these ferries, you'll probably want to head out of town immediately – the ferries are usually met by minibuses to Puerto Aisén, from where you can catch buses to Coyhaique (with Buses Don Carlos, Sargento Aldea 1090; ☎67/332918).

San Rafael glacier

From Chacabuco, a 200-kilometre boat ride through the labyrinthine fjords of Aisén brings you to the dazzling **San Rafael glacier**, spilling into the broad **Laguna San Rafael**. The journey is a spectacle in itself, as the boat edges its way through narrow channels hemmed in by precipitous cliffs, dripping with vegetation. You get little sense of entering the Pacific, as the chain of islands which form the Chonos archipelago blends into one seething mass of mottled green, creating a natural barrier between the mainland and the open sea. After sailing down the long, thin Golfo de Elefantes, the boat enters the seemingly unnavigable río Témpanos, or "Iceberg River", before emerging into the Laguna San Rafael. Floating in the lagoon are dozens of **icebergs**, fashioned by wind and rain into monumental Henry Moore-style sculptures, holes and all, with such a vibrant electric-blue colour that they appear to be lit from within. Their precarious balance is upset by the gentlest of wakes from a passing boat, whereupon, brought suddenly to life, they bob up and down in the water before finding a new equilibrium.

Sailing through these icy phantoms, you approach the giant **glacier** at the far end of the lagoon. Over 4km wide, and rearing out of the water to a height of 70m, it really is a dizzying sight. While the cruise boat keeps at a safe distance, to avoid being trapped by icebergs, you'll probably be given the chance to get a closer look on board an inflatable motor dinghy – but not too close, as the huge blocks of ice that, with a deafening roar, calve off into the water create dangerous, crashing waves. What you can see from the boat is in fact just the tip of the glacier's "tongue", which extends some 15km from its source. If you look at the rocks that encircle the lagoon, either side of this tongue, you'll see a series of white markers, painted by scientists over the last couple of decades to monitor the position of the glacier's edge. It is, unmistakeably, retreating fast. Early explorers reported that, in 1800, the glacier filled three-quarters of the lagoon, and archive photographs from the beginning of the twentieth century show it as being far longer than it is today. It is estimated that within thirty years, the glacier will be gone.

Stretching beyond the shores of the lagoon are the 1.7 million hectares of land that make up **Parque Nacional Laguna San Rafael**, of which the eponymous *laguna* forms just a tiny fraction. Almost half this vast area is covered by the immense icefield known as the **Campo de Hielo Norte**, which feeds eighteen other glaciers on top of this one, and which contains over 250 lakes and lagoons. Towering over the frozen plateau is **Monte San Valentín** which, at 4058m, is the highest peak in the southern Andes. The Laguna San Rafael is the only accessible part of the park, though – to Conaf's continual frustration – the thousands of tourists who visit the glacier each summer by boat are exempt from the CH$2500 entrance fee, payable only if you land. A mere 500 or so per year do so, most of them on the light aeroplanes that fly tourists over the glacier and touch down for a couple of hours. Spending longer on the park is very difficult to arrange; for those who manage to, Conaf offers accommodation in a *refugio* with hot water and light (CH$10,000 per person). The Conaf *Guardería* is close to the glacier, by the shores of the *laguna*. From here, a seven-kilometre trail leads to a breathtaking viewpoint over the sprawling, icy tongue, taking around two hours up and slightly less coming down – too long to fit in if you only have a couple of hours between plane rides.

VISITING THE SAN RAFAEL GLACIER

The glacier is accessible only by aeroplane or sea. **Flights** from Coyhaique in five-seater planes are offered by three companies, from US$150 per person: Aerohein, Baquedano 500, Coyhaique (☎ & fax 67/232772); Transportes San Rafael, 18 de Septiembre 469, Coyhaique (☎67/232048, fax 233408); and Transportes Don Carlos, Subteniente Cruz, Coyhaique (☎ & fax 67/231981). Flying over the icefield is an unforgettable experience, but the most sensational views of the glacier are from the small dinghies that thread through the icebergs towards its base, usually included as part of a visit to the *laguna* **by sea**. Scheduled departures leave from Chacabuco and Puerto Montt (via Chacabuco) from December to March.

Iceberg Expedition, Providencia 2331, oficina 602 (☎2/335 0579, fax 335 0581; *hotelsa@chilesat.net*). The latest outfit on the scene, offering day-trips to the *laguna* from Chacabuco (5hr each way) onboard its catamaran, the *Iceberg*, including three meals and an open bar. Operates in January and February.

Navimag, Av El Bosque Norte 0440, Santiago (☎2/203 5030, fax 203 5025; *www.australis.com*); Angelmó 2187, Puerto Montt (☎65/253318, fax 258540). Navimag's huge ferry, the *Evangelistas*, visits the *laguna* from December to March, either as a two-night trip from Chacabuco (16hr each way; from CH$90,000); as a three-night one-way trip from Puerto Montt to the *laguna* and Chacabuco (from CH$100,000), or as a four-night round-trip from Puerto Montt (from CH$110,000). The price includes all meals. The boat has 23 bunks and 300 reclining seats. Cars can be carried from Puerto Montt to Chacabuco.

Patagonia Express, Fidel Oteíza 1921, oficina 1006, Santiago (☎2/225 6489, fax 274 8111; *patagonia@chilnet.cl*). This long-established luxury catamaran visits the *laguna* on a day-trip from Chacabuco (5hr each way) every Friday in January and February (US$250); the price includes three meals and an open bar. From September to March, the excursion is combined with a stay at the *Termas de Puyuhuapi* (see p.368) on four- or six-day packages (from US$1500).

Skorpios, Agusto Leguia Norte 118, Las Condes, Santiago (☎2/231 1030, fax 232 2269; *skorpios@tmm.cl*) and Angelmó 1660, Puerto Montt (☎65/256619, fax 258315); *www.skorpios.cl*. Six-day luxury cruises from Puerto Montt to the Laguna San Rafael and back, from US$750 per person.

TransMarChilay, Agustinas 715, oficina 403, Santiago (☎ & fax 2/633 5959); Angelmó 2187, Puerto Montt (☎65/270416, fax 270415); O'Higgins s/n, Chacabuco (☎ & fax 67/351144). The state-run ferry company now offers weekly summer excursions (Jan & Feb) to the *laguna*, either as a two-night trip from Chacabuco (16hr each way), from CH$97,000, or a four-night round-trip from Puerto Montt, from CH$133,000. The boat has a few bunks, but most accommodation is on reclining seats.

Coyhaique and around

From Chacabuco, a good paved road heads 15km east to Puerto Aisén, from where it continues 67km to the city of **Coyhaique**. It's a very scenic route, holding fast to the río Simpson as it rushes through the **Reserva Nacional Río Simpson**, sandwiched between tall, craggy cliffs. Thirty-two kilometres out of Puerto Aisén, a small wooden sign by the road (saying "Museo") points to the reserve's administration and attached **museum** (daily 8.30am–1pm & 2.15–6.30pm; CH$300) which focuses on local wildlife and flora, of which the best exhibit is the huge stump of a 400-year-old lenga tree in the garden. The reserve's main attractions are conveniently located right by the road: 1km on from the museum, you pass the **Cascada de la Virgen**, a tall, graceful waterfall that drops in two stages, separated by a pool of water; a further 8km east you pass another waterfall, the **Velo de la Novia**, or "bride's veil", so named for its diaphanous spray. Shortly after, the road leaves the río Simpson and turns south, giving sweeping panoramic views onto Coyhaique, sitting in a wide, golden valley at the foot of the towering basalt bluff known as Cerro Macay.

Coyhaique

After the smattering of half-dead villages scattered down the Carretera Austral, Aisén's thriving regional capital, **COYHAIQUE**, comes as a bit of a shock, with its smart boutiques, lively cafés, and streets packed with traffic and pedestrians. The city's forty thousand inhabitants make up half the region's population, and it's the only place along the Carretera that offers a wide range of services, from pharmacies and banks to laundries and car-rental outlets. Although resolutely urban, it's also a good launchpad for some great **day-trips** that will give you a taste of the region's wilderness – for more details see p.379.

Arrival and information

Most **buses** pull in at the centrally located terminal on the corner of Lautaro and Magallanes, though a few arrive at and depart from their company office, separate from the terminal. Coyhaique's nearest airport is **Aerodromo Teniente Vidal**, 5km west of town, but it's a small affair, used only by local small-plane companies flying in from

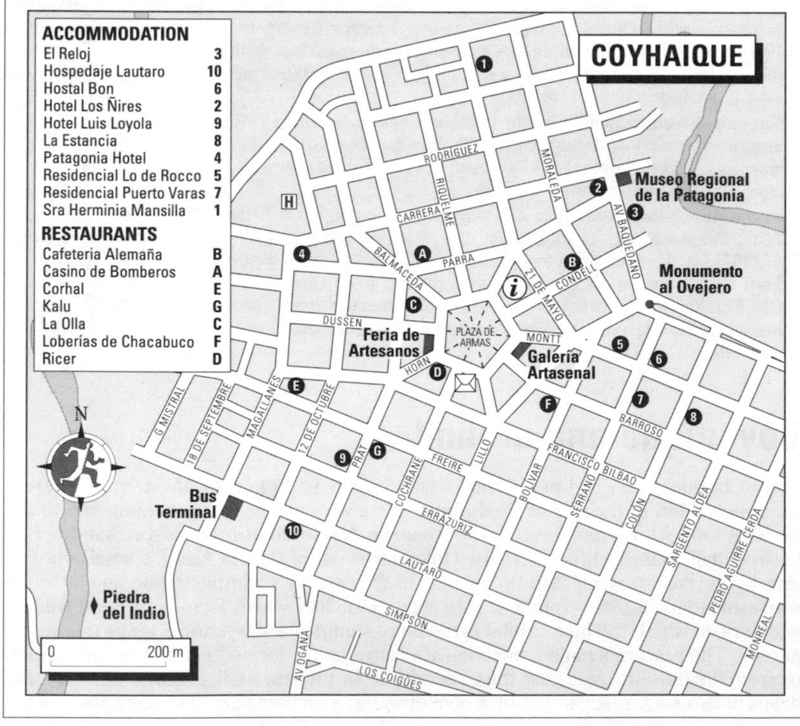

regional aerodromes. All Lan Chile, Ladeco and Avant flights land at the **Aeropuerto de Balmaceda**, 55km south, and are met by **minibuses** that take passengers to their hotels for around CH$3000–4000.

You can pick up information on the city and the region at the very helpful **Sernatur** office, at Bulnes 35 (Dec–Feb Mon–Fri 8.30am–9pm, Sat & Sun 11am–8pm; March–Nov Mon–Fri 8.30am–1pm & 2.30–7pm; ☎ & fax 67/231752), which produces printed lists of Coyhaique's accommodation (with prices), restaurants, transport facilities and tour operators. For information on Aisén's national parks and reserves, visit **Conaf**'s Oficina Patrimonio Silvestre at Bilbao 234 (Mon–Fri 8.30am–noon & 3–5.30pm; ☎67/212125).

Accommodation

Coyhaique offers a wide choice of places to stay, from simple *hospedajes* to upmarket hotels. Prices are very reasonable at the lower end of the scale, but many mid- and upper-range hotels are decidedly overpriced. **Camping** facilities are available at *Ogana*, on Avenida Ogana, pasaje 8, set in a small orchard with a hut for cooking and hot showers (CH$2000 per person), and at *HI Albergue Las Salamandras* (listed below; CH$5000 per site).

El Reloj, Baquedano 444 (☎ & fax 67/231108). A spotlessly clean, comfortable house with en-suite rooms and its own restaurant. Good value if you want a private bathroom. ④.

HI Albergue Las Salamandras, Carretera Teniente Vidal, km 1.5 (☎67/234700, fax 237923). Set in a wood by a river 1.5km along the road to Teniente Vidal, this popular hostel offers the use of a kitchen, laundry facilities, mountain-bike rental and a range of excursions. ③.

Hospedaje Lautaro, Lautaro 269 (☎ & fax 67/238116). An attractive old house in a quiet garden with single, double and triple rooms and a bunk dormitory. The helpful owners have their own minibus and organize local tours, including horse trekking. ③.

Hostal Bon, Serrano 91 (☎ & fax 67/231189). Small hotel with thin partition walls and a mixture of shared-baths and en-suite rooms, some of which are a little cramped. It's a friendly place, though, with a good restaurant that specializes in hearty *parilladas*. ③–④.

Hotel Los Ñires, Baquedano 315 (☎67/232261, fax 233372). One of the older hotels in town with a slightly dreary atmosphere and a large, good restaurant. ⑤.

Hotel Luis Loyola, Prat 455 (☎ & fax 67/234200). A modern hotel with eighteen en-suite rooms, all with cable TV and central heating. Probably the best choice in this price range. ⑤.

La Estancia, Colon 166 (☎67/250193). Contrary to the images conjured up by its name, this is a tiny house with two or three simple, tidy rooms, one with private bath. ③.

Patagonia Hotel, General Parra 551 (☎ & fax 67/236505). This smart new hotel features lots of pale wood and pastel-coloured furnishings, an attractive dining area, and some of the highest prices in town. ⑦.

Residencial Lo de Rocco, 21 de Mayo 668 (☎67/231285). A family house with neat, basic rooms and comfortable beds; note that those upstairs are inconveniently separated from the bathroom by a steep wooden staircase. ③.

Residencial Puerto Varas, Serrano 168 (☎67/233689, fax 235931). Clean, well-maintained *residencial*, offering spacious doubles and a few tiny singles, mostly with shared bath. The front en-suite room is good value if you want a private bathroom without the added frills. ③.

Sra Herminia Mansilla, 21 de Mayo 60 (☎67/231579) Neat and tidy family house, slightly out of the centre, with light, airy rooms and a friendly owner who is very proud of the long list of foreign visitors in her guest book. ②.

The Town

After the rigid grid layout of Chile's other towns and cities, Coyhaique's infuriating pentagonal street plan tends to throw most visitors, who can be spotted wandering around, map in hand, hopelessly lost. At its centre is the large, five-sided **Plaza de Armas**, whose densely planted trees provide shade or shelter, depending on the weather. On the southwest corner with Horn, the small **Feria de Artesanos** sells jewellery and leather goods, while, just across the plaza on the corner with Montt, the **Galería Artesenal de Cema Chile** has a wide range of handicrafts, including knitwear, weavings, wooden carvings and ceramics. Continue up Montt, walking away from the plaza, and you'll come to Baquedano, the city's main thoroughfare. Immediately to your right stands one of Coyhaique's quirkiest landmarks, the **Monumento Al Ovejero**, a large white sculpture of a shepherd and a flock of sheep. A couple of blocks left along Baquedano, at no. 310, is the **Museo Regional de la Patagonia** (Jan & Feb daily 9am–1pm & 3–8pm; March–Dec Mon–Fri 8.30am–1pm & 2.30–6.30pm; CH$500), where an excellent collection of black-and-white photographs vividly captures the "Wild West" frontier atmosphere during the opening up of Aisén at the turn of the century. Other exhibits include archeological finds that prove that the Tehuelche people once roamed this far north, while Chonos fishing groups inhabited the coastal islands and channels. Finally, you could make the half-hour walk out to the **Piedra del Indio**, a large rock outcrop weathered into the form of a profile – popularly believed to be that of a former Tehuelche chieftain. It sits next to the bridge over the río Simpson, reached by following Avenida Simpson south out of town.

Eating and drinking

Although Coyhaique's **restaurants** are, on the whole, no more adventurous than those in most other Chilean cities, they're a real treat after the limited choice along the rest of the Carretera Austral. As for **drinking** and **nightlife**, there are several pub-discos to choose from, of which *Pub El Zorro*, at Morelada 420, is probably the best. Another popular drinking hole is *Bar West* at Bilbao 110, done up like a Wild West saloon. If you're after something more authentic, check out *Café Peña Quilantal* at Baquedano 791, for live *música folklórca* and *boleros*. Nightlife is quiet everywhere through the week, and at the weekend doesn't warm up until after midnight.

Cafeteria Alemana, Condell 119. With its scrubbed pine tables and floral furnishings, this is an attractive place for a snack, though there's nothing remotely German about the menu, which offers the usual *lomos*, pizzas and sandwiches – plus above-average pancakes and home-made ice creams.

Casino de Bomberos, General Parra 365. Slightly hidden away, Coyhaique's firemen's canteen is one of the best places in town for lunch, with excellent-value set meals and a packed-out, lively atmosphere.

Corhal, Bilbao 125. A good restaurant which does enormous *parilladas* for CH$5000 including wine. On Friday and Saturday nights there's a disco downstairs until 5am.

Kalu, Prat 402. One of the most popular cafés with locals, particularly at lunchtime when they flock in for the cheap set meals.

La Olla, Prat 176 (☎67/234700). Run by a charming old man from Extremadura, this cosy, old-fashioned restaurant does excellent paellas every Sunday (and through the week if you phone in advance), and first-class *estofado de cordero* (lamb stew).

Loberìas de Chacabuco, Barroso 553. An unassuming little café-restaurant whose owner prides himself on the freshness of his seafood, and more often than not cooks and serves it himself – at a rather unhurried pace.

Ricer, Horn 48. Just off the plaza, this bright and cheerful café attracts a lot of gringos, and is a good meeting place. There's a more formal restaurant upstairs, decorated with evocative photographs of the early pioneers, and knick-knacks from the turn of the century.

Listings

Airlines Avant, General Parra 202 (☎67/237570); Ladeco, Prat 18 (☎67/231300); Lan Chile, General Parra 211 (☎67/231188).

Banks and exchange Banco Santander has an ATM at Condell 184, and there are several *cambios*, including Cambio Mendoza at Condell 140; Emperador at Bilbao 222; Lucia Saldivia at Condell 140; and Turismo Prado at 21 de Mayo 417.

TOURS FROM COYHAIQUE

Adventure tour companies come and go quite frequently in Coyhaique – check with Sernatur, as it's very clued-up as to what's around, which ones are good, and what they offer. You can expect to pay something in the range of CH$15,000–20,000 for a day excursion, around CH$80,000 for two days, and CH$200,000 for five-day trips. *Ricer*, at Horn 48 (☎67/232920), is a good bet for arranging **half-day** and **day-tours** to the nearby lakes (see overleaf), to see local rock art (see p.383) and to Reserva Nacional Cerro Castillo (see p.381), among other destinations. Aventura Turismo, at General Parra 222 (☎ & fax 67/234748) concentrates on places south along the Carretera Austral, including the marble caves at **Puerto Tranquilo** (see p.383), and five-day excursions to the **Campo de Hielo Norte**. Several operators are particularly strong on **fishing** excursions, including Expediciones Coyhaique, Portales 195 (☎ & fax 67/232300) and Patagonia Tours, Colón 203 (☎ & fax 67/232522); for more on fishing in the region, see p.368. For **horse trekking**, try Turismo Aysén at Barroso 626 (☎67/233216, fax 235294), and 45° Latitud Sur at Lillo 194 (☎67/234599, fax 235294). A good choice for guided **mountaineering** in the region is Cochrane Patagonia at Teniente Merino 750 (☎ & fax 67/522197).

Car rental AGS, Av Ogana 1298 (☎67/235354, fax 231511); Aisén, Bilbao 926 (☎67/231532); Arriendo de Jeep, O'Higgins 501 (☎ & fax 67/411461); Automóvil Club de Chile, Bolívar 194 (☎ & fax 67/231649); Automundo, Bilbao 510 (☎67/231621, fax 231794); Travel Car, Colón 190-B (☎ & fax 67/236840).

Hospital The regional hospital is on calle Hospital 68 (☎67/233171).

Internet access There's a terminal at Entel, Prat 340, and at the local community centre at Bilbao 144.

Laundry There's a reasonably priced laundry on the corner of Bilbao and 12 de Octubre.

Outdoor equipment Patagonia Outdoors, at Horn 47, has a wide selection of camping and fishing gear, plus outdoor clothes.

Telephone centres There's a CTC *centro de llamados* at Horn 40; Entel is at Prat 340.

Around Coyhaique

You can do a number of rewarding day-trips from Coyhaique, dipping into Aisén's back-country and getting back to a comfortable bed at night. The nearest target is **Reserva Nacional Coyhaique**, just north of the city, which has several trails. To the south, side tracks lead both east and west off the paved road to a spread of lakes, of which **Lago Elizade** and **Lago Atravesado** are the most impressive. Slightly further afield, continuing south down the paved road, the **Reserva Nacional Cerro Castillo** encompasses the magnificent silhouette of its namesake mountain.

Reserva Nacional Coyhaique

Just 4km north of the city – about a 45-minute walk – the **Reserva Nacional Coyhaique** (daily 8.30am–6pm; CH$600) is an easily accessible slice of wilderness, featuring areas of native forest, a couple of lakes and fantastic views down to the city, huddled at the foot of towering Cerro Makay. Thanks partly to the efforts of locally based Operation Raleigh volunteers, a series of clear, well-maintained paths weaves through the reserve – they're displayed on a large map in the *Guardería* by the entrance, alongside a scale model of the reserve. **Sendero Los Leñeros** leads almost 2km from the *Guardería* through native lenga and ñirre trees to a **camping** area (CH$3500 per site), from where the path continues for another 1.8km through pine trees to **Laguna Verde**, a small lake with a few picnic tables on its shore. From here, you pick up with a jeep track which if you follow it north for a couple of hundred metres will take you to the

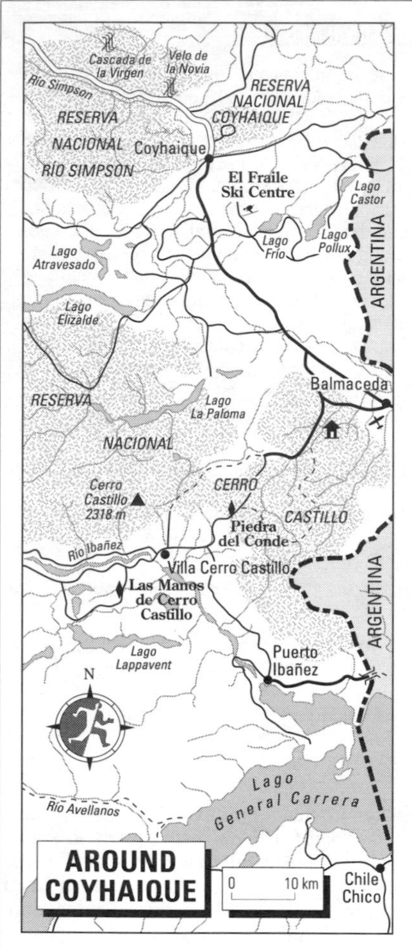

trailhead of **Sendero Las Piedras**, which leads 13km up to and across a ridge, giving breathtaking views for miles around. This is by far the best hike in the reserve, and, though steep in parts, isn't too difficult, taking around four hours to complete. After descending at the other end, a side path branches off to Lago Venus, an attractive lake 1km beyond, reached by walking through dense native forest. Alternatively, keep on going another couple of hundred metres and you'll join up with **Sendero El Chucao**, which leads 2.6km back to the *Guardería*.

Lakes south of Coyhaique

South of Coyhaique two separate round trips of around 100km apiece take you through wild and totally contrasting scenery, via a series of picture-postcard lakes. All have superb fishing and make a great backdrop for a stroll, though there are no proper hiking trails around here. Note, too, that the roads are poor and almost totally unsigned, so take a good map with you if you're in your own vehicle.

Heading southwest, if you cross the bridge out of town past the Piedra del Indio (see p.378) and keep going straight for 20km, you'll get to the remote and very beautiful **Lago Atravesado**, set among steeply forested hills whose deep-green shades are mirrored in the water. Double back on your tracks for 4km and take the first right turn, which leads through rolling farmland past the **Seis Lagunas** – a group of six little ponds, nestling in the fields. Carry on down the track and turn right for long, slender **Lago Elizalde**, spectacularly set amongst lush forest and mountains. From here, you can return to the paved road to Coyhaique via the rather run-down little village of **Villa Frei**.

The second route takes you through a very different landscape of flat Patagonian steppe, carpeted with golden *coirón* grass. Following the paved road south out of Coyhaique, the first left turn leads to little **Lago Frío**, tucked at the foot of the rustic El Fraile ski centre. A few kilometres further east is **Lago Pollux**, enclosed by dense reeds, which provide a haven for nesting birds. Just beyond, **Lago Castor** stretches right to the Argentinian border. From the lake's shore, the road turns north towards the international road to Argentina – take the left (west) turn to get back to Coyhaique.

Reserva Nacional Cerro Castillo

About an hour's drive south of Coyhaique, the Carretera Austral crosses the (unsigned) northern boundary of **RESERVA NACIONAL CERRO CASTILLO**. In stark contrast to the rich grazing land you've left behind, you're suddenly faced with a wild, windswept landscape with scenery to gasp at. Spread out below you is a broad river valley flanked by densely forested lower slopes that rise to a breathtaking panorama of barren, rocky peaks. Dominating the skyline is the reserve's centrepiece, **Cerro Castillo**, whose needle-point spires loom over the valley like the turrets of a Transylvanian castle. Further down the road, exactly 64km from the city, you pass the *Guardería* on your left (daily 8.30am–6.30pm), which has a basic **camping** area (CH$2500) with a covered grill for cooking. You can also pick up a map of the reserve here, showing the two **long-distance hiking trails** that branch off from the Carretera Austral.

The first, 36-kilometre **Sendero Río Blanco**, forks left (east) some 3km south of the *Guardería*, and follows the río Blanco up the fairly steep slopes of Cerro Pico Gancho, through forests of native lenga. It then loops back down, rejoining the Carretera Austral at the **Piedra del Cónde**, a curious rock formation 16km from the *Guardería*. This hike takes two days to complete. The second, more rewarding, route is the challenging three- to four-day **Sendero Valle La Lima**, which branches right (west) from the road 6km south of the *Guardería*, and follows the río La Lima towards the peak of Cerro Castillo. On the way, you pass the stunning **Laguna Cerro Castillo**, at the foot of a glacier suspended from the mountainside, before descending to the village of **Villa Cerro Castillo** (see p.383), where you can find comfortable accommodation and catch a bus back to Coyhaique. Note that both trails are very poorly marked, and not always easy to follow – you can get more detailed route advice from the *guardaparque*, who should be informed before you set off. You can get here on any of the **buses** from Coyhaique to Villa Cerro Castillo.

Across Lago General Carrera to Chile Chico

Just beyond the southern boundary of Reserva Nacional Cerro Castillo, a 31-kilometre side road shoots south from the Carretera Austral to the tiny village of **Puerto Ibáñez**, on the northern shore of **Lago General Carrera**. This deep-blue lake encircled by rocky, sharp-peaked mountains is the second-largest in South America, and stretches east into Argentina, where it is known as Lago Buenos Aires. Regular ferries connect Puerto Ibáñez with the small town of **Chile Chico**, opposite, making an attractive alternative to following the Carretera Austral *around* the lake. From Chile Chico, a 128-kilometre road skirts the lake's southern shore, joining the Carretera just beyond the village of Puerto Gaudal.

Puerto Ibáñez

Sitting in a green, fertile plain that contrasts sharply with the barren hills around it, **PUERTO IBÁÑEZ** is a shrinking and somewhat lifeless village, worth visiting only to

FERRIES ACROSS LAGO GENERAL CARRERA

Ferries are operated by **Sotramín**, based at Portales 99, Coyhaique (☎67/234240). The crossing takes 2hr 15min and costs CH$1800 for passengers, and CH$21,000 per vehicle. In January and February ferries set off from Puerto Ibáñez at 9am from Monday to Friday, and at 10am on Saturday, and from Chile Chico at 5.30pm from Monday to Friday and at 3pm on Sunday. During the rest of the year, they leave Puerto Ibañez on Monday, Wednesday, Friday and Saturday at 9am, and Chile Chico on Tuesday, Wednesday, Friday and Sunday at 3pm.

catch the ferry across Lago General Carrera. Founded in 1908, it was once an important harbour for boats plying the lake with produce from the remote *estancias* at the eastern end, but it fell into decline when the construction of the Carretera Austral provided nearby villages with direct access to Coyhaique. These days it makes its living from agriculture, made possible by the warm microclimate that surrounds the entire lake. There's nothing much to do here, though you could check out the village's *artesanía* shops that do a curious line in pottery clad in sheeps' and goats' leather. Puerto Ibáñez has several places to **stay**: at the far end of Bertrand Dickson, the village's only street, *Residencial Ibáñez* (☎67/423227; ③) has simple but comfortable rooms looking out across the lake; at no. 282, *Residencial Vientos del Sur* (☎67/423208; ③) is a clean, modern family house, offering decent set meals; finally, María Turnena at no. 66 (②) wraps up the choice with five basic beds and no hot water. Transport to Puerto Ibáñez from Coyhaique is provided by **minibuses** which leave from calle Prat (opposite the shop Calaforte) or will collect passengers from their homes or hotels and get here in time for the ferry; phone to book a place as far in advance as possible with: Colectivos Sr Parra (☎67/251073) or Yamil J Ali M (☎67/250346).

Chile Chico

Sitting on the southern shore of Lago General Carrera, the small agricultural town of **CHILE CHICO** has a slightly abandoned feel to it, an impression enhanced by the layer of ash deposited by the eruption of nearby Volcán Hudson in 1991, that still fills the streets with grey clouds when the wind gets up. It was settled by farmers who crossed over from Argentina in 1909, causing a conflict known as the "Chile Chico war" when they refused to hand over land to the concessionaires given land grants by the government. The new settlement depended entirely on Argentina until a road was built between Coyhaique and Puerto Ibáñez in 1952, after which Chile Chico's orchards became Coyhaique's main source of fresh fruit. While the fruit trees haven't really recovered from the volcanic eruption, the town's fortunes have been boosted slightly by the recent influx of mine workers and tourists.

There's a helpful **Oficina de Turismo** (Mon–Fri 8.30am–noon & 3–6pm; ☎67/411359) on O'Higgins at the corner of Lautaro, where you can pick up a town map. Upstairs, a small **museum** (variable hours) displays a few Tehuelche artefacts and fossils of giant molluscs and other marine animals, reminders that thousands of years ago this area was covered by the sea. There's nothing else to do in town, but the wide choice of **accommodation** makes it a good place to break your journey. *Hostería de la Patagonia* at Chacra 3-A (☎ & fax 67/411337; ④) is a charming, old-fashioned house tucked away in a large garden on the eastern edge of town. Opposite, *No Me Olivdes* (no phone; ②) is popular with backpackers, with seven basic, good-value rooms and room to camp in the large orchard, while *Residencial Don Luís* at Balmaceda 175 (☎67/411384; ③) is slightly sprucer. Perhaps the best place to stay and **eat** in town is the new and very comfortable *Hostería Austral* at O'Higgins 501 (☎ & fax 67/411461; ④) – a true family concern, designed by the son, built by the father, decorated by the daughter and run by the mother.

Moving on from Chile Chico, Transportes Ales, Rosa Amelia 820 (☎67/411739) operates a **bus** service west to the Carretera Austral and down to Cochrane on Tuesdays and Fridays. There are daily flights to Coyhaique (CH$18,000) with Aero Don Carlos, at O'Higgins 264 (☎67/231981). If you've got your own transport, you might want to make a detour to the **Reserva Nacional Lago Jeinimeni** (daily 8.30am–6.30pm; CH$600) before rejoining the Carretera Austral. Reached by a sixty-kilometre rough road running parallel to the border with Argentina, the reserve is a wild, scarcely visited region of forests, glaciers and lakes, with a sizeable population of *huemul* (native deer). Its centrepiece is **Lago Jeinimeni**, a striking, indigo lake enclosed by densely forested hills.

Around Lago General Carrera to Puerto Bertrand

Crossing Lago General Carrera to Chile Chico is a very scenic route, but looping around the lake along the Carretera Austral offers equally impressive, if not better, panoramas – in this case of the grey-and-pink mountains west of the road, plus a few glimpses of the Campo de Hielo Norte (northern icefield). Nine kilometres on from the turn-off to Puerto Ibáñez, you pass **VILLA CERRO CASTILLO**, a dreary, lifeless new town whose sole attraction is its dramatic views onto the jagged silhouette of Cerro Castillo. There are a few grocery shops and places to **stay** here, including friendly *Residencial El Castillo* at O'Higgins 241 (no phone; ②) by the turning into town, run by a delightful woman offering tasty home cooking. Just across the bridge outside the town, a signed two-kilometre track leads to **Las Manos de Cerro Castillo**, a dense collection of over 100 handprints, in three separate panels, at the foot of a sheer basalt rockface. The images, which are mostly negative prints against a red background, are thought to have been left by the Tehuelche people between 5000 and 8000 years ago, and are now preserved as a national monument (there's no viewing fee, but most people leave a small donation with the guide in the wooden hut).

Continuing along the Carretera Austral, the next sign of life – about 100km on from Villa Cerro Castillo – is the 5km side-road to **PUERTO MURTA**, a tiny cattle-farming community (and former logging centre) sitting on a long, thin arm of Lago General Carrera, with a couple of simple places to **stay** including shoreside *Hostería General Carrera* (☎67/419601; ③). Bypassing Puerto Murta, shortly beyond the turn-off, the Carretera hits the shore of the lake and clings to it for the next 75km, giving striking views across the gleaming, emerald water. Some 25km south of the turning for Puerto Murta you'll reach **PUERTO TRANQUILO**, a picturesque lakeside hamlet with basic services including **accommodation** at *Hostal Los Pinos*, 2 Oriente 41 (☎67/411637; ④), and *Residencial Carretera Austral*, 1 Sur 223 (☎67/419500; ③). The latter runs short boat rides (CH$25,000 per boat) across the lake to the **Capilla de Mármol** ("Marble Chapel"), a heavily eroded limestone cliff looming out of the water, streaked with blue-and-white patterns and gashed with caves which can be entered by boat.

Twenty kilometres south of Puerto Tranquilo, the road crosses a bridge over the río Leones – look west here for distant views onto the dazzling white glaciers of the Campo de Hielo Norte. A further fifteen kilometres down the road you reach the outlet of Lago General Carrera, which drains into the adjacent Lago Bertrand. A cluster of upmarket timber *cabañas* has sprung up around here, including *Cabañas Bahía Catalina* (☎67/232920; ⑤) and *Cabañas Mallín Colorado* (☎67/411443; ⑦). Pushing on, about 25km further south, you reach the charming village of **PUERTO BERTRAND** sitting near the head of the turquoise río Baker, Chile's longest river. There's a highly recommended tour agency here, Patagonia Adventure Expeditions run by a dynamic North American (☎ & fax 67/411330; *riobaker@entelchile.net*) offering white-water rafting, fishing, horse riding and kayaking classes in the pristine wilderness around the village. There are a couple of attractive, upmarket places to **stay** – *Río Baker Lodge* (☎67/411499; ⑥) and *Hostería Campo Baker* (☎67/411447; ⑧) – plus the more affordable *Residencial Quimey* (☎67/419900; ③).

Cochrane and beyond

Fifty kilometres south of Puerto Bertrand, **COCHRANE** is the first proper town since Coyhaique and the last major stop on the Carretera Austral. It was founded by the government in 1930 in an attempt to create a southern urban centre in the newly opened region, but it remained a backwater until it was made provincial capital in 1954 when it quickly filled up with civil servants and their families. There's nothing to do here, but the paved, orderly streets spreading out from the neat Plaza de Armas, and array of efficient services make this an appealing place to rest up after the wildness of the Carretera Austral. The best place to **stay** in town is smart new *Hotel Ultimo Paraíso* at Lago Brown 455 (☎67/522361; ⑤), followed by the older and more faded *Hotel Wellmann* at Las Golondrinas 36 (☎67/522171; ④). Simpler, less expensive options include *Residencial Sur Austral* at Prat 334 (☎67/522150; ③) and *Hospedaje Paola* at Lago Brown 150 (☎67/522215; ③). All of these places provide **meals**, though you could also try *El Fogón* at San Valentín 651 for filling *parilladas* and *Café El Farolito* at Teniente Merino 546 for sandwiches and other light snacks. While in town, you could make a day-trip to the **Reserva Nacional Tamango** (daily 8.30am–6.30pm; CH$1500), 9km east, set on the banks of **Lago Cochrane**, a skinny, twisting lake that straddles the Argentinian border. The reserve is notable for its population of wild *huemul* (an endangered species of native deer), which can be observed on five-hour guided walks with Conaf rangers (around CH$5000 per person). You can get more information from Conaf in Cochrane on the northwest corner of the square (☎67/422164).

South of Cochrane, the road continues for 125km to the tiny, bleak settlement of **PUERTO YUNGAY**, winding past emerald lakes and fast-flowing rivers, and giving sporadic but clear views onto the Campo de Hielo Norte. Other than for a sense of completion, or the reward of getting to the utmost end of one of the most isolated highways in the world, there's not much point in going to Puerto Yungay, which consists of little more than a military camp housing the construction team extending the Carretera Austral to Villa O'Higgins, 100km south. There's no place to stay, nowhere to eat, and apart from camping wild, your only option is to turn around and head back to Cochrane.

travel details

Buses

Chaiten to: Coyhaique (2–4 weekly; 12hr); Futaleufú (6–7 weekly; 3hr 30min); La Junta (3 weekly; 3hr).

Coyhaique to: Chaitén (2–4 weekly; 12hr); Cochrane (4 weekly; 10hr); La Junta (2 weekly; 6hr); Puerto Aisén (15 daily; 1hr); Puerto Cisnes (1 daily; 4hr); Puerto Ibáñez (1 daily; 2hr 30min); Punta Arenas (1 weekly Jan & Feb; 24hr).

Ferries

Caleta Gonzalo to: Hornopirén (Jan & Feb 1 daily; 5hr).

Caleta Puelche to: La Arena (7–10 daily; 30min).

Chacabuco to: Laguna San Rafael (Dec–March 2 weekly; 5–16hr); Puerto Montt (2–4 weekly; 24hr); Quellón (1–3 weekly).

Chaitén to: Puerto Montt (1–4 weekly; 10hr); Quellón (1–4 weekly; 5hr).

Hornopirén to: Caleta Gonzalo (Jan & Feb 1 daily; 5hr).

La Arena to: Caleta Puelche (7–10 daily; 30min).

Flights

Balmaceda (Coyhaique) to: Puerto Montt (4 daily; 1hr); Santiago (4 daily; 3hr).

CHAPTER NINE

CHILEAN PATAGONIA AND TIERRA DEL FUEGO

A country of windswept bleakness, whose settlements seem to huddle with their backs against the elements, **Chilean Patagonia** and the **Tierra del Fuego** archipelago, tucked away right on the bottom of the South American continent, exercise a fascination over the minds of many travellers. Some come to hike in Chile's most famous national park, **Torres del Paine**, a massif crowned with otherworldly granite towers; others want to follow in the footsteps of the region's famous travellers, such as the navigator Ferdinand Magellan, the naturalist Charles Darwin, or more recently, the author Bruce Chatwin. Others just want to look at the **glaciers** that calve into the sea, or visit the **penguin sanctuaries**, or just see what it's like, down here at the end of the world.

The far south of Chile was originally inhabited by the hunters of the bleak Patagonian desert and the seafaring canoeists of the hundreds of rainy islands, fjords and shores of the western coast. The first European to discover the area was Ferdinand Magellan, a Portuguese navigator in the service of the Spanish crown, searching for a westerly sea route to the legendary Spice Islands and their untold wealth. The area was quickly colonized by the Spanish, and by 1584 there were two settlements, both of which failed catastrophically (see box p.396). No European tried to settle the place again for another two hundred and fifty years.

It was the voyages, from 1826 to 1834, of the ship *The Beagle* that renewed interest in the area. *The Beagle* was sent out by the British admiralty to explore the Magellan Strait, and on board as naturalist was none other than the young Charles Darwin. This foreign interest disturbed the Chileans, who had always considered this land theirs, and so in 1843, they sent their first settlers to the area. This disturbed the Argentinians, who had considered the area *theirs*, and in the 1870s the two narrowly avoided war over the territory. But it wasn't until the discovery of gold and the realization that the land was excellent for sheep farming, that the settlements of either the Argentinians or the Chileans amounted to much. The goldrush didn't last long, but sheep farming did, and the late-nineteenth century was a time of great wealth for the owners of sheep *estancias*.

Wool is no longer the big earner it was, and these days has been replaced by oil as the region's main resource. The territorial squabbles have for the most part settled down

ACCOMMODATION PRICE CODES

Prices are for the cheapest **double room** in high season. At the lower end of the scale, **single travellers** can expect to pay half this rate, but mid- and upper-range hotels usually charge the same for a single as for a double. For more information see p.27 in Basics.

① Less than US$10/CH$4800
② US$10–20/CH$4800–9600
③ US$20–30/CH$9600–10,080
④ US$30–50/CH$10,080–24,000
⑤ US$50–75/CH$24,000–36,000
⑥ US$75–100/CH$36,000–48,000
⑦ US$100–150/CH$48,000–72,000
⑧ over US$150/over CH$72,000

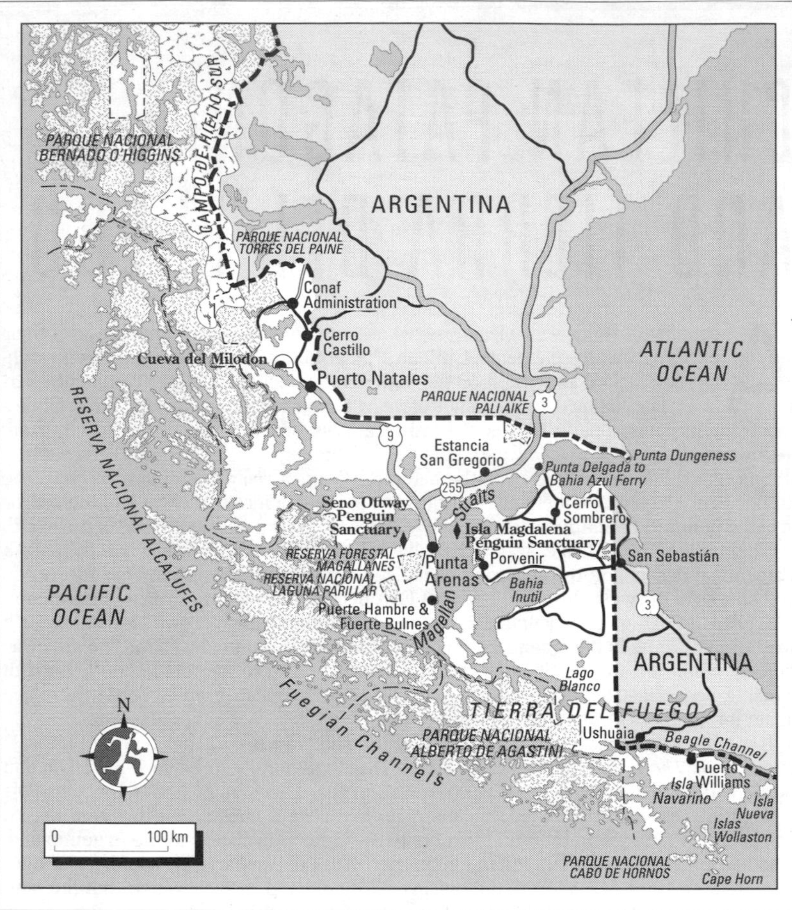

(although Argentina and Chile almost went to war in 1978 over a couple of small uninhabited islands), and Chile now occupies all land either side of the Magellan Strait (right the way across to the Atlantic Ocean) and half of Tierra del Fuego. The Chileans call the area the province of **Magallanes**, and it's one of the least inhabited areas in Chile. Magallanes' capital is the city of **Punta Arenas**, and the only other towns of any size are **Puerto Natales** in the northwest, gateway to Torres del Paine, and **Porvenir** in Chilean Tierra del Fuego, shivering on the opposite side of the Magellan straits to Punta Arenas.

CHILEAN PATAGONIA

Patagonia is a wide area of steppe to the east of the Andes, mostly in Argentina but shared at the bottom of the continent with Chile, separated from Tierra del Fuego by the Magellan Strait. It's cursed by a persistent wind, and trees grow horizontally here, sculpted by the gales. It's still pretty much as it was when described by the eccentric nineteenth-century English traveller, Lady Florence Dixie: "Nowhere else are you so completely alone. Nowhere else is there an area of 100,000 square miles which you may gallop over, and where, whilst enjoying a healthy, bracing climate, you are safe from the persecution of fever, friends, savage tribes, obnoxious animals, telephones, letters and every other nuisance you are elsewhere liable to be exposed to."

Chilean Patagonia is made up of four distinct areas: the region around **Punta Arenas**; the region around **Puerto Natales** containing **Parque Nacional Torres del Paine**; the broad expanse of frigid grassland between the two, stretching to the Atlantic coast and the **Parque Nacional Pali Aike**; and the remote, hardly visited **islands** of the western coast. Punta Arenas and Puerto Natales are linked by an excellent and frequent **bus** service, and the area around Parque Nacional Pali Aike is served by the occasional bus. However, there's no realistic way of getting to the islands of the western coast without your own boat.

Punta Arenas and around

Seen from the air, **PUNTA ARENAS**, 3090km south of Santiago, seems lost in the flat barren plains and vast expanses of water that surround it, a sprawling patchwork of galvanized tin roofs, struggling up from the shores of the Magellan Strait. On the ground, however, the city looks much more substantial and modern, especially in the centre where glass and concrete office-blocks have replaced the ramshackle wooden houses, paid for in part by the oil that's been flowing into the city since the first wells went on-stream in 1945.

Punta Arenas started life 60km south of where it is now, at a place called **Fuerte Bulnes**, the first Chilean settlement along the Magellan Strait. Fuerte Bulnes was founded in 1843 by Captain John Williams, a seaman from Bristol in the service of the Chileans, to forestall any other country's attempts at colonization. In 1848 the new settlement moved to a more suitable location to the north, named by an English sailor "Sandy Point", which became Punta Arenas in Spanish. It was originally envisaged as a penal colony, but it ran into trouble just three years after the move when the prisoners revolted, executed the governor, captured two visiting ships (marooning their passengers), and attempted to escape to Brazil. It was only because of the courage of the American skipper of one of the captured boats, and the fact that the mutineers got blind-drunk on looted French brandy, that they were recaptured.

Punta Arenas blossomed in the nineteenth-century sheep boom, when thriving immigrant communities sprang up and left their marks – the British built **St James' Church** and the **British School**, and other nationalities constructed the magnificent houses around the central **Plaza Muñoz Gamero**. Today Punta Arenas is enjoying another boom of sorts, with oil revenues flowing into the town and the **Zona Franca** ("duty free zone") attracting shoppers and some tourists, and some good museums, especially the **Museo del Recuerdo**.

Despite these attractions, Punta Arenas is not the most scintillating of places – Lady Florence Dixie opined: "I suppose there may possibly be drearier places but I do not think it is probable" – but it *is* the only city in the south, well-equipped with services, and a useful base for exploring Chilean Patagonia and Tierra del Fuego. It's also close to a handful of charming local attractions – the two nearby **penguin sanctuaries** of **Isla Magdalena** and **Seno Otway**, and to the west, the **Reserva Forestal Magallanes**.

Arrival and information

Most travellers arrive at the **airport**, 20km north of town. It's quite a busy little place, with ATMs and car-rental desks. Taxis to the centre charge CH$5000, minibuses CH$2000 and

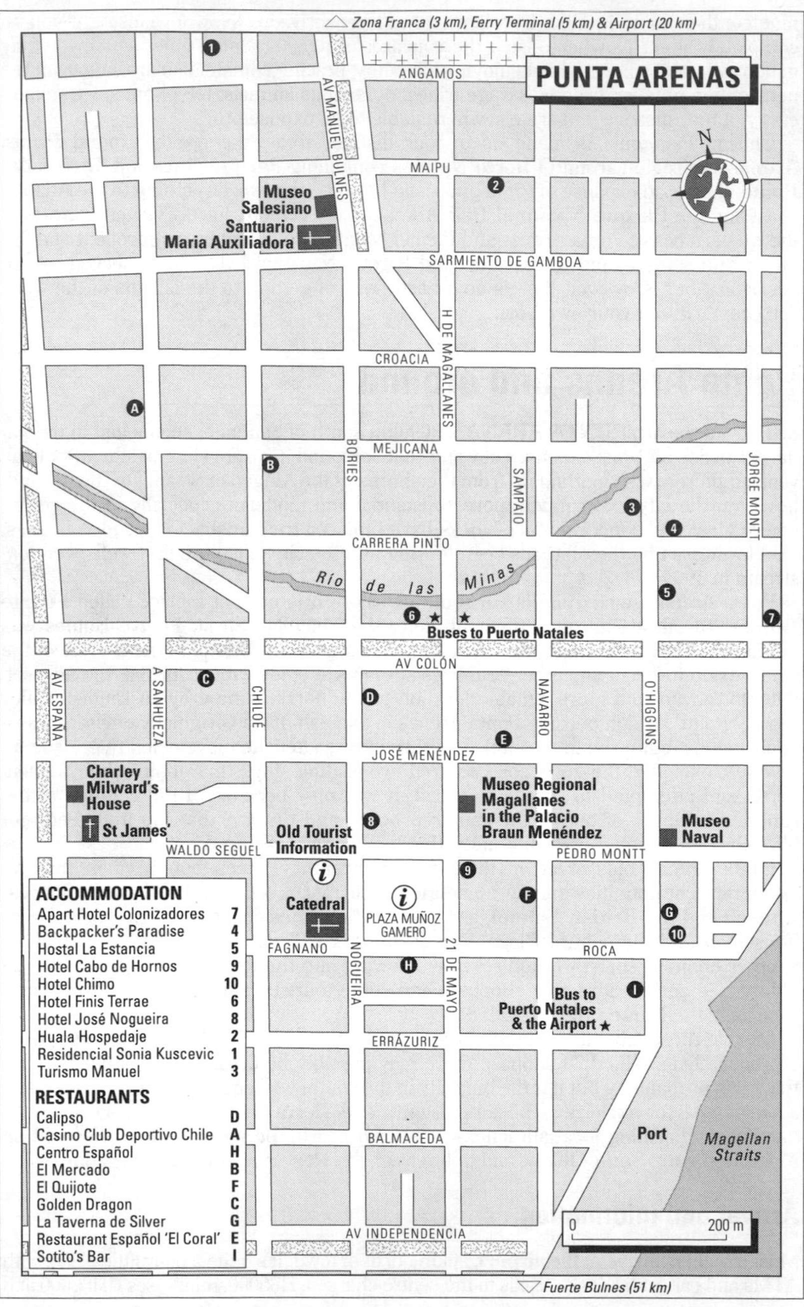
Zona Franca (3 km), Ferry Terminal (5 km) & Airport (20 km)
PUNTA ARENAS
N
ANGAMOS
AV MANUEL BULNES
MAIPU
Museo Salesiano
Santuario Maria Auxiliadora
SARMIENTO DE GAMBOA
H DE MAGALLANES
CROACIA
MEJICANA
BORIES
SAMPAIO
JORGE MONTT
CARRERA PINTO
Río de las Minas
Buses to Puerto Natales
AV COLÓN
AV ESPAÑA
A SANHUEZA
CHILOÉ
NAVARRO
O'HIGGINS
JOSÉ MENÉNDEZ
Charley Milward's House
St James'
Museo Regional Magallanes in the Palacio Braun Menéndez
Museo Naval
WALDO SEGUEL
Old Tourist Information
PEDRO MONTT
Catedral
PLAZA MUÑOZ GAMERO
FAGNANO
NOGUEIRA
21 DE MAYO
ROCA
Bus to Puerto Natales & the Airport
ERRÁZURIZ
BALMACEDA
Port
Magellan Straits
AV INDEPENDENCIA
0
200 m
Fuerte Bulnes (51 km)
ACCOMMODATION
Apart Hotel Colonizadores 7
Backpacker's Paradise 4
Hostal La Estancia 5
Hotel Cabo de Hornos 9
Hotel Chimo 10
Hotel Finis Terrae 6
Hotel José Nogueira 8
Huala Hospedaje 2
Residencial Sonia Kuscevic 1
Turismo Manuel 3
RESTAURANTS
Calipso D
Casino Club Deportivo Chile A
Centro Español H
El Mercado B
El Quijote F
Golden Dragon C
La Taverna de Silver G
Restaurant Español 'El Coral' E
Sotito's Bar I

buses – run by a company called Transfer (☎61/223205) – charge CH$1000. The bus meets most flights, and normally hangs around on the far side of the car park.

Punta Arenas doesn't have a single bus terminal, so different bus companies drop passengers at various points around town, though all within five blocks of the Plaza Muñoz Gamero. The other way to get to Punta Arenas is by **ferry** from Tierra del Fuego – the ferry terminal is a taxi-ride from the Plaza, on the outskirts of Punta Arenas to the north.

Information

Punta Arenas has an excellent joint **Sernatur** and **Oficina de Turismo** kiosk in the Plaza Muñoz Gamero (Nov–March Mon–Fri 8.15am–8pm, Sat & Sun 10am–8pm; April–Oct Mon–Fri 8.15am–1pm & 3–6.30pm; ☎61/221644), with helpful staff and lots of information on both the city and the region. **Conaf** is at José Menéndez 1147 (Mon–Thurs 8.30am–5.50pm, Fri 8.30am–4.50pm; ☎61/223420) – it's informative about the area's national parks and reserves, though rather surprisingly doesn't have any maps.

Accommodation

Punta Arenas boasts a wide range of hotels, hostels and *residenciales* in all price ranges. However, the cheapest places fill up quickly and don't take bookings, so to be sure of a budget room you'll need to arrive early.

Apart Hotel Colonizadores, Av Cristóbal Colón 1108 (☎ & fax 61/226587). Modern, clean, fully equipped two-bedroom apartments. ⑤.

Backpacker's Paradise, Ignacio Carrera Pinto 1022 (☎61/222554). The most popular backpackers' hostel in town, with 30 bunks in two open-plan rooms. Cable TV, Internet access and use of the kitchen. CH$3000 a bunk.

Dinka's House, Caupolicán 169 (☎61/226056). Run by a large, Germanic-looking woman with small fragile servants, this velvet-curtained family house overflows with people, who seem to spend most of their time eating. It's very welcoming, but it can be noisy and it's eight blocks from the Plaza. ②.

Hostal La Estancia, O'Higgins 765 (☎61/249130). Excellent little place, warm and hospitable, with bright rooms on the first floor of a house, all set around a communal landing. ③.

Hotel Cabo de Hornos, Plaza Muñoz Gamero 1025 (☎ & fax 61/242134). A monolithic edifice, dominating the city centre, that contains a good hotel. The depressing bar is only slightly cheered by a stuffed orange ostrich. ⑦.

Hotel Chimo, Roca 1038 (☎61/244259). It's a little overpriced, some rooms have broken glass in the windows, plywood walls and no heaters, but the lounge is comfy, the people are friendly, and it's very central. ②.

Hotel Finis Terrae, Av Cristóbal Colón 766 (☎61/228200, fax 248124). A spanking new modern hotel with a penthouse restaurant which has good views over the city. ⑧.

Hotel José Nogueira, Bories 959 (☎61/248840, fax 248832; *nogueira@chileaustral.com*; *www.hotelnogueira.com*). A beautiful location on the Plaza, in the Palacio Sara Braun. The rooms are a little cramped because of the restrictions of converting this old building into a hotel, but it's still the most stylish place to stay in Punta Arenas. ⑧.

Huala, Maipu 851 (☎61/244244). A very good little hostel – perhaps a little far out at seven blocks from the centre – with a double room and a bunk room, kitchen for residents' use and a friendly English-speaking owner. This is where the volunteers for the Seno Otway penguin sanctuary stay when they're in town. ②.

Residencial Sonia Kuscevic, Pasaje Darwin 175 (☎ & fax 61/248543). Established twenty years, a compact *residencial* in a 1970s building with parking. Discount for IYHA members. ③.

Turismo Manuel, O'Higgins 648 (☎61/220567, fax 221295). The cheapest place in town, basic, noisy and a bit squalid, but friendly. Cable TV, Internet access and use of the kitchen. CH$25000.

The City

Set on a bleak windy edge of the Magellan Strait, Punta Arenas – disturbingly for a Chilean city – faces eastward to the ocean. The city has four main streets, all designed to be wide enough to drive sheep down: the north–south streets are avenidas España and Bulnes, the east–west are avenidas Independencia and Colón. Contained within these streets, the centre of town is quite compact, and focused around the central **Plaza Muñoz Gamero**. The main shopping street, **Bories**, which runs north from the west of the Plaza, bustles with people especially when the sun's out, but the rest of town has a Sunday-afternoon feeling even midweek.

Around the Plaza

The **Plaza Muñoz Gamero** is a tranquil place, with shady pathways under magnificent hundred-year-old Monterey cypresses, thronged with strolling couples of an evening. In the middle is an imposing **monument to Ferdinand Magellan**, donated by the sheep baron José Menéndez, who modestly ensured that his name was just about as big as Magellan's. You'll notice that the toe of one stylized Ona Indian has been polished to a shine – if you touch it (some say kiss it), the tradition is that you'll return to Punta Arenas.

Around the Plaza are several grand houses dating from the wool boom. The only one you can visit is the **Palacio Sara Braun** (Mon–Fri 3–6pm; CH$500), on the northwestern corner, now divided between the Club de la Union and the *Hotel José Nogueira* (see "Accommodation", overleaf). Designed by a French architect, Numa Mayer, for Sara Braun, widow of one of the great sheep barons, it originally rivalled the great houses of Santiago. It was built over nine years from materials imported from Europe at great expense, and after forty years of renovation is once again full of marble fireplaces and crystal chandeliers.

If you walk along the northern edge of the square to calle Hernando de Magallanes and turn north, you'll find another glorious house: the **Palacio Braun Menéndez**. It's no longer a family house, donated to the nation some years ago to form the home of the **Museo Regional Magallanes** (Nov–March Tues–Fri 11am–5pm, Sat & Sun 11am–2pm; April–Oct Mon–Fri 11am–1pm; CH$800, free on holidays). Overshadowed by ancient evergreen trees, the exterior looks rather gloomy in contrast to the brilliance of the interior, which is naturally lit by a glass cupola in the roof. After donning soft overshoes to protect the polished wooden floors, you can visit the beautifully preserved private quarters which reveal a time-capsule turn-of-the-century French family home. Lavishly decorated and filled with European furniture and paintings, the dining room, bedrooms and sitting rooms recall a wealthy middle-class lifestyle achieved by few who came to Patagonia in search of it. Standing in his gleaming snow-white bathroom, you can easily imagine the larger-than-life Russian immigrant Braun Hamburguer enjoying a good hot soak after supervising the shearing of his two million sheep out on the desolate pampas.

Seven of the fourteen rooms in the museum are devoted to a permanent exhibition detailing the colonization of Patagonia and Tierra del Fuego. The rooms leading off the hall contain sepia photographs of the city, depicting its ramshackle and temporary appearance during the early years, while dusty old account books and documents reveal that the founding families controlled not only the sheep trade, but an immense range of other commercial activities. In effect, they *were* the city.

Half a block downhill is the **Museo Militar** at José Menéndez 961 (Tues–Fri 9am–12.30pm & 3–7pm; free), whose display of army uniforms and weapons will only interest the enthusiast, and, another block south, the more interesting **Museo Naval y Maritimo** at Pedro Montt 989 (Tues–Sat: Jan–March 9.30am–12.30pm & 3–6pm; April–Dec 9.30am–12.30pm & 2–5pm; CH$300), with a collection of minutely detailed scale-models of Chilean naval ships and, to emphasize the Chilean claim to the Antarctic, a glass freezer containing a blue lump of Antarctic ice.

FERDINAND MAGELLAN

Ferdinand Magellan was born in about 1480 in Portugal, and had an adventurous early life: in his twenties he saw service with the Portuguese fleets in their wars against the Muslims of the Indian Ocean, and by 1515 he was a veteran of the campaigns in Morocco, where he picked up a wound which made him limp for the rest of his life. In 1516, as a result of being refused a rise in his pension by the king of Portugal, Magellan took his services to Spain.

These days were the beginning of European exploration, prompted mainly by the desire to seek out new routes to the east, and its valuable Spice Islands (the Moluccas of Indonesia). The Portuguese had an early start, and managed to dominate the sea lanes around the coast of Africa, prompting other European powers to search for alternative routes. Magellan believed that the answer lay to the west, under or through the newly discovered American continents, and he asked the king of Spain, Charles I, to fund his search. Charles agreed, eager to prove that the Spice Islands lay in the half of the New World that the pope had just assigned to Spain.

On September 20, 1519, Magellan sailed west as admiral of a fleet of five ships. They crossed the Atlantic Ocean, entered the bay of Río de Janeiro on December 13, and started to search the coast of South America for the elusive passage. It was a long and hard hunt, and not all Magellan's fleet believed there was a strait: on Easter Day 1520 Magellan had to quash a mutiny by his Spanish captains. But on October 21, 1520, his flagship, the *Trinidad,* finally rounded Cabo Virgenes and entered the strait that now bears his name. Thirty-six days later the open seas of an ocean were sighted, and Magellan wept for joy. They named the new ocean "the Pacific" for its calmness after the storms of the strait, and set out across it. They did not expect it to be so wide.

They sailed for four months without seeing land. Their food and water ran out: "We ate only old biscuit reduced to powder, which stank from rat droppings ... and we drank water that was yellow and stinking. We also ate the ox hides that were under the main yard... and sawdust, and rats each of which cost a ducat." Then Magellan himself was killed in a fight with the natives of Mactán Island, but the fleet didn't turn back, petrified of attempting to go through the straits at the bottom of South America for a second time. Three years after they'd set out, just one of Magellan's original five ships finally limped back to Spain. It was loaded with spice (cloves and nutmeg) and manned by only eighteen of the original crew, men wasted and half-dead, "weaker than men have ever been before". The voyage's chronicler said he could not imagine the journey ever being repeated.

Three blocks south of Pedro Montt, is the shabby **port**. Dotted along the shore to the south, the remains of rusting wrecks are reminders of the treacherous southern waters and fierce winds that scourge Punta Arenas: the most impressive are the bare ribs of the *Lord Lonsdale*, beached here in 1942. There are, however, no remains of the most spectacular wrecking of a ship at Punta Arenas, that of the Royal Navy cruiser *HMS Dotterel*. On April 26, 1881, the *Dotterel* was anchored out in the bay when its ammunition exploded. The ship was blown into thousands of pieces, which were scattered over Punta Arenas, along with three hundred of the ship's company. Every window in Punta Arenas was broken by the blast. One of the five survivors was the ship's captain who noticed a small detonation while relaxing in a hot bath in his cabin, and, realizing that something was amiss, squirmed out of his porthole and dived into the sea. When the mammoth secondary explosion struck, he'd swum some distance from the ship and escaped unharmed, apart from having all his hair singed off.

St James' Church and the British School

Three blocks west of the Plaza, along Waldo Seguel, are two modest but finely proportioned buildings, **St James' Church** and the **British School** (neither of which would be out of place in an English market town), which recall the days when the British influence in Punta Arenas was at its zenith. In those days, the town was still called Sandy Point, sterling was widely accepted as currency, and the community was dominated by one Charley Milward, distant relative of the author **Bruce Chatwin**. Chatwin wrote his travelogue *In Patagonia* about his trip here to learn more about Milward, ex-sea captain and adventurer, who helped discover a chunk of a deep-frozen prehistoric ground sloth in the Cueva del Milodon (see p.404). Around the corner at España 959 you can see Milward's old house (not open to the public), part Victorian parsonage, part castle. It was here that the famous explorer Sir Ernest Shackelton stayed in 1914, and planned the rescue of his stranded crew, after his ship the *Endurance* was crushed by ice in the Antarctic.

If you cross Avenida España and climb some steps up to the **Mirador Cerro la Cruz**, there's a pretty view over the city's multicoloured roofs.

Museo Salesiano Maggiorino Borgatello and around

Seven blocks north of the plaza, on the west side of the wide Avenida Manuel Bulnes, is the **Santuario María Auxiliadora**, a grimy, grim-looking neo-gothic church and convent. The bland interior of the church contains more than its fair share of grotesquely tormented statuary, complete with toupees made from human hair. To the right of the church is the **Museo Salesiano Maggiorino Borgatello** (Tues–Sun 10am–1pm & 3–6pm; CH$1000). Amongst the cases of geological samples, jars of pickled marine animals and trays of mounted insects, displays vividly depict the daily life of the extinct Fuegian Indians. The weapons used by these accomplished hunters varied amongst the different tribes: the Alacaluf and Yahgan canoe Indians made long spears with viciously barbed heads for catching fish while the Ona (Selk'nam) and Haush were expert bowmen and used different types of arrows depending on their prey. The Europeans regarded the Tehuelches as the finest horsemen they had ever seen, and marvelled at the skill with which they could bring down a guanaco or rhea (a type of ostrich, locally called a *ñandú*) using *bolas* (a throwing weapon of heavy balls linked with string). The museum has a large collection of these weapons and the stone tools used to make them.

One room of the museum is completely taken up by a full-size copy of the **Cave of Hands**, near Chile Chico, 1600km north of Punta Arenas (see p.382). The 11,000-year-old rock paintings are typical of the nomadic art found throughout Patagonia. The hand paintings, which give most of these caves their name, were created in two ways: either by wetting the rock with blood and pressing a hand on it, or by blowing ground rock around a hand, creating a silhouette. The other paintings include purely geometric designs and delicately illustrated guanacos and rheas.

Two blocks north of the Museo Salesiano, on the other side of Avenida Bulnes, is the **cemetery** (daily 7.30am–10pm; free), which covers four city blocks. Amidst the network of footpaths lined with immaculately clipped cypresses, this eclectic necropolis reflects the turbulent history of Patagonia in marble and stone. The simple statue of a solitary Fuegian Indian, and the solemn epitaphs on the headstones of the pioneers and sailors interred far from their native soil, are dwarfed by the ostentatious mausoleums constructed at the end of last century. In 1919, 25 years after the cemetery opened, Sara Braun commissioned the imposing Neoclassical entrance to the cemetery, but even this is but a modest attempt at immortality in comparison with José Menéndez's colossal replica of Victor Emmanuel II's wedding-cake tomb in Rome.

The Museo del Recuerdo and Zona Franca

Take one of the many buses or *colectivos* from the centre with "Zona Franca" written on the front and you'll arrive 3km north of the centre of town at Punta Arenas' **Zona Franca**. An industrial park with shops, the Zona is Punta Arenas' duty-free shopping zone, and the south's temple to consumerism. There's a big shopping mall, mainly packed with electrical retailers, and a street of large shops with a quite bewildering array of whisky, including bizarre brands like Dunhill and Burberrys.

Outside the Zona, on the grass in the middle of Avenida Bulnes, is a life-size statue of a shepherd, his dog, a horse and some sheep. Realistically portrayed struggling into the teeth of a gale, these figures represent the first three hundred ewes brought to Punta Arenas in 1876. On the other side of the Avenida is the **Instituto Patagonia**, a centre for cultural and scientific research set in extensive grounds which also contain the **Museo del Recuerdo** (Mon–Fri 8.30–11.30am & 3–6pm, Sat 8.30am–1pm; CH$500). This "museum of recollections" is an open-air display of horse-drawn vehicles, farm machinery, steam engines and cars used in the region at the turn of the century. There is also a small-scale replica of the reconstructed Fuerte Bulnes (see p.387) and some timber-framed buildings from an old *estancia*, built between 1870 and 1930. These old pioneers' houses, originally sited 50km south of the city, were declared national monuments in 1974, and were brought here ten years later. There's also a *trinero*, or sledge, a common form of transport in southern Chile because of the wet climate and steep terrain. Two of the other exhibits show the Chilean love of nicknames: the municipal refuse cart was also used to pick up stray dogs, and therefore became known as the *perrera* ("dog-catcher's wagon"); while the cumbersome steamroller was dubbed *la bicicleta del Alcalde* or the Mayor's bicycle.

Eating and drinking

It's an affordable pleasure to eat out in Punta Arenas, and the local speciality of *centolla* (king crab), either on its own or in a chowder (*chupe*) is a delight. All the country's excellent wines are widely available, and due to the Zona Franca, imported lagers are easier to find in Punta Arenas than elsewhere.

Calipso, Carlos Bories 817. Good value three-course set lunches in the week for CH$2000, and enormous Calipso Burgers, double hamburger with all the trimmings and chips, for CH$3400.

Casino Club Deportivo Chile, Armando Sanhueza 546. A friendly place, though not used to tourists, specializing in cheap but well-cooked traditional Chilean dishes like *curanto* (meat and seafood stew) and *cazuela de cordero* (lamb broth).

Centro Español, Plaza Muñoz Gamero 771. You get a lovely view over the Plaza from the tables by the window, and the food's served by efficient (if brusque) waiters. Standard Chilean fare.

El Mercado, Mejicana 617, second floor. A 24-hour restaurant serving first-class seafood. There's a full-size *centolla* mounted on the wall so you can see just how big these monsters really are.

El Quijote, Lautaro Navarro 1087. Red neon in the window, and polished chrome tube seats inside make this place look seedier than it really is. The set lunches are good and cheap (CH$2000), and they also do shellfish.

Golden Dragon, Av Cristóbal Colón 529. A lovely old building which has been plastered with a standard Chinese-restaurant interior with good, gooey food, swimming in MSG.

Hotel José Nogueira, Carlos Bories 959 (☎61/240040). The restaurant in the vine-draped conservatory is beautiful. Relax with a pisco sour or enjoy a reasonably priced fillet steak with crab sauce (around CH$5200).

La Taverna de Silver, O'Higgins 1037. They've not spent much on the decor here, but they do a magnificent *centolla* chowder.

Restaurant Español "El Coral", José Menéndez 848. Excellent traditional restaurant, with an imaginative menu: try *conejo escabechado* (stew of marinaded rabbit), *cochinillo* (roast suckling pig), or *pescado al capricho* (fish in an elver and gill sauce), all at under CH$4000.

Sotito's Bar, O'Higgins 1138 (☎61/221061). Recently refurbished, so that the bare brick walls and starched linen tablecloths resemble a New York or London brasserie, this restaurant has attentive waiters serving large portions of meat and seafood – the *milanese de pollo* is fresh, big and tasty. Booking's a good idea at peak times.

Nightlife and entertainment

In summer it gets dark around 10.30pm in Punta Arenas, so the evening only really begins well past midnight. As a result, most places don't open their doors until around 1am and don't take off for another couple of hours.

Discotheque Abracadabra, Bories 655. When Puerto Montt's fashionable youth get bored of *Studio 54* they drift down to the *Abracadabra*, which is almost identical.

Discotheque Torreones, Km 5½-Sur. Described by the tourist office as "a disco for adults", it plays more Latin and Seventies music than its rivals.

Pub 1900, Bories 793, on the corner of Colón. Tinted glass and thick carpets, this laid-back café-bar is part of the average *Hotel Tierra del Fuego*, and is a good place to chill out a little.

Studio 54, Bories 448. Named after the famous club in New York, this place is popular with a young crowd, and plays techno music.

Listings

Airlines Avant, Broom Travel, Roca 924 (☎61/228312, fax 228322); DAP, O'Higgins 891(☎61/223340, fax 221693); Lan Chile, Lautaro Navarro 999 on the corner of Pedro Montt (☎61/241232 or 247079).

Banks and exchange Most of the banks are clustered around the Plaza. There are many *cambios*: El Conquistador, José Menéndez 556; Sur Cambios, Lautaro Navarro 1001; Tour América, Lautaro Navarro 1109.

Books There's a small shop in the Instituto Patagonia (see p.393), Av Bulnes, which sells recent issues of the institute's magazine and expensive, beautifully illustrated books. The institute's library is also open to visitors. Also try Southern Patagonia, Bories 404, and local 122-A in the Zona Franca.

Bus companies Bus El Pingüino, Armando Sanhueza 745 (☎61/221812), for Río Gallegos in Argentina; Bus Sur, Magallanes on the corner of Colón (☎61/244464), for tours to Seno Otway penguin colony, Puerto Natales, Coyhaique, Puerto Montt, and Chiloé; Buses Fernández, Armando Sanhueza 745 (☎61/242313), for Puerto Natales; Buses Ghisoni, Lautaro Navarro 971 (☎61/223205, fax 222078), for Río Gallegos in Argentina; Buses Punta Arenas, Pinto 457 (☎61/249868), for Puerto Montt and Chiloé; Transfer, Pedro Montt 966 (☎61/244475), for the airport, Puerto Natales and tours to the Seno Otway penguin colony; Buses Tecni Austral, Lautaro Navarro 975 (☎61/222078), for Ushuaia in Argentina; Turibus, Armando Sanhueza 745 (☎61/227970), for journeys throughout Chile. Remember that buses for anywhere north of Puerto Natales travel through Argentina.

Car rental América Rent a Car, José Menéndez 631 (☎ & fax 61/240852); Avis (Emsa) Roca 1044 (☎61/241182); Budget, O'Higgins 964 (☎61/241696); Hertz, O'Higgins 987 (☎61/248742); International, Waldo Seguel 443 (☎61/228323); Lubag Magallanes 970 (☎61/242023). Because there are so many loose stones on Patagonian roads, you are almost guaranteed to get a shattered windscreen or headlight, so it's a good idea to ask how much you'll have to pay if the car's glass gets damaged. Some companies (for example International) charge a fixed fee per crack, and don't ask you to pay for a whole new windscreen.

Consulates Argentina, 21 de Mayo 1878 (☎61/261912 or 261532, fax 261264); Belgium, Roca 817, Of. 61 (☎ & fax 61/241472); Brazil, Arauco 769 (☎61/241093, fax 226290); Denmark, Av Colón 819, Dpto. 301 (☎61/221488); Italy, 21 de Mayo 1569 (☎61/221596); Netherlands, Sarmiento 780 (☎61/248100); Paraguay, Av Bulnes 0928, Dpto.14, first floor (☎61/211825); Spain, José Menéndez 910 (☎61/243566, fax 226516); UK, Roca 924 (☎61/228312); Uruguay, José Nogueira 1238 (☎61/241053, fax 226822).

Hospital Hospital Regional, Angamos s/n between Señoret and Zenteno (☎61/242432).

Internet access CTC, O'Higgins 1099; Austrointernet, Bories 687, second floor, office 3; both CH$2000 an hour.

Laundry Lavasol, O'Higgins 969.

Photographic processing Foto Arno, Roca 974; Foto Centro, Bories 789.

Telephone offices CTC, O'Higgins 1099; Entel Baquedano 270.

Travel agents To visit the Torres del Paine national park, you're better off travelling up to Puerto Natales and visiting a travel agent there (see p.403). To visit the penguin sanctuaries or any of the sights near Punta Arenas, it's cheaper to use one of the bus companies' tours or ask in your hotel – trips cost around CH$4000 for a half-day. If you want to arrange a boat trip to Antarctica or the Falkland Islands, contact Turismo Cabo de Hornos, Plaza Muñoz Gamero 1039 (☎61/241321), which also has an office in Santiago at Augustinas 814, office 706 (☎2/633 9119, fax 633 8480; *hornos@chilepac.net*); or COMAPA, Av Independencia 830, second floor (☎61/224256, fax 225804),

MOVING ON FROM PUNTA ARENAS

The **ferry** for **Porvenir** in Tierra del Fuego is the *Barcaza Melinka*, an old tub-like landing craft with a three-storey metal house stuck on the back. It leaves from the ferry terminal, 5km north of town, Tuesdays through Saturdays at 9am, and on Sundays at 9.30am. It returns from Porvenir on Tuesdays, Thursdays and Saturdays at 12.30pm, on Wednesdays at 2pm, on Fridays at 3.30pm, and Sundays at 5pm. It costs CH$3100 for a foot passenger and CH$18,500 for a car.

Buses to **Puerto Natales** (4hr) leave regularly throughout the day from Avenida Colón, two blocks north of the plaza, and cost CH$3000 one way, CH$5000 return. There are also buses to Río Gallegos and Ushuaia in Argentina, Coyhaique, Puerto Montt and Chiloé – see "Listings" opposite.

The usual **airlines** (see "Basics" p.21) leave Punta Arenas' airport for every major Chilean city, and in summer, a small operator called **DAP** runs daily flights to Porvenir (CH$24,000 return) and bi-weekly flights to Puerto Williams (CH$67,000 return) and Río Grande (CH$86,500). In winter, the flights are half as frequent.

which also runs the Barcaza Melinka, the boat that visits the Isla Magdalena penguin sanctuary for CH$15,000. For a large, well-established general operator, contact Aventur, José Nogueira 1255 (☎61/241197, fax 243354) or Turismo Yamana, Av Colón 568, (☎61/221130, fax 240056).

South of Punta Arenas

Shortly after leaving Punta Arenas' city limits, the road becomes dirt, and as you drive south you're treated to views out over the Magellan straits to Tierra del Fuego – if it's not raining, that is. After 26km you come to a *Carabineros* checkpoint by an old, slightly rotting monument to Swiss settlers, where a signed road to the right (west) leads 16km past thousands of silver-black tree-stumps to the **Reserva Nacional Laguna Parrillar** (Jan–March Mon–Fri 9am–5pm; CH$900). A popular fishing and picnic spot, the wide, grey-black lake is surrounded by low bleak hills covered in a dense scrub, and flanked by stubby, withered trees. You can see fishermen wading out in all weathers attempting to catch salmon or trout, as fierce winds whip up white horses across the water. There are a couple of *fogóns*, which cost CH$1800 to use, and a fairly poor half-hour nature walk in a forest of lenga near the reserve's entrance. There's no public transport here, and camping's prohibited.

Returning to the main road, and continuing south, the next settlement is **PUNTA CARRERA**, just a couple of fishermen's shacks by the sea. It was here that some of the first *estancias* in the area were built, now transported to Punta Arenas (see p.393). There's a tiny historical **graveyard** by the side of the road, which is so small – only an enclosed patch of turf with a couple of modern crosses – that you'd never notice it but for the massive great signpost. Just south of here, 48km from Punta Arenas, there's a large **white obelisk** around which the road forks. Vaingloriously, this is a monument to the geographical centre of Chile, right here by the toe of South America. It takes into account, of course, Chilean Antarctic territory right down to the South Pole, most of which is claimed also by Argentina and (a little bizarrely) the UK.

The road to the left of the obelisk leads 12km south to **Puerto Hambre** ("Port Famine"). Puerto Hambre is the site of one of the first two Spanish colonies on the Magellan Strait and one of the saddest stories in the history of the Spanish empire (see box, overleaf). All that's left is a plaque, a concrete dolmen, and the ruins of a church, sitting forlornly on a little promontory exposed to the elements. The road to the right of the obelisk leads to **Fuerte Bulnes** (no set opening hours; free), a 1940s reconstruction of the first Chilean settlement in the area. Fuerte Bulnes was founded in September 1843 by a boatload of sailors from Ancud in Chiloé, captained by one John

HOW PUERTO HAMBRE GOT ITS NAME

In the sixteenth century, the Magellan Strait was one of the most important secrets in the world, guarded carefully by the Spanish, but by 1578 it had been discovered by the Englishman Francis Drake. The Viceroy of Peru, determined to close the strait to all but the Spanish, sent off his most skilled navigator, Pedro Sarmiento de Gamboa, to hunt Drake down and take him, dead or alive. Drake gave Sarmiento the slip, but Sarmiento realized that if the Spanish were to keep the strait for themselves, it had to be fortified and settled. He proposed to Charles I that the area be colonized, and in 1581 set sail from Spain with a massive expedition of 23 ships and 3000 people (the conquistador Pizarro had vanquished the Incas with a mere 168). Storms took some ships, others were sunk by English pirates, while yet more gave up and returned to Spain, but in 1583 Sarmiento made it to Cabo Virgenes, the Atlantic entrance to the strait, with a mere five ships and 500 men and women. However, as he was unloading his supplies a tempest blew up and forced four of his ships out to sea. For two weeks these ships attempted to sail back to the stranded colonists, before having to admit defeat and return to Spain, battered and almost wrecked.

Sarmiento was not disheartened, and started by founding a city half a league from Cabo Virgenes, calling it Nombre de Jesus. He continued on and founded another city, calling it Rey Don Felipe, building a wooden curtain wall, a chapel, a town hall and a monastery. Land was cleared and seed sowed. In time, Sarmiento decided to visit his first colony, and in his sole remaining ship set sail for Nombre de Jesus. Another storm blew up, and forced him out to sea, and despite all his efforts he could not return to the strait. "Seeing how desperate was their plight," he wrote, describing himself in the third person, "the Governor grieved more than at the loss of life itself, and could not contain his tears at the thought that he could not even take leave of his friends and companions."

He made for Brazil, intending to send the colonists help. He sent one ship, and it sank. He led another and it too sank – he himself only just survived by clinging to the wreckage. On the third attempt the crew mutinied, and he had to return to Brazil, from where he sent impassioned requests to the Spanish court that his colonists might be relieved or resupplied. These were refused. He resolved to travel to Spain and in 1585 embarked for Europe, but was captured by English pirates and taken to England. There he charmed Walter Raleigh into pleading his case, and Queen Elizabeth I released him. Sarmiento, still with his settlers in his heart, set off once more for Spain, and was promptly captured by French Huguenots. They didn't release him for two years. He finally secured his liberty, and in 1890 arrived at the Spanish court. No one listened to him. He died, old, scarred, worn by care, and not knowing what happened to his colonists.

What did happen is almost as sad as the fate of Sarmiento himself. By the end of 1586, only eighteen colonists were alive, the rest having starved. A year later they sighted a ship, and were aghast when they discovered that it wasn't a friendly Spanish galleon, but belonged to a squadron of corsairs under the English buccaneer Thomas Cavendish. Only one of the remaining colonists, a soldier called Tomé Hernández, trusted the Englishman enough to accept his offer of transport to Europe, and then the winds changed, and Cavendish sailed on. All the other settlers died. Cavendish, shocked by the wretched sight of the village, scored out the words "Rey Don Felipe" on his sea-chart and renamed it with the name it bears today: "Port Famine" ("Puerto Hambre" in Spanish).

Williams. They came to pre-empt colonization from Europe, and only just made it, because a few hours after they arrived a French warship, the *Phaeton*, turned up and planted the tricolour on the shore. After Williams protested the French moved off, and annexed Tahiti in the Pacific instead. A number of old cannon, sturdy but empty log cabins and a lookout tower have a decidedly neglected air, and the whole looks more like a children's adventure playground than an important national monument. Standing slightly apart is a small wooden **chapel**, adorned inside with gifts and supplications left by visitors, giving it a shrine-like atmosphere. In good weather you can see across the strait from the fort, and rising up behind Dawson Island are the 2000-metre peaks of the snow- and ice-covered Cordillera Darwin (further south in Tierra del Fuego), dominated by the majestic, solitary peak of Mount Sarmiento.

There's no public transport down here, and to reach Fuerte Bulnes without your own car you have to take a tour from Punta Arenas.

East and west of Punta Arenas

Just 10km west of Punta Arenas lies the **Reserva Forestal Magallanes** (Jan–March Mon–Fri 8.30am–5.30pm, Sat & Sun 8.30am–8.30pm; CH$900), 196 square kilometres of protected Magellanic forest. It's used mainly as a picnic centre, with dozens of *fogóns* hidden away in the trees or standing alone in the occasional glade. There's no camping here, and no public transport. The forest has two entrances, both of which provide wonderful views back over the city, across the Magellan Strait and towards Tierra del Fuego.

A road to the north leads to the reserve's main entrance, at a dense forest of short, stubby trees. There are a couple of hikes here, but the only one that's in any condition to use is the **Sendero las Lengas** (3km, 1hr) to the **ski centre**, the site of the second entrance, reached along the road to the south. Known as **Club Andino** or the Centro de esquí Cerro Mirador, the ski centre boasts a nature trail, with labels describing different tree species, and café that's open all year round (Tues–Sun). In winter, from June to August, it's a fabulous place to ski, with eleven runs through the forest, a chair-lift (CH$10,000 a day) and equipment for rent (CH$8500 per day).

Thirty-five kilometres east of Punta Arenas, two hours away by boat, there's the penguin sanctuary of **Monumento Natural Isla Magdalena**, one of the largest penguin colonies in southern Chile, with an estimated 120,000 birds. It's a small island, just one square kilometre, topped by a pretty red lighthouse, and surrounded by fifteen-metre-high cliffs. The cliffs are covered in tufts of grass, and it's under this that the penguins dig their burrows. They tend to be more frightened of humans than the penguins in Seno Otway (see p.397), so you can't get too close, but there are many, many more of them here. Isla Magdalena is visited by the *Barcaza Melinka*, operated by Turismo COMAPA (see p.394) on Tuesday, Thursday and Saturday at 3.30pm; a five-hour round trip costs CH$15,000.

North of Punta Arenas

To the north of Punta Arenas, just after the airport, there's a thin strip of pebbly beach, steep cliff and withered-tree forest, called **Parque Chabunco**, where locals come to picnic: the section by the road is very noisy, but down towards the beach it's better. Twenty-seven kilometres out of Punta Arenas there's a *Carabineros* checkpoint, at which the road forks, and a good dirt road strikes out to the left (west) across the open pampa towards the Seno Otway penguin sanctuary. The road crosses flat, bleak plains of brown-green grass, and passes the massive **Mina Pecket**, thought to be the world's largest surface coal reserve, an enormous complex of high, dark slag heaps and dirt and noise. After 65km, a couple of shacks appear over the brow of a hill, marking the **Seno Otway penguin sanctuary** (Sept–April 8am–8.30pm; CH$1800). A nesting site of 3000 Magallanic penguins (also called jackass penguins because of the braying noise they make), this is a non-profit-making organization, staffed by knowledgeable volunteers who give talks in Spanish, English, French and German. The area's divided into two zones, and there's a rope fence to keep you away from the penguins and give them some privacy.

In about September each year, the birds return to Seno Otway and find their mate – they're monogamous and remain faithful to one partner all their lives. They start burrowing, and lay two eggs in the nest, and when the chicks hatch they nurture the young, one adult remaining with the chick, the other going fishing. In late January the ground is covered with drifts of white down, blown about by the wind, as the hatched chicks shed their baby feathers ready for their first trips into the ocean. You'll get within a metre of the birds – they're remarkably tolerant of humans – as they half hide in the waving grass, but be careful if they start to cock their head from side to side, because you're disturbing them.

The best time to see the penguins is in the morning (before 10am) or evening (after 5pm), before or after they go fishing. Beachfront hides (you're not allowed on the beach itself) let you watch them amble out of the water, particularly amusing when they're en masse. However, penguin traffic jams are developing at about 5pm, because too many people are coming in the evening, and the penguins won't cross human paths if there's anyone around. They wait, sometimes for up to an hour, while the chicks get very hungry, so try if you can to make it here in the morning.

There's no public transport out to the Sanctuary, and most of the traffic out here is made up of tours, who don't like giving lifts to hitchers. Cyclists who try biking it will be punished by the persistent wind. The easiest way to get here, then, is to drive or join a tour, which take three hours and cost around CH$4000 to CH$5000. Tours are run by any of the operators listed on p.394, by many of the bus companies and by most hotels.

Northeast to the Atlantic Ocean

Heading northeast from Punta Arenas, you pass through grassland that's desolate, barren and harsh, formed by an elemental wind that colours the sky with ever-changing clouds, and blows with a persistence and ferocity that has to be felt to be believed. As you drive you can catch sight of grey, dowdy *ñandús*, and large brown-and-white guanacos, while if you're very lucky you might see a hairy armadillo, or *peludo*, which can only be closely approached from downwind because, although almost blind, it has a very acute sense of smell. When frightened, a *peludo* will dig itself into the ground at incredible speed. In the past, hungry *huasos* would try and dig out these little animals, usually a fruitless task, which has led to the job of extracting a vehicle from the mud being known locally as *peludiar*.

Sixteen kilometres after the turning to Seno Otway, you pass a semi-abandoned hotel called the *Hotel Cabeza del Mar*, wonderfully sited on a sheltered lagoon and looking like a French country *brasserie*. Shortly after this is a crossroads (48km from Punta Arenas), the left (northwest) fork leading to Puerto Natales. The right-hand fork leads to the Atlantic, through miles and miles of Patagonian steppe, past dozens of little piles of blue glass that are the remains of shattered windscreens. The large oil terminal of San Gregorio looms on the right, and with it the only petrol station within 340km.

A short distance further is the **Estancia San Gregorio**, once owned by José Menéndez, and part of his Sociedad Explotadora de Tierra del Fuego, which controlled 13,500 square kilometres of grazing land and owned two million sheep. All that's left are the weathered ochre bricks and peeling paintwork of several imposing old buildings, dominated by the escarpment behind. Dating back to 1882 these storehouses, shearing sheds and *huasos*' sleeping quarters have survived vandalism and revolution, but are now slowly rotting, accompanied on the seashore by the ribs of the sailing barque *Ambassador* and the steamship *Amadeo*, skeletal reminders of the Menéndez fleet.

The only buildings that are maintained are the pretty church – visible from the road but locked – and the old *estancia* house, off the road, at the end of a kilometre-long avenue of blasted trees which were once delicate topiary. At the end of the avenue is a gate flanked by pillars, crowned with a couple of eroded stone sheep. The gardens beyond are still prim and well-kept, surrounded by a high wooden fence for protection against the wind, and the house beyond is shut to the public.

Further down the main road there's the *Hotel Sanhueza* (no phone; ②), a wonderful place to thaw out after wandering around the *estancia*. You can warm yourself by a large old cast-iron stove, meet the hotel's friendly hairy dog, and eat well-prepared food – a set lunch costs CH$2500. The only other accommodation is the *Hostería El Tehuelche* (☎61/211245; ④), 30km further on, by the turning to the Primera Angostura (see below). The *hostería* was built a hundred years ago by an English *estancia* family, and retains its atmosphere of colonial opulence, with high airy rooms, polished wood floors and a large conservatory.

The Primera Angostura ("First Narrows") is the narrowest point of the Magellan Strait, and it's here that the **ferry to Tierra del Fuego** crosses from the mainland. The ferry leaves from the port of Punta Delgada 16km from the main road (not to be confused with the town of Punta Delgada 11km up the road towards Monte Aymond). It runs during daylight hours, and leaves about once every twenty minutes in summer, and once every ninety in winter, except at **low tide**, when it doesn't run at all – check with the ferry company, Transbordadora Austral Broom, Av Bulnes 05075, Punta Arenas (☎61/218100) or at Sernatur in Punta Arenas. The crossing takes thirty minutes, and costs CH$8000 for a car (foot-passengers are carried free).

Parque Nacional Pali Aike

Eleven kilometres beyond the turning for the ferry is the small town of Punta Delgada and the road heading 18km north to Chilean Patagonia's *other* national park, the small and pretty much unvisited **Parque Nacional Pali Aike** (dawn–dusk; free). The park's entrance looms up out of the barren rolling plains, green roof first, as if rising from the bowels of the earth. In sharp contrast to the rock castles of Torres del Paine over in the west, this is an area of flat heathland, very like Dartmoor in England, with tussocks of beige grass and enormous skies. Around the heath are scattered strange volcanic formations, pimples and towers, and either side of the road, there's the odd depression filled with evaporating water and ringed by white tide-marks, where you can occasionally see flamingos.

Almost half of the park, the eastern side nearer Argentina, is covered by fields of jagged black rock, the **Escorial del Diablo** ("Devil's slag heap"), surrounding a burst crater called the **Morada de Diablo** ("dwelling of the Devil"). To the south of the Escorial is a ridge of congealed lava, ten metres high, covered in black, orange and lime-green lichen and so full of holes and air bubbles that it looks like a piece of baroque carving, or a Japanese drawing of a wave, or a fractal. In this wall of rock, 8km from the park entrance, is **Pali Aike**, a cave excavated by the famous archeologist Junius Bird in 1937. He discovered a two-metre-deep sediment containing evidence of prehistoric inhabitation, including bones of the Milodon (prehistoric ground sloth) and an extinct American horse, dating from 9000 years ago. A nine-kilometre (2hr 45min) **walk** leads from the cave to remote **Laguna Ana** to the northwest, across flat, windy, exposed terrain (carry water).

Wild camping's not permitted in the park and there's no public transport here – the nearest you'll get is the main road, 25km away, on buses heading towards Río Gallegos in Argentina or Tierra del Fuego.

Back on the main road, it's another 22km before the **border crossing** at **Monte Aymond** (daily: Dec–March 24hr; April–Nov 8am–10pm). There's a basic, but decent nameless **hotel** here (☎61/694413; ③) which changes money.

Puerto Natales and around

Two hundred and forty-seven kilometres north of Punta Arenas, Patagonia's second city, **PUERTO NATALES**, has a stunning location at the edge of the pampa, sitting by a body of water fringed by tall peaks. There's not much in the town itself except travel agents, restaurants and accommodation, but its usefulness as a base for visiting the **Parque Nacional Torres del Paine**, the nearby **Cueva del Milodón**, the glaciers of the **Parque Nacional Bernardo O'Higgins**, and, over the border, the Argentinian Parque Argentino Los Glaciales, means it's flush with tourist dollars and filled with nylon-clad, Gore-tex-booted hikers. It's also a good transport hub, home to the terminal of the **Navimag** ferry from Puerto Montt in the Lake District, and linked to Punta Arenas by a good, regular bus service. Daily buses head up to Torres del Paine, and

there are also regular services over the border to Argentina and frequent tourist boats to the glaciers.

Arrival and information

The Navimag ferry terminal is on the Costanera, five blocks west of the Plaza de Armas (☎61/411421, fax 411642). There's no bus terminal, so each bus pulls in outside their company's offices, all a couple of blocks from the Plaza de Armas (see "Listings" for addresses).

A desk in the Museo Historico at Bulnes 286 (Mon–Fri 8.30am–12.30pm & 2.30–6pm, Sat & Sun 2.30–6pm; ☎61/411263) provides some **tourist information**, but you're better off at the good **Sernatur** office housed in a forlorn-looking shack a little out of town on the coast road from Punta Arenas (Dec–March Mon 8.30am–1pm & 2.30–6.30pm, Tues–Fri 8.30am–8pm; April–Nov Mon–Fri 8.30am–1pm & 2–6pm; ☎61/412125). The **Conaf** office, O'Higgins 584 (Mon–Fri 8.30am–6pm; ☎61/411438), is often woefully ill-equipped, so for information about Torres del Paine, visit Path@gone, the travel agent which runs the park's refuges (see box p.403).

Accommodation

There's no shortage of **accommodation** in Puerto Natales as many people let out rooms in their houses – you'll be offered half a dozen as you step off the bus. There's a good choice of more expensive hotels, too.

Almirante Nieto, Bories 206 (no phone). A good basic, bed and breakfast with a friendly welcome. ②.

Amerindian Concept, Ladrilleros 105 (☎61/410678, fax 410169). A large blue-and-yellow building right by the water, this hostel-cum-travel agency has top-floor rooms with unparalleled views towards the mountains, but when the wind picks up you can feel the walls shake. ③.

Café Melissa, Blanco Encalada 258 (☎61/411944). Primarily a café, but with some snug, bright rooms on the first floor. Beware the gold lamé bed-covers. ④.

Costaustralis, Av Pedro Montt 262 (☎61/412000). The best hotel in town, right on the waterfront, with modern rooms and all mod cons. ⑧.

Glaciares, Eberhard 104 (☎61/411452). Inside a building that can't make up its mind whether it's faux-Tudor or Swiss chalet-style, there's a clean and friendly modern hotel. ⑥.

Hospedaje Cecilia, Tomás Rogers 54 (☎ & fax 61/411797). A warm, cosy *hospedaje* with good beds, a decent breakfast and tasty, home-baked bread. ②.

Lady Florence Dixie, Bulnes 659 (☎61/411158, fax 411943). A long-established place, set back from the road like a motel. ⑥.

Niko's Residencial, E Ramirez 669 (☎61/412810). A firm favourite with backpackers, this is a good place to meet other travellers, and a handy alternative if *Patagonia Adventure*'s full. ②.

Patagonia Adventure, Tomás Rogers 179 (☎61/411028). A truly excellent hostel, right on the plaza, with good beds, warm rooms and friendly young owners who are into hiking. ②.

The Town

Puerto Natales is beautifully sited on Seno Ultima Esperanza ("Last Hope Sound"), a narrow turquoise channel that regularly gets whipped up with white horses. Grey mountains line the other side, coated with ice and snow, a contrast to the flat pampa to the east of the town. The name "Seno Ultima Esperanza" comes from the 1557 explorer, Juan Ladrilleros, who named it when he was at the end of his tether while searching for the western entrance to the Magellan Strait. He found it, but almost all his crew died in the attempt. Following in his footsteps is a little easier these days, as boats sail three times a day to the **Balmaceda** and **Serrano** glaciers, two rivers of ice that flow into the sea – see box on p.403.

Puerto Natales is a small town, centred, as ever, on a few blocks surrounding its **Plaza de Armas**. While hardly packed with distractions, it's a pleasant spot to prepare for a trek or unwind after it. Its most interesting feature is the **church** on the plaza, a bit uninspiring from the outside, but with a very beautiful altarpiece inside, occupying one entire wall and showing local Indians, dignitaries, the Madonna and Child, and, behind their shoulders, a delicate painting of the Torres del Paine.

Three blocks west of the Plaza, there's a small but well laid-out **Museo Historico Municipal** on Bulnes 285 (Mon–Fri 8.30am–12.30pm & 2.30–6pm, Sat & Sun 2.30–6pm; free). A carved Milodon (see p.404) with a silly smile guards the entrance to a room full of photos of Aonikenk and Kaweshkar Indians, the area's original inhabitants: some look unkempt and nervous, others quite noble, and all wear thick, heavy cloaks, clasped at the groin. The next room holds a collection of memorabilia relating to the region's first settler, a rather fierce-looking German called Herman Eberhard – look out for his ingenious collapsible boat. Next door to this are some relics of the Bories sheep packing plant (the ruins of which can still be seen on the outskirts of town) which used to process 300,000 sheep a year, such as a ceramic hot water bottle, a couple of firemen's helmets and a partially squashed trumpet. In a shed out the back there's the usual collection of stuffed animals: a black-necked swan, a *ñandú*, a condor (note the chicken-like feet – the stories of condors carrying away sheep and small children are all myths). If you're still interested in stuffed animals, then visit the one-room stuffed zoo of the **Museo Colegio Salesiano** at Padre Rossa 1456 (daily 10am–1pm & 3–6pm; free), down in the southeast of town.

Eating, drinking and nightlife

Puerto Natales is well served with restaurants, which cater for the thousands of tourists passing through each year. Because of this, like Pucón in the Lake District, the quality of food is surprisingly good for such a small town, and indeed is better than in many other places in Chile. However, unlike Pucón, Puerto Natales isn't blessed with bars and clubs – exhausted trekkers seem to prefer to collapse into bed rather than drink and dance.

Amerindian Concept, Ladrilleros 105. Sandwiches on wholemeal baps as big as dinner plates, and good pizzas in the evening, but it's all a little expensive.

Café Melissa, Blanco Encalada 258. A bit antiseptic, but with enormous windows which look out onto the main street, and enormous sandwiches to match.

Costaustralis, Pedro Montt 262. The hotel has two restaurants, both with beautiful views out over the Sound. The cafeteria serves standard Chilean food and is reasonable value (though *El Maritimo* is better, and you get the same view), and the upmarket restaurant serves international food at international prices.

Cristal, Bulnes 433–440. Pleasantly decorated in yellow and green, this is a good fish restaurant which offers, remarkably for Chile, fish prepared in other ways than frying. The salmon in butter is particularly good.

El Maritimo, Pedro Montt 214. The best place to come and refuel after a long trek, with truly enormous *lomo a la pobre*, and a glorious view to stare at while you digest.

La Esquina, Eberhard 301. The only nightclub in town, packed with exhausted trekkers feebly trying to dance.

La Tranquera, Bulnes 579. A popular meeting place, with decent standard Chilean fare served by surly waiters, walls covered with junk-shop paraphernalia, and a front strewn with flags.

Midas, Tomás Rogers 169. Cheerful café on the square, the only place in windswept Patagonia that attempts to keep tables and umbrellas upright outside on the pavement despite the gales.

Supermercado San Sebastian, Baquedano 570. A corner shop that sells good, cheap *empanadas* for a filling snack lunch.

Listings

Banks and exchange There's an ATM in Banco Santiago, Bulnes 436, and a whole string of *cambios* on Blanco Encalada, including Andes Patagónicos at no. 226, Latino Americana at no. 189 and Omega at no. 238.

Bus companies Austral Bus, Baquedano 384 (☎61/411859); Buses Fernandez, Eberhard 555 (☎61/411111); Bus Sur, Baquedano 534 (☎61/411325); Buses Transfer, Baquedano 414 (☎61/410681); Turismo Zaahj, Arturo Prat 236 (☎61/412260, fax 411355).

Camping equipment Most of the travel agents rent equipment, but try Path@gone, Eberhard 212, which has a wide range from stoves (CH$500 a day) and sleeping bags (CH$1500 a day) to kayaks. For butane cylinders, try the hardware shop Casa Pivcevic, Bulnes 613.

TOUR COMPANIES

There are a handful of standard tours run by every one of the dozens of travel agents in town: a half-day trip to the **Cueva del Milodon** (CH$3000), see overleaf; a day-trip to the Argentinian town and national park of **El Calafate** and the **Parque Argentino Los Glaciales** (from CH$28,000 – park entrance extra); a day-trip to **Torres del Paine** (CH$15,000 – park entrance extra), see p.405; and a boat trip up the Ultima Esperanza Sound to the **Balmaceda and Serrano glaciers**, see overleaf. For this last trip, there are two types of boat running: the *21 de Mayo* (CH$25,000) which is a slow single-hulled craft, and it also gives you the opportunity of travelling in small inflatable boats up the Serrano River to the Torres del Paine national park (see Onas, under Path@gone, below); and the two catamarans, *Campo de Hielos Sur* and *Our Lady of the Snows* (CH$28,000), which are pricier but get you to the glaciers more quickly, and allow you an extra hour to explore and perhaps go for an ice hike (see Amerindian below).

As usual, many of the operators offering standard tours are pretty indistinguishable, but we've selected some of the more reliable names. However, just because a company's not listed doesn't mean it's no good. There are also a few organizations in town offering a little more.

Amerindian Concept, Ladrilleros 105 (☎61/410678, fax 410169; *amerindi@entelchile.net*). As is obvious from the climbing wall bolted onto the outside of the building, this tour operator specializes in climbing. A day's ice-climbing costs US$50, a day's mountaineering from US$120. It also offers three days' kayaking down the río Serrano for US$380, and a five-hour ice-hike on the Grey glacier (see p.409) for US$50.

Aventur, Bulnes 698 (☎ & fax 61/410825). A Punta Arenas company that's recently expanded into Puerto Natales, and is now running one of the catamarans.

Baquedano Zamora, Cerro Castillo (☎61/412911). Based in the village of Cerro Castillo (see p.405), near the Torres del Paine park, these people can arrange horse trekking in Torres del Paine from a couple of hours (at around US$40 an hour), to longer hikes of up to four days.

Kundsen, Blanco Encalada 284 (☎ & fax 61/411819). A friendly old company.

Patagonia Ice, Blanco Encalada 183 (☎ & fax 61/410630). Runs the basic tours, changes money and deals with flights.

Path@gone, Eberhard 212 (☎61/413290; *pathgone@chileaustral.com*). The shared office of three of the biggest companies in Puerto Natales. **Andescape** and **Fantastico Sur** run the *refugios* in the Torres del Paine park, and are the first stop if you want to book a bed there, while the third company, **Onas**, specializes in water-based activities, especially trips up the Serrano river in a Zodiac inflatable boat (CH$30,000) and two days' sea kayaking (US$200).

Servitur, Arturo Prat 353 (☎61/411858, fax 411328). An established local company, specializing in tours to Torres del Paine.

MOVING ON FROM PUERTO NATALES

Buses to **Punta Arenas** (4hr) leave regularly throughout the day, from the various companies' addresses (see "Listings", overleaf) and cost CH$3000 one way.

The Navimag **ferry** to Puerto Montt leaves once a week and costs from CH$140,000. For more details, see p.401 and 26.

Buses to the Torres del Paine (3hr) leave every morning at 7am to 8am, and every afternoon at 1pm to 3pm. They're run by Andescape, JB, Buses Gomez, Servitur and Turexpress and cost CH$8000 return. They stop at three places in the park – the entrance at Laguna Amarga, the Lago Pehoe *Guardería* and the Park Administration. The trip takes three hours. From October to April, on Fridays and Saturdays, Turismo Zaahj, Prat 236 (☎ & fax 61/412260) runs buses from Puerto Natales to **El Calafate** in Argentina (CH$9000 one way). The trips take five hours. They leave El Calafate for Puerto Natales on Saturday and Sunday at 8am.

Car rental Andes Patagónicos, Blanco Encalada 266 (☎61/411594); EMSA at the *Hotel Martín Gusinde*, Ramírez 278 (☎61/410775).

Hospital Hospital Puerto Natales, Ignacio Carrera Pinto 537 (☎61/411582 or 411581).

Internet access Amerindian Concept, Ladrilleros 105 (6–11pm), and the rather unfriendly Rincon de Tata, 236 Pratt.

Laundry If you've a lot of washing, the cheapest place is at Bories 218 (CH$3000 for a large basket). If you've only got a couple of things to do, Lavendería del Milodón, Baquedano 642 will work out cheaper as it charges per item.

Photographic processing Foto Austral, Bulnes 5.

Puerto Natales to Torres del Paine

From Puerto Natales, a fast 150-kilometre road runs through flat Patagonian desert to the Torres del Paine national park. It's a dull drive, except for the **Cueva del Milodón** (8.30am–6pm; CH$2000), an obligatory stop after 21km.

Marked by a large plastic monster at the end of a five-kilometre dirt road left off the main route, the cave itself isn't much more than a hole in the ground, but it's a site of some importance. In 1895 the German settler Herman Eberhard, who owned the land bordering the cave, discovered a human skull and a large piece of skin from an unidentifiable animal. Over the next few years explorers systematically excavated the cave, and dug up an assortment of bones and more fragments of skin, which they eventually traced to a giant sloth called a *Milodón*. This creature was thought to be long extinct, but the excavated skin looked so fresh that rumours began to circulate that it might still be alive. In 1900 an expedition sponsored by London's *Daily Express* arrived to investigate, but no live creatures were found. The skin, it turned out, was so well preserved because it had been deep-frozen by the frigid Patagonian climate. However, the discovery of a stone wall across the cave, and of neatly cut grass stalks in the animal's faeces, led researchers to conclude that ten thousand years ago, a group of Tehuelche Indians had captured a giant sloth and kept it confined here. (Modern scientists disagree, and think that the Tehuelche herded guanacos here, not mylodons. Shortly afterwards, an unscrupulous gold prospector and Charley Milward (see p.391) dynamited the cave's floor, uncovering and then selling the remaining skin and bones. Two pieces made their way to Britain: one to the British Museum, the other to Charley Milward's family.

To the northwest of the cave, the Seno Ultima Esperanza continues on for about 100km until it meets the río Serrano, which, after 36km, arrives at the **Balmaceda** and **Serrano glaciers**. A boat trip here (run by most of the tour operators in Puerto Natales

– see p.403) is one of the most beautiful in the whole of the area – it takes seven hours and you pass a colony of cormorants and a slippery mass of sea-lions. The glaciers themselves make an impressive sight, especially when a chunk of ice the size of a small house breaks off and crashes into the water. They form the tip of the **Parque Nacional Bernardo O'Higgins**, the largest and (in terms of people per area) least visited national park in the whole of Chile. The east of the park is almost entirely made up of the Campo de Hielo Sur (the Southern Icefield), the west of fjords, islands and untouched forest. The Navimag boat (see p.404) passes through, but the only way of exploring the park in any detail is to have your own boat.

Back on the main road, after travelling north for 39km you reach the border village of **Cerro Castillo**. There really is nothing here except the frontier (Dec–Mar 8am–midnight), and the most that the tourist leaflet can boast of is the dizzy glories of a 1943 sheep-shearing shed.

Parque Nacional Torres del Paine

Fifty-six kilometres after Cerro Castillo, rising above the flat brown pampa, is a small range of mountains topped by weird twisted peaks and unfeasibly smooth towers. This is the **Paine massif**, centrepiece of the **PARQUE NACIONAL TORRES DEL PAINE** (daily 8.30am–8pm; CH$6500 for foreigners, CH$2500 for Chileans) and one of the world's stunning geographical features. Wandering around the giants' castles and demons' lairs of this mountain is one of the highlights of any trip to Chile – on the eastern side are the soaring, unnaturally elegant **Torres del Paine** ("Paine Towers"), the icon of the park, and further west, the dark-capped, sculpted **Cuernos del Paine** ("Paine Horns"), which rise above the moonscape of the **Valle del Frances** ("French Valley"). To the east of the park is the broad river of ice of **Glacier Grey**, and on the plains at the mountains' feet large herds of **guanacos** and the odd *ñandú* still run wild.

That said, if you're coming here to taste wilderness you'll be disappointed, as the park is usually full of people and fully equipped with *refugios*, campsites and hotels. The compensation for this development, though, is that it's well managed, and there's hardly any litter on the trails, people generally camp only in designated sites, and erosion is being kept to a minimum. And should you get lost, the *guardeparques* will come out to look for you, as all the campsites and refuges in the park are linked by radio.

Arrival and information

The entrance to the park for those coming by road is 116km from Puerto Natales at **Laguna Amarga**. The Conaf station (*Guardería*) here isn't much more than a hut with a map on the wall where you pay your entrance fee and give your name, but a regular bus connects it with the *Hostería las Torres* (CH$1500), 7km to the west, the starting point of the two most important trails. The buses from Puerto Natales continue along to the south of the massif and arrive at the **Lago Pehoe** *Guardería* after another 19km, near the impressive cataract of Salto Grande (Large Waterfalls). After 18km the bus reaches the **Park Administration**, around which there's a visitor centre, a refuge, a grocery store, a *hostería* and even a post office. On the map, it looks like you can continue on along this road and eventually return to Puerto Natales, but you can't because the road's not open to the public. You can also enter the park on the **inflatable boats** that travel up the Serrano river (see Onas, under Path@gone, in box on p.403). These arrive at *Hostería Cabañas del Paine*, where they're met by a bus which takes them 9km north to the Park Administration.

The best place for general **information** is the Park Administration, although all the *Guarderías* can provide information about the state of the trails. Most also have a large

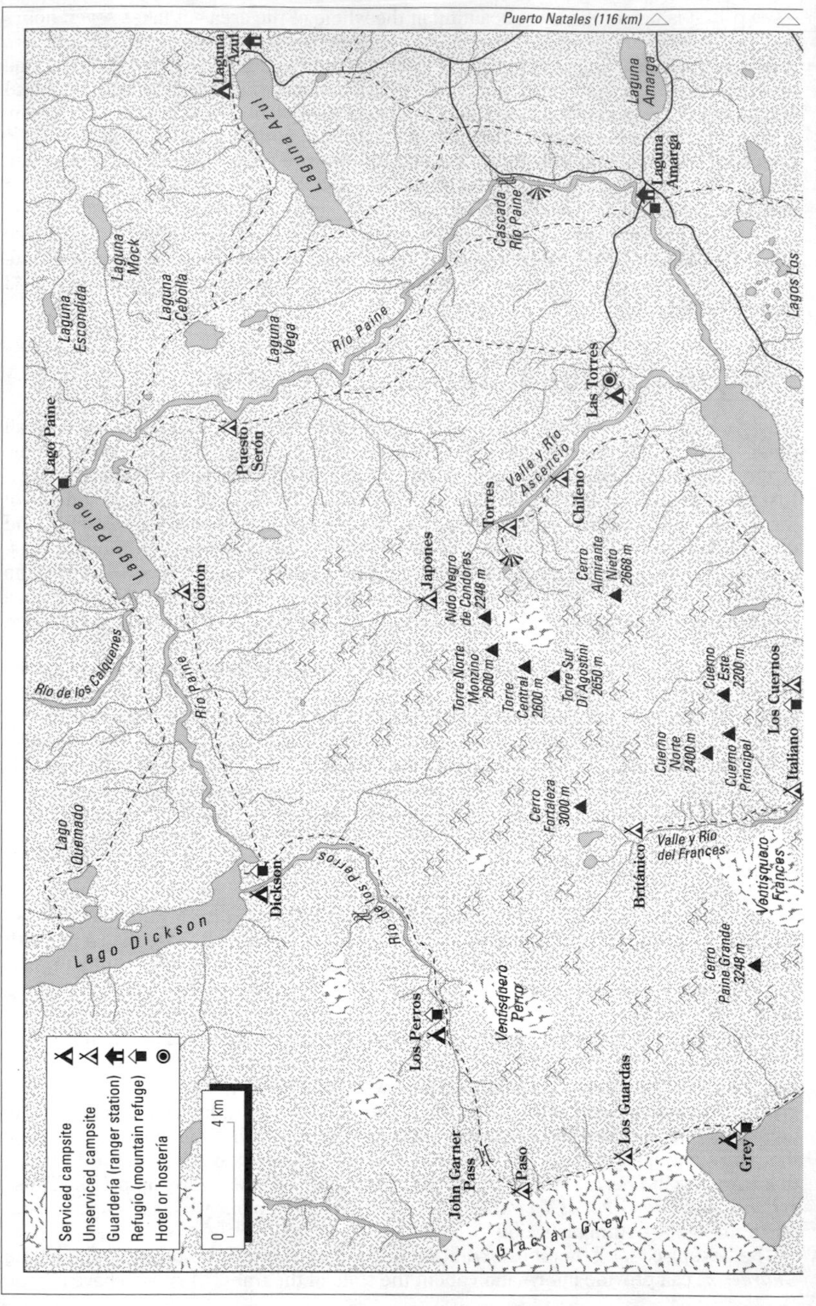

Puerto Natales (116 km)
Serviced campsite
Unserviced campsite
Guardería (ranger station)
Refugio (mountain refuge)
Hotel or hostería
0
4 km
Laguna Azul
Laguna Azul
Laguna Amarga
Laguna Amarga
Cascada Río Paine
Laguna Escondida
Laguna Mock
Laguna Cebolla
Laguna Vega
Río Paine
Lagos Los
Lago Paine
Lago Paine
Puesto Serón
Las Torres
Valle y Río Ascencio
Torres
Chileno
Japones
Nido Negro de Condores 2248 m
Cerro Almirante Nieto 2668 m
Coirón
Río de los Calquenes
Río Paine
Torre Norte Monzino 2600 m
Torre Central 2600 m
Torre Sur Di Agostini 2650 m
Cuerno Este 2200 m
Los Cuernos
Cuerno Norte 2400 m
Cuerno Principal
Italiano
Lago Quemado
Cerro Fortaleza 3000 m
Dickson
Río de los Perros
Valle y Río del Frances
Británico
Ventisquero Frances
Lago Dickson
Cerro Paine Grande 3248 m
Ventisquero Perro
Los Perros
Los Guardas
John Garner Pass
Paso
Grey
Glaciar Grey

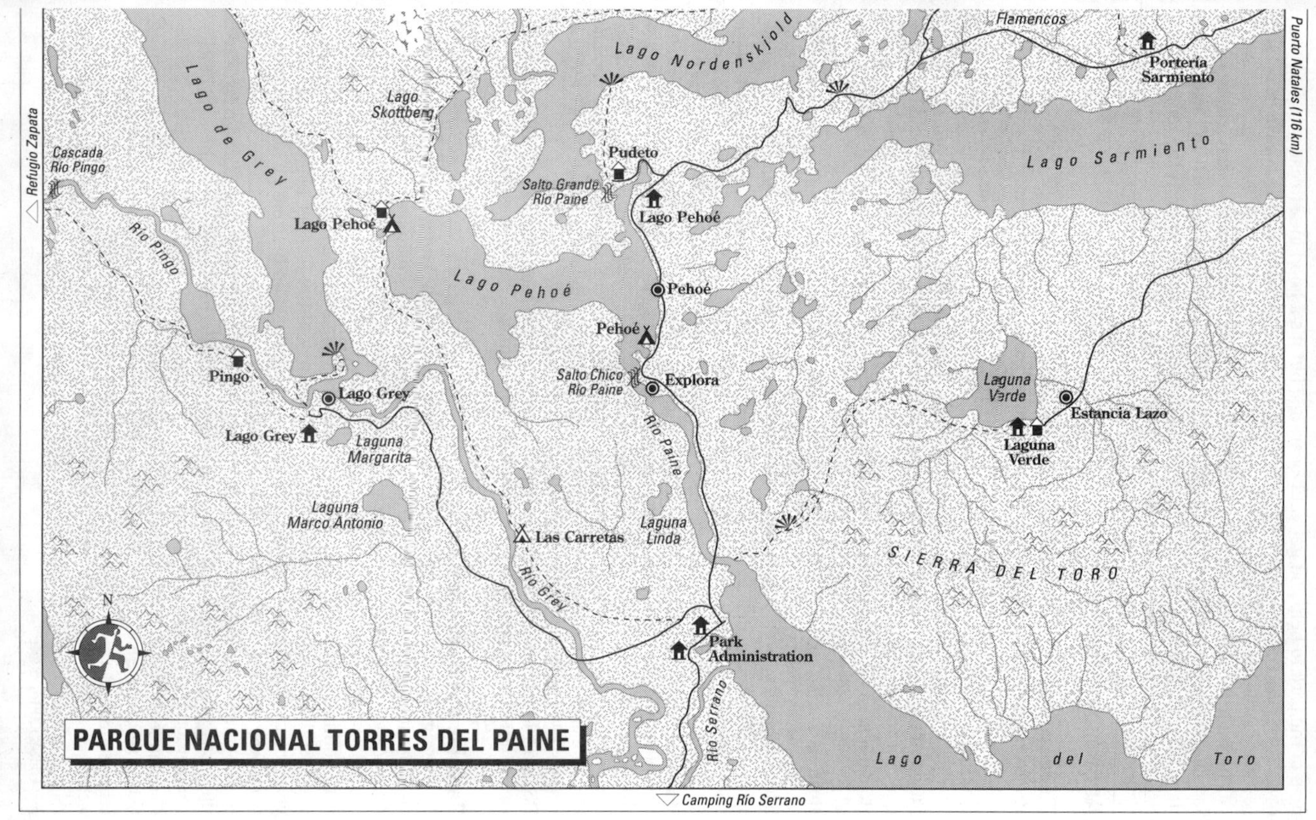
Puerto Natales (116 km)
Flamencos
Portería Sarmiento
Lago Nordenskjold
Lago Skottberg
Lago de Grey
Refugio Zapata
Cascada Río Pingo
Río Pingo
Pudeto
Salto Grande Río Paine
Lago Pehoé
Lago Sarmiento
Lago Pehoé
Lago Pehoé
Pehoé
Pehoé
Pingo
Salto Chico Río Paine
Explora
Lago Grey
Lago Grey
Laguna Margarita
Laguna Verde
Estancia Lazo
Laguna Verde
Río Paine
Laguna Marco Antonio
Las Carretas
Laguna Linda
SIERRA DEL TORO
Río Grey
N
Park Administration
Río Serrano
PARQUE NACIONAL TORRES DEL PAINE
Lago del Toro
Camping Río Serrano

map of the park to help you get your bearings, but it's a good idea to carry one of your own: *Torres del Paine*, number 13 in the JLM/ Entel series, covers the area in detail and is widely available in Puerto Natales.

The **best months to visit** the park are November, December, March and April. In January and February the park is crammed with Argentinians and Chileans taking their summer holidays, and in winter the park can be shut by snow as the temperature falls to -12°C (and it feels colder still out in the Patagonian wind).

Accommodation

There are four different types of accommodation in the park: unserviced campsites, serviced campsites, *refugios*, and *hosterías*. Wild camping isn't permitted.

Hosterías

The park's **hosterías** are expensive in comparison with those in Puerto Natales or Punta Arenas – the rooms are mostly decent enough but unimaginative, and the same goes for the food in the restaurants.

Hostería Lago Grey (☎ & fax 61/222681). This *hostería* has a beautiful view of Glacier Grey, across a lake dotted with floating icebergs. ⑧.

Hostería Las Torres (☎61/411572). Spread out across a couple of fields, *las Torres* has the feel of an *estancia*, and good views up to the Torres del Paine. It sometimes arranges sheep-shearing exhibitions followed by barbecues, so you can shave your meal before you eat it. ⑧.

Hostería Mirador del Payne (☎61/226930, fax 225167; *j.iglesias@EntelChile.net*; *www.chileaustral.com/vientosur*). Formerly known as the *Hostería Lazo*, a colonial-style house with a veranda and eight *cabañas* near Laguna Verde, in a quiet corner of the park. ⑧.

Hostería Pehoe (☎61/411390). Beautifully sited on a small island in Lago Pehoe looking out to the highest peaks of the Paine massif, with a warm bar and restaurant. ⑦.

Hotel Explora, Salto Chico (☎2/206 6060 or 208 0664, fax 228 4655; *explora@entelchile.net*; *www.interknowledge.com/Chile/explora*). Probably the best hotel in Patagonia. It overlooks the Salto Chico (Small Waterfalls), and has designer rooms decorated with local woods. It's really aimed at package tours, as the minimum stay is four nights. ⑧.

Posada Rio Serrano (☎61/410684). The cheapest *hostería* in the park, in an attractive old building on the site of the first *estancia* near the Park Administration. No en-suite rooms. ⑤.

Refugios and campsites

The **refugios** in the park are open from September to May, and generally closed by the weather during the rest of the year. Most are run by two companies, Fantastico Sur and Andescape, who share an office in Puerto Natales (Eberhard 212; ☎61/413290 or 413291, *pathgone@chileaustral.com*; see box p.403). Buildings range from a bare hut with nothing but a wood-fired stove, to modern chalets with a restaurant. None comes with bedding, although you can rent a sleeping bag at the flashier places. Most of the year you can just turn up and get a bunk, but in January and February everywhere gets very busy and you'll need to book in advance.

The unserviced **campsites** are free, and are just a flat path of land and a *fogón*. All the serviced campsites cost money, but they provide firewood, have ablution blocks, and sometimes even a small shop.

Campamiento Los Perros (Andescape). Last campsite before the John Garner pass – there used to be a *refugio* here too, but it was burnt down by careless trekkers. CH$1700 per person.

Campamiento Seron (Fantastico Sur). At the end of the first day's hike on The Circuit (see below), a campsite at the bottom of the northeast corner of the massif. CH$2000 per person.

Camping Azul (☎61/411157). On the shores of a little-visited lake to the northeast of the park, costing CH$8500 for a site.

Camping Serrano (no phone). Out of the way, south of the Park Administration, this campsite is on a bend in the río Serrano, and is accessible from the road. A site costs CH$6000.

Refugio y Campamiento Lago Pehoe (Andescape). The *refugio* is a cramped, two-floored wooden hut with a small kitchen. It's surrounded by grassy fields where people camp, and there's a small shop nearby. Camping costs CH$1600 per person, and a *refugio* bed is CH$7500.

Refugio y Camping Chileno (Fantastico Sur). Halfway up the Valle Ascencio, at the foot of the Torres del Paine. CH$6000 a bed, CH$2000 a person to camp.

Refugio y Camping Grey (Andescape). A popular *refugio* thanks to its position by Glacier Grey, this place gets full very quickly. CH$7500 a bed, CH$1700 per person to camp.

Refugio y Camping Los Cuernos (Fantastico Sur). An isolated modern hut in a forest beneath the Cuernos del Paine, with a restaurant and campsite. CH$7500 a bed, CH$2000 each to camp.

Refugio y Camping Los Torres (Fantastico Sur). Near the park entrance at Laguna Amarga and the *Hostería Las Torres*, this place is a first-night stop for those who are taking it easy. CH$7500 a bed, CH$2000 per person to camp.

Refugio Dickson (Andescape). The most remote refuge in the park, on the shores of Lago Dickson. Quiet and peaceful. CH$7500 a bed, CH$1700 per person to camp.

Refugio Lago Torro (no phone). The Conaf-run *refugio* near the Park Administration, just a hut with a wood stove. CH$2000 per bed.

Exploring the park

You'll have seen photographs of the park long before you visit, as the pristine-smooth rock towers that are the actual **Torres del Paine** feature on just about every piece of tourist literature produced in Chile, and beautify calendars the length and breadth of the country. And yet nothing really prepares you for your first sight of it all. Travelling across the barren featureless expanses of Patagonia your eye gets accustomed to dreary flatness, when suddenly the **Paine massif** rises up from the grasslands like a mirage. In your shock, it's easy to shoot off a roll of film before you even get a good view of these chiselled turrets, but it's best to wait until you're closer, as the finest views are from the south, where the waters of Lago Nordenskjöld act as a great reflecting mirror.

What you see is one very large mountain, or set of mountains, the main body of which is made up of the twin peaks of **Monte Almirante Nieto** (2668m and 2640m). The massif is essentially an enormous rectangle of rock, 22km long and 14km wide, cut into by two valleys – the **Valle Ascencio** in the east, and the **Valle del Frances** in the middle. From every angle the massif looks different, and reveals hidden peaks, valleys and cliffs. The western edge is fringed by **Glacier Grey**, which is over 7km wide at its largest point and stretches back into the **Campo de Hielo Sur** ("Southern Icefield"), over a million hectares of ice-cap and one of the largest ice-fields outside the poles.

The best way to explore the massif is on foot, and there are two hikes (see box overleaf) which take in most of the main features. Both start in the east, at the foot of the **valle Ascencio**, up which hide the three **Torres del Paine – Torre Monzino** (2600m), **Torre Central** (2800m) and **Torre D'Agostini** (2850m). Further west, guarding the entrance to the Valle del Frances, are the **Cuernos del Paine**, a set of incredibly carved towers capped with dark rock peaks (**Cuerno Principal** at 2600m, **Cuerno Este** at 2200m and **Cuerno Norte** at 2400m). The **Valle del Frances** itself is one of the glories of the park, a high-altitude valley ringed by a rock curtain-wall, broken by peaks whose names describe them well: Catedral ("Cathedral"), Castillo ("Castle") and Aleta de Tiburon ("Shark's Fin"). Both hikes also visit the icy fastness of the **Glacier Grey**.

Around the massif lie large pools and rivers of glacial meltwater, which flow to the nearby fjords of the Seno Ultima Experanza. The main river is the río Serrano, a freezing torrent which plunges through uninhabited rainforest and leads to the glaciers **Serrano** and **Balmaceda** in Parque Nacional Bernardo O'Higgins (see p.405).

HIKES IN THE PARK

THE CIRCUIT

The Circuit is the traditional way of seeing the park, a six- to seven-day walk around the whole of the massif, longer if you're tempted up the Valle del Frances or the Valle Ascencio. It's not as daunting as it sounds, as for the most part it's pretty flat. That said, there's one nasty pass where you have to climb 600m, and a couple of steep climbs if you're heading up either of the two valleys. Though you can obviously tackle it in either direction, the counterclockwise route is arguably easier.

You should aim to be at the *Hostería Las Torres* at 11am (if you catch the 7am bus from Puerto Natales you should be fine). If you want to see the **Torres del Paine**, then you should start up the **Valle Ascencio** in the afternoon, otherwise head off northeast in the direction of *Campamiento Seron*, a hike which takes four to five hours (go back down the road along which you've just come, and the path strikes off to the north 1km from the *hostería*). The second day takes you to *Refugio Dickson*, a five- to six-hour slog through boggy mud along the río Paine, and the third will walk you to *Campamiento Los Perros*, past a pretty little waterfall. At *Los Perros*, you need to wait for the weather before starting on a four-hour climb up to the top of **Paso John Garner** (1250m), and there's no way of escaping the freezing streams and bogs through which you'll have to walk. The reward for all this is the staggering view from the top of the pass over the **Campo del Hielo Sur** (Southern Icefield). On the other side the path descends steeply, and is overgrown by beech forest or scourged by the wind, and its easy to get lost here. Ideally you want to reach *Refugio y Camping Grey* tonight, six or seven hours from the pass, but if the weather's foul that won't be possible. Don't worry if you're not going to make it, as there's a small unserviced campsite at the foot of the pass called *Campamiento Paso*.

Refugio y Camping Grey is beautifully sited at the foot of **Glacier Grey**, and you can take the day off and go for ice-hikes over the glacier (organized by Amerindian Concept in Puerto Natales, see p.403). From here, it's a long day around the corner of the massif and back along to the mouth of the **Valle del Frances**. You can either head up the valley, or continue on for another two hours to *Refugio y Camping Los Cuernos*, nestling under the shadow of the strangely weathered **Cuernos del Paine**. After *Los Cuernos* you've almost made it, and there's only a three-hour stroll along the side of Lago Nordenskjöld to your starting point at the *Hostería Las Torres*.

THE W

The W is the current favourite hike. It's called "The W" because the route you follow looks like a W, up three valleys and along the bottom of the southern face of the massif. It takes four to five days to complete.

From the *Hostería Las Torres*, you start by heading west along the foot of the massif. Just after a bridge you head uphill, up the Valle Ascencio, and sleep the first night in the

Other ways of exploring the park

If you want to explore the park but don't want to walk, there are a few options. You can hire **horses** from the *Hostería Las Torres* and trek to the Torres, the Cuernos, or along the shore of Lago Nordenskjöld – prices start at CH$17,000 for three hours. For the same price, you can ride in a **four-wheel-drive car** on the tracks to Lago Paine in the north, or Lago Azul in the south. The *Hostería Las Torres* can arrange this, as can Andescape (see p.408). Alternatively, Zodiac inflatable **boats** run up and down the río Serrano (prices start at CH$30,000; see Onas p.403), while a large, conventional boat makes a three-hour return trip (CH$14,000) to Glacier Grey from the Lago Grey *Guardería* when the lake's not blocked by ice.

To **climb** in the park, you'll need to get a permit from the Dirección de Fronteras y Limites (see "Basics" p.53 for details), and Conaf; the latter costs CH$40,000, and covers any ascent.

Refugio y Camping Chileno. It's a hard climb, but the worst bit is at the beginning and just about anyone can manage it if they pace themselves. If you find yourself at *Chileno* with time to burn, press on to the *Campamiento Torres*, a free, unserviced campsite, 90 minutes further up the valley at the foot of the **Torres**. From *Campamiento Torres* most people turn west and head up the small valley to the foot of the peaks, where there's a small lake and – if the clouds clear – a stunning view up to the three strange statuesque towers. There's an alternative, though, and that's to press on north for an hour to the *Campamiento Japones*, another free and unserviced site. Here you'll find a hidden valley which also heads west, called the **Valle del Silencio**, much less visited than the Torres and a great place to escape the crowds.

You then head downhill again towards the *Hostería Las Torres*, and after you reach the bridge where you turned up the valley, turn right (west) and continue along the foot of the massif. After three hours you'll reach the *Refugio y Camping Los Cuernos*, which is an excellent place to stay the night, or you can press on another two hours to the *Campamiento Italiano*. At the *Italiano*, head north again up the **Valle del Frances**. It takes three hours to reach a campsite, *Campamiento Britanico*, and another hour or two to reach a viewpoint at the head of the valley. Then you turn around and head south again.

Back down at *Campamiento Italiano*, carry on to the west, and after two hours you'll reach *Refugio y Campamiento Pehoe*, where you should spend the night. From here head northwest up the side of **Lago Grey** to *Refugio y Camping Grey*, snug by Glacier Grey a three-hour walk away. From *Grey*, the route out is back the way you came, to *Pehoe*. Here there are two options. First, you can pick up a **boat** across Lago Pehoe (CH$6000, tickets sold at the shop in the campsite) to *Refugio Pedeto*, half a kilometre from the main road, from where you can catch a bus to Puerto Natales. The boat normally makes three one-hour trips a day across the lake, but if there's a wind it can't sail. The alternative way out is the five-hour hike to the Park Administration along the long, flat pampa to the south of Lago Pehoe. From the Park Administration there are regular buses to Puerto Natales, the last leaving at 6.30pm.

OTHER TRAILS

These two walks by no means exhaust the park. There's a three and a half hour walk from Laguna Amarga to **Laguna Azul**, a secluded and little-visited lake in the northeast. From Laguna Azul there's a four-hour trail to **Lago Paine**, where there's a refuge, and it's another three and a half hours to *Refugio Dickson*, which you can reach only if the ferry across the río Paine is working. **Laguna Verde** is another remote lake, five hours' walk to the east of the Park Administration (also served by a spur from the Torres del Paine–Puerto Natales road). The most remote lake is **Lago Pingo**, five and a half hours from the southern tip of Lago Grey, itself a four-and-a-half-hour walk from the Park Administration.

TIERRA DEL FUEGO

TIERRA DEL FUEGO, across the Magellan Strait from Patagonia, is badly named. The fault is that of the King of Spain, who didn't like Magellan's original *Tierra del Humo* ("Land of Smoke"), prompted by the smoke seen rising from numerous fires on Isla Grande, and considered "Land of Fire" much more poetic. In fact, Tierra del Fuego is a land of wind and cold.

Its main island, **Isla Grande**, is divided almost equally between Chile – in the east – and Argentina – in the west. The main Chilean town is **Porvenir**, huddled on the opposite coast of the Magellan Strait from Punta Arenas, while the main Argentinian town is Ushuaia in the south. To the south of Isla Grande, across the Beagle Channel is **Isla Navarino**, on which **Puerto Williams** is the southernmost permanently inhabited

CHARLES DARWIN, THE BEAGLE AND JEMMY BUTTON

In the early nineteenth century, the land around the Magellan Strait was all but unknown, so in 1826 the British Admiralty sent two ships, *The Adventure* and *The Beagle*, to explore it. The expedition's leader, Robert Fitzroy, was a liberal man, and for the most part encouraged his men to be friendly and careful in the way they dealt with the Fuegian Indians. However, when one of his ship's boats was stolen, Fitzroy retaliated by kidnapping four Indians and holding them hostage. The boat was never returned, so Fitzroy took the Indians back to England.

The sailors couldn't pronounce the Indians' names, and poetically rechristened them "Boat Memory", "York Minster", "Jemmy Button" and "Fuegia Basket". Boat Memory, described as an intelligent young man, died of smallpox on reaching London, but the others survived, and were educated into English society. The only woman, Fuegia Basket, was presented at court and charmed the King and Queen, who gave her a lace cap and a golden ring. Jemmy Button became a dandy, and Darwin described him as: "…short, thick and fat, but vain of his personal appearance; he used to wear gloves, his hair was neatly cut, and he was distressed if his well-polished shoes were dirtied. He was fond of admiring himself in a looking glass…"

Some years later in 1831, Fitzroy returned to Tierra del Fuego on *The Beagle*, with the three Fuegian Indians on board, and Charles Darwin as his naturalist. Fitzroy intended to return the Indians to their homeland with a missionary, in an attempt to "civilize" and evangelize the rest of the Fuegians. The missionary didn't last more than three days before asking to be taken back on board, but it was hoped that Jemmy Button, York Minster and Fuegia Basket might be a kernel of Britishness in this far-off corner of the world. Unsurprisingly, however, when *The Beagle* returned in a year's time, the natives had returned to their traditional lifestyles.

place in the world (except for bases on Antarctica). To the west of Tierra del Fuego are the remote **Fuegian channels**, where the sea winds its way between hundreds of uninhabited islands, all that's left of the mighty Andes as they slip gently under the sea. To the south of Isla Navarino are the **Wollaston islands**, better known as Cape Horn.

As with Patagonia, Tierra del Fuego was pretty much ignored by Europeans until the late nineteenth century when first gold, and then the land's sheep-rearing potential were discovered. And again, as with Patagonia, oil is now the big earner. Today, tourists come to hike or fish in the scrubby Magellanic forest around **Lago Blanco**, to visit Ushuaia in Argentina, or to just look around.

Getting there

There are **two ferries** to **Isla Grande**. The *Barcaza Melinka* leaves from Punta Arenas (see p.395) and arrives at Porvenir, while the *Ferry Bahía Azul* crosses the Primera Angostura (see p.399) and arrives at Puerto Espora in Bahía Azul. Both are run by Transbordadora Austral Broom, Av Bulnes 5075 in Punta Arenas (☎61/218100). You can also **fly** from Punta Arenas to Porvenir with DAP (see p.395), or take the bus to Ushuaia (see p.395).

Getting to **Isla Navarino** is more difficult. The easiest way is to fly with DAP to Puerto Williams (see p.395), but there's also a ferry, the *Barcaza Crux Australis*, which leaves Punta Arenas three times a month on Wednesdays at 7pm (31hr, and one-way from CH$56,400, including food). COMAPA (see p.394) also runs a luxury cruise on the *Terra Australis*, which takes four days and costs from US$1244.

Isla Grande

ISLA GRANDE is the biggest island of Tierra del Fuego, and the most developed. That isn't to say that there's a lot here – in Chilean Tierra del Fuego, there's just the main town of **Porvenir** and the inevitable string of oil settlements. Evidence of the importance of oil is everywhere, from pipelines that follow the road, to little piles of blue glass, the remains of windscreens shattered by the flying stones kicked up by the wheels of enormous oil trucks. These trucks thunder across the northern half of the island, a wasteland of windswept steppe. Further south, ranges of hills gradually become higher and less barren, and in the south they become the densely forested 2000-metre peaks of the Cordillera Darwin. Beneath these mountains, glaciers meander through narrow valleys then break up in the Beagle Channel.

There's precious little public transport, and traffic's very light, so travelling without your own car is difficult. Cycling is not an option, as the blistering wind makes it almost impossible to make any progress.

Porvenir

PORVENIR, 35km east of Punta Arenas across the Magellan Strait, is a collection of brightly painted corrugated iron houses. The town gives off the impression of order stamped on nature, with neat topiary leading down the main street, Phillippi, from an immaculate Plaza de Armas. On the seafront there's a little plaza with a curve of flagpoles, the painted skeleton of a steam engine and the broken, but mounted stern of a boat.

The town started life in 1883 as a police outpost in the days of the Fuegian gold rush, and has since been settled by foreigners. First came the British managers of sheep farms, and then refugees from Croatia after World War II. You can read the history of the town in the names of the dead in the **cemetery** (daily 8am–6pm) four blocks north of the Plaza: Mary Montgomery Mackenzie lies with Neil Morrison Morrison opposite Rosenda Manquemilla Muñoz, who lies beside Juan Senkovic Restovich. It's not only the names that are fascinating, and at the far end of the trees there's the tomb of the family Mimica Scarpa, designed to resemble a miniature mosque, complete with a scaled-down minaret. The only other site of interest in Porvenir is the **Museo Regional** on the north corner of the Plaza (Mon–Thurs 9am–1pm & 2.45–5pm, Fri 9am–1pm & 2.45–4pm; free), with photographs of miners and machinery from the goldrush years, a collection of cine cameras from the early days of Chilean film and the usual collection of stuffed animals. None of this is enough to attract you here – most people pass through Porvenir quickly on their way to Ushuaia or Punta Arenas.

Practicalities

Ferries from Punta Arenas arrive at Bahía Chilota, 5km to the west of Porvenir along the bay, from where a taxi into town will cost CH$1500, and a *colectivo* CH$400. There are some bright fishermen's houses out here, a restaurant staffed by a couple of taciturn women, and an absurd one-way system (there are only two streets). Coming by **bus**, you'll arrive on the corner of Riobo and Sampaio, a couple of blocks northeast of the Plaza. The **aerodrome** is 5km north of town, and flights are met by taxis who charge CH$2000 to take you into Porvenir.

There are a number of reasonable **places to stay**. *Hostal Patagonia*, Jorge Schythe 230 (☎61/580088; ③), is a modern hostel with good quality en-suite rooms, while *Residential Colón*, Riobo 198 (☎61/580593; ②), is a friendly bed and breakfast with a large, bright dining room, use of the kitchen and camping on a patch of ground outside (CH$2000). The best choice is offered by *Hotel España*, Croatia 698 (☎61/580160; ③–④), a deceptively large old building run by a formidable woman, with basic rooms with shared bathrooms and plush new en-suite doubles. The *Hospedaje* (no sign) at

Guerrero 43 (☎61/580509; ①) is the cheapest option in Porvenir. It smells a bit, but the room's pretty clean and the family's friendly. There aren't that many **places to eat** in town, and the best is probably *Club Croatia*, Señoret 542, which serves well-prepared standard Chilean fare (but do check your bill). *Hotel España* does good sandwiches and set meals.

You can change money at Chile Express next door to the *España*, and there are CTC and Entel telephone offices on Croatia near Phillippi.

Buses Gesell at Sampaio 300 (☎61/580162) runs a service to Río Grande in Argentina (CH$8000) on Tuesday and Sunday at 1pm, and returns on Wednesday and Saturday at 7am. (These times change regularly, so it's a good idea to check them before you travel.) From Río Grande, you can catch a bus to Ushuaia or Punta Arenas.

You can buy tickets for the **ferry** or the **aeroplane** back to Punta Arenas from a kiosk on the *costanera* (Mon–Fri 9am–noon & 2.30–5pm; Sat 9am–noon & 3–6pm). If that's shut, the restaurant at Bahía Chilota sells tickets for the ferry an hour before it's due to leave (departures Tues, Thurs & Sat 12.30pm, Wed 2pm, Fri 3.30pm, Sun 5pm).

Northeast to Cerro Sombrero and Bahía Azul

The first 20km out of Porvenir heading north is lined with large shallow lakes, ranging in colour from turquoise to sapphire, and often dotted with dazzling pink flamingos. After that excitement, there's not much for the next 86km until you reach the turning to the right which leads to Chilean Tierra del Fuego's other town, **CERRO SOMBRERO**.

Cerro Sombrero is 42km from the coast. It's a small oil town, looming up out of the moonscape, snugly ensconced on the top of a small flat hill, and bristling with aerials like something out of the *Mad Max* movies. It's not worth travelling to the ends of the earth to visit, but if you're passing it's friendly enough – a good place to stop at if you need petrol, or just want a break. Being an oil town, it's not short of heating, and the Plaza de Armas is blessed with a plant-filled conservatory. There's one place to stay, *Tunkelen* (☎61/212757; ③), which is just at the bottom of the hill – a pleasant truck stop, run by a hospitable family. They have a good quality en-suite room in the *hostería*, and a large outside block of rooms with one shared bathroom. Best of all, they have an enormous efficient water heating system. Such things become very important in Tierra del Fuego.

Forty-three kilometres north of Cerro Sombrero (139km from Porvenir), there's the **ferry** across the Primera Angostura, at a place known locally as **Bahía Azul**. There's nothing at the ferry terminal except a telephone and a couple of buildings.

East across the Baquedano Hills to the border

A little-used road heads east from Porvenir across the **Baquedano Hills**, where most of the region's gold was discovered. It starts with a beautiful view, 20km outside Porvenir, down to the town and across the strait to Punta Arenas. All around, the landscape bears the reminders of the gold that was mined here – 41km from Porvenir you pass a gold washer, and then the road crosses the río del Oro (Gold River), by which you can see the rusting remains of an original dredge. After a steep descent, you come to the main Porvenir–San Sebastian road, and after another 84km of flat wilderness you reach the **San Sebastian frontier**. (Slightly confusingly, there are two San Sebastians – the Chilean border post and a town further on in Argentina.) All there is here is a hotel and the crossing post (daily: Dec–March 24hr; April–Nov 8am–10pm).

South to Lago Blanco

While the north of Isla Grande is flat, bleak wasteland, there are areas of forest in Tierra del Fuego where you can trek, fish and camp. They're mostly unknown, down in the south around the beautiful **Lago Blanco**, and tend to be ignored by travellers who set their minds on visiting the Argentinian town of Ushuaia.

Sadly there's no public transport and little traffic down here, so the only realistic means of travelling is in a rental car. The prettiest road is the one which follows the coast. It starts by running along the northern shore of **Bahía Inutil**, a wide bay which got its curious name through being a useless anchorage for sailing ships. After 99km you reach a crossroads, and turn south, and a little past the village of Onaisin you pass a little **English cemetery**. Like the cemetery in Tiliviche in the Norte Grande (see p.219), the desolate landscape is at stark odds with the English gravestones of the cemetery, which carry short inscriptions that hint at tragic stories: "killed by Indians", "accidentally drowned" and "died in a storm".

The coast road then skirts around the south of Bahía Inutil, giving beautiful views across to **Isla Dawson**. It passes the occasional small cluster of bare fishermen's huts – keep an eye out for the windlasses with which they draw up their small boats out of the reach of the furious sea. (Be careful of taking photos here, as the whole area is a military zone.) When the tide's out, you can see a more ancient way of catching fish – underwater stone *corrals* (pens) built by the Ona Indians to trap fish when the tide turned. Just before the village of **Camerón**, the road turns inland and leaves the bay. Camerón was once a Scottish settlement, and is built either side of the río Shetland. Once it was a thriving town, the centre of the largest sheep farm on the island. Nowadays all that's left are some neat little workers' houses and a large shearing shed.

From here, the land begins to lose its Patagonian severity, and as you travel inland it becomes densely forested. Thirty-seven kilometres in you pass another rusting reminder of the goldrush, a 1904 dredge, now preserved as a national monument. Some 20km later, the road forks north to San Sebastian, and south to a place called Sección Río Grande, where an iron bridge crosses the river. You are now surrounded by Magallanic forest, occasionally interspersed with open grassland, all of which resembles a well-tended park. If you're lucky you'll see guanacos.

Twenty-one kilometres further is **Lago Blanco** itself, majestic and brooding, encompassed by steeply forested hills and snow-covered mountains. The lake's being developed, with *cabañas* springing up around its edge and a romantic fishing lodge on an island in the middle. In five years or so, it might resemble some of the over-developed resorts of the Lake District, but at the moment, it's a place of isolation and escape. Arranging somewhere to stay is difficult (there are no telephones down here, only radio phones). There are two lodges, sharing one contact number in Punta Arenas: *Tierra del Fuego Lodge* in Río Rassmusen and *Refugio Isla Victoria* in Lago Blanco itself (☎61/241197; Sept March; ⑦)

Isla Navarino

Apart from the small settlement and naval base at **Puerto Williams** and a few *estancias* along the northern coast, **ISLA NAVARINO**, the island to the south of Isla Grande, is an uninhabited wilderness studded with barren peaks and isolated valleys. Covering about four thousand square kilometres, Navarino is dominated by a range of peaks, the **Cordón Dientes del Perro** ("Dog's Teeth Rampart") through which weaves a seventy-kilometre hiking trail called the **Los Dientes circuit**. A sign of the remoteness of the island is the fact that this trail is more the result of wandering indigenous guanacos than of man.

Puerto Williams

Nestling in a small bay on the north shore of Isla Navarino is **PUERTO WILLIAMS**. A military outpost, it looks tranquil and idyllic on a fine day, colourful roofs surrounded by the jagged peaks of **Los Dientes**. It's a tiny place, and the centre is not much bigger than a single square kilometre. The only thing to visit is the **Museo Martín Gusinde**, Comandante Aragay 1 (Mon–Fri 10am–1pm & 3–6pm, Sat & Sun 3–6pm; CH$1000), which contains photographs and maps charting the history and exploration of the region, from the days of the Fuegian Indians, through the goldrush, to the commercial shipping of today. There's also a collection of knick-knacks donated by modern kayakers who've paddled around Cape Horn.

There's an **Oficina de Turismo** at Ibáñez (Dec–March Mon–Fri 10am–1pm & 3–6pm; ☎61/621011) who are useful and have copies of hiking maps. A twenty-minute walk west of town is the best **hotel**, *Hostería Wala* (☎61/621114; ⑥), packed with horrid little decorations made of wool, but with good views and en-suite rooms. Everything else is crowded around the centre – try *Residencial Onashaga*, Uspashun on the corner of Nueva (☎61/621081; ③), for a family bed and breakfast. The hotels are the best **places to eat**, but if you're bored of their food then try *Los Dientes del Navarino*, a small, friendly restaurant in the centre where you'll probably have to go into the kitchen and point out what you want to eat. You can change money in the bank, and make telephone calls from the CTC centre on Plaza El Ancla or the post office. There are a couple of tour agencies, the oldest being Karanka Expeditions, Austral 05 (☎61/621127).

Around Puerto Williams

The seventy-kilometre **Los Dientes** trekking circuit leaves from the statue of the Virgin Mary, about one kilometre **west** of town on the road to the airport. There you'll find a turning uphill, which leads to a waterfall and a dammed stream, to the left of which is a marked trail. Further along the coast, beyond the Virgin, are numerous picturesque little bays and islands with an abundance of birdlife, both along the shore and in the edge of the forest, and near **Bahía Virginia** are large middens of mussel and clam shells left by what must once have been a large settlement of Yahgans, the local Fuegian Indians. Twelve kilometres out of town, an *estancia* owned by the very Chilean-sounding MacLean family has been developed into a *centolla* and shellfish processing factory, and there you can eat in the friendly workers' café.

Two kilometres to the **east** of Puerto Williams is the town of **Ukika**, a small collection of houses where the last dozen or so of the Yahgan Indians live. Beyond them the road continues, giving beautiful views across the Beagle Channel until it ducks into the forest and inland. It emerges once again at **Puerto Toro**, the end of the last road in South America, looking out at **Picton Island**, and beyond, into the endless seas of the Atlantic Ocean.

travel details

Buses

Porvenir to: Río Grande (2 weekly; 3hr 30min); Ushuaia, Argentina, only via Río Grande (2 weekly to Río Grande connect with daily buses to Ushuaia; 7hr).

Puerto Natales to: Cerro Castillo (4 weekly; 1hr 30min); El Calafate, Argentina (2 daily; 6hr); Parque Nacional Torres del Paine (12 daily; 2hr 30min–3hr 30min); Punta Arenas (hourly; 4hr); Río Gallegos, Argentina (3 weekly; 5hr).

Punta Arenas to: Estancia San Gregorio (1 daily; 3hr 30min); Monte Aymond (1 daily; 5hr, including formalities); Puerto Natales (every hour; 4hr); Río Gallegos in Argentina (1 daily; 7hr); Río Grande in Argentina (1 daily; 8hr 30min); Ushuaia, Argentina (2 weekly; 12hr).

Ferries

Puerto Natales to: Puerto Montt (weekly; 66hr).

Punta Arenas to: Porvenir (1 daily except Monday; 3hr); Puerto Williams (3 monthly; 31hr).

Punta Delgada to: Bahía Azul, Tierra del Fuego (every half-hour, but only when it's not low tide; 30min).

CHAPTER TEN

THE PACIFIC ISLANDS

Chile is the proud possessor of two Pacific territories, both of them national parks, and both singled out by UNESCO for special protection. Closest to the mainland, at 674km from Valparaíso, the **Juan Fernández Archipelago** is, ironically, the most difficult to reach, served only by a couple of tiny five- and ten-seater light aircraft. With their sharp, jagged peaks soaring dramatically out of the ocean, coated in a thick tangle of lush, deep-green foliage, the islands' topography is among the most spectacular in Chile. On top of this comes a compelling history, spilling over with adventure and romance. The archipelago's largest island – **Isla Robinson Crusoe** – started out as a pirates' refuge, when notorious freebooters like Bartholomew Sharp and William Dampier used it as a watering spot during their raids on the Pacific seaboard in the seventeenth century. In 1709 the faraway island was thrust into the public gaze when the Scottish seaman Alexander Selkirk was rescued from its shores, after spending four years and four months marooned there. Selkirk's story was to go down in literary history when Daniel Defoe used it as the basis for his classic novel, *The Adventures of Robinson Crusoe*. These days, the island's small community (descended from Chilean and European colonizers) milks the Crusoe connections to death in an attempt to boost the tourist trade, but this remains very low-key, and the Juan Fernández Archipelago is still an adventurous destination, well off the beaten track.

Far beyond, lost in the vastness of the Pacific, tiny **Easter Island** was annexed by Chile in 1888, but over a century later it remains a world unto itself, surrounded on all sides by thousands of kilometres of empty ocean. Its closest inhabited neighbour is Pitcairn Island, 2250km northwest, while to the east it's separated from the Chilean coast by 3878 kilometres – the distance between Spain and Canada. Isolation on this scale is barely comprehensible, though you begin to feel something of the island's remoteness during the five hours it takes to fly there from Santiago or Tahiti (the closest international airports). Once there, you're faced with a windswept land of low, gently rolling hills and steep cliffs riddled with caves, pounded on all sides by crashing waves. Spanning just 23km at its longest stretch, the island is triangular in shape, with low-lying extinct volcanoes rising out of each corner. Scattered between these points, running parallel to the shore, are the unique monuments that have made this little island so famous – the hundreds of monolithic stone **statues** of squat torsos and long, brooding heads looming sombrely over the coast. These are the Easter Island **moai**,

ACCOMMODATION PRICE CODES

Prices are for the cheapest **double room** in high season. At the lower end of the scale, **single travellers** can expect to pay half this rate, but mid- and upper-range hotels usually charge the same for a single as for a double. For more information see p.27 in Basics.

① Less than US$10/CH$4800
② US$10–20/CH$4800–9600
③ US$20–30/CH$9600–10,080
④ US$30–50/CH$10,080–24,000
⑤ US$50–75/CH$24,000–36,000
⑥ US$75–100/CH$36,000–48,000
⑦ US$100–150/CH$48,000–72,000
⑧ over US$150/over CH$72,000

among the most arresting and intriguing prehistoric sculptures in the world. Their fascination lies not only in their visual impact, but also in the many questions that surround them. Like, why were they made? When? What did they signify? And how on earth were they transported and erected? Such questions are indicative of the extent to which Easter Island's past remains unknown, and the lack of information available to us on the society that created these statues is both frustrating and deliciously tantalizing, creating a sense of mystery and intrigue that constitutes one of the island's abiding attractions.

THE JUAN FERNÁNDEZ ARCHIPELAGO

The **JUAN FERNÁNDEZ ARCHIPELAGO** is formed by the peaks of a submerged volcanic mountain range rising from the sea bed. It's made up of two principal islands, a third, much smaller, island, and numerous rocky islets. The archipelago takes its name from the Portuguese sailor who discovered it in 1574, while straying inland to avoid winds and currents in an attempt to shorten the journey between Lima and Valparaíso. The most easterly of the two main islands was called, quite simply, Mas a Tierra ("Nearer Land"), while the other, 187km further west, was known as Mas Afuera ("Farther Out"). Fernández made a brief attempt to colonize the three uninhabited islands, and introduced vegetables and goats, which multiplied in great numbers (the third, smallest, island was later known as Goat Island). These were still flourishing when British buccaneers started making occasional calls here to stock up on water and fresh meat between their raids on the mainland.

Following Alexander Selkirk's much-publicized rescue, more and more buccaneers began calling here, prompting the Spanish Crown to take official possession of the archipelago in 1742, building a series of forts around Mas a Tierra. The island was then used as a penal colony for many years, and it wasn't until the mid-nineteenth century that a mixture of Chilean and European colonizers formed a permanent settlement here. In 1966, with an eye on the islands' potential as a tourist destination, the Chilean government changed Mas a Tierra's name to **Isla Robinson Crusoe**, while Mas Afuera became **Isla Alejandro Selkirk**. Today, only a few hundred tourists make it out

ALEXANDER SELKIRK

Daniel Defoe's story of Robinson Crusoe, the world's most famous literary castaway, was inspired by the misadventures of the real-life Scottish mariner Alexander Selkirk, who was marooned on Isla Robinson Crusoe (then Mas a Tierra) in 1704 while crossing the Pacific on a privateering expedition. Unlike Crusoe, who was shipwrecked, Selkirk actually asked to be put ashore following a series of quarrels with his captain. The irascible sailor regretted his decision as soon he was deposited on the beach with a few scanty supplies, but his cries from the shore begging to be taken back onboard were ignored. Selkirk spent four years and four months on the island, with only his Bible and dozens of wild goats for company. During that time he was transformed into an extraordinary athlete, as he hunted the goats on foot, and a devout Christian, addicted to his Bible. Following his rescue by a British ship in 1709, however, Selkirk lost no time in reverting to his buccaneering ways, joining in attacks on Spanish vessels all the way home. Back in Fife, the former castaway became something of a celebrity, and threw himself into a life of drink and women. Fourteen years after his rescue Selkirk finally met his end when he took up the seafaring life once more, set off on another privateering expedition, and died of fever in the tropics.

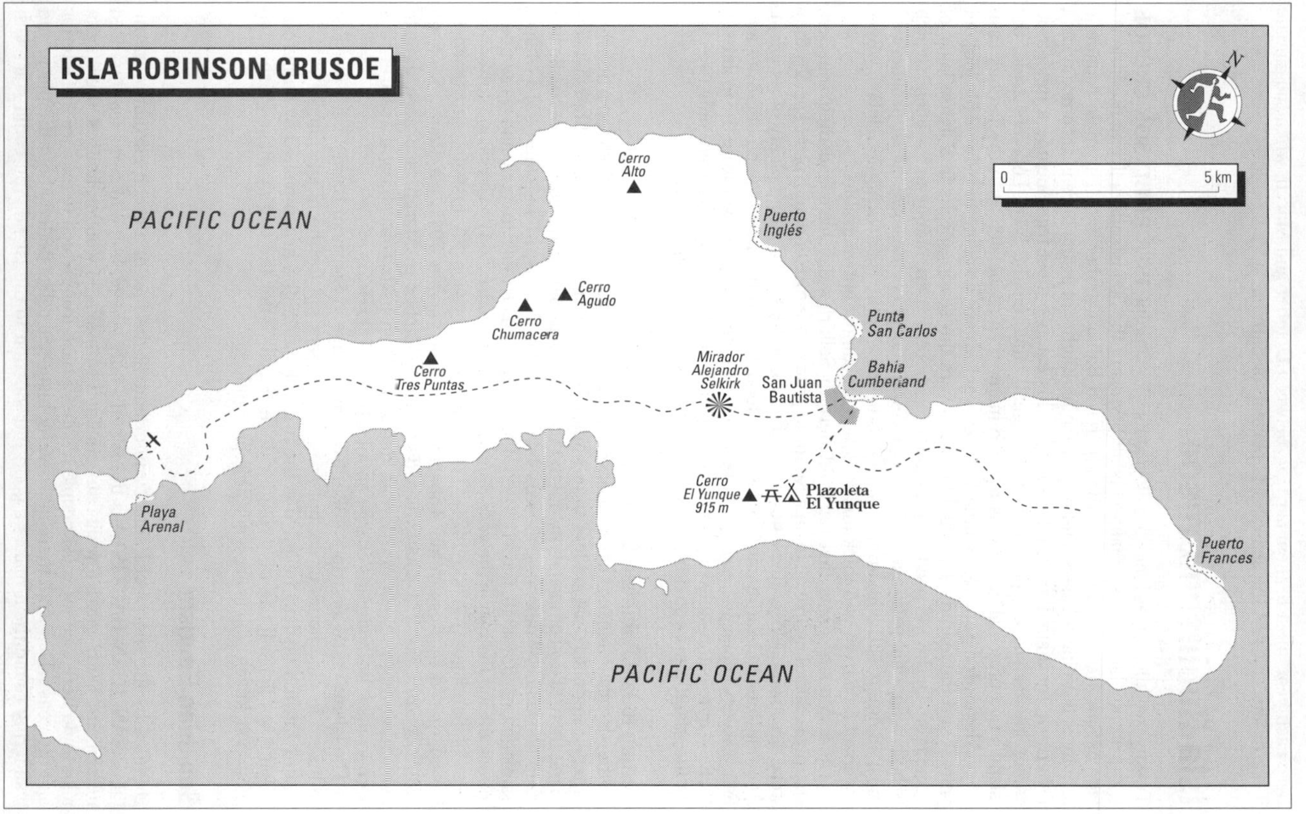
ISLA ROBINSON CRUSOE
N
0
5 km
PACIFIC OCEAN
Cerro Alto
Puerto Inglés
Cerro Agudo
Cerro Chumacera
Cerro Tres Puntas
Punta San Carlos
Mirador Alejandro Selkirk
Bahia Cumberland
San Juan Bautista
Cerro El Yunque 915 m
Plazoleta El Yunque
Playa Arenal
Puerto Frances
PACIFIC OCEAN

here each year, most of them arriving between October and March, when the climate is warm and dry, and the seawater is perfect for bathing.

Isla Robinson Crusoe

Twenty-two kilometres long, and 7km at its widest point, **ISLA ROBINSON CRUSOE** is the archipelago's only inhabited island. Most of the 509 islanders live in the little village of **San Juan Bautista**, on the sheltered Bahía Cumberland. The main economic activity is trapping lobsters, and one of the highlights of a stay here is accompanying a fisherman, for a small cost, out to haul in his catch – most trips include a fresh-as-it-comes lobster supper, prepared over a small stove on the boat. Lobsters aside, the island's two principal attractions are the many sites associated with the famous castaway **Alexander Selkirk** – from the replica of his cave dwelling to his real-life lookout point – and the abundant **plant life** that covers the soaring peaks in a dense layer of vegetation. Of the 146 plant species that grow here, 101 are unique to the island, which is both a national park and a UNESCO World Biosphere Reserve. Most prolific, and most stunning, is the luxuriant rainforest that covers the island's higher slopes, where the giant fern trees and thick undergrowth are almost impenetrable.

The legendary goats that ran wild here in Selkirk's day have had their numbers sharply reduced by Conaf, in an attempt to protect the rare endemic plant species they were devouring. Mosquitoes, however, abound, so be sure to bring plenty of repellent. Another thing to bear in mind is that basic foodstuffs, with the exception of lobster and fish, are very expensive, so it might be worth bringing a supply over from the mainland. If you plan to camp, note that petrol is very difficult to come by (there are only two cars on the island), and you'd be much better off with a butane gas stove.

Getting to Isla Robinson Crusoe

Getting to Isla Robinson Crusoe is an adventure in itself, involving a **flight** on a tiny five- or ten-seater plane that judders and wobbles for most of the two and a half hours it takes to get there. Two companies fly out to the island, both of which have a strict 10-kilo luggage allowance. Transporte Aéreos Isla Robinson Crusoe, Monumento 2570 Maipú, Santiago (☎2/531 4343, fax 531 3772), flies daily from October to April, and three times a week during the rest of the year, departing from Aerodromo Los Cerrillos, 8km southwest of Santiago (☎2/533 1424). Línea de Aeroservicios SA (usually shortened to Lassa), based at Aerodromo Tobalaba, Avenida Larraín 7941, La Reina, Santiago (☎2/273 5209, fax 273 4309), flies daily from October to March, and according to demand during the rest of the year, departing from both Tobalaba and Los Cerrillos aerodromes. Both airlines charge about CH$190,000 return.

The island's little airstrip is 13km from the village of San Juan Bautista; it's possible to hike it in nine hours or so, but most passengers opt for the ninety-minute ride by **motor launch** (usually included in the price of your flight) accompanied by numerous yelping sea lions. It can be a rough ride, especially after the bumpy plane journey, so motion sickness tablets are a sensible precaution.

San Juan Bautista

Huddled by the shores of Bahía Cumberland, at the foot of a green curtain of mountains, **SAN JUAN BAUTISTA** is the island's only village, home to some five hundred inhabitants. With only a few dirt streets lined with simple wooden houses, there's not a lot to do here, and for most people it's just a base from which to explore the interior and the coast. That said, there are several historical relics dotted about the place, and wandering round them makes a good introduction to the island. You could start with

the **Fuerte Santa Barbara**, a small stone fort perched on a hillside just north of the plaza. Heavily restored in 1974, it was originally built by the Spanish in 1749 in an attempt to prevent enemy buccaneers from using the island as a watering point. Right next to the fort, the **Cuevas de los Patriotas** is a group of seven dank caves formerly inhabited by 42 independence fighters who were banished to Mas a Tierra after the Battle of Rancagua in 1814.

Down on the shore, follow the path to the north end of the bay and you'll reach the cliffs of the **Punta San Carlos**, embedded with unexploded shells fired by British warships at the German *Dresden* during World War I. The Germans surrendered, but sank their ship rather than let it go to the British, and the wreck still lies 70m under the sea, in Bahía Cumberland. Nearby, you'll find the graves of the naval battle's casualties in the island's **cemetery**, next to the lighthouse. At the southern end of the bay, a five-minute walk from the village, the small rocky beach of **El Palillo** is good for swimming and diving, and has a few picnic tables.

Around the island

Striking out from San Juan Bautista, the first place to head for is the **Mirador Alejandro Selkirk**, the famous lookout point where Selkirk lit his daily smoke signals and scoured the horizon for ships. It's a three-kilometre uphill hike from the village, taking about ninety minutes; the path starts north of the plaza, extending from subida El Castillo, snaking through lush native forest, dense with overhanging ferns. At the top you'll be rewarded with stunning, panoramic views of almost all of the island. Note, too, the two metal memorial plaques set in the rocks, one donated by the officers of *HMS Topaze* in 1868, the other by one of Selkirk's descendants in 1983, pledging to remember his forefather "Till a' the seas gang dry and the rocks melt i' the sun". From the Mirador the trail continues for a further 10km to the airstrip, at the southwestern tip of the island (allow about eight hours there, and take plenty of water).

Another three-kilometre trail leads from the village (continuing from calle El Yunque; allow 45min) through native forest to **Plazoleta El Yunque**, a lookout point and picnic site at the foot of Cerro El Yunque, the island's tallest mountain at 915m. The stone ruins near the site are the remains of the house of Hugo Weber, the "German Robinson Crusoe" who spent twelve years living as a hermit here after escaping from the *Dresden* in 1915. Most other destinations are reached by **boat**, either on the municipal *Blanca Luz*, or with fishermen, who'll drop you off in the morning and pick you up at the end of their day's work, around 8pm – it's a good idea, as a precaution, not to pay for your return journey until *after* you've been picked up. At **Puerto Inglés**, a fifteen-minute boat ride (around US$10 round trip) from the village, you'll find a mock-up of the cave where Alexander Selkirk took refuge. The terrain is very rugged around here, and it makes a beautiful place to camp, though be sure to choose a reliable fisherman to come and pick you up the next day, or else you'll have to fight your way though dense overgrowth and up steep hillsides to get back to the village. Just south of the airstrip, **Playa Arenal** is the island's only sandy beach, and is a glorious place to spend a couple of days, with its warm, transparent waters. Two hours and thirty minutes by boat through islets and seal colonies, it can also be reached on foot along the trail to the airstrip from the Mirador.

Island practicalities

All services, and most accommodation, are based in San Juan Bautista. The Municipalidad (Mon–Fri 9am–1pm & 3–6pm; ☎32/701045, fax 751047), off the southwest corner of the plaza, hands out tourist **information**, including maps. To find out more about the island's trails, flora and fauna, visit the Conaf information centre (☎32/751022) at Sendero El Pangal 130, just south of the village. **Accommodation**, on the whole, is simple but very expensive. On the west side of the plaza, *Residencial Villa Green* (☎32/751044; ⑥) offers clean, comfortable doubles with private bath, while *Hostería Daniel Defoe*, at Larraín Alcalde 449 (☎32/751075; ⑥), has a few weather-beaten but spacious and well-equipped *cabañas* overlooking the ocean. Further south along the shoreline, *Hostal Charpentier* at Ignacio Carrera Pinto 256 (☎32/751010, fax 751020; ⑥) has a few decent rooms with lovely views. Three kilometres south of the village, at Caleta El Pangal, the Lassa-run *Hostería El Pangal* (☎ & fax in Santiago 2/273 4309; ⑥) is the largest (with 24 rooms) and smartest option on the island.

A far cheaper alternative is to **camp**, either at the free municipal campsite, *Camping Lord Anson*, in the woods on the path up to the Conaf information centre (with picnic tables and a rather foul pit toilet) or out at Plazoleta El Yunque. Most visitors **eat** at their hotel, but if you're camping, or fancy a change, try *La Bahía* on Larraín Alcalde, for first-rate lobster and fish (it's a good idea to get your orders in a few hours before you plan to eat). There's a **post office** just off the plaza, next to the Municipalidad (don't go home without getting a couple of Isla Robinson Crusoe stamps) with a direct dial public **telephone**. Be sure to take plenty of cash with you as there are no **banks** or *cambios* on the island.

EASTER ISLAND

One of the loneliest places on earth, tiny **EASTER ISLAND**, or **Rapa Nui** as it is known by its people, is home to some 2700 islanders, of whom around seventy percent are native *pascuenses*, with the rest being mainly *continentales* (Chilean immigrants). The *pascuenses*, with their fine-boned Polynesian features, are unmistakeably distinct from the Chileans, and speak their own Polynesian-based language, Rapanui, although Spanish is the official language. Virtually the entire population is confined to the island's single settlement, **Hanga Roa**, and just about all the islanders make their liv-

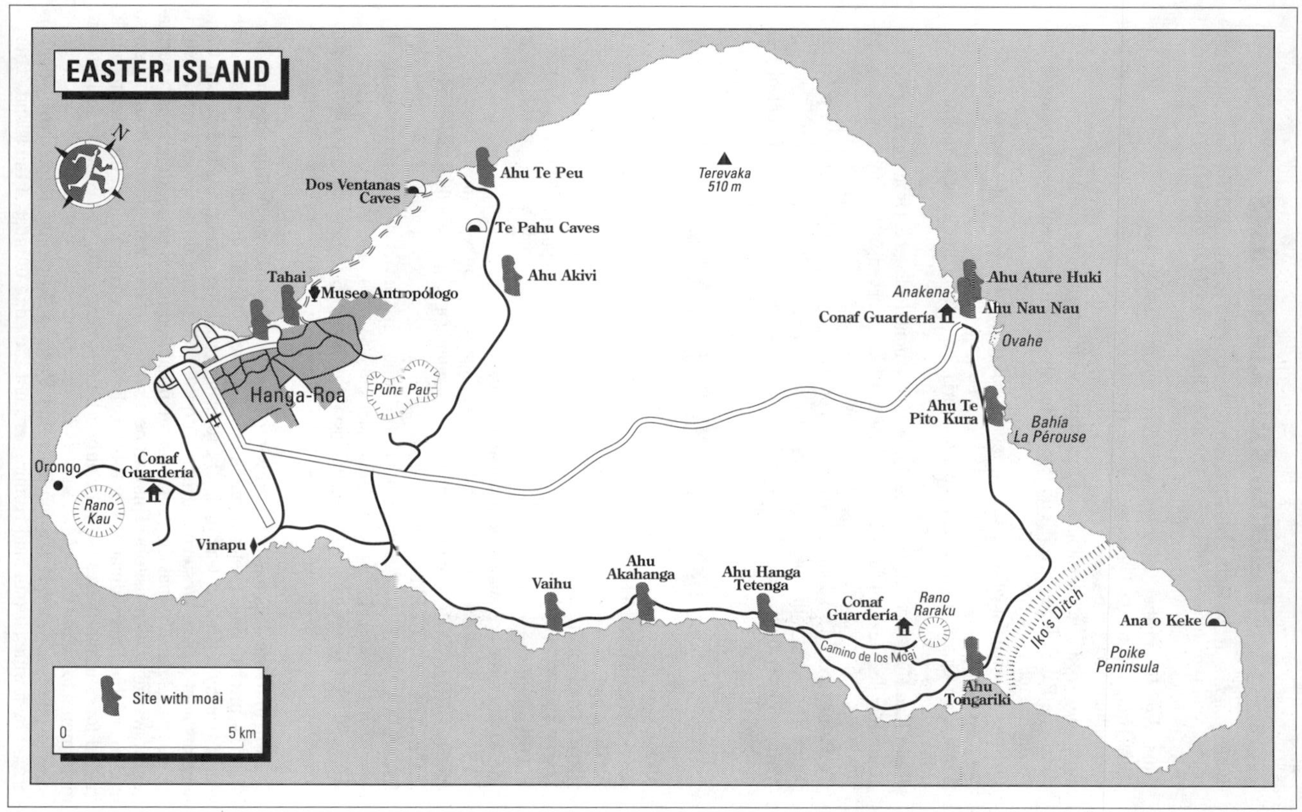
EASTER ISLAND
N
Ahu Te Peu
Terevaka
510 m
Dos Ventanas
Caves
Te Pahu Caves
Ahu Akivi
Tahai
Museo Antropólogo
Ahu Ature Huki
Anakena
Ahu Nau Nau
Conaf Guardería
Ovahe
Hanga-Roa
Puna Pau
Ahu Te
Pito Kura
Bahía
La Pérouse
Orongo
Conaf
Guardería
Rano
Kau
Vinapu
Vaihu
Ahu
Akahanga
Ahu Hanga
Tetenga
Conaf
Guardería
Rano
Raraku
Iko's Ditch
Ana o Keke
Camino de los Moai
Poike
Peninsula
Ahu
Tongariki
Site with moai
0
5 km

THE MAIN SITES AT A GLANCE

When you first arrive on the island, it can be hard to get to grips with the long list of site names, and remember what's what. The following is a brief rundown of the major attractions, to remind you what you'll find where.

Ahu Akivi Inland ahu with seven well-preserved moai; see p.441.

Ahu Hanga Tetenga The largest moai transported to a platform, now lying on the ground in ruins; see p.434.

Ahu Tongariki The largest ahu on the island, with fifteen moai; see p.435.

Anakena Palm-fringed beach, and site of ahu with seven moai, some with topknots and reconstructed eyes; see p.439.

Orongo Ceremonial village used during annual rituals devoted to the cult of the birdman; see p.441.

Puna Pau Quarry used to extract red scoria for carving the moai's "topknots"; see p.441.

Rano Kau Huge volcanic crater, and site of ceremonial village of Orongo; see p.441.

Rano Raraku Quarry where almost all the moai were carved, with many remaining statues; see p.435.

Te Pahu Caves Two underground caves, connected by a 150m lava tube; see p.441.

Tahai Three ahu with moai, a short walk from Hanga Roa village; see p.440.

Vinapu Finely built ahu made of precisely fitted blocks of stone, reminiscent of Inca stonework; see p.434.

EASTER ISLAND GLOSSARY

ANA Cave

AHU Platform on which the moai stand

ARIKI Chief

ARIKI HENUA Highest leader

HARE PAENGA Low stone dwelling place, shaped like an upturned boat

MANA Spiritual, supernatural power

MOAI Carved stone images of heads and torsos

PUKAO Cylindrical red stone "hats" or "topknots" placed on some moais' heads

RONGORONGO Undeciphered symbols resembling a script carved on tabled of wood

TANGATA HONUI Elderly man of high status

TANGATA MANU Translated as "Birdman", who was the victor of the annual competition to find the first egg of the sooty tern, part of a sacred ritual

TAPU Sacred, taboo, often referring to objects that may only be touched by certain people

ing from tourism. This has been growing steadily ever since an airstrip was built here in 1967 – prior to that, Easter Island's only contact with the outside world was a once-yearly visit by a Chilean warship, sent to bring provisions and mail. Today, Lan Chile deposits a jet-load of Western tourists onto the little island three times a week, which means, paradoxically, that the most remote inhabited island on earth is almost permanently swarming with visitors. This can be a serious fly in the ointment, though it's also true to say that the vast majority of tourists limit their exploration of the sites to quick, guided tours in minibuses, so with only a little patience you can contrive to have the monuments to yourself.

Most points of interest are found within **Parque Nacional Rapa Nui**, which is formed by a wide strip of land running around the edge of most of the island. There's open access to all the park's land at all times, and the only place where a visitor's fee is charged is at Orongo (CH$4000, valid for your whole trip). If you're pushed for time and need to prioritize, you should, as an absolute minimum, visit **Rano Kau** and **Orongo**, **Rano Raraku**, **Ahu Tongariki** and **Playa Anakena**. With a little more time to spare, try, also, to include **Ahu Akivi**, the **Te Pahu caves**, **Ahu Tahai** and **Ovahe**. These suggestions are really just a starting point – the whole island is highly rewarding, and there are plenty of opportunities for getting off the beaten track and exploring the less obvious attractions like **Terevaka**. With a vehicle, you can see the major sites quite comfortably in three days, but a few extra days would allow you to take your time and soak up the atmosphere. If you plan to visit most places on foot, leave yourself a week.

There's no ideal time to visit the island; the **weather** is fairly constant year-round, with an average temperature of 23°C in January and February, and 18°C in July and August, with moderate rainfall throughout the year. February is the busiest month, but is also the most exciting, when the islanders put on an extravagant display of singing, dancing and feasting in their annual festival, "Tapati Rapa Nui". **Getting to** Easter Island is possible only with Lan Chile, which flies here from Santiago's international airport three times a week. **Fares** are much cheaper if you buy your ticket in conjunction with a long-haul Lan Chile flight to Chile: this way, the return flight to Easter Island works out at US$525, compared to the standard fare of US$898. In addition, the airline occasionally offers low-season promotional fares for as little as US$350 for tickets bought with a long-haul Lan Chile flight.

Post-contact history

Easter Island clearly enjoyed a long, rich history before it was "discovered" and named by the Dutch naval commander **Jacob Roggeveen** on Easter Sunday, 1722, but in the absence of any written records left by the islanders (or any that we can read), Roggeveen's **log** is the earliest written account we have of the island. In it, he colourfully describes the excited inhabitants who, visiting the ship, "were so bold that they took the hats and caps of the sailors from their heads and jumped with their plunder overboard." His party spent only a single day on land, long enough, however, to observe the "particularly high erected stone images" which "caused us to be struck with astonishment, because we could not comprehend how it was possible that these people, who are devoid of heavy thick timber for making any machines, as well as strong ropes, nevertheless had been able to erect such images, which were fully thirty feet high and thick in proportion." After their departure, it was another 48 years before Easter Island was revisited, this time by the Spanish commander **Felipe González**, who mapped the island and claimed it for King Carlos III of Spain during his six-day stay. Four years later, **Captain Cook** anchored here in the hope of restoring the health of his crew, who had developed scurvy during their long search for the "southern continent". As there were few provisions to be found, Cook stayed only four days, but he too observed with incredulity the "stupendous figures" erected on the island, though he noted that some lay strewn on the ground, toppled from their platforms. Later visitors reported an increasing number of fallen statues, and by 1825, all of the moai on Hanga Roa bay had been destroyed. When the English doctor Linton Palmer visited in 1868, he confirmed there wasn't a single statue left standing on the island.

The mass destruction of statues suggests serious internal strife, but the biggest threat to Easter Island's civilization was to come from outside. In 1805 the island was raided by the first of the **slave traders** when an American schooner captured twelve men and ten women to be used as seal hunters on the Juan Fernández Islands. After three days at sea the prisoners were released from captivity and allowed onto the deck, whereupon they promptly threw themselves overboard in a desperate attempt to swim back to the island. All of them drowned. The following years saw many similar acts of cruelty, reaching a peak in 1862 when the island's population was almost annihilated. The tragedy was set in motion on December 12, when ninety Peruvian sailors landed on the island and enticed the inhabitants onto the bay with a large display of gifts. They then attacked and captured over a thousand people, who were shipped off to work as slaves in the Peruvian guano mines. After nine hundred islanders had died from disease and appalling work conditions in the mines, the Bishop of Tahiti, Tepano Jaussen, finally managed to persuade the Peruvian government to repatriate the remaining pris-

WHERE DID THEY COME FROM?

The details of Easter Island's pre-contact history remain, now, and probably forever, outside our full knowledge. The island's centuries-long isolation, added to the absence of written historical records and the decimation of the indigenous population in the nineteenth century conspire to leave few clues that might explain the settlement and development of this people. Instead, archeologists, scientists, linguists and anthropologists have had to painstakingly gather what evidence there is in an attempt to piece together the jigsaw puzzle and gain a clearer picture of the island's past. At the same time, the legends and chronicles passed orally from generation to generation over hundreds of years – and assiduously documented by several European investigators – provide their own versions of the island's history. Subject as oral history is to exaggeration, embellishment, confusion and reinvention during the course of the years, it would be unwise to read these legends as pure facts, but they do, at the very least, provide us with a glimpse of how the old Easter Islanders viewed their world and their ancestry.

WHAT THE ISLANDERS SAY: THE ARRIVAL OF HOTU MATU'A

The islanders claim that the original colonizer of Easter Island was **Hotu Matu'a**, a great *ariki henua*, or chief, who lived in a (now unknown) place called Hiva. Hotu Matu'a was forced to flee Hiva when the sexual misdemeanours of his brother aroused the anger of a rival chief, who declared war on Hotu Matu'a's tribe. It had been revealed to Hotu Matu'a's tattooist in a dream, or "spirit voyage", that an island with craters and fine beaches awaited his master, so the chief dispatched a reconnaissance party to find this promised land, following on some time later with his family, servants and fellow colonists in a large double canoe. He arrived safely on Anakena beach, just as his wife was giving birth to their first son. Hotu Matu'a and his family lived in a cave on this beach while his servants built him a house; meanwhile, the colonists set to work planting the seeds and shoots they'd brought with them, living only from fish until the resultant taros, yams, bananas and sugar cane could be eaten. They had also brought many kinds of livestock, of which only chickens and rats survived and bred on the island.

As *ariki henua*, Hotu Matu'a's role was not that of political leader, but rather of a revered and important person in possession of great supernatural qualities, or *mana*. Accordingly, he and the place where he lived were *tapu*, or sacred and untouchable, and so Hotu Matu'a and his family lived in seclusion at Anakena while the rest of his party dispersed around the island, where their families expanded and new communities began to spring up. Eventually these grew into eight separate kin-groups, each with its own *tangata honui*, or leader. As time passed and generation after generation was born, these groups became more sophisticated and stratified, made up of a diverse collection of priests, fishermen, farmers and craftsmen. It appears that everyone lived in close co-operation and relative harmony until conflict broke out between warring clans, leading to the toppling of the statues and the breakdown of society (see p.437).

WHAT THE EXPERTS SAY: EAST OR WEST?

Central to any discussion of Easter Island's settlement are the controversial theories of **Thor Heyerdahl**, the Norwegian explorer-archeologist whose widely-publicized expedi-

oners – most of whom died on the return voyage home. Tragically, the fifteen who made it back infected the rest of the islanders with smallpox and TB, reducing the population to a few hundred. Critically, the loss of life was accompanied by the loss of a crucial part of the island's culture and collective memory, for the last *ariki henua* (high chief), *moari* (keepers of sacred knowledge), and *tangata rongorongo* (specialist readers) were among those who perished.

A certain degree of stability arrived when the first **missionary**, Eugène Eyraud, settled on the island in 1864 and set to converting its people to Christianity – a

tions, best-selling books, and prolific TV series made him a household name in the 1960s, and, more importantly, generated an enormous amount of academic interest in the island's history. It was in 1936, while living in the Marquesas Islands, that the subject first caught Heyerdahl's attention, when he heard a legend claiming that the first settlers of the Marquesas had arrived from an eastern land on the other side of the sea, under the leadership of a king called Tiki. Further investigations unearthed an old Peruvian legend of a ruler known as **Kon Tiki** who, following military defeat, fled to the Peruvian coast where he built a raft and sailed west with his supporters. Was this the same Tiki of the Marquesan story? Could such a voyage be possible? In 1948 Heyerdahl proved, quite spectacularly, that it was indeed possible when he and five companions successfully sailed a traditionally constructed balsa raft (the *Kon Tiki*) from Peru to an island east of Tahiti in a 101-day voyage.

This was followed up, in 1955, with a ground-breaking expedition to Easter Island where Heyerdahl and a team of professional archeologists spent five months excavating the monuments, houses and other sites. The archeologists drew different conclusions from his, but Heyerdahl was convinced that Easter Island had been colonized by South Americans. He backed up his theory with some persuasive but highly selective details, concentrating on the fact that winds and currents in the Pacific move in a westward, not an eastward, direction; on the presence in Polynesia of the sweet potato, indisputably of South American origin; on the resemblance between the close-fitting stonework of some Easter Island platforms and some types of Inca masonry; and on the ancient Peruvian custom of artificially extending the ear lobes, just like the islanders at the time of European contact. He failed to explain, however, the total absence in Polynesia of South American pottery and textiles – pivotal elements of that continent's culture – and the fact that no trace of any South American language had been found there.

Seductive as Heyerdahl's theories were, they never really gained currency in the academic world. The view of most experts, then and now, is that Easter Island was colonized by Polynesians from the west – an opinion backed by linguistic evidence, physical anthropology, including bone analysis, and the proliferation on Easter Island of Polynesian plants such as taro, yam, bananas and sugar cane. Which precise part of Polynesia these settlers came from is still open to debate, though the Marquesas is thought to be the most likely point of departure (for the settlement not only of Easter Island, but also of Hawaii and New Zealand). As for the date of the settlers' arrival, all we can be sure of is that they were constructing *ahu* (ceremonial platforms) by 690 AD – the earliest reliable radiocarbon date – but the sophistication of the platforms associated with that date suggests that the islanders had by then been building for several centuries. No one knows for sure if this culture developed in complete isolation, or if another wave of colonists arrived at a later date, as suggested in some of the oral traditions. Most scholars tend to think that Easter Island's archeological remains point towards an unbroken line of cultural development, interrupted only by European discovery. What they still can't explain, however, is the presence of the South American sweet potato, which remains a perplexing archeological mystery – letting in a tiny chink of hope for Thor Heyerdahl, who to this day holds firmly to his convictions.

mission fully accomplished by the time of his death, four years later. The peace was disrupted, however, when the French plantation owner, **Jean-Baptiste Doutrou-Bornier**, bought up large tracts of land and proceeded to run the island as his personal ranch, paying the islanders a pittance for their hard labour, and resorting to violence when they wouldn't co-operate. When the missionaries opposed Doutrou-Bornier's exploitation of the islanders, he instigated armed attacks on their missions, forcing them to evacuate the island. He dealt a further blow to the island's slowly recovering population by sending all but a hundred islanders to Tahiti to work on his partner's plantation. His autocratic rule finally came to an end in 1877, when he was murdered by the oppressed islanders. The **Chilean government** acquired the lands that had belonged to Doutrou-Bornier, and went on to purchase most of the remaining land on the island, leaving only the village of Hanga Roa in the possession of the

RONGORONGO

In 1864, in his account of his nine-month residence on Easter Island, the French missionary Eugène Eyraud wrote of an intriguing form of writing he'd come across in the islanders' homes.

> *In all the houses are encountered tablets or staffs of wood covered with hieroglyphics. These are figures of animals unknown in the island which the people inscribed with sharp stones. Each figure has its name but the little account that they take of these tablets inclines me to believe these signs, the remains of primitive writing, are for them today a usage which they preserved without enquiry into their meaning.*

This was the first the outside world had heard of the inscribed wooden tablets, known by the Rapa Nui as "*ko hau motu mo rongorongo*" or "lines of script for recitation". The revelation of this unheard-of script prompted a flurry of academic interest, but, predictably, the rongorongo tablets remained firmly beyond the grasp of the scholars who came to study them, for none of the islanders knew how to read them, though a few had heard them recited in their childhood. Almost 130 years later, no one has succeeded in deciphering them.

The script consists of tiny, tightly packed symbols carved in straight lines across the wooden boards. The symbols, which include representations of people, animals, birds and plants, are upside down on each alternate line, requiring the reader to turn the board around at the end of each line. Late nineteenth-century oral testimonies suggest that the tablets contained records of genealogies, creation myths, wars and deaths, and religious hymns. They claim that the knowledge of reading and writing the script was in the hands of a few specialists, the last of whom were probably killed off with the slave raids and TB epidemics in the 1860s.

Of the numerous tablets noted by Father Eugène, the vast majority have disappeared. Many of them were destroyed by their owners for fear that the strictly tapu objects would pass into foreign hands, invoking the rage of the ancestors. Others were hidden in secret underground caves where they decomposed in the damp air. Today, only 29 rongorongo tablets remain in existence, all of them spirited off to overseas museums. Modern scholars are scarcely any further on than they were when the tablets were first brought to light. Some believe that the script was developed after the first European contact, inspired by the written documents that the Spaniards made the island's chiefs sign in 1770. Others dispute the fact that it is a script at all. The most widely accepted theory is that, rather than representing grammatical sentences, the symbols were mnemonics for use in recitals and chantings. While it seems unlikely that the rongorongo code will ever be cracked, we are at least left with the outstanding craftsmanship of the exquisitely carved tablets, which deserve equal attention as works of art as of repositories of lost information. You can see rongorongo tablets in Santiago's Museo de la Merced (see p.78) and Museo Nacional de Historia Natural (see p.85).

islanders. Then, on September 9, 1888, the Chilean navy officially **annexed** Easter Island, and declared it Chilean territory. Chile, however, took no real interest in the place, and leased it off to a wool-trading company, which virtually governed the island according to its own needs and interests, an arrangement that continued until 1953 when the company's lease was revoked and the navy stepped in to resume command. Still the islanders were given no say in the running of their affairs, and seemed to be regarded more as property than as citizens – it was not until 1966, eighty years after annexation, that they were granted full citizenship and entitled to vote. The last few decades have thankfully seen a more enlightened approach on the part of the Chilean government, which has finally transferred the management of most local affairs to the islanders. Many inhabitants still feel badly done by, however, and land rights remain a contentious issue, as expressed in the large placard hanging on the wall of Hanga Roa's church: "*Rapa Nui demands the restitution of its lands usurped by the state of Chile.*"

Hanga Roa

Nestling in the southwest corner of the island, the village of **HANGA ROA** is somewhat low on attractions (even the island's single **museum** is out of town – see p.440) but high on accommodation and other services, and, unless you're camping, is almost certainly where you'll be based. Its long, sprawling streets, lined with single-storey houses and fragrant eucalyptus trees, are mostly unpaved, giving the place the unfinished feel of a recently settled frontier town. In fact it's been the island's main residential sector since the 1860s, when Catholic missionaries relocated the islanders here to facilitate their conversion. A relic of those early days is the small stone **church** in the northeast corner of town, where islanders still congregate every Sunday morning – join them, if you're around, for an unforgettable rhapsody of Polynesian hymns. In addition to the church there are the other community staples, like the Gobernación (government building), the post office and the bank, all close to each other down towards the *caleta*. Also down here, overlooking the harbour, you'll find a couple of badly fractured **moai** erected on an ahu – quite exciting when you've just arrived, but nothing compared to what's ahead of you. The rest of town is made up principally of the very long main street, Policarpo Toro, lined with souvenir shops and small supermarkets, and the undisciplined, winding lanes that surround it.

Arrival and information

The **airport** is about 1km from the southern edge of Hanga Roa. When you emerge from the aeroplane you'll be met by every single *residencial* owner on the island, all of them trying to snap up your custom, and many eager to adorn you with hand-threaded garlands of flowers. It's possible to walk into town in less than half an hour, but most of the *residenciales* are widely dispersed around the village, and it can be a drag traipsing from one to another, particularly as many owners don't return from the airport for some time as they wait to fill up their jeeps with guests. In light of this it's probably a good idea to sort your accommodation out while you're here at the airport, thus securing a lift into town from the owner – make it clear, though, that you'll take the room only if you like it when you see it.

Sernatur has an office down towards the *caleta* (Mon–Fri 8am–1pm & 2.30–5.30pm; ☎32/223255). Very little of its printed information is on display, so you'll have to ask for the lists of the island's accommodation (with room rates), restaurants and car-rental outlets. **Conaf**'s administration centre is in calle Atamu Tekana (Mon–Fri 9am–noon & 3–6pm; ☎32/223236).

Accommodation

Accommodation on Easter Island is very expensive for what you get – a typical double room in a *residencial* costs around US$50–60 (almost always with private bath), while a smart hotel room costs up to US$120. There are over thirty **residenciales** on the island – most of them family homes (invariably bungalows) with a few extra rooms added on – and about ten proper **hotels**, which tend to earn their living from package-tour block bookings. Most places offer evening **meals** at a set rate, usually around US$15–25 in *residenciales* and US $25–30 in hotels. Room rates are usually quoted in US dollars, and can be paid for either in dollars or pesos. Always try **bargaining** the price down but note that the Rapa Nui are astute negotiators, and will generally try to charge you as much as they think you're prepared to pay. Finally, bear in mind that addresses are rarely used, so the best way to find a hotel or *residencial* listed below is to use the map above. Many establishments have no name, and even when they do it's usually better to give the owner's name when you're asking for directions (we've included this in each listing, where necessary).

Residenciales

Ana Rapu, Av Apina (☎ & fax 32/100540). Always-busy *residencial* in a beautiful location, down by the coast. Some rooms are light and airy, with good views, while others are dark, dingy and crumbling. Shared and private bath, and access to shared kitchen. ③–④.

Kona Tau, Av Avareipua (☎32/100321). Simple, good-value rooms in a friendly family home, close to the airport but inconvenient for the rest of town. ④.

Martín y Anita, calle Simón Paoa (☎ & fax 32/100593). Attractive house offering six pleasant, sun-filled rooms set in a lovely garden with a patio and garden chairs. ⑤.

Mirú, Av Policarpo Toro (run by Sandra & Janet; ☎32/100365). New addition to the crop of *residenciales*, offering brightly coloured, fairly spacious rooms on Policarpo Toro. It's run by two cheerful sisters, who also cook good meals and snacks in the attached café-restaurant. ⑤.

Pedro Atan, Av Policarpo Toro (☎32/100329). Plain but fresh, clean rooms built around a yard, owned by the son of the famous mayor who features prominently in Thor Heyerdahl's *Aku Aku* – note the signed photo of Heyerdahl hanging proudly on the wall of the dining room. ⑤.

Rapa Nui Inn, Av Policarpo Toro (owned by Rebeca Tepano; ☎32/100228). Fairly basic but adequate rooms, cheaper than most, conveniently located on the main street, towards the airport. ④.

Sofia Gomero, calle Tuukoihu (☎32/223313). A high standard of comfort and decor at this peaceful *residencial*, efficiently run by a Pascuense-Austrian couple. Good food, too, served in a smart new dining area with great views, but a bit of a walk from the centre. ⑤.

Tahai, sendero Tahai (owned by Maria Hey; ☎32/100395). Spacious, slightly neglected but very tranquil rooms about a 10min walk from the village. There's a large wooden veranda where you can sit and admire the garden, overflowing with flowers and banana trees. ⑤.

Tahiri, calle Ara Roa Rakei (owned by Tutti Pakomio; ☎32/100263). Spotless bungalow rooms with white walls and bright floral prints looking onto a lush, green garden. Its young owner is very welcoming, too, making this a good choice. ⑤.

Tekena Inn, Av Policarpo Toro (owned by Juan Nahoe Calderón; ☎32/100289). The rooms here, set well back from the main street, feel a little dated, but they're clean, with private bath, and better value than many others of a similar standard. ④.

Vai Kapu, off Av Te Pito Ote Henua (owned by Ines Paoa; ☎32/100377). Friendly *residencial* close to the church offering a pretty garden and tidy rooms. ⑤.

Villa Tiki, Av Pont (owned by Georgina Paoa; ☎32/100327). Spacious, neat rooms with sweeping views onto the hills and a large, well-tended garden, great to relax in. A little overpriced, however. ⑥.

Hotels

Chez Joseph, Av Avareipua (owned by Jose Pakomio; ☎32/100281). Small, family-run hotel with light, spacious rooms and a pleasant dining area. There's no sign by the drive; look out for the moai carving by the door. ⑤.

Iorana, off Av Atamu Tekena (☎32/100312). The rooms of this upmarket hotel aren't as smart as you'd expect for the price but the secluded location, looking down to the ocean, is unbeatable. As well as a regular outdoor pool, there's a "natural" pool enclosed by rocks and filled with seawater. ⑦.

O'Tai, Av Pito Te Henua (owned by Rosita Cardinali; ☎32/100250). Smart, well-furnished bungalow rooms with patio doors set in a large, flower-filled garden in a central location. ⑥–⑦.

Victoria, Av Pont (owned by Jorge Edmunds Rapahango; ☎32/100272). Small hotel with eight bungalow-style rooms, a decent restaurant and an outdoor terrace giving splendid views out to sea. ⑤.

Camping

Hanga Roa's first official **campsite** is due to open down by the beach, run by Ana Rapu, close to her *residencial*. The site should be up and running by the time you read this, and is to include cold water showers and the use of a kitchen. In addition, many *residencial* owners have allowed camping in their gardens for years, charging around US$10 per tent or per person, depending on their mood – *Tekana Inn* is a good bet. You're also allowed to camp for free next to the rangers' huts at **Playa Anakena** (see p.439) and at **Ranu Raraku** (see p.438), both of which have limited supplies of water.

Eating, drinking and entertainment

There isn't a large concentration of **eating** places on Easter Island, as so many tourists eat at their *residencial* or hotel, which means demand isn't that high. That said, what's

RAPA NUI ROMEOS

Rapa Nui men have a well-deserved reputation as lovers and schmoozers and breakers of hearts. With their chiselled features, flowing black locks (set off by the *de rigueur* red bandana) and purring motorbikes, they've turned the holiday romance into an art form. Add to their innate charms the palm-fringed island setting, with its ancient, mysterious statues, and it begins to be clear why every year hundreds of foreign women fall hook, line and sinker for these Rapa Nui Romeos. Not that it's a problem – these guys are in it for nothing more sinister than the fun, and most women go home with happy memories and a big smile. Where things go wrong, however, is when the women start believing their island Casanovas. One of Rapa Nui's most recent casualties was a no-nonsense British government economist whose newfound lovemate had talked longingly of marriage. At the airport, about to board the plane, she impulsively forfeited her return flight to Chile and turned back, combing the airport crowds for her lover – only to catch a glimpse of him speeding off on his motorbike with a newly arrived gringa installed on the back. This particular woman spent three weeks trying to get off the island on the overbooked Lan Chile flights. During that time, she encountered twelve cases not wildly dissimilar from her own. So, female travellers, be on your guard. Enjoy, for sure – but don't believe a word they say.

on offer is pretty good, including several excellent, though expensive, fish restaurants, and a number of cheaper outlets serving quick snacks like pizzas, *empanadas* and burgers. There's a small but lively local **nightlife** scene, focused on a couple of **bar-discos** – namely *Piriti*, on Avenida Hotu Matu'a, near the airport, and *Toroko*, north of the *caleta*. These are good places to meet the islanders, as they're geared more towards young Rapa Nui than tourists, though the strong local feel can be slightly daunting when you first walk in. Less authentic, but more exotic, entertainment is offered in the form of regular **hula dances** (beautiful women, grass skirts, swaying hips) held at various restaurants and hotels – keep your eye open for fliers, or ask at Sernatur. These are tame, soulless offerings, however, compared to the genuine hulas you'll see for free at **Tapatai Rapa Nui**, the annual festival held in the first two weeks of February, celebrating Rapa Nui culture, tradition and history. As well as dancing there are body painting competitions, sculpture competitions, choral recitals, surfing displays, re-enactments of old legends and huge earth-oven feasts.

Restaurants and snack bars

Averei Pua, Caleta Hanga Roa. Modest, no-frills, restaurant serving inexpensive, filling fish and meat dishes in generous portions.

Gringo's, Av Policarpo Toro, towards the airport. Good-value, home-cooked snacks like *empanadas* and pizzas served up by two delightful sisters. Great pineapple milkshakes, too.

Ki Tai, near the *caleta*. Down-to-earth little restaurant in a lovely location by the beach, serving excellent-value fish and meat dishes.

Kona Koa, near Entel. Fancy restaurant serving overpriced but good steaks and fish, sometimes accompanied by a hula show. It offers a free taxi service from your hotel – call on ☎32/100415.

La Taverne du Pecheur, Caleta Hanga Roa. The best restaurant on Easter Island, run by a dour Frenchman. Don't let this put you off, though – his Pacific lobster *aioli* is outstanding, not to be missed on any account.

Mamá Sabina, Av Policarpo Toro, opposite the Lan Chile office. Reliable, friendly and good-value place offering a range of snacks and meals.

Pea, Caleta Hanga Roa. Beautifully situated, with great views across the ocean. Busy and popular, serving the usual fish specialities. Good service.

Listings

Banks and exchange The best place to change travellers' cheques (US dollars only) is at the petrol station on Av Hotu Matu'a, which gives reasonable rates and charges no commission. The Banco del Estado de Chile (Mon–Fri 8am–noon), down by the *caleta*, charges a hefty commission and its rates are poor.

Camping As you can't bring fuel on the plane, you'll need to buy it on the island. White gas (*bencina blanca*) is hard to come by, but is usually stocked at Kai Nene supermarket on Policarpo Toro. For Camping Gaz, try Maitai, on the same road.

Car and motorbike rental In addition to the car-hire firms, many souvenir shops and even supermarkets on Policarpo Toro hire jeeps as a sideline, usually with just a couple of vehicles available. Average daily rates range from US$50 to US$80. Outlets include Easter Island Rent a Car (☎32/100326); Hertz; Insular (☎32/100480); Kioa Koe (☎32/100282); Tekena Inn (☎32/100289).

Hospital The island's only clinic is at the end of the plot east of the church.

Lan Chile Midway up Policarpo Toro (☎32/223279).

Laundry The only laundry is on Policarpo Toro, up from Residencial Pedro Atan, but it's very expensive, priced by item, not by weight. Try asking the *señora* at your *residencial*, which would be a lot cheaper.

Mountain bikes These are available for hire at several shops on Policarpo Toro, including Kodak and Via Mona.

Post Office The island's single *correo* is down towards the *caleta*, opposite *Hotel O'Tai*. The cost of postage is the same from Easter Island as from mainland Chile.

Telephone office There's an Entel office round the corner from the bank, with faxing facilities.

GETTING AROUND EASTER ISLAND

The layout of the island's roads encourages you to visit the sites on three or four different trips: one taking in the south coast, Rano Raraku and Anakena on a long circular route; another going inland to Ahu Akivi, either returning along the west coast, via Tahai, or else covering the coastal path on foot in a separate trip; and finally climbing up to Rano Kau and Orongo.

It's worth putting some thought into how you want to **get around** the island, as the type of transport you choose can make a big difference to your experience of the place. The easiest, most hassle-free choice is to take an **organized tour**, but while this ensures you get to see a large number of sites, with guided commentary (and without getting lost), you can feel you're on a sightseeing conveyer belt – and it seems a shame to visit the most remote inhabited island in the world with a crowd of other tourists. Tours usually cost around US$35–45 for a full day, and US$20–25 for a half-day. The two main **tour companies** on the island are Kia Koe (☎ & fax 32/100282), on Policarpo Toro, and Mahina Tur, at Hotu Matu'a with Policarpo Toro (☎ & fax 32/100220), both of which have comfortable vehicles and guides fluent in Spanish, English, French, Italian and German. In addition to these, numerous hotels, *residenciales* and local people offer jeep or minibus tours. If you want more solitude and independence you can hire a **jeep** or a **motorbike** (see "Listings", above) which can be quite an adventure as the roads are so dreadful. This is a very popular option so you should book your vehicle as soon as you can after arrival, before the rest of your plane beats you to it. Another alternative is to visit the island on **horseback**. You'll find a lot of places offering horses, from *residenciales* to souvenir shops, but they're often badly cared-for and rather mangy – for sleek, healthy beasts, contact Roberto (☎32/100474), or French-born Patrice (☎32/100518), or ask Sernatur for a recommendation. Finally, you could consider visiting some sites on a **mountain bike** (see "Listings", above) or **on foot**, though walking round the whole island would be quite a challenge. Easy targets include Ahu Tahai (30min), Rano Kau (1hr) and Vinapu (1hr 30min); if you're prepared to carry a tent, food and water, you could also hike out to Rano Raraku (5hr) and Playa Anakena (6hr inland, 8hr along the coast).

The southeastern circuit

The loop formed by the sixteen-kilometre southern coast road and the thirty-kilometre paved road from Anakena to Hanga Roa lends itself to a convenient sightseeing route that takes in some of the island's most impressive sights – including Vinapu, Tongariki, Rano Raraku and Anakena. The road bypasses the Poike peninsula, though it's possible (if not terribly rewarding) to explore this area on foot. Most visitors do this circuit with a rental vehicle or on a tour; it's too far to do on horseback in a single day, but you could hike it in three days, camping by the Conaf huts at Rano Raraku and Anakena.

Vinapu

From Hanga Roa, follow Avenida Hotu Matu'a down to the southern coast road then turn right, just after the oil containers, and you'll reach **Vinapu**, the site of two large ahus. Anyone who's seen Macchu Pichu or other Inca ruins can't fail to be startled by the masonry of Vinapu's main ahu, made of huge, mortarless blocks of stone described by Thor Heyerdahl as "cut like cheese and fitted carefully to one another without a crack or a hole". It's easy to imagine the thrill Heyerdahl must have felt on seeing this stonework, given his conviction that Easter Island had been settled from South America, and it's not surprising he begged the question: "Could it be the master masons from Peru who had been busy out here too?" Close to this platform, known as Vinapu I, is another ahu, Vinapu II, whose stonework is vastly inferior to its neighbour, consisting of roughly hewn stones and boulders fitted loosely together.

The sequence of the two ahus' construction has been vigorously debated. The Norwegian expedition was the first to excavate the site and, with radiocarbon dating, concluded that the precisely carved Vinapu I (the famous stone that caused so much ink to flow) was among the earliest built on the island, and that Vinapu II was a much later construction. This supported Heyerdahl's theory that the island's first settlers imported the highly specialized stone-carving techniques of Peru, and that later platforms, after a period of degeneration, were built by "far less capable architects, who were no longer masters of the complicated Inca technique". Modern archeologists, however, believe that this impressive masonry is simply a perfected example of a style developed locally on Easter Island, and more recent radiocarbon tests have given Vinapu I a new date of 1516 AD, and Vinapu II a date of 857 AD – the reverse of Heyerdahl's sequence. Both ahus once supported moai, now lying in fragments behind the platforms, and another moai stands half-buried in the ground in front of Vinapu I, perhaps intended to be raised to the platform, which bears a pedestal that was never filled.

Along the southern coast

Back on the coast road, heading northeast towards Poike, you'll pass site after site of toppled moai, all knocked from their ahu and lying prostrate on the ground. Many lie flat on their faces in a position of humiliation, evoking, quite intensely, a sense of the violence, destruction and tragedy that marked the final phase of the island's pre-history, when warring clans desecrated and destroyed the sacred sites of their enemies. Above all there's an acute impression of futility, and of wasted human effort. The first site you pass is **Vaihu**, where eight tall statues lie face-down on the ground, their red stone topknots strewn along the coast. Three kilometres further along, **Ahu Akahanga** presents an equally mournful picture of a row of fallen moai; according to some oral traditions, it's also the burial place of Hotu Matu'a, the island's first settler and king. Further up the coast, **Ahu Hanga Tetenga** is the site of the largest moai – 9.94m – ever transported to a platform. It's not clear if the statue was successfully erected, as its eye sockets were never carved (usually the finishing touch). In any event, it now lies shattered at the foot of its ahu, leaving no clues as to whether it fell during erection or was toppled at a later date.

Just beyond Ahu Hanga Tetenga, the road forks. The left-hand branch, known as the **Camino de los Moai**, leads to the quarry of Rano Raraku. It's thought to have been the main roadway along which the statues were transported from the quarry, and is still littered with abandoned statues, fallen by the wayside en route to their platforms. The right-hand branch continues up the coast to the magnificent Ahu Tongariki. Note that Rano Raraku can also be approached from Tongariki.

Ahu Tongariki

The fifteen colossal moai lined up on **Ahu Tongariki** make a sensational sight. This was the largest number of moai ever erected on a single ahu, and the platform, some 200m long, was the largest built on the island. It was totally destroyed in 1960 when a massive tidal wave, caused by an earthquake in Chile, swept across this corner of the island, dragging the platform blocks and the statues 90m inland – a remarkable distance, given that the statues weigh up to thirty tonnes each. The whole site has been recently restored by a Japanese project, and today the statues stand tall and proud on their ahu, the very picture of dignity. One of them's wearing a red topknot, and several have holes in their earlobes, which perhaps had obsidian disks inserted in them. The most curious feature, though, is the faint outline of goatee beards carved on some of these moai – among the very few on the island with such facial decoration.

Rano Raraku

North of Tongariki, **Rano Raraku** rises from the land in a hulking mass of volcanic stone. This is where almost all of the island's statues were produced, carved directly from the "tuff" (compacted volcanic ash) of the crater's outer slopes. The first surprise, on approaching the crater from the car park, are the dozens of **giant heads** sprouting from the ground. Tall, thin and angular, with long noses and hollow cheeks, these are the island's most widely photographed statues and have become the classic image of Easter Island presented to the outside world. It was originally thought that these heads were bodyless, but when archeologists began digging earlier this century they discovered whole torsos and arms buried beneath the ground. They are, in fact, finished moai brought down from the quarry, and were probably placed in shallow pits (that gradually built up) until they could be transported to their ahu. Clearly these were the last of the moai to be completed, and one of them bears an image on its chest of a three masted sailing ship, suggesting that they were carved *after* European contact.

As you move higher up Ranu Raraku's slopes, you gradually become aware that you are surrounded by hundreds of **unfinished statues** carved out of the very rock you're walking on. Of all the marvels on Easter Island, this is the one that will make you gasp with astonishment, as you realize that the ledge you just sat on is an arm, and that this overhanging rock is a nose. It's an extraordinary spectacle, vividly described by Thor Heyerdahl in this passage from *Aku Aku*:

> *We were surrounded, as in a hall of mirrors, by enormous faces circling about us, seen from in front, in profile and at every angle. . . We had them above us, beneath us and on both sides. We clambered over noses and chins and trod on mouths and gigantic fists, while huge bodies lay leaning over us on the ledges higher up. As our eyes gradually became trained to distinguish art from nature, we perceived that the whole mountain was one single swarm of bodies and heads.*

Among this mass of shapes, still attached to the rock face, is **El Gigante**, the biggest moai ever carved, stretching over 20m from top to bottom. Experts believe it would

THE MOAI OF EASTER ISLAND

The enduring symbol of Easter Island always has been, and doubtless always will be, the monolithic **statues** that line its shores. That's not to say there's nothing else to command our attention on the island. On the contrary, its elaborate rock carvings, ceremonial platforms, intriguing architecture and spectacular volcanic geography are all compelling attractions in their own right. And yet, inevitably, they're overshadowed to the point of oblivion by the overwhelming presence of the moai, whose haughty features stare at us from every corner of the island. These moai astonish for a good many reasons, not least because they are utterly unique, and can be found nowhere else in the world. A neolithic statue cult on this scale would impress in any location, but the fact that it developed in total isolation on a tiny island in the middle of the Pacific almost defies belief. How did this stone-age people, with no cross-cultural contact or outside influence, create such a specialized and advanced carving industry? And why did they take it to such extremes? There are some 400 finished statues scattered around the island, and almost as many in the statue quarry, in varying stages of completion. Clearly the people of Easter Island were in the grip of an extraordinary obsession – that led them, it would seem, to accomplish towering artistic achievements, but also, ultimately, to wreak devastation on their own society.

The Easter Island moai range in height from 2m to almost 10m, and while no two statues are identical, all are carved in the same highly stylized manner. Each figure – probably male – is represented down to the level of the hips. Their bellies are gently rounded, their nipples clearly marked, and their arms are held tightly by their sides, with their strange, long-fingered hands placed across their abdomens. Their heads are long and rectangular, with pointed chins, prominent, angular noses and thin, tight lips curled into an expression of disdain. According to the assertions of the islanders, which are consistent with widespread Polynesian tradition, it would seem that these figures represented important **ancestors**, such as chiefs and priests, and were erected on the ancestral land of the kin-group these individuals belonged to, which they would watch over and protect with their *mana* (almost all the moai are looking inland, rather than gazing out to sea). It's possible, also, that some statues were commissioned during the lifetime of the people they were destined to commemorate, who presumably wanted their memorials to be as impressive as possible, perhaps leading to intense competition over their size and splendour. Almost all the statues were carved out of the quarry at Rano Raraku, one of the island's volcanic craters. It's impossible to establish exactly when the first were carved, as radiocarbon dating works only on organic material, but archeologists have proposed tentative dates of around the seventh century AD for the early statues, and around the fifteenth century for the bulk of the statues, when production was at its peak. What we do know, however, is *how* they were carved, as the hundreds of abandoned tools and unfinished statues in Rano Raraku demonstrate quite clearly how their forms were chiselled out of the rock face until they were attached to it by only a thin keel running down their spine. When all was completed but their eye sockets, they were freed from their keel and slid down the slope of the quarry, then temporarily erected in a pit until they were transported to their ahu.

Just how they were **moved** across the island remains a mystery. Not only were the statues extremely heavy (weighing, on average, some 18 tonnes), but many were embellished with delicate carvings in bas relief representing tattoos or loin cloths. These were carved before transportation, and must have required very careful handling not to be damaged. The island's oral histories offer no clues as to how the moai were moved, claiming that the statues' *mana* enabled them to walk a short distance each day until they reached their platforms. Some modern theories have been even less convincing – the French writer Francis Mazière suggested in 1969 that they were moved by "certain men" using "electro-magnetic or anti-gravitational forces", while the Swiss Erich Von Däniken was convinced they were moved by the humans with birds' heads – which he interpreted as "unknown space travellers" – depicted in the island's rock art. More plausible theories have included horizontal swivelling and vertical swivelling, but since it was established in the 1980s that the island was once densely covered by two species of tree – the shrublike toromiro and a large palm – it's been assumed that they were dragged either on wooden sledges, or on top of rollers, probably heavily padded by palm fronds.

How the statues were **erected** onto their platforms in the absence of any type of machinery is another enigma, though much light was thrown onto this in a now-famous experiment conducted by Thor Heyerdahl in 1955. Heyerdahl challenged the island's mayor to raise a fallen, 25-tonne statue at Anakena beach and, under the mayor's supervision, twelve islanders raised the statue in eighteen days, using two levers and slipping layer after layer of stones underneath the horizontal statue. Little by little, it was raised on the bed of stones until it was level with its platform; at this point, the layers of pebbles were placed only under its head, until the statue was nearly vertical and could be slipped into place. Archeologists agree that this method is highly likely to have been used when the statues were first raised. In contrast, no one has been able to demonstrate how the large, heavy "topknots" were placed on the raised statue's head – a monumental feat, achieved only with the use of a crane in modern times.

Quite clearly, the mass production, the transportation and the erection of these monoliths must have involved an enormous amount of work. Oral traditions and archeological records suggest that there was no central controlling power on Easter Island, and that its society was based around independent clans, or **kin-groups**, each with its own high-ranking members. Presumably, then, the statue-carvers were not forced to work by a central authority, but worked voluntarily for their kin-group – indeed, it seems they were highly revered members of a privileged class who were exempt from food production, and were supported by farmers and fishermen on the island. Such a system must have involved a great deal of economic co-operation, which appears to have been successfully maintained for hundreds of years. Then, in the later stages of the island's pre-history, something went wrong and the system collapsed. Groups that had worked peacefully, if competitively, alongside each other at Rano Raraku withdrew from the quarry and exchanged their tools for weapons, as the island became engulfed by internal strife and warfare. The island's archeological record reveals a sudden, dramatic proliferation of obsidian weapons during the eighteenth century, as well as the remains of violently beaten skulls, and evidence of the widespread use of caves as refuges. Fragments of teeth found in human bones even indicate the possibility of cannibalism – something that features prominently in the island's oral traditions. The most dramatic testimony of this period of conflict, however, is provided by the hundreds of fallen statues littering the island, deliberately and systematically toppled from their platforms, as enemy groups set out to desecrate each other's sacred sites. The Spanish expedition, under González, reported no toppled statues in 1770 after a fairly thorough exploration of the island, but just four years later, Captain Cook saw many overturned figures lying next to their platforms. Almost a century later, in 1868, a visiting English doctor found that not a single statue remained standing on the island.

So what went wrong on Easter Island? What caused this highly organized and productive civilization to self-destruct? Why was a culture of interdependence and collaboration exchanged for one of violence and conflict? It seems likely that the seeds of social collapse lay, paradoxically, in the statue cult – or rather the extremes it was taken to by the islanders. In the words of William Mulloy, a member of the Norwegian expedition: "[statue carving] came to take up so much of the force of the culture that such important activities as farming and fishing were neglected, and the people didn't have enough to eat. You can carry statue-making only so far." It seems that as the impulse to produce moai required more and more hands, the delicate balance between food distribution and statue-carving was destroyed. This situation was profoundly aggravated by the growing scarcity of food brought about possibly by overpopulation, and certainly by deforestation, following centuries of logging for boat-building, fuel consumption and statue-transportation. By the time the Europeans arrived in the eighteenth century, there was scarcely a tree left on the island, and the large palm, shown by pollen samples to have been once abundant, had become extinct. This must have had a catastrophic effect on the islanders' ability to feed themselves: deep-sea fishing became increasingly difficult, and eventually impossible, due to the lack of wood available for new canoes, and even land cultivation was affected, as the deforestation caused soil erosion. In this climate of encroaching deprivation, it begins to be clear why the system broke down, and why the farmers and fishermen were no longer willing or able to pool their spoils – and why the Easter Island civilization descended into anarchy, dragging its majestic monuments with it.

have been impossible to transport, let alone erect, this monster, and it's been suggested that it was never intended to be moved. A faint path leads up to the top of the crater rim where you'll find, on the other side, more buried moai, staggered down the green slopes of the interior. At the bottom, a large, murky lake is covered with floating reeds, adding to the strangeness of the scene.

There's free **camping** at Rano Raraku, by the Conaf ranger station west of the quarry – useful if you want to climb among the statues at sunrise, before any other tourists get there.

The Poike peninsula

East of Rano Raraku, the Poike peninsula is a green, gently rounded plateau bound in by steep cliffs. Few people venture onto this part of the island, which is fenced off and used for cattle grazing. You can, however, hop across quite easily, and walk round the edge of the peninsula in about four hours, but there's no shade, no path and little to see but cows and ocean. Poike's main interest lies in the myths and legends associated with it. One tells of the **cave of the virgins**, *Ana o Keke*, where a number of young girls were confined for months on end, so that their skin should remain as pale as possible. Another one, more famous, is of the battle of the **Long Ears and Short Ears** (see box below). This battle is supposed to have taken place in the 3.5-kilometre-long ditch separating the peninsula from the rest of the island, known as *Ko te Ava o Iko*, or "Iko's ditch". Early investigators thought it was a natural geographic feature, and that the islanders had simply invented a myth to explain its presence, but the Norwegian expedition was able to prove that the trench was either an artificial extension of a natural feature, or else entirely man-made. Moreover, they discovered traces of intense burning which radiocarbon dating placed at 1676 AD, corresponding to estimates, based on oral traditions, of when this battle took place. Modern archeologists, however, are far from convinced, mainly due to the complete absence of weapons and mass human remains in the ditch. They speculate that the evidence of burning could easily be asso-

THE BATTLE OF THE LONG EARS AND THE SHORT EARS

According to an oft-repeated oral tradition, the island's population, in the time just before the toppling of the statues, was divided into two principal groups: the *Hanau Momoko*, or **Short Ears**, and the *Hanau Eepe*, or **Long Ears**, the latter so called because they pierced their ears and used wooden disks to extend their lobes right down to their shoulders – a practice still current at the time of the first European visitors. It seems that the Long Ears were extremely domineering, and that the Short Ears resented them intensely. Things came to a head when the Long Ears tried to force the Short Ears to clear the island of the many loose stones that covered its surface and throw them into the sea, to make more land available for agriculture. This was the final straw for the Short Ears, who rebelled, forcing the Long Ears to retreat to the **Poike** peninsula at the eastern end of the island. Here the Long Ears dug a series of deep ditches separating the peninsula from the rest of the island, and filled them with branches and grass, intending to force their enemies inside and set them alight. Their plans were thwarted, however, when a Short Ears woman who was married to one of the Long Ears alerted her people to this scheme, and, with a secret signal, allowed them to pass into the peninsula and surround their enemies while they were sleeping. When the Short Ears attacked, the Long Ears had nowhere to run but straight into their own ditch, which the Short Ears gleefully set fire to. The Long Ears roasted to death in the pits, but three of them escaped, and fled into hiding. Two of them were caught and executed, but one, a certain Ororoina, was allowed to live, and went on to father many children – whose descendants, to this day, are proud of their Long Ear heritage.

ciated with cooking (the islanders commonly cooked in holes in the ground), or even with agriculture.

North to Anakena

From the southern coast, the road turns inland, cutting past the Poike peninsula, and leads directly to Ovahe and Anakena. On the way, look out for **Ahu te Pito Kura**, down by Bahía La Perouse (signed). This is the site of **Paro**, probably the largest moai successfully erected on a platform, at 9.8m tall (it's just a fraction smaller than the moai transported to Ahu Hanga Tetenga on the southern coast, which seems not to have been successfully erected). Paro is thought to have been one of the latest moai to be moved and erected, and is estimated to weigh a staggering 82 tonnes. No one has attempted to restore and re-erect the giant, which still lies face down before its ahu, surrounded by rubble.

Further north, **Ovahe** is a tiny, secluded and exquisitely beautiful beach, its white sands lapped by crystal-clear waters at the foot of a large volcanic cliff. There's just about room to pitch a tent on the grassy patch next to the cliff – locals swear the tide never comes in this far, though it certainly gets unnervingly close. A little further up the coast, **Playa Anakena** is much larger, and presents a picture-postcard scene of powdery golden sands fringed by swaying palm trees. It's great for an afternoon of swimming or sunbathing, but camping here is *not* recommended unless you don't mind sharing the place with the mass of cockroaches that come out to play after dark – instead, camp by the **Conaf** office across from the beach, which offers more shade and limited water.

Anakena has a special place in Rapa Nui oral history, which holds it to be the landing site and dwelling place of Hotu Matu'a, the island's first colonizer (see p.426). It's also home to the splendid moai of **Ahu Nau Nau**, which were so deeply covered in sand until their restoration in 1978 that they were largely protected from the effects of weathering. Their haughty facial features are particularly fine, and some of them have delicate spiral designs carved in bas relief on their buttocks, perhaps representing tattoos. What makes these moai really striking, though, are the large, gleaming white eyes inserted into their eye sockets, fixed in a slightly up-turned gaze towards the sky. Archeologists had always assumed that the statues' eye sockets had remained empty, but when fragments of white coral and a circular red pebble were discovered here in 1978, it was found that they fitted together to form an oval eye with a red iris. It's not known if all the statues on the island had such eyes, as the only other fragments found have been at Vinapu. The reproduction eyes of the Nau Nau moai completely transform their faces, almost bringing them to life.

Just up the hillside by the beach you'll find the squat and rather corpulent moai of **Ahu Ature Huki**. This was the first moai to be re-erected on the island in the experiment carried out by Thor Heyerdahl in 1955, when twelve islanders showed they could raise a 25-tonne statue in eighteen days (see box on p.437).

The northern circuit

Although the triangle formed by Vinapu, Tongariki and Anakena contains the densest concentration of sites, the western and northern parts of the island are also well worth exploring. Attractions include the impressive moai of **Tapai** and **Ahu Akivi**, plus a network of underground **caves**. There are two roads serving this area: one runs inland to Aku Akivi, then continues to Ahu Te Peu on the coast; another follows the shoreline from Hanga Roa north to Ahu Te Peu, where it joins the inland road. You can cover both roads in a circular route, either on foot (about 6hr), on horseback, or in a vehicle; if you're driving, note that the coastal track is difficult to make out and extremely rough, and should only be attempted in a high clearance 4x4. An alternative is to do two separate day-trips, perhaps driving up the inland road, and walking along the coast. The very northern corner of the island is scarcely visited by anyone, as there's no access for vehicles beyond Te Peu. You can, however, continue up the coast on foot, following it all the way round to Anakena – a long, hot hike (8hr from Hanga Roa) but immeasurably peaceful, and offering good views.

Tahai and the Museo Antropólogo Sebastian Englert

To get to Tahai, walk north from the *caleta* past the cemetery, taking the path that hugs the coast. After about ten minutes you reach the ceremonial centre of **Tahai**, composed of three ahus. The first, **Ahu Vai Uri**, supports four broad, squat moai, two of which have badly damaged heads, and the stump of a fifth statue. In front of the ahu is the outline of a flattened esplanade, presumed to have been used as a ceremonial site. Archeological remains suggest that some individuals – possibly chiefs and priests – used to live near these ceremonial sites, in several locations on the island, in stone, oval houses called *hare paenga* that looked like an upturned canoe. You can see the foundations of one of these houses near Ahu Vai Uri. The second platform is **Ahu Tahai** itself, topped by a lone, weathered moai. Finally, **Ahu Kote Riku** is the site of a well-preserved moai fitted with white, glinting eyes and a red topknot.

About half a kilometre further north, set well back from the coastal path, the **Museo Antropólogo Sebastian Englert** (Tues–Fri 9.30am–12.30pm & 2–5.30pm, Sat & Sun 9.30am–12.30pm; CH$800) is housed in a modern, rotunda-shaped building. Its contents focus on the daily life of the Rapa Nui, and include a very evocative collection of black-and-white photographs of islanders from about 1915 onwards. In addition, there are several displays on language, crops and bones pointing to the Polynesian origin of the Rapa Nui people, as well as some examples of carvings and spearheads, and fragments of original moai eyes. It's not unmissable, but is worth a look-in if you're walking up the coast.

Dos Ventanas caves and Ahu Te Peu

Back on the coast road, continue north for about 3km – until you reach the point where you're standing opposite two little islands out at sea – and look out for the stone cairn by the left-hand side of the road signalling a track down towards the cliffs. At the end of the track, a tiny opening in the ground is the entrance to a pitch-black passage (take a head torch) which continues 50m underground to the adjoining **Dos Ventanas caves**. Both caves are flooded with light streaming in from the "windows", or gaping holes, that open out of the cliff wall. Prepare for a rush of adrenaline as you approach the edges, as both drop vertically down to a bed of sharp rocks and pounding waves many metres below. It's very easy to miss the path down to the cave, never mind find the opening, and your best hope is that a tour van's parked outside.

About 1km further up the coast you reach **Ahu Te Peu**, a large platform made of big, well-fitted rocks. The moai that once stood on the ahu still lie flat on the ground, left as they were during the period of warfare. Scattered around the ahu are the remains of many boat -shaped *hare paenga*, including one that's sixty metres long. It's thought that this was the site of the village of the Miru clan, the direct descendants of Hotu Matu'a.

At Ahu Te Peu, most people join up with the inland road and head back to Hanga Roa via Ahu Akivi. You can, however, continue north, either heading up the gentle volcanic cone of **Terevaka**, where you'll be rewarded with fine views across the island from its 510-metre summit, the highest point of the island (no path; 1hr up), or else follow the coastline round to Playa Anakena (4–5hr). The latter is clearly only an option if you're carrying a tent, food and water, and plan to camp at Anakena. On the way, you'll pass many fallen moai, none of them restored, as well as the ruins of stone houses and chicken pens.

Inland to Puna Pau, Ahu Akivi and the Te Pahu caves

From Hanga Roa, heading up the inland road to Ahu Akivi (first left from the paved road to Anakena) you'll pass a signed track branching left to **Puna Pau**, a low volcanic crater made of rusty-coloured rock, known as "scoria". It was out of this rock that the islanders carved the **pukao** for their statues – the cylindrical "topknots" worn by up to seventy of the moai standing on ahu. No one knows for sure what these cylinders represented, and suggestions have ranged from grass hats and turbans through to topknots (of hair) and feather headdresses. Up in the quarry, and along the track to the top, you can see thirty or so finished *pukao* lying on the ground; it's not the most exciting of Easter Island's sites, but is worth a quick detour – for the fine views, as well – if you have time to spare.

Back on the road, continue north and you'll reach **Ahu Akivi**, whose seven moai are the only ones to have been erected inland, and the only ones that look towards the sea. In fact, it's been discovered that they are oriented directly towards the rising summer solstice, along with several other ahu, suggesting that solar positions were of significance to the islanders. These curious facts aside, Ahu Akivi is a great collection of statues, in excellent condition. They were raised in 1960 by William Mulloy and Gonzalo Figueroa, two of the archeologists recruited by Heyerdahl in 1955, both of whom went on to devote their entire career to Easter Island.

From Ahu Akivi, the road turns towards the coast, where it meets Ahu Te Peu (see p.440). On the way, look out for the second path branching left from the main road, and follow it towards the thick, green leaves apparently sprouting from the ground. On closer inspection you'll find that they belong to tall bamboo trees growing in a magical underground garden at the bottom of a deep cave. Clamber down and you'll find that the cave leads properly underground into a tunnel that you can follow without any fear of getting lost. About 150m further on, you'll emerge into another huge cave (once used as a dwelling place) where blinding shafts of sunlight announce the exit above ground. These are the **Te Pahu caves**, and the corridor connecting them is a lava tube created by volcanic activity millions of years ago, along with many other underground channels that riddle this part of the island.

Rano Kau and Orongo

The ceremonial village of **ORONGO** enjoys the most spectacular location on the island, perched high on the rim of the giant volcanic crater of **Rano Kau**. On one side, a steep slope descends to the bottom of the crater, which holds a vast lake covered in a bright-green mat of floating reeds. On the other side, a near-vertical drop plunges 300m down to the dark-blue ocean. Orongo is easily reached from Hanga Roa, either by car or taxi in ten minutes, or on foot in about an hour (follow the footpath branching right from the main road, just after the Conaf sign, continuing up the hill through the eucalyptus trees). Either way, you'll end up at the Conaf hut at the top, where you're supposed to pay your park fee (unfixed hours; CH$4000) but often don't have to, as it's frequently unstaffed. The village, a short distance beyond, consists of the partially restored remains of some 48 low-lying, oval-shaped huts made of thin stone slabs, each with a tiny entrance just large enough to crawl through. A few steps from the houses, on the face of some basalt outcrops looking out to sea, you'll find a dense group of exquisitely carved **petroglyphs** depicting curled-up human figures with birds' heads and long curved beaks. These bas-relief images honour an important annual ceremony dedicated to the **cult of the birdman**. Unlike much of the island's heritage, a great deal is known about this ceremony, as it was practised right up to 1878 (though no one knows when it began).

It took place in September, when the chiefs of the various kin-groups on the island assembled at Orongo – the only time of year the village was occupied – to take part in a ritual competition. The object of this competition was to find the first egg laid by the sooty tern (a migratory bird) on Motu Nui, the largest of three islets sitting opposite Orongo, 2km out to sea. The chiefs could either seek the egg themselves or choose a servant to act as their representative. Most chiefs chose the latter option, which is no surprise, given the dangers the egg-hunter had to face – first scaling down the sheer cliff to the ocean, then swimming through shark-infested waters out to the islet. It could take several weeks for the egg to be found; meanwhile, the chiefs would remain in Orongo, where they participated in ritual dances, songs and prayers. When the sacred egg was finally found, its discoverer would bellow the name of his master across the sea, and then swim back to the island with the egg tucked into a headband. The victorious chief now became the new *tangata manu*, or **birdman**. The privileges conferred by this position were curious, to say the least: the new birdman would first have all the hair shaved off his head, including eyebrows and eyelashes; he would then be taken off, with his egg, to a sacred house at the foot of Rano Raraku, where he would live in strict seclusion for a whole year. He was allowed to eat only certain foods prepared by a special servant, and was forbidden to bathe or cut his nails. His kin-group, meanwhile, was endowed with a special, high status, which was often taken as an excuse for members to dominate and bully their rival groups. At the end of the year, the sacred powers of the egg vanished, and the ritual would begin all over again.

PART THREE

THE CONTEXTS

A BRIEF HISTORY OF CHILE

Enclosed within the mighty barriers of the Andes, the Atacama desert and the Pacific Ocean, Chile has evolved almost as an island, relatively undisturbed by the turbulence that has punctuated much of South America's history over the years. Though inhabited by indigenous groups for millennia, the country's recorded history dates only from the arrival of the Spaniards in the sixteenth century. The colonial society that emerged, and the ensuing struggle for independence, form part of a history shared by the whole continent, but from its early days as a republic Chile took on its own political shape, distinct from that of its neighbours. With its largely ordered, constitutional model of government, and a healthy respect for the law, Chile earned itself the sobriquet of "the England of South America" in the nineteenth century. More recently, however, it was the repressive military regime of General Augusto Pinochet in the 1970s and 1980s that brought Chile to the attention of the outside world. Today, with democracy firmly back in place, Chile is an outward-looking country boasting political and economic stability, albeit with some serious social inequalities and unresolved political legacies lurking beneath the surface.

THE BEGINNINGS

Chile's history, like that of all the Americas, began when the first groups of Asians crossed the land bridge connecting Siberia to Alaska before the end of the last Ice Age, when the sea level was 70–100m lower than it is today. Archeologists are unable to tell us exactly when this **first migration** occurred, but it's generally thought to have been between 25,000 and 40,000 years ago.

What *is* known is that by 12,000 BC the descendants of these people, supplemented by further waves of migration from Asia, had spread down the whole of North and South America as far as the southern tip of Patagonia. While some devoted themselves to fishing, the majority were probably nomadic hunters living off the animals that inhabited the region at the time – mastodons (prehistoric elephants), mammoths, giant armadillos and wild horses. When the Ice Age came to an end around 11,000 BC the climate changed abruptly and many of these animals became extinct. The hunters were forced to adapt, supplementing their diet by gathering fruits and seeds. Eventually this led to the deliberate cultivation of foodstuffs and the domestication of animals, and along with these incipient agricultural practices came more stable communities and important cultural developments, such as pottery and burial practices. Slowly, distinct cultural groups emerged, shaped by their very different environments and the resources available to them.

THE PRE-COLUMBIAN CULTURES

In the absence of written records, archeologists have had to piece together information about Chile's **pre-Columbian cultures** from what these groups have left behind, principally funerary offerings found in burial sites and domestic objects left in former dwelling places. The strata in which the remains are buried (plus the use of radiocarbon dating) indicates the chronology in which these developments took place. However, Chile's contrasting geography from north to south presents unequal conditions for the preservation of artefacts, and has led to a far greater knowledge of the cultures of the north than of the south.

THE NORTE GRANDE

More is known about the pre-Columbian cultures of Chile's Norte Grande – the far north – than of any other part of the country, thanks to the extreme dryness of the Atacama desert, which has preserved archeological remains for thousands of years. One of the earliest peoples to leave its mark was the **Chinchorro culture** (see p.224), a collection of nomadic fishing groups that lived along the desert coast some 8000 years ago, where by 5000 BC they had developed the practice of mummifying their dead – 2000 years earlier than the Egyptians. Their technique, which involved removing internal organs and tissues and replacing them with vegetable fibres and mud, survived for 4000 years, and is the oldest known in the world.

By around 500 BC life in the far north was based largely on agriculture, supplemented by fishing in the coastal areas, and herding llamas and alpacas in the Andean highlands. Although vast tracts of the region are taken up by barren desert, a number of oases provided fertile land where agricultural communities were able to dedicate themselves to the cultivation of maize, beans, squash, chillis and potatoes. They lived in permanent dwellings, usually consisting of circular huts surrounding a shared patio, and often with a cemetery nearby.

Among the most important (and longest-lasting) of these early agricultural groups was the **San Pedro culture** (also known as the Atacameño culture), which settled along the salt flat oases around San Pedro de Atacama around 500 BC. They produced ceramics, textiles, and objects in copper and stone, along with delicately carved wooden snuff tablets and tubes used for inhaling hallucinogenic substances – a practice probably introduced by the **Tihuanaco culture** around 300 AD. This latter was a powerful religious state based near the southern shores of Lake Titicaca in present-day Bolivia, and its influence extended over most of northern Chile and much of Peru for many centuries. Its influence was most visible in the spread of its ceramics and textiles, often decorated with images of cats, condors and snakes, which probably had religious significance. The culture also fostered an active trading system, encouraging the exchange of goods between regions, which brought about increased social stratification, with those at the top controlling the commercial traffic. Sometime between 900 and 1200 AD the Tihuanaco culture declined and collapsed, for reasons unknown today. The regional cultures of the Norte Grande were then free to reassert their individual authority and identity, expressing their independence with a series of *pukarás* (fortresses) dotted around the altiplano. This period of *desarollo regional* ("regional development"), as it is known, was halted only by the arrival of the Incas in the late fifteenth century (see p.448).

THE NORTE CHICO

Around 300 AD, when the peoples of the Norte Grande had been living in fixed agricultural communities for several centuries, those of the Norte Chico were just beginning to abandon their lives of hunting and gathering, and turning to cattle herding and farming. What emerged was the **El Molle culture**, composed of communities that settled along the river valleys between Copiapó and Illapel, where they developed a system of artificial irrigation to cultivate maize, beans, squash and possibly cotton. They also herded llamas, a practice recorded in numerous petroglyphs, and produced the first ceramics of the Norte Chico. Between 700 and 800 AD the El Molle culture declined and was replaced by a new cultural group known as **Las Animas**, which probably originated in the Argentinian highlands. The changes introduced by this culture included rapid developments in metalworking, new, more decorative, styles of pottery, and – most curiously – the practice of ritual sacrifice of llamas.

Towards 1000 AD an important new group appeared in the Norte Chico – the **Diaguita culture** – that dominated the region over the next five centuries until the Spanish invasion. The Diaguitas tended to live in large villages along the river valleys, presided over by a chief and a shaman. Each valley was divided into two sections: a "lower" section, towards the coast, which was ruled by one chief, and a "higher" section, towards the mountains, ruled by another. Their economy was based on agriculture, herding, mining and metalworking, and was supplemented by fishing on the coast, aided by the invention of inflated sealskin rafts. Their greatest achievement, however, was their outstandingly fine pottery, characterized by intricate white, black and red geometric patterns.

CENTRAL CHILE

The first agricultural groups to settle in central Chile were the **El Bato** and **Llolleo** peoples, from around 300 AD. The El Bato group occupied the zone between the río Choapa (near Illapel) and the río Maipo (south of Santiago); its highly polished monochrome pottery indicates that it was strongly influenced by the El Molle culture from the Norte Chico. The Llolleo settlements were spread along the coastal plains between the río Aconcagua (just north of Santiago) and the río Maule (near Talca). One of the most striking characteristics of this culture was their practice of burying their dead under their own houses, with small children buried in clay urns. Later, around 900 AD, the **Aconcagua** emerged as the dominant culture in Central Chile; these people lived in houses made of branches and mud, and dedicated themselves to growing beans, maize, squash and potatoes; they also developed far more specialized ceramics than had previously existed in the region.

ARAUCANIA

Relatively little is known about the development of the cultures of the south of Chile, owing to a scarcity of archeological remains, but it's generally agreed that the first group to adopt cultivation was the **Pitrén** culture, around 600 AD. This comprised small family groups spread between the Bío Bío and Lago Llanquihue, where they grew maize and potatoes on a small scale, as well as hunting and gathering. They also produced ceramics, often decorated with zoomorphic and anthropomorphic images, which they usually buried with their dead. Around 1000 AD a new community, known as **El Vergel**, emerged in the region between Angol and Temuco. Its economy combined hunting and gathering with the cultivation of potatoes, maize, beans and squash, and it's likely that its people were the first to domesticate guanacos. Other new practices these people brought to the region included burying their dead in ceramic urns, which they decorated with red and white paint. They also developed a very beautiful style of pottery, known as Valdivia pottery, characterized by parallel zigzag lines and shaded triangles.

Sometime in the fourteenth century a group of nomadic hunters called the *moluche* (people of war) arrived from Argentina and occupied the land between the Itata and Toltén rivers. They absorbed the existing Pitrén and El Vergel cultures to form a new entity called **Mapuche** (People of the Earth). While engaging in fishing, hunting and gathering, their lifestyle was based principally on herding and farming – labour was divided between the sexes, with men responsible for preparing the fields, and women for sowing and harvesting. The basic social unit was the family clan, or "lov", which were independent from each other and autonomous. Their isolation meant the Mapuche culture didn't develop any further until forced to unite in the face of the Spanish invasion.

THE FAR SOUTH

The narrow channels, fjords, impenetrable jungles and wild steppes of the far south have never encouraged communities to settle in one place. Accordingly, the peoples that inhabited this region led a more primitive lifestyle than those further north – they could not adopt agriculture as their main economy, and so maintained their tradition of hunting and fishing in nomadic groups. Groups like the **Selk'nam** and the **Tehuelche** hunted guanaco and rhea on the Patagonian steppes, and lived in temporary wigwam-like structures covered in guanaco skins. The **Yámanas** and **Chonos** hunted seals, otters, birds and gathered shellfish in their canoes, constantly moving from place to place. None of the Patagonian or Fuegian groups produced ceramics, manufacturing instead bows, arrows, lassoes, baskets and warm skin capes. Their understanding of the world was rich in mythology and symbolism – the Selk'nams, for instance, believed that many birds and animals were spirits that had once been human; they also practised elaborate initiation rites marking the passage from boyhood into manhood, involving physical tests and secret ceremonies. Unlike the other native peoples of Chile, these groups were never incorporated into Spanish colonial society, and their lifestyles remained virtually unchanged until the twentieth century, when the clash with seal hunters and sheep farmers led to their disappearance.

THE INCA CONQUEST

While the native peoples of Chile were developing relatively simple communities based on agriculture, herding and fishing, a great civilization was emerging further to the north – that of the **Incas**. This people arrived in Cuzco around 1200 AD and by the fifteenth century had developed a sophisticated and highly organized society that boasted palaces, temples and fortresses of great architectural sophistication. In 1463 the Inca emperor, Pachacuti, initiated a period of massive **expansion** which saw the conquest of lands stretching north to present-day Quito and south as far as the río Maule in Chile, where its progress was halted by the fierce resistance of the Mapuches. The impact of the Incas in Chile was considerable: they constructed a breathtaking network of roads connecting the conquered lands to the capital of the empire in Cuzco (later very useful to the Spanish *conquistadores*), and forced the subjugated peoples to pay tribute to the Inca ruler and to use Quechua as their official language. While the Incas tolerated indigenous cults, they required their subjects also to adopt the **cult of the sun**, a central tenet of the Inca religion. Sun-worship usually took place at altars built on high mountain peaks where the sun's first rays were received; it sometimes involved human sacrifice, but more commonly animals or objects like silver figurines were offered as substitutes. Remains of Inca worship sites have been found on numerous mountains in Chile, the most famous being Cerro El Plomo, near Santiago, where the frozen body of a small child was discovered in 1954, undoubtedly offered as a sacrifice. The Inca occupation of Chile spanned a relatively short period of time – about 70 years in the Norte Grande and perhaps just 30 in Central Chile. It was interrupted first by civil war in Cuzco, caused by the struggle between two rivals over succession to the throne. Then, in 1532, the Spanish arrived in Peru, marking the beginning of the end of the Inca empire.

THE SPANISH CONQUEST

It was while seeking a westward route to Asia across the Atlantic that **Christopher Columbus** unwittingly discovered the Americas in 1492. His patron, Queen Isabella of Spain, supported him on two further expeditions, and sent settlers to colonize the Caribbean island of Hispaniola (today's Haiti and Dominican Republic). It gradually became apparent that the islands were not part of Asia, and that a giant landmass – indeed a whole continent – separated them from the East. After colonizing several other islands, the explorers and adventurers, backed by the Spanish Crown, turned their attention to the mainland and the period of conquest began in earnest. In 1521 **Hernán Cortés** defeated the great **Aztec Empire** in Mexico and then in 1524 **Francisco Pizarro** and his partner **Diego de Almagro** set out to find the rich empire they had been told lay further south. After several failed attempts, they finally landed on the coast of **Peru** in 1532, where they found the great **Inca Empire** racked by civil war. Pizarro speedily conquered the empire, aided by advanced military weapons and tactics, the high morale of his men, their frenzied desire for gold and glory and, most significantly, the devastating effect of Old World diseases on the indigenous population. Within a few years, Peru was firmly in Spanish hands.

Diego de Almagro was entrusted with the mission of carrying the Conquest further south to the region named **Chile**, spoken of by the Peruvian natives as a land rich in gold and silver. In 1535 Almagro and his four hundred men set off from Cuzco and embarked on a long journey down the spine of the Andes (following an Inca road) as far as the Aconcagua valley, suffering extreme deprivation and hardship along the way. To make matters worse, the *conquistador* found none of the riches the Peruvians had spoken of. Bitterly disappointed, Almagro returned to Cuzco, where his deteriorating relations with Pizarro led to armed combat and death at the hands of Pizarro's brothers.

Three years later, **Pedro de Valdivia** (one of Pizarro's most trusted officers) applied for and was granted license to colonize Chile. Due to its lack of gold and the miseries of the first expedition, Chile was not an attractive destination, and so it was with just ten men, a group of native porters and his mistress, Inés Suarez, that Valdivia set off from Cuzco in 1540. Almost a year later, having picked up 150 extra men en route, Valdivia reached the río Mapocho in the Aconcagua valley where he officially founded **Santiago de la Nueva Extremadura** on February 12, 1541. The new "city" was hastily put together, with all the trappings of a colonial capital, including church, prison, court and *cabildo* (town council), which elected Valdivia as Governor. It was a humble affair, regularly attacked and destroyed by local Picunches, but the new colonists were determined to stay and did not return to Peru.

Over the next decade, Valdivia attempted to expand the colony, founding the cities of La Serena in the north in 1544 and Concepción in the south in 1550, followed by a handful of other centres in the south. It was here that the Spaniards faced the fierce resistance of the **Mapuches** (known by the Spanish as Araucanians) who successfully prevented the spread of colonization south of the Bío Bío river, which became known as **La Frontera**. It was in a confrontation with the Mapuches that Valdivia met his death in 1553, at the hands of the famous chief Lautaro. The details of his execution are believed to be particularly grisly – some versions claim he was forced to swallow molten gold, others that he was lanced to death by a crowd of warriors, one of whom sliced through his breast and ripped out his heart.

In the panic caused by Valdivia's death, the southern colonists retreated to Santiago, leaving only Concepción as a garrison outpost, occupied mainly by soldiers guarding La Frontera. A new Governor – don García Hurtado de Mendoza – was dispatched from Peru, and by the time his term of office ended, in 1661, the natives in the central region had been subjugated and colonization was effectively complete.

COLONIAL CHILE

The new colony was a marginal, isolated and unprofitable addition to Spain's empire in the Americas, which revolved around the viceroyalties of Mexico and Peru. The need to maintain a standing army to guard La Frontera, and the absence of large quantities of precious metals to fund it, meant that Chile ran at a deficit for most of the colonial period. Administratively, it was designated a "captaincy-general", ruled by a Governor with the help of an *audiencia* (a high court, whose function included advising the Governor). All high officials were sent from Spain as representatives of the king, whose authority was absolute, and whose instructions were communicated via the *Consejo de Indias* (Council of the Indies). Chile, however, received little attention and, enclosed within the mighty barriers of the Atacama desert and Andean cordillera, was more or less left to its own devices.

Growth was very slow, amounting to no more than five thousand settlers by 1600. Most of these lived from the farming of land handed out by the Governor in grants known as *mercedes de tierra*, spreading over the valleys near Santiago and in the Central Valley. At the same time, large "grants" of indigenous people were given to the colonists in what was known as the **encomienda** system – the *encomienda* being the group of natives allocated to an *encomendero*. In theory, the *encomenderos* were supposed to look after the well-being of their charges and convert them to Christianity in exchange for tribute (by means of work) offered to the Spanish Crown. In practice, the system simply provided the colonists with a large slave workforce that they could treat however they pleased, which was often appallingly. From the very beginning, then, the *mercedes de tierra* and *encomiendas* established a pattern that was to dominate Chile's rural society until modern times: namely, large estates owned by seigniorial landlords at the head of a dependent, disempowered workforce.

During the **seventeenth century** this pattern became more clearly defined with the emergence and economic dominance of the **hacienda**. Enclosed within thick, protective walls, haciendas were self-sufficient, self-contained entities, whose buildings – arranged around numerous courtyards – comprised workshops, wine *bodegas*, dairies, a chapel and the *casa patronal*, the landowner's home. Initially the workforce was provided by *encomiendas*, but, with tragic inevitability, the indigenous population rapidly decreased through exposure to Old World diseases. In its place there sprang up a new generation of **mestizos**, the result of miscegenation between the Spanish colonists (almost exclusively male in the early years) and indigenous women. In time, a more or less homogeneous mestizo population came to make up the bulk of the Chilean workforce, presided over by a ruling, landowning elite made up of "**peninsulares**" (Spaniards born in Spain) and "**creoles**" (those of Spanish blood born in the colony). Most mestizos were incorporated into the haciendas either as peons or as **inquilinos** – labourers allowed to farm a small plot of land in return for year-round service (a practice that continued until the twentieth century). The main activities on the haciendas were livestock-raising and the cultivation of cereals and fruit. Production was healthy but never reached particularly high levels, owing to Spanish trading restrictions, which prevented the colonies from trading freely with each other or with Spain.

Along with the haciendas, the other main shaping force in Chilean society was the **Catholic Church**. From the colony's earliest days, missionaries from most orders poured into Chile and embarked on a zealous programme of conversion in the farthest flung corners of the territory, erecting chapels and crosses wherever they went. Their success was rapid and set the seal on the "pacification" of the Indians, who were less likely to cause trouble if they could be incorporated into the Hispanic culture and their sense of separate identity diminished. The Catholicism that emerged wasn't an altogether orthodox version, as many pre-Hispanic elements of worship – such as ritual dancing and sacrificial offerings – were incorporated into this new religion, and even now survive in Chile's more remote communities, especially in the north. Nonetheless, both *indígenas* and mestizos embraced the symbolic elements of the Catholic faith with enthusiasm, and several cults sprang up around supposedly miraculous icons, such as the Cristo de Mayo in Santiago, which was believed to have bled real blood after an earthquake in 1647.

The most influential element of the Church was the **Jesuit order** (Compañía de Jesús), which arrived in Chile in 1593 and quickly established itself as one of the colony's largest landowners. In a paternalistic arrangement, the Jesuits gathered hundreds of indigenous families to their missions where they were fed, clothed, converted, taught Spanish and instructed in many skills from weaving to glass manufacturing. As a result, the order's numerous workshops were the most productive and profitable in the country, as was the case throughout Spanish America – until the Jesuits were suddenly expelled from the Spanish empire in 1767, when the Crown was persuaded that they had become too powerful to tolerate.

The first half of the **eighteenth century** saw little real advance in Chile's development. Patterns that had been established earlier on were simply reinforced: the mestizo population grew, and the dominance of the great landed estates (often known as "latifundia") was bolstered by the creation of **mayorazgos**, a system of entailment which allowed (at a price) the wealthiest landowners to pass on their property without having to divide it among their heirs. The bulk of the population was rural and attached to the estates, principally spread between the Aconcagua valley and the Maule valley, with only a very limited urban population outside of Santiago.

Things did change noticeably, however, with the reign of **Charles III** from 1759. The most progressive of the Bourbon monarchs (who had replaced the Habsburg dynasty in Spain in 1700), the king set about improving the management of the American colonies and increasing their productivity, so as to augment revenues. Among his reforms was the relaxation of the stifling trade restrictions that had hampered economic growth throughout much of Spanish America. Suddenly, the colonies were able to trade freely with each other and with Spain. There was no overnight miracle, but Chilean trade did expand considerably, particularly with neighbouring Río de la Plata (Argentina). At the same time, imports soared, and the need to pay for them in gold or silver stimulated a small **mining boom** in the Norte Chico. Settlements sprang up around the mining centres, and some, such as Copiapó, Vallenar and Illapel, were granted official city status. All in all, there was an emerging spirit of change and progress, which gave a sense of empowerment to Chile's Creoles, who had always been barred from the highest colonial offices. But while Chile's commercial horizons were widening, the king's administrative shake-ups – which involved sending a number of "Intendants" to the colonies to tighten up administration and eradicate abuses of local power – was experienced as unwanted interference – creating a tension that would soon find a more focused channel.

THE STRUGGLE FOR INDEPENDENCE

Chile entered the **nineteenth century** with a burgeoning sense of its own identity. The Creole elite, while fiercely loyal to the Spanish king, was becoming increasingly alienated from the *peninsulares* dispatched from Spain to administer the colony, and the gap between them was widening with each successive generation. Creole aspirations to play a more active role in government (and thus look after their own interests, not just the Crown's) were given a sudden, unexpected opportunity for fulfillment when Napoleon invaded Spain in 1808 and deposed the Spanish king (Ferdinand VII). **Local juntas** sprang up in Spain's main cities to organize resistance to Napoleon, and were soon followed by a number of locally elected juntas in the American colonies – including Chile when, on September 18, 1810, over four hundred leading citizens gathered in Santiago and elected a six-man **junta**, made up of Chileans. It must be stressed that the junta's initial objective was to "preserve the sovereignty of Ferdinand VII" in the absence of legitimate authority, and few entertained thoughts of independence at this stage. The junta did, however, go on to implement several far-reaching reforms: trade was liberalized; a Congress was elected; and the *real audiencia* (royal court) was replaced by a Chilean tribunal, with Chilean judges.

Over time, it became clear that a minority of Creoles sought a far greater degree of autonomy for the colony, and whispers of independence began to circulate. This small tide was given dramatic impetus in November, 1811, when **José Miguel Carrera**, a member of one of the wealthiest and most influential Creole families in Chile, seized power, dissolving Congress and appointing himself head of a new, more radical, junta. His actions were swift and bold, and included the creation of a Chilean flag and the drafting of a provisional constitution which declared all rulings issued outside Chile to be illegitimate. The viceroy of Peru – where the colonial machinery remained intact – was greatly alarmed by these subversive measures, and early in 1813 sent troops down to the old-guard strongholds of Chiloé and Valdivia to prepare for an assault on Santiago. In response, Carrera charged down to confront them with Chilean troops (whose generals numbered one **Bernardo O'Higgins**, the son of a former viceroy of Peru) and war was effectively declared. Loyalties were now thrown sharply into focus with the **Royalists** on one side, made up of Spaniards and pro-Spanish Chileans, and the **Patriots** on the other, made up of Creoles who supported some form of self-government.

When Carrera's military leadership did not produce impressive results the junta voted to replace him with Bernardo O'Higgins, who proved far more adept at holding off the Royalist forces. In July 1814 the power-hungry Carrera returned to Santiago and overthrew the government once more, reinstating himself at its head and causing considerable upheaval. In October that year Royalist troops, taking advantage of the chaos, began to advance on Santiago. O'Higgins mounted a desperate and heroic defence at Rancagua, attempting to hold them back, but Carrera's promised reinforcements never arrived, and the Patriots were overwhelmingly defeated. The **"Disaster of Rancagua"**, as it is known, marked the end of La Patria Vieja (the name given to the fledgling independent nation) and its leaders fled across the Andean border to Mendoza in Argentina, as the Royalist troops marched triumphantly into Santiago.

The victory coincided with the defeat of Napoleon in Spain and the restoration of Ferdinand VII on the throne. The king immediately set out to crack down on all insurgent elements in his American colonies: in Chile, some forty Patriot Creoles were exiled to the Juan Fernández Islands, where they were to live in caves, and every reform instigated by the junta was reversed. The Spanish Crown's attempt to turn back the clock and revert to a centralized, interventionist colonial government was felt as repressive and authoritarian by Creoles throughout the continent. For many, it was this **Spanish reconquest**, as it's been termed, that convinced them that independence was the only way forward.

Meanwhile, just as the great general **Simón Bolívar** was preparing anti-Spanish campaigns in Venezuela, which would liberate the northern half of the continent, so too was **José de San Martín**, the Argentine general, masterminding his plans for South American emancipation from his base in Mendoza, near the Chilean border. San Martín knew that independence could never be assured until the Spanish were ejected from their heartland in Peru, which he planned to achieve by first liberating Chile, from where he would launch a naval attack on Lima. To this end, San Martín was rigorously recruiting and training an army – known as the **Army of the Andes** – whose numbers were considerably increased by the Chilean Patriots who fled across the border after their defeat at Rancagua. After more than two years of preparation, and with O'Higgins placed in command of the Chilean division, San Martín's army scaled the cordillera over four different passes in February 1817. Nothing was left to chance and the campaign unfolded like clockwork: on February 12, Patriot forces surprised the Spaniards and defeated their forces at the battle of Chacabuco, just north of Santiago. The

Royalists fled to the south, and the Patriots entered the capital in triumph. Fighting continued after Royalist reinforcements were sent from Peru, but when San Martín inflicted devastating losses on their army at the battle of Maipú in April 1818, the Patriot victory was complete, setting the final seal on Chilean independence. Leadership of the new country was offered to San Martín, but he declined – instead, the job went to Bernardo O'Higgins, who was elected Supreme Director by an assembly of Chile's leading Creoles.

O'Higgins' immediate task was to put together a national navy with which to clear the southern coast of remaining Royalist troublemakers and launch the seaborne attack on Peru. A flotilla was equipped and placed under the command of a British admiral, **Lord Thomas Cochrane**, who successfully captured Callao, the port of Lima, in 1820. With the colonial nerve centre effectively toppled, the days of the Spanish American empire were drawing to an inescapable close. Turning his attention from liberation to government, however, O'Higgins was confronted with a whole set of new problems, not least the near bankruptcy caused by crippling war costs. Resentment at the stiff taxes imposed to recoup these costs caused widespread discontent, and after five years of difficult rule O'Higgins was forced to step down. The former hero exiled himself in Peru, where he remained until his death in 1842, leaving the new republic of Chile with the challenge of building itself into a nation.

THE EARLY REPUBLIC

The transition from colony to republic was not a smooth one. In its first thirteen years of independence, Chile got through five constitutions and eleven changes of government, marked by continual tussles between **Liberal** and **Conservative** factions. Then, in 1829, the Conservatives, with the support of the army, imposed an authoritarian-style government that ushered in a long period of political stability, making Chile the envy of Latin America. The chief architect of the regime was **Diego Portales**, who never stood for presidency himself, preferring to run the show from various cabinet posts. Convinced that Chile could only move forward under a strong, centralist government able to maintain rigorous order, Portales designed, in 1833, the Constitution that was to underpin Chilean government for 92 years. It granted enormous powers to the president, allowing him, for instance, to veto any legislation passed by Congress, and protecting him from impeachment until his term of office had expired (two five-year terms were allowed). The system in many ways replicated the autocratic approach of the Spanish Crown, with the Crown's vested interests simply replaced by those of the landowning oligarchy, staunch supporters of the new constitution, who were extremely satisfied by this arrangement.

Portales was not, however, without his detractors and in 1837, in protest at the government's invasion of Peru (which had been forcibly annexed by the Bolivian president), he was brutally gunned down by political opponents. This atrocity led to increased support for the government, who went on to defeat the Peru-Bolivia Confederation – to the great pride of Chilean citizens.

The growing self-confidence of the nation, added to the political and social stability within it, created conditions that were favourable to growth. Between the 1830s and 1870s international trade took off rapidly, with hugely increased wheat exports fuelled by the Californian and Australian goldrushes, and, more significantly, a silver- and copper-mining boom in the Norte Chico. At the same time, advances in technology and communications saw railways, roads, steamships and telegraphs opening up the country. Its populated territory expanded, too: a government programme encouraged Europeans to come over and settle the lakeland region of the south, which was duly cleared and farmed by some four thousand German immigrants. Meanwhile, Santiago and Valparaíso were being transformed – with avenues, parks, palaces and mansions, and an ever-expanding population. Only the countryside in the Central Valley heartland showed no real change, dominated as it was by haciendas whose owners frequently neglected their estates in favour of other business interests.

In time, the nation began to tire of the authoritarian model of government established by Portales and the influence of Liberal politics began to gain ground. In 1871 the election of **Federico Errázuriz Zañartu** as president marked the beginning of twenty years of Liberal government. Many of the Liberals' reforms were aimed at reducing the undiminished power of the Church: they legalized free worship in private places; they introduced civil cemeteries, where persons of any faith could be buried; and they instituted civil marriages and registries. The Liberals also went some way towards reducing the individual power of the president, and giving Congress a stronger role in government. The breath of fresh air and sense of optimism produced by these reforms suffered a deathblow, however, when a world recession between 1876 and 1878 sent copper and silver prices tumbling and brought wheat exports to a virtual halt, plunging Chile into economic crisis.

THE WAR OF THE PACIFIC

Rescue was at hand in what at first appeared to be yet another calamitous situation. Ever since the 1860s, when two enterprising Chileans started exploiting the vast nitrate deposits of the Atacama desert, Chilean capital and labour had dominated the region's growing **nitrate** industry. Most activity took place on the pampas around Antofagasta, which Chile had formally acknowledged as Bolivian territory in 1874 – following lengthy border disputes – in exchange for an assurance from Bolivia that export tariffs would not be raised for 25 years. Many of Chile's most prominent politicians had shares in the nitrate companies, so when Bolivia flouted its agreement by raising export taxes in 1878 – directly hitting shareholders' pockets – they were up in arms, and determined to take action.

In February 1879, following mounting tension, Chilean troops invaded Antofagasta and soon took control of the surrounding coastal strip. Within two weeks Chile and Bolivia were **at war**, with Peru drawn into the conflict on Bolivia's side within a couple of months. It soon became clear that success would depend on **naval supremacy** – Bolivia did not have a navy, leaving Peru and Chile pitted against each other, and fairly evenly matched. Following a series of early losses, Chile secured an overwhelming maritime victory in August 1979, when it captured Peru's principal warship, the *Huáscar*. The coast was now clear for the invasion of Peru's nitrate territories, and the emphasis shifted to land fighting. Casualties were heavy on both sides, but by June 1880 Chile had secured control of these areas with a resounding victory at El Morro, Arica.

With the nitrate fields theirs, the Chilean government would doubtless have been happy to bring the war to a close, but the public was clamouring for blood: it wanted Peru brought to its knees with the capture of Lima. In January 1881 Peru's humiliation was complete when Chilean troops occupied the capital. Peru was still not ready to give up, though, and the war dragged on for two more years, resulting in heavy human loss and exhausting both sides. Eventually, Peru accepted defeat, sealed by the **Treaty of Ancón** in October 1883 (an official truce with Bolivia was not signed until April the following year).

By the conclusion of the war, Chile had extended its territory by one-third, acquiring the Peruvian province of Tarapacá, and the Bolivian littoral (thus depriving Bolivia of sea access). Its new, nitrate-rich pampas yielded enormous, almost overnight wealth, refilling government coffers and restoring national confidence.

ARTURO PRAT

Nothing has captured the Chilean imagination like the heroic, and tragic, efforts of Arturo Prat in the Battle of Iquique. On the morning of May 21, 1879, the *Esmeralda* – an old wooden boat under Prat's command – found itself under attack from Peruvian artillery on one side, and from the ironclad warship, the *Huáscar*, on the other. The two vessels could not have been more unevenly matched: the *Huáscar* boasted 300lb cannons, while those of the *Esmeralda* were only 40lb. When the *Huáscar* rammed the *Esmeralda*, Prat refused to give in, instead leaping aboard the enemy's vessel, sword in hand, determined to fight to the end. The gesture was futile, and Prat was killed on the warship's deck, but the commander's dignity and self-sacrifice have made him Chile's favourite national hero, in whose honour a thousand avenues and squares have been named.

CIVIL WAR AND THE PARLIAMENTARY REPUBLIC

The War of the Pacific had rescued Chile from its economic crisis and transformed the nation's fortunes. Now unfettered by war, the nitrate industry began to boom in earnest, and by 1890 export taxes on nitrates were providing over 50 percent of government revenue. With national confidence running high and the economy in such good shape, the government's position looked unassailable. Within a short time, however, cracks began to appear in the constitutional framework, expressed by mounting tension between the legislature (Congress) and the executive (chiefly the president).

The conflict came to a dramatic head under the presidency of **José Manuel Balmaceda** (1886–1891), a Liberal but autocratic leader who believed passionately in the president's right to run a strong executive – an approach jarringly at odds with the political trend of the previous couple of decades. One of the unifying objectives of the various Liberal parties was the elimination of electoral intervention (which had been standard practice since independence), and when Balmaceda was seen to influence Congressional elections in 1886, many Liberals were outraged and withdrew their support. Equally antagonistic was the president's determination to insist on his right to pick and choose his cabinet, without the approval of Congress – whose response was to refuse to pass legislation authorizing the following year's budget until Balmaceda agreed to appoint a cabinet in which they had confidence.

Neither side would give way, and as the deadline for budget approval (January 1, 1899) drew close, it became obvious that Balmaceda would either have to give in to Congress's demands, or act against the constitution. When he chose the latter option, declaring that he would carry 1890's budget through to 1891, Congress revolted, propelling the two sides into war. Balmaceda held the army's support, while Congress secured the backing of the navy. Operating out of Iquique, where they established a junta, Congress were able to use nitrate funds to recruit and train an army. In August that year their troops landed near Valparaíso where they defeated Balmaceda's army in two long, bloody battles. The president, whose refusal to give in was absolute, fled to the Argentine embassy where he wrote poignant farewell notes to his family and friends before shooting himself in the head.

The authoritarian model of government established by Diego Portales in the 1830s, already undermined over the previous two decades, had now collapsed. Taking its place was a system – dubbed the **Parliamentary Republic** – based on an all-powerful legislature and an extremely weak executive. Now, it was Congress who imposed cabinets on the president, not the other way round, with frequent clashes and constantly shifting allegiances seeing cabinets formed and dissolved with breathtaking frequency – between 1891 and 1915 the government got through more than sixty ministries. This chronic instability seriously hampered government action although, ironically, the one arena where great progress was made was the public works programme vigorously promoted by Balmaceda, which saw rapid construction of state railways, roads, bridges, schools, hospitals, prisons and town halls.

All this was taking place against a background of momentous social and economic change which the government, bound up with its continual infighting, seemed scarcely aware of. One of the by-products of the nitrate industry was increased **industrialization** elsewhere in Chile, as manufacturing stepped up to service increased production in the north. This, combined with the growth of railways, coal mining, education, construction and banking, saw a period of rapid **social diversification**. A new group of merchants, managers, bureaucrats and teachers formed an emerging middle class, while the increasingly urban workforce – usually living in dire poverty – formed a new working class more visible than its counterpart on the large rural estates. It was in the nitrate fields of the north that an embryonic **labour movement** began to take root, as workers protested against the appalling conditions they were forced to live and work in. With no political representation to voice these grievances, strikes became the main form of protest, spreading from the mining cities of the north to the docks of Valparaíso. The government's heavy-handed attempts to suppress the strikes – reaching a peak of brutality when almost two hundred men, women and children were shot dead in Iquique, in 1907 – were symptomatic of its inability to deal with the social changes taking place in the country. When the nitrate industry entered a rapid decline with the outbreak of World War I in 1914, leaving thousands of workers unemployed and causing inflation to soar, Chile's domestic situation deteriorated further.

1920–1970

The first leader committed to dealing with the republic's mounting social problems was **Arturo Alessandri**, elected in 1920 on the strength of an ambitious reform programme. The weakness of his position, however, in the face of an all-powerful and obstructive Congress, prevented him from putting any of his plans into action, and after four years hardly anything had been achieved. Then, in 1924, a strange set of events was set in motion when an army junta – frustrated by the lack of government action – forced the cabinet to resign and had Alessandri appoint military men to key cabinet positions. The president appeared quite willing to accommodate the junta, which used its muscle to ensure that Congress swiftly passed a series of social reform laws, including legislation to protect workers' rights. After several months, however, the relationship between the president and his military cabinet began to unravel and Alessandri fled to Argentina in exile.

More drama was to follow when, on January 23, 1925, a rival junta led by Colonel **Carlos Ibañez** staged a coup, deposed the government and invited Alessandri to return to Chile to complete his term of office. With Ibañez's weight behind him, Alessandri set about redrafting the constitution, with the aim of restoring authority to the president and reducing the power of Congress. This was achieved with the **1925 Constitution**, which represented a radical departure from the one of 1833, incorporating protective welfare measures among other reforms. Despite this victory, however, tensions between Ibañez and Alessandri led to the president's resignation. The way was now clear for the military strongman, Ibañez, to get himself elected as president in May 1927.

Ibañez's presidency was a curious contradiction, at once highly autocratic, with severe restrictions on freedom of expression, and refreshingly progressive, ushering in a series of badly needed reforms promoting agriculture, industry and education. His early years were successful, bringing about improvements in living standards across all sections of society, and stimulating national prosperity. But when the Wall Street Crash of 1929 sparked off a worldwide depression, Chile's economy virtually collapsed overnight, producing deep social unrest. Faced with a wave of street demonstrations and strikes, Ibañez was forced to resign in July 1931. His departure was followed by eighteen months of political and social chaos, involving nine changes in government, further military intervention, a mutiny in the navy, a socialist coup and several huge strikes. The task of restoring stability to the nation fell to the old populist, Alessandri, who was re-elected in 1932.

Military interference in government affairs was now at an end (for a few decades, at least) and the country settled down to a period of orderly political evolution, no longer held back by a weak executive. What emerged was a highly diverse multi-party system embracing a wide spectrum of political persuasions. From 1938 the government was dominated by the **Radical Party**, a centre-right group principally representing the middle classes. Radical presidents like Pedro Aguirre Cerda, Juan Antonio Ríos and Gabriel Gonzalez Videla took an active role in regenerating Chile's economy, investing in state-sponsored steelworks, copper refineries, fisheries and power supplies. In the 1950s left-wing groups gained considerable ground as the voting franchise widened, but old-guard landowners were able to counter this by controlling the votes of the thousands of peasants who depended on them for their survival, thus ensuring a firm swing back to the right. Nonetheless, it was by a very narrow margin that the socialist **Salvador Allende** was defeated by the Conservative Jorge Alessandri (son of Arturo) in the 1958 elections, causing widespread alarm among the wealthy elite. As the next election approached in 1964, the upper classes, with the discreet backing of the USA (still reeling from the shock of the Cuban missile crisis), threw all their efforts into securing the election of **Eduardo Frei**, the candidate of the rising young **Christian Democrat** party.

In power, Frei turned out to be a good deal more progressive than his right-wing supporters could have imagined, initiating – to their horror – bold **agrarian reforms** which allowed the expropriation of all farms of more than 180 hectares. The other memorable achievement of the Frei administration was the "Chileanization" of the **copper industry**, which had replaced nitrates as the country's dominant source of revenue, and which was almost exclusively in the hands of North American corporations. Frei's policy gave the state a 51 percent stake in all the major copper mines, providing instant revenues to fund his social reform programme. These, which included the introduction of a minimum wage and impressive improvements in education, made Frei's government popular with the working classes, though his reforms were unable to keep pace with the rush of expectations and demands. At the same time, Conservative groups became increasingly alarmed at the direction in which Frei was steering the country, prompting Liberals and Conservatives to join forces and form the new **National Party**, aimed at putting a check on reform. As Chile approached the 1970s its population was becoming sharply polarized between those who clamoured for further social reform and greater representation of the working class, and those to whom this was anathema and to be reversed at all costs.

ALLENDE AND THE UNIDAD POPULAR

On September 4, 1970, 62-year-old **Salvador Allende** was elected as Chile's first socialist president, heading a coalition of six left-wing parties, known as the **Unidad Popular** (UP). His majority, however, was tiny, and while half the country rejoiced, full of hopes for a better future, the other half feared a slide towards communism. Allende was passionately committed to improving the lot of the poorest sectors of society, whose appalling living conditions had shocked him when he had encountered them in his training as a doctor. His government pledged, among other things, to nationalize Chilean industries, to redistribute the nation's wealth, to increase the people's participation in government, and to speed up agrarian reform, though there were disagreements as to how fast these changes should be made. Within a year, over eighty major companies had been nationalized, including the copper mines, which were expropriated without compensation. The following year, radical agrarian reform was enforced, with over 60 percent of irrigated land – including all haciendas with more than 80 hectares – taken into government hands for redistribution among the rural workforce. In one fell swoop, the latifundia system that had dominated rural Chile for over 400 years was dismantled, never to be restored.

In the short term, Allende's government was both successful and popular, presiding over a period of economic growth, rising wages and falling unemployment, but it wasn't long before strains began to be felt. For a start, government expenditure was exceeding income by a huge margin, creating an enormous deficit. The looming economic crisis was dramatically accelerated when the world copper price fell by some 27 percent, cutting government revenue still further. Inflation began to rise uncontrollably, with wages unable to keep pace, and before long food shortages became commonplace.

Part of the UP's failure stemmed from the sharp divisions within the coalition, particularly between those who, like Allende, were in favour of a measured pace of reform, and those pressing for rapid, revolutionary change. The internal disunity led to a lack of co-ordination in implementing policy, and an irreversible slide towards political chaos. Making matters worse were the extremist far-left groups outside the government – notably the Revolutionary Left Movement, or **MIR** – which urged the workers to take reform into their own hands by seizing possession of the haciendas and factories where they worked.

Opposition to the government rose sharply during 1972, both from political parties outside the coalition (such as the Christian Democrats, who had previously supported Allende) and from widening sectors of the public. Panic was fuelled by the right-wing press, and reinforced behind the scenes by the CIA, who, it later emerged, had been given a US$8 million budget with which to destabilize the Allende government. Strikes broke out across the country, culminating in the truckers' strike of October 1972, which virtually paralysed the economy. By 1973, with the country rocked by civil disorder, it was clear to all that the government could not survive for much longer.

MILITARY RULE

On the morning of September 11, 1973, tanks rolled through the capital and surrounded the presidential palace, La Moneda, marking the beginning of the **military coup** that Chile had been expecting for months. La Moneda was evacuated and Salvador Allende was offered a safe passage to exile. He refused, and in an emotional speech broadcast live on radio from the palace, vowed that he would never give up, and that he was ready to repay the loyalty of the Chilean people with his life. In this unique moment of history, citizens heard their president declare "I have faith in Chile and in its destiny. Other men will overcome this dark and bitter moment . . . You must go on, safe in the knowledge that sooner rather than later, the great avenues will open once more, and free men will march along them to create a better society . . . These are my last words, but I am sure that my sacrifice will not be in vain." Shortly afterwards the signals were cut short, and jets began to drop their bombs. At the end of the day, Allende was found dead in the ruins of the palace, clutching a submachine gun, with which, it is widely believed, he had killed himself.

The coup was headed by a four-man junta of whom **General Augusto Pinochet**, chief of the army, quickly emerged as the dominant figure. Although Chile had seen military intervention in government affairs on two occasions in the past, these had been the exception to a highly constitutional norm. Nothing in the country's political history prepared its people for the brutality of this operation. In the days and weeks following the takeover, at least seven thousand people – journalists, politicians, socialists, trades union organisers and so on – were herded into the national football stadium, where many were executed, and still more were tortured. Curfews were imposed, the press was placed under the strict control of the junta, and military officers were sent in to take charge of factories, universities and other seats of socialist support. Before long, Congress had been dissolved, opposition parties and trade unions banned, and thousands of Chileans had fled the country.

General Pinochet saw his mission – and it was one in which he was supported by a sizeable portion of the population – as being that of rescuing Chile from the economic and political chaos into which it had undoubtedly fallen. To achieve this, he planned not to hand the country over to a right-wing political party of his approval, but to take it into his own hands and rule it himself. His key strategy was to be the adoption of a radical **free-market economy**, which involved a complete reversal of Allende's policies and a drastic restructuring of government and society. In this he was influenced by a group of Chilean economists known as "the Chicago boys", who had carried out postgraduate studies at the University of Chicago, where they'd come into contact with the monetarist theories of Milton Friedman. Almost immediately, price controls were abolished, government expenditure was slashed, most state-owned companies were privatized, import tariffs were reduced, and attempts were made to liberalize investment and attract foreign capital.

Such measures would take time to work, and called for a period of intense austerity. Sure enough, unemployment soared, wages plummeted, industrial output dropped, and the lower and middle classes became significantly poorer. At the same time, as Pinochet strove to reduce the role of the state in society, social welfare became increasingly neglected, particularly health and education. By the late 1970s the economy was showing signs of growth and inflation was finally beginning to drop – from an annual rate of 900 percent in 1973 to 65 percent in 1977 and down to a respectable 9.5 percent in 1981. Soon, there was talk of the Chilean "economic miracle" in international circles. The boom did not last, however, and in 1982, Chile found itself, along with much of Latin America, in the grip of a serious **debt crisis** which swept away the previous advances: the country was plunged into recession, with hundreds of private enterprises going bankrupt and unemployment rising to over 30 percent. It wasn't until the late 1980s that the economy recovered and Pinochet's free-market policies achieved the results he sought, with sustained growth, controlled inflation, booming, diversified exports and reduced unemployment. This prosperity, however, did not benefit all Chileans, and 49 percent of Chile's private wealth remained in the hands of 10 percent of its population.

Pinochet's free-market experiment had only been possible with the tools of ruthless repression at his disposal. His chief instrument was the secret police known as the **DINA**, which carried out surveillance on civilian (and even military) society, brutally silencing all opposition. Although the wholesale repression which followed the coup diminished in scale after the first year, regular "disappearances", torture and executions continued throughout Pinochet's regime. In the absence of any organized political opposition, only the Catholic Church spoke out against the government's human rights violations, providing assistance and sanctuary to those who suffered, and vigilantly documenting all reports of abuse. Pinochet held the country in such a tight, personal grip – famously claiming "there is not a leaf that stirs in Chile without my knowing it" – that it doubtless became difficult for him to conceive of an end to his authority. The constitution that he had drawn up in 1980 – ratified by a tightly controlled plebiscite – guaranteed him power until 1988, at which point the public would be given the chance to either accept military rule for another eight years, or else call for elections.

From the mid-1980s **public protest** against Pinochet's regime began to be voiced, both in regular street demonstrations (particularly in Santiago's shanty towns) and with the reformation of political opposition parties (still officially banned). Open repression was stepped down as international attention became increasingly focused on the Chilean government's behaviour, and the US (a major source of foreign investment) made clear that it favoured a return to democracy. In this climate, the opposition parties were able to develop a strong, united strategy in their efforts to oust the dictator. As the referendum in which Chile would decide whether or not to reject military rule drew closer, the opposition forces banded together to lead a highly professional and convincing "no" campaign, having secured crucial guarantees that the ballot would be totally secret. Pinochet remained convinced of his own victory, and with control of all media, and the intimidation tactics of a powerful police state at his disposal, it is easy to see why. But when the plebiscite took place on **October 5, 1988**, 55 percent of the nation voted "no" to continued military rule, 43 percent voted "yes", and 2 percent of votes were null and void.

After sixteen years in power, the days of Pinochet's dictatorship were now numbered. Much to everyone's surprise, he accepted his defeat without resistance, and prepared to step down. But the handover system gave him one more year in power before democratic elections would be held – a year in which he hastily prepared **amnesty laws** that would protect both himself and the military from facing any charges of human rights abuses levied by the new government, and that would make his constitutional model extremely difficult to amend. A year later on December 14, 1989, the Christian Democrat **Patricio Aylwin**, at the head of a seventeen-party centre-ground coalition called the **Concertación de los Partidos por la Democracia**, became Chile's first democratically elected president in seventeen years.

RETURN TO DEMOCRACY

The handover of power was smooth and handled with cautious goodwill on all sides, including the military. Aylwin was in the fortunate position of inheriting a robust economy and a buoyant, optimistic public. He did, of course, face serious challenges, including the need to channel substantial funds into those areas neglected by the previous regime while sustaining economic growth, and to address the human rights abuses of the past seventeen years without antagonizing the military and endangering the transition to democracy.

Pinochet's **economic** model was by now accepted as being the only realistic way forward, and was vigorously applied, with some protectionist modifications, in an effort to promote "growth with equity" (the Concertación's electoral slogan). Foreign investment poured into the country and exports continued to rise, keeping economic growth at levels that gave Chile much international prestige. This allowed Aylwin to divert resources into welfare sectors run down by Pinochet, with state spending on health and education increasing by one-third during his government. He proposed no quick fixes for eliminating poverty, but was, at least, seen and felt to be making genuine efforts to alleviate the problems faced by the poorest members of society.

On the matter of **human rights** issues, progress was more difficult to achieve. One of the new government's first actions was the establishment of a National Commission for Truth and Reconciliation to investigate and document the abuses committed by the military regime. The commission's report, published in 1991, confirmed 2279 executions, disappearances, and deaths caused by torture, and listed a further 641 suspected cases. But although compensation was paid to the families of the victims, the few attempts made to bring the perpetrators to justice were unsuccessful, due to the protective amnesty laws passed by Pinochet before he relinquished power.

After a successful four-year term, the Concertación was in 1993 once again elected to power, this time headed by the Christian Democrat **Eduardo Frei** (son of the 1964–70 president). Frei's policies have essentially been a continuation of his predecessors', with a firmer emphasis on tackling human rights issues and eradicating severe poverty. His success has been mixed. His National Programme for Overcoming Poverty, established in 1994, has been seen as inconsistent and ineffective. More progress has been made on **human rights**, with courts finally willing to find ways of getting round Pinochet's amnesty laws. In 1995, there were breakthrough convictions of six former *Carabineros*, two former DINA (secret police) agents, and most significantly, of General Manuel Contreras and Brigadier Pedro Espinoza, these last sentenced to life imprisonment in "Punta Peuco", a new jail built purposely for former members of the armed forces and other high-profile human rights criminals.

In its final couple of years, Frei's government has run into unexpected problems. Firstly, the Asian economic crisis of 1998 has had serious repercussions on the Chilean economy, hitting exports, foreign investment (much of which came from Southeast Asia) and the value of the peso. At the same time, the unresolved tensions over lack of justice for Pinochet erupted afresh when the general retired from his position of Commander-in-Chief of the Army in March 1998 and immediately took up a seat in Congress as life senator, a post he had created before stepping down. A few months after the protests had died down, Pinochet was dramatically thrust into the spotlight once more when he was arrested in a London hospital on October 16, following a request for his **extradition** to Spain to face charges of murder and torture, filed by the prominent Spanish judge Baltasar Garzón. The arrest provoked strong reactions in Chile: families of Pinochet's victims rejoiced euphorically; supporters of the general were outraged, burning British flags in the streets; while the government, in a difficult position, denounced the arrest as an affront to national sovereignty, and demanded Pinochet's immediate return to Chile – whereupon, they claimed, his alleged crimes would be dealt with in the Chilean courts.

In what has turned out to be a protracted and complex legal battle, the general was first told by the English High Court that he was immune from prosecution as a former head of state, only to see this ruling overturned by a panel of five Law Lords, Britain's highest legal authority. In a sensational move, however, the ruling was declared invalid when Pinochet's lawyers pointed to links between one of the Law Lords, Lord Hoffmann, and Amnesty International, casting doubts on his impartiality. After almost two months of deliberation, a new panel of Law Lords ruled that Pinochet could face extradition proceedings only on alleged crimes committed after 1988, when Britain signed the International Convention Against Torture – which reduced the number of charges from over three hundred to just three. The final decision now lay with Britain's Home Secretary, **Jack Straw**, who, in April 1999 (six months' after Pinochet's arrest) announced that proceedings could go ahead.

These events, while polarizing Chilean public opinion once more, have proved that Chile's democracy is more than capable of dealing with such disturbances, with the general's detainment prompting no military or civil unrest. These testing circumstances however, have not been ideal for the government as it approaches the next round of presidential elections, this time with left-wing **Ricardo Lagos** (of the Socialist Party) as the Concertación's candidate.

LANDSCAPE, WILDLIFE AND THE ENVIRONMENT

One of South America's smaller countries, Chile is roughly the same size as France and Britain combined – but stretched over the equivalent distance of Vancouver to Panama. This sliver of land, on average just 180km across, spans 4350km from the desert of the north to the subantarctic icefields in the south, and encompasses almost every kind of natural habitat along the way, hosting an incredible diversity of wildlife.

GEOGRAPHY

Geographically, Chile is divided into a number of latitudinal **zones**, each of which shows clear differences in terms of climate, vegetation and fauna. These zones only tell part of the story, though, with Chile's three principal landforms – the Andes, the central depression and the coastal range, running the length of the country – all having a significant impact on the local ecology. The **Andes**, in particular, straddle all of Chile's disparate regions. Characterized by precipitous slopes with ravines cut deep into the rock, at points the range acts as a great, impenetrable wall dividing Chile from neighbouring Argentina and Bolivia. Scores of **volcanoes**, many topping 6000m, line these borders, where episodic eruptions and seismic activity are everyday realities. The country's highest peak, Ojos de Salado (6893m), is also the world's highest active volcano; Aconcagua (6959m), the world's tallest peak outside the Himalayas, lies a few kilometres over the Argentine border.

In the far north, the **Norte Grande** region stretches from the Peruvian border over 1000km south to the Copiapó river valley. Covering the central depression between the Andes and the coastal range here is the **Atacama desert**, thought to be the driest place on earth. Surprisingly, the desert is unusually temperate, due to the moderating influence of the Humboldt Current, a cold-water sea current just off the coast. While thick fog banks, known as *camanchaca*, accumulate along the coast where the cold water meets the warm air, a high-pressure zone prevents the cloud from producing rain and from moving inland.

A search for wildlife is a pretty fruitless activity in these barren northern wastes. The frustrated ornithologist A.W. Johnson remarked that the desert was "without doubt one of the most completely arid and utterly lifeless areas in the whole world". It's a very different story, however, up in the Andes bordering the Atacama, where a high plateau known as the **altiplano** is home to a diverse wildlife population and an otherworldly landscape of volcanoes, lakes and salt flats.

The semi-arid **Norte Chico**, bounded roughly by the Copiapó valley and the Aconcagua valley, just north of Santiago, forms a transitionary zone, where the inhospitable northern desert gives way to scrubland and eventually forests further south, as precipitation levels increase. The heat of the sun here is tempered by air humidity, making the land suitable for irrigation farming. The crops of tobacco and cotton that predominated in the colonial era have since been replaced by more lucrative exotic fruits, such as papaya and *cherimoya*. Throughout the north mining has also long been prevalent, thanks to the high levels of nitrates, copper, silver and other minerals in the soil.

Beyond Santiago, the region known as the **Central Valley** extends south to the Bío Bío river. Mineral-rich earth coupled with warm dry summers and short humid winters have provided ideal conditions here for growing grapes, peaches, pears, plums, mangoes, melons and apricots. As the country's primary agricultural zone, as well as a major centre of industry, it is no surprise that this region is home to around 80 percent of the population, almost half based in the capital.

Towards the southern end of the Central Valley, forests signal a marked increase in precipitation levels. Systematic **afforestation**, begun over a hundred years ago in Arauco province, has seen the introduction of a variety of foreign trees, such as eucalyptus and Australian myrrh. No species has flourished as well as the radiata pine, however, which far exceeded the rate of development normal in its native California; concern is mounting that its success is damaging Chile's fragile endemic forest habitats.

In the **Lake District**, between Temuco and Puerto Montt, precipitation reaches 2300mm a year, allowing luxuriant native forests to predominate over the rolling foothills of the coastal range. To the east, azure lakes, remnants of the last glacial age are backed by conical, snow-capped **volcanoes**. Amongst the many volcanoes still active, both Villarrica and Llaima have erupted ten times in the last hundred years.

Beyond Puerto Montt the central depression submerges into the sea, while the tops of the coastal mountains nudge through the water in a mosaic of **islands** and **fjords**. It is here, in this splintered and remote region, that continental Chile finally runs out of dry land: the Carretera Austral, the highway that runs south from Puerto Montt, is cut short after 1000km by two massive ice-fields, the largest in the southern hemisphere outside Antarctica. South of here, **Chilean Patagonia** is an inhospitable place, with continual westerly winds roaring off the sea and dumping up to 7m of snow, sleet, hail and rain on the western slopes every year. Even so, the glaciated scenery, with its perfect U-shaped valleys and rugged mountains, has an indisputable grandeur. In stark contrast, the monotonous grasslands of the Patagonian pampa, which lies in the rain shadow on the eastern side of the Andes, describe the beginning of a quite different habitat.

Tierra del Fuego ("Land of Fire") is separated from mainland Chile by the Magellan Strait. Mountains and forests dominate the south of the island, while the north hosts little more than windswept grasses. From Cape Horn, the tip of the South American continent, Antarctica is a mere 1000km away.

WILDLIFE

Chile's political boundaries are echoed by its geography. Its natural barriers of sea, desert and mountains have proved insurmountable obstacles to many species, preventing contact with their counterparts on the rest of the continent. So it's not surprising that Chile has such a high degree of endemism – one-third of its mammals are not found anywhere else in the world. Many of these species are now at risk of extinction, due to the continuing destruction of their habitats.

MAMMALS

The ferocity of the arid northern climate inhibits both population and diversity, except at its margins. High in the altiplano, herds of **llamas** and **alpacas** graze on the *bofedal* (spongey grass). The latter is uniquely adapted to these high altitudes, able to increase the amount of red blood cells in its body to facilitate oxygenation. As well as these two domesticated camelids, the altiplano is also home to the **vicuña**, whose exceptionally fine coat has long attracted the attention of hunters. In pre-colonial times, only Inca royalty was allowed to wear their highly prized fur, but by the 1970s public demand had brought the vicuña population down to only a few hundred in Chile. Protected as an endangered species, numbers are steadily recovering.

Thought to be the common ancestor of the other three South American camelids, the once-abundant wild **guanaco** survive in isolated herds in the altiplano and in Chilean Patagonia. The large, deer-like **huemul**, an endemic mammal in danger of extinction, may be seen darting around the rocky Patagonian outcrop, all the time alert to highland predators such as mountain cats and foxes. **Geoffroy's cat**, the continent's smallest wild feline, hunts equally well at the fringes of the desert as in the bushlands and mountains, enjoying the near-invisibility afforded by its grey-black spotted coat.

A natural target for predators are the **rodents**, which dominate the temperate grasslands and mountains. The endemic **mountain vizcacha** sports long furry ears and nests in crags at altitudes of over 3000m. At the first sign of danger, they emit a high-pitched whistle to alert the colony and propel themselves to safety on powerful hind legs. Its relative, the **chinchilla**, used to live in huge numbers throughout the Andean altiplano – early explorers described rock faces teeming with the creatures. Like the vicuña, its downfall has been its exceptionally soft, thick coat. From each follicle grows not one but eighty hairs, so close that fleas cannot penetrate them, creating a formidable barrier against the cold. Once discovered, chinchillas were soon being trapped in their thousands to satisfy worldwide demand for their fur. With over 150 pelts required for a single coat, by 1905 it's recorded that 216,000 chinchilla skins were distributed from the port of Coquimbo alone. Thirteen years later an embargo was declared, but by then the chinchilla was almost extinct. It took a team of 23 men over 3 years to find just 11 chinchillas, most of which died in transit from their natural habitat. Although now a popular pet, the chinchilla remains extremely rare in the wild.

Further south in the pampas and low savannahs, the **mara** or **Patagonian cavy**, which resembles a hare, is difficult to approach, as it will break into a run, zigzagging at speeds of 45km per hour to escape hunters such as the **puma**. Wildcats including the **colo-colo** – the spitting image of a ginger tom – and **guiña** also stalk these grasslands. The **grison**, a grey marten-like predator with a black nose, leaves shelter at dusk and steams through the surrounding countryside in search of rodents, birds, eggs, reptiles and molluscs. When threatened, it squirts a foul-smelling vapour from its anal gland.

The forested regions of the south are populated by small mammals such as rabbits, hares, cats and mice. In the marshy areas, the predominantly aquatic, otter-like **coypu** makes its home in burrows extending over 15m into the riverbank. The temperate rainforest habitat harbours several unfamiliar and rarely seen animals, such as the **monito del bosque**, an arboreal marsupial, while in the woodland of Chiloé, the unusual-looking, endemic **pudú**, a miniature red deer about the size of a dog, lives on the verge of extinction.

A variety of marine mammals inhabit Chile's expansive coastline, including the **southern sea lion**, which can be seen the length of the coast, while the **southern fur seal** prefers the cooler waters around Tierra del Fuego. Further south you may see **dolphins** and blue **whales** sifting for krill.

REPTILES, AMPHIBIANS AND INSECTS

There are no venomous **snakes** in Chile. The six species that exist here, including the **long-tailed snake** which can reach 2m in length, feed on nothing larger than lizards, mice, frogs, toads and occasionally small birds. The only poisonous creatures are the **brown corner spider** and the **corn spider**, identified by its black body with a red mark, but an encounter with either is highly unlikely. **Lizards** abound from the arid regions to the temperate forests and many, like the **Chilean iguana**, are peculiar to the country.

The **amphibians** prefer the humidity of the south, where **Darwin's frog** undergoes its extraordinary breeding process. The male swallows the fertilized eggs, which gestate inside him until ejected through his mouth as tadpoles. In the Andes **leptodactylid** (thin-fingered) **frogs** are roasted and eaten whole. Farming of these creatures has proved impractical since they take so long to develop.

Chile's reptiles and amphibians rely on a variety of **insects** once plentiful in the vegetation and native temperate forests. Following widespread deforestation and the introduction of foreign conifers, many insect species have suffered, failing to adapt to the changes in habitat. The **stag beetle**, for instance, a colossus at 9cm long, depends on these dwindling forests for its survival.

BIRDS

With its contrasting habitats, geographical isolation and 5337km of coastline, Chile's birdlife is as diverse as in any non-tropical region in the world. Newcomers to the southern hemisphere will encounter a curious mix of the familiar and the unknown, seeing for example, the common **house sparrow** alongside such oddities as the **red-breasted blackbird**. Other old acquaintances are the 37 species that migrate from the north to Chile, including **sandpipers**, **curlews**, **plovers** and **godwits**. But the country's many endemics and peculiarities more than compensate. One such is the unmistakeable **Inca tern**, with its scarlet legs and bill, and brilliant-white forked moustache, or the **chestnut-throated huet-huet**, the **chucao** and **churrin de la mocha**, three furtive woodland foragers, whose shrill calls ring through Chile's temperate rainforests.

Chile's northernmost tip is populated by a few truly tropical birds which have never managed to cross the arid Atacama desert. In many respects these birds, including the **slaty finch**, the **white-winged dove**, the **Pacific scarlet flycatcher** and **D'Orbigny's ground-dove**, have more in common with those of coastal Peru than the rest of Chile. In the desert zone itself, only a handful of birds manage to eke life from such limited resources: for example, the **desert-coloured** and **shore miners**, the **tit-like spine-tail** and the **Peruvian grey gull**.

In the Mediterranean-like areas of central Chile, commonly seen birds are the **Chilean parakeet**, the **Chilean black croke** and the **giant hummingbird**, a summer visitor. Further south, as the landscape changes with the increased levels of rainfall and forestation, woodland and river-based birds, such as the **Chilean pigeon**, the **giant red-headed** and **black woodpeckers**, the **southern ringed kingfisher** and the **spectacled duck** become more apparent. On the edges of the forests the gregarious **crested caracara** calls its loud greetings so heartily that it arches its head all the way onto its back. Further south still, in Chilean Patagonia, waterfowl begin to predominate, including the elegant **coscoroba** and **black-necked swans**, which build their bulky, partly floating nests from a thick bed of rushes.

In the mountains the mighty **Andean condors**, among the world's largest birds with a wingspan of over 3m, can be seen wheeling overhead, buoyed by the upward thermals. High in the Andes near the Bolivian border, three species of **flamingo** gather at remote saltwater lakes: the **Chilean flamingo**, recognizable for its grey-green feet with red joints, the yellow-legged **Andean flamingo** and lastly **James's flamingo**, which was thought to be extinct for 50 years until its rediscovery in 1957. Often described as the most beautifully coloured of the flamingoes, it has a delicate pinkish tinge, bursting into red at the base of the neck that gradually fades over the wings. **Darwin's rhea** or **ñandú** also inhabits the highland regions and parts of the far south. Resembling the ostrich or emu, it hides its periscopic head and neck under its bushy feathers to blend in with the surrounding brush. If this doesn't work, it can run faster than a galloping horse, with its neck stretched out horizontally in front. Here in the highlands you may also see the **Andean sheldgoose**, the **crested duck**, **D'Orbigny's seedsnipe** and several species of **tyrant bird**.

The cold Humboldt Current supports a wealth of marine life, due to the myriad microscopic organisms that thrive in its cooler water. Over 225 fish species proliferate in the current, along with large stocks of anchovy, tuna, corvina and congrio. With such bountiful supplies, Chile enjoys one of the richest and most varied population of **sea birds**, including many endemic species. The **Peruvian pelican**, a dapper sight with its pronounced yellow crest, is only found around the current, as are the **Humboldt penguin**, **Peruvian booby** and four species of **storm petrel**. But **skuas**, **gulls**, **fulmars**, **cormorants**, **shags**, **shearwaters** and **terns** are encountered along much of the coastline and in the subantarctic areas. Amongst the many gawky-looking **petrels** that swarm behind fishing boats awaiting the ejection of galley waste, the **southern giant petrel** has been aptly described as "a pugnacious, ungainly and uncouth scavenger". Not so the striking **black skimmer**, whose masterly flight enables it to glide just above the water, tilling a perfect furrow with its longer lower beak as it goes. But perhaps the most eye-catching is the largest of all the seabirds, the **albatross**, eight species of which migrate through Chilean waters.

Nine species of **penguin** inhabit Chilean territory, including the **Magellanic** and **rockhopper penguin**, so called for its peculiar, stuttering gait. The **Emperor penguin**, the tallest of them at over a metre, can withstand temperatures of minus 40°C and gale-force winds on the ice floes of Antarctica, and is the most southerly breeding of any bird.

FLORA

Extraordinary diversity of altitude, latitude and precipitation inevitably leads to an extraordinary diversity of flora. Only humid tropical forest fails to feature in Chile's rich and varied ecology. The tropical area in the far north is stricken with aridity too severe to support most plant life, except at higher altitudes, where **xerophytes** ("dry growers"), such as **cacti**, begin to appear. Ninety percent of Chile's vascular plants are from the cactus family, many of them endemic and endangered. On the altiplano, **tough grasses** and **brush** associated with minimal rainfall support the herds of grazing alpaca.

Moving south towards Central Chile, where the climate is more balanced and water less scarce, **sclerophyllous** ("rigid leaf") shrubs and trees feature leathery leaves that help them retain water. As rainfall increases towards the south, these plants begin to blend with **temperate rainforests**. In the heavily populated areas of this central region, such woodlands have suffered widespread deforestation to clear land for farming and housing, and only patches remain. Near Santiago, for example, in Parque Nacional La Campana, stands the last forest of endangered **Chilean palm**, sole reminder of a time when millions of the trees covered the area, favoured as they were for the flavour of their sap.

Further south the **temperate rainforests** have fared a little better, constituting almost a quarter of this type of habitat worldwide. Over 95 percent of the fifty tree species found here are endemic, including the **araucaria** (*araucaria araucana*), known in English as the **monkey puzzle**, Chile's national tree, and rare **southern beeches** (*Nothofagus*) – principally coïgue, ñirre, raulí and lenga – which vie for sunlight, towering up to 40m into the air to break clear of the canopy. The **alerce** or **Chilean false larch** (*Fitzroya cupressoides*), a relative of the North American sequoia, takes several hundred years to reach maturity and can live for 4000 years, providing the loggers don't get there first. The tree is best seen in the areas around Puerto Montt.

In Chilean Patagonia, **evergreen beeches** (*Nothofagus betuloides*) grow in the sheltered areas bordering the great fields of ice, while its **deciduous** cousins *Nothofagus pumilio* and *antarctica* prefer the drier eastern flanks of the Andes. Where the canopy is broken, dazzling scarlet *Embothrium*, yellow *Berberis* bedecked with mauve berries and deep-red *pernettya* emblazon the ground. Rare **orchids** and pink **oxalis** interweave in a tapestry of colour. Such brilliant displays are impossible on the coastal Magellanic **moorland** where high levels of precipitation drown all but the sphagnum **bog** communities and **dwarf shrubs**. Here, the wind-beaten **Magellanic gunnera** grows only a few centimetres high, a tiny fraction of what its relative Brazilian gunnera is capable. Meanwhile, the rain shadow effect on the eastern Patagonian steppe supports little more than coarse tussocks of *Festuca* grasses.

ENVIRONMENTAL ISSUES

The slow destruction of Chile's environment was set in motion by the Spanish in the sixteenth century, though it wasn't until the early twentieth century, with widespread settlement and increased industrialization, that the scale reached damaging levels. Today, although Chile has suffered less environmental degradation than most other countries with comparable resources, there are few habitats that have not been affected in some way by human activity, and it's debatable whether the government is prepared to prioritize future protection over financial exploitation.

There was little interest in environmental issues in Chile until large-scale disruption caused by the appalling **smogs in Santiago**, considered by Greenpeace to be the third most polluted city in Latin America, mobilized public concern. Most years the capital's schools are suspended for days on end and people are warned to stay indoors as a dense cloud of toxic gases hangs over the capital, caught between the two surrounding mountain ranges. The problem is worsened in dry weather, when the concentration of contaminated air is not dissolved by rain. Pressure from the urban middle-class has forced the government to introduce (many say weak) measures to lessen air pollution in Santiago, and has encouraged politicians to include environmental elements to their policies.

The most important new **environmental law**, following a guarantee in the 1980 Constitution that all Chileans have "the right to live in an environment free of pollution", is the Environmental Act of 1994, which has standardized procedures for assessing environmental damage, while encouraging public involvement by allowing citizens to bring charges against violators, even if they have not been directly affected by them. One successful application of this new law occurred in 1997, when the Chilean Supreme Court overturned a government-approved project involving the logging for woodchips of centuries-old, endangered forests of native lenga, a cherry-like beech found in the Tierra del Fuego.

Chile's precious **temperate rainforests** have been threatened for many years by intensive logging and the introduction of harmful foreign species, with large tracts razed in the free-

THE EL NIÑO EFFECT

Nature's footnote to the end of the millennium, the **1997–98 El Niño** wreaked havoc with global climate patterns and brought chaos to the world. In parts of Chile, Peru and Ecuador, floods and landslides engulfed people and animals, houses, farms and factories, while torrents swept away bridges, roads and railways. Elsewhere, severe droughts scorched the earth, drying up forests and bushland and creating the tinderbox conditions that sparked off raging fires. Clouds of poisonous smoke billowed into the atmosphere, affecting 70 million people in Southeast Asia, while millions of others risked starvation following widespread crop failure. As the Pacific countries affected by El Niño pick up the pieces, conservative estimates of the cost of reparation put it at around US$20 billion.

In Chile, **flooding** was the worst it had been for a decade, as 80,000 people were made homeless in June 1998 alone. The warm coastal water associated with El Niño drove fish stocks to cooler places, crippling the fishing industry and killing millions of marine animals. But while some watched their crops and livestock drown, the rains also filled irrigation basins that had been at a critically low level for years and water surges saved the hydroelectric companies from having to ration their power output. In the Atacama desert, freak rainfall woke up the barren soil, causing it to burst into blossom.

The phenomenon itself is no new thing. Records document such events over 400 years ago, but it was only in the 1960s that the Norwegian meteorologist Jacob Bjerknes identified the processes that lead to such an event. He saw that the El Niño (meaning "the Little Boy" or "the Christ Child", a name given by Peruvian fishermen to the body of warm water that would arrive around Christmas) was intimately connected to extremes in the so-called **Southern Oscillation**, a feature where atmospheric pressure between the eastern equatorial Pacific and the Indo-Australian areas behaves as a seesaw, one rising as the other falls.

In "normal" years easterly trade winds blow west across the Pacific, pushing warm surface water towards Indonesia, Australia and the Philippines, where the water becomes about 8°C warmer and about 50cm higher than on the other side of the ocean. In the east, the displacement of the sea allows cold nutrient-rich water, known as the Humboldt or Peru Current, to swell up from the depths along the coast of South America, providing food for countless marine and bird species.

An El Niño event occurs when the trade winds fall off and the layer of warm water in the west laps back across the ocean, so warming up the east Pacific and cooling the west. Consequently, air temperatures across the Pacific begin to even out, tipping the balance of the atmospheric pressure seesaw, which further reduces the strength of the trade winds. Thus the process is enhanced, as warm water continues to build up in the eastern Pacific, bringing with it abnormal amounts of rainfall to coastal South America, while completely starving other areas of precipitation. The warm water also forces the cold Humboldt Current and its micro-organisms to deeper levels, effectively removing a vital link in the marine food chain, killing innumerable fish, sea birds and mammals. Meanwhile, the upset in the Southern Oscillation disturbs weather systems all around the world, resulting in severe and unexpected weather.

In the past twenty years, El Niño-Southern Oscillation (ENSO) events seem to have become stronger, longer and more frequent, leading many to suggest that human activity, such as the warming of the earth's atmosphere through the greenhouse effect, could well be having an influence. If this is true, failure to cut emissions of greenhouse gases may in the end cost the lives and livelihoods of millions of people across the world.

for-all scramble to colonize remote areas. The worst damage occurred in the prewar years, but illegal clearance is still common today. The alerce, an evergreen with a life span of 4000 years, has been a target of international campaigning as it continues to be logged because of the high commercial value of its wood, despite a law passed in 1976 making it illegal to cut live alerces. Yet landowners burn the trees or strip their bark to kill them first, thus evading the hands of the law. Many thousands of hectares of alerce forest are wiped out in this manner every year.

Meanwhile in the central regions native trees have been wiped out to make space for the commercial planting of more profitable foreign species. In many areas the practice has left only islands of indigenous forest in an ocean of introduced eucalyptus and radiata pine. The result is genetic isolation of both flora and fauna, leaving many mammals with distinct ecological needs imprisoned in small pockets of native woodland. The few thin strips that connect such pockets are the only way for many species to maintain communication with the rest of their population. If these corridors are destroyed countless endemic organisms face extinction.

In the north **mining** is a major cause of environmental concern. Chuquicamata, near Antofagasta, is the biggest open-pit copper mine in the world and continues to grow. Now visible from space, the giant pit threatens to swallow up the town that grew with it, as 600,000 tons of rock are dug up every day, spewing arsenic-rich dust into the air. The plume from the smelting works carries 200km to San Pedro de Atacama, a pre-colonial village in the east. The country's mines consume vast quantities of water, often contaminating it in the process. In tandem with agricultural irrigation, reckless water usage is taking its toll on wildlife, as animals find the search for drinking places increasingly difficult. Even the human population has been put out, relying in some northern villages on an ingenious invention that turns fog into drinking water.

Overexploitation of the land and sea have brought further problems. Incompetent or negligent farming, either through overgrazing or the clearing of vegetation has resulted in extensive **desertification**, particularly in the north. Meanwhile, careless practices in the fishing industry are upsetting the fragile balance of Chile's **marine life**. A leaked government report shows that some fish stocks have been depleted by as much as 96 percent between 1985 and 1993.

On a global level, many believe human-induced climate change to be a leading cause of the **El Niño phenomenon**, which badly damaged Chile's fisheries, agriculture and marine species (see box overleaf). Moreover, the expansion of the hole in the ozone layer over Antarctica has put many people, especially in Patagonia, on guard against the harmful ultraviolet rays that seep through it.

Chile has been more effective than most Latin American countries in its opposition to the damage brought about by the excesses of unfettered capitalism, and awareness of the delicacy of the country's habitats and its unique species is growing. However, environmentalists continue to bemoan the lack of concerted pressure, claiming that many merely respond occasionally and emotionally to images churned out in the media, rather than pushing consistently for action and reform.

by Harry Adès

CHILEAN MUSIC: NUEVA CANCIÓN

Chile has produced a wide range of music genres, from cueca to bolero, but none has been so important and influential as Nueva Canción, the "New Song" movement that developed in Chile in the 1960s, along with parallel movements in Argentina, Uruguay and also Cuba. A music rooted in the guitar traditions of the troubadour, the songs could be love lyric or chronicle, lament or call to action, and, as such, they have played a part of Latin America's political and cultural struggles. In Chile, the great singer-songwriter Víctor Jara was murdered for his art by Pinochet's thugs, while groups like Inti Illimani were forced into exile. In an extract taken from the *Rough Guide to World Music*, Jan Fairley looks at the history and legacy of this music of "guitar as gun".

Latin America's revolutionary politics have found expression in many of the continent's musics, but never more directly than in **nueva canción**. This "new song" emerged at the end of the 1960s in Argentina and Chile, and over the next three decades it fulfilled an important role in countries from Uruguay to Nicaragua, and (in a different relationship to government) across the Caribbean in Cuba. It was brought to international attention, above all, through the lyrical songs of Chilean theatre director and singer-songwriter **Víctor Jara**, who was murdered by the military in Chile during the 1973 coup d'état.

PITY THE SINGER . . .

"Pity the singer who doesn't risk his guitar and himself ... who never knew that we were the seed that today is life."

Cuban **Pablo Milanés** "Pobre del cantor"

Nueva canción as a movement spans a period of over thirty years, from the early 1960s, when its musicians became part of the political struggle to bring about change and reform in their own countries. As a result of their activities, many of their number were arrested or forced into exile by dictatorships which through murder, torture and disappearance wiped out so much of a generation. The sense of a movement grew as the musicians involved met one another at festivals in Cuba, Nicaragua, Peru, Mexico, Argentina and Brazil, visited each others' countries, and occasionally sang each others' songs. At the end of the 1990s, with the return to democracy on the continent, the singers continue to pursue their careers in different ways, while maintaining long-term friendships and exchanges.

The 1960s was a time of politics and idealism in South America – far more so than in Europe or North America. There was a stark challenge presented by the continent's obvious inequalities, its inherited power and wealth, its corrupt regimes, and by the denial of literacy and education to much of the population. It is within this context that nueva canción singers and writers must be understood. With voice and guitar, they composed songs of their own hopes and experiences in places where many of those involved in struggles for change regularly met and socialized.

It is a music that is now, in some ways, out of time: the revolutionary past, the 1960s rhetoric of guitar as gun and song as bullet. Yet the songs – poems written to be perfomed – are classic expressions of the years of hope and struggle for change, their beauty and truth later nurturing those suffering under dictatorship, and those forced into exile. They are still known by heart by audiences throughout the continent and exile communities in Europe.

Nueva canción was an expression of politics in its widest sense. It was not "protest song" as such. The musicians involved were not card-carrying members of any international organization and were often independent of political parties – although in the early 1970s the Chilean musicians were closely linked with the Popular Unity government of Salvador Allende, the first socialist president and government to be legitimately elected through the ballot box.

What linked these and other musicians of the movement was an ethical stance – a commitment to improve conditions for the majority of people in Latin America. To that end they sang not only in concerts and clubs but in factories, in shanty towns, community centres and at political meetings and street demonstrations. People in protest the world over have joined in the Chilean street anthems *El Pueblo Unido Jamás Sera Vencido* (The People United Will Never Be Defeated) and *Venceremos* (We Will Win).

YUPANQUI AND VIOLETA PARRA

The roots of the nueva canción movement lie in the work of two key figures, whose music bridged rural and urban life and culture in the 1940s and 50s: the Argentine **Atahualpa Yupanqui** (1908–1992) and the Chilean **Violeta Parra** (1917–1967). Each had a passionate interest in their nation's rural musical traditions, which had both an Iberian and Amerindian sensibility. Their work was in some respects paralleled by the Cuban Carlos Puebla.

Atahualpa Yupanqui, spent much of his early life travelling around Argentina, collecting popular songs from itinerant *payadores* (improvising poets) and folk singers in rural areas. He also wrote his own songs, and during a long career introduced a new integrity to Argentine folk music – and an assertive political outlook which ultimately forced him into exile in Paris.

Violeta Parra's career in Chile mirrored that of Yupanqui. She travelled extensively, singing with and collecting songs from old *payadores* and preserved and popularized them through radio broadcasts and records. She also composed new material based on these rural song traditions, creating a model and repertoire for what became nueva canción. Her songs celebrated the rural and regional, the music of the peasant, the land-worker and the marginalized migrant.

Musically, Parra was also significant in her popularization of **Andean or Amerindian instruments** – the armadillo-shelled charango, the quena (bamboo flute) and panpipes, and in her enthusiasm for the **French chanson** tradition. She spent time in Paris in the 1960s with her children Angel and Isabel, where they met Yupanqui, Edith Piaf and the flautist Gilbert Favre, who was to found the influential Andean band, Los Jairas, and with whom Violeta fell in love. Returning to Buenos Aires, she performed in a tent in the district of La Reina, which came to be called the Carpa de La Reina (The Queen's Tent). However, with a long history of depression, she committed suicide in 1967.

Parra left behind a legacy of exquisite songs, many of them with a wry sense of humour, including the unparalleled *Gracias a la vida* (Thanks to life), later covered by Joan Baez and a host of others. Even her love songs seem informed by an awareness of poverty and injustice, while direct pieces like *¿Qué dirá el Santo Padre?* (What does the Sainted Pope Say?) highlighted the Church's responsibility to take action. As Parra wrote (in the décima form she often used in her songs) in her autobiography:

"I sing to the Chilean people
if I have something to say
I don't take up the guitar
to win applause
I sing of the difference there is
between what is certain
and what is false
otherwise I don't sing."

THE MOVEMENT TAKES OFF

Nueva canción emerged as a real force in the mid-1960s when various governments on the continent were trying to effect democratic social change. The search for a Latin American cultural identity became a spontaneous part of this wider struggle for self-determination, and music was a part of the process.

The first crystallization of a nueva canción ideal in Chile emerged with the opening of a crucial new folk club. This was the legendary (and now reopened) crucible of nueva canción, the **Peña de los Parra**, which **Angel and Isabel Parra**, inspired by the Paris *chanson* nightclubs, opened in downtown Santiago in 1965. Among the regular singer-songwriters performing here were **Víctor Jara** and **Patricio Manns**. Their audiences, in the politically charged and optimistic period prior to the election of Allende's government, were enthusiastic activists and fellow musicians.

VÍCTOR JARA

The great singer-songwriter and theatre director **Víctor Jara** took nueva canción onto a world stage. His songs, and his life, continue to reverberate, and he has been recorded by rock singers like Sting, Bruce Springsteen, Peter Gabriel and Jackson Brown, and (memorably) by the British singer Robert Wyatt. All have been moved by Jara's story and inspired by his example.

Jara was born into a rural family who came to live in a shanty-town on the barren outskirts of Santiago when Víctor's father died; he was just eleven. His mother sang as a *cantora* for births, marriages and deaths, keeping her family alive by running a food-stall in the main Santiago market. It was from his mother and her work that Jara gained his intuitive knowledge of Chilean guitar and singing styles.

He began performing his songs in the early 1960s and from the beginning caused a furore. During the government of Eduardo Frei, for example, his playful version of a traditional piece, *La Beata* – a send-up of the desires of a nun – was banned, as was his accusatory *Preguntas por Puerto Montt* (You ask for Puerto Montt), which accused the Minister of the Interior of the massacre of poor landless peasants in the South of Chile. Working with Isabel Parra and the group **Huamari**, Jara went on to create a sequence of songs called *La Población*, based on the history and life of Santiago's shanty-town communities. His great gift was a deceptively simple and direct style applied to whatever he did.

One of his best-loved songs, *Te recuerdo Amanda* (I remember you Amanda), is a good example of the simplicity of his craft. A hauntingly understated love song, it tells the story of a girl who goes to meet her man Manuel at the factory gates; he never appears because of an "accident" and Amanda waits in vain. In many of his songs, Jara subtly interwove allusions to his own life with the experiences of other ordinary people – Amanda and Manuel were the names of his parents.

Jara's influence was immense, both on nueva canción singers and the Andean-oriented groups like **Inti Illimani** and **Quilapayún** (see p.471), whom he worked with often, encouraging them to forge their own new performance styles. Enormously popular and fun-loving, he was nevertheless clear about his role as a singer: "The authentic revolutionary should be behind the guitar, so that the guitar becomes an instrument of struggle, so that it can also shoot like a gun." As he sang in 1972 in his song *Manifiesto*, a tender serenade which with hindsight has been seen as his testimony, "I don't sing just for love of singing, but for the statements made by my guitar, honest, its heart of earth, like the dove it goes flying. . . Song sung by a man who will die singing, truthfully singing his song."

Like many Chilean musicians, Jara was deeply involved with the Unidad Popular government of Salvador Allende, who in 1970, following his election, had appeared on an open-air stage in Santiago surrounded by musicians

PLEGARIA UN LABRADOR (PRAYER TO A LABOURER)

Stand up and look at the mountain
From where the wind comes, the sun and the water
You who direct the courses of the rivers
You who have sown the flight of your soul
Stand up and look at your hands
So as to grow
Clasp your brother's, in your own
Together we will move united by blood
Today is the time that can become tomorrow

Deliver us from the one who dominates us through misery
Bring to us your reign of justice and equality
Blow like the wind the flower of the canyon
Clean like fire the barrel of my gun

Let your will at last come about here on earth
Give to us your strength and valour so as to fight
Blow like the wind the flower of the canyon
Clean like fire the barrel of my gun

Stand up and look at your hands
So as to grow
Clasp your brother's, in your own
Together we will move united by blood
Now and in the hour of our death
Amen.

Víctor Jara

under a banner saying "There can be no revolution without song". Three years later, on September 11, 1973 – along with hundreds of others who had legitimately supported the government – Jara was arrested by the military and taken to the same downtown stadium in which he had won the First Festival of New Chilean Song in 1969. Tortured, his hands and wrists broken, his body was found with five others, riddled with machine-gun bullets, dumped alongside a wall of the Metropolitan Cemetery; his face was later recognised amongst a pile of unidentified bodies in one of the Santiago mortuaries by a worker. He was just 35.

Jara left behind him a song composed during the final hours of his life, written down and remembered by those who were with him at the end, called as a poem of testimony *Estadio Chile* (Chile Stadium). It was later set a cappella to music as *Ay canto, que mal me sales*, by his friend and colleague Isabel Parra.

EXILES AND ANDEAN SOUNDS

After Pinochet's coup d'état anything remotely associated with the Allende government and its values came under censorship, including books and records, whose possession could be cause for arrest. The junta issued warnings to musicians and folklorists that it would be unwise for them to play nueva canción, or indeed any of the Andean instruments associated with its sound – charangas, panpipes and *quenas*.

It was not exactly a banning but menacing enough to force the scene well underground – and abroad, where many Chilean musicians lived out the junta years in exile. Their numbers included the groups Inti Illimani and Quilapayún and later Illapu (see below), Sergio Ortega,

DISCOGRAPHY

Nueva canción has had a raw deal on **CD** – it peaked in the decades before shiny discs – and for many classics, you'll need to search secondhand stores for vinyl. If you travel to Chile, you can also obtain **songbooks** for Víctor Jara (the Fundación Víctor Jara publish his complete works), while most other songs of the period are featured in *Clasicos de la Musica Popular Chilena Vol 11 1960–1973* (Ediciones Universidad Catolica de Chile).

COMPILATIONS

Music of the Andes (Hemisphere EMI, UK).
Despite the title, this is essentially a nueva canción disc, with key Chilean groups Inti Illimani, Quilapayun and Illapu to the fore. There is also an instrumental recording of *Tinku* attributed to Víctor Jara.

ARTISTS

ILLAPU

Illapu, with a track record stretching back over 25 years, and a big following in Chile, play Andean instruments – panpipes, quenas and charangos – along with saxophones, electric bass and Caribbean percussion. Their music is rooted in the north of the country where most of the band hail from.

Sereno (EMI, UK).
This enjoyable collection gives a pretty good idea of what Illapu have got up to over the years and includes strongly folkloric material, as well as dance pieces influenced by salsa, romantic ballads and the earlier styles of vocal harmony.

INTI ILLIMANI

The foremost Chilean "new song" group who began as students in 1967, bringing the Andean sound to Europe through their thousands of concerts in exile, and taking European influences back home again in the late 1980s. The original band, together for thirty years, featured the glorious-voiced José Séves.

Lejanía (Xenophile, US).
The focus is on Andean themes in this celebration of their thirtieth anniversary and their original inspiration.

Arriesgaré la piel (Xenophile, US).
A celebration of the music the Intis grew up with, from creole-style tunes to Chilean cuecas, most lyrics by Patricio Manns with music by Salinas. This was the final album to be made with the core of the original band before Séves left.

Grandes Exitos (EMI, Chile).
A compilation of seventeen songs and instrumental pieces taken from the band's thirty-year history.

Patricio Manns, Isabel and Angel Parra, and Patricio Castillo. They were not the only Latin Americans forced from their country. Other **musician exiles** of the 1970s included Brazilian MPB singers Chico Buarque, Caetano Veloso and Gilberto Gil; Uruguay's nueva canción singer Daniel Viglietti; and Argentina's Mercedes Sosa.

In Chile, the first acts of musical defiance took place behind church walls, where a group of musicians who called themselves **Barroco Andino** started to play baroque music with Andean instruments within months of the coup.

It was a brave act, for the use of Andean or Amerindian instruments and culture was instinctively linked with the nueva canción movement. Chilean groups like **Quilapayún** and **Inti Illimani** wore the traditional ponchos of the peasant and played Andean instruments such as panpipes, bamboo flutes and the charango, and the maracas and shakers of Central America and the Caribbean. That these were the instruments of the communities who had managed somehow to survive slavery, resist colonialism and its aftermath had a powerful symbolism. Both the "los Intis" and "los Quilas", as they became familiarly known, worked closely with Víctor Jara and also with popular classical composers Sergio Ortega and Luís Advis.

In 1973 both groups travelled to Europe as official cultural ambassadors of the Allende government, actively seeking support from governments in Europe at a time when the country was more or less beseiged economically by a North American blockade, its economy being undermined by CIA activity. On September 11 when General Pinochet led the coup d'état in which

QUILAPAYÚN

This key Chilean new-song group worked closely in their early years with Víctor Jara and in 1973 – the year before the coup – they split into multiple groups in order to get their message across on as many stages as possible. They co-authored, with Sergio Ortega, the street anthem *El Pueblo Unido Jamás Sera Vencido* (the People United Will Never Be Defeated). Although they disbanded in the late 1990s, their influence lives on.

Santa María de Iquique (Dom Disque, France).
Chilean composer Luis Advis's ground-breaking Cantata, composed for Quilapayún, tells the emblematic and heroic tale of the murder of unarmed nitrate workers and their families in 1971.

VÍCTOR JARA

The leading singer-songwriter of his generation, Víctor Jara was murdered in his prime by Pinochet's forces in September 1973. His legacy is an extraordinary songbook, which can be heard in his original versions, as well as a host of Latin and Western covers.

Manifesto (Castle, UK).
Reissued to mark the 25th anniversary of his death, this is a key disc of nueva canción, with *Te recuerdo Amanda*, *Canto libre*, *La Plegaria a un labrador* and *Ay canto*, the final poem written in the Estadio Chile, before his death. Includes Spanish lyrics and English translations.

Vientos del Pueblo (Monitor, US).
A generous 22-song compilation that includes most of the Jara milestones, including *Te recuerdo Amanda* and *Preguntas por Puerto Montt*, plus the wonderful revolutionary romp of *A Cochabamba me voy*. Quilapayún provide backing on half the album.

Víctor Jara Complete (Plane, Germany).
This four-CD box is the definitive Jara, featuring material from eight original LPs. Plane have also released an excellent single disc selection of highlights.

La Poblacion (Alerce, Chile).
Classic Jara: a project involving other musicians, but including most of all the lives and experiences of those celebrated here, who lived in various shanty towns (*poblaciones*) including the one where Jara himself grew up.

VIOLETA PARRA

One of South America's most significant folklorists and composers, Violeta Parra collected fragments of folklore from singers, teaching them to the next generation and influencing them with her own superb compositions. Parra's songs have also been superbly recorded by Argentinian Mercedes Sosa.

Canto a mi America (Auvidis, France).
An excellent introduction to Parra's seminal songs.

Las últimas composiciones (Alerce, Chile).
A reissue of Parra's 1965 release which turned out to be her last as well as latest songs ("últimas" means both in Spanish).

Salvador Allende died, the Intis were in Italy and the Quilas in France. For the Intis the tour ("the longest in history", as Intis member Jorge Coulon jokes) turned into a fifteen-year and fifty-four days European exile for the group, an exile which put nueva canción and Amerindian music firmly on Europe's agenda of Latin American music.

The groups were the heart and soul of a worldwide Chilean (and Latin American) solidarity movement, performing almost daily for the first ten years. Both also recorded albums of new songs, the Intis influenced by their many years in Italy, creating some beautiful songs of exile, including the seminal song *Vuelvo*, with key singer-songwriter and musician **Patricio Manns**.

The impact of their high-profile campaigning against the military meant that the Intis were turned back on the airport tarmac long after politicians and trade union leaders were repatriated. They eventually returned on September 18, 1988, Chile's National Day, the day of one of the biggest meetings of supporters of the "No" vote to the plebiscite called by Pinochet to determine whether he should stay in office. Going straight from the airport to sing on a huge open-air stage and to dance the traditional cueca (Chile's National Day dance), the group's homecoming was an emotional and timely one. In 1998, after ten years of rebuilding their lives, making music and supporting various projects, including the Víctor Jara Foundation, the group's personnel, almost unchanged since 1967, is now adapting to the amicable departure of Max Berrú and Jose Séves to pursue other projects.

The Andean instruments and rhythms used by Quilapayún (who disbanded in the 1980s) and Inti Illimani have been skilfully used by many other groups whose music is equally interesting – groups like **Illapu**, who remained popular throughout the 1980s (with a number of years in forced exile) and 1990s.

THE FUTURE AND LEGACY

Times have changed in Chile and in Latin America generally, with revolutionary governments no longer in power, democracy restored after dictatorships, and even Pinochet placed under arrest. The nueva canción movement, tied to an era of ideals and struggle, and then the brutal years of survival under dictatorship, would seem to have lost its relevance.

Its musicians have moved on to more individual concerns in their (always poetic) songwriting. But the nueva canción form, the inspiration of the song as message, and the rediscovery of Andean music and instruments, continues to have resonance and influence. Among a new generation of singers inspired by the history of "new song" are **Carlos Varela** in Cuba and the Bolivian singer, **Emma Junaro**.

And there will be others. For Latin America, nueva canción is not only music but history. As the Cuban press has said of the songs of Silvio Rodríguez: "We have here the great epic poems of our days." Or as the Dominican Republic's merengue superstar Juan Luís Guerra, put it, "they are the master songwriters – they have influenced everyone."

BOOKS

Unfortunately, some of the best and most evocative books written on Chile have long been out of print, but we include some of them – mainly travel narratives or general accounts – below (marked by o/p in the parentheses after the title), as they can often be found in public libraries. Modern publications are inevitably dominated by analyses and testimonies of the Pinochet years, much of which makes compulsive reading. There are relatively few up-to-date general histories of Chile in English, with those available focusing more on the academic market than the general reader. Chilean fiction, meanwhile, is not very widely translated into English, with the exception of a handful of the country's more famous authors. Its poetry, on the other hand, or more specifically the poetry of its famous Nobel laureate, Pablo Neruda, has been translated into many languages and is widely available abroad. Note that in the list below, where two publishers are given, these refer to UK/US publishers respectively. If just one publisher is listed, and no country is specified, the book is published in both the UK and the USA.

IMPRESSIONS, TRAVEL AND GENERAL ACCOUNTS

GENERAL INTRODUCTIONS

Stephen Clissold *Chilean Scrapbook* (Cresset; o/p). Beautifully and evocatively written, taking you from the top to the bottom of the country via a mixture of history, legend and anecdote.

Augustin Edwards *My Native Land* (Ernest Benn; o/p). Absorbing and vivid reflections on Chile's geography, history, folklore and literature; particularly strong on landscape descriptions.

Benjamin Subercaseaux *Chile: A Geographic Extravaganza* (New York; o/p). This seductive, poetic meander through Chile's "mad geography" is still one of the most enjoyable general introductions to the country, if a little dated.

RECENT TRAVELS/ACCOUNTS

Bruce Chatwin *In Patagonia* (Vintage/Penguin). The cult travel book that single-handedly enshrined Patagonia as the ultimate edge-of-the-world destination. Witty and captivating, this is essential reading for visitors to Patagonia, though unfortunately concentrates far more on the Argentinian side.

John Pilkington *An Englishman in Patagonia* (Century; o/p). A fun-to-read and sympathetic portrayal of Patagonia and its people by the co-author of Bradt's *Backpacking in Chile and Argentina*. Includes some wonderful black-and-white photographs.

Rosie Swale *Back to Cape Horn* (Collins; o/p). An extraordinary account of the author's epic 408 day journey on horseback from the Atacama desert down to Cape Horn – which she'd last visited while sailing around the world ten years previously in 1972.

USEFUL ADDRESSES

Canning House Library, 2 Belgrave Square, London SW1X 8PH (☎0171/235 2303). An exhaustive collection of books on Chile (and other Hispanic countries). Also produces a quarterly bulletin detailing new publications on Latin America and Brazil.

Latin American Bureau, 1 Amwell St, London EC1R 1UL (☎0171/278 2829). Publishers of books on Latin America, available by mail order along with a wide selection of titles produced by other publishers.

South American Explorer's Club, 126 Indian Creek Rd, Ithaca, NY 14850, US (☎607/277-0488; *explorer@samexplo.org*). Among its mountain of resources on South America, this long-established organization produces a free catalogue containing a wide choice of books available by mail order. The service can be used by members and non-members alike.

Sara Wheeler *Travels in a Thin Country* (Abacus/Modern Library). A pacy, amusing account of the author's six-month solo journey zigzagging the entire length of Chile in the early 1990s.

NINETEENTH- AND EARLIER TWENTIETH-CENTURY ACCOUNTS

John Arons and Claudio Vita-Finzi *The Useless Land* (Robert Hale; o/p). Four Cambridge geography students set out to explore the Atacama desert in 1958 and relate their adventures along the way in this highly readable book.

Charles Darwin *Voyage of the Beagle* (Penguin/Wordsworth Editions Ltd). This eminently readable (abridged) book contains some superb, evocative descriptions of nineteenth-century Chile, from Tierra del Fuego right up to Iquique.

Maria Graham *Journal of a Residence in Chile During the Year 1822* (o/p). *The* classic nineteenth-century travel narrative on Chile, written by a spirited, perceptive and amusing British woman.

Che Guevara *The Motorcycle Diaries* (Fourth Estate/Verso Books). Comic, picaresque narrative taken from the diaries of the future revolutionary as he and his buddy travelled around South America – including a large chunk of Chile – by motorbike, just out of medical school.

E B Herivel *We Farmed a Desert* (o/p). Entertaining account of the fifteen years spent by a British couple on a small farm in the Huasco valley in the 1930s and 1940s.

Alistair Horne *Small Earthquake in Chile* (Macmillan; o/p). Wry description of a visit to Chile during the turbulent months leading up to the military coup, written by a British journalist.

Bea Howe *Child in Chile* (o/p). A charming description of the author's childhood in Valparaíso in the early 1900s, where her family formed part of the burgeoning British business community.

HISTORY, POLITICS AND SOCIETY

GENERAL

Leslie Bethell (ed) *Chile Since Independence* (CUP). Made up of four chapters taken from the *Cambridge History of Latin American History,* this is rather dry in parts, but rigorous, comprehensive and clear.

Nick Caistor *In Focus: Chile* (Latin American Bureau/Interlink Books). Brief, potted introduction to Chile's history, politics and society, highlighting the social problems bequeathed by Pinochet's economic model.

Simon Collier and William Sater *A History of Chile, 1801–1994* (CUP). Probably the best single-volume history of Chile from independence to the 1990s; thoroughly academic but enlivened by colourful detail along with the authors' clear fondness for the country and its people.

John Hickman *News from the End of the Earth: A Portrait of Chile* (Hurst & Co./St Martin's Press). Written by a former British ambassador to Chile, this concise and highly readable book makes a good (if conservative) introduction to Chile's history, taking you from the conquest to the 1990s in some 250 pages.

Brian Loveman *Chile: the Legacy of Hispanic Capitalism* (OUP). Solid analysis of Chile's his tory from the arrival of the Spanish in the 1540s to the 1973 military coup.

Sergio Villalobos *A Short History of Chile* (Editorial Universitaria, Chile). Clear, concise and sensible outline of Chile's history, from pre-Columbian cultures through to the past decade, aimed at the general reader with no prior knowledge of the subject. Available in Santiago.

THE PINOCHET YEARS

Sheila Cassidy *Audacity to Believe* (Darton, Longman & Todd; o/p). Distressing account of the imprisonment and horrific torture of a British doctor (the author) after she'd treated a wounded anti-Pinochet activist.

Paul Drake (ed) *The Struggle for Democracy in Chile* (University of Nebraska Press). Excellent collection of ten essays examining the gradual breakdown of the military government's authority. The pieces, which offer contrasting views both in support of and opposition to the regime, were written in 1988, during the months around the plebiscite.

Diana Kay *Chileans in Exile: Private Struggles, Public Lives* (Longwood Academic). Although written in a somewhat dry, academic style, this is nonetheless a fascinating study of Chilean exiles in Scotland, with a strong focus on women. The author looks at their attempts to reconstruct their lives, their sense of dislocation, and the impact exile has had on their attitude to politics, marriage and the home.

Grino Rojo and John J Hasset (ed) *Chile, Dictatorship and the Struggle for Democracy* (Ediciones Hispamérica). A slim, accessible volume containing four essays written in the months approaching the 1986 plebiscite, in which the country would vote to reject or continue with military rule. Contains contrasting analyses of the impact of the dictatorship on the country and its people.

Jacobo Timerman *Chile: Death in the South* (Vintage Books; o/p). Reflections on the Pinochet years by an Argentinian journalist, written thirteen years into the military regime. Particularly compelling are the short personal testimonies of torture victims that intersperse the narrative.

Thomas Wright and Rody Oñate *Flight from Chile: Voices of Exile* (University of New Mexico Press). Detailed and affecting account of the exodus after the 1973 coup, when over 200,000 Chileans fled their homeland.

SPECIAL-INTEREST STUDIES

George McBride *Chile: Land and Society* (Kennikat Press; o/p). A compelling and exhaustively researched examination of the impact of the hacienda system on Chilean society, and the relationship (up to the mid-twentieth century) between landowners and peasants.

Colin McEwan, Luis Borrero and Alfredo Prieto (eds) *Patagonia: Natural History, Prehistory and Ethnography at the Uttermost End of the Earth* (British Museum Press/Princeton University Press). Brilliant account of the "human adaptation, survival and eventual extinction" of the native peoples of Patagonia, accompanied by dozens of haunting black-and-white photographs.

William Sater *The Heroic Image in Chile* (University of California Press; o/p). Fascinating, scholarly look at the reasons behind the near-deification of Arturo Prat, the naval officer who died futilely in battle in 1879, described by the author as "a secular saint".

Richard W Slatta *Cowboys of the Americas* (Yale UP). Exhaustively-researched, highly entertaining and lavishly illustrated history of the cowboy cultures of the Americas, including detailed treatment of the Chilean *huaso*.

CHILEAN WOMEN

Marjorie Agosin (ed) *Scraps of Life: Chilean Arpilleras: Chilean Women and the Pinochet Dictatorship* (Zed Books/Red Sea Press). A sensitive portrayal of the women of Santiago's shanty towns who, during the dictatorship, scraped a living by sewing scraps of material together to make wall hangings, known as *arpilleras*, depicting scenes of violence and repression. The *arpilleras* became a symbol of their protest, and were later exhibited around the world.

Jo Fisher *Out of the Shadows* (Latin American Bureau/Monthly Review Press). Penetrating analysis of the emergence of the women's movement in Latin America, with a couple of chapters devoted to Chile.

Elizabeth Jelin (ed) *Women and Social Change in Latin America* (Zed Books). A series of intelligent essays examining the ways women's organizations have acted as mobilizing forces for social and political change in Latin America.

FICTION AND POETRY

FICTION

Marjorie Agosin (ed) *Landscapes of a New Land: Short Fiction by Latin American Women* (White Wine Press). This anthology includes four short stories by Chilean women authors, including the acclaimed Marta Brunet (1901–67) and María Luisa Bombal (1910–80). Overall, the book creates a poetic, at times haunting, evocation of female life in a patriarchal world. Also edited by Agosin, *Secret Weavers: Stories of the Fantastic by Women of Argentina and Chile* (White Wine Press; o/p) is a spellbinding collection of short stories interwoven with themes of magic, allegory, legend and fantasy.

Isabel Allende *The House of the Spirits* (Black Swan/Bantam Books). This baroque, fantastical and best-selling novel chronicles the fortunes of several generations of a rich, landowning family in an unnamed but thinly disguised Chile, culminating with a brutal military coup and the murder of the president. Allende's *Of Love and Shadows* (Black Swan/Bantam Books) is set against a background of disappearances and dictatorship, including a fictional account of the real-life discovery of the bodies of fifteen executed workers in a Central Valley mine. The author was a relative of Salvador Allende.

José Donoso *Curfew* (Picador/Grove Atlantic). Gripping novel about an exiled folk singer's return to Santiago during the military dictatorship, by one of Chile's most outstanding twentieth-century writers. Other works by Donoso translated into English include *Hell Has No Limits* (Sun and Moon Press), about the strange existence of a transvestite and his daughter in a Central Valley brothel, and *The Obscene Bird of Night* (Godine), a dislocated, fragmented novel narrated by a deaf-mute old man as he retreats into madness.

Ariel Dorfman *Hard Rain* (Readers International). This complicated, thought-provoking novel is both an examination of the role of the writer in a revolutionary society, and a celebration of the "Chilean road to socialism" – not an easy read, but one that repays the effort. Dorfman later became internationally famous for his play *Death and the Maiden* (Penguin), made into a film by Roman Polanski.

Alberto Fuguet *Bad Vibes* (o/p; St Martin's Press). Two weeks in September 1980 as lived by a mixed-up Santiago rich kid. A sort of Chilean *Catcher In the Rye* set against the tensions of the military regime.

Alicia Partnoy (ed) *You Can't Drown the Fire: Latin American Women Writing in Exile* (Virago/Cleis Press). Excellent anthology bringing together a mixture of short stories, poems and essays by exiled Latin American women, including Veronica de Negri, Cecila Vicuña, Marjorie Agosin and Isabel Morel Letelier from Chile.

Luis Sepúlveda *The Name of a Bullfighter* (Allison & Busby Ltd). Fast-paced, rather macho thriller set in Hamburg, Santiago and Tierra del Fuego, by one of Chile's leading young novelists.

Antonio Skármeta *The Postman* (Hyperion), formerly *Burning Patience* (Minerva). Funny and poignant novel about a postman who delivers mail to the great poet Pablo Neruda, who helps him seduce the local beauty with the help of a few metaphors. It was also made into a successful film, *Il Postino*, with the action relocated to Capri. Also by Skármeta, *I Dreamt the Snow Was Burning* (Readers International) is a tense, dark novel evoking the suspicion and fear that permeated everyday life in the months surrounding the military coup, while *Watch Where the Wolf is Going* (Readers International) is a collection of short stories, some of them set in Chile.

POETRY

Vicente Huidobro *The Selected Poetry of Vicente Huidobro* (W.W. Norton & Co./New Directions). Intellectual, experimental and dynamic works by an early twentieth-century poet, highly acclaimed in his time (1893–1948) but often overlooked today.

Gabriela Mistral *Selected Poems* (Johns Hopkins UP). Mistral is far less widely translated than her fellow Nobel laureate, Neruda, but this collection serves as an adequate English-language introduction to her quietly passionate and bittersweet poetry, much of it inspired by the landscape of the Elqui valley.

Pablo Neruda *Twenty Love Poems and a Song of Despair* (Jonathan Cope/Penguin); *Canto General* (French & European Publications/ University of California Press); *Captain's Verses* (New Directions). The doyen of Chilean poetry seems to be one of those poets people love or hate – his work is extravagantly lyrical, frequently verbose, but often very tender, particularly his love poetry. Neruda has been translated into many languages, and is widely available.

Nicanor Parra *Emergency Poems* (W.W. Norton & Co../New Directions). Both a physicist and poet, Parra pioneered the "anti-poem" in Chile during the 1980s: bald, unlyrical, often satirical prose poems. A stimulating read.

BIOGRAPHY AND MEMOIRS

Fernando Alegría *Allende: A Novel* (Stanford UP). Basically a biography, with fictional dialogue, of Salvador Allende written by his former cultural attaché, who was busy researching the book while the president died in the coup. Also of note by Alegría is *The Chilean Spring*, a fictional diary of a young photographer coming to terms with the coup in Santiago.

Ariel Dorfman *Heading South, Looking North* (Hodder & Stoughton/Penguin). Recently published memoirs of one of Chile's most famous writers, in which he reflects on themes such as language, identity, guilt and politics. Intelligent and illuminating, with some interesting thoughts on the causes of the Unidad Popular's failures.

Joan Jara *Víctor: An Unfinished Song* (Bloomsbury; o/p). Poignant memoir written by the British wife of the famous Chilean folksinger Víctor Jara, describing their life together, the Nueva Canción movement (see p.467), and their optimism for Allende's new

Chile. The final part, detailing Jara's imprisonment, torture and execution in Santiago's football stadium, is almost unbearably moving. The story is to be made into a feature film written by and starring Emma Thompson.

R L Mégroz *The Real Robinson Crusoe* (Cresset Press; o/p). Colourful biography of Alexander Selkirk, who spent four years and four months marooned on one of the Juan Fernández islands, inspiring Daniel Defoe to write *The Adventures of Robinson Crusoe*.

Pablo Neruda *Memoirs* (Penguin). Though his occasional displays of vanity and compulsive name-dropping can be irritating, there's no doubt that this is an extraordinary man with a fascinating life. The book also serves as a useful outline of Chile's political movements from the 1930s to the 1970s.

PACIFIC ISLANDS

Paul Bahn and John Flenley *Easter Island, Earth Island* (Thames & Hudson; o/p). Richly illustrated with glossy photographs, this scholarly but accessible book provides an up-to-date and comprehensive introduction to the island's history and archeology. Interestingly, it also suggests that Easter Island could be a microcosm representing a global dilemma – that of a land so despoiled by man that it could no longer support its civilization.

Sebastian Englert *Island at the Centre of the World* (Hale; o/p) . Based on a series of lectures broadcast to the Chilean navy serving in Antarctica, this is perhaps the clearest and most accessible (though now somewhat dated) introduction to Easter Island, written by a genial German priest who lived there for 35 years from 1935.

Thor Heyerdahl *Aku Aku* (George Allen & Unwin; o/p). This account of Heyerdahl's famous expedition to Easter Island in 1955 makes a cracking read, with an acute sense of adventure and mystery. Dubious as the author's archeological theories are, it's hard not to get swept along by his enthusiasm. In contrast, his *Reports of the Norwegian Archeological Expedition to Easter Island and the East Pacific* is a rigorous and respected documentation of the expedition's findings.

Alfred Métraux *Easter Island* (André Deutsch; o/p). Key study of Easter Island's traditions, beliefs and customs by a Belgian anthropologist, based on exhaustive research carried out in the 1930s. Métraux's *The Ethnology of Easter Island*, published in periodical format, is available from Periodicals Service Company, 11 Main St, Germantown, NY, USA (☎518/537-5899).

Catherine and Michel Orliac *The Silent Gods: Mysteries of Easter Island* (Thames & Hudson; o/p). Pocket-sized softback, densely packed with colour illustrations and surprisingly detailed background on the island's explorers, statues, myths and traditions.

Katherine Routledge *The Mystery of Easter Island* (Adventures Unlimited Press). Recently back in print, this compelling book chronicles one of the earliest archeological expeditions to the island, led by the author in 1914. Routledge interviewed many elderly islanders and recounts their oral testimonies as well as the discoveries of her excavations.

Ralph Lee Woodward *Robinson Crusoe's Island* (University of North Carolina Press; o/p). There's a good deal more drama to the Juan Fernández Islands' history than the famous four-year marooning of Alexander Selkirk, all of it enthusiastically retold in this lively book.

FLORA AND FAUNA

Sharon R Chester *Birds of Chile* (Wandering Albatross). First-rate, easy-to-carry softback guide with over 300 colour illustrations of the birds of mainland Chile.

Claudio Donoso Zegers *Chilean Trees Identification Guide/Arboles Nativos de Chile* (Marisa Cúneo Ediciones, Chile). Handy pocket guide to Chile's main native trees, with commentary in Spanish and English. Produced for Conaf (the National Parks administration), and part of a series that includes *Chilean Bushes, Chilean Climber Plants* and *Chilean Terrestrial Mammals*. Available in Conaf's information office in Santiago (see p.69).

LANGUAGE

Relatively few Chileans speak English, and since the tourist industry has traditionally been directed at Argentinians or Chileans themselves, you'll find this to be equally the case among hotel-owners, waiters and even tourist office staff. Bus drivers, taxi drivers and shop assistants will almost certainly speak no English, so, to get by in Chile, you really need to equip yourself with a bit of basic Spanish. It's not a difficult language to pick up and there are numerous books, cassettes and CD-ROMs on the market, teaching to various levels – *Teach Yourself Latin American Spanish* is a very good book-cassette package for getting started, while for an old-fashioned, rigorous textbook, nothing beats H. Ramsden's *An Essential Course in Modern Spanish*, published in the UK by Nelson.

The snag is that Chilean Spanish does not always conform to what you learn in the classroom or hear on a cassette, and even competent Spanish-speakers will find it takes a bit of getting used to. The first thing to contend with is the dizzying **speed** with which most Chileans speak; another is **pronunciation**, especially the habitual dropping of consonants. In particular, "s" is frequently dropped from the end or middle of a word, so *dos* becomes *do*, *gracias* becomes *gracia*, and *fósforos* (matches) becomes *fóforo*. "D" has a habit of disappearing from past participles, so *comprado* is *comprao*, while the "gua" sound is commonly reduced to *wa*, making the city of Rancagua *Rancaawa*.

Another way in which Chilean differs from classic Castilian Spanish is its borrowing of words from other languages, mainly Quechua, Aymara and Mapuche, but also German (*küchen*) and even English ("plumber" in Chile is *el gasfiter*). Adding to the confusion is a widespread use of **slang** and **idiom**, much of which is unique to Chile. None of this, however, should put you off attempting to speak Spanish in Chile – Chileans will really appreciate your efforts, and even faltering beginners will be complimented on their language skills. Chilean Spanish is, moreover, a particularly melodious version of the language, enjoyable to listen to even with only a limited understanding.

PRONUNCIATION

The rules of **pronunciation** are pretty straightforward and, once you get to know them, strictly observed. Unless there's an accent, words ending in d, l, r, and z are **stressed** on the last syllable, all others on the second last. All **vowels** are pure and short.

A somewhere between the "a" sound of back and that of father.

E as in get.

I as in police.

O as in hot.

U as in rule.

C is soft before E and I, hard otherwise: *cerca* is pronounced "serka".

G works the same way, a guttural "h" sound (like the ch in loch) before E or I, a hard G elsewhere – *gigante* becomes "higante".

H is always silent.

J is the same sound as a guttural G: *jamon* is pronounced "hamon".

LL sounds like an English Y: *tortilla* is pronounced "torteeya".

N is as in English unless it has a tilde over it (ñ), when it becomes NY: *mañana* sounds like "manyana".

QU is pronounced like an English K.

R is rolled, RR doubly so.

V sounds more like B, *vino* becoming "beano".

X is slightly softer than in English – sometimes almost SH – except between vowels in place names where it has an "H" sound – for example México (Meh-Hee-Ko).

Z is the same as a soft C, so *cerveza* becomes "servesa".

On the following page we've listed a few essential words and phrases, though if you're travelling for any length of time a dictionary or phrase book is obviously a worthwhile investment. If you're using a **dictionary**, bear in mind that in Spanish CH, LL, and Ñ count as separate letters and are listed after the Cs, Ls, and Ns respectively.

IDIOM AND SLANG

As you travel through Chile you'll come across a lot of words and expressions that crop up again and again, many of which aren't in your dictionary, or, if they are, appear to have a different meaning from that given. Added to these day-to-day **chilenismos** is a very rich, exuberant and constantly expanding vocabulary of **slang** (*modismos*). This is near impossible to get to grips with, but mastering a few of the most common examples will help you get by and raise a smile if you drop them into the conversation.

EVERYDAY WORDS AND EXPRESSIONS

Some of the words and expressions listed below are shared by neighbouring countries, while others are uniquely Chilean. As well as these peculiarities, we've listed a few other expressions you're likely to encounter very frequently.

Al tiro: "right away", "immediately" – though this can mean anything up to several hours.

Boleto: as Chilean law requires that customers must not leave shop premises without their *boleto* (receipt), you will frequently hear "*¡su boleto!*" yelled at you as you try to leave without it.

Calefónt (pronounced "calefón"): "water heater" – not a Chilean word, but one you'll need on a daily basis if you're staying in budget accommodation, where you'll have to remember to light the *calefónt* with *fósforos* (matches) before you take a shower.

Carné: nothing to do with meat, this means "identity card".

Cédula: interchangeable with *carné*.

Chao: by far the most common way of saying "goodbye" among friends; in slightly more formal situations, *hasta luego* is preferred over *adiós*.

Confort (pronounced "confor"): A brand name, and now the de facto word for toilet paper (which is correctly *papel higiénico*).

De repente: in Spain this means "suddenly"; in Chile it means "maybe", "sometimes" or "occasionally".

Flojo: "lazy", frequently invoked by northerners to describe southerners and southerners to describe northerners.

Guagua: (pronounced "wawa"): baby, derived from Quechua.

Harto: "loads of"; a more widely used and idiomatic alternative to *mucho*.

Listo: literally "ready", and used as a response to indicate agreement, or that what's been said is understood, something like "sure" or "right".

Plata: literally "silver" but meaning "money", used far more commonly than *dinero*, except in formal situations.

Qué le vaya muy bien: "May everything go well for you", frequently said when saying goodbye to someone you won't see again.

Rico: "good", "delicious", "tasty", usually to describe food and drink.

Ya: Chilean equivalent of the Spanish *vale*; used universally to convey "OK", "fine", "sure" or (depending on the tone) "Whatever".

SLANG

The few examples we give below barely scrape the surface of the living, constantly evolving lexicon of Chilean slang – for a crash course, get hold of the excellent *How to Survive in the Chilean Jungle* by John Brennan and Alvaro Baboada, published by Dolmen and available in the larger Santiago bookshops.

Buena onda: "cool!"

Cachai: "you know?", "are you with me?", liberally scattered through conversations.

Chabela: slang version of *chao*.

Cuico: wealthy young Santiaguino – the type that dresses conservatively, carries a mobile phone and lives in Las Condes.

Huevón: "asshole" or "fucker", but so commonly and enthusiastically used it's no longer particularly offensive (though it should not be used by foreigners).

Los pacos: the police.

Pololo/a: boyfriend, girlfriend.

Sí po: abbreviation of *sí pues*, meaning "yeah", "sure".

Taco: traffic jam.

BASICS

yes, no	*sí, no*	with, without	con, sin
please, thank you	*por favor, gracias*	good, bad	*buen(o)/a, mal(o)/a*
where, when	*dónde, cuando*	big	*gran(de)*
what, how much	*qué, cuanto*	small	*pequeño/a, chico*
here, there	*aquí, allí*	more, less	*más, menos*
this, that	*este, eso*	today, tomorrow	*hoy, mañana*
now, later	*ahora, más tarde*	yesterday	*ayer*
open, closed	*abierto/a, cerrado/a*		

GREETINGS AND RESPONSES

Hello, Goodbye	*Hola, Adiós*	My name is . . .	*Me llamo . . .*
Good morning	*Buenos dias*	What's your name?	*¿Como se llama usted?*
Good afternoon/night	*Buenas tardes/noches*	I am English	*Soy inglés(a)*
See you later	*Hasta luego*	. . . American	*americano(a)*
Sorry	*Lo siento/discúlpeme*	. . . Australian	*australiano (a)*
Excuse me	*Con permiso/perdón*	. . . Canadian	*canadiense (a)*
How are you?	*¿Como está (usted)?*	. . . Irish	*irlandés (a)*
I (don't) understand	*(No) Entiendo*	. . . Scottish	*escosés (a)*
Not at all/You're welcome	*De nada*	. . . Welsh	*galés (a)*
Do you speakEnglish?	*¿Habla (usted) inglés?*	. . . New Zealander	*neozelandés (a)*
I don't speak Spanish	*(No) Hablo español*		

NEEDS – HOTELS AND TRANSPORT

I want	*Quiero*
I'd like	*Querría*
Do you know. . .?	*¿Sabe. . .?*
I don't know	*No sé*
There is (is there)?	*(¿) Hay (?)*
Give me. . .	*Deme. . .*
(one like that)	*(uno así)*
Do you have. . .?	*¿Tiene . . .?*
the time	*la hora*
a room	*una habitación*
with two beds/ double bed	*con dos camas/ cama matriomonial*
It's for one person	*es para una persona*
(two people)	*(dos personas)*
for one night	*para una noche*
(one week)	*(una semana)*
It's fine, how much is it?	*¿Está bien, cuánto es?*
It's too expensive	*Es demasiado caro*
Don't you have anything cheaper?	*¿No tiene algo más barato?*
Can one. . . ?	*¿Se puede. . ?*
camp (near) here?	*¿acampar aqui (cerca)?*
Is there a hotel nearby?	*¿Hay un hotel aquí cerca?*
How do I get to. . .?	*¿Por dónde se va a. . .?*
Left, right, straight on	*Izquierda, derecha, derecho*
Where is. . .?	*¿Dondé está. . .?*
the bus station	*el terminal de buses*
the train station	*a estación de ferro carriles*
the nearest bank	*el banco más cercano*
the post office	*el correo*
the toilet	*el baño*
Where does the bus to. . . leave from?	*¿De dónde sale el camión para. . .?*
Is this the train for Santiago?	*¿Es éste el tren para Santiago?*
I'd like a (return) ticket to. . .	*Querría pasaje (de ida y vuelta) para. . .*
What time does it leave (arrive in. . .)?	*¿A qué hora sale (llega en. . .)?*
What is there to eat?	*¿Qué hay para comer?*
What's that?	*¿Qué es eso?*
What's this called	*¿Como se llama este en*

NUMBERS AND DAYS

1	*un/uno/una*	17	*diecisiete*	500	*quinientos*
2	*dos*	18	*dieciocho*	1000	*mil*
3	*tres*	19	*diecinueve*	2000	*dos mil*
4	*cuatro*	20	*veinte*		
5	*cinco*	21	*veitiuno*	first	*primero/a*
6	*seis*	30	*treinta*	second	*segundo/a*
7	*siete*	40	*cuarenta*	third	*tercero/a*
8	*ocho*	50	*cincuenta*		
9	*nueve*	60	*sesenta*	Monday	*lunes*
10	*diez*	70	*setenta*	Tuesday	*martes*
11	*once*	80	*ochenta*	Wednesday	*miércoles*
12	*doce*	90	*noventa*	Thursday	*jueves*
13	*trece*	100	*cien(to)*	Friday	*viernes*
14	*catorce*	101	*ciento uno*	Saturday	*sábado*
15	*quince*	200	*doscientos*	Sunday	*domingo*
16	*dieciséis*	201	*doscientos uno*		

GLOSSARY

ADOBE Sun-dried mud.

ALTIPLANO High plateau region in the Andes of the far north.

APU Mountain god.

ARRIERO Muleteer, or horseman.

AYLLU Kinship group or clan.

BARRIO District, quarter or suburb.

BOFEDAL Spongey green grass or peat bog in the altiplano.

CAMANCHACA Coastal mist.

CASA PATRONAL Hacienda-owner's house.

CHICHA Cider; fermented grape or maize drink.

CHOCLO Corn.

COLECTIVO Collective taxi.

CORDILLERA Mountain range.

CRIOLLO "Creole": used historically to refer to a person of Spanish blood born in the American colonies, but nowadays as an adjective to describe something (such as food or music) as "typical" or "local".

ENCOMENDERO Possessor of an *encomienda.*

ENCOMIENDA A grant of indigenous labourers to landowners during colonial times.

ESTANCIA Ranch, or large estate.

FUNDO Estate or farm.

HACIENDA Large estate.

HOJA DE COCA Coca-leaf.

HUASO Chilean "cowboy", or mounted farm worker.

JUNTA A ruling council; usually used to describe small groups who've staged a coup d'état.

LATIFUNDIA Entailed estates.

LLARETA Deep-green, rock-hard woody plant in the altiplano.

LOCAL "Unit" or "shop" in shopping centre or mall.

MAYORAZGO Entailment system of large etates.

MESTIZO Person of mixed Spanish and indigenous blood.

MICRO City bus.

PAMPA Plain.

PEÑA Restaurant or nightclub where live folk music is performed.

POBLACION Poor suburb.

PORTAZUELA Mountain pass.

PUKARA Fort.

PUNA Barren Andean heights, sometimes used interchangeably with altiplano.

QUEBRADA Ravine, dried-out stream.

SOROCHE Altitude sickness.

INDEX

Z

Stay in touch with us!

I would like to receive ROUGH*NEWS*: please put me on your free mailing list.

NAME . . . .

ADDRESS . . . .

Please clip or photocopy and send to: Rough Guides, 62–70 Shorts Gardens, London WC2H 9AB, England or Rough Guides, 375 Hudson Street, New York, NY 10014, USA.